FLOYD V. FILSON

A NEW TESTAMENT HISTORY

FLOYD V. FILSON

A NEW
TESTAMENT
HISTORY

SCM PRESS LTD
BLOOMSBURY STREET LONDON

A note about British editions appears on pp. 429-432

334 01142 6

First British Edition 1965
Second impression 1971
Third impression 1974

© W. L. Jenkins 1964

Typeset in the United States of America
Printed in Great Britain by
REDWOOD BURN LIMITED
Trowbridge & Esher

CONTENTS

Part Four

PAUL THE APOSTLE TO GENTILES

Part Five

THE CHURCH ANCHORED IN HISTORY

PREFACE

This New Testament history has been written for ministers, theological students, and lay teachers and leaders who are ready to undertake a serious study of the origin and emergence of the Christian church. The story necessarily covers an extensive area, as the main divisions and chapter subjects in the Contents clearly show. To make it possible to understand each division of the total story some repetition of material is justified and essential, but the main aim has been to provide a clear and connected account of the crucial three hundred years of history that are involved.

Bibliographical references, provided throughout the book, direct attention to works in English wherever possible. In itself this is misleading, for much of the significant work in the field studied is written in German, French, and other languages. But the works in English are much more widely accessible, and the main aim of the footnotes has been to help the reader find works that carry further the discussion this book has begun.

I am greatly indebted to McCormick Theological Seminary for the sabbatical leave during which I wrote the first draft of this book; to Mrs. Burton W. Hales for making available a grant to enable me to visit again many Biblical sites and important museums in Europe and the Near East; to my friend and colleague, Prof. Paul E. Davies, for his thoughtful reading of the manuscript; and to my wife for her loyal encouragement and her professional skill in typing the manuscript.

F. V. F.

INTRODUCTION

The emergence of the church is a story significant in itself and influential in later history. It is so important that it usually is not treated as a whole but is broken up into a series of intensive studies. Either the life of Jesus, for example, or the career of Paul is significant enough to justify book-length discussion. But such partial studies are not sufficient. The student, the minister, and the serious general reader need a connected account of how the church emerged. It is such a historical picture which the present book attempts to give. The attention is focused not merely on the documents of the New Testament but on the history out of which these writings came and for which they are the most important witnesses.

To understand the situation in which Jesus Christ appeared and the church was founded, we must first survey the geographical, political, social, and religious background. This essential background can be provided if we start our story about 175 B.C., trace the Maccabean movement among the Jews, and go on to sketch the development of Judaism through the New Testament period in the setting of current world history.

How far must we trace the early Christian history in order to deal thoroughly with the New Testament story and describe the emergence of the church? We cannot stop with the end of the book of The Acts, for at that time at least half of the books of the New Testament had not yet been written; we must include the history of the period in which these later writings were composed. For much the same reason we cannot stop with the fall of Jerusalem in A.D. 70. Even the close of the first century is too soon to end our story, for probably the latest of the New Testament writings had still not been produced, and the role which these writings were to play in later history had not yet been clarified.

The most satisfactory solution is to continue the story to the middle of the second century. By that time the emerging church had begun to understand that its faith, worship, and life must be grounded in the apostolic witness as reliably recorded in the writings that were being assembled to form our New Testament. Our purpose is not to write a

1*

complete history of the ancient world, but to describe the essential facts and forces that give the setting for the rise of the church and then go on to tell and interpret the New Testament story.

It must be admitted that we lack sufficient data to write a detailed and connected story of how the church emerged. Even in the period covered by the book of The Acts the data are sketchy; they by no means cover all that went on in the first decades of the apostolic church. Once the book of The Acts ends, the important decades that follow are but meagerly portrayed in our sources. We must resist the temptation to pretend that a clear, complete, and connected story can be written.

In view of this deficiency of material, we must use every literary source that promises to throw light on the Christian story. Some clues to the history of our period survive in later writings. They must be used with care but with gratitude. Archaeology rarely gives direct Christian data, but it can help in reconstructing the setting and in attesting a limited number of details. In the use of both literary and archaeological material we must watch for clues to the common life of that time, for the church in its earliest decades was confined mostly to the middle and lower classes; few outstanding individuals of the day figured directly in its history. We are interested not merely in the thought and teaching of the church but in its entire life—its faith, worship, social pattern, economic status, leadership, and witness.

For two reasons, the references to Judaism in this book have a special importance. Most important for our purpose is the fact that the Old Testament and the Jewish heritage was the dominant background factor in the origin and growth of the Christian movement. The other reason is that it was precisely in the period covered by our study that Judaism emerged in the essential form it has held in succeeding centuries.

It is often thought by Christians that the Judaism of the days of Jesus and Paul was a finished product which stood in a static way over against the emerging Christian church. Such an idea is quite wrong. It was during the period we are to study that the Jewish parties known from the New Testament emerged; the apparent domination of the Sadducees, effective only to a limited degree and radically challenged by the Pharisees even in the days of Jesus, was broken by the fall of Jerusalem; Pharisaism emerged as the continuing form of Judaism; and the oral tradition, which later was embodied in the Mishnah and so became the core of the Talmud, was taking form. The fall of Jerusalem in A.D. 70 and the failure of the Bar-Cochba rebellion in A.D. 132–135 practically marked the end of all Jewish sects except the Pharisees, whose rabbinical leadership and tradition developed into Talmudic Judaism and so in time became the orthodox Judaism of our day. Thus a minor contribution of the present book should be to note how during the period under study Judaism as well as Christianity took its classic position.

One question of method calls for comment. The commonly accepted procedure in writing history is to describe the human situation in the light of the natural world. This method recognizes that man is more than an animal; he is gifted with intellectual and spiritual capacities that make him truly human. But history on this view is the story of human experience, and religion is described as man's experience in the observable world of nature. All of this is undoubtedly an integral part of history, but it is a question whether this is the whole of it. Our story deals mainly with Biblical material, and for the Biblical writers, God is the chief actor in history; his will and action are decisive. Can we do justice to the Bible history if we reject or ignore or are neutral toward its central faith and outlook? Can we adequately describe Biblical history in a way that excludes God's role? For every New Testament leader and writer, it would be radically misleading to do so.

Quite obviously the modern writer who accepts the New Testament gospel and writes as an involved person is in constant danger of warping the data and conforming the story to his understanding of the New Testament message. The danger is real. The scholar usually tries to escape from it by dealing with the data from an objective, neutral, detached viewpoint. This attitude, I repeat, suggests indifference to or suspicion of the religious message so central in this history. Is there another way to write this history? There is. This history, if it is to be fairly presented, has to be told from the standpoint of personal involvement. In fact, a writer who clearly states and then vigorously rejects the driving concern of this Christian movement is closer to an understanding of it than one who tells about it as though he can be neutral toward it. To the Biblical writers, these events in which God is believed to have been purposefully active permit no neutrality.

But how then can the involved writer avoid the danger of bias and distortion? Probably he never can avoid the danger completely; no one can, regardless of his method and point of view. But the point often overlooked is that the Christian has an urgent reason for honesty in his historical study as in every other area of his life. His obligation to rigid honesty, accuracy, and fairness is a debt he owes not only to scholarly standards but above all to God. Critical study, continual distrust of one's own understanding and method and conclusions, are a Christian possibility and a Christian duty in presenting a New Testament history in which God is active and central.

Part One

THE BACKGROUND

Chapter 1

THE HISTORICAL BACKGROUND
175 B.C.–A.D. 30

ON THE FIRST half of the second century B.C., Judaism underwent a serious crisis. The outcome of that crisis shaped the development of all later Judaism and so determined in part the setting for the emergence of the church. The issue at stake was the role that Hellenistic civilization and culture were to play among Jews.

When the Persian king Cyrus overthrew the Babylonian empire in 539 B.C., he gave permission for the captive Jews in Babylonia to return to Palestine (Ezra, ch. 1). Only a courageous minority did so. For the next two hundred years this small group, and fellow Jews who had not been in captivity, led a rather obscure life, mainly in and near Jerusalem.

Even before these Jews returned from exile, Greek wares and culture had begun to make their way into Palestine. When Alexander the Great invaded the Near East and took over Palestine, the impact of Greek culture increased. Alexander died in 323 B.C. after a brief but spectacular career. His leading generals divided his empire, and by 275 B.C. three main kingdoms, all Hellenistic in leadership, had emerged.[1] Of direct significance for Palestine were the Ptolemaic kingdom in Egypt and the Seleucid empire, which centered in Syria and extended from Asia Minor eastward to Parthia and Bactria.

Palestine came under the Ptolemaic dynasty. But the Seleucid rulers, whose capital city was Antioch in Syria,[2] schemed to annex Palestine. In 217 B.C. this was attempted by Antiochus III (223–187 B.C.), but he was soundly defeated at Raphia by Ptolemy V (203–181 B.C.). About 200 (or 198) B.C., however, at Paneas, near the foot of Mt. Hermon in Northern Palestine, he decisively defeated Ptolemy V, and Palestine became linked with the Seleucid kingdom (*Ant.* XII.3.3).[3]

---

[1] See Map D, Plate XI, *The Westminster Historical Atlas to the Bible*, rev. ed., by G. Ernest Wright and Floyd V. Filson (The Westminster Press, 1956).

[2] See Glanville Downey, *A History of Antioch in Syria* (Princeton University Press, 1961).

[3] Flavius Josephus, the Jewish historian who lived from about A.D. 37 to at least the

3

Antiochus III gave the Jews official permission to live according to their ancestral laws (*Ant.* XII.3.4). Probably by his time, and certainly not later than Seleucus IV (187–175 B.C.), there emerged the Jewish group called the Hasidim or Hasideans, the "pious" or "godly" ones (I Macc. 2:42).[4] They were earnestly loyal in observing the Mosaic law and diligent in applying it to Jewish life. Probably the Hasidim movement developed in reaction to the tendency of some Jews to neglect the Mosaic law and accept Hellenistic ways of life.

Both Antiochus III and Seleucus IV, as Hellenistic rulers, naturally dealt mainly with the Greek-speaking and Hellenistically inclined leaders of the Jews. Certainly the Jewish high priest, as titular head of the Jews, carried on official dealings with the king, and in the king's eyes was a political appointee. Seleucus IV, it appears, even assumed authority to confiscate funds in the Temple treasury in Jerusalem. This treasury, considered by Jews a sacred place under divine protection and priestly management, served as a kind of "safe-deposit vault," not only for Temple funds but also for assets of individual Jews. On one occasion when the king needed money for military and governmental expenses, he apparently, according to a legend-clouded story, tried to seize some of these funds, but somehow was prevented (II Macc., ch. 3).

ANTIOCHUS EPIPHANES AND THE JEWS

Under Antiochus IV Epiphanes (175–163 B.C.) the question of Jewish acceptance of Greek culture reached a crisis. The problem, as already stated, was not new. Traces of Greek influence in Palestine date back to the seventh century B.C.[5] They increased after the conquest by Alexander the Great. Both the Ptolemies and the Seleucids were Greek in origin and cultural interests. Under the Ptolemies the Hebrew language had fallen into such disuse among the Jews in Egypt that by the middle of the third century B.C. it was necessary to translate the Pentateuch into Greek for use in Jewish worship and teaching,[6] and the translation of

---

end of the first century, wrote *The Jewish War* (which we refer to as *War*) a few years after A.D. 70 and his *Antiquities* (which we refer to as *Ant.*) about A.D. 95. On Josephus, see H. St. J. Thackeray, *Josephus, The Man and the Historian* (Jewish Institute of Religion Press, 1929).

4 On the Hasidim, see *A History of Israel*, Vol. II, by W. O. E. Oesterley (Oxford, Clarendon Press, 1932), pp. 315 ff., and *Hellenistic Civilization and the Jews*, by Victor Tcherikover, tr. by S. Applebaum (The Jewish Publication Society of America, 1959), pp. 125 f., 196 ff.

5 Evidence and further bibliography in Tcherikover, *Hellenistic Civilization and the Jews*, pp. 40 f., 417 f. (notes 4–8).

6 For *The Letter of Aristeas*, an introduction, translation, and commentary by H. T. Andrews is available in R. H. Charles (ed.), *Apocrypha and Pseudepigrapha of the*

the other Old Testament books was completed not much more than a century later.[7] Greek had become the native language of Jews in Egypt, and it gave access to Greek ways of thought and life.[8]

A similar openness to Hellenistic culture developed among the Jews of Palestine.[9] There, however, the development was less extensive; it occurred chiefly among the rich aristocratic circles, especially the priestly leaders at Jerusalem. It involved not only use of the Greek language and social contacts with Gentiles but also some toleration of Greek gods recognized in Hellenistic society, business, and government. Many influential Jewish leaders were ready to be thus broad-minded. To do so, they thought, would advance the prestige and welfare of their people.

It was at the request of such Jews that Antiochus Epiphanes took the steps that provoked the Maccabean rebellion.[10] The Jewish leader in this move was the priest Jason. By an offer of a total of four hundred and forty talents he induced the king to appoint him to replace Onias III as high priest (II Macc. 4:8; a talent was a little less than a thousand dollars). To the king this was a financially profitable and politically justified move. To Jews loyal to the ancestral customs, it was an outrage for a pagan king thus to depose God's high priest.

Jason took a still more fateful step. He promised the king an additional one hundred and fifty talents for permission "to establish . . . a gymnasium and a body of youth for it, and to enroll the men of Jerusalem [i.e., selected, Hellenistically interested Jews there] as citizens of Antioch" (II Macc. 4:9). This does not mean that he wanted to enroll these men as citizens of Antioch in Syria; he proposed to change the political status of Jerusalem itself. By decree of Antiochus III, Jerusalem had been organized according to the Jewish ancestral customs, but Jason planned to make it a Hellenistic city named Antioch, in which the

---

Old Testament, Vol. II (Oxford, Clarendon Press, 1913), pp. 83–122. On the Septuagint, see H. B. Swete, *Introduction to the Old Testament in Greek* (Cambridge, University Press, 2d ed., 1914).

7 This is indicated by The Prologue to Ecclesiasticus.

8 See Victor A. Tcherikover and Alexander Fuks, *Corpus Papyrorum Judaicarum*, Vol. I (Harvard University Press, 1957), pp. 1–111, for "a general survey of the historical development of the Jewish people in Egypt during the Hellenistic-Roman-Byzantine age."

9 Tcherikover, *Hellenistic Civilization and the Jews*, Part I, deals with "Hellenistic Civilization in Palestine," and gives bibliographical references.

10 The two main narrative sources for the Maccabean period are I Maccabees, written in Hebrew about 100 B.C. and covering the period from about 175 to 134 B.C., and II Maccabees, written in Greek to summarize in a conscious literary style the five books by a Jason of Cyrene and covering the period from just before 175 to 160 B.C. I Maccabees appears more factual. It avoids saying "God," using "Heaven" instead. It centers attention on the Maccabees, probably minimizing the role of the Hasidim. II Maccabees is more legendary in content, but preserves valuable historical material.

gymnasium would provide Greek athletic and social activities and selected youths would be trained in the Hellenistic way of social and political life. "The king assented," and Jason "shifted his countrymen over to the Greek way of life." (II Macc. 4:10.) The Hellenistic Jews, particularly the priests of Hellenistic sympathies, participated enthusiastically in Jason's program.

If Jason could buy the high priesthood, another Hellenistic-minded Jewish priest could outbid him and obtain the office by the king's appointment. This is what Menelaus did, "outbidding Jason by three hundred talents of silver" (II Macc. 4:24); he then drove Jason from office, and Jason took refuge in Ammon. Menelaus stole gold vessels from the Temple to give as gifts and sell for funds, and arranged for the deposed high priest Onias III, who was in refuge at Antioch in Syria, to be murdered; but by clever scheming he escaped punishment by the king for such acts (II Macc. 4:23–50).

In 169 and 168 B.C., Antiochus Epiphanes made expeditions against Egypt, in an attempt to add it to his kingdom. On his way back to Syria each time he visited Jerusalem.[11] While in Egypt on his second expedition, a rumor that he had died reached Jason in Ammon. Jason believed it. With a thousand men he marched to Jerusalem to regain the high priesthood, but was defeated by Menelaus (II Macc. 5:5–7). Word of the fighting reached the king. He had just been ordered out of Egypt by the Roman legate Popilius Laenas, whose presence and blunt action show Roman influence being extended into that region.[12] "Raging inwardly" at this humiliating rebuff more than at the supposed revolt in Palestine, he returned to Jerusalem, took the city, killed great numbers of men, women, and children, entered the Temple, confiscated with Menelaus' approval the holy vessels and offerings he found there (or did he do that to get funds on his visit the year before?), and left Philip, a Phrygian, to govern the Jerusalem area (II Macc. 5:11–23). Later the king sent to Palestine a "chief collector of tribute," probably Apollonius (I Macc. 1:29; II Macc. 5:24). He built a strongly fortified citadel in the "city of David," on the western hill of Jerusalem, and garrisoned it with "lawless men," Syrian troops and others loyal to the king but indifferent to the Mosaic law.

Only then did Antiochus Epiphanes take steps to end the ancestral

---

[11] This is disputed. Perhaps the king himself did not come to Jerusalem in 168 B.C., but sent his army to take the city. Cf. Elias Bickermann, *Der Gott der Makkabäer* (Berlin, Schocken Verlag, 1937), pp. 161 ff. Tcherikover, *Hellenistic Civilization and the Jews*, pp. 186, 473 f., argues that Dan. 11:28, 30, clearly describes two visits by the king.

[12] Polybius, *Histories* 29.27. Cf. Dan. 11:29 f.

Jewish worship at Jerusalem. I Macc. 1:41–42 asserts that "Then the king wrote to his whole kingdom that all should be one people, and that each should give up his customs." This sounds like a program of complete religious and cultural unification. But II Macc. 6:1 f. knows only of the king's attempt, through an Athenian emissary, to force the Jews of Palestine to give up the ancestral law.

In December, 167 B.C., "a desolating sacrilege," an altar to Zeus, was erected on the altar of burnt offering in the Temple court, and "abominable offerings which were forbidden by the [Mosaic] laws" were offered there (I Macc. 1:54; II Macc. 6:5). The Temple became a temple of Olympian Zeus; Jewish worship and sacrifices were prohibited and offensive pagan rites were substituted for them. Jews were compelled to partake of the pagan sacrifices on the monthly celebration of the king's birthday, and were forced to walk in the procession at the annual feast of the god Dionysus. Possession of a copy of the law was made a capital offense, as was the circumcision of new-born Jewish boys; observance of the Sabbath and of Jewish feasts was prohibited (I Macc. 1:54–61).

We may conclude that the king's edicts were directed against the Jews alone. His reason for these measures was not religious, due to evangelistic desire to convert Jews to pagan religion; it was, rather, political, prompted by determination to force the Jews to cooperate peaceably with royal officials. He knew that some Jews were pro-Egyptian and hostile to him, and he was determined to have a loyal Palestine as his southern border province. He wanted a steady payment of tribute and tax money from the Jews, and this required a peaceable, obedient people. No doubt he thought that common acceptance of Hellenistic culture would give unity to his empire, that the monotheistic zeal of Jews was unreasonable, and that the Jews were lacking in respect for their king.[13] But he was not a religious reformer; he was an egotistical, exasperated king who faced troubles all over his empire and finally determined to end by ruthless force what he considered the senseless bickering and rebellious acts of the Jews. In effect he determined to stamp out the Jewish religion, at least in Palestine (it is not clear what the numerous Jews in other parts of his empire were to be required to do).

Numerous Jews, undoubtedly mainly the Hasidim, offered courageous and stubborn resistance. They knew that they faced a life-and-death struggle to preserve their ancestral faith. II Maccabees gives examples

[13] Antiochus IV took the title "Epiphanes." It meant "Manifest," and seems to refer to him as Zeus-Manifest. For a coin that describes King Antiochus as "God-Manifest" and shows an image typical of Zeus, see Florence A. Banks, *Coins of Bible Days* (The Macmillan Company, 1955), p. 59.

of stirring heroism: Eleazar, an aged scribe "in high position," who died rather than eat swine's flesh, and a mother and seven sons who in a similar situation were tortured and martyred (II Macc. 6:18 to 7:41). I Maccabees tells of no specific heroes except the Maccabees, whom it was written to glorify, but it reports that "many in Israel stood firm" and "chose to die rather than to be defiled by food or to profane the holy covenant." Women who had their children circumcised in defiance of the king's decree were put to death (I Macc. 1:60–63).

But the situation called for more than heroic martyrdoms. Leadership was needed. It did not come from the Hellenistic priestly circles of Jerusalem; there is no hint that they acted to defend the Jewish faith. It came from a previously obscure priestly family in the town of Modein, and from at least one writing, The Book of Daniel, which strengthened the spirit of resistance.

THE MACCABEAN REVOLT

The king's decree required a pagan altar to be set up in each town. His officers were to force the Jews of the town to offer pagan sacrifices on it. They came to Modein, some twenty miles northwest of Jerusalem, and assembled the men of the city. Among them were the priest Mattathias and his five sons (John, Simon, Judas, Eleazar, and Jonathan). Since it was an influential family, the king's officers asked Mattathias to be the first to offer the pagan sacrifice, and promised him special honor and rewards from the king. Mattathias boldly refused. He and his sons were determined to "live by the covenant" of their fathers; they would not "desert the law and the ordinances."

Other Jews were not so brave. One stepped forward to offer the required sacrifice. Mattathias, incensed by this apostasy, rushed upon him and "killed him upon the altar." The Greek word "killed" can refer to slaying a sacrifice. Perhaps I Maccabees with grim irony means that Mattathias, who "burned with zeal for the law," did offer a sacrifice—not the one the king required, but the renegade Jew! Then he and his sons fled to the hills (I Macc. 2:1–28).

This overt act lighted the flame of active revolt. Many loyal Jews, with their families and livestock, "went down to the wilderness" to join the rebel movement. The king's officers pursued the fugitives and found them hiding in wilderness caves. On the Sabbath Day the pursuers confronted one group of fugitives and demanded that they surrender. The trapped group refused, and since to fight would be work and the law prohibited work on the Sabbath, they were slain. When Mattathias and his sons heard of this, they decided that during the war the prohibition of work on the Sabbath must be interpreted to permit self-defense (I Macc. 2:29–41).

The king's officers were resisted, not only by Mattathias and his sons and friends, but also by the "Hasideans, mighty warriors of Israel," and by other fugitives. The Hasideans were thus ancestors not only of the Pharisees and Essenes but also, as their militant action showed, of the later Zealot party, which refused to accept the rule of Rome. These Hasideans "organized an army" and attacked "lawless men," including Jews who had given up the practice of their ancestral religion. The group led by Mattathias tore down pagan altars, circumcised uncircumcised Jewish boys (as should have been done on the eighth day; Lev. 12:3), and "hunted down the arrogant men" who were carrying out the king's decree. This was both revolt against the king and civil war among the Jews (I Macc. 2:42–48).

When Mattathias, worn by the rigor of guerrilla warfare, saw death approaching, he gave his sons final instructions. Disregarding their age ranking, he urged them to look to Simon for wise counsel and follow Judas in military action (I Macc. 2:65 f.). For the next few years Judas was the active leader of the revolt. He showed remarkable ability to strike sudden blows that disorganized disciplined armies; by unexpected attacks he defeated forces many times as large as his poorly armed troops.

THE BOOK OF DANIEL

Early in the revolt The Book of Daniel was written by an unnamed Hasidean.[14] Speaking in the name of a proverbial wise man referred to in Ezek. 14:14, 20; 28:3, he wrote an appeal to the persecuted Jews to stand fast in loyalty to the God of their fathers. He knew that only loyal Jews ready for martyrdom could preserve their faith. He wrote to promise that God would soon give victory to his loyal people.

His book has two main parts. The first six chapters give examples of how God can vindicate and defend his people even when the situation seems hopeless. The refusal to eat unclean food (Dan., ch. 1), God's gift of wisdom to interpret the king's dream and explain the course of history (ch. 2), the refusal to worship the king's image (ch. 3), the judgment on the kingdom weighed in the balances and found wanting (chs. 4; 5),

14 On the historical situation reflected in The Book of Daniel, see James A. Montgomery, *The Book of Daniel*, in the *International Critical Commentary* (Charles Scribner's Sons, 1927), pp. 57 ff.; John Bright, *A History of Israel* (The Westminster Press, 1959), pp. 401 ff.

and the protection of Daniel in the lions' den (ch. 6), show that God will honor and defend the faithful who loyally serve him.

The last six chapters of the book (and also ch. 2) present a philosophy of history. History has meaning because God is at work in it; God's people may have confidence, because he certainly will bring his divine plan to completion and vindicate his faithful servants. The successive earthly kingdoms, symbolically presented, will give way to God's perfect and eternal Kingdom in which his loyal people will have eternal security (ch. 2). The historical sketch comes to a climax as it presents God's certain judgment on the "little horn," Antiochus Epiphanes (chs. 7:8; 8:9; 11:21–45). "One like a son of man," that is, a being in human form, will receive the Kingdom (ch. 7:13 f.). This description, used later in the Book of Enoch to describe a specific leader of God's forces, and still later adapted by Jesus as a self-designation, is here explained to mean "the people of the saints of the Most High" (ch. 7:27); "their kingdom shall be an everlasting kingdom," and so it is worth all the suffering that may come before God gives them that eternal privilege. There is repeated assurance that the time of persecution will be short (ch. 12:11); with such immense issues at stake God's people must hold fast, no matter how agonizing the trials they must endure. And if they ask what good it will do to hold fast if they die for their faith, ch. 12 assures them not only that God's people will be delivered but that "those who are wise," the faithful martyrs, will arise "to everlasting life" (ch. 12:2 f.). The blessings of God are for those who endure.

This stirring message must have helped greatly to sustain the spirit of indomitable resistance in the Maccabees and Hasideans. It has had remarkable influence in later times of crisis. It was the first full writing of the type we call "apocalyptic," that is, the type that in time of crisis lays bare in vivid pictorial language the eternal issues at stake and appeals to God's people to stand fast. Used in this sense by Jesus, New Testament writers, and later Christians, the book has shown that it can speak with power to severely tried believers. But it is wrongly used when regarded as an outline of world history down to our own days; the writer's interest focused on the time of Antiochus Epiphanes.

THE FIGHT FOR RELIGIOUS FREEDOM

When Judas assumed active leadership of the revolt against the king, the situation looked almost hopeless. Judas had neither numbers nor arms to risk open battle with a large Syrian army. Fortunately for him he did not have to do so. At first, it appears, the king thought a small force could crush the rebels. But he and his leaders were taught better by the sudden, repeated, and smashing blows struck by Judas. For such tactics, it seems, Judas received the title Maccabeus. It probably means "the hammer" and recalls his sudden striking power, especially in his early days of guerrilla warfare. From Judas the name Maccabee then passed on to other members of his family; they were called the Maccabees. (The family was also referred to as the Hasmoneans, from the name of a family ancestor, according to Josephus.)[15]

I and II Maccabees, our two main sources for this period, differ somewhat in their account of the attempts by Antiochus to crush the revolt led by Judas. It is clear that at first armies of modest size, and then larger and better equipped forces, were sent against the rebels. The Syrian generals Apollonius, Seron, (Nicanor?), Gorgias, and Lysias successively tasted defeat, and the Jewish forces gained supplies and confidence from each succeeding victory (I Macc. 3:10 to 4:35; cf. II Macc. 8:9–36). Yet despite this series of setbacks, Antiochus led an army east to Persia, no doubt to deal with threats in that region, but also to confiscate resources for his costly military program (I Macc. 3:31; II Macc. 9:2).

After Judas defeated Gorgias at Emmaus and Lysias at Beth-zur, Lysias returned to Antioch to raise a larger army and renew the campaign. In this interim, Judas and his brothers led the army to Jerusalem; they rebuilt the Temple, removed the defiled stones of the altar of burnt offering, built a new altar of unhewed stones, and made new vessels for the Temple ministry and sacrificial rites. On the morning of the twenty-fifth of Chislev, three years to the day, we are told, after Antiochus had profaned the Temple and offered pagan sacrifice on the altar, sacrifice was resumed on the new altar (December, 164 B.C.). The Jewish Feast of Hanukkah, or Dedication, celebrated annually thereafter (I Macc. 4:59), is still an important annual festival in Jewish life.[16]

Much of Palestine was not under the control of Judas. He and his brothers next moved to rescue groups of Jews who wanted to remain true to their ancestral faith but found themselves among Gentiles or hostile Jews. Judas, Jonathan, and Simon led forces to Idumea, Gilead, and Galilee to rescue hard-pressed fellow Jews, whom they led back safely to Mt. Zion (I Macc., ch. 5). When, however, Joseph and Azariah, left to guard Jerusalem, rashly undertook to take the city of Jamnia, Gorgias, stationed there with Syrian troops, routed them. To the writer of I Maccabees this was inevitable; only the Maccabean family would God bless

15 Greek *Asamōnaios* (*Ant.* XII.6.1).
16 Cf. John 10:22 f.

with victory (I Macc. 5:62). All this time the citadel in Jerusalem was still in the hands of the king's garrison. Judas held the Temple area and Mt. Zion, but Antiochus held the citadel.

Antiochus Epiphanes met a reverse in Persia, and on his way home fell sick and died. Before his death he directed that his young son Antiochus should become king when old enough. and in the meantime his friend Philip was to rule. But when news of Antiochus' death reached Antioch, his general Lysias, who was in charge of the young son, proclaimed him king with the name Antiochus V Eupator (163–162 B.C.). This left Lysias as the actual ruler. He continued preparations to renew the war with the Jews (I Macc. 6:1–17).

Judas besieged the citadel at Jerusalem, but some of the Syrians there, and some Jews who sided with the king, escaped and went to the king (in effect, to Lysias) and demanded decisive action to crush the army of Judas. In the resulting major expedition Judas was defeated and Eleazar his brother killed. The young king and Lysias went to Jerusalem and there took over Mt. Zion. They besieged the Temple itself, so strongly built that it was a real fortress; its defenders were hard pressed. Beth-zur, which the forces of Judas had captured earlier, had to be given back to the king's army (I Macc. 6:18–50).[17]

At this critical time news reached Lysias that Philip, returned from Persia with the armies of the deceased Antiochus Epiphanes, intended to rule as regent, as the dead ruler had appointed. Lysias had to return to Antioch immediately or lose his position. So he induced the young king and the other commanders to make peace with the Jews and give them freedom to practice their religion as their law prescribed (I Macc. 6:51–63; cf. II Macc., ch. 11). More than once the weakness of the Seleucid rulers and strife between contending aspirants for the Seleucid throne enabled the Maccabees to advance the Jewish cause.

The grant of religious freedom to the Jews marks the end of the first main period in the Maccabean struggle. Threatened with the loss of religious freedom and with the extinction of their faith and worship, the Jews had fought against overwhelming odds and vindicated their right to worship God according to their law. But the Maccabees did not stop there. They considered the religious freedom precarious as long as the Seleucids ruled Palestine, so they enlarged their original aim to include political freedom.

17 On the history and excavation of Beth-zur, see Ovid R. Sellers, *The Citadel of Beth-zur* (Board of Christian Education, Presbyterian Church U.S.A., 1933).

The Fight for Political Freedom

That there was some basis for their view immediately became clear. Shortly after Lysias returned to Antioch and repulsed Philip's attempt to seize the throne, Demetrius, who as son of Seleucus IV had been held in Rome as a hostage, arrived at Tripoli and became the Seleucid king (162–150 B.C.). He did not feel bound by the agreements of Lysias with Judas Maccabeus. Furthermore, Alcimus, whom Demetrius appointed high priest, desired to bring Jewish life into close touch with the Hellenistic life and culture of the empire. He induced the new king to send an expedition, headed by Nicanor, to crush Judas and his forces. Nicanor was soundly defeated (I Macc. 7:1–48; II Macc. 14:1 to 15:35).

To the Maccabeans this victory was of crucial importance; the day of victory, the thirteenth of Adar (about March), was declared an annual day of glad remembrance (I Macc. 7:49), and II Maccabees ends its story with the declaration that from that time the city of Jerusalem "has been in the possession of the Hebrews" (ch. 15:36 f.).

But in fact the picture was not so promising. The Seleucid king was certain to take further military measures to establish effective control of Palestine. Judas and his friends knew this, and sought help from the Romans. They sent an embassy to Rome to establish an alliance of friendship. The Romans, who were extending their influence eastward, were glad to do this (I Macc., ch. 8). They had already taken much of Asia Minor from the Seleucids. They had ordered Antiochus Epiphanes out of Egypt in 168 B.C. When Antiochus Eupator and his general Lysias had granted religious freedom to the Jews, the Romans wrote giving their consent (II Macc. 11:35), implying their right to intervene in Palestinian affairs. But Rome was not yet ready to intervene actively in Palestine; it did not do so until Pompey took over that region in 63 B.C.

The Romans gave Judas no immediate help, and among his own people his position was not strong. When Alcimus was appointed high priest, the Hasideans were ready to accept him and only his cruel slaughter of many of their number changed their mind (I Macc. 7:12–18). This shows that the Maccabeans could no longer be certain of Hasidean help. Probably many Hasideans, formerly staunch allies of Judas, lost interest in the struggle once religious freedom seemed assured by royal decree. The withdrawal of the Qumran sect to their retreat near the western shore of the Dead Sea came at this time or not many years later, in protest at the political aims of the Maccabees.[18] But Judas and his friends evidently held that as long as the Jewish high priest shared in the

[18] For bibliography on Qumran and Dead Sea Scrolls, see note 31 in Chapter 2.

tolerant acceptance of Hellenistic culture, the religious heritage of Judaism was in danger. They wanted political freedom and a high priest ready to break with the Hellenizing aims of the Seleucid rulers.

Alcimus, threatened by Judas and his forces, appealed to the king, who sent Bacchides to give Alcimus military support. The army of Judas melted away. Friends urged Judas to avoid open battle and resume guerrilla warfare, at which he was a genius, until the situation became more favorable. He refused, saying that now as before he had to trust God for victory. He fought bravely against overwhelming odds, but he was killed (160 B.C.) and his army scattered (I Macc. 9:1–18).

As I Maccabees puts it (ch. 9:23–27), "the lawless [mainly Jews ready to compromise their ancestral faith] emerged in all parts of Israel" and Bacchides "put them in charge of the country." Many friends of Judas were searched out and tortured to death. The survivors chose Jonathan to succeed Judas. Bacchides tried to seize Jonathan, who fled to the wilderness and tried to send his camp followers and possessions to the Nabateans for safekeeping, but people from Medeba in Transjordan seized and killed his brother John, who was in charge of the group, and confiscated the possessions. Bacchides, eluded by Jonathan and his warriors, fortified Jerusalem and other important points of Judea. Then the death of Alcimus and the feebleness of Jonathan's group led to a two-year respite from war (I Macc. 9:28–57).

The uneasy peace was broken when the "lawless" Jews appealed for a Syrian army to come and capture Jonathan. Jonathan learned of it, struck back at the "lawless" men, withdrew to the wilderness, and defeated Bacchides at Bethbasi. Bacchides withdrew to Syria; before his departure Jonathan obtained the release of captives, settled at Michmash, and in Old Testament fashion began to "judge the people" (I Macc. 9:58–73).

In the following years the almost constant rivalry of claimants for the Seleucid throne enabled Jonathan and later his brother Simon to play one claimant off against the other and obtain concessions for the Jews.

In 152 B.C., Alexander Balas, son of Antiochus Epiphanes, landed at Ptolemais and "began to reign" over Syria. The Syrian king Demetrius I, to hold Jonathan's loyalty, gave him permission to recruit troops, to become the king's ally, and to receive back the hostages held by the Syrian garrison in the citadel at Jerusalem. Jonathan began to rebuild Jerusalem and its walls; the foreign troops and anti-Maccabee Jews began to abandon strongholds in surrounding Judea, except Beth-zur (I Macc. 10:1–14).

Then Alexander Balas outbid Demetrius; he appointed Jonathan high priest (a position Judas had not held) and made him "the king's friend," a position of special privilege. Jonathan transferred his loyalty to Alexander, refused a counteroffer of still greater gifts from Demetrius, and assumed the high priesthood at the Feast of Tabernacles (152 B.C.; within a year Alexander defeated and killed Demetrius). Later when "pestilent men from Israel, lawless men," charged Jonathan with disloyalty, Alexander "paid no attention." Instead, he clothed Jonathan in purple "and made him general and governor of the province" (I Macc. 10:15–66).

In 145 B.C., Demetrius II, son of Demetrius I, appeared in Syria to take the throne from Alexander Balas. He sent Apollonius to take over Palestine for the new regime, but Jonathan defeated Apollonius near Azotus (I Macc. 10:67–89). Then Ptolemy VI of Egypt (181–145 B.C.), renewing the old struggle with the Seleucids, seized the coastal cities of Palestine and Phoenicia and even captured Antioch in Syria. Alexander Balas returned from quelling a revolt in Cilicia and faced Ptolemy, but was defeated (he fled to Arabia and was killed there). Ptolemy held both Egypt and Syria, but three days later he suddenly died, and Demetrius II ruled Syria. He confirmed Jonathan in the high priesthood and other honors, freed Judea and three districts of Samaria from tribute, and later, at Jonathan's request, promised to withdraw the Syrian troops from the citadel at Jerusalem (but did not do so). The situation seemed stable; Demetrius dismissed most of his army to their homes; he kept only his foreign mercenaries (I Macc. 11:1–53).

This was his mistake. The soldiers and their officers resented being discharged. Trypho, one of the generals, obtained the young son of Alexander Balas and crowned him Antiochus VI (145–142 B.C.); this gave the real power to Trypho. Jonathan was confirmed in his position and honors, and his brother Simon was made governor over the coastal region from the Ladder of Tyre to the borders of Egypt. But soon afterward Jonathan, not Simon, besieged and captured Gaza on the coast, while Simon captured Beth-zur in southern Judea; the two brothers evidently worked together, with Jonathan in charge. Jonathan warded off attempts of Demetrius II to maintain rule over Palestine, renewed the alliance with Rome, and made an alliance of friendship with the Spartans on the pretense that they were both of the family of Abraham (I Macc. 11:39 f.; 11:54 to 12:38).

At this point Trypho dropped the pretense that Antiochus VI was king, and claimed the throne (142 B.C.). He undertook to take over Palestine. When Jonathan met him with a large army, Trypho invited him to a parley at Ptolemais and treacherously took him captive. Simon assumed leadership in place of his brother Jonathan. Trypho demanded as the price of Jonathan's release a hundred talents of silver and two sons of Jonathan's as hostages. Simon did not dare refuse, but Trypho, as suspected, did not release Jonathan. Instead, using Jonathan as a bait, he moved southward, aiming at Jerusalem. Simon kept his army between Trypho and Jerusalem, and finally Trypho, prevented from attacking the city, marched northeast to Gilead and there put Jonathan to death. Once back in Syria he also killed Antiochus VI (I Macc. 12:39 to 13:32).

Demetrius II was still trying to retain the kingship. On Simon's appeal and to hold Simon's loyalty, he wrote to Simon and the Jewish elders granting them all previous privileges and complete release from tribute and taxation (142 B.C.). The Jews regarded this letter as granting them independence; "the yoke of the Gentiles was removed from Israel" (I Macc. 13:41). This year was taken as the first year of a new era, and documents were dated from it. Simon was called "the great high priest and commander and leader of the Jews"; the priestly, military, and political power was united in one man. This had become the fact under Jonathan; it was formally acknowledged under Simon. But Trypho did not concede independence to the Jews, nor did Demetrius really mean to do so, for he kept the citadel in Jerusalem until Simon by siege starved the garrison, regained the citadel, and fortified the city. Demetrius, trying to defend the eastern portion of the empire and obtain resources with which to oppose Trypho, was captured (ca. 138 B.C.) and held prisoner by Arsaces, the Parthian king (I Macc. 13:34 to 14:3).

Palestine enjoyed a brief period of peace. Letters of sympathy came from Rome and Sparta on word of Jonathan's death, and Simon sent a gift to confirm the alliance with Rome. The Jews set up bronze tablets on pillars on Mt. Zion, paying tribute to Simon and his brothers, declaring him "their leader and high priest for ever, until a trustworthy prophet should arise," making him governor, and providing that "he should be clothed in purple and wear gold." They did not give him the formal title of king; he was "high priest" and "commander and ethnarch of the Jews and priests"; but this gave him supreme religious, military, and political authority (I Macc. 14:4–49).

This marked the high point of recognition of the Maccabees. Later rulers of this family had wider territory under their control, but after Simon there is no real religious leadership by the Maccabees. And as the Qumran sect and other indications show, there were always those who thought that the combining of religious, military, and political leadership in one man was wrong.[19] The later record of the Maccabees seems to prove that they were correct.

With Demetrius II taken captive, Trypho seemed to have the throne,

[19] On the views of the Qumran sect, cf. "The Two Messiahs of Aaron and Israel," by Karl Georg Kuhn, in *The Scrolls and the New Testament*, edited by Krister Stendahl (Harper & Brothers, 1957), pp. 54 ff.; Matthew Black, *The Scrolls and Christian Origins* (Charles Scribner's Sons, 1961), pp. 145 ff. See also note 31 in Chapter 2.

but the brother of Demetrius expelled Trypho from Syria and became Antiochus VII (138–129 B.C.). He promised Simon all former privileges and some new ones to get his support, but after the Romans by letter warned Antiochus not to trouble the Jews (they sent similar letters to other kings and to many cities of the Eastern Mediterranean region), he rejected Simon's offer of military help and charged him with unlawfully holding cities that belonged to the king. Cendebeus was sent to subdue the Jews, but John Hyrcanus, son of Simon, dealt him a severe defeat (I Macc. 15:1 to 16:10).

Just when the position of Simon seemed secure, disaster struck. Ptolemy, the son of Abubus, governor over the plain of Jericho and Simon's trusted son-in-law, determined to kill Simon and his sons and take over their authority. At Dok, near Jericho, he received Simon and two sons as guests, got them drunk, and had them killed. Simon's other son, John Hyrcanus, governor of Gazara, west of Jerusalem, learned of the murders, seized the men Ptolemy sent to kill him, and took control of Jerusalem before Ptolemy could do so. He was accepted by the people as their high priest and leader (I Macc. 16:11–22).[20]

TERRITORIAL EXPANSION

The political freedom claimed under Simon soon proved precarious. Hyrcanus assumed leadership (134–104 B.C.), but Antiochus VII Sidetes (138–129 B.C.) promptly besieged him in Jerusalem, and forced him to ask for terms. Antiochus was generous, but the Jews had to give up their arms and the cities outside of Judea that Simon had held, pay taxes and tribute, and give hostages. Hyrcanus, in other words, was subject to the Syrian king, and so continued until 129 B.C. In that year the king, who had forced Hyrcanus to march with him against the Parthians, was killed in battle, and Demetrius II, long a captive in Parthian hands, again ruled Syria (129–125 B.C.). Because the Seleucid kingdom was unstable, however, Hyrcanus could assert his independence and expand his rule. He took Medeba east of Jordan, Scythopolis in the Plain of Jezreel, Sichem (Shechem) and Gerizim in Samaria, and Idumea south of Judea. He destroyed the Samaritan temple on Mt. Gerizim (it was never rebuilt), and by military force converted the Idumeans to Judaism.[21]

20 At this point I Maccabees ends, and Josephus becomes our only narrative guide to the Jewish history that follows. His sources probably included the writings of Strabo and Nicolaus of Damascus, but we are not sure what other sources were available to him. His account of the later Maccabean period is much fuller in the *Antiquities*, written ca. A.D. 95, than in *The Jewish War*, written a few years after A.D. 70, the year Jerusalem fell.

21 On Hyrcanus, see *War* I.2.5–7; *Ant*. XIII.8–10.

By the time of Hyrcanus the two main Jewish sects had clearly emerged.[22] They had not yet taken definite form when the Maccabean revolt began. At that earlier time, it seems, the Hasideans included those Jews banded together to observe and defend the Mosaic law in the face of the disintegrating forces of Hellenistic assimilation. Though they were most like the later Pharisees, their group was not called by that name. When religious freedom was won by the Maccabees and Hasideans, its preservation had at least two aspects. One was faithful observance of the sacrifices and other Temple rites; with this activity the priests especially were concerned. The other was constant attention to observe the law in regular worship and daily life; this called for careful study and teaching of the law and its application to the varied conditions of life. Around the Temple and its worship the Sadducee group developed, always under temptation to worldliness due to inevitable contacts with the political authorities. Loyalty to regular observance of the law stimulated the development of the synagogue and the rise of the Pharisees.

It is ironical that when the later Maccabeans, whose ancestors had fought the worldly and Hellenistic tendencies in the Seleucid-appointed high priesthood, tried to combine religious, military, and political power, and maintain contacts with neighboring (Hellenistic) rulers, they succumbed to those same tendencies. So the Pharisees, emerging as a definite party to oppose this liberal and secularizing tendency, looked with disfavor on a high priest involved in political and military life. Did they note the loss of the religious devotion that had moved Mattathias and Judas? Though Josephus says that no Maccabean assumed the title of king until Aristobulus I did in 104 B.C., Hyrcanus may have done so, and thus aggravated the Pharisee distaste for his political activities. Josephus says of Hyrcanus that he had been "accounted by God worthy of three of the greatest privileges: the rule of the nation, the office of high priest, and the gift of prophecy" (*Ant.* XIII.10.7). But he admits that the Pharisees asked Hyrcanus, who obviously would not give up the political rule, to give up the high priesthood. Instead, Hyrcanus joined the Saducean party and canceled the regulations the Pharisees had established for Jewish life.

When Hyrcanus died, his son Aristobulus I became high priest (104 B.C.). Hyrcanus had intended his widow to be the ruler of the Jews, but Aristobulus imprisoned her and starved her to death, killed his brother Antigonus, and took the title of king.[23] He extended the borders of his kingdom to include Galilee.

---

[22] Hyrcanus at first followed the Pharisees but later turned to the Sadducees, according to *Ant.* XIII.10.5–6.

[23] On the reign of Aristobulus I, see *War* I.3; *Ant.* XIII.11. His Hellenistic leaning is

On his death his widow Salome Alexandra released his surviving brothers, appointed one of them, Alexander Janneus, as king and high priest (103–76 B.C.), and married him. Under his rule the Maccabean kingdom reached its greatest extent. By conquest he took over most of Transjordan and the coastal region of Palestine as far south as Raphia as well as the great central area from Galilee south through Samaria and Judea to Idumea. Rivalries of competing candidates for the Seleucid throne gave room for such successful expansion. But by carelessness in high-priestly duties Alexander alienated great numbers of Jews. Once when he was officiating as high priest at the Feast of Tabernacles, the Jews in attendance pelted him with the citrons that they held on such an occasion; this indicates indignation at his lack of concern for the priestly duties. He retaliated by killing six thousand Jews, according to Josephus (*Ant.* XIII.13.5). Late in his reign he was forced to see a Seleucid king, Antiochus XII Dionysus, fight on Jewish soil with the Nabatean Aretas (ca. 85 B.C.). Aretas defeated Antiochus; he then defeated Alexander at Adida, but came to terms with him and withdrew from Judea.

Before his death Alexander, who had fought the Pharisees, advised his wife, whom he designated to succeed him on the throne, to make peace with them and follow their wishes in religious and governmental matters.[24]

After his death his widow Alexandra reigned as queen (76–67 B.C.). Since a woman could not serve as high priest, she appointed her son Hyrcanus II to that post. He was of quiet disposition, but his brother, Aristobulus II, had a restless lust for power and resented his mother's rule. She followed Alexander's advice and "permitted the Pharisees to do as they liked in all matters. . . . And so, while she had the title of sovereign, the Pharisees had the power," which they exercised like "absolute rulers" (*Ant.* XIII.16.2). Aristobulus II denounced his mother and defended those harassed by the Pharisees. She did not withdraw the power from them; her one concession was to give their opponents control of certain fortresses so that they could escape from the Pharisees when threatened.

The administrative role that Alexandra gave to the Pharisees shows that by this time—how much earlier is hard to say—the Pharisees had won an important place in the Sanhedrin (called in Greek *Gerousia*). The Sanhedrin, originally an aristocratic body and essentially in control of the Sadducees, had been forced to receive Pharisees into their council

---

shown by the fact that he was titled Philhellene. This was the trend among the later Hasmonean rulers.

24 On Alexander Janneus, see *War* I.4; *Ant.* XIII.12–15.

in such numbers that with the queen's backing they could make public policy and control civil and criminal administration.[25]

When the queen was on her deathbed, Aristobulus began to assert power. He seized numerous fortresses in Judea, and though the Pharisees appealed to her to oppose him, she had no strength left to organize resistance. At her death Hyrcanus II, the lawful successor to the throne, assumed power (67 B.C.), but Aristobulus defeated him in battle and became king and high priest. Hyrcanus retired to private life.[26]

Rome Takes Over Palestine

At this point, Antipater, an Idumean, became a key figure. He was already governor of Idumea. (His father, Antipas or Antipater, had previously held this position by appointment of Alexander Janneus.) He distrusted Aristobulus, was the friend of Hyrcanus, and wanted more power for himself. By continual persuasion he induced Hyrcanus to try to regain his position. To this end he enlisted the help of Aretas III, the Nabatean ruler at Petra, who was promised twelve cities the Jews had taken from him. Antipater and Hyrcanus fled to Petra, and returned with Aretas and his army. Aristobulus was defeated in battle and besieged in Jerusalem.

At this time Pompey was pushing Rome's boundaries eastward. He had subjugated Mithridates in Pontus and Tigranes in Armenia, and moved into Syrian Antioch. His general Scaurus came to Damascus, learned of the fighting in Judea, and went to take advantage of the situation. Both Aristobulus and Hyrcanus promised four hundred talents for his support; Aristobulus, it was said, also offered the Roman Gabinius three hundred talents. Scaurus sided with Aristobulus, who held Jerusalem, was king and high priest, and more likely could pay the promised money; he commanded Hyrcanus to withdraw from the siege. When Hyrcanus did, Aristobulus pursued and defeated him and Antipater.

This did not settle the dispute. When Pompey reached Damascus in 63 B.C., he summoned both brothers and promised to come to Jerusalem and settle the issue after punishing the Nabateans. Aristobulus prepared to resist, so Pompey went at once to Jerusalem, besieged it three months, and took it. Though he entered the Holy Place of the Temple, he disturbed nothing and permitted resumption of the sacrifices. But he required payment of annual tribute to Rome and took from the Jews

[25] Cf. George Foot Moore, *Judaism in the First Centuries of the Christian Era: The Age of the Tannaim*, Vol. I (Harvard University Press, 1927), pp. 260 f.
[26] On Alexandra and the succession, see *War* I.5.1 to I.6.1; *Ant.* XIII.16 to XIV.1.2.

the Hellenistic cities of Transjordan, Samaria, and the coastal plain. However, he left Galilee, Judea, Idumea, and Perea under Jewish government, and Hyrcanus, though he could not call himself king, was both ethnarch and high priest. Antipater actually exercised the political power; Rome depended on him for stable administration. To ensure peace Pompey took the fiery Aristobulus and his sons to Rome; the elder son, Alexander, escaped en route, an event prophetic of the further trouble this family was to cause.[27]

About this time or soon after was formed the Decapolis,[28] that is, the ten-city league of Hellenistic cities; it was still known in Jesus' day (Mark 5:20; 7:31). Except for Scythopolis, they were located east of the Jordan. This league was formed to ward off Arab attacks from the east, to further Hellenistic city life in the area, and to provide centers of resistance to Jewish influence.

In the Roman view, Palestine was part of Syria, so the ethnarchy of Hyrcanus became part of the new Roman province of Syria. When Scaurus, its governor, on an expedition against the Nabateans, needed supplies, Antipater sent them to him (in the name of Hyrcanus), and thus began a series of helpful acts that won him Roman favor.

In 57 B.C., Gabinius became proconsul of Syria. Alexander, son of Aristobulus II, tried to conquer Judea, but was soundly beaten, forced to surrender, and then set free (to revolt again, as it later proved). Gabinius, to check this renewed disturbance in Judea, reorganized the administration of the region, leaving Hyrcanus as high priest, but dividing Palestine into five districts. Then Aristobulus II escaped from Rome and with his son Antigonus went to Judea to try to regain his kingdom. He was defeated, captured, and again taken to Rome as a prisoner. In 55 B.C., while Gabinius was in Egypt to help Ptolemy XI regain his throne, Alexander again raised an army and revolted against Rome. Gabinius again defeated him, but still did not execute or imprison him. Clearly, Gabinius considered Antipater the real governor of Judea; the Maccabean royal line had become a chronic evil, to be endured but not treated too harshly for fear of offending Jewish feelings. During all this time, of course, tribute was being exacted.

When Gabinius was recalled (54 B.C.), Crassus, proconsul of Syria, took over the governing of Judea. He plundered the Temple treasury

---

27 On Antipater's rise to power and the taking over of Palestine by Pompey, see *War* I.6.2 to 7.7; *Ant.* XIV.1.3 to 4.5.

28 On the Decapolis, see George Adam Smith, *A Historical Geography of the Holy Land*, 18th ed. (Hodder and Stoughton, n.d.), pp. 593–608; F.–M. Abel, *Géographie de la Palestine*, 2d ed. (Paris, J. Gabalda et Cie, 1938), Vol. II, pp. 145 f. The league later included more than ten cities.

of two thousand talents. When Cassius succeeded him, Pitholaus, a former supporter of Aristobulus, led a revolt and was captured. Cassius, on Antipater's advice, put him to death.[29]

In 49 B.C. civil war broke out between Pompey and Julius Caesar. Pompey, defeated, fled to Macedonia, and Caesar began to figure in Palestinian history. He released Aristobulus II and gave him troops to take to Syria to oppose Pompey. Supporters of Pompey in Rome, however, poisoned Aristobulus and got his son Alexander executed. The defeat and death of Pompey (48 B.C.) brought crisis to Antipater and Hyrcanus, who had been Pompey's friends. But when Caesar, in Egypt to war with Ptolemy XII, ran into trouble, Antipater sent troops to help Caesar and induced Jews in Egypt to support him. This won Caesar's friendship; Antipater was continued as procurator of Judea, made a Roman citizen, and released from obligation to pay taxes to Rome; Hyrcanus was continued as high priest and made ethnarch of the Jews for life. Full religious freedom was assured, rebuilding of the walls of Jerusalem was permitted, and a series of letters to other Roman regions stated clearly the right of the Jews to practice their religion. The Jews throughout the Roman world were regarded as under the government of their ethnarch Hyrcanus. In fact, however, Antipater was in control of Palestine and formulated policy for Hyrcanus.

But things were not harmonious in Palestine. Though Rome gave privileges to Jews in Palestine and elsewhere, it was to most Jews a hated foreign conqueror. And they resented being ruled by Antipater, an Idumean. Moreover, Antipater gave his sons authority. He appointed Phasael governor of Jerusalem and Herod governor of Galilee. Brigands, lawless plunderers who were hostile to Idumean government, were active in Galilee, and Herod with courage and skill destroyed them. He captured and executed Hezekiah, a ringleader, but the Jewish authorities in Jerusalem summoned him for trial for inflicting the death penalty, which only the Sanhedrin could impose. Herod came, but when Hyrcanus seemed ready to hand him over to the Sanhedrin, he fled and appealed to the Roman Sextus Caesar at Damascus, who appointed him governor of Coelesyria—a position not clear in scope, but obviously giving him Roman support against the Sanhedrin. Herod returned to Judea to take vengeance on his accusers, but his father and brother dissuaded him; he bided his time.[30]

The political scene then became chaotic. Caesar was assassinated (44

---

29 The dealings of Scaurus, Gabinius, Crassus, and Cassius with Palestine and the Hasmoneans are told in *War* I.8; *Ant.* XIV.5.1 to 7.3.

30 On the relations of Julius Caesar with Palestine through Antipater and his sons, see *War* I.9.1 to 10.10; *Ant.* XIV.7.4 to 9.5. The letters of Caesar and the decrees of various cities protecting the Jews are given in *Ant.* XIV.10.

B.C.). Cassius assumed the proconsulship of Syria; needing money, he demanded seven hundred talents from Judea. Antipater had to raise the money; he appointed Phasael and Herod, and a certain Malichus, to do the distasteful work. The latter, ambitious to displace Antipater, had him poisoned; Herod then had Malichus stabbed to death. In 42 B.C., at Philippi, Cassius and Brutus met Octavian and Mark Antony in a battle for Roman rule, and were defeated. Hyrcanus, Phasael, and Herod were now suspect, since by necessity they had supported Cassius. Antigonus, son of Aristobulus II, tried to gain control of Judea, but Herod's vigorous resistance repulsed him. About this time Herod, already married, made plans to marry Mariamne, daughter of Alexander, the son of Aristobulus II; this would link him with the royal Hasmonean line.

Antony took control of the eastern part of the Roman world. To him went the rivals for the religious and political leadership of Palestine. The Sadducees and others wanted the Idumean governors expelled; Herod wanted the political leadership, leaving Hyrcanus as high priest; Antigonus wanted full rule. Antony made Herod and Phasael tetrarchs, and continued Hyrcanus as high priest.

But Antony was too harassed by supporters of Cassius to enforce his decisions. His demands for money increased Jewish hostility. His infatuation for Cleopatra of Egypt kept him from prompt action. And the Parthians were eager to push westward into Syria and Palestine. By promising them a thousand talents and five hundred women Antigonus won their help, and took Jerusalem. He captured Phasael, who committed suicide, and Hyrcanus, whose ear he bit off to make him ineligible to act as high priest (Hyrcanus was then carried captive to Parthia). He himself became high priest and took the title of king.

His apparent triumph led to his downfall. The Parthians could not maintain control of Palestine, and the inevitable Roman recovery of the land would oust Antigonus. For the moment, however, Herod's position seemed hopeless. Only by a courageous rearguard action did he hold off the Parthians and partisans of Antigonus and get his family safely to Masada, a fortress on the western side of the Dead sea.[31] When Malchus, king of the Nabateans, refused to help him, he went to Alexandria and thence on stormy, wintry seas to Rome. There he appealed to Antony and Octavian, rulers of the Romans; on their recommendation the Roman senate voted (40 B.C.) to make Herod king of the land Antigonus held. He was a vassal king, under Rome.

Not until 37 B.C. did Herod win full control of his kingdom. The

---

[31] For the main facts on Masada, see *The Interpreter's Dictionary of the Bible* (cited hereafter as *IDB*), edited by George A. Buttrick, 4 vols. (Abingdon Press, 1962), K–Q, pp. 293 f.

Roman general Ventidius, sent to expel the Parthians, did nothing because he had been bribed by Antigonus. Herod, landing at Ptolemais, gathered a fighting force and began to subdue the land. Ventidius then became active and defeated the Parthians. Herod took troops to Syria and helped Antony take Samosata; then Antony made Sosius governor of Syria and instructed him to help Herod. Sosius at once sent two legions to Judea. Thus reinforced, Herod defeated Antigonus at Jericho, and besieged him in Jerusalem. After Herod had left the siege long enough to go to Samaria and marry Mariamne, he returned and, with help from Sosius, who had now arrived with the rest of his army, captured Jerusalem and executed Antigonus, the last ruler of the Hasmonean family.[32]

HEROD THE GREAT

Herod had proved himself a leader of courage and energy, with personal qualities that could lead to greatness. He was unfailingly loyal to Rome, and at times showed genuine concern for his subjects. When Jerusalem was taken, he protected the Temple to conciliate the Jews; out of his own funds he paid the soldiers not to plunder it (*Ant.* XIV.16.3). When a famine caused great suffering, he took heroic measures to give relief and preserve life (*Ant.* XV.9.1–2). He made attempts to win the loyalty and support of the Jewish religious leaders.

Yet other factors kept him from attaining real greatness. One was the strong and stubborn hatred the Jews had for him. He was not a Jew but an Idumean, and so was not acceptable. This was not merely a racial issue, for as shown by Herod's later building of pagan temples with money raised by taxing Jews (*War* I.21.11; *Ant.* XV.8.5), he did not share the Jewish faith and was ready to further polytheistic worship. In addition, his reign represented the control of Rome, and in Jewish eyes the Romans had no right to hold God's people in subjection. Another reason for Jewish opposition was his cruelty; he killed forty-five leading Jews for resisting his occupation of Jerusalem. He confiscated the wealth of certain Jews and laid heavy taxation upon his subjects. He did try to improve relations with the Jews by bringing Hyrcanus II back from Parthia and by marrying Mariamne of the Hasmonean family, but these acts did not overcome the hostility. His marriages to both Jewish and Gentile women so complicated his home life as to cast doubt on his good sense and make one wonder how he retained any sanity.

32 On the death of Caesar and Antipater, the rise of Antony and Octavian to power, the Parthian invasion of Palestine, and Herod's coming to the throne there, see *War* I.11.1 to 18.3; *Ant.* XIV.11.1 to 16.4. This ended Hasmonean rule in Palestine.

He had ten wives, and they, with his sister Salome, his brother Pheroras, and other relatives, filled his palace with slander, intrigue, and plots.[33] This inevitably produced emotional disturbance and weakened administrative ability. Each wife was jealous for the rights of herself and her children, and the entire group was divided into two main factions, Idumean and Jewish. Within the Jewish faction those of Hasmonean descent asserted their rights with special arrogance. Everyone seemed to accuse the others of plotting for self-advancement and against Herod. Some charges were slanders, but many were true. The total story told by Josephus is confusing; one is never sure who if anyone was innocent of criminal plotting against Herod. In the entire "harem" there was no one who protected Herod and served his welfare with unselfish motive and religious dedication to the God of Israel. There was much rivalry for the high priesthood, but no hint that it was regarded as a religious ministry; it was a political plum, sought by sordid ambition and scheming.

When Herod gained control of his puppet kingdom, his personal loyalty was to Antony, who ruled the eastern part of the Roman Empire while Octavian ruled the western portion. In one early action Herod defeated the Nabateans. But Herod's real threat was from Cleopatra, the seductive queen of Egypt with whom Antony was infatuated. Cleopatra wanted Palestine and all other territory that had once belonged to the Ptolemaic empire. Antony needed Herod's ability in Palestine, and resisted her full demand, but he gave her with other land most of the coastal cities of Palestine and Phoenicia (not Tyre and Sidon), and also the famous balsam groves near Jericho. Herod had to lease them from her at a stiff annual rental (cf. *Ant.* XV.4.2).

All of this changed in 31 B.C. when Antony and Octavian clashed at Actium in a decisive battle for the sole rule of the Roman Empire. Herod of necessity supported Antony, but took no part in the battle because Antony needed him in Palestine to keep out the Parthians and Nabateans. The defeat of Antony and Cleopatra placed Herod in an embarrassing position. But he convinced Octavian, known henceforth as Augustus (31 B.C. to A.D. 14), that he was loyal to the Romans and could be trusted to support the new ruler. His word was good; Augustus never had reason to doubt his loyalty.

In recognition of Herod's loyalty and ability Augustus gave him the parts of Palestine that Cleopatra had held, and also other cities: Gadara, Hippos, Samaria, Gaza, Anthedon, Joppa, and Strato's Tower, which last city Herod later rebuilt and renamed Caesarea. (These and other

[33] See the genealogical chart of the Herodian family in the back of this book.

coastal cities were mainly Hellenistic cities and not part of what in
Maccabean days was called Judea. They could be entrusted to Herod,
who was actively favorable to Hellenistic culture and tolerant of pagan
religions.) Later, about 23 B.C., Augustus added to Herod's kingdom
regions east and northeast of the Sea of Galilee: Trachonitis, Batanea,
and Auranitis. About 20 B.C. Herod received territory located between
Galilee and (northern) Trachonitis. A puzzling reference in Josephus
says that Augustus made Herod "procurator of all Syria" (*War* I.20.4).
Roman procurators governed Syria; Josephus understands Herod's position to give him supervisory power over them—which seems doubtful.

JEWISH SECTS

During Herod's reign the four Jewish sects commonly noted in New
Testament study come clearly into view.[34] Since the Sadducees had the
official leadership of Jewish Temple worship, Herod inevitably had
dealings with them. As high priest he appointed, not one of the Hasmonean line, but Hananel, a priest from Babylonia—a hint of the
strength of Jewry in that eastern area. That strength had roots in the
sixth-century B.C. exile of Judah, and continued into Rabbinic times,
when the Babylonian Talmud was completed and became the classic
formulation of Rabbinical Judaism. Alexandra, mother of Mariamne I,
got Herod to depose Hananel and appoint as high priest the Hasmonean
Aristobulus, whom Herod later found unworthy and put to death (*Ant.*
XV.2.7 to XV.3.3). Like the Seleucids, Herod regarded the high priest
as his political appointee. Toward the middle of his reign he deposed
the high priest Jesus[35] and appointed Simon, whose daughter Herod
wished to marry (*Ant.* XV.9.3).

With the Pharisees, Herod had no real rapport. He could not understand their aloofness and their ardent determination to live by the
Mosaic law and its oral interpretation. He tried to conciliate them, but
never succeeded. At the start of his reign he did receive support from
at least two Pharisees, Pollio and Sameas (*Ant.* XV.1.1), but Josephus tells
how later the Pharisees, "greatly opposing kings," would not swear loyalty
to Caesar but came to "open fighting" and predicted the overthrow of
Herod's government (*Ant.* XVII.2.4); Herod fined them for refusing to
swear allegiance to him and the emperor.

---

[34] These sects are described in more detail in Chapter 2.
[35] The Greek word "Jesus" (*Iēsous*) translates the Hebrew word "Joshua." It was a
frequent name among Jews of Herod's day. Josephus mentions some twenty men
named Jesus.

For some reason Herod honored the Essenes and did not make them swear allegiance as he expected the Pharisees and other Jews to do. Perhaps the fact that the Essenes were not so active in Jerusalem made Herod more lenient with them.

Whether the Zealots, extremist patriots active in the Jewish revolt of A.D. 66–70, were already a definite group in Herod's day is doubted. Certainly the view that God's people should not be ruled by a pagan nation but should resist the foreign power was already present and on occasion was expressed even by the Pharisees. But the Pharisees usually were more quietist, and it was mainly other Jews who as a religious duty refused allegiance to foreign rule. Herod did not attempt to regulate the religious rites or community life of Judaism; as long as his rule was accepted and taxes paid, he let the high priests control most aspects of Jewish life.

HEROD'S BUILDING PROJECTS

The building activity of Herod is noteworthy. It extended beyond Palestine to Ptolemais, Sidon, Tyre, Berytus, Tripolis, Syrian Antioch, Rhodes, Athens, and other places, and it included gymnasiums, temples, marketplaces, aqueducts, baths, fountains, colonnades, and pavements. He endowed the Olympic games in Greece. His building activity in Palestine was even greater. In Samaria he built the city of Sebaste; on the hilltop was a massive temple dedicated to Caesar Augustus. At Paneas, at the foot of Mt. Hermon, he built a temple of white marble. At Jericho he built new grounds and buildings for his palace there; ruins recently excavated probably go back in part at least to his time. Among his most spectacular projects was the rebuilding of Strato's Tower on the Palestinian coast. He renamed it Caesarea after the emperor.[36] Since the coast of Palestine offered no good harbor, he created one by running moles out into the Mediterranean in a large semicircle, with an entrance for ships on the north side. Underwater exploration has recently followed the course of this sea wall and thrown fresh light on what Josephus tells of it. In Caesarea itself he built a large temple to Rome and Augustus, and in addition an amphitheater, theater, and other public structures. At various sites he built strong fortresses, in some cases including a palace. This remarkable building program he carried out at great expense to his heavily taxed subjects.

36 On recent exploration at Caesarea, see Charles T. Fritsch and Immanuel ben-Dor, "The Link Expedition to Israel, 1960," in *The Biblical Archaeologist*, XXIV (1961), pp. 50 ff.

From the point of view of Judaism and New Testament study, his greatest project was the rebuilding of the Temple at Jerusalem.[37] Begun about 20–19 B.C. and carried out by specially trained priests so as not to profane the sacred area, the main Temple building, housing the Holy Place and the Most Holy Place, was completed in eighteen months. Herod continued work on the other structures of the Temple area, but they were completed only about A.D. 64, shortly before the complete destruction of all the Temple buildings. At the northwest corner of the Temple area Herod built the fortress and tower named Antonia, and on the west hill, the "upper city," he built a palace.

HEROD'S LAST DAYS

The wives and sons of Herod seem to have been interested mainly in who would succeed to his throne. Early in his reign he chose Antipater, son of Doris, to be his heir. The chief plotters against Antipater were Alexander and Aristobulus, whom Antipater diligently slandered or justly condemned; they were insolently determined to avenge the death of their mother, Mariamne I (Herod had put Mariamne and her mother, Alexandra, to death for plotting against him). After Herod had wished to condemn the two brothers but was reconciled to them by Augustus, he planned that Antipater, Alexander, and Aristobulus should succeed him as "three kings." Later, on renewed evidence of plotting, he had the two brothers tried before Varus, the Roman governor of Syria, and put to death. Antipater, too, was finally executed for plotting, and Antipas, son of Malthace the Samaritan, was to succeed Herod. But later Herod changed his will; he named Archelaus, another son of Malthace, to be king of Judea, Samaria, and Idumea; Antipas was to be tetrarch of Galilee and Perea; Philip, son of Cleopatra of Jerusalem, was to rule the districts east and northeast of the Sea of Galilee; his sister Salome, veteran master of palace plot and intrigue, was to rule the cities of Jamnia, Ashdod, and Phasaelis.

In his last years Herod fell sick of an incurable disease. Neither doctors nor health resorts, such as Callirhoe on the east side of the Dead Sea, did him any good. He was deprived of his last grim joke; as death neared, he had all the chief Jews gathered in the hippodrome at Jericho; when he died, they were to be killed; this, he thought, would ensure universal mourning at the time of his death. But his sister Salome and her husband Alexas had them released before his death was announced.

[37] For compact discussion and good bibliography, see W. F. Stinespring, "Temple, Jerusalem," *IDB*, R–Z, pp. 550–560.

He was buried at Herodium, four miles southeast of Bethlehem; it was a huge artificial mound of earth on which he had built a palace.

It is difficult to assess Herod's achievement. He served Rome well and kept the political life of Palestine and its neighbors fairly stable; he protected Palestine from invasion and confusion. He preserved order almost everywhere except in his polygamous palace. He was imperious and could be cruel; whether or not he massacred the little children at Bethlehem (Matt. 2:16), he had the temperament to do so. He generally respected the religious freedom of the Jews, but he was an outsider to their worship and faith, and there is no clear light on his own religious faith. His willingness to build pagan temples as well as the Jewish Temple suggests that he had no specific religious motivation. He set the political stage for the coming of Jesus, but the real preparation for that coming he never understood.[38]

HEROD'S SONS AND ROMAN GOVERNORS

Herod could make a will, but as his son Archelaus told the crowd when he announced Herod's death, the final word rested with the emperor Augustus. So Archelaus said he would go to Rome to ask Augustus to approve the will and confirm him as king. The crowd urged immediate tax relief and release of Jewish political prisoners. He agreed. They returned to demand that he remove the incumbent high priest, appointed by Herod, and punish Herod's friends to atone for the Jews whom Herod had executed for tearing down the golden eagle on the gate of the Temple. Archelaus, unable to quiet the people, finally quelled the riot with force; three thousand were killed. Then, leaving his half brother Philip in charge, he left for Rome.

On the way he met Sabinus, the Roman financial officer of Syria. Sabinus had heard of Herod's death and was coming to take over Herod's personal possessions and fortresses, ostensibly to hold them until the succession was determined, but perhaps also to seize part of the wealth for himself. Archelaus appealed to Varus, Roman governor of Syria, who also had come to Palestine, and he forbade Sabinus to carry out his plan; but when Varus returned to Antioch, Sabinus seized Herod's palace in Jerusalem and robbed the Temple treasury. A period of turbulent unrest followed.

[38] The long and important reign of Herod the Great receives detailed attention from Josephus in *War* I.18.4 to 33.9; *Ant.* XV.1.1 to XVII.8.1. Rebuilding of the Temple: *Ant.* XV.11. See further on Herod, A. Momigliano, "Herod of Judea," *The Cambridge Ancient History*, Vol. X (Cambridge, University Press, 1934), Ch. 11; also Stewart Perowne, *The Life and Times of Herod the Great* (Abingdon Press, n.d.).

2*

It was not only Archelaus who went to Rome. Leading Jews went to ask Augustus to deny the Herodian family any rule in Palestine and appoint instead a Roman governor. But not all Jews wanted Roman rule. At least three Jews stirred up rebel movements at this time: Judas in Galilee, Simon at Jericho, and Athronges, a shepherd who set himself up as king; there were also "other disorders" and "Judea was full of robberies" (*War* II.4; *Ant.* XVII.10.4–8). Varus returned and restored some order; he crucified two thousand captured rebels. Josephus treats these as political disturbances. They were in part expressions of religious zeal, probably aroused by eschatological expectation that God was about to act to deliver his people.

Herod Antipas also followed Archelaus to Rome. Herod the Great had at one time designated Antipas as his successor, and Antipas argued that he should succeed his father as king. Philip, who also had come to Rome, supported Archelaus and defended his own right to rule the region assigned him in his father's will. Augustus heard all parties. He decided that Archelaus should govern Judea, Samaria, and Idumea, but not as king until he had proved his ability; for the time being he was ethnarch of the Jews. Herod Antipas was to be tetrarch of Galilee and Perea. Philip was to be tetrarch of the region east and northeast of the Sea of Galilee. Salome, also present, was given Jamnia, Azotus, and Phasaelis as Herod had willed; the emperor added the palace of Ascalon.[39]

The least important of the three main assignments fell to Philip. His territory was the least Jewish and most sparsely populated. He proved loyal to Rome, and although his administration until his death in A.D. 34 was uneventful, it was wise, conscientious, and efficient. His chief known achievement was in building projects, always a favorite activity of the Herods. He rebuilt Paneas, at the foot of Mt. Hermon, and named it Caesarea; since so many cities had that name, it was known as Caesarea Philippi, Philip's Caesarea (cf. Mark 8:27). He also rebuilt Bethsaida, on the north shore of the Sea of Galilee, and made it a city named Julias (called Bethsaida in the gospel story).[40]

Herod Antipas also was long in office. He kept order in turbulent Galilee; this indicates real ability. He too undertook building projects, particularly the building of the city Tiberias, on the west shore of the Sea of Galilee; he named it after the emperor Tiberius (A.D. 14–37). But he ran into difficulty, as had his father, by his marriages. He was married

---

[39] On Herod's will and the unrest in Palestine and the decision of Augustus, see *War* II.1–6; *Ant.* XVII.8–11.

[40] Cf. *War* II.9.1; *Ant.* XVIII.2.1; 4.6.

to the daughter of Aretas, the Nabatean king, but fell in love with Herodias, the wife of his half brother Herod of Rome (also called Philip or Herod Philip, as has been claimed; or do Mark 6:17 and Matt. 14:3 confuse this Herod with Philip the tetrarch?). Herodias agreed to marry Herod Antipas provided he divorce the daughter of Aretas. He did so, and Herodias divorced her husband (contrary to Jewish law, under which only the husband could divorce) and married Herod Antipas. This outraged not only the Jews, to whom the action of both Herod and Herodias was abhorrent, but also Aretas. Later a border dispute arose between Antipas and Aretas, and Aretas severely defeated Antipas. The Jews, Josephus says, considered this a divine retribution for Antipas' wickedness in executing John the Baptist.

Antipas appealed to Rome for help against Aretas, who was not under Roman rule and so in attacking Antipas was threatening Roman territory. Vitellius, the legate of Syria, was sent to help Antipas, but the death of Tiberius (A.D. 37) stopped the expedition. In A.D. 39 Herodias, jealous of honors shown to others, induced Antipas to go to Rome and ask for the title of king. But Agrippa, son of Aristobulus and grandson of Herod the Great, and others accused Antipas of plotting revolt, and Caligula, the new emperor of Rome (A.D. 37–41), deposed Antipas and banished him to Gaul (A.D. 39). His wife Herodias was not banished, but she went into exile with him.[41]

Archelaus, of course, had the most difficult task, for he faced the problems of "church and state" at Jerusalem. He lacked the ability and tact to make himself acceptable to the Jews. He shocked them by divorcing his wife Mariamne and marrying Glaphyra, the widow of his brother Alexander, by whom she had had three children. (Josephus notes that the Jewish law forbade such a marriage; cf. Lev. 18:16; 20:21.) He further offended the Jews by removing the high priest Joazar from office on charge of aiding the opposition to his rule. He continued Herod's practice of keeping the high priest's robes when not in actual use; this was a resented sign of political control of the priesthood.

The accumulation of his "barbarous and tyrannical" actions led to renewed complaints, and in A.D. 6 the emperor deposed him and banished him to Gaul. From that date until A.D. 41 Judea, Samaria, and Idumea were under a Roman procurator. This area, however, was not a separate province; it was loosely attached to Syria, whose legate could act in crisis without prior instruction from Rome.[42]

The first Roman procurator was Coponius (A.D. 6–9). At the beginning

[41] Cf. War II.9.1,6; Ant. XVIII.2.1,3; 5.1–2.
[42] Cf. War II.7.3; Ant. XVII.13.1–3.

of his administration a census was made by the Roman legate of Syria, Quirinius (known in the KJV as Cyrenius; Luke 2:2). Its purpose was to provide the basis for taxation. This expressed Jewish subjection to Rome, and aroused wide resentment among the Jews. Judas the Galilean (or Gaulonite) and a Pharisee named Zadok headed a revolt, but it failed. Josephus dates at this time the founding of the Zealots, the "fourth sect of Jewish philosophy" (*Ant.* XVIII.1.6); some scholars think, however, that the actual Zealot party emerged only in A.D. 66. Quirinius removed the high priest Joazar, whom Josephus says the multitude had appointed (apparently out of resentment at his deposition by Archelaus a few years before); in his place Quirinius appointed Ananus. About this time certain Samaritans defiled the Temple at Jerusalem. As a result and contrary to previous custom, the Samaritans were excluded from the Temple precincts.

The next Roman procurators were Marcus Ambibulus (A.D. 9–12) and Annius Rufus (A.D. 12–15), who was in office when Augustus died and Tiberius became emperor (A.D. 14–37). Valerius Gratus (A.D. 15–26) removed from office the high priest Ananus or Annas (A.D. 6–15) and appointed in succession four other high priests; his fourth appointee, Joseph Caiaphas (A.D. 18–36), plays a prominent role in the gospel story (cf. John 18:13, 24).[43]

The next procurator was Pontius Pilate (A.D. 26–36), notorious thereafter—though he no doubt thought the event a minor incident—for condemning Jesus of Nazareth to be crucified. He was not wise or tactful, and understood neither the leading Jews nor Jesus. At his first entry into Jerusalem the troops who escorted him carried their ensigns bearing the emperor's image. He knew this would seem idolatry to the Jews, but he insisted on doing as the Romans did elsewhere. The Jews entreated him to remove the ensigns. He refused and threatened to kill the protesters. They were ready to die, so he finally did as they asked; he could not begin his rule with a massacre.

He improved the water supply of Jerusalem by building an aqueduct into the city from the south, but he paid for this project with money taken from the Temple treasury, an act that earned him further hostility. This time he resisted public protests; his soldiers beat the crowd with clubs.

His experience with the Samaritans was even more disastrous. A Samaritan promised to lead his people to the spot where their sacred vessels had been placed by Moses. A strong force gathered and brought weapons. Pilate took this to be a revolt and broke up the procession, killing some

43 On Quirinius and the first three Roman procurators, see *War* II.8.1; *Ant.* XVIII.1.1 to 2.1–2.

and capturing others. The Samaritans protested to Vitellius, the legate of Syria. Clearly the Roman legate of Syria had authority over the procurator of Judea; Vitellius removed Pilate from office (A.D. 36) and sent him to Rome to answer for his actions.[44]

It was under Pilate that the ministry, arrest, trial, and execution of Jesus of Nazareth occurred. The present text of Josephus, *Ant.* XVIII.3.3, tells of the prophecy-fulfilling ministry, truthful teaching, miracles, death, resurrection, and continuing influence of Jesus. But Josephus was no Christian, and we must say either that Josephus cynically repeated what he did not believe, or that this explicitly Christian passage was inserted, or at least revised into its present form, by a Christian scribe who copied his works. Since it was the Christians and not the Jews who for over a thousand years preserved and copied Josephus' writings, we may conclude that this passage was revised to its present form or even inserted as a whole by some pious Christian scribe.[45]

---

[44] On Pilate's ten years in Palestine, see *War* II.9.2–4; *Ant.* XVIII.3.1 to 4.2.
[45] Cf. Maurice Goguel, *The Life of Jesus*, Eng. tr. by Olive Wyon (The Macmillan Company, 1933), pp. 75–82. He considers it "very probable that this passage has been either expanded or modified by Christian writers" (p. 78).

Chapter 2

THE RELIGIOUS SETTING

$\mathcal{F}$OR THE STUDY of New Testament history, it is essential to know the political background. The earlier Maccabean movement in Seleucid times, the Roman rule of the Mediterranean area, the Roman and Herodian role in Palestine, the Nabatean activity to the immediate east and south, and the Parthian threat on the east and northeast give the setting for the rise and westward spread of the Christian faith. But still more important is the religious setting of the emerging Christian religion. No political ruler of the first Christian generation shared that faith.[1] Few priestly leaders of the Jews threw in their lot with the disciples of Christ (Acts 6:7). Christianity did not take its rise or draw its strength from the ruling classes. But it was deeply rooted in vital religious currents of the first century. The study of these currents will help one to understand how the church emerged and made its impact on the ancient world.

The religious situation in Palestine demands our first attention. In that small land the situation was quite complex. Chapter 1 has shown that Palestine in the first half of the first century was a meeting place of varied cultural and religious streams. Naturally, Judaism was by far the most prominent factor; this was the solid result of the Maccabean revolt. But Greek language, architecture, and culture, and the Roman and Herodian promotion of Greco-Roman culture with its polytheistic overtones, challenged Judaism in its homeland. Still other Near Eastern trends (e.g., Iranian influence) brought syncretistic currents into the land.

The Jews varied in their reaction to the presence of Gentile culture and religion in their homeland. As in the days when the Maccabean revolt was brewing, there were Jews—and some of the most eager were priests—ready to adapt or sacrifice their ancestral faith to Greco-Roman culture and its religious aspects. Others were passive, content to avoid Gentile contacts as much as possible. Still others reacted with fiery resistance to

---

[1] On "The Abgar Legend" that King Abgar V of Edessa asked Jesus to visit him and Jesus sent Thaddaeus, see Edgar Hennecke, *New Testament Apocrypha*, Vol. I: *Gospels and Related Writings*, edited by Wilhelm Schneemelcher; Eng. tr. edited by R. McL. Wilson (The Westminster Press, 1963), pp. 437–444.

34

invading foreign influences. These Jews, precisely because the pagan influences were so plain and pervasive, put increased stress on the practices (circumcision, the Sabbath, food laws) that separated them from the Gentiles; they actively opposed every foreign influence that threatened the purity and permanence of their ancestral faith.

One thing is clear. If in the days of Jesus the Jew clung to his ancestral faith, it was not because he was too remote from the Gentile world to know any alternative to Judaism. The Jew who remained loyal to his inherited faith did so by choice and not by merely yielding to environmental pressure. His faith was under visible, vigorous challenge even in Palestine itself. Just as the Jews who were dispersed in Gentile lands saw almost daily the signs and practices of pagan cults, so the Jews in Palestine inevitably came into frequent contact with persons and places that represented Greco-Roman culture and religion.

The Jewishness of Jesus

Thus when Jesus, like other loyal Jews of Palestine, stood firmly for his faith, he did so by choice.[2] His parables drawn from nature show his deep appreciation for his native land. He watched with understanding the varied types of persons—rich and poor, Jew and Gentile—who walked the streets and roads of Palestine; they live in his parables. He had no impulse to travel widely, to "go to the Dispersion among the Greeks and teach the Greeks" (John 7:35); he stayed in Palestine. The one apparent exception, when he "went away to the region of Tyre and Sidon" (Mark 7:24), is often misunderstood. Mark does not say that Jesus went into those Gentile cities, but says that he withdrew briefly from Galilee into the neighboring rural regions of Phoenicia to be with his disciples; he carried on no ministry there, and healed the Syrophoenician woman's daughter only with reluctance, since that act ended his retirement and hastened his return to the region of the Sea of Galilee (Mark 7:25–31). Even in Palestine he ministered to the Jewish towns and cities. The places named in the Gospels were either all Jewish or partly Jewish; hardly an incident brings him into clear contact with a Gentile.[3] Quite exceptional is the healing of the centurion's servant (or son? See Matt. 8:5–13; Luke 7:1–10; compare John 4:46–54).

Equally Jewish in focus is the thinking of Jesus. He reflects this in his

---

[2] "The Jewishness of Jesus" is emphasized, e.g., by Joseph Klausner, *Jesus of Nazareth*, Eng. tr. by Herbert Danby (The Macmillan Company, 1925), pp. 363–368.

[3] On the geographical setting of Jesus' ministry, see G. Ernest Wright and Floyd V. Filson, *The Westminster Historical Atlas to the Bible*, p. 94.

word about verbose praying: "In praying do not heap up empty phrases as the Gentiles do" (Matt. 6:7). His disciples were impressed with the beauty and massive strength of the Temple built by Herod the Great: "Look, Teacher, what wonderful stones and what wonderful buildings!" But Jesus, with true prophetic focus on the divine judgment due to strike this place, replied: "There will not be left here one stone upon another" (Mark 13:1 f.). What impressed him was not architectural beauty but the impending judgment on Israel's sin. Such words on prayer and judgment serve to illustrate his tie with the religious heritage and outlook of Judaism.

Israel the People of God

The Judaism in which Jesus gratefully lived was a life of community. Israel was the people of God. It was as a member of that people that the individual had his privilege and responsibility. Jesus was no lone religious hermit; he was one of his people. One must realize this to sense the spirit in which he came to the baptism (Mark 1:9 and ||s). Israel needed to repent in preparation for the imminent coming of the Kingdom (Mark 1:15); Jesus, as a member of Israel, could not stand aside and leave all the preparation to others. His life and work were unique, but he lived his religious life as a member of God's covenant people.

It has sometimes been said that although ancient Israel lived with a strong sense of solidarity, it later, led by Jeremiah and Ezekiel, came to understand religion as an individual experience (Jer. 31:29 f.; Ezek., ch. 18).[4] Jesus, on this view, was an individualist, and so were his followers. The social ties in their religious living were optional and of minor importance.

One could hardly misunderstand more completely the Old Testament prophets and Jesus. The renewed life to which Jeremiah and Ezekiel looked forward was a life in the community of God's people, where later Jesus and his first followers gratefully lived. He did not secede from Judaism; he did not ask his followers to do so. He went to the synagogue as long as he could get a hearing there; at the end of his life he went to Jerusalem and the Temple to make his final appeal; his final appeal had to be at the center of the religious life of his people. He gathered disciples not to form a separate new church but as the nucleus of a renewed Israel.

4 For a restrained statement of this view, see A. B. Davidson, *The Theology of the Old Testament* (Charles Scribner's Sons, 1904), pp. 283–285.

God's Acts in History for Israel

This community of Israel was a covenant community based on God's acts in history.[5] The tie that bound this people of God together had deep roots in history. But it was not merely a history of great ancestors in whom they could take pride. They did remember with gratitude many notable ancestors, such as Abraham, Isaac, and Jacob; Moses; Joshua; Samuel; David; Amos, Isaiah, and Jeremiah; and Ezra. But the greatness of these leaders was not their unaided human achievement; many of them were honored in spite of weakness or glaring faults frankly told in the Biblical story. The distinctive thing about them all was that God had used them as his agents in his special dealings with Israel.

This community's basic bond was this unique action of God with them and for them. He had chosen, redeemed, judged, disciplined, forgiven, taught, and trained them. He had made them his covenant people, brought them into the Promised Land, given them judges and then a king, and promised them that a Son of David would sit on the throne and rule God's people (II Sam. 7:12–16). In this special history he had made known to them his ways and his will. This community could continue only by remembering its history and by being loyal to the one God, who had made his covenant with them and been true to his covenant even when his people had ignored or broken the covenant bond. The constancy of God had upheld Israel, and it was his purpose and promise to bring his wayward people to fulfill willingly their obligation to the God who had brought them "out of the land of Egypt, out of the house of bondage" (Ex. 20:2).

The Vital Role of the Scripture

This grounding in history explained why the Old Testament meant so much in Jesus' day. Israel—and in particular Jesus—did not live merely by the present gifts and leading of God; they lived by their roots in God's past work and by the revelation recorded and interpreted in their Scripture. It told the story of God's acts with his people; in it Israel and Jesus could find God's revelation, his law, his promise. By the time of Jesus the Old Testament—as we Christians call it; it was of course the sole Scripture for loyal Jews—was practically completed.[6] The Penta-

---

[5] "The Covenant" and "God's Action Within Israel" are chapter headings in *A Christian Theology of the Old Testament*, by George A. F. Knight (John Knox Press, 1959).

[6] On the Old Testament canon, see Floyd V. Filson, *Which Books Belong in the Bible?* (The Westminster Press, 1957), Ch. 3.

teuch, the Torah or instruction containing God's law for his people, had been completed and recognized as authoritative for over four centuries. The Prophets, including the Former Prophets (which we misleadingly call historical books) and the Latter Prophets, had been brought together in their present form for perhaps three centuries. The Writings, as the third division of the canon was called, had been known as a collection for almost two centuries,[7] and the list of books it included was almost fixed.

Of these three divisions of Scripture, the Pentateuch was both the first to be completed and the first in importance. Jewish life was based on these five books, which we often call the Law. But they are not a code of law in any rigid sense; they contain history and varied teaching. The word "Torah," which was applied to them, means "instruction"; it indicates that although law is definitely an important part of their contents, the total content includes a wider range of instruction and guidance for life.

The Scripture was used not only to direct the leaders but also to guide the entire community. It was read to the people. Few Jewish homes had copies; it was mainly by hearing the Scripture read in public gatherings for worship that most Jews learned its content. Relatively few Jews had access to copies for intensive study; for most Jews, it was alert attention and retentive memory that gave them a grasp of what God had done for Israel and what he wanted Israel to do.

It was so important for Israel to know the content of their Scripture that these books, originally written in Hebrew (except for a few passages in Aramaic),[8] had been translated into Greek because many Jews had learned Greek and lost their ability to use Hebrew or Aramaic. This need was first felt in the Dispersion (groups of Jews scattered in Gentile lands), and probably most keenly in Egypt, where Jews were numerous and Greek was the prevailing language.[9] But by the time of Jesus, Greek was spoken in Palestine not only by numerous Gentiles but also by many Jews. Some of them had returned to Palestine from other lands and brought with them their knowledge of Greek; others had learned Greek in Palestine in necessary business and community contacts with their

---

[7] The Prologue to Ecclesiasticus (The Wisdom of Jesus the Son of Sirach) refers to "the law and the prophets and the other books of our fathers." These "other books" included at least most of the Writings mentioned above. This Prologue was written about 125 B.C., when the grandson of the author of Ecclesiasticus was in Egypt making a translation of Ecclesiasticus from Hebrew into Greek.

[8] Ezra 4:8 to 6:18; 7:12–26; Dan. 2:4b to 7:28; Jer. 10:11, are in Aramaic.

[9] The Greek version preserved for us is called the Septuagint (LXX) from the Latin word *septuaginta*, "seventy." The name comes from the tradition in the Letter of Aristeas that seventy-two scholars translated the Pentateuch from Hebrew into Greek. This number was later shortened to "seventy" in referring to the Greek version.

Gentile neighbors. To know their own history and face God's will for his people, the Jews needed the Scripture in the language they spoke. This was true also of Aramaic-speaking Jews. Because they were not fully at home with Hebrew, the practice had arisen, when the Scripture lesson was read, of adding an oral Targum,[10] a restatement of the Scripture passage in Aramaic.

The regular reading of the Law and the Prophets according to a planned cycle of readings ensured systematic attention to the basic Scripture content.[11] Most of the Writings received attention at certain times of year.

RELIGIOUS INSTITUTIONS: THE HOME

In the days of Jesus, Jewish worship and instruction centered in three basic institutions. One was the home. Though perhaps least obviously a religious institution, its role in Jewish worship and teaching was basic and unsurpassed. Certain specific rites were there observed. Circumcision, the mark of belonging to the covenant people, was performed there on the eighth day after the birth of a Jewish boy. The Christian who wonders why Jewish Christians hounded Paul for his refusal to require circumcision of Gentile converts to Christianity should read Gen. 17:9–14, and remember that this rite symbolized to Jews their special status as members of God's covenant people.

Another outstanding home observance was the Passover meal. It was observed at Jerusalem by those who could make the pilgrimage there (Deut. 16:6), and on such occasions the Passover lamb was slain in the Temple. Elsewhere the usual practice was for the meal to be eaten in the home, where the father presided and the oldest son asked the meaning of the rite. It recalled with joy and gratitude the past redemptive action of God when he brought his people out of Egypt. It bound the family group together with Israel past and present and it gave them renewed hope for the future. In this annual celebration it was clear that the home was a vital factor in the life of Israel. When later Paul referred to "the church in their house" (I Cor. 16:19; cf. Philemon 2), his words would have had special meaning for a Christian Jew who knew how deeply the home is bound up with the life of the people of God.[12]

It was a point of strength in Israel's religious life that it did not leave

10 On Targums, see G. F. Moore, *Judaism*, Vol. I, pp. 100 ff., 302 ff.
11 There were weekly lessons from the Pentateuch and Prophets. Cf. G. F. Moore, *Judaism*, Vol. I, pp. 296–302; W. O. E. Oesterley and G. H. Box, *The Religion and Worship of the Synagogue* (London, Sir Isaac Pitman and Sons, 1907), pp. 351 ff.
12 On Jewish home observances, cf. G. F. Moore, *Judaism*, Vol. II, pp. 16 ff., 40 ff.

all religious training to a community institution but placed much of it in the home. The people of Israel were to talk of their divinely given law at night, in the morning, at home, and when on a walk (Deut. 6:7). Practice of their faith was to be built into everyday life. The father in particular was responsible for careful training of his sons in their religious heritage and rites.[13]

RELIGIOUS INSTITUTIONS: THE TEMPLE

The second major institution of Israel was the Temple. Since the law prescribed a system of sacrifices, no loyal Jew had clear ground to question their necessity. Deuteronomy made obligatory the concentration of this system in one place (e.g., Deut. 12:5–7).[14] If any Jew did not support the Temple services at Jerusalem, he might appeal to Scripture passages that seemed to reject sacrifices in favor of obedience to God's will (Isa. 1:12 f.; Amos 5:22, 25), but this was not convincing, for the law explicitly prescribed such sacrifices. Some Jews refused to participate in the Temple sacrifices because of the corruption of the priesthood, but because the law commanded sacrifices, those who rejected the sacrifices offered at the Temple could do so only on a temporary basis and with readiness to resume participation when priestly abuses were corrected.[15] The Pentateuchal rules for the Tabernacle and its sacrifices, and the role of the Temple in the Old Testament, led the Jews of Jesus' day to support the Temple and its sacrifices or at least to stand ready to do so when abuses were rectified.

The Temple of Jesus' day had been built by Herod the Great.[16] The ground plan he had used was new. The Temple built by Solomon was in one respect a "royal chapel," closely associated with the king's palace and other royal buildings, which included the house Solomon built for his wife, the daughter of Pharaoh of Egypt (cf. I Kings 7:1–8). It appears that not merely the priests but all the people could approach the altar. The vision of Ezekiel tried to prevent foreigners from profaning the

---

13 Cf. G. F. Moore, *Judaism*, Vol. II, pp. 127 f.

14 We hear in the Elephantine Papyri of a Jewish temple in Egypt, built in the sixth century B.C., destroyed in the late fifth century B.C., and apparently rebuilt; cf. Bright, *A History of Israel*, pp. 359 f., 389 ff. In the second century B.C. a Jewish temple was built at Leontopolis in Egypt (*Ant.* XIII.3.1–3). But most of the Jews in Egypt regarded the Temple in Jerusalem as their temple.

15 On the way the Qumran sect handled this problem, see Lucetta Mowry, *The Dead Sea Scrolls and the Early Church* (The University of Chicago Press, 1962), pp. 219–222.

16 F. J. Hollis, *The Archaeology of Herod's Temple* (London, J. M. Dent & Sons, Ltd., 1934).

Temple area; it allowed only the people of Israel to share in its rites, and the priests alone were to enter the inner court and carry out the rites at the altar (Ezek. 44:9–16).

We know too little of the Temple that Zerubbabel built after the Jewish return from exile to say just how it was planned. But from Josephus (*War* V.5.1–7; *Ant.* XV.11), the Rabbinical tractate *Middoth,* and other sources we know the plan of Herod's Temple. He began the work about 20–19 B.C. To keep the sacred place from being profaned by workmen not qualified to be in the Temple area, he had priests specially trained to carry out the construction work. The main Temple building was completed in eighteen months, but the entire complex of courts, walls, and special buildings was not completed until about A.D. 64, long after Herod's death.

The ground plan was ambitious. To give adequate space, Herod extended the hilltop and greatly enlarged the area of the outer court. This large outer court, accessible to all people of any race or faith, was the new and distinctive feature of the Herodian Temple; it deliberately provided for Gentile access to the Temple area. Perhaps Herod wanted to encourage tourists and spread the knowledge of his interest in architecture. Or possibly, in the time since the earlier temples had been built, the dream of Isa. 56:7 that Gentiles would come to the house of the Lord had led to a desire for a temple that would provide a place for Gentiles to worship. According to Mark 11:17, this was the concern Jesus had for the outer court; he was indignant that the only Temple court into which Gentiles could enter was rendered unfit for such worship by the noise and graft that accompanied the sale of sacrificial animals (but Matt. 21:13 and Luke 19:46 do not report that Jesus had this concern for Gentiles).

Yet the Temple plan permitted only Jews to share in the actual rites of the Temple. Between the outer court and the inner courts rose a wall or embankment. Nine gates led from the outer court into the inner courts, and only Jews could enter these gates. In fact, as Josephus says and two Greek inscriptions that have been discovered confirm, a large sign at each gate warned Gentiles that death would strike the Gentile who entered. The inscription read:

> "No foreigner may enter inside the barrier and embankment. Whoever is caught doing so will have himself to blame for his ensuing death."[17]

---

[17] G. Ernest Wright, *Biblical Archaeology* (The Westminster Press, 1957), p. 225, reproduces this inscription.

It was because of the mistaken idea that Paul had violated this rule by bringing a Gentile into the inner court that the Jews started the riot that led to his arrest (Acts 21:28). So in a real sense the Jewish Temple did not include the outer court, but only the inner courts.

In that inner area, on the east side, was the Court of the (Jewish) Women; this was as far as they could go into the Temple area. Jewish laymen, however, could go on westward into the Court of Israel, which let them observe the priests as they carried out the sacrifices and other rites in the Court of the Altar of Burnt Offering. From this latter court the priest appointed to carry out the daily ministry in the Holy Place (Luke 1:9) could proceed through the vestibule or porch of the main Temple building into the Holy Place, where the altar of incense and the "showbread" or "bread of the Presence" were placed. Just west of the Holy Place, in the same main Temple building, and separated from the Holy Place by a curtain, was the Most Holy Place, into which only the high priest might enter, and he only one day a year, the Day of Atonement (cf. Heb. 9:1-7, which speaks of the Tabernacle in the wilderness and wrongly places the altar of incense in the Most Holy Place).

Thus beginning with the outer court, the Court of the Gentiles, each stage of the plan led to a more sacred area, and the increase in holiness of each stage was marked by steps that led up to the next inner stage of the total plan. Perhaps the increasing elevation at each stage was meant to suggest to the Jews that the dwelling of God is not confined to any spot, even the most sacred spot, for he is Lord of heaven and earth and his most adequate dwelling place is in heaven (cf. I Kings 8:22-30).

The priests carried out the offerings; the Temple was the center of the priestly ministry of Israel. The high priest alone could enter the Most Holy Place; this function made him the supreme minister in the Jewish Temple system. But Jewish laymen regularly were present in the Court of Israel to observe the sacrifices and represent the people of Israel. It was not thought adequate for the priest alone to minister at the altar.

The Temple services meant much in the life of ancient Israel. In the first place, since these services were prescribed in the law, it was an act of obedience to fulfill them. In the second place, these acts of worship were carried on with praise and prayer and so fostered and expressed the devotion of God's people. Also, there was a teaching and judicial ministry committed to the priests, and this ancient priestly activity was still to some extent carried out at the Temple in Jesus' day. The Sanhedrin, the highest religious and official court of the Jews, met in the Temple area, was presided over by the high priest, and had strong priestly (Sadducee) representation in its membership of seventy.

Furthermore, the Temple cultus symbolized the unity of God's people. Its rites were carried out on behalf of the entire people; the few laymen present represented them all; every Jew knew that in the daily sacrifices and times of prayer (cf. Acts 3:1) their people as one whole rendered worship to their God. By payment of the annual Temple tax, and by pilgrimages as they were able to make them, Jews who lived far from the Temple could participate in its worship and feel their oneness with all Israel.

The Temple cultus, however, had severe limitations. Serious to Jews, but not the chief limitation, was the foreign control of the Temple. The pagan ruler assumed the right to appoint and replace the high priest, and thus assumed the superiority of the foreign rule over the priestly ministry. The fact that the Temple with its strong walls served as a treasury and military stronghold compromised it by involving it in activities of government, business, and war. The political interests of the high-priestly family, which necessarily had contacts with pagan civil officials and took over responsibility for many aspects of civil administration, kept its leadership from being helpfully spiritual. The further fact that most Jews lived too far from Jerusalem to take any part in the Temple services kept the Temple from being an adequate expression of the unity and community of Israel. Most of all, the great emphasis on animal sacrifice meant that the Temple services could never be a worthy and complete expression of the deepest meanings of Israel's faith. The destruction of the Temple by the Romans in A.D. 70 seemed to the Jews an unspeakable tragedy, which they have lamented for centuries. But in reality it was an immense blessing. If the Jews today could resume animal sacrifices, it would at once become evident that the Temple represents an antiquated and inferior way of expressing God's grace and his fellowship with Israel.

RELIGIOUS INSTITUTIONS: THE SYNAGOGUE

The third main religious institution of Israel was the synagogue.[18] Its origin is obscure. But as soon as Israel centered its sacrificial worship in one central temple (cf. Deut. 12:5 ff.), every other community was left without an adequate local center of worship and instruction. The home alone could not fulfill all the worship needs of a local community. More-

---

[18] The name comes from the Greek word *synagōgē,* which means "assembly." It referred primarily to the assembly and then came to be used of the place of assembly. Cf. Floyd V. Filson, "Synagogue, Temple, and Church," in *The Biblical Archaeologist Reader,* edited by G. Ernest Wright and David Noel Freedman (Doubleday & Company, Inc., 1961), pp. 185–200.

over, the exiles in Babylon keenly felt the need of some way of keeping the communities in faith and loyalty to the ancestral God (cf. Ps. 137). This need was not less urgent when those exiles who returned to Palestine found themselves a subject people surrounded by hostile groups. Such situations inevitably led, no doubt by stages, to the development of the synagogue, which for many generations before Jesus had been the common center of worship and community life for at least most if not all Jewish communities. Jesus would find one in every Jewish community of Galilee, Perea, and Judea (cf. Mark 1:39).

In establishing the synagogue there was no intention of displacing the Temple. The law prescribed sacrifices in the place that God would choose. It was the common Jewish conviction that Jerusalem was that place, and a temple there was necessary to fulfill God's will. But the synagogue still had a function to fulfill; it supplied a local center of worship, teaching, and community ties. Even in Jerusalem the need of such an institution was felt. We cannot trust the late Jewish tradition that there were 480 synagogues there,[19] but Jerusalem did have many synagogues.

Among them was one now known from a Greek inscription found at Jerusalem. It attests the existence of a synagogue there, built by a certain Theodotus, for the use of Greek-speaking Jews; some of them no doubt lived in Jerusalem, but the inscription's reference to guest quarters connected with the synagogue shows that Greek-speaking pilgrims present in Jerusalem were expected to share in the life and worship of that particular synagogue.[20] This suggests that there were other Greek-speaking synagogues in Jerusalem; Acts 6:9 evidently refers to Greek-speaking synagogues[21] and so confirms what the Theodotus inscription indicates. No doubt the greater number of Jerusalem synagogues were Aramaic-speaking, but the presence there of Greek-speaking ones tells us much about the language(s) spoken by the earliest apostolic church; Greek was certainly included. In the smaller Jewish cities and towns of Palestine, however, Aramaic must have been the common language of Jewish communities and synagogues.

In its basic form the synagogue was a simple institution.[22] Any ten

---

[19] This tradition is quoted in Emil Schürer, *A History of the Jewish People in the Time of Jesus Christ*, Eng. tr. by Sophia Taylor and Peter Christie (Charles Scribner's Sons, n.d.), Part II, Vol. II, p. 50.

[20] Jack Finegan, *Light from the Ancient Past* (Princeton University Press, 1946), gives the inscription in Fig. 105 and in English translation on p. 228.

[21] It is not clear how many synagogues are here in mind; possibly only one, but probably four.

[22] See G. F. Moore, *Judaism*, Vol. I, pp. 281–307.

Jewish men banded together for worship and sharing a concern to learn and fulfill God's will as made known in the law constituted a synagogue. It was essentially a lay institution; a priest was honored if present and would be asked to pronounce the benediction, but no priest was necessary. The functions of worship and instruction could be carried on by laymen. The central concern was to carry out God's revealed will by worship, study of his law, and application of it to the life of the local Jewish community whose common life centered in the synagogue. Women and children might be present at services of worship, but they apparently did not sit with the men and took no active part in the conduct of the service. The synagogue was an organization of Jewish men.

The presiding officer was called the ruler of the synagogue (Luke 13:14); there might be more than one "ruler" (Mark 5:22). Probably the elders, that is, the older men rather than elected leaders chosen for recognized administrative competence, chose the "ruler(s)." It is not clear precisely what functions the ruler(s) exercised. They must have assigned to individual men parts in the regular synagogue worship, and invited visitors to speak when they thought it wise (Acts 13:15).

Essential to every service of worship in the synagogue was prayer, usually offered by one of the laymen present. A second equally essential part was the reading of the Scripture, including the Law and the Prophets (cf. Luke 4:16–20). At special seasons of the year other Scripture books were read. If someone competent was present, a third feature of the service could be included, an exposition of the Scripture lesson or an address that applied the lesson or exhorted the congregation to worthy living (cf. Acts 13:15).

Such a service was held regularly every Sabbath. Other gatherings were held at special times. In addition, boys were taught to read, so that on reaching manhood (later, at least, this meant thirteen years of age) they could take part in the synagogue service by reading the Scriptures. This called for a school and a teacher (a man) connected with the synagogue. How universal such schools were in the time of Jesus is not certain, but it was at least the usual arrangement. Only by such care for literacy was the synagogue's tremendous program of lay education possible and effective. And of course what boys read in such a school was the Scriptures; to learn to read meant to learn to read and know the Scriptures.[23]

The group most concerned for the effectiveness of this program were the Pharisees. Hence, when Jesus was challenged in the synagogues of Galilee it was by the Pharisees and by the scribes, most of whom were Pharisees (e.g., Mark 2:16, 24).

23 On elementary schools, see G. F. Moore, *Judaism*, Vol. I, pp. 316 ff.

SPECIAL DAYS IN THE YEAR'S WORSHIP CALENDAR

All three of these institutions, the home, the Temple, and the synagogue, promoted the regular observance of the prescribed special days of Jewish religious life. Such observances were in addition to the regular prayers and blessings spoken daily in every loyal Jewish home and to the daily offerings and praise in the Temple. The regular weekly day of rest and worship was the Sabbath. The reason most commonly given for its observance was that the Lord, after creating all things in six days, rested on the seventh day, and directed his people to rest on every seventh day (Gen. 2:2; Ex. 20:8–11). Deuteronomy 5:15 adds that the day commemorates God's deliverance of his people Israel from Egypt. The day was observed strictly by good Jews as a day of rest; the Hebrew verb *shābath* means "cease," "rest."

To prevent gradual intrusion of work into the Sabbath period of rest, numerous specific restrictions were devised. For some, these rules were cramping, but this should not obscure the willing observance of other Jews, and there were rabbis who shared with Jesus a concern that in an emergency human welfare should take precedence over formal requirements (Mark 2:23 to 3:5).[24]

In earlier history the new moon was a special festival, particularly when the lunar calendar was followed. It was a festival day with special offerings (Num. 28:11–15; II Kings 4:23; Isa. 1:13; Amos 8:5; Ezek. 46:6 f.). It still played some part in first-century Jewish life (cf. Gal. 4:10; Col. 2:16), but by then it had no such importance as the weekly Sabbath observance.

One annual festival was the new year celebration in the early fall, on the first day of the seventh month, Tishri (September–October; cf. Lev. 23:23–25; Num. 29:1–6). At first sight its celebration at the beginning of the seventh month is puzzling. It reflects an early calendar in which the first month was in the early fall. But it was later fitted into the calendar used in the Old Testament, in which the first month began in the spring. Galatians 4:10 probably attests new year observance by Jewish Christians.

The most solemn day of the Jewish year was the Day of Atonement, on the tenth day of the seventh month, Tishri (September–October). It was "a sabbath of solemn rest," "a day of atonement," "a time of holy convocation," on which the Israelites were to "afflict" themselves and special sacrifices were offered to cleanse sanctuary and people (Lev. 16:29–34; 23:26–32). This affliction was understood to call for fasting, and this was the only day of the year on which fasting was prescribed by the

24 On the Sabbath, see G. F. Moore, *Judaism*, Vol. II, pp. 21–39.

written law. National fasts might be called in time of crisis, and individuals or groups might choose to fast at other times. The fasting of the disciples of John the Baptist and the Pharisees (Mark 2:18), and the fasting twice weekly of the Pharisee in Luke 18:12 (cf. Didache 8:1), were self-imposed and not prescribed by the written law.

THREE CHIEF FESTIVALS

Three basic festivals of the Jewish year were the Passover and Feast of Unleavened Bread, celebrated in Jesus' day as practically one festival; the Feast of Weeks; and the Feast of Tabernacles.[25] In very ancient times the Passover may have been the festival when shepherds offered the firstlings of the flock, but by the first century it commemorated the deliverance of the Israelites from Egypt (Deut. 16:1), and in days of subjection it aroused hope of a new and final deliverance. It celebrated God as the Redeemer of his people; the Old Testament thus presents God as the Redeemer before he gives his law at Sinai (Ex. 20:2).

The Passover was usually celebrated in the homes of Israelites on the evening of the fourteenth day of the first month (Abib, March–April). It could be celebrated in Jerusalem with a lamb slain in the Temple courts, but this, although specially significant for Jews in Jerusalem on pilgrimage, was not necessary, and in most cases a family, perhaps with friends present, celebrated the festival at home, with the father presiding at the table. According to all four Gospels, the Last Supper of Jesus with his disciples was eaten at Passover time (cf. I Cor. 5:7), either as a Passover meal (Mark 14:12–16; Matt. 26:17–19; Luke 22:7–13) or on the evening before the Passover (John 13:1; 18:28); the Passover imagery and atmosphere colored the celebration. The Gospel of John places the entire ministry of Jesus in the setting of a series of three (some would say four) Passovers (John 2:13; [5:1]; 6:4; 11:55).

The seven-day Feast of Unleavened Bread immediately followed the Passover (Lev. 23:5 f.). In Mark 14:12 the day on which "they sacrificed the Passover lamb" is actually called "the first day of Unleavened Bread." The two festivals had become practically one. In origin agricultural, marking the beginning of the grain harvest, this Feast came to carry reference to the deliverance from Egypt. But the offering of a sheaf of the first grain to be harvested (Lev. 23:10–14) kept the Feast tied in part at least to the agricultural situation and expressed gratitude for the new harvest.

About fifty days later came the Feast of Weeks (Lev. 23:15–21; Deut.

16:9–12). It was later called the Feast of Pentecost, from the Greek word *pentēkostē*, "fiftieth" (cf. Acts 2:1). It originally marked the end of the grain harvest, but later the rabbis connected it with the giving of the law at Mt. Sinai.

The third great festival of the year, the Feast of Booths, or Tabernacles, was observed for eight days beginning the fifteenth day of the seventh month (Lev. 23:33–36; cf. John 7:2). It originally celebrated the grape harvest. In the first century the Temple was illuminated on the first night (cf. John 8:12), and on seven days a libation of water was made in the Temple (cf. John 7:37). This festival, like the Passover and Pentecost, was considered a time specially suited for pilgrimage to the Temple in Jerusalem.

MINOR FESTIVALS

Three minor feasts deserve brief mention. The Feast of Purim, on the fourteenth and fifteenth of the twelfth month Adar (February–March), commemorated the deliverance of the Jews from a plot to exterminate them (Esth. 9:15–32). The Feast of Nicanor, on the thirteenth of Adar, commemorated the victory of Judas Maccabeus over the Syrian general Nicanor (I Macc. 7:49; II Macc. 15:36). The Feast of Dedication, celebrated for eight days beginning the twenty-fifth day of Chislev (December), celebrated the recovery of the Temple and the renewal of the altar sacrifices by Judas Maccabeus (I Macc. 4: 59; II Macc. 10:6–8; cf. John 10:22).

THE CHIEF JEWISH SECTS

Up to this point we have described the religious life of the Jews as a people. They shared a common history and a common revelation recorded in Scripture; by and large they shared a basic loyalty to Jewish institutions—home, Temple, and synagogue—and observed the same festivals. But not all Jews understood their faith and duty in the same way. The differences led to the formation of parties or sects, which shaped the Judaism Jesus knew. To be sure, not all Jews belonged to one of these parties. Most of them belonged to no special group; they were content to practice their ancestral religion without sectarian connection. Moreover, no one of these sects was clearly normative and obviously destined to be the Judaism of future centuries. Looking back, we can see that the Pharisees had the vitality and the way of life that would mark the

Judaism of later centuries. But that was not yet clear. We must study the leading groups.[26]

1. *The Sadducees*. At the time of Jesus one might have concluded that the Sadducees were and would continue to be the leading group in Judaism. They were the priestly party. The high priest, the leading religious minister of Judaism and the presiding officer of the Sanhedrin, was one of their number. They were in control of the Temple, the center of the religious life of Judaism. Their leaders lived mainly in and near Jerusalem, the key city of their people, though as a group their outlook was shaped somewhat by rural homes and land holdings. They had social standing; the Sadducees or at least their dominant portion belonged to the aristocratic upper level of society.[27] To them the Romans through the high priesthood entrusted the routine political administration of the Jewish sections of Palestine; thus they had both religious and political supremacy (a fact that some Jews held against them). Conservative in their views, they seemed to be the solid members of the ongoing community.

Their name is often thought to be derived from the Zadok who was the leading priest in David's time (I Kings 1:32). Others derive the party name from a later priestly leader. Much more important than the origin of the name is the attitude of the party in Jesus' day. As the aristocratic party in power, linked with Rome in the rule of Palestine, they were exposed to Hellenistic influences which their foreign rulers promoted, and they became more worldly than befitted their priestly position. Their religious outlook was conservative; as Acts 23:8 reports, they did not join the Pharisees in faith in the resurrection of the body or hold that angels and spirits had an active role in human life. Their emphasis was on the Pentateuch, which gave the regulations for their priestly ministry; they gave less authority to other writings. Undoubtedly they had an oral tradition; every religious group, even if it has a Scripture, quickly develops one. But they did not accept the Pharisees' oral tradition, which for Pharisees was equally authoritative with the Scripture itself. This was a deep cleavage between the two groups.

Not all priests belonged to the Sadducee party. Some were Essenes; priests clearly had a leading role in the Qumran sect, to be described shortly.

In the arrest and trial of Jesus, the Sadducees, and especially the high

---

26 See J. W. Lightley, *Jewish Sects and Parties in the Time of Jesus* (London, The Epworth Press, 1925).

27 See Louis Finkelstein, *The Pharisees* (The Jewish Publication Society of America, 1940), Vol. I, pp. 80–83.

priest, played the main part (Mark 11:27; 14:1, 53; 15:1), and in the earliest days of the church it was the Sadducees who started the persecution of Jesus' followers (Acts 4:1). The reason is clear. As long as Jesus was in Galilee he did not directly threaten their leadership and prestige. But as soon as he came to Jerusalem and presumed to interfere in the Temple management by driving the profiteering sellers of animals and birds from the outer court (Mark 11:15–18), he challenged the position of the Sadducees and they determined to put him out of the way. Similarly, when Peter and John healed the lame man at the Beautiful Gate of the Temple and thus caused an excited crowd to gather, the Sadducees again saw their control of the Temple threatened and acted to imprison the disciples (Acts 3:1 to 4:3). They fought whatever struck at their Temple control and priestly prestige.

2. *The Pharisees*.[28] The name of this group is usually thought to be derived from the Hebrew root *pārash* and to mean "separated." (Cf. Paul's reference to himself in Rom. 1:1 as "separated" or "set apart"; he was a former Pharisee, and may mean that now as a Christian apostle he is truly set apart or separated by God for his apostolic ministry.) This sect, highly respected by the people, was not numerous; Josephus says that in Herod's day it numbered "above six thousand" (*Ant.* XVII.2.4). But their influence was much larger than small numbers might suggest. This was due to the dedication with which they lived. They held no lucrative position; they served their cause without thought of financial profit or personal advantage.

Their concern was to further the knowledge and practice of the law. For this purpose, the synagogue was their chief instrument. They had obtained a considerable proportion of the seventy seats in the ruling Sanhedrin in Jerusalem, and this gave them influence in national affairs, but their main influence was through the synagogues found in every Jewish community. This in itself gave them widespread influence, for although the Sadducee influence was centered chiefly in the Temple at Jerusalem, the Pharisees could exercise direct influence wherever there was a synagogue.

In teaching and practicing the law, they had to decide how to apply the ancient law in their day. Though the conditions of life continually changed, they were committed to live by the law and teach the people to observe it. To do this, they developed a continually adapted oral tradition ("the tradition of the elders" of Mark 7:3; etc.). In their view this tradition was given (at least implicitly) when the law was given to

---

28 See R. Travers Herford, *The Pharisees* (The Macmillan Company, 1924); Louis Finkelstein, *The Pharisees*, Vols. I and II.

Moses, and it had been handed down faithfully from the fathers, so it was as authoritative as the written law.[29] This in effect gave the oral tradition more importance than the written law, and this was a chief point of difference not only between the Pharisees and the Sadducees but also between the Pharisees and Jesus, who radically downgraded this oral tradition and considered it a merely human tradition (Mark 7:6–8).

This must not obscure the strength and vitality of the Pharisaic position. It was necessary to bring the law up to date. Only by continuous new application of the ancient Scripture could it continue to be a vital and controlling guide in the present. The Pharisees were in a real sense progressive. They accepted the hope of the resurrection of the body, which was not taught by the law, and they believed in the presence and activity of angels and other spirits as factors in human life (Acts 23:8). They constantly carried on the study and application of the law. Most of the scribes, who gave themselves not merely to the copying of the law but also to the study and teaching of it, were Pharisees.

A number of passages in the Gospels reflect the serious clash between Jesus and the Pharisees. Some scholars have thought that this clash was really between the Pharisees and the early church, which then mistakenly ascribed the same clash to Jesus. This view is untenable. Jesus rejected the oral tradition of the Pharisees. He thereby struck at their entire system of teaching and practice, and inevitably brought on an open break with the essential Pharisaic position. Jesus shared with other Jews the conviction of the authority of the written law, but he broke sharply with the Pharisees by denying to their oral tradition an authority equal to that of the written Scripture.

3. *The Zealots.* This name describes a group of Jews so zealous for their people's independence and so certain that God wanted them to be free from foreign control that they were ready to die rather than submit to Roman rule. It is not certain when this group emerged as a distinct sect. Josephus suggests that it occurred when the Romans took a census of Palestine in A.D. 6 (*Ant.* XVIII.1.1, 6). The Romans then took over direct rule of Judea, Samaria, and Idumea, and the census was taken to give them a basis for taxation. Two Jewish patriots, Judas the Galilean (or Gaulonite) and Sadduk, a Pharisee, led a revolt against the humiliating census. This may be the origin of the Zealots. In modern times, however, some scholars have dated their origin as a definite sect

---

[29] On this "Oral Law," cf. Aboth I.1: "Moses received the Law from Sinai and committed it to Joshua, and Joshua to the elders, and the elders to the Prophets, and the Prophets committed it to the men of the Great Synagogue." See Herbert Danby, *The Mishnah* (Oxford, Clarendon Press, 1933), p. 446.

in A.D. 66, when the Jews revolted against Rome. Be that as it may, Jewish resentment against Roman rule was a constant fact. It flared into rebel action in A.D. 6 and found continual expression among Palestinian Jews in the first century. To some degree at least, Josephus rightly indicates that the movement had a continuous existence beginning in A.D. 6. Such rebel spirits held that if God's people would rise in resistance against the foreign oppressor, God would support them and enable them to defeat the pagan enemy; all of God's people, on this view, should give every possible resistance to the enemy and should refuse to pay him tribute.

Jesus had to face this viewpoint when asked about paying taxes to Caesar (Mark 12:13–17). It is often said that he evaded the question and escaped the dilemma. This is not correct. His answer permitted payment of taxes to Rome, and so was bound to alienate Zealot Jews.

The Zealot question could not escape Jesus' attention.[30] One of the Twelve he chose was called "Simon the Cananaean" (Mark 3:18; Matt. 10:4), or "Simon who was called the Zealot" (Luke 6:15; cf. Acts 1:13). The word "Cananaean" transliterates the Aramaic word for "Zealot." The word might mean that this Simon was a hothead, particularly enthusiastic or zealous. But more likely he had been a Jew dedicated to resisting Rome in every possible way.

Some have thought that Judas also had been a Zealot and lost faith in Jesus when he found that Jesus did not share this view. This idea would be supported if his title Iscariot came from the Latin word *sicarius*, "dagger," and he was thus a "dagger man." But the word "Iscariot" may, rather, mean "man of Kerioth" (a place in Judea). In any case it seems clear that Jesus had among his disciples Jews hot in hostility to Roman rule. He must have heard their position discussed and he had to take a position on this question. He turned his back on armed revolt as a possible way to serve God's cause and help God's people. Perhaps he remembered that Maccabean might had obtained political independence but had lacked the spiritual strength to renew the people and produce in them radical obedience to God.

4. *The Essenes.* This group is never mentioned in the New Testament, and its origin is nowhere clearly described. But the Essenes probably emerged from the Hasidim or Hasideans ("pious ones") active in Maccabean days. Some of these Hasidim continued to take part in the religious life of their people and tried to make it conform to their interpretation of the law (the Pharisee position). Others, largely of priestly background but out of sympathy with the increasingly worldly Maccabeans, withdrew

[30] Cf. Oscar Cullmann, *The State in the New Testament* (Charles Scribner's Sons, 1956), pp. 8–23.

from public life to keep true to their ancestral faith. They may have opposed the Maccabeans as not belonging to the priestly family that was entitled by law to the priestly leadership. Or they may have been repelled because the Maccabees combined political, military, and religious leadership in one man and became increasingly secularized by adopting Hellenistic ways of life. Since Josephus (*Ant.* XIII.5.9) mentions the Essenes first in the time of the Maccabean leader Jonathan (160–142 B.C.), before Maccabean rulers became so obviously secular, it was probably the combination of political, military, and religious leadership in one man that initially repelled the priestly nucleus of the Essenes, and led them to withdraw into a separated and ascetic life.

THE QUMRAN SECT

Our understanding of the Essenes will be greatly affected by the view we take of the ancient ascetic group that lived at Qumran, near the northwest shore of the Dead Sea.[31] The ruins there point to a withdrawal sect; the manuscripts (Dead Sea Scrolls) and other objects found in some dozen nearby caves testify that the group settled there possibly as early as the latter half of the second century B.C. and finally left the site about A.D. 66.

Features of the Dead Sea Scrolls recall what Josephus and Philo have told us of the ancient Essenes,[32] and Qumran is just where Pliny the Elder would lead us to look for their home. In his *Natural History* (V.15) he locates their residence near the Dead Sea north of En-gedi; this is just where Qumran lies. Josephus says the Essenes lived by themselves, but "many of them dwell in every city" (*War* II.8.4), and Philo says that a somewhat similar group, the Therapeutae, lived in Egypt,

---

[31] Of the great number of books on this subject, we mention H. H. Rowley, *The Zadokite Fragments and the Dead Sea Scrolls* (Oxford, Basil Blackwell, 1952); Millar Burrows, *The Dead Sea Scrolls* (The Viking Press, Inc., 1955) and *More Light on the Dead Sea Scrolls* (The Viking Press, Inc., 1958); Theodore H. Gaster, *The Dead Sea Scriptures in English Translation* (Doubleday & Company, Inc., 1956); Krister Stendahl (ed.), *The Scrolls and the New Testament* (Harper & Brothers, 1957); Frank Moore Cross, Jr., *The Ancient Library of Qumran and Modern Biblical Studies* (Doubleday & Company, Inc., 1958); J. T. Milik, *Ten Years of Discovery in the Wilderness of Judaea*, Eng. tr. by J. Strugnell (London, SCM Press, Ltd., 1959); Kurt Schubert, *The Dead Sea Community* (Harper & Brothers, 1959); Matthew Black, *The Scrolls and Christian Origins* (Charles Scribner's Sons, 1961); A. Dupont-Sommer, *The Essene Writings* (Oxford, Basil Blackwell, 1961); Lucetta Mowry, *The Dead Sea Scrolls and the Early Church* (The University of Chicago Press, 1962).

[32] Josephus, *War* II.8.2–13; *Ant.* XIII.5.9; XVIII.1.5; Philo, *Every Good Man Is Free*, XII to XIII (on the Essenes); *On the Contemplative Life* (on the Therapeutae, whom Philo explicitly distinguishes from the Essenes).

3

but Pliny seems to know only a settlement of Essenes who lived where we find these ruins. At the least the Qumran sect was an Essene-type sect, and it may be better to say that it was a prominent Essene center or the chief Essene center. From a study of this sect and a critical use of what Josephus and Philo tell us we should get a fairly accurate idea of the Essenes.

The sect was a withdrawal sect. Even its members who lived "in every city" did not live in normal fellowship with other Jews, but kept to their own group and discipline. We call them a withdrawal sect rather than a monastic sect, for although Philo says flatly that they did not marry, Josephus says that one group in the Essene movement did permit marriage (*War* II.8.13), and the burials found at Qumran include female as well as male skeletons. The withdrawal was a reaction partly against the ruling priestly class, the Maccabean priesthood, and partly against the unsatisfactory religious and moral conditions among the Jews.

This withdrawal had a purpose; under the leadership of an unidentified "Teacher of Righteousness" and in obedience to Isa. 40:1-3, these Jews withdrew into the wilderness to prepare for the expected action of God who would soon judge his people and honor those who proved faithful and prepared. The group looked for the coming of "The Prophet" (cf. Deut. 18:15) and a priestly Messiah of Aaron as well as a kingly Messiah of Israel.

The initial group were all or mainly of the priestly class, but later, if not from the start, other equally serious Jews who regarded with horror the current evil conditions and met the test of a severe probationary period were admitted to full membership and lived under the strict discipline and rigid organization of the community. But those Jews who saw no danger and refused to act in repentance and self-discipline were regarded by these earnest-minded ascetics as "children of darkness," and the sect was at least as hostile to them as to the Gentiles. The imminent judgment of God would strike all who were not prepared by repentance and self-discipline to meet the impending crisis.

Yet though these people lived under strict discipline and a strongly legalistic regime, the Thanksgiving Psalms found at Qumran show a keen awareness of sinfulness and a grateful dependence on the undeserved grace of God. Since modern men often think that legalism and grace are mutually exclusive, the finding of both themes in the Qumran literature deserves close attention.

Obviously the Qumran sect did not represent normal Judaism. The life of withdrawal, the ascetic tendency, and the apocalyptic teaching were not characteristic of most Jews. But these people thought themselves the true Israel, the "children of light," the only Jews really ready for the impending judgment of God.

THE QUMRAN SECT AND CHRISTIAN BEGINNINGS

It has been suggested that the emerging Christian church borrowed heavily from the Qumran sect. John the Baptist was of priestly ancestry, spent years in the wilderness, lived an ascetic life, apparently never married, quite likely connected his ministry with the demand of Isa. 40:1-3, expected the Kingdom of God to come soon, and emphasized repentance in preparation for this imminent event. So some have thought that John was for a time a member of the Qumran group.[33] He certainly had views that they also held. But at least some of such views were shared by still other Jews.

There is no real evidence that John was ever in close touch with the Qumran community. It took two or three years of probation to join that group, and to join it meant to commit oneself completely to its discipline. There is no evidence that John had done that and then become a renegade. His preaching to all who came to hear was quite unlike the withdrawn attitude of the Qumran sect. He admitted Jews to baptism without probation or withdrawal from normal community life; this was contrary to Essene probationary requirements. What we know of John differs in essentials from the Qumran group's teaching and way of life. He was no Essene.

There is even less reason to regard Jesus as an Essene. He did go to hear John, submitted to baptism by John, and spent a brief time in the wilderness, but alone and not as a member of an Essene group. He shared in part the urgent eschatological expectation of the Essenes; he seems to have thought of John as Elijah (Mal. 4:5; Mark 9:13), so he shared their expectation that "The Prophet" would come at the end of history; he spoke favorably of poverty (Matt. 6:24; Luke 6:20), which recalls the voluntary poverty of the Qumran sect. But he was not a priest and had no close ties with the priestly group. He went to the Temple in Jerusalem and spoke of it as God's house (Mark 11:17); this differed from the withdrawal of the Qumran sect. He disowned the legalistic way of life so stressed at Qumran, and his freedom in eating with ceremonially careless common people must have shocked the Essenes as it did the Pharisees. His sense of the seeking love of God was not matched in Essene outlook and practice. His love of neighbor had a breadth quite unlike the

[33] So, W. H. Brownlee, "John the Baptist in the New Light of Ancient Scrolls," in *The Scrolls and the New Testament* (cited in note 31), pp. 33–53.

hostility of the Qumran sect toward Jews outside their sect; to them the common people were "children of darkness" but to Jesus they were beloved children of God and he was their friend and helper. The Qumran sect does not give us the setting of Jesus' life and ministry.

There are points of contact between the Qumran group and the early church. The "communism" of the early Jerusalem community (Acts 2:44; 4:32), the common meal of the disciples (Acts 2:42, 46), and the leadership of the Twelve have been cited as examples. But the "communism," a passing phase, was not complete and mandatory (Acts 5:4). The disciples had no common work program. Their breaking of bread was not presided over by a priest, nor did it follow a rigid procedure (common meals were by no means peculiar to the Essenes). The twelve apostles were not priests; the Qumran sect had twelve laymen and three priests as a judicatory.[34] The early church went freely to the Temple in a way the Qumran sect would have thought wrong (Acts 3:1; 5:12). The Christians spoke not of two Messiahs but of one, and he was not still to come but had already come in Jesus. It is barely possible that the priests who became disciples (Acts 6:7) had been Essenes, but this is quite unlikely.

The early church showed similarities to the Essenes, but the differences were far more significant, and the early Christian worship, thought, and way of life were not essentially shaped by the Essene pattern.

THE PIOUS POOR

In addition to the sects just described, some scholars have thought they could identify another less organized, less clearly definable group of pious poor people, "the quiet in the land," who without making a public stir cherished the faith and hope of Israel in a simple and unpretentious way.

Undoubtedly there were undistinguished people who looked to God for help and prayed for the welfare of their people. That they were organized in any way or constituted in the public eye a separate group is much more doubtful. The reference to them, however, reminds us that not all Jews were included in the four parties or sects named above; Jewish piety, patriotism, and hope were not limited to those groups. There was elsewhere a hunger, a readiness for spiritual response, as Jesus found. In none of the organized forms of Jewish religion did he find an adequate preparation and instrument for God's message.

[34] See the Manual of Discipline, viii.1 ff.

UNREST AND EXPECTANCY

From the variety of sects in Judaism in the first half of the first century A.D. it is clear that the religious situation was fluid. Obviously it was a time of unrest. There was political resentment at the rule of Rome; heavy taxation and other difficulties made the economic lot of most people hard and precarious; advanced education and other social privileges were confined to the few; and there were signs of religious hunger and searching.

To this unrest there was no one answer. The Sadducees by and large were in a favored position and were content to maintain the *status quo*. The hotheads, the fierce nationalists, were for revolt against the Roman rule. The prudent were more inclined to live a cautious life, upright but calculating, such as we find in the Wisdom writings of Ecclesiasticus and the Wisdom of Solomon. Devout, simple folk, such as the "pious poor" just discussed, knew mainly that their constant duty was unswerving trust in God. The Pharisees as a rule did not look for help from political or military action; through the faithful keeping of the law they expected to open the way for God's fulfillment of his promises to his people. The Essenes, and in particular the group of ascetics at Qumran, had withdrawn from normal society to prepare themselves by rigid discipline for God's intervention to fulfill his purpose. In their group and in other groups of earnest Jews the eschatological hope was vivid that God would intervene, decisively crush evil, and reward his chosen people. The Book of Daniel encouraged this point of view; other writings, such as I Enoch,[35] the Sibylline Oracles, and the Testaments of the Twelve Patriarchs encouraged hope for God's imminent action to establish his perfect order.

Into such a situation the gospel came. In a time of unrest, coupled with expectancy that God would act to do what men could not do for themselves, there appeared the spokesman of a new, crucial, and effective word of God.

JOHN THE BAPTIST

The immediate setting for the ministry of Jesus was the ministry and movement of John the Baptist.[36] The New Testament reflects John's

[35] Chapters 37 to 71 of I Enoch are of chief importance in the study of the Jewish eschatological hope. But the date of the writing of these chapters is disputed, especially because no remnant of them is present among the many fragments of the Book of Enoch found at Qumran. See Frank Moore Cross, Jr., *The Ancient Library of Qumran,* p. 150, who notes also the absence of the Testaments of the Twelve Patriarchs (another, probably earlier, draft of the Testaments of Levi and Naphtali has been found at Qumran).

[36] The best thorough study available is by Carl H. Kraeling, *John the Baptist* (Charles

importance; only Jesus, Peter, and Paul are mentioned more often than John.

John was of priestly descent, and Luke, ch. 1, suggests that his family shared the deep and earnest hope that God would visit his people. As John came to manhood, he turned from the priestly career his father had followed and withdrew into the wilderness near the Jordan River or Dead Sea, rejecting the current Jewish religious life and priestly leadership. Of his life in the wilderness we know little. It was a religious retreat, lasting for years and ending in a divine call to preach to all Jews who would come to the wilderness to hear him. In this ministry it was not his priestly background but only his call to speak as a prophet that counted. His dress and diet were later so described as to recall Elijah, the fiery prophet of earlier times (Mark 1:6), and possibly he was conscious of following in Elijah's steps, but perhaps it was Jesus and the early church who first pictured him as a second Elijah (cf. Mal. 4:5; Mark 9:13).

His message was eschatological. The God of Israel was about to judge his people; without delay they should prepare for that judgment. Whether John described the coming situation as the coming of the Kingdom of Heaven, as Matt. 3:2 suggests, is not certain, since the other Gospels do not say that he did, but in fact he expected the judgment as the prelude to God's righteous, effective, and decisive rule, so that regardless of what specific terms he used, he did expect God's effective rule to be established in the very near future.

Deeply conscious of his people's sinfulness, he summoned all to repent (Mark 1:4; Matt. 3:2; Luke 3:3). Descent from Abraham would not protect them in the impending judgment; only by repentance and changed life could one escape condemnation and enter God's righteous and eternal realm. John himself would not execute that judgment; a mightier one would soon come and put men on the threshing floor of God's judgment, separating the grain from the chaff and burning the chaff (the wicked) in Final Judgment (Matt. 3:12; Luke 3:17).

Those ready to repent and turn from their evil ways John baptized, evidently by immersion, in the Jordan River (Mark 1:5; Matt. 3:6). Did John derive the idea of baptism from foreign (possibly Iranian) sources? Probably not. There was a definite tendency in Judaism to increase the number of ritual washings, and it appears that proselyte baptism for

Scribner's Sons, 1951). On p. 191 he cites important earlier works by Dibelius, Goguel, Lohmeyer, and others. Unfortunately, Kraeling wrote before the Dead Sea Scrolls could be studied in their relation to John the Baptist. For this problem, see W. H. Brownlee, "John the Baptist in the New Light of Ancient Scrolls," in *The Scrolls and the New Testament*, pp. 33–53.

Gentiles converted to the Jewish faith was already being practiced.[37] Yet John's baptism differed from proselyte baptism; he baptized Jews; their membership in God's people did not suffice; they must repent and be baptized. John's baptism was administered to a person only once and had an eschatological reference: it was to prepare for the coming judgment.

To John, baptism was evidently a purifying rite,[38] although the strong ethical note in his preaching keeps us from supposing that the rite was automatically effective. Real repentance and dedication followed by "fruit that befits repentance" were necessary (Matt. 3:8; Luke 3:8); active compassion and justice were imperative (Luke 3:10–14).

John's ministry evoked a sensational response. Even allowing for exaggeration in the Gospel accounts, great numbers heard him and responded (Mark 1:5; Matt. 3:5 f.). This hints at a widespread sense of crisis and spiritual need. It also indicates that John's ministry lasted for months or more than a year; the impact of his preaching and baptism had time to permeate throughout Palestine.

Most of the baptized evidently returned home to their usual tasks. But some became John's disciples and continued with him. To all he apparently gave rules for living. These included regular fasting and special prayers (Mark 2:18; Luke 11:1).

It is not clear what title his followers gave him. The title Baptist or the Baptizer may have been a popular description of John rather than a title given him by his followers. But since not all of his disciples went over to Jesus when he appeared, they perhaps thought of John as the Messiah expected by the Jews. The hymn in Luke 1:68–79 refers to John as the one in whom redemption had come to Israel; this pictures him not merely as a great forerunner but as God's final decisive leader. Perhaps the narrative and hymns in Luke, ch. 1, come at least in part from John's followers, who thought him the climactic figure of history.

JESUS AND JOHN THE BAPTIST

Although John deserves attention as a prophet in his own right, it is as the forerunner of Jesus that he has become most widely known.[39] To

---

[37] On proselyte baptism, see G. F. Moore, *Judaism*, Vol. I, pp. 331 ff.; Kraeling, *John the Baptist*, pp. 99 ff.

[38] Josephus says that John's baptism was only "for the purification of the body" (*Ant.* XVIII.5.2), but this is an inadequate statement of its significance. The Gospels connect it with forgiveness of sins, which the rite symbolized as a cleansing.

[39] On the relation of John to Jesus, see Goguel, *Life of Jesus*, pp. 264–279; Kraeling, *John the Baptist*, pp. 123–157.

judge by his reported teaching, he himself claimed not to be the decisive figure of history but to be preparing the way for that final climactic leader (Mark 1:7 f.; Matt. 3:11; Luke 3:16). We cannot decide this from the Gospel of John; it reads the final full Christian estimate of Jesus back into the earliest paragraphs of the narrative, and so its indication in ch. 1:19–36 that, even before Jesus began his ministry, John expressed the full Christian view of Jesus is a dramatic way of presenting the meaning of Jesus' coming; it is not a literal historical picture of how things developed. But the Synoptic Gospels make it sufficiently clear that John did not claim to bring in the Kingdom but only to prepare men for it; another was to be the judge and inaugurate the Kingdom.

Jesus was among those stirred by the reports of John's preaching. He went to the Jordan to hear for himself. Impressed and convinced, he was baptized and continued briefly with John. At his baptism Jesus had an experience of the claim of God on his life which meant that he could not be merely John's follower (Mark 1:10 f.). Yet he always spoke with respect of John, and regarded John's ministry as the dividing line of history, the event after which the decisive action of God began (Matt. 11:7–14; Luke 7:24–30; 16:16). Indeed, Jesus came to regard John as the Elijah who in accordance with Mal. 4:5 was to come just before the great Final Judgment Day (Mark 9:9–13; Matt. 17:9–13).

John never became a follower of Jesus, and to Jesus he was not a part of the Kingdom movement. But Jesus said no greater man had lived, and for the early church, John's unique ministry was an integral part of the total gospel story; the common preaching message began with the story of John's preaching and baptism (cf. Acts 10:37; 13:24).

John's manner and message were not those of Jesus. He shunned the cities and towns; Jesus went to the people. He emphasized the stern note of judgment; Jesus kept that note, but his main accent was a more tender note. To John, God's judgment and action were imminent but future; Jesus was conscious of being part of God's present action. John did no miracle, as far as the records show (cf. John 10:41); Jesus' healing ministry expressed the Kingdom's presence in him and his work. For all their differences, Jesus respected John as a true prophet of God, indeed, as the great final prophet before God's decisive action.

JOHN'S DEATH AND CONTINUING INFLUENCE

John's prophetic rebuke struck not only the Jews, including their leaders, but also Herod Antipas, tetrarch of Galilee and Perea (Mark 6:17 f.; Matt. 14:3 f.). Herod had divorced his lawful wife and married the wife of his brother. For this marital laxity, repugnant to Jewish teaching, John rebuked Herod. This specific rebuke was probably why Herod had John arrested, though Josephus explains it only by Herod's fear that John might use his popularity to lead a revolt against Herod (*Ant.* XVIII.5.2). Possibly John went to the court of Herod to utter this rebuke, but perhaps John spoke thus while preaching in Perea, east of the Jordan, where Herod could arrest him.

Josephus says that John was kept prisoner at Machaerus, on the eastern side of the Dead Sea. But his followers were able to visit him; John could send them to question Jesus; and when Herodias, Herod's wife, plotted against John's life, John was not far away and could be executed at once (Mark 6:19–29; Matt. 14:5–12). All this suggests that he was kept prisoner in a more accessible place, perhaps in Galilee. In any case, he died as a martyr, and his disciples were permitted to take and bury his body.

His death did not end his influence.[40] His ministry found a permanent place in the gospel story. Some of his followers continued to regard him as their leader and won new disciples to follow him. His influence spread outside of Palestine. When Apollos, a Jew of Alexandria, came to Ephesus (Acts 18:24–26), he knew of John's ministry and rite of baptism, and he practiced baptism as one who followed John. (It seems that he did not know the Christian message.) Whether he heard of John in Egypt or elsewhere, and so most likely in Palestine, we cannot say. Later, at Ephesus, Paul found twelve Jews who had been baptized into John's baptism (Acts 19:1–7). Probably they had been baptized by Apollos. If not, they are evidence that others besides Apollos had brought the message of John to Ephesus. The attention given to John in the Gospel of John shows that his influence still continued when that Gospel was written, late in the first century; its author felt bound to emphasize that John was subordinate to Jesus (John 1:6–8, 15, 19–27; 3:27–30). All this indicates that for decades there were non-Christians who considered John the Baptist to be the climactic prophet of history.

[40] On "The Later History of the Baptist Movement," see Kraeling, *John the Baptist*, pp. 158 ff. On this and on the ministry of John the Baptist, see also the careful study of Charles H. H. Scobie, *John the Baptist* (London, SCM Press, Ltd., 1964).

3*

Part Two

JESUS THE CENTRAL FIGURE

Chapter 3

THE HISTORICAL JESUS

CHIS CHAPTER deals mainly with the way the gospel tradition about Jesus was preserved and used in the first decades of the church. This discussion is necessary before we can study the ministry and message of Jesus; we must know whether our sources can be trusted. But this is not merely a literary question. The use of the gospel tradition in the church is an important part of the process by which the church emerged and took form.

Jesus of Nazareth lived in the first third of the first century. A few scholars have asserted that no such person ever lived, and that "Jesus" was only the creation of pious imagination or social process, but such claims are false. There is no reason to doubt that Jesus lived a human life in Palestine. Roman, Jewish, and early Christian testimony unite to make that conclusion certain.[1]

It is not so easy, however, to determine exactly what Jesus did and said. We have no direct evidence dating from his lifetime; Jesus himself wrote nothing, and there were no newspapers or other news organs to preserve a contemporary record of his life and words. Centuries later certain writings appeared that claim to give official records of governmental authorities, but these are undoubtedly pious fiction.[2] No written records come to us from the days of his ministry.

One may unconsciously assume that the Gospels are reliable documents from the very time of Jesus. They are not quite that early. Their early date and immense importance are clear, but they date from later decades of the first century, and are not contemporary accounts of the deeds and words of Jesus.

How then can we learn what Jesus did and said and what kind of

[1] A good survey of the evidence is found in Maurice Goguel, *Jesus the Nazarene: Myth or History?*, tr. from the French by Frederick Stevens (D. Appleton and Company, 1926); and in H. G. Wood, *Did Jesus Really Live?* (The Macmillan Company, 1938).

[2] For an English translation of the fanciful Acts of Pilate and related writings, see Montague Rhodes James, *The Apocryphal New Testament* (Oxford, Clarendon Press, 1924), pp. 94–165.

person he was? Much light is thrown on his life and work by a knowledge of his political, social, and religious background, of which the two preceding chapters give a partial picture. To understand Jesus, it is necessary by study and informed imagination to become at home in that first-century setting in which he lived and worked. But this will not carry us far. More specific information is needed.

SCANT HELP FROM ROMAN AUTHORS

The earliest Roman writings that mention Jesus come from the early second century. Tacitus, in his *Annals* XV.44, written about A.D. 115, tells of the burning of Rome when Nero was emperor, and reports that the Christians in Rome were accused of setting the fire; he adds: "Christus, from whom their name is derived, was condemned to death in the reign of Tiberius by the procurator Pontius Pilate." Tiberius was the Roman emperor from A.D. 14 to 37; Pilate was the Roman governor of Judea, Samaria, and Idumea from A.D. 26 to 36. So Tacitus dates the death of Jesus between A.D. 26 and 36, reports that Pilate condemned him to death, and makes it clear that when he wrote, Jesus was called Christ in Rome by his followers.

In the first third of the second century, Suetonius wrote his *Life of Claudius* (the Roman emperor A.D. 41–54). In paragraph 25 he says that Claudius "banished from Rome the Jews, who were making an incessant uproar at the instigation of Chrestus." It is not certain that Suetonius here refers to Jesus Christ. He speaks of Chrestus as a rabble rouser in Rome, and he spells the name with an *e*: Chrestus. But in the Greek of his day *Christos* and *Chrēstos* were pronounced in the same way. So it is possible and even probable that what happened in Rome was a series of riots or excited disputes between Jews who believed in Jesus as the Christ and Jews who rejected that claim; Suetonius mistakenly thought that the riots were stirred up by a Roman Jew named Chrestus.

The third Roman author to refer to Jesus was Pliny the Younger. In A.D. 111, while governor of Bithynia in Asia Minor, he wrote a letter to the emperor Trajan (A.D. 98–117), asking how he should treat the numerous Christians of Bithynia. He indicates that Christians had been there for decades, and says that they "sing together a hymn to Christ as to a god."[3] This tells us something about their faith and worship in the early second century, but gives no facts about the life of Jesus himself.

[3] *Epistles* X.96–97.

INFORMATION FROM JEWISH SOURCES

Jewish sources tell us more than do the Roman historians. Josephus, in his *Antiquities,* written about A.D. 95, has two passages about Jesus. One (XX.9.1) is a brief passing reference; it speaks of James, the leader of the church in Jerusalem, as "the brother of Jesus who was called Christ." This indicates that Jesus actually lived and that his followers thought he was the expected Jewish Christ or Messiah ("Christ" transliterates a Greek word, and "Messiah" a Hebrew word; both mean the same thing: "Anointed").

The other passage (XVIII.3.3) in its present form could only have been written by a Christian. Josephus, as all agree, was not a Christian, so a Christian scribe must have inserted this passage or at least altered or expanded it. This was quite possible; for many centuries it was the Christians and not the Jews who preserved Josephus and the other ancient Jewish writings in Greek, and so a Christian scribe could have changed the passage.[4] Here is a translation of the passage as now extant (the parts that Klausner and others think are Christian insertions are printed in italics):

> "Now there was about this time Jesus, a wise man, *if it be lawful to call him a man.* For he was a doer of wonderful works, a teacher of such men as receive the truth with pleasure. He drew over to him both many of the Jews and many of the Gentiles. *He was the Messiah;* and when Pilate, at the suggestion of the principal men among us, had condemned him to the cross, those that loved him at the first ceased not (so to do), *for he appeared to them alive again the third day, as the divine prophets had foretold these and ten thousand other wonderful things concerning him;* and the race of Christians, so named from him, are not extinct even now."[5]

The italicized words can hardly have been written by the sophisticated Jew Josephus; indeed, some other statements, such as the assertion that Jesus did miracles and that many Gentiles believed in him during his ministry, may not come from him. It is entirely possible that Josephus

---

[4] A similar alteration of Josephus appears in the Slavonic version of *The Jewish War;* see a translation and discussion of two important alterations, given in Maurice Goguel, *Life of Jesus,* pp. 82–91. A translation of twenty-two alterations is given by H. St. J. Thackeray, *Josephus,* Vol. III, in The Loeb Classical Library (G. P. Putnam's Sons, 1928), pp. 635–658. The theory that these Slavonic passages are at least in part from Josephus himself is usually and rightly rejected.

[5] See Klausner, *Jesus of Nazareth,* pp. 55 f.

wrote something about Jesus as a good man and helpful teacher, but if so, he thereby indicted the leaders of his people for prompting the execution of a good man. Would he have done that? Perhaps the entire paragraph is, rather, the work of a Christian scribe.

Clearly authentic, though not so favorable to Jesus, are the references in Rabbinical sources.[6] Though written down considerably later than the time of the rabbis quoted, these statements by common consent give views expressed in the decades immediately following the fall of Jerusalem (A.D. 70).

The rabbis are hostile witnesses. For example, they know the story of the virgin birth, but deduce from it that Jesus was an illegitimate child of a Jewish woman; they tell of his execution, but to show that it was deserved they say that forty days of delay and public proclamation inviting testimony in his defense brought forth no evidence to justify acquittal. Nevertheless, such reports have historical value. They give the name, Jesus of Nazareth; this is indisputable testimony that he actually lived. Their statement that he "practiced sorcery" attests that he did remarkable deeds. (It is also attested that his disciples healed the sick in his name.) The charge that he mocked at the words of the wise shows that he was critical of the Jewish leaders of his day, and the claim that he beguiled and led Israel astray reveals that he had a wide following. The report that he had five disciples is puzzling, but shows that he did have special disciples. The reported saying that he had not come to cancel or add to the law recalls Matt. 5:17; Luke 16:17. The statements that he was hanged as a false teacher who misled Israel, and that this execution occurred on the eve of a Passover which occurred on a Sabbath, agree with the timing of the execution in the Gospels. The Rabbinical evidence shows a polemical spirit, but it confirms in some important respects the evidence of the Gospels.

NONCANONICAL CHRISTIAN SOURCES

Neither Roman nor Jewish sources, however, provide any detailed information about Jesus. It is only from Christian sources that we get such detailed data. This means that we must look to the New Testament. It is true that in ancient papyri and in writings of ancient church fathers we find sayings attributed to Jesus and meager hints about his actions. For the most part this material consists of rather meager fragments of apocryphal "gospels"; among the most important and earliest of these apocryphal "gospels" are The Gospel of the Nazareans, The Gospel of the Ebionites, The Gospel of the Hebrews, The Gospel of the Egyptians,

6 For an excellent survey of such references from the age of the Tannaim (the first two centuries of the Christian era), see Klausner, *Jesus of Nazareth*, pp. 18–47.

and The Gospel of Peter; it appears from their surviving portions that they were written about the first half of the second century. A careful sifting of this material, therefore, makes it clear these writings are all later than the New Testament Gospels and are a baffling mixture of items that ring true and items obviously not authentic. And if we ask how to determine what items can be trusted, the New Testament has to be the standard of comparison and judgment. From these later fragments of tradition, little solid information can be derived to add to the New Testament evidence.[7]

Recent manuscript discoveries have brought to light writings called "gospels" which promise more help. For example, an interesting fragmentary work, published as *Fragments of an Unknown Gospel and Other Early Christian Papyri*,[8] contains incidents and sayings resembling but differing from both the Synoptic Gospels and the Gospel of John. When first discovered this "gospel" seemed to its editors to have been written earlier than the Gospel of John. But further study shows that it dates later than our canonical Gospels, and has no independent value. Recently there has come to light in Egypt a group of over forty Christian writings in the Coptic language.[9] They include so-called "gospels": The Gospel of Truth, The Gospel of Thomas, and The Gospel of Philip. But The Gospel of Truth[10] is a meditation in Gnostic terms, with practically no information about the historical Jesus. The Gospel of Philip,[11] likewise deeply Gnostic, gives no trustworthy account of the deeds and words of Jesus. The Gospel of Thomas[12] is the writing of the group that most

[7] An excellent sifting of such material has been made by Joachim Jeremias, *Unknown Sayings of Jesus,* tr. by Reginald H. Fuller (The Macmillan Company, 1957). The sayings in the recently published Coptic Gospel of Thomas could not be included in Jeremias' study. The most comprehensive collection of all noncanonical evidence is Edgar Hennecke, *New Testament Apocrypha,* Vol. I: *Gospels and Related Writings,* edited by Wilhelm Schneemelcher; Eng. tr. edited by R. McL. Wilson (The Westminster Press, 1963).

[8] Edited by H. Idris Bell and T. C. Skeat (London, British Museum, 1935).

[9] A description and preliminary study of all these manuscripts, with an English translation of The Gospel of Thomas, has been published by Jean Doresse, *The Secret Books of the Egyptian Gnostics,* Eng. tr. by Philip Mairet (The Viking Press, Inc., 1960). I have given a nontechnical description and evaluation of these Coptic "gospels" in *The Biblical Archaeologist,* XXIV (1961), pp. 7–18.

[10] Coptic text and English translation in *Evangelium Veritatis,* edited by M. Malinine, H.-Ch. Puech, and G. Quispel (Zürich, Rascher Verlag, 1956). English translation and commentary in Kendrick Grobel, *The Gospel of Truth* (Abingdon Press, 1960).

[11] For English translation, introduction, and commentary see R. McL. Wilson, *The Gospel of Philip* (Harper & Row, Publishers, Inc., 1962).

[12] Coptic text and English translation by A. Guillaumont, H.-Ch. Puech, G. Quispel, W. Till and †Yassah 'Abd al Masîh, *The Gospel According to Thomas* (Harper & Brothers, 1959). For an introduction, English translation, and Commentary, see Robert M. Grant, David Noel Freedman, and William R. Schoedel, *The Secret Sayings of Jesus* (Doubleday & Company, Inc., 1960).

resembles our canonical Gospels. It consists of some 113 sayings attributed
to Jesus but varying greatly in the degree to which they resemble his
sayings found in the New Testament. None of these Coptic "gospels" contains an account or outline of the events of his life. Possibly, as has been
asserted, The Gospel of Thomas can add to our knowledge of what
Jesus said. But this fourth-century Coptic "gospel" is a revision and expansion of a second-century Greek "gospel"; it depended on the gospel
tradition, which is more authentically preserved in our canonical Gospels.
Even if a few of the sayings in The Gospel of Thomas should prove to
contain new and truthworthy information about Jesus' teaching, this
could only be determined by their basic agreement with our New Testament Gospels. We are always driven back to the New Testament as the
one source of detailed material for the life of Jesus.

NEW TESTAMENT EVIDENCE OUTSIDE THE GOSPELS

In the New Testament this material is found mainly in the Gospels.
For an interesting example of this, one may compare the Gospel of Luke
and the book of The Acts. Both were written by the same writer; the
author of The Acts knew all that the Gospel of Luke says, and so could
have drawn on it in writing The Acts. But in The Acts he does not
quote once from the gospel material he had used in Luke, and apart
from words dated after the resurrection (ch. 1:4–8), the book of The Acts
contains only one saying of Jesus' (ch. 20:35)—a saying not found in Luke.
Clearly this writer knew a great deal about the life and teaching of Jesus
which it did not suit his purpose to use in writing The Acts. This nonuse
of gospel tradition is noticeable in the New Testament letters (and the
book of The Revelation). Among these other non-gospel writings, Paul
is the one who gives the most clues to the historical Jesus. Other writings
speak of his suffering and death (Heb. 5:8; 9:11–28; I Peter 1:19; 4:1;
Rev. 5:6, 9), and Heb. 2:18; 4:15 speaks of his temptation, but Paul gives
more specific information.[13]

Paul, who was converted only a few years after Jesus' death, knows that
Jesus was of Davidic ancestry (Rom. 1:3). He knows teachings of Jesus',
and for him that teaching carries full authority; he mentions, for example, that Jesus prohibited divorce (I Cor. 7:10) and taught that
preachers of the gospel are entitled to support (I Cor. 9:14; cf. Matt.
10:10; Luke 10:7; cf. also I Tim. 5:18). He reports the action and words
of Jesus at the Last Supper (I Cor. 11:23–25), speaks frequently of his

13 For a study of "The Pauline Evidence," see Maurice Goguel, *Life of Jesus*, pp. 105–
127.

crucifixion (and burial), and refers often to his resurrection, giving in I Cor. 15:3–8 an account of the appearances of the risen Christ to his followers. All this is not much; it deals mostly with the closing events of Jesus' ministry; and oddly enough it appears mostly in I Corinthians. In still other passages Paul may reflect sayings of Jesus', but they give no new information as to what Jesus said. They at best confirm items found in the Gospels.

ARE THE GOSPELS TRUSTWORTHY?

Thus to study the life and teaching of Jesus we must go mainly to the Gospels.[14] They come from the latter third of the first century A.D. Can we be sure that they give us a substantially trustworthy picture of Jesus? Their trustworthiness has been and is challenged, and we must ask whether knowledge of the career of Jesus was faithfully preserved during the decades between his death about A.D. 30 and the writing of the Gospels about A.D. 65 to 95. To get back from the Gospels to the historical Jesus we must form an idea of what happened to the gospel tradition in the earliest decades of the church.

One answer to this question is that no problem exists; the Gospels are completely trustworthy; God himself dictated the words of the Gospels; the human author wrote down what God told him to write. There is vivid presentation of this view in a frontispiece found in some medieval manuscripts of the Gospel of John. John stands in the center, listening, with left hand cupped to his ear. In the upper corner of the picture, to John's left, is a cloud from which rays of light flash forth and a hand reaches down; this indicates that God is dictating to John. On John's right, at his feet, sits Prochorus, his scribe. John gestures to him with the right hand—to indicate that he is speaking to Prochorus what the divine voice dictates. The Gospel of John is thus a divinely dictated book; it can have no flaw or error. The trouble with this view is that when we compare the four Gospels, we see that each one has its own distinctive vocabulary and style. Thus in the writing of each Gospel there was a human factor which that pictorial theory of inspiration failed to recognize.

---

14 Survey studies of the work of scholars in their search for the historical Jesus, especially in the Gospels, are provided by Albert Schweitzer, *The Quest of the Historical Jesus*, tr. by W. Montgomery (London, A. & C. Black, 1910); Chester Charlton McCown, *The Search for the Real Jesus* (Charles Scribner's Sons, 1940); James M. Robinson, *A New Quest of the Historical Jesus* (London, SCM Press, Ltd., 1959). A recent reflection of scholarly views on the Gospels and their light on the historical Jesus is *Studia Evangelica*, edited by Kurt Aland, F. L. Cross, Jean Danielou, Harald Riesenfeld, and W. C. van Unnik (Berlin, Akademie-Verlag, 1959). It contains in 813 pages papers read at an International Congress on "The Four Gospels in 1957."

Another view that asserts the dependable quality of the Gospels ascribes each of them to an apostle of Jesus or to an immediate assistant of an apostle. The apostles Matthew and John were companions of Jesus; John Mark, according to ancient church tradition (Eusebius, *Church History* III.39.15; cf. I Peter 5:13), was the companion of the apostle Peter, and Luke was the companion of the apostle Paul (Col. 4:14). So all four Gospels, written independently, should be trustworthy. Apart from the plain fact that neither Luke nor Paul[15] knew Jesus in the days of his ministry, a comparison of the Gospels indicates that they were not all written independently; between the first three Gospels (called the Synoptic Gospels, since they give a common view of the life of Jesus), there are so many agreements in content, order, and wording that there must be some connection between them.

Moreover, there are signs that these Gospels are not merely stenographic or factual eyewitness reports of what took place; they record a tradition that has been interpreted in the telling. This is particularly true of the Gospel of John; as we shall see in more detail in Chapter 14, and as both Clement of Alexandria[16] and John Calvin[17]—to name just two Christian scholars—have clearly discerned, this Gospel, though it contains valuable historical information about Jesus, blends theological interpretations with the tradition as to what Jesus did and said. But the same thing is true of the Synoptic Gospels. So the problem is too complicated to be solved by regarding each Gospel as an independent account of what happened. The conviction has grown and must be accepted that in some way the origin of the Gospels involved many Christians who had a part in selecting, preserving, handing on, and writing the tradition about Jesus. Thus to learn what Jesus did and said we must first study what went on in the early church.

A Fixed Oral Tradition?

1. One view, not in vogue today, is that there was a fixed oral tradition which was handed down carefully under control of the leaders of the church. This does not mean merely that the tradition about Jesus was preserved for years in oral form; that is almost universally agreed. It

---

15 As the RSV rightly indicates, II Cor. 5:16 refers not to Paul's knowing the historical Jesus but to a way of thinking about Jesus that Paul had used at an earlier time, before conversion.

16 Reported by Eusebius, *Church History* VI.14.7.

17 *Commentary on the Gospel According to John*, Eng. tr. by William Pringle (Wm. B. Eerdmans Publishing Company, 1949), p. 21: "John dwells more largely on the doctrine . . . also devotes a portion of his work to historical details."

means that the tradition was given a fixed and official form, that this fixed form was preserved not only when the gospel tradition was in Aramaic but also when that tradition was translated into Greek. It means that the leaders of the church, especially its teachers, controlled and watched over this tradition to make sure that it remained dependable and accurate.

This would explain the agreements between the three Gospels, but it would not explain the places in which these Gospels differ in content, order of sections, and wording. Moreover, there is no evidence that any authority so controlled the tradition that there was one fixed wording of it. No evidence exists that the Jerusalem leaders, who on this view would have controlled the gospel tradition, had any real control over its exact content and wording, especially in the Greek-speaking Gentile churches.

But this theory may remind us that among the Jews oral tradition was common and was carefully handed down. It was usual especially among Pharisees to give tradition a compact form and memorize that basic tradition for use in study and community life. Thus the natural thing in the early Palestinian church, composed as it first was of Jews, would be to memorize key sayings of Jesus and stories of what he did. It would not be left entirely to the choice of any and every Christian speaker to word the tradition according to his individual interest. The tradition was more stable than that.[18]

WRITTEN SOURCES?

2. Thus there was a period of oral tradition and some attention to memorizing important items, but the idea of a fixed and officially controlled oral tradition from which each Gospel writer derived the wording of his material is too rigid. So a second view has been suggested: one Gospel depends on another or all depend on a still earlier written source. Some such theory would explain the agreements in Greek between the three Synoptic Gospels. It is not likely that an earlier gospel large enough to contain all the material in these three Gospels could have existed, been used by the Synoptic authors, and then disappeared without a trace and without even a mention of it in any extant ancient source. A more reasonable theory is that the one of these Gospels written first was then used by the other two as a written source.

From our modern point of view this may not seem a legitimate way to write a gospel; for us, literary ethics and copyright protection prevent

[18] There is thus a limited truth in the argument of Birger Gerhardsson, *Memory and Manuscript; Oral Tradition and Written Transmission in Rabbinic Judaism and Early Christianity* (Uppsala, C. W. K. Gleerup Publishers, 1961).

extensive copying of another document. But ancient statements show that in those days it was considered quite proper to do this; in II Macc. 2:23 the writer frankly says that he used the history by Jason of Cyrene as a written source, and scholars generally agree that Josephus used Nicolaus of Damascus and other written sources. So the latter two of our Synoptic Gospels could have used the earliest Gospel as a written source, and they could also have used one or more other written sources that they found trustworthy.

One such view, particularly favored in Roman Catholic circles, is that Matthew was the first Gospel written[19] and was used by the writers of Luke and Mark. On this view, a Gospel by an apostle and eyewitness was then used as a source by two Christian writers who were not apostles or eyewitnesses. This supposed priority of Matthew, though it has ancient tradition in its favor,[20] is highly doubtful. When the three Synoptic Gospels are compared, the Gospel of Mark appears more original than either of the other two, and its priority explains best the choice of material, the order in which the Gospels place it, and the agreements in wording.

For this reason the so-called two-document theory has been widely accepted; Mark is the oldest Gospel, and the writers of Matthew and Luke used Mark as their basic document, and as their second written source used an early document (usually called Q), consisting mainly if not entirely of sayings of Jesus. This theory, however, leaves unexplained where the writers of Matthew and Luke obtained the material that only one of them contains. Even if part of it came from Q, with one Gospel taking certain sayings from Q whereas the other did not, there is other material that certainly did not come from Q. So the two-document theory has been enlarged, notably by B. H. Streeter, to a four-document theory: Matthew and Luke used Mark and Q, and in addition Matthew used a written source M and Luke used a written source L. One form of this theory holds that Luke first gathered his special material L, combined it with Q to form a Proto-Luke, and finally supplemented Proto-Luke by using Mark and so obtained our present Gospel of Luke.[21]

19 On June 19, 1911, the Pontifical Biblical Commission issued authoritative decisions as to the apostolic authorship of the Gospel of Matthew and its date prior to the Gospels of Mark and Luke. See John E. Steinmueller, *A Companion to Scripture Studies*, Vol. III (Joseph F. Wagner, Inc., 1943), pp. 66–68.

20 Eusebius in his *Church History* reports this, quoting Irenaeus in V.8.2–4 and Origen in VI.25.4; he agrees with this view in III.24.6–7, and may have found the same view in Papias, whom he quotes in III.39.16 as saying that "Matthew compiled the oracles in the Hebrew language."

21 On the two-document theory, the four-document theory, and the Proto-Luke theory, see the classic argument by Burnett Hillman Streeter, *The Four Gospels*, Fourth Impression, rev. (London, Macmillan and Co., 1930). His diagram on p. 150 shows his total view.

This four-document theory has the advantage that it tries to explain the source of all the material in both Matthew and Luke (it allows that other written items or oral tradition provided a few small units of each of these Gospels). Streeter assumed that each main source represented gospel tradition known in some prominent center of the church, and so he related each source and each Synoptic Gospel to the ongoing life of one local church.

This directed attention to a point that source theories had too much neglected. What had happened to the gospel material in the years before any written sources were composed? What was the intended use of the written sources and the written Gospels? We can only understand the origin of the Gospels when we study their origin, and the origin of their written sources, in the actual life situation in which the material was preserved, used, and handed on. It is to the credit of the method of study known as form criticism that it has taken this task seriously.

FORM CRITICISM

3. Form criticism[22] does not exclude the theory that the writers of our Synoptic Gospels used written sources. But it holds—rightly—that back of the written records of the life of Jesus lay an earlier period when what was known of Jesus was preserved and handed on in oral form. It undertakes to study that oral period. In so doing, it takes the spotlight from the writers of our Gospels and their written sources and puts it on the far larger number of early Christians who had a part in preserving and handing on the oral tradition about Jesus. The Gospels result from a social process in which countless Christians made oral use of the gospel tradition and determined to a large extent what our Gospels would contain and how it would be worded.

In this oral period the gospel tradition was not preserved in a carefully arranged chronological order. It was not preserved as a connected story but in separate units. Each unit was used as needed in the life of the church, and for such use it was not important to know when most events happened or most sayings were spoken. What counted was that the unit was useful in the life of the church; it was recalled and used in connection

---

22 Basic for all later publications of form criticism are Karl Ludwig Schmidt, *Der Rahmen der Geschichte Jesu* (Berlin, Trowitsch & Sohn, 1919); Martin Dibelius, *From Tradition to Gospel*, tr. by Bertram Lee Woolf (Charles Scribner's Sons, 1935); Rudolf Bultmann, *The History of the Synoptic Tradition*, Eng. tr. by John Marsh (Harper & Row, Publishers, Inc., 1963). Two leading works critical of the excesses of form criticism are Vincent Taylor, *The Formation of the Gospel Tradition* (London, Macmillan and Co., Ltd., 1933); Laurence J. McGinley, *Form-Criticism of the Synoptic Healing Narratives* (Woodstock College Press, 1944).

with actual current needs. Such tradition about Jesus was used in worship, in teaching, in solving problems of daily life, and in controversy with opponents of the Christians.

The purpose for which the unit of tradition was recalled and used determined the way in which it was worded, and sometimes led the Christians to alter its wording to meet explicitly new needs of the church. At times—according to some form critics—such needs even led the church to appropriate from other sources material considered consistent with what was remembered about Jesus. Or the church, needing help in some special situation and convinced that it had "the mind of Christ," added new items of tradition ascribed to the risen Christ or considered consistent with what Jesus had done and said.

Continuous use of this tradition through a period of time—at least two decades—gave it a more or less fixed form in most items.[23] In thinking of this continuous process the form critics, especially in the early development of their method, tended to use the laws of oral tradition discovered in the transmission of folk tales through generations of storytelling. After this oral period the tradition that had been remembered, used, shaped, and expanded to meet the needs of the church was written down, first in written sources and then in our canonical Gospels.

Such study of the forms that the gospel tradition took on as a result of this assumed process implies that the Gospels are witnesses first of all for the faith and life of the early church, and that the elements altered or added cannot be used to determine what Jesus of Nazareth did and said. But this method of study does not in itself decide how much of the exist-

[23] In studying the gospel tradition, Bultmann divides the sayings of Jesus into these groups: (1) Logia or wisdom sayings. (2) Prophetic and apocalyptic sayings. (3) Legal sayings and church rules. (4) I-sayings, in which Jesus speaks of himself. (5) Parables. (6) Apothegms, a decisive saying as climax of a brief narrative. Supplemental to the sayings is the narrative material, with two main groups: (1) Miracle stories. (2) Historical narratives and legends.

Martin Dibelius divides the narrative material of the Synoptic Gospels into five types or forms: (1) Paradigms (the same as Bultmann's apothegms). (2) *Novellen* or wonder stories. (3) Legends, edifying stories of a holy person. (4) The Passion Story, the one part of the gospel story thought to have been told from the earliest times as a connected narrative. (5) Myths, telling of the invasion of human life by a supernatural power. Dibelius did not attempt to classify the sayings of Jesus in so detailed a way as did Bultmann. He centered attention particularly on the hortatory aspects of the teaching of Jesus, and noted some seven types or forms of teaching: (1) Wisdom sayings. (2) Comparisons or similitudes. (3) Narrative parables. (4) Prophetic utterances. (5) Concise commands. (6) More elaborate commands. (7) Sayings concerning the nature of the speaker.

A less elaborate analysis of forms found in the gospel material is proposed by Vincent Taylor: (1) Passion narratives. (2) Pronouncement stories: brief narratives, each climaxing in an authoritative saying. (3) Sayings and parables. (4) Miracle stories. (5) Stories about Jesus.

ing gospel material is trustworthy evidence for the life and ministry of the historical Jesus, and that historical life and ministry are our concern in this present chapter.

There are scholars who use this method of study and find the Gospels substantially trustworthy for the study of Jesus' life. But other form critics, notably Rudolf Bultmann, hold that the early church had no clear historical interest. The church's concern was with the risen Christ preached and believed in, and the first Christians had no concern to determine what Jesus really did and said. The gospel tradition was formed by the church in creative response to its needs. This does not deny that Jesus lived, but his earthly life was not of interest to the believers, and so the gospel tradition formed by such faith-controlled use tells us what the church believed and taught but not what Jesus did and said. We cannot go back of the Christ preached in the church; we cannot recover a detailed and trustworthy story of the historical Jesus.[24] So Bultmann and others.

TRUTH AND ERROR IN FORM CRITICISM

It is important to recognize the truth in form criticism. The gospel tradition was indeed preserved not merely by a few individuals, not merely in a scholar's notebook or a research library, but in the vibrant life of the church and as a constant resource for its worship, teaching, guidance, and defense. The selection and form of the material tells us much about the faith, thought, and activity of the church in those earliest years, for which we have no adequate direct contemporary witnesses. The narratives of The Acts is sketchy and meager, and to realize that the church was using this gospel tradition in its daily life adds to our knowledge of the church. The Gospels thus attest an ongoing process in the earliest church; they are documents of faith; they reflect how the church defended and expressed its faith by recalling Jesus' life and teaching and using them in its regular worship and life.

Furthermore, the gospel tradition was preserved at first in oral form; the individual incidents, parables, and sayings were preserved as separate units and used as needed in the life of the church; the continual use of this material gave it a form and focus that stayed with it in its written form. This means, as form criticism says, that the Gospels have not preserved a clear and connected chronological order of material; the

---

24 A recent 710-page symposium by forty-eight scholars deals with this issue; see Helmut Ristow and Karl Matthiae, editors, *Der historische Jesus und der kerygmatische Christus* (Berlin, Evangelische Verlagsanstalt, 1960).

time when most of these events and sayings occurred was not remembered and was of no importance for the helpful use of the tradition. As a result we can never reconstruct a detailed chronology of the events in Jesus' ministry.

Thus there is great truth in form criticism. But the picture some form critics give of the wholesale creation of gospel tradition in the early church is unconvincing. Their radical negative results are due more to their presuppositions than to the data with which they deal. When the form critic judges the transmission of the gospel tradition by comparing the oral transmission of popular folk tales, he forgets that folk tales pass on from generation to generation and have much time in which to be shaped and changed by popular ideas, whereas the gospel tradition was preserved in oral form for hardly more than twenty years before it began to be written down. This gives no time for the operation of such laws as govern oral transmission from one generation to another.

Furthermore, in that one generation when the tradition was preserved only in oral form, it was not a folk tale that was being transmitted. It was the story of a historical person whose place of ministry was known. It was the story of one whom the church considered the Lord and future judge of his followers; they expected to be judged by their response to what he had taught and done, so they had urgent reason to remember what he had done and said and to govern life by that tradition.[25] It was a story which in that first generation could be checked by eyewitnesses; in fact, some of the most important early preachers were eyewitnesses who were telling what they had "seen and heard" (Acts 4:20). It was a story not left to chance telling; in large part it was told and its meaning taught by teachers,[26] whose task was to convince, train, and guide those they taught by use of this gospel tradition. The tradition was never told out of mere historical interest; the driving impulse to tell the story was religious; but the religious interest was directed to a quite recent history, which was told because of its supreme importance for every hearer.

The early church would have been astounded at the idea that they had no historical interest and had themselves created the gospel tradition. They knew that they had received this crucial story; it was Jesus, not themselves, whom they regarded as the creative instrument of God's

[25] This point is noted by Burton Scott Easton, *Christ in the Gospels* (Charles Scribner's Sons, 1930), p. 30.
[26] A study of a concordance will show that teaching is as prominent as preaching in the Gospel accounts of Jesus' ministry, and Acts 13:1; I Cor. 12:28; and Eph. 4:11 illustrate the prominent role of the teacher in the apostolic age. Their special role in preserving and handing on the gospel tradition must not be neglected.

revelation and saving action. A radical rejection of the historicity of the gospel tradition is not justified.

EARLY PALESTINIAN TRADITION

Our Gospels come to us in Greek, but they have such a strong Semitic tone that the basic tradition they contain must have come from Palestine and from the earliest days of the church. Greek-speaking Gentile Christians naturally said things differently and no doubt unconsciously reflected their interests in the final form given the gospel tradition in our Greek Gospels. But the extensive Semitic language patterns and thought forms, present in the Gospel of John as well as in the Synoptic Gospels, show that the basic setting of the gospel material is not Hellenistic but Semitic; it is rooted in the Old Testament, the Palestinian ministry of Jesus, and the early Aramaic-speaking church.[27]

That the Synoptic Gospels preserve an essentially early Palestinian tradition about Jesus may be illustrated by three examples. The most common title for Jesus during the apostolic age was "Lord"; the basic early confession of the church was that "Jesus Christ is Lord."[28] But the Synoptic Gospels show very sparing use of this title during Jesus' ministry; their writers know it was not used much at that time. This is not what one would expect of a church that had no historical sense.

Again, the term "the Son of Man," which raises many questions, is found in the New Testament, except for a single use in Acts 7:56, only in the Gospels and only on the lips of Jesus. If the titles of Jesus in the Gospels were the creation of the apostolic church, the dominance of this title in the Gospels and its almost complete absence from the other writings of the apostolic age would be inexplicable. The church knew that Jesus had used this title himself; it also knew that this title was not clear to Gentiles, so it did not use it much when it was speaking of Jesus independently of the gospel tradition.

A third example is the parables. Jesus is known in the world's literature as the matchless teacher through parables. Others had used this way of illustrating truth—it was a well-known teaching method in ancient

---

27 This is the solid truth in the exaggerated claim of Charles Cutler Torrey that all four canonical Gospels were written in Aramaic. See his books, *The Four Gospels* (Harper & Brothers, 1933), and *Documents of the Primitive Church* (Harper & Brothers, 1941). A more balanced view is presented by Matthew Black, *An Aramaic Approach to the Gospels and Acts*, 2d ed. (Oxford, Clarendon Press, 1954).

28 See Oscar Cullmann, *The Earliest Christian Confessions*, Eng. tr. by J. K. S. Reid (London, Lutterworth Press, 1949).

Judaism[29]—but Jesus was the unique master of its use. If the parables in the Gospels had been the creation of the early church, we would expect to find in the other New Testament writings, written in the same general period, equally skillful use of the same teaching method. But such is not the case. No other leader or writer in the New Testament story even attempts to match Jesus in the use of parables. The church knew that Jesus taught in parables; they were able to distinguish his method and message from their own method and teaching.[30]

FROM JESUS TO THE SYNOPTIC GOSPELS

It will be well to summarize now in chronological order the entire process that led from the life and ministry of Jesus to the final writing of the Synoptic Gospels. Jesus himself wrote nothing, and he held no official position that would have caused a record of his life and message to be preserved. What he had said and done was remembered by his followers, not primarily out of historical interest, but because after his resurrection these things were of vital importance for their faith and life. What they remembered they used in the life and mission of their group: in their worship and preaching, their teaching, their decisions as to how to live, and their defense of their Master and their faith against hostile attacks.

As they remembered and used this tradition, the form in which it was handed on was shaped by their needs and their aims. It was continually used for a practical religious purpose, and this purpose left its mark on the tradition. One way in which the story was shaped to bring out a point may be noted in passing; because of the conviction, shared by the early church with their Master himself, that his ministry and work was the climactic fulfillment of Old Testament promise, the tradition was so handed on as to make plain how this promise found fulfillment in Jesus.[31]

This practical use of the gospel tradition to meet the immediate needs of the church did not require that Christians know the exact time and place that every event and teaching occurred. Most incidents and sayings could be preserved as separate items. So there was no geographical loca-

---

[29] Cf. W. O. E. Oesterley, *The Gospel Parables in the Light of Their Jewish Background* (The Macmillan Company, 1936), pp. 3–18.

[30] Cf. Burton Scott Easton, *The Gospel Before the Gospels* (Charles Scribner's Sons, 1928), p. 109: "The primary historic value of the Synoptists is not for their own age but for the tradition of the teachings of Jesus."

[31] The beginning of the process that led to our Gospels was the gathering and explanation of Old Testament passages fulfilled in Christ, according to B. P. W. Stather Hunt, *Primitive Gospel Sources* (Philosophical Library, Inc., 1951).

tion or fixed sequence of most items in the oral tradition, and the actual historical sequence of most of them was lost beyond recovery. For the understanding of what Jesus had said and accomplished, this was not a serious loss. But the result was that it is not now possible to write a biography of Jesus and put the happenings of his life in an established sequence. And as a result of the shaping of the material to meet the needs of the church the Gospels do not provide an inerrant and infallible story of Jesus' life and message.

But the broad lines of his ministry, message, and purpose can be discerned. The broad framework stands out: the ministry of John the Baptist, the baptism of Jesus, his initial preaching and first disciples, his strong appeal to the crowds and the gathering hostility of Jewish leaders, the growing discernment of his unique role, the increasing clouds of danger, the final preaching and challenge to Israel and her leaders at Jerusalem; the arrest, trial, crucifixion, and resurrection. Within this general and trustworthy framework we have preserved a large number of incidents and sayings that could have happened early or late in the ministry; their dating is not a crucial matter.[32]

The church had a real historical sense when it was important to have it, but was not concerned primarily with dating events and sayings. Nor was it interested in Jesus' psychological processes. Its basic concern was religious loyalty to Jesus Christ the Lord and the need to know enough about him to guide it in worship, teaching, life, and evangelistic witness. But this religious loyalty and purpose were linked with historical sense to such a degree that the Gospels are not merely testimonies to the faith and life of the early church—they are that—but are also sources for essential knowledge of the Jesus of history.[33]

At an early date, which we cannot fix, the practice began of writing down some of the gospel tradition that was in use. These writings were produced not merely for literary reasons or personal satisfaction, but for use in worship and for the guidance of those who had the special task of teaching in the church.

Probably one early type of document was a selection of Scripture passages that the church saw had been fulfilled in the life and work of Jesus. Such a topical collection of Scripture passages may now be illus-

32 That a broad general outline of the ministry was preserved in the church's teaching has been rightly argued by C. H. Dodd in "The Framework of the Gospel Narrative," available in his *New Testament Studies* (Charles Scribner's Sons, 1954), pp. 1–11.

33 Recognition of this fact by the Bultmann school is found to some degree not only in James M. Robinson, *A New Quest of the Historical Jesus*, but also in Günther Bornkamm, *Jesus of Nazareth*, tr. by Irene and Frazer McLuskey with James M. Robinson (Harper & Brothers, 1960).

trated by manuscripts found at Qumran;[34] this non-Christian parallel shows that such a use of Scripture would seem natural and useful among Jews, and the earliest Christians were Jews.

Another early document may well have been a brief account of the passion and resurrection of Jesus. It is widely agreed that even in the early days of oral teaching, when most gospel tradition was preserved and used in separate units, the essential passion narrative was already told as a connected story. Because of its importance to the church, this narrative could have been written down rather early.

Collections of sayings of Jesus, sometimes of just one type of teaching such as the parables, may have been made. The finding in The Gospel of Thomas of a noncanonical writing containing practically nothing but a series of sayings of Jesus supports the view that such a document as the hypothetical Q document could have seemed useful and fitting.

These suggestions about early written records cannot be proved. Nevertheless, they can be correct. Certainly not long after A.D. 50, and possibly some years earlier, the writing down of the gospel tradition began. The use of oral tradition did not cease at once; even in the second century we hear that Papias preferred to hear through oral tradition what the original apostles had told of the life and message of Jesus.[35] But the first writing of the gospel tradition must be dated rather early, and it gave to the tradition a stable form that would resist radical change.

THE GOSPEL OF MARK

Such early documents were produced before any of our canonical Gospels were written. Then, probably between A.D. 65 and 70, John Mark wrote the first Gospel. To us the gospel type of writing is a natural thing, but it was then a new literary form. A gospel is not a biography, though it deals with an actual human life. It is not just a collection of one man's teachings; it puts the teaching in a narrative framework. Essentially a gospel presents the ministry and message which for the writer constitute God's decisive action through the unique figure of

---

[34] See J. M. Allegro, "Further Messianic References in Qumran Literature," *Journal of Biblical Literature* (cited hereafter as *JBL*), Vol. LXXV (1956), pp. 174–187; see also Hunt, *Primitive Gospel Sources*.

[35] Papias' lost writing is quoted on this point by Eusebius, *Church History* III.39.4. Papias may be opposing second-century writings rather than our canonical Gospels. But his high estimate of oral tradition is clear. See R. P. C. Hanson, *Tradition in the Early Church* (The Westminster Press, 1960), for the conclusion that "nothing highly significant nor crucially important can have survived in the oral tradition preserved by Papias" (p. 39), and in general "such oral tradition as did survive was scattered, casual and insignificant" (p. 50).

human history; through him God acted to save all who will believe in and follow him.

As far as we know, John Mark wrote the first such Gospel.[36] He probably wrote in Rome. There is no reason to doubt the ancient church tradition that in writing he used information from Peter, whom he had assisted in his work.[37] But this tradition is misleading when it implies that Peter was Mark's sole source of information. Mark knew the oral tradition in the church, and no doubt had used it in his own teaching. He may have had some written documents—a collection of controversies Jesus had had with opponents, to show what the church should believe and do on disputed points (cf. chs. 2:1 to 3:6; 11:27–33; 12:13–40); a collection of parables, to show what Jesus taught about the Kingdom of God (cf. ch. 4:1–34); a brief written sketch of the passion story (cf. chs. 14:1 to 16:8). That he had such documents we cannot prove. But that Mark originated the written Gospel pattern as we know it is a reasonable conclusion. He wrote to show that God had acted through Jesus of Nazareth, his Son, the expected Christ of Old Testament promise and the Suffering Servant of God's people, and thus had given men the glad news of the beginning and imminent full coming of God's Kingdom and had provided the way of forgiveness and salvation for those who repent and believe.[38]

The Gospel of Matthew

There were other Christian teachers who could realize the practical usefulness of a written Gospel, and Mark's example and achievement was a stimulus to at least two of them. One was a Jewish Christian. He was deeply appreciative of his Jewish heritage and knew how deeply the gospel was rooted in it, but he recognized that the gospel was for "all nations" (Matt. 28:19). He knew the Gospel of Mark and also a collection consisting mainly—almost entirely—of sayings of Jesus. This collection, called Q by scholars, may have been the work of the apostle Matthew; this would explain how Matthew's name came to be connected with this Gospel. (Or possibly Matthew had made a collection of Scripture passages

36 As already stated in note 19, the Roman Catholic position is that Matthew wrote the first Gospel. See also, Basil C. Butler, *The Originality of St. Matthew* (Cambridge, University Press, 1951); Pierson Parker, *The Gospel Before Mark* (The University of Chicago Press, 1953).

37 Eusebius, *Church History* III.39.15.

38 On the Gospel of Mark, see Frederick C. Grant, *The Gospels: Their Origin and Their Growth* (Harper & Brothers, 1957), Chs. 6 to 9; Vincent Taylor, *The Gospel According to St. Mark* (London, Macmillan and Co., Ltd., 1952).

fulfilled by Jesus, and the use of this collection in writing this Gospel gave reason for his name to be connected with it.)

In any case, if the writer of this Gospel used the Gospel of Mark, whose author was not an apostle, it is not likely that he himself was an apostle. He was a Jewish Christian, writing in Syria or Phoenicia (or Palestine) somewhere about A.D. 85. He was a teacher, and probably aimed chiefly to provide Christian teachers with a Gospel useful in the teaching work of the church. He grouped the teaching of Jesus in a topical way. For example, he composed five main "discourses" by bringing together sayings not thus connected in earlier tradition. This method is clear in the Sermon on the Mount (chs. 5 to 7), which groups with still other teaching sayings found in six different chapters of Luke. A similar topical grouping of teaching occurs in the Charge to the Twelve Disciples (ch. 10), the Parables of the Kingdom (ch. 13), the Instructions for Community Life (ch. 18), and the Eschatological Discourse (chs. 24; 25). All five of these "discourses" end with the same formula: "And it happened that when Jesus had finished these sayings," etc.; by this repeated formula the author calls attention to this series of five discourses.[39]

THE GOSPEL OF LUKE

The Gospel of Luke is a consciously literary product. It is the only canonical Gospel with a formal literary preface (ch. 1:1–4). In all probability the writer was Luke, the physician and traveling companion of Paul (Col. 4:14). He had at hand previously written documents, and his aim was to write an orderly and accurate work. He apparently used Mark as one source and Q as another. In addition, he used other material, oral or written, and in arranging his material he laid great stress on the significance of the journey of Jesus to Jerusalem; this journey starts at ch. 9:51, and continues until the arrival in ch. 19:45.[40]

At first sight the Gospel seems complete in itself, and perhaps was originally written to stand alone, but Acts 1:1 shows that either originally or later Luke undertook by his two-volume work to provide a complete

---

39 Benjamin W. Bacon, *Studies in Matthew* (Henry Holt and Company, 1930), argued that the author composed these five "discourses" and made them basic in the structure of his Gospel in order to express his view that Jesus was the new Moses and that his teaching replaced the five books of the law as the authoritative statement of God's will. On the authorship, date, structure, and purpose of this Gospel, I have stated my conclusions in *The Gospel According to St. Matthew* (Harper & Brothers, 1960).

40 This journey to Jerusalem is used by Luke as a literary framework for a large number of incidents and sayings about whose date and place of occurrence tradition gave no clue.

history of the church's origin and establishment in the Roman Empire and in Rome itself. He stresses the Jewish background and the significance of Jerusalem in the emergence of the church, but he indicates both in the Gospel and in The Acts that the gospel message is for all men "to the end of the earth" (Acts 1:8). The date of the Gospel depends on the date assigned to The Acts; if The Acts was written while Paul was still in prison at Rome and before his case was decided (Acts 28:30), Luke must be dated in the early sixties of the first century (and Mark, one of the sources of Luke's Gospel, must be dated in the fifties), but if The Acts may be dated about A.D. 90, as seems more likely, then the Gospel of Luke may be dated in the late eighties or a little earlier.[41] So little is known of Christian history in the latter third of the first century that exact dating of the Gospels is impossible.

THE SCOPE OF THE GOSPEL STORY

A comparison of the Synoptic Gospels will show the scope which the gospel message had when publicly presented in the first decades of the church. Mark has no story of the birth and infancy of Jesus. Matthew and Luke both do, but their accounts differ so much that they clearly use independent sources of information. The common tradition of the three Synoptic Gospels obviously starts with the appearance of John the Baptist and the baptism of Jesus. All three then report his ministry in Galilee, his visit to Jerusalem, his Last Supper, arrest, crucifixion, burial, and resurrection. This, then, was the scope of the common gospel presented in the regular preaching and teaching of the church.

This is confirmed by other evidence. Much as the Gospel of John differs from the Synoptic Gospels, it still has the same scope and builds upon much the same framework. The replacement chosen for Judas had to be able to witness to the gospel story "beginning from the baptism of John until the day when he was taken up from us" (Acts 1:22), and this is the scope common to the three Synoptics. When we examine the "sermons" of The Acts (such short compact summaries, of course, were not complete sermons as actually preached by apostles), we get the same result. For example, Acts 10:36–43 notes the fulfillment of prophecy, begins the story with the work of John the Baptist, and carries it forward to the resurrection, after which the obligation of the apostles to preach

---

41 On the literary study of the Gospel of Luke, see Henry J. Cadbury, *The Making of Luke-Acts* (The Macmillan Company, 1927); Frederick C. Grant, *The Gospels*, pp. 117–133. Recent study of Luke has been directed to its reflection of church thinking; cf. Hans Conzelmann, *The Theology of St. Luke*, Eng. tr. by Geoffrey Buswell (Harper & Brothers, 1960).

4

this message is stated. The common public message about Jesus Christ, then, covered the period from the ministry of John the Baptist and the baptism of Jesus to his resurrection (and ascension or exaltation).

THE FUNCTION OF THE BIRTH STORIES

What, then, was the role of the birth and infancy stories, which are so prominent by their very position at the start of Matthew and Luke?[42] They were not part of the common public message taught by the church. Through messages divinely given in dreams or through angels they attest not only the divine causation of the birth of Jesus but also God's saving purpose in Jesus' coming. They anchor the gospel story in the Old Testament heritage and by poetic imagination and theological hints they interpret God's act in sending Jesus.

The attention of the church has often been so concentrated on the physical miracle of the virgin birth that many have missed its spiritual message. Some have rejected the miracle and regarded Jesus' birth as an ordinary natural birth of a Jewish son of pious but socially undistinguished parents. This is to miss (or to deny) what the story is really trying to say, for the story confesses in faith that this birth cannot be explained as a natural event. Here, God was at work to bring into human life the one who was to carry out God's unique saving purpose for men. Whatever may be thought of the physical origin of Jesus, whether he had a human father or not, his coming and career cannot be explained by reference to human parentage and heritage. Indebted as he was to his Jewish heritage and home, he was brought into the world by God's special act for the unique saving purpose that God was determined to accomplish. If he had a human father, that does not exclude the unique action of God to bring this life into the world. If he had no human father, as the narratives indicate, that still does not by physical conditions provide a sinless and effective Savior; it is the action of God that is the key factor and the decisive event in bringing this life into human history.

This is the real point of these stories. They were not part of the common public preaching and teaching of the early church. But those who knew Jesus as the Christ, the living Lord, the Suffering Servant and effective Savior of men, could understand this story of his human birth; they could join in the confession that only by special action in the earthly origin and life of Jesus could God achieve his divine purpose.

The birth and infancy stories root this life of Jesus in the life and

[42] J. Gresham Machen, *The Virgin Birth of Christ*, 2d ed. (Harper & Brothers, 1932); Thomas Boslooper, *The Virgin Birth* (The Westminster Press, 1962).

heritage of the Jewish people; the genealogies (Matt. 1:1–17; Luke 3:23–38) have this meaning, and so do the Old Testament phraseology and references that recur in these chapters. But these stories also say that Jesus can never be explained by reference to his human parentage and his Jewish heritage. Only by the divine initiative and the specific action of God did this life come into history and fulfill this ministry.

The aim of the present chapter has been to determine what resources we have to tell us what the historical Jesus did and said. It is clear that while non-Christian sources attest the historicity of Jesus, they give us little detailed information. Even the New Testament books from The Acts to The Revelation supply only meager data about his life and teaching. The Gospel of John yields much more information and must not be ignored in writing the history,[43] but it is so deeply combined with interpretation that it is not our best resource for concrete historical data. The Synoptic Gospels, though they too are documents of faith that teach us much about the faith and life of the apostolic church, remain our chief witnesses to the ministry and message of Jesus. They come from a church whose faith in Jesus Christ the risen Lord was concerned at the same time to preserve and attest the work of God in and through the historical Jesus of Nazareth. The church was to emerge through the fact and the achievement of his ministry, and the Gospels, especially the Synoptic Gospels, enable us to discern the essentials of his life and message.

[43] For example, John 3:22–24 suggests that the early ministry of Jesus may have paralleled the closing part of John the Baptist's ministry; Jesus' early disciples, as John 1:37 suggests, may have been previously disciples of the Baptist (Acts 1:22 indicates this was true of the Twelve); Jesus probably went to Jerusalem at the time of the Jewish feasts, as John 2:13; 5:1; 10:22 f. state, and had disciples there or at least in Bethany (cf. Mark 11:11; John 11:1, 5; 12:1). See C. H. Dodd, *Historical Tradition in the Fourth Gospel* (Cambridge, University Press, 1963)..

Chapter 4

THE GALILEAN MINISTRY

$\mathcal{A}$ BIOGRAPHY tries to present a clear picture of the historical and family background of the person studied. To trace his educational and personal development is also considered essential for an understanding of his character and actions. Such a specific tracing of background and growth is not possible for Jesus or, indeed, for any ancient Jew. What was considered important was not the childhood, training, and development, but the career and sayings of the grown man. We may discern some aspects of the background and preparation of Jesus, but they do not give us a clear, specific picture of his childhood, training, and psychological traits. His ministry and message were the real interest of the Gospel writers; they must be our main interest also.

UNCERTAIN CHRONOLOGY

As though to underline our lack of information, the chronology of Jesus' life is uncertain.[1] To be sure, we divide world history into two parts, before and after the birth of Jesus Christ.[2] But, ironically, this widespread method of dating events is in error; Jesus was born at least 4 B.C.! It is said that he was born "in the days of Herod the king" (Matt. 2:1). Herod died in 4 B.C.; so Jesus' birth is usually dated about 8 to 4 B.C.

The dating of his ministry and death is no more certain. The one elaborate dating in the Gospels dates not the ministry or death of Jesus but the beginning of John the Baptist's ministry (Luke 3:1 f.). The data there given place this event between A.D. 26 and 34. If, as seems best, we reckon the fifteenth year of the Roman emperor Tiberius from his accession to full power when Augustus died in A.D. 14, John did not begin his ministry until about A.D. 28. If, however, the reign of Tiberius is reckoned from the time he became coruler with Augustus in A.D. 11, then

---

1 For a survey of the problems, see George Ogg, *The Chronology of the Public Ministry of Jesus* (Cambridge, University Press, 1940).

2 On this system of dating and its relatively late adoption, see Oscar Cullmann, *Christ and Time: The Primitive Christian Conception of Time and History*, tr. by Floyd V. Filson, 2d ed. (The Westminster Press, 1950), pp. 17 f.

John began his preaching about A.D. 26. We cannot say how long John preached before word of his ministry drew Jesus from Galilee to the Jordan, where John was preaching. Probably, Jesus entered on his own ministry in the year A.D. 28, and not later than A.D. 29. How long did his ministry last? The mention of at least three Passovers in the Gospel of John (chs. 2:13; 6:4; 11:55) has led to the widespread view that the ministry lasted more than two but less than three complete years; if John 5:1 speaks of still a fourth Passover, the ministry is thought to have lasted over three years. A ministry of a little over two years is our best estimate, and if we date the crucifixion A.D. 30, we may date the ministry A.D. 28–30. But its actual length cannot be fixed with certainty, and may have been less than two years.[3]

BOYHOOD AND EARLY MANHOOD

Concerning Jesus' boyhood, youth, and early manhood we know little. He lived during those years at Nazareth in Galilee (Mark 1:9), a small and unimportant town not mentioned by the Roman historians, the Jewish historian Josephus, or the Talmud. In all probability the word "Nazarene" comes from this place name Nazareth. Some think that Nazarene refers to Jesus either (1) as a Nazirite (Num., ch. 6); or (2) as the fulfillment of the idea of Isa. 11:1, where *Netzer* in Hebrew means "branch," "shoot"; or (3) as a member of a pre-Christian sect; but the best, simplest, though not certain explanation is (4) that it designates Jesus as a man from Nazareth.[4]

There he grew up. It seems that Joseph, his legal father, was a carpenter in Nazareth, and that Jesus, as was customary among Jews as among other peoples, had learned his father's trade.[5] It was his father's responsibility to instruct his son in the law and ways of their people. In addition, Jesus probably went to the village school and learned to read the Hebrew

[3] An estimate of one year has had strong supporters; see Ogg, *The Chronology of the Public Ministry of Jesus*, Ch. 6. A duration of less than a year has been proposed, but if the reference to green grass in Mark 6:39 is trustworthy, it would date the incident in springtime, at least a year before the springtime of Jesus' death, and since the incident fits best a date at least months after his ministry opened, a ministry of something like two years seems indicated.

[4] George F. Moore, Appendix B, "Nazarene and Nazareth," in *The Beginnings of Christianity: Part I, The Acts of the Apostles*, 5 vols., edited by F. J. Foakes-Jackson and Kirsopp Lake (London, Macmillan and Co., Ltd., 1920–1933), Vol. I, pp. 426–432. Less decided is Black, *An Aramaic Approach to the Gospels and Acts*, pp. 143–146; he thinks the title "Nazorean" may be original and have been a title for a follower of John the Baptist.

[5] See Chester Charlton McCown, "*ho tektōn*," in *Studies in Early Christianity*, edited by Shirley Jackson Case (The Century Co., 1928), pp. 173–189.

Scriptures. Joseph probably died before Jesus reached manhood, since he never appears during Jesus' ministry and in Mark 6:3, contrary to usual Jewish custom, Jesus is called the son of Mary rather than the son of Joseph.

There were at least six other children in this family (Mark 6:3; Matt. 13:55 f.). The four brothers are named: James, Joses, Judas, Simon; the reference to sisters in the plural indicates that there were at least two of them. Mark 3:20 f. and John 7:5 show that the brothers were not sympathetic with Jesus during his ministry, but the risen Christ appeared to James (I Cor. 15:7), and the brothers were active in the apostolic church from early days (Acts 1:14; 12:17; I Cor. 9:5), so they clearly changed their attitude. Were these brothers and sisters younger than Jesus? Probably so; this is implied in Matt. 1:25 and Luke 2:7, and seems to fit all the Gospel evidence. But a Christian tradition, which can be traced back to the second century, holds that these other children were the children not of Mary but of Joseph by an earlier marriage, and so were all older than Jesus.[6]

It may be taken for granted that from early boyhood Jesus absorbed the Jewish heritage and Old Testament content through training at home and through worship and school at the village synagogue. He knew also the Jewish aspirations, the discontent under Roman rule, and the hopes that God would deliver his chosen people. But no evidence tells us in detail precisely what he learned and what he thought. At the age of twelve, Luke 2:41–52 tells, his parents took him to Jerusalem to celebrate the Passover. This was the last year of parental responsibility for his observance of Jewish rites.[7] The story thus implies faithful instruction throughout his boyhood and an early tie with the Temple (ch. 2:46, 49). His later ministry is a testimony that between the age of twelve and his public appearance when about thirty years old (ch. 3:23) he had "increased in wisdom and in stature, and in favor with God and man" (ch. 2:52). This general statement, however, gives no direct biographical information about the years before his public appearance.

6 There are three views about these brothers: 1. Helvidian: they were children of Joseph and Mary and born after the birth of Jesus. 2. Epiphanian: they were children of Joseph by a former marriage. 3. Hieronymian: they were cousins of Jesus. The views are named after the protagonists in a fourth-century controversy on the subject: Helvidius, Epiphanius, and Hieronymus (Jerome). The Epiphanian view is found essentially in Papyrus Bodmer V, *Nativité de Marie* (Cologny-Genève, Bibliothèque Bodmer, 1958). This third-century manuscript is a copy of a second-century work.

7 See Hermann L. Strack and Paul Billerbeck, *Kommentar zum Neuen Testament aus Talmud und Midrasch*, Vol. II (München, C. H. Becksche Verlagsbuchhandlung, 1924), pp. 144–147.

THE BAPTISM AND TEMPTATION

Jesus apparently was living an outwardly uneventful life in Nazareth, supporting his widowed mother and fatherless brothers and sisters, when news of the preaching of John the Baptist reached him. Did the spirit, message, and dress of John remind men of Elijah? Since in view of Mal. 4:5 the return of Elijah was a current expectation, this may have been the case. Certainly the Christians later saw the parallel (Mark 1:6; Matt. 3:4), and John, conscious of a prophetic role at the end of the history of God's people, may have thought of himself in this way and by use of Mal. 3:1 may have led to the spread of the report. This would explain the electric excitement which ran through the Jewish cities and towns of Palestine and stirred the mind and imagination of Jesus. John's announcement of impending divine judgment and his appeal for repentance, faith, baptism, and upright living must have compelled attention in Nazareth as elsewhere. How far it disrupted life in Jesus' Nazareth home for him to leave to hear John we do not know, but the dissatisfaction of his family with his religious zeal hints that such a problem did result (Mark 3:20 f., 31–35). How long Jesus was with John at the Jordan River is likewise unknown, but it is clear that Jesus accepted John's preaching as God-given and was baptized by John (Mark 1:9–11 and ||s).

This baptism was a decisive event in Jesus' life. The Gospels have little direct interest in the inner experiences of Jesus and his followers, but since all four Gospels describe this experience in vivid terms and since it led Jesus to take up his own ministry, early tradition must have reported it as an epochal experience. Mark 1:11 implies that the vision and the Voice were experienced by Jesus and not by John or the bystanders.[8] The event is often described by modern Christians as a Messianic experience, in which Jesus realized that he was the Messiah his people were expecting. (The word "Messiah" comes from a Hebrew word that means "anointed"; the word "Christ" comes from a Greek word of the same meaning; both words, identical in meaning, were used to refer to the anointed leader whom Jews awaited to deliver them from political bondage and to be their perfect spiritual leader.) That was one way to interpret the experience, but as it is described, in pictorial language, it expresses his realization of his unique filial relation to God his Father. The vision, however, was concerned with far more than the static status of Son; the gift of the Spirit was not for quiet self-enjoyment; it was the gift of the

---

[8] Matt. 3:16 f. and Luke 3:21 f. describe the event in more objective terms, with a hint, especially in Matthew, that it was in part for the benefit of the bystanders. In John 1:32–34 the point of the event is to identify Jesus to John the Baptist.

Father's presence and power, given for a unique and active ministry, such as the Messianic expectation had in mind.

Given the Spirit and a sense of mission, Jesus needed to know what his task was and how it should be undertaken. The temptation story is pictorial (Matt. 4:1–11; Luke 4:1–13. Mark 1:12 f. is much briefer); there is no mountain on earth from which one could see "all the kingdoms of the world." The story asserts in a figurative way that Jesus faced two questions: Was he really in a special sense God's Son? How could he properly use his newly given role and power? The story, whether reported by Jesus or formulated by the early church, sums up the decisions he made and points out the path he took. He refused to aim for personal honor, advantage, and security; he would not use his gifts to seek a leading role in nationalistic and military activities; he determined to teach and win people to recognize God's urgent claim, await God's coming Kingdom, and accept God's offer of grace and power for his repentant, believing, and obedient people.

The Ministry Centered in Galilee

Just when and where Jesus opened his ministry are questions on which the Gospels do not agree. The Gospel of John dates it while John the Baptist was still carrying on his active ministry (John 3:23; 4:1). In this Gospel, even before Jesus enters upon his public ministry, he wins disciples and is identified as "the Lamb of God, who takes away the sin of the world" (ch. 1:29), "the Messiah" (ch. 1:41), "the Son of God . . . the King of Israel" (ch. 1:34, 49). In addition, this Gospel says that before John was imprisoned Jesus carried on a ministry in Galilee (ch. 2:1–12; cf. ch. 4:43–54), Jerusalem (chs. 2:13 to 3:21), Judea (ch. 3:22), and Samaria (ch. 4:1–42).

This is quite different from the picture in the Synoptic Gospels; in them Jesus begins his ministry only after John is imprisoned, and he goes to Galilee to do so (Mark 1:14; Matt. 4:12; Luke 3:19 f.). Does the Gospel of John simply supplement this Synoptic account? It clearly does more than that. With an eye on dramatic effect, the Gospel of John brings forward every major title of Jesus and every field of Jesus' total ministry, and presents them all early in the story. The actual historical development is reflected more accurately by the other three Gospels.

The basic ministry of Jesus centered in Galilee. It may be reasonable to accept the Gospel of John's report that Jesus made more than one visit to Jerusalem during his ministry, but if we ask where he began his own ministry and where it centered, the answer is Galilee. The chief local center was Capernaum (cf. Mark 1:21; 2:1; 9:33), and references to "the sea" show that he was often found on the northern or western shore of the Sea of Galilee, even crossing once to the east shore (Mark 5:1); but mention of Nain (Luke 7:11), Nazareth (Mark 6:1; Luke 4:16), Cana (John 2:1; 4:46), and Chorazin (Matt. 11:21; Luke 10:13) indicate travel throughout Galilee.

This is highly significant for the understanding of Jesus. He did not go at once to Jerusalem, the focal center of Judaism and the place where the official leadership of his people was found. (Compare Paul, who after his conversion did not go at once to Jerusalem to get the approval and support of the apostles there; Gal. 1:17.) As a result of his experience at the baptism, Jesus assumed an independent leadership. This is an indication that in his view the need of Israel was not merely reform in organization and official leadership but a radical change of mind and spirit in all the people. So he returned to the people he knew and the region he understood best, and began to preach and teach.

The Seeking Ministry of Jesus

His method was quite different from that of John the Baptist. He did not stay in the wilderness and let people come to him; he went to the people. His outlook was not merely local; he went from place to place in Galilee to preach his message. In the places to which he went, as far as we learn, he went to Jews; he did not go to Gentiles but went from place to place to reach the Jews.[9] When he could, he spoke in the synagogue (e.g., Mark 1:21; Luke 4:16 ff.). The synagogue was essentially a lay institution, and could permit qualified laymen to speak after the reading of the Scripture and the offering of the prayers. So Jesus could use the synagogue to reach the people. But in addition, and later as a substitute when the synagogues were closed to him, he talked with people on the streets and roads and in the homes and fields of Galilee.

This shocked "respectable" Jews. Many Jews, out of carelessness or business pressure or sheer wickedness, did not keep the Jewish law, and as a result were unclean in the sight of pious people. Such lax or sinful people were shunned by those who wanted to keep the law and the strict tradition. To keep these Jewish standards of ceremonial cleanness required a kind of self-quarantine, and the Pharisees of a community led the way in avoiding contacts with the Jewish "tax collectors and sin-

---

[9] He sometimes, as in Jericho (Mark 10:46–52; Luke 19:1–10), went to cities that had both Jews and Gentiles, but where he went he dealt with Jews, and in the two or three instances where he healed a Gentile, he did so at a distance and as an obvious exception (Mark 7:24–30 = Matt. 15:21–28; Matt. 8:5–13 = Luke 7:1–10; cf. John 4:46–54).

4*

ners."[10] Jesus took quite another course. He went especially to these people regarded by most "good" people as social and religious outcasts.

In doing this he obviously disregarded the prevailing standards of ceremonial cleanness, and so in the view of those who upheld those standards he broke the law of God. He thought differently; he thought that he was doing God's will and advancing God's cause by his friendship and association with these outcasts; he went to all of his people who would respond to him, and many such outcasts were touched by his friendship and responded in faith. One of the miracles of his ministry was that he could disregard prevailing barriers and win the friendship and response of such people without giving them the idea that he was indifferent to sin. Many of them took his message seriously; they believed it and turned to obey his teaching about God's will. His attitude and outreach to the outcasts did much to determine the course of later events; in the end it raised the question whether his movement could be confined within the bounds of inherited Judaism. But for the time being, this question did not arise.

The Kingdom: Its Nature and Coming

Central in this seeking ministry was the preaching of Jesus. He opened his ministry with the message, already implied if not explicitly stated in the preaching of John the Baptist, that the Kingdom of God was just at hand. Here again the question arises as to where we most clearly find the central message of Jesus. In the Synoptic Gospels the central theme is the Kingdom; in the Gospel of John it is eternal life through faith in Jesus Christ the Son of God. The term "eternal life" occurs in the Synoptic Gospels—but only two or three times in each one; it occurs seventeen times in the Gospel of John. The term "Kingdom of God" occurs twice in the Gospel of John (ch. 3:3, 5; cf. ch. 18:33–37). Jesus evidently used both terms, but his usual theme was clearly the Kingdom.

The Gospel of Matthew speaks usually of the Kingdom of Heaven (thirty-four times), but also speaks four times of the Kingdom of God, which occurs fourteen times in Mark and thirty-two in Luke. Outside of the Gospel of Matthew, the term "Kingdom of Heaven" never occurs in the New Testament. If, then, we ask which term Jesus used, it would seem

10 The tax collectors of the Gospels were not the "tax farmers" who in ancient times purchased from the ruler the right to collect the taxes or the tax on a specific commodity, in a certain district, but were the Jewish subordinate officers who actually collected the taxes. Such subordinates were hated by Jews not merely because they collected as much as they could but also because they collected it for a foreign power and could not remain ceremonially clean while thus serving a pagan government.

that he spoke of the Kingdom of God, and the Gospel of Matthew, with its strong Jewish-Christian background, followed a well-known Jewish tendency to avoid frequent use of the word "God" and so usually substituted the word "Heaven." I Maccabees illustrates such a substitution; it refers to God often and with earnest reverence, but it never uses the word "God," and in a few cases uses the word "Heaven" to refer to him. The usual practice of the Gospel of Matthew follows a similar tendency to avoid the word "God" out of reverence.

More important than the exact wording of this theme is the meaning Jesus gave to it.[11] The Kingdom of God did not refer essentially to the territory God rules or to administrative organization, but to his reign or rule over his people; this phrase for Jesus meant the kingly rule of God. So when he opened his ministry by announcing that "the time is fulfilled, and the kingdom of God is at hand" (Mark 1:15), he meant that God was just on the point of establishing his effective rule over his people. Such a message conceded that at present that kingly rule was not effectively in operation. In other words, the background of Jesus' preaching was the fact of sin and rebellion against God by his chosen people Israel, and so Jesus followed his announcement by a summons to "repent." This appeal was urgent, for God was beginning to act to set up his effective rule, which would be established not by man's brilliance and action but by God's decisive intervention.

The atmosphere of this preaching was thus eschatological; that is, Jesus was convinced that God's decisive action to realize his purpose and establish his perfect Kingdom was getting under way and would be completed in a short time. Unlike the modern tendency to think of centuries or thousands of years still to come in world history, Jesus saw history coming to a climax, with men facing the crucial choice whether to recognize and prepare for the impending crisis or continue indifferent and be struck by ruin for their sin and indifference. The urgency of Jesus' ministry came largely from this eschatological note in his thought and ministry.[12]

Jesus did not doubt that this decisive action of God would bring judg-

11 See T. W. Manson, *The Teaching of Jesus* (Cambridge, University Press, 1931); Rudolf Otto, *The Kingdom of God and the Son of Man*, tr. by Floyd V. Filson and Bertram Lee Woolf (London, Lutterworth Press, 1938); K. L. Schmidt, H. Kleinknecht, K. G. Kuhn, and Gerhard von Rad, "*Basileia*," in *Bible Key Words*, Vol. II (Harper & Brothers, 1958); Norman Perrin, *The Kingdom of God in the Teaching of Jesus* (The Westminster Press, 1963).

12 On the strong eschatological note in Jesus' message, see Otto, *The Kingdom of God and the Son of Man;* Werner Georg Kümmel, *Promise and Fulfilment: The Eschatological Message of Jesus*, tr. by Dorothea M. Barton, 3d rev. ed. (London, SCM Press, Ltd., 1957).

ment on the wicked. Of this he was as sure as was John the Baptist.[13] But to a much greater degree than John he discerned in God's action eager forgiveness and free grace. In John's preaching the stern note predominated; the gracious note prevailed in the preaching of Jesus. The Kingdom could not be earned; the pious people of his day could not claim it on the basis of their record; all men had sinned and needed to repent and believe that through him God was offering the one way of escape from their threatened doom. Those who humbly responded in repentance and faith, with no claim that they had earned or could earn a place in the Kingdom, would receive that place as an undeserved gift. This meant that because "good" people found it hard to admit their need while "tax collectors and sinners" more easily recognized their faults, Jesus was able to win common people and people of doubtful reputation more easily than he could reach "the good church people" of his day. It was clearer to the outcasts that if they were to enter the Kingdom, it had to be a gift.

But the message that the Kingdom was a gift did not exclude stringent ethical teaching; the gift of God was not a permit for continued moral indifference or perversion. Those who knew God, and understood what a miracle his gracious gift of the Kingdom was, understood also that to repent and believe meant to turn from the old way of life and live in faith and obedience. It will be emphasized later that Jesus' urgency about the impending Kingdom only made more urgent his extensive teaching about how God wants his people to live. In his message the gift of God contained an obligation that man must recognize and fulfill.

The Kingdom was both present in its beginnings and future in its full realization. It is clear from the opening preaching of Jesus (Mark 1:15) that he did not think the Kingdom had been present all along.[14] Certainly God had not lost control of the world he had made, but the persistence of sin and disobedience was so obvious, and in the existing world God's will was so far from being done on earth as it is in heaven (Matt. 6:10), that the Kingdom as the effective rule of God over his obedient people had to *come* to replace the present rebellious situation. So the Kingdom in any full sense was future. At the start of his public ministry, it was "at hand" (Mark 1:15);[15] it was not far in the future, yet it was still future.

---

13 On the relation between John the Baptist and Jesus, see Kraeling, *John the Baptist*, Ch. V.

14 That Jesus talked of God as King in terms of "eternal sovereignty" is the one point to question in the otherwise outstanding discussion of the Kingdom by T. W. Manson, *The Teaching of Jesus;* see his Ch. VI.

15 C. H. Dodd has argued that for Jesus the Kingdom had come (realized eschatology); see *The Parables of the Kingdom* (Charles Scribner's Sons, 1936), p. 44. Later, in *The Interpretation of the Fourth Gospel* (Cambridge, University Press, 1953), p. 447,

But in the ministry and movement of Jesus, the Kingdom began to come. The parables of growth indicated this. Jesus was sure that his healings of mind and body showed its coming to those with spiritual eyes to see what was happening (Matt. 12:28; Luke 11:20). The puzzling reference to violent pressing into the Kingdom since the days of John the Baptist (Matt. 11:12; Luke 16:16) likewise indicated that for Jesus the new era had begun to come in his ministry.[16] Luke 17:20 f. may mean that the Kingdom was there in the midst of the Pharisees.[17] The kingdom of Satan had now met a Stronger One and was coming to an end (Mark 3:22–27); by the Stronger One, Jesus meant the Spirit of God, whom his critics blindly misinterpreted to be Beelzebul, the prince of the demons. The Kingdom had begun to come, and his followers were privileged to see this, a privilege the prophets and saints of earlier generations had not had (Matt. 13:16 f.; Luke 10:23 f.).

We shall note later the pictorial imagery in which Jesus described the final triumph of God's cause. Here we note that in Jesus' teaching the Kingdom's coming was both present and future.

GOD AS FATHER

This message about the Kingdom was a message about God. He is the great fact, the central actor in Jesus' picture of human life and history. He is the God of the past; his work and will are recorded in the Scripture, which is his revelation that men should heed. It is against him, the Creator and rightful Lord of all men, that men have sinned. It is he who chose Israel; to him Israel must answer for their failure to fulfill his will for them. He has been and is the Judge whom men must face. Thus he is also the God of the future.

But he is not merely the God of the past and the future. He is the living God of the present, and the sense of God's present claim and action marks the gospel story. He has begun to act; he opens the way to forgiveness; he is about to establish his full rule; and he admits to his Kingdom those who repent and obey him. He has been patient, but it is urgent that men face the crisis and respond in repentance and faith. For man's hope is not in himself or in other men or in any magical rites, but only in God. God must have man's single and complete loyalty; man cannot serve God and also a rival lord, whether possessions (Matt. 6:24) or any other worldly loyalty.

Dodd expressed a liking for a word by Joachim Jeremias, *"sich realisierende Eschatologie,"* which means eschatology in actual process of being realized.

16 On this saying, see Kümmel, *Promise and Fulfilment*, pp. 121–124.

17 This is the view of T. W. Manson, *The Teaching of Jesus*, pp. 123 ff.; Kümmel, *Promise and Fulfilment*, pp. 32–36.

In a way not usual in Judaism, Jesus spoke of God as Father.[18] We must not overstate this fact, for as T. W. Manson pointed out, most of the cases where Jesus calls God "Father" occur in the Gospel of John and in sayings found only in the Gospel of Matthew. But each Gospel contains at least a few instances. In some cases Jesus uses the term "Father" to express his own special relation to God and his special role in God's cause. Significant for this is the fact that he never says "our Father" in a way that includes himself; he speaks rather of "your Father" and "my Father." There was no Greek metaphysical meaning in his references to God as his Father; he was not stating the doctrine of the Trinity, even in part; he was referring to his special relation to the Father in his worship and work. But such references reflect deep awareness of his unique relation to the Father and his unique task in God's plan.

In two ways Jesus' teaching about God as Father of men is often misunderstood. For one thing, it is often ignored that Israel had long been aware that God was their Father and had chosen them as his special people. We may think of God as the Father only of individuals, but Jesus, although concerned for the individual, knew that God had been and was the Father of Israel. It was as members of his people that they knew God's concern for each of them. The other mistake commonly made is to think that Father means a sentimental, weak, and pliable God. One could learn better from Jewish synagogue prayers, whose essential form probably goes as far back as the days of Jesus. They often address God as "Our Father, Our King."[19] We distrust kings and glorify individualism, so this may seem to us an odd combination. But it is not, once we sense the authority and discipline of the Father and the personal concern of the King for his people. The two terms largely overlap. The Father of whom Jesus spoke was the Lord and the Judge; he was gracious but not to be trifled with. This underlines the seriousness of Jesus' ethical teaching. It does not deny God's gracious care of his people, but that care is the care of a righteous God who keeps control of his world and regardless of human rebellion will realize his will.

THE CALL OF SPECIAL DISCIPLES

Noteworthy in Jesus' ministry was his calling of disciples. He summoned all men to repent and promised forgiveness to all who sincerely responded. But he called some men to stay with him and be his special

[18] See T. W. Manson, *The Teaching of Jesus*, Ch. IV; Bornkamm, *Jesus of Nazareth*, pp. 124–129.
[19] See Israel Abrahams, *A Companion to the Authorised Daily Prayer Book*, 3d ed. (London, Eyre and Spottiswoode, 1932), pp. lxxiii f.

disciples (the Greek word for disciples, *mathētai*, means "learners," "pupils"). They were to be with him, learn his teaching, catch his spirit, and later extend his ministry (Mark 3:13; 6:7). What did this imply? He was more than a rabbi whose disciples followed him and learned his teaching. He was not merely an individualist gadfly trying to arouse men to face their duty to God. He wanted to reach his people and lead them to confess their failure and turn to God in repentance. This group of disciples was the nucleus and spearhead of a renewed Israel. Jesus aimed to build up within Israel a brotherhood who would be the true Israel, the rallying center of God's people. He did not try to organize a separate church; he set loose a new force in Israel to make it truly the special people of God.[20]

Common tradition identifies the first of those thus called as two pairs of brothers: Simon and Andrew, and James and John, the sons of Zebedee (Mark 1:16–20 and ||s). The Gospel of John dates too early the explicit perception of Andrew (and Peter) that Jesus fulfilled their people's Messianic hopes (John 1:41), but the New Testament evidence gives these four a leading role during Jesus' life and after his death.[21] (The selection of twelve disciples for a special role will be noted in the next chapter.)

JESUS' TEACHING: IMPORTANCE AND METHOD

It is clear that Jesus preached the coming of the Kingdom of God and called men to repent and believe. Such an evangelistic appeal called for a basic decision and dedication. It is also clear that Jesus, for all his urgency in preaching, spent a great proportion of his time in teaching how God wanted men to live. He could not do his work merely by preaching the imminent coming of the Kingdom and living an exemplary life; he needed to help people to face life and discern what it means to obey God with a willing spirit in all situations. It was not enough to repent and believe the gospel message; people needed to be taught how to show their obedience in a true and helpful way and so fulfill God's will for them in daily life.[22]

Basic in Jesus' teaching method was unmistakable independence. In view of the importance of tradition among the Jews and the role of a rather fixed oral tradition, it surprised people to hear him say, "You have heard that it was said, . . . but I say to you" (Matt. 5:21 f.; etc.). This

20 On "Discipleship," see Bornkamm, *Jesus of Nazareth*, Ch. VI.
21 Andrew is the only one of the four who plays no personal role in the book of The Acts.
22 On the teaching of Jesus, see C. G. Montefiore, *Rabbinical Literature and Gospel Teachings* (London, Macmillan and Co., 1930); T. W. Manson, *The Teaching of Jesus;* Ernest Cadman Colwell, *An Approach to the Teaching of Jesus* (Abingdon Press, 1947); Bornkamm, *Jesus of Nazareth*, Ch. V.

independence carried with it the note of a personal authority not subject
to any other man. But though marked by independence and authority, his
teaching was not confined to formal pronouncements.[23] He used the
synagogue whenever the opportunity offered, and this, it seems, was
mainly in the earlier part of his ministry, before opposition closed such
doors to him. But he also spoke to groups in the towns and fields and
on the shores of the Sea of Galilee. He was not too busy or formal for
private conversation with interested people; he even sought such contacts (Luke 19:5). By eating with tax collectors and notorious sinners,
he taught that God had a deep concern for them as for all men (Mark
2:15–17 and ||s).

His teaching method varied. He often used Scripture as the basis of
what he said, for to him the Old Testament was God's revelation and
therefore had real authority. He commented on Scripture in the synagogue service and in more informal teaching situations. Sometimes his
teaching started from questions others asked or from questions he himself
raised. He pointed to common things in nature and human life, and used
common events to illustrate truth. He used exaggerations, warnings,
denunciations, laments, beatitudes, proverbs, parables. His direct and
urgent approach, his concern for human welfare, and his pushing aside
of merely conventional piety won him an eager hearing and gave vitality
to his teaching. What were the main themes he treated?

Themes of the Teaching

1. The axiom back of all he said was God. The central theme of all his
teaching was *the Kingdom of God*. That has already become clear. All
other themes or areas of teaching are tied to that controlling theme.

2. *Repentance* was basic and indispensable (Mark 1:15; Matt. 4:17).
As surely as Paul, though with no labored argument, Jesus recognized the
sinfulness of men and their need to repent at once. It is often noted that
the Greek word for repentance, *metanoia*, means "a change of mind."
But Jesus normally spoke Aramaic, and the verb he used for "repent" was
in all probability *tub*, which like the Hebrew word *shub* meant "to turn,"
and so called for a complete turning of the entire life to follow the right
way.

---

23 The Sermon on the Mount (Matt., chs. 5 to 7; cf. Luke 6:20–49), one of the justly
classical passages in world literature, may have a nucleus in a tradition of connected
teaching given on a specific occasion, but as it stands it is mainly a compilation of
teaching on the life of the true disciple, including his relation to his Old Testament
and Jewish heritage. For recent studies of the Sermon, see Harvey K. McArthur,
Understanding the Sermon on the Mount (Harper & Brothers, 1960), and W. D.
Davies, *The Setting of the Sermon on the Mount* (Cambridge, University Press,
1964).

The slowness of his hearers to repent amazed Jesus; such stubborn resistance to his pleas, he was sure, would not have been shown by wicked Tyre, Sidon, Sodom, or Nineveh (Matt. 11:21–24; 12:41; Luke 10:13 f.; 11:32). He denied that natural calamities proved the unusual sinfulness of those who suffered them, but urged that such calamities could and should teach men how transient and uncertain life is; in view of the eternal consequences of rejecting God, they should repent before it is too late (Luke 13:1–9). For Jesus there clearly is no neutrality in life; persistent sin leads to terrible consequences; man does not have unlimited time to change his way of life. The thing to do is to repent at once.[24]

3. *Faith,* in Jesus' use of the word, included the conviction of the truth of his preaching. But it meant far more. Faith accepts the Lordship of God. It is trust in God. It is a trust free from worry and anxiety (Matt. 6:25–34; Luke 12:22–31), and it is certain that God's care will prove sufficient to hold his people steady and save them to the end. A coldly calculating, stingily rationed faith will not help, but an honest faith small as a grain of mustard seed will win God's aid (Matt. 17:20; Luke 17:6; cf. Mark 9:24). Jesus was convinced that men have not realized the immense possibilities of human achievement open to faith (Mark 11:22 f.). Faith ensures answer to prayer (Mark 11:24), and is the key to all good living.[25]

4. In the life of faith *worship* has an integral, indispensable place. Real faith and trust in God are expressed in grateful worship and earnest *prayer*. Prayer must never be offered publicly merely for show, to get credit for being pious; to avoid the temptation thus to parade one's piety, one should not merely share in public worship but also pray in private (Matt. 6:5 f.). The number of words is not decisive; men will not be heard simply "for their many words" (Matt. 6:7); sincerity is what counts. Least of all should one think that pious pose and words will cover up or cancel such social injustice as grasping men sometimes show to helpless widows (Mark 12:40). One should pray in honest humility with a sense of need; if the answer does not come at once, one should remain sure that God answers prayer and so persist in asking (Luke 11:5–8; 18:1–14). In praying with others a great multitude is not necessary; numbers alone do not determine the power of prayer; two or three disciples earnest and united in prayer are sure of an answer (Matt. 18:19 f.).

The experience of Jesus in Gethsemane, where after three prayers for deliverance from impending death he finally had to pray the basic prayer, "Not what I will, but what thou wilt" (Mark 14:36), underlines the truth

---

24 See William Douglas Chamberlain, *The Meaning of Repentance* (Board of Christian Education, Presbyterian Church U.S.A., 1943), pp. 51 ff.
25 Bornkamm, *Jesus of Nazareth*, pp. 129–137.

that God's answer may not be what man with his human limitations thinks best. But the fundamental fact about prayer is that God in his wisdom does hear and answer.

The Lord's Prayer, given for the disciples to use, includes crucial areas of prayer. The exact form of this prayer which Jesus taught his disciples cannot be determined with certainty; Matt. 6:9–13 and Luke 11:2–4 differ considerably. A brief study of the Lucan form, with side glances at the additions in Matthew, will show the common content.

It is not a prayer that Jesus himself prays; it is for his disciples. So the addition of "our" in Matthew is correct in meaning, and points up the fact that the disciples are to pray this prayer as a group, or at least with awareness that they are members of the group. They pray in trust to God as Father and in reverent desire that his name may be regarded as holy. Just as the basic theme of Jesus' preaching was the Kingdom of God, so the basic prayer of the disciples is that God's kingly rule may come and his will be perfectly realized. All of men's wants may be brought to God in prayer; "bread" represents the essential needs of man's physical life; the disciples are to pray in trust that God will provide for their needs. Because even the disciples, though committed to follow Christ, fail to give full obedience to God and constantly meet testing in life, they are regularly to pray for forgiveness and for preservation from temptation as far as possible; but only as they forgive others can they ask and receive forgiveness.[26] (The Doxology with which the Lord's Prayer closes in most Protestant church usage was no part of the original Gospel of Matthew and is not found in the Gospel of Luke; it was added later, probably on the basis of I Chron. 29:11, to give the prayer a fitting conclusion when used in public worship by the church.)

5. *Humility* Jesus emphasized as essential. No other attitude is in place when sinful man daily faces God. But men are likely to lose that spirit when comparing themselves with other men. The Pharisee in the parable of Luke 18:9–14 is typical of the "religious" man whose faithfulness in religious observance tempts him to think that he is better than others and that God is fortunate to have so worthy a worshiper; such a man lets his outward obedience lead him to despicable contempt of others and false pride in himself. To use acts of worship to parade one's piety is always wicked (Matt. 6:1–18). To seek the best places at banquets or in services of worship or in any group reveals a false idea of greatness; true greatness is willing and consistent helpfulness to others with no thought of self-promotion (Matt. 23:5–12; Mark 9:33–37 and ||s).

6. *The family* was a real concern in Jesus' teaching; it was divinely established, and marriage is to be a permanent monogamous union

26 This point is strongly emphasized in Matt. 6:14 f.; 18:21–35; cf. Luke 6:37.

(Mark 10:2–12; Matt. 5:31 f.; 19:3–11; Luke 16:18; I Cor. 7:10).[27] Jesus spoke strongly against both adultery and lustful looks and desires (Matt. 5:27–32). Possibly because of the early loss of his father, he denounced with special feeling those who took advantage of widows for financial gain (Mark 12:40). He showed his interest in children and was not too important or busy to give attention to them (Mark 10:13–16). But he explicitly put the family second in comparison with the claims of discipleship. The bond of common faith in God and dedication to the Kingdom was the supreme bond; he expressed this clearly in relation to his own family (Mark 3:31–35); when a choice had to be made, the obligation of discipleship to Christ came first (Matt. 10:34–37; Luke 12:51–53).

7. In family and *social relations* the command to love is the central and controlling duty (Matt. 5:38–48; 7:12; Mark 12:28–31).[28] Love to others is as important as the love of God (Matt. 22:34–40). The disciple will not use others to serve his personal advantage but will serve and help them; he will always forgive whoever has wronged him; he will further reconciliation rather than retaliation and revenge (Mark 9:35; 11:25; Matt. 6:12, 14 f.; 18:21–35; Luke 17:3 f.). To be last of all and servant of all (Mark 9:33–37 and ||s; 10:42–45), to be a guest who shows deference to other guests and a host who invites guests without choosing them to promote his social advancement (Luke 14:7–14), to be in society as salt in food (Matt. 5:13), to refrain from harsh judgment (Matt. 7:1 f.), to give alms without receiving or wanting credit, with the sole purpose of helping those in need (Matt. 6:2–4)—this self-effacing, helpful life Jesus described as that of the true disciple.

8. *Possessions* Jesus saw to be a special temptation. They could make one self-centered and callous to the needs of others (Luke 16:19–31), and for Jesus whatever makes one indifferent to the needs of others is spiritually ruinous. He puts this danger in another way; possessions, "mammon" or wealth, can and often do become the grim rival of God for man's loyalty. Man can become so obsessed with physical needs and the gaining of wealth that God is crowded out of his life. But God tolerates no rival; he claims complete loyalty; man cannot serve both God and mammon (Matt. 6:24; Luke 16:13). Man is a fool not to see this, for in the end, if he fails to see it, he will lose both his possessions and his own soul; true wealth is to be "rich toward God" (Luke 12:13–21).

9. *The future* was of great concern to Jesus. With faith in God's pur-

---

27 It appears that Matthew adapts Jesus' unqualified condemnation of divorce as contrary to the divine will for married people. See Ernest F. Scott, *The Ethical Teaching of Jesus* (The Macmillan Company, 1924); McArthur, *Understanding the Sermon on the Mount*, pp. 45 ff.

28 Anders Nygren, *Agape and Eros*, tr. by Philip S. Watson (The Westminster Press, 1953), pp. 61–109; Bornkamm, *Jesus of Nazareth*, pp. 109–117.

pose and power he was certain that by great impending actions God would soon establish his effective kingly rule. The urgency of that impending world transformation reached into all his teaching and gave it added earnestness.[29] The disciple cannot live as though things will continue as they are and man may delay indefinitely his response to God's claim. The time is short; the Kingdom is already coming; the demand for repentance, faith, grateful worship, and loyal living is an urgent issue that no alert, intelligent person can ignore. At the end of his life Jesus had special reason to emphasize these matters, and the next chapter will speak further of them, but in all study of Jesus' teaching one must keep in mind the importance for him of this already beginning decisive action of God.

THE PARABLES: THEIR NATURE AND PURPOSE

One teaching tool of Jesus' deserves special attention. He was the master in the use of parables to make his teaching vivid and effective.[30] Most definitions of a parable say that it is a story. In the parables of Jesus, however, the word has a wider range of meaning. The word does not occur in the Gospel of John (the word translated "parable" in the KJV of John 10:6 and 16:26 is a different Greek word from the one used for parables in the Synoptic Gospels). In the Synoptic Gospels, "parable" can be used of a proverb (Luke 4:23, where the Greek word is "parable"), or of a comparison from nature (Mark 4:26–29) or from human life (Luke 15:11–32), or of an example story to show how one should act in a similar situation (Luke 10:30–37), or of an illustration with at least something of the nature of an allegory (Mark 12:1–12). Since the Gospels call all of these illustrations "parables," our definition should do justice to them all.

So a parable in Jesus' use is an illustration of spiritual or moral truth; he used it to make that truth vivid and convincing to the hearers; it may be a story, but that is not essential; the essential thing is that it illustrates and clarifies truth, challenges the imagination and will of the hearer, and so demands that he face the claims of the truth presented. It is a teaching tool to make truth live and to change lives.

This raises a question. In Mark 4:10–12 it appears that parables are

---

29 It is important to note, however, that Jesus disclaimed knowledge of the exact time of the end of the present age (Mark 13:32; Acts 1:7), and discouraged an overeager expectancy that allowed no margin of delay in its thought of the end (Matt. 25:5; Mark 13:35; Luke 12:38).

30 Among the good books on the parables of Jesus are C. H. Dodd, *The Parables of the Kingdom*; Charles W. F. Smith, *The Jesus of the Parables* (Board of Christian Education, Presbyterian Church U.S.A., 1948); and Joachim Jeremias, *The Parables of Jesus*, tr. by S. H. Hooke (Charles Scribner's Sons, 1955).

used to conceal truth. But the parables as a group are clear in meaning; on at least one occasion the Jewish leaders condemned in a parable see clearly Jesus' meaning (Mark 12:12 and ||); his concern was to teach so as to help people, and because they understood him, people heard him gladly (Mark 12:37). So it is impossible to think that he used parables to keep people from understanding and responding to the gospel message. Either his words as given in Mark 4:10–12 are ironical (as is Isa., ch. 6, which Mark is using), or they were garbled in translation from Aramaic into Greek, or the church forgot the setting in which Jesus spoke them and misunderstood their purpose. In historical fact, Jesus did not use parables to conceal truth; he "spoke the word to them as they were able to hear it" (Mark 4:33).

When it is observed that in the rest of the New Testament and in later Christian writings Jesus has no rival in the effective use of parables, the authenticity of the parables of the Synoptic Gospels and the skill of Jesus in using them stand out. They were his distinctive though not exclusive method of teaching. To waken men to the added dimension that faith senses in this world, to make spiritual truth live, to challenge men to decision, parables are a fit instrument, and Jesus was master of their use.

THE MIRACLES AND THEIR MEANING

To many modern students the miracles are a separate problem and not an integral part of the ministry of Jesus.[31] One thing is clear: for the Gospel writers they are an essential part of that ministry.

Two things hinder their ready acceptance by many modern readers. One is that these stories are written in a prescientific or nonscientific atmosphere, and so to an age steeped in the thought forms of modern science they seem discredited. There is truth in this, but we must not take the modern scientific world view as the complete and final truth or define a miracle as a breaking of natural laws. Another difficulty is that some stories have grown in the telling. One can test this by asking whether Jairus' daughter was sick or already dead when Jairus left his home to ask Jesus for help. In Mark 5:23 she is "at the point of death," but is still living, and Jairus only gets word of her death later, whereas in Matt. 9:18 the father comes and says that his "daughter has just died." Mark seems the earlier form of the story; Matthew's shortened form is secondary. Thus we cannot defend every detail of every story. But that Jesus did

[31] On the miracles, see Alan Richardson, *The Miracle-Stories of the Gospels* (London, SCM Press, Ltd., 1941); S. Vernon McCasland, *By the Finger of God: Demon Possession and Exorcism in Early Christianity in the Light of Modern Views of Mental Illness* (The Macmillan Company, 1951); Ethelbert Stauffer, *Jesus and His Story*, tr. by Richard and Clara Winston (Alfred A. Knopf, Inc., 1960), pp. 8–12.

remarkable deeds should be clear from the abundant evidence of the Gospels. That Jesus healed disturbed minds and diseased bodies need not be doubted, and the healing ability of our day is no final standard as to the scope of his power.[32]

What is a miracle to the Gospel writers? We may define it as a remarkable event in which the eye of faith sees the purposeful working of God to further his cause. It is not an inevitably convincing occurrence. Opponents of Jesus could not deny the exorcisms, in which Jesus gave mental health to deranged or troubled minds, but they ascribed them to the working of Beelzebul, the prince of the demons (Mark 3:22). They could not deny the power of Jesus to work decisive changes in such troubled minds, but they asserted that the power was not that of the Spirit of God in Jesus but the power of Beelzebul controlling Jesus for his evil ends. Jesus was conscious that the Spirit of God was present and active in his ministry and especially in such deeds of power as we call miracles. It outraged him to have opponents say that such beneficent works, done by the power of God's Spirit, were the work of the devil. He saw no hope for people so perverted and prejudiced in their attitude (Mark 3:23–30).

To Jesus the miracles had deep meaning. It was not simply that they were acts of compassion, though they certainly did show his concern for human suffering. Nor was it simply that the miracles would convince those spiritually open-minded that God was with him and was working through him. Jesus refused to give men a "sign" in the sense of a remarkable deed done to overcome doubt and compel acceptance of his claims; he knew that men could stand in the presence of beneficent healing power and still be unconvinced that God was present and at work; it took a spiritual openness to grasp his aim. The deepest meaning of the miracles for Jesus was that in them the coming of the Kingdom was discernible to faith: "If it is by the finger of God that I cast out demons, then the kingdom of God has come upon you" (Luke 11:20; cf. Matt. 12:28). Not only in word but also in effective deed the victory of God over sickness was making itself felt; the establishing of God's perfect order, the final Kingdom, was under way. The stories of the raising of the dead have the same meaning (e.g., Mark 5:22–43; Luke 7:11–17; John 11:1–44). They were preliminary actions in the effective inauguration of the realm of blessed eternal life. In the ministry of Jesus, the Kingdom was preached; in his mighty deeds its establishment was going forward—and those with understanding hearts could share in it.

---

[32] The fact of miraculous deeds by Jesus is paralleled by the explicit testimony of Paul that he, too, had done such "signs and wonders." Cf. Rom. 15:19; II Cor. 12:12; Gal. 3:5. In two of these passages Paul is writing to churches which had witnessed his miracles.

Chapter 5

FROM GALILEE TO JERUSALEM

THE MINISTRY of Jesus did not conform to the usual success story. His busy life of preaching, teaching, and healing did not climax in a general triumph. To be sure, numerous signs show that Jesus was widely popular and eagerly sought both because of his new teaching and especially for his healing power. But the Gospels, whose dark hints of gathering opposition undoubtedly were written in the light of the passion story, rightly suggest that this popularity was not universal. The Galilean ministry was of limited duration; it was not an unqualified success; there followed, it seems, a period of undefined length in which Jesus withdrew from his itinerant ministry and was not yet ready to go to Jerusalem for the final decision on his message and claim.[1] This intermediate period requires our attention in this chapter.

THE NOTE OF URGENCY

The urgency that marked the earlier stages of his ministry was still with him. This was not just a personality trait, although the modern picture of Jesus as a calm, patient, relaxed person is misleading. His ministry was marked by energy, vigorous criticism of opponents, deep regret at the slowness of so many to grasp and accept his preaching, and determination to force men to face the claim of God and the message of the Kingdom. If Jesus changed his plans or method of ministry, it was not due to distaste for public contacts or desire for a more quiet life. The note of urgency continued. Why?

His motive was not to avoid personal danger; his aim was not to get away from Galilee before someone hurt him. His final visit to Jerusalem, where concentrated opposition was sure to be met, shows that considerations of personal safety did not motivate his urgency or his period of withdrawal. He did plan for the decisive crisis of his ministry to occur at

---

[1] It is not possible to trace with any confidence the exact sequence and duration of the successive stages of this period of Jesus' ministry. But a withdrawal period and a visit to Phoenicia and the region of Caesarea Philippi have a place in the story.

Jerusalem rather than in some minor town of Galilee, but this was not due to fear of danger.

The urgency at every stage of his ministry came from his impelling sense of vocation, or more specifically, from his awareness that since his baptism he had worked by the power and guidance of the Spirit of God. When scribes charged that it was by the power of Beelzebul (Satan) that he expelled demons from human lives, his indignant response expressed his consciousness that it was not Satan but the Spirit of God who led him and gave him power for such beneficent acts (Mark 3:22–27). This incident and the preceding charge of his family[2] that he was "beside himself," that is, so urgently active in his ministry that he had lost balance and sanity (Mark 3:21), reveal his great urgency and earnestness, which he ascribed to the working of the Spirit.

His eschatological message led to such urgency. His deep conviction that in his ministry the Kingdom of God was beginning to be established and that its full coming was not far distant left him little time to complete his ministry. He had to reach all he could as quickly as possible. He had to help his people sense the seriousness and urgency of their personal situation before God. How could he best bring the greatest possible number to realize the present crisis and act while there was time? The basic way was to reach as many as possible with his personal appeal of preaching and teaching. He could also send out selected followers to spread his message. Even if, as good tradition indicates, synagogue leadership gave determined opposition to him and his followers, his disciples could still find abundant opportunities to teach and warn the people.

THE CHOICE OF THE TWELVE

For this purpose Jesus chose twelve disciples to form a special group (Mark 3:13–19 and ‖s). They were selected, it seems, from a larger group who regularly followed him and were ready to support him in his ministry. A few scholars suggest that Jesus never chose the Twelve; on this view, the Twelve were a group of leaders who emerged only in the early days of the apostolic church. This reverses the facts. The Twelve play no extended or prominent role in the apostolic church; they are rarely mentioned. Who are the prominent leaders in the book of The Acts? They include only one member of the Twelve, Peter (John is his silent partner, not an independent leader). The other outstanding figures of the

---

2 The Greek phrase *hoi par autou*, literally "the ones from beside him," is admittedly vague, but when connected with Mark 3:31–35, it seems to point not to some entirely unidentified "friends" (RSV) but to "his family" (*The New English Bible New Testament*).

first generation, Barnabas, Stephen, Philip (one of the Seven), Paul, and James, the brother of Jesus,[3] are not numbered among the Twelve.

If the Twelve had emerged only in the apostolic age, it is hard to see how the story of the defection of Judas (Mark 14:10 f. and ||s) and his replacement by Matthias, who is never mentioned again (cf. Acts 1:15–26), could have arisen. The references to the Twelve make sense only when it is accepted that Jesus chose them, that they were with him during his ministry, and that he used them to extend its outreach.

Their names are given in four New Testament passages: Mark 3:16–19; Matt. 10:2–4; Luke 6:14–16; and Acts 1:13 (where Judas, now dead, naturally is not included). Simon Peter was the leading member, and the two pairs of brothers, Peter and Andrew, James and John, were prominent. Judas is mentioned last in all three Synoptic lists. The others are little more than names; whatever their contribution—and there is no reason to belittle them or think them worthless—they were not prominent in later times; the abundant legends of the later church about their leadership in various parts of the church must not mislead us.[4]

As if to underline the inconspicuous role of many of the Twelve, the name of one of them is uncertain.[5] Matthew and Mark call him Thaddaeus (though some evidence, especially in Matthew, calls him Lebbaeus instead of Thaddaeus). Luke and The Acts give instead the name Judas the son of James. Rather than say that Thaddaeus (and possibly Lebbaeus) was an alternate name of Judas the son of James, it is better to say that though the Twelve had a real role during Jesus' ministry, they had a decreasing role after the very first days of the apostolic church, and the identity of one of the Twelve is uncertain; indeed, most of them were not known for individual contributions.

None of these Twelve, as far as we can learn, were of priestly origin; all were Jewish laymen. They were of Galilean origin; if the word "Iscariot" comes from the Hebrew and means "man of Kerioth," as has been held,[6] then Judas would appear to be of Judean origin, since Kerioth was a place in Judea;[7] but the Galilean origin of the remaining eleven may be assumed (cf. Acts 2:7).

---

[3] James the brother of Jesus is sometimes identified with James the son of Alphaeus and considered one of the Twelve. But the evidence is that the brothers of Jesus did not believe in him at the time the Twelve were chosen (Mark 3:21, 31–35; John 7:5).

[4] Such legends receive attention in Carl A. Glover, *With the Twelve* (Cokesbury Press, 1939).

[5] Cf. Goguel, *Life of Jesus*, p. 339.

[6] Cf. William F. Arndt and F. Wilbur Gingrich, *A Greek-English Lexicon of the New Testament and Other Early Christian Literature* (The University of Chicago Press, 1957), p. 381.

[7] See *IDB*, K-Q, article on "Kerioth-Hezron."

Why did Jesus choose the Twelve? Mark 3:14 f. says it was "to be with him, and to be sent out to preach and have authority to cast out demons." "To be with him" implies not merely to give him human companionship but also to learn his message and purpose and help him as he directed. The number twelve seems meant to recall the twelve tribes of Israel. It is not meant that the Twelve included one member from each tribe; the number simply symbolized the complete Israel which Jesus wanted to reach.

Within the group, three formed an inner circle particularly close to Jesus. Peter, James, and John were with him at critical times and thus had a special importance. That Peter was the outstanding individual[8] and that these three were the central trio is confirmed by the book of The Acts. There Peter alone of the Twelve speaks and acts as a visible leader; John goes with Peter (Acts 3:1, 11; 4:13, 19; 8:14); and James, John's brother, was martyred, which shows that he was active enough to draw the attention and opposition of the Jewish leaders (Acts 12:2).

THE MISSION OF THE TWELVE

These Twelve, Jesus sent out to preach and heal throughout Galilee (Mark 6:7–13 and ||s). He himself was not able to go to all the cities and villages of that region; time did not permit it. This means that the Galilean ministry must not be thought of as lasting for years. The Twelve were not sent out merely to get "field education" for a later ministry. Their urgent task was to preach that the Kingdom was at hand and that men should repent at once. Like Jesus, they were to heal and so show the actual presence of the power of the Kingdom in Israel. Since their aim was to reach as many as possible, they were to travel light, preach wherever they could get a hearing, but move on when rejected. The geographical area that their ministry covered is not stated, but it must have included numerous Jewish settlements of Galilee.

The group did not go out singly; they were sent out two by two.[9] This could hardly have been for safety, although danger from robbers and opponents may have existed. It might have been in part for mutual encouragement and help; two might make the message more effective

---

8 See Oscar Cullmann, *Peter: Disciple, Apostle, Martyr*, tr. by Floyd V. Filson, 2d rev. and expanded ed. (The Westminster Press, 1962).

9 Cf. Mark 6:7. Luke 10:1 says that the Seventy went out two by two. Was the mission of the Seventy an actual second mission or was it, rather, a duplicate story of the mission of the Twelve, described as a mission of seventy disciples to symbolize the church's mission to the (traditionally seventy) nations after the mission of the Twelve to Israel?

than one could do alone. But perhaps the Old Testament principle that two witnesses are needed for a valid testimony was mainly in mind (cf. Deut. 17:6; 19:15).

INSTRUCTIONS TO THE TWELVE

It would be instructive to learn just what directions Jesus gave to the Twelve. This, however, is difficult to discover. One reason is that the church, in preserving the tradition of what Jesus said, was so concerned to apply such instruction to their own day that it is hard to be sure what Jesus said to the Twelve. His teaching about their mission and about what would happen later was not kept separate; note that Mark 13:9–13, which refers to what the disciples will face after the end of Jesus' ministry, is used in Matt. 10:17–22 as teaching given to the Twelve when sent out during Jesus' ministry.[10] In particular, the sayings about persecution, beatings, and martyrdom, even if they have a limited basis in Jesus' words to the Twelve, reflect in their present form the use of Jesus' teaching in the life of the apostolic church to guide his disciples.

The other reason we have so little knowledge of Jesus' specific instructions to the Twelve at the time of their mission is that the Gospels have little interest in organization, method of work, and specialized training. Most of their content is solid instruction as to how all disciples are to live; and it presupposes that all of Jesus' followers will be active and vocal witnesses to him and his message. Every disciple is to repent and believe and pray and live as Jesus has taught. Each is to serve the others, to be the "last of all and servant of all" (Mark 9:35). It is not enough to say, "Lord, Lord," to Jesus; it is necessary to do what he has taught is the will of God for his people (Matt. 7:21; Luke 6:46). Actual fruits in daily living are what count; they identify the genuine disciple (Matt. 7:16–20; Luke 6:43–45). The disciple is to have no reservations in his faith and dedication. He must put the claim of Jesus even before family obligations when necessary (Matt. 10:37; Luke 14:26).[11] He is to live with self-discipline, holding steadily to the narrow way and cutting out of his life whatever prevents full loyalty (Mark 8:34 and ||s; Matt. 7:13 f.; Luke 13:24).

Other instructions apply to all disciples but with greater force to those given special tasks. Perhaps it is chiefly those who went with Jesus all the

10 See G. R. Beasley-Murray, *Jesus and the Future: An Examination of the Criticism of the Eschatological Discourse, Mark 13, with Special Reference to the Little Apocalypse Theory* (St. Martin's Press, Inc., 1954).

11 The command to "hate" the members of one's own family is a strong instruction to keep loyalty to Jesus and the Kingdom in first place.

time, the Twelve above all, who are to deny themselves, take up their cross, and follow their Master (Mark 8:34 and ||s).[12] The leaders especially must be ready to confess their loyalty to Jesus and defend it when challenged. They particularly must be faithful when they meet denunciation or ill treatment. They must not be ashamed when public disapproval strikes or danger comes. Some of these teachings referred at least in part to what lay ahead for Jesus' followers in future days, but in view of the gathering opposition to Jesus, there is no reason to doubt that the Twelve as soon as sent out would meet similar hostility if they persisted in urgent preaching of his message. We must not imagine that they had a pleasant, peaceful tour of Galilee and found a friendly welcome and grateful hearing in every town. We have to allow for hostility to their mission.

It is time to study more directly the opposition to Jesus and see what effect it had on the course of his ministry.

OPPOSITION TO JESUS

The fact of opposition to Jesus cannot be denied, nor can its radical nature be minimized. Attempts have been made to belittle its role. But the idea—rarely expressed—that Jesus got into difficulty only or mainly because he did not understand his opponents is unconvincing; he could go to the heart of an issue, and his alert intelligence cannot be questioned.

The usual way of brushing aside the serious conflict between Jesus and Jewish leaders is to say that the church has read back into the lifetime of Jesus the later clash between the church and the synagogue.[13] No doubt the church did see Jesus in the light of the conflicts of its own time. But the preaching of Jesus was based on the premise that his people (as well as Gentiles) were sinners and needed to repent and change their way of life. His teaching indicted the current practices of his people and their leaders. History has yet to produce a generation or people or group of leaders who welcome wholesale condemnation, and a prophet inevitably directs the keenest and deepest criticism at the leaders, for they do most to determine the direction and character of the common life. To pretend that Jesus lived in congenial fellowship with the Jewish leaders of his day is futile. The thing to do is to ask with whom he clashed and what the issues were.

First of all, his freedom of attitude and the note of authority in his

---

[12] Mark 8:34 directs this teaching to the multitudes, but its specific setting includes Peter's misunderstanding of his mission and Jesus' concern to set his special disciples straight.

[13] On this issue, see R. Travers Herford, *The Pharisees,* especially pp. 201 ff.

message evoked a hostile reaction from almost all who had positions of
leadership and authority. This was inevitable; the only possible question
is who was in the right. Every person bested in argument—and Jesus was
clearly a formidable opponent in debate—would join in the hostile
reaction.

The rich and all those hit by his denunciations of the antisocial evils
inherent in a life of wealth and luxury would line up with his opponents,
except for the few who, confessing their sin, changed their way of life.[14]
The socially elite were struck by his criticism of those who entertain as a
means of social climbing instead of as a way to befriend and help others
(Luke 14:12–14). The references to unbelief in Nazareth, Capernaum,
Chorazin, and Bethsaida show that those in opposition more than once
combined to offer a community hostility to his message (Matt. 11:20–24;
Mark 6:1–5; Luke 10:13–15). His special sympathy and friendship for
the poor, the sick, the outcasts, and despised people lowered his social
rating in the eyes of the "important" and "best" people.

These factors, however, do not go to the root of the matter. The basic
opposition to Jesus was religious, and so it went deep. It affected every
sect in Judaism. The opposition of the Sadducees comes into clear view
only in Jerusalem, where this priestly party centered in the Temple
worship; on its attitude, see the next chapter. The Essenes are never
mentioned in the New Testament, but their withdrawal from society to
escape contamination from sinners (who in their view included almost all
other Israelites) makes it certain that they would not champion one who
befriended and ate with tax collectors and sinners (cf. Luke 15:1 f.). The
Zealots, or anti-Roman group in Judaism, would not have understood
one who rejected violent revolution and stressed love of neighbor and
even of enemies (Matt. 5:43–48; Luke 6:32–36); to them he would have
been an impractical dreamer who had not faced the realities of political
slavery and pagan domination of God's people. The continuing group of
disciples of John the Baptist, who had a more rigid way of life than Jesus
favored, would perhaps have felt some sympathy with Jesus, but would
have resented his assumption of a role superior to that of their master
John. Of all groups in Judaism, however, the Pharisees furnished the
most prompt, persistent, and deep-seated opposition to Jesus. Why was
this?

---

14 The Gospel of Luke (chs. 6:24; 12:15–21, 33; 16:1–9, 19–31; 19:1–10) lays special
   emphasis on the spiritual danger in wealth and possessions, but this idea is present
   in Matthew (ch. 6:24) and Mark (ch. 10:17–31 and ||s), and was a clear accent in the
   teaching of Jesus.

Jesus and the Pharisees

The Pharisees were honestly concerned to keep the Mosaic law and apply it to contemporary life.[15] In a real sense they were the liberal wing of Judaism; they tried constantly to keep the law up to date. In their theory not only had the law come down to them in written form but their oral tradition had been transmitted through the generations from the time of Moses. This means that the oral tradition was consistent with the written law and was as truly Mosaic in origin as was the Pentateuch. So it was fully authoritative. Yet this oral tradition, continuously discussed and often newly defined by group action, gave an opportunity to bring the law up to date on points where it was no longer workable or had previously had nothing to say. Once accepted, an item of oral tradition was to the Pharisees as authoritative as the written Pentateuch, and in fact more influential, since the oral tradition in practice altered, canceled, and supplemented the written law. The Pharisees considered it their duty to preserve, observe, and defend this oral tradition; no Pharisee would have felt authorized to act individually to change the accepted tradition.

With the Pharisee position Jesus was in irreconcilable conflict. In the first place, his tacit claim of authority to forgive sinners seemed to Pharisees an assumption of divine prerogatives (Mark 2:1–12 and ||s). The Pharisees did not doubt that God forgave sinners, but no one of them dared to forgive as did Jesus. They sensed in him a personal authority and claim that they considered unjustified and blasphemous.

Even more far-reaching, perhaps, was the freedom with which Jesus set aside the oral tradition, which to Pharisees was part of the law of God. To him it was merely "the tradition of men" (Mark 7:8); he recognized no binding authority in the decisions by which the Pharisee leaders had built up the oral tradition that they made the organizing basis of worship and life. Around the Sabbath, for example, had grown up a large number of regulations intended to ensure the reverent observance of the day. But Jesus saw this tradition keep people from helping human beings in need on the Sabbath, and to him this discredited the entire body of such traditions (Mark 3:1–6 and ||s; Luke 14:1–6).

The freedom of Jesus reached into the very content of the written law.[16] What we call the ceremonial law was an integral part of the

---

15 See Chapter 2, pp. 50 f.
16 See Bennett Harvie Branscomb, *Jesus and the Law of Moses* (Richard R. Smith, 1930).

Mosaic law in the Pentateuch. It might seem above criticism, but Jesus regarded it as possessed of no ultimate authority. Most striking, and most shocking to the Pharisees, was his assertion that "there is nothing outside a man which by going into him can defile him; but the things which come out of a man are what defile him" (Mark 7:15; Matt. 15:11). As Mark notes, "Thus he declared all foods clean" (ch. 7:19), or as we might say, he canceled the entire kosher system of clean and unclean foods. Not that he explicitly intended to do this, but in effect this was what his saying finally meant. In usual practice Jesus evidently observed the familiar Jewish rites, which he no doubt had learned at home and in the synagogue; but when these rites prevented practical human helpfulness, he promptly discarded them.

This freedom toward the oral tradition, toward the ceremonial features of the written law, and even to the idea that the Pentateuch is really a rigid code of law, enabled Jesus to associate with "tax collectors and sinners." He freely offered the grace of God to the careless and wicked people of his generation. He insisted upon repentance and faith, but he allowed no merit to the "good" people, since no one can do more than he owes to God and all in fact do less; and he let no legalism bar the way that led even gross sinners from wickedness to reconciliation with God. To the Pharisees this free spirit showed a lack of respect for moral standards. They were ready to accept sinners who repented, put their house in order, and thus showed that they were prepared to enter into fellowship with good people. But the idea of going to sinners and living in friendly fellowship with them without first requiring them to accept and practice the ceremonial and moral laws was repugnant to the Pharisee group.

Thus the radicalism of Jesus was alien to the spirit and method of the Pharisees. We may note this by a study of Matt. 5:21–48. The material of this passage has been editorially organized in a systematic way; some of it has a less formal pattern in the parallel passages of the Gospel of Luke.[17] But the section makes clear how Jesus looked for God's deepest intent and did not stop with the letter of even the Scripture.

God's law in reality forbids not only the act of murder but also hate-filled, contemptuous words and thoughts. It forbids not only the act of adultery but even the lustful look. It is not content with forbidding hasty, unrecorded divorces (which Jewish husbands could grant at will), but brands all divorce as contrary to God's will and plan for marriage.

---

[17] A part of this passage is paralleled in Luke's Sermon on the Plain; see Luke 6:27–36. Other parts are paralleled in Luke 12:57–59; 16:18. Still other parts have no parallel in Luke.

It rejects the division of speech into oaths, which must be truthfully made and faithfully kept, and other speech in which man may play fast and loose with the truth; it requires truthful speech at all times. It forbids equal retaliation for wrongs received; it requires nonresistance to evil treatment. It forbids limiting love to one's neighbor and extends it even to enemies.

All this means radical, complete obedience to God in all of life and in all relations with others. The Pharisees, aiming to obey the will of God given in Scripture and oral tradition, did not share this radicalism that brushes past the letter of Scripture to lay hold of its full intent.

All these points document a deep-going difference in spirit and thought between Jesus and the Pharisees. The opposition that Jesus encountered in the synagogues of Galilee (and the synagogue was the center of Pharisaic influence) was not accidental but inevitable. The Pharisees on the basis of their position had to work to discredit Jesus and his teaching.

A PERIOD OF WITHDRAWAL?

With this background it is easier to understand why after a period of public ministry that included teaching in Galilean synagogues, Jesus apparently decided on a period of withdrawal.[18]

There is no real indication that he lost his popularity with the common people. It is sometimes said that after a period of Galilean popularity Jesus was quite rejected and widely shunned. That does not seem accurate.

The problem that Jesus encountered concerned mainly two points. On the one hand, the crowds, though interested in his teaching and even more in his healing power, showed a limited response. The rigor of his demands they did not really accept. Thus the extent of his Galilean success must not be overstated. On the other hand, the religious leaders —the scribes and Pharisees, and in particular the rulers or elders of the synagogue, many of them Pharisees—probably closed most synagogues against him. He probably could attend, but the local authorities could keep him from speaking. Under their leadership the bulk of whole cities rejected his message (Matt. 11:21–24; Luke 10:13–15).

In this situation it appears that for a time Jesus did not push his direct appeal to the people in the cities and villages of Galilee. Possibly his

18 See Ch. Guignebert, *Jesus*, tr. by S. H. Hooke (Alfred A. Knopf, Inc., 1935), pp. 223 ff., on "The Itinerary of Jesus." On "The Withdrawal from Galilee," see also Vincent Taylor, "The Life and Ministry of Jesus," Section III, in *The Interpreter's Bible*, Vol. VII (Abingdon Press, 1951), pp. 128 ff.

mission and that of the Twelve aroused political excitement among the people, so that they pined for the Kingdom as deliverance from subjection to Rome (cf. John 6:15). Perhaps Jesus wanted to protect the Twelve from the hostile teaching of the scribes and Pharisees, and give them further teaching himself; but though he may have done such further teaching, he could hardly have withdrawn mainly because he feared that his closest disciples would desert him and side with his opponents. Nor was he afraid of Herod Antipas, tetrarch of Galilee and Perea. When Herod imprisoned John the Baptist, Jesus did not avoid the region Herod governed, but boldly went into Galilee and continued, though with some difference of emphasis, the message that the Baptist had preached until Herod had arrested him (Mark 1:14); and when Pharisees warned Jesus, out of friendliness or to trick him into leaving the region, that he should leave Galilee, since Herod intended to seize him, he refused to fear the tetrarch and alter his plan of action (Luke 13:31–33).[19]

The real reason for withdrawal probably was that Jesus realized that his preaching, teaching, and healing were not achieving his aim: the winning of Israel to the repentance and faith that alone would prepare it for the coming Kingdom. What should he do? In a period of partial withdrawal he could reshape his course of action.

One thing is clear; the aim of such a withdrawal, to the extent that it did occur, was not to undertake a ministry to Gentiles or even to Jews in Gentile lands (cf. John 7:35). It is clear throughout the Gospels that Jesus considered himself "sent only to the lost sheep of the house of Israel" (Matt. 15:24; cf. ch. 10:5 f.). This verse in Matthew has often been discounted because this Gospel was written by a Jewish Christian who emphasized the Jewishness of Jesus. But in fact all four of the Gospels show that Jesus concentrated his ministry on an effort to win his own people. When he was drawn by special appeal into contact with a Gentile, it was strictly an exception, and—an interesting point—the rare healings of Gentiles are performed at a distance; Jesus never enters a Gentile home (Matt. 8:5–13 = Luke 7:1–10; Mark 7:24–30 and ||; cf. John 4:46–54). He felt sent to his people; whatever mission to Gentiles he foresaw was to be undertaken through a repentant and obedient Israel. He did not withdraw from Galilee to minister to the Gentiles.[20]

Two Gospels tell of an apparently brief visit, undertaken incognito,

---

[19] Goguel, *Life of Jesus*, pp. 346–358, ascribes to Herod Antipas' decision to kill Jesus the crisis that arose in Galilee.

[20] See Joachim Jeremias, *Jesus' Promise to the Nations*, tr. by S. H. Hooke (London, SCM Press, Ltd., 1958), pp. 25–39.

5

into the region of Phoenicia, just northwest of Galilee (Mark 7:24–30; Matt. 15:21–28).[21] The vague expression "the region of Tyre" or "the district of Tyre and Sidon" means that Jesus did not go to the city or cities named, but into the mountainous region near them. Only the persistent appeal of a mother desperate over the mental derangement or severe illness of her daughter led him to heal the child (from a distance),[22] and the incident apparently led him to abandon his attempt to find quiet in that region; he returned to the Sea of Galilee. Perhaps he went east and then came down from the north to the east side of that sea, for "the region of the Decapolis" was on that side (Mark 7:31); if so, he still was in largely Gentile areas and desired to continue his withdrawal, for to return to Galilee would at once bring him into public attention among the Jews.

It is difficult to fit the stories of Jesus' feeding the multitude into the events of this intermediate period of his ministry. Indeed, it is difficult to determine what actual event lay back of these stories. The Gospels of Matthew and Mark tell of two such feedings, first of five thousand (Matt. 14:13–21; Mark 6:30–44) and then of four thousand (Matt. 15:32–39; Mark 8:1–10). But the Gospels of Luke and John have only the former story (Luke 9:10–17; John 6:1–15), and the introduction of the second story gives no hint that such an event had happened before in Jesus' ministry, so that the two accounts are probably variants of one story, widely told and regarded as particularly significant (the feeding of the five thousand is the only miracle done by Jesus that is told in all four Gospels).[23]

Later followers of Jesus, in the apostolic age and to this day, have seen in the story a preview of the Lord's Supper, and the language that describes the event shows that the Gospel writers already took this view, most strongly presented in John, ch. 6. But the prior question is what Jesus actually did and what the multitude saw happen.

The story as it now reads says that Jesus by miraculous power so multiplied a few small loaves of bread and a few fish that the entire hungry multitude had more than enough to eat. This is one of the nature miracles, most unlike what men today can do, and so most often doubted.

21 It is curious that Luke, who obviously was interested in the gospel as a message for Gentiles as well as for Jews, does not parallel these passages. He must have realized that this withdrawal, even including the healing of the Syrophoenician woman's daughter, was not for a Gentile ministry but only for withdrawal, and could be omitted without serious loss to his particular purpose.

22 On exorcism, see McCasland, *By the Finger of God.*

23 The exact time of the event back of the two feeding narratives cannot be fixed. It may best be dated in the period when Jesus tended to withdraw from the active Galilean ministry.

In its basic meaning the event was symbolic of fellowship in the impending Kingdom. Did it literally take place as reported? Or was the event, rather, a token meal in which the sharing of a meager supply of food, perhaps augmented by others as the spirit of participation spread through the crowd, proved sufficient to satisfy men's needs and unite them in expectation of the imminent coming of God's kingly rule? It seems highly probable that in either case the note of eschatological anticipation was present.

The occasion was one in which Jesus had contact with the Galilean crowds. It shows that at this stage of his ministry Jesus tried at times to withdraw from such contact, but his popularity was still so great as to make such withdrawal difficult to manage. It shows that Jesus still looked forward to the Kingdom, and his action expresses his determination to unite responsive men with him in preparation for it.[24]

JESUS NEAR CAESAREA PHILIPPI

Such suggestions as to what the feeding of the multitude may have meant cannot be described as proved facts but only as an honest attempt to grasp the meaning of this period of Jesus' career. The Gospels give a clearer picture of the incident near Caesarea Philippi (Mark 8:27–30 and ||s). They do not say that Jesus entered that Hellenistic city, but only that he came to the region around it. This, however, is significant. The region was not Jewish; its population was mostly Gentile. In other words, Jesus was still following mainly a withdrawal policy. The disciples, meaning here the Twelve, were with him.

The gospel tradition preserved the memory that on this journey Jesus questioned the disciples concerning what the Jews were saying about him. At an earlier time, according to Mark 6:14–16 and ||s, Herod Antipas had spoken of Jesus as John the Baptist returned from the dead; others thought that Jesus was Elijah or some other Old Testament prophet returned to the scene of history. The disciples give Jesus similar reports. People, they say, regard him as John the Baptist, or Elijah, or some other Old Testament prophet.

They hardly meant that Jesus was the very same person as John the Baptist; they surely knew that these two leaders had lived at the same time and were two different men. They must have meant that for all their differences of emphasis both expressed the same prophetic vigor

---

24 On this miracle story, see Alan Richardson, *The Miracle-Stories of the Gospels*, pp. 94 ff. The event need not be dated during the period of withdrawal; it might fit at the end of that period.

and boldness, the same stern call to repentance in view of God's impending action, the same strong call to change the life direction while there was time.

Related to this identification with the Baptist was the view that Jesus was Elijah. John the Baptist had worked to prepare for God's final action, just as Elijah was expected to return and prepare men for that climactic divine action (Mal. 4:5). Many people, recognizing a similarity between John the Baptist and Jesus, thought of Jesus, as his message of the impending Kingdom could lead them to do, as the great final prophet of the last days (cf. also Deut. 18:15; John 1:21). The other suggestion, that Jesus was one of the Old Testament prophets,[25] underlines the conviction common to all views: he was a divinely sent prophet. The prevailing view of the people was that Jesus was the great prophet of the last days, sent to prepare for the coming of the Kingdom of God.

Matt. 11:2–19 and Luke 7:18–35 report that at an earlier time John the Baptist had already raised a further question. While in prison he heard of Jesus' miraculous deeds. He himself was already acting as the prophet of the final days; quite possibly he thought of himself as the Elijah who was to come, as Mal. 4:5 had promised. So, if Jesus fitted into the scheme given by Scripture, then Jesus had to be the one for whom John was preparing the way; he had to be God's anointed King to bring in the Kingdom. If we were to accept the chronological outline of the Gospel of John, the Baptist knew from the time of Jesus' baptism that Jesus was the Lamb of God, the Son of God, and so the climactic figure of all history (John 1:29, 34, 36). But the Gospel of John, for dramatic purposes, pushes forward to the very beginning of the Gospel every great title of Jesus; all such titles used by this Gospel occur in ch. 1. Such early and explicit identification of Jesus by John the Baptist must be discounted. So when John asks in Matthew and Luke: "Are you he who is to come, or shall we look for another?" the question is rather a dawning of faith that Jesus may be the very leader for whom he had been preparing the way. If the eschatological expectation was as vivid as we have said, that question was bound to rise, and if the Baptist regarded himself as the Elijah of the last days, the inevitable answer was that Jesus, as his mighty works indicated, was the expected Greater One.[26]

---

25 Matt. 16:14 mentions a report that he was Jeremiah. II Esdras 2:18 speaks of God's promise to send Isaiah and Jeremiah. But Strack-Billerbeck, *Kommentar zum Neuen Testament aus Talmud und Midrasch*, Vol. I, p. 730, can find no evidence in ancient Jewish literature that Jeremiah was to be a forerunner of the Messiah. They think that this statement in II Esdras comes from a Christian writer who was prompted by Matt. 16:14.

26 On "John the Baptist and Jesus," see Kraeling, *John the Baptist*, Ch. V; John A. T.

Jesus, however, did not give John a direct answer. He pointed to what was happening, in words that reflect the work of God promised in Isa. 29:18 f.; 35:5 f.; 61:1 f. He implies that since he is doing what Scripture has said will be done in the last days, he is the one endowed with the Spirit of God to carry out that final work (cf. Luke 4:16–21). The Synoptic Gospels give no hint that John the Baptist accepted this implication. He did not. His followers continued as a separate movement in the apostolic age (Acts 18:25; 19:3), and words of Jesus indicate that John stayed outside of the Kingdom (Matt. 11:11; Luke 7:28).[27] But the incident shows that what happened near Caesarea Philippi was not without preparation.

PETER'S MESSIANIC CONFESSION

Jesus' main interest was not in what other men were saying but in what the disciples thought. When he asked them this question, Peter as usual spoke for the group: "You are the Christ" (Mark 8:29). That is, you are the expected anointed leader, the Messiah, of our people Israel; you are the promised leader sent to act for God to set up and rule his Kingdom. After perhaps a year or two with him, they feel compelled to give him this title.

The narratives raise two main questions. One is: Just what did Peter say? Instead of the simple title, "the Christ," with which "the Christ of God" in Luke 9:20 closely agrees, Matt. 16:16 reads: "the Christ, the Son of the living God."[28] The Messianic King was thought of as the Son of God, so this fuller title is not essentially different from the one in Mark unless one wrongly reads into it the Greek substance philosophy. It is a Jewish phrase (cf. Hos. 1:10), and here designates Jesus as Messiah. However, the simpler title of Mark is likely to be what Jesus heard from Peter.

The other question is: Did Jesus accept the title of Messiah? All three Synoptic Gospels indicate that the title was in some way unsatisfactory to Jesus; it suggested to people a military, nationalistic leadership that he had no intention of giving. He considered the basic need to be spiritual and moral renewal rather than the regaining of political freedom or the establishing of Jewish rule over the Gentiles. So he commanded his

Robinson, *Twelve New Testament Studies* (London, SCM Press, Ltd., 1962), Ch. 2, on "Elijah, John, and Jesus."

[27] See Kraeling, *John the Baptist*, Ch. VI, on "The Later History of the Baptist Movement."

[28] Cf. John 6:69: "You are the Holy One of God." In John 1:41, Andrew identifies Jesus as "the Messiah" before Peter has seen Jesus.

disciples to say nothing of his Messianic role. But did he agree that the title was correct? Did he accept the title of Messiah or Christ?

As we have said, the title was unsatisfactory. In current Jewish thought it often implied political and nationalistic aspirations that obscured what Jesus wanted to keep central. It did not force Israel to face its sin and see that its real need was repentance, faith in the gospel message, and dedication to do God's will in every aspect of life. It pointed to a worldly kingdom rather than the Kingdom of God where love and integrity ruled. In widespread current thought the great leader was indeed to be a spiritual as well as a national leader, but the heavily nationalistic content kept the title from proper emphasis on what Jesus had to say. So in part at least Jesus rejected the title; he was not the kind of leader the title suggested to most Jews.

Yet it was not satisfactory to reject the title completely. Jesus, like other Jews, accepted the Scripture as the revelation of God's ways and promise. In them God had promised a great leader. The fulfillment of God's promise would bring that leader. Jesus as a student of Scripture and its promises accepted that Messianic hope as sure to be fulfilled. If he was doing the work that the Spirit of God was to lead the climactic leader of history to do, he could and should accept the title. He did so.[29] But he found other titles more congenial, since they expressed better what he really had set out to do.

THE ROLE OF PETER

The words to Peter in Matt. 16:17–19 have no parallel in any other passage of the Gospels, and it is not likely that Jesus uttered them all on this occasion.[30] He did expect Peter to take the leading role among his disciples; this is clear from his instruction to Peter in Luke 22:31 f. The Matthew passage expresses Peter's faith and loyalty, his recognition of Jesus' central and climactic role in history, and Peter's responsibility as central leader in the crucial earliest days of the church. It says nothing that Jesus could not have uttered, provided we do not read into it more than it says. It does not speak of the later organized church;[31] it says nothing of formal organization or of successors of Peter. It recognizes

29 So Burton Scott Easton, *Christ in the Gospels*, pp. 164 ff.
30 Cf. Oscar Cullmann, *Peter: Disciple, Apostle, Martyr*, pp. 164 ff. The Gospel of Matthew is known for its topical grouping of sayings which were spoken on various occasions; that can be true of these verses.
31 The word "church" occurs in the Gospels only in Matt. 16:18 and 18:17. In the latter passage it refers to a local congregation of disciples; in the former, it refers to the whole group of followers of Christ, but does not specify a church polity.

Peter's leadership among the Twelve in both thinking and active leadership, and the early chapters of The Acts show that Peter was just such a leader as these words promise.

The Son of Man Must Suffer

Since Jesus was not the kind of Messiah or Christ commonly expected, the title could easily mislead, and so Jesus did not use it of himself or let his disciples use it of him. It could have given the impression that as a nationalist military leader he intended to solve Jewish problems and give Jews their proper place by leading an open revolt against Rome. To describe what he really was doing and still had to do he used other titles. The title of prophet had great truth for him; according to Luke 4:24 he used it of himself.[32] But it did not express adequately his unique role in the bringing of the Kingdom.

He found more meaning in the title "Son of Man." The New Testament indicates that he used it frequently of himself, but others rarely or never used it of him. To modern men this title expresses his humanity, his sharing of the human lot. To Jesus this was part but by no means all of its essential meaning. It meant much more than that. He was more than a frail human being used of God for the divine purpose (cf. Ezek. 2:1; etc.). With a background in The Book of Daniel, especially ch. 7:13, and on the basis of such development in meaning as the Book of Enoch shows, Jesus could use the title to refer to himself as God's special representative, closely linked with the Father, and destined to fulfill God's purpose and establish God's Kingdom in the impending eschatological crisis.[33] The title combined lowly situation, stirring leadership, and full vindication in the climactic days just ahead.[34]

But even this title was not fully satisfactory to Jesus. The public ministry in Galilee had revealed widespread unwillingness to accept his message. He was left with the harsh fact that preaching, teaching, and healing were not adequate to bring in the Kingdom. A smooth transition from a lowly ministry to a glorious triumph was not possible. How could

[32] Cf. Paul E. Davies, "Jesus and the Role of the Prophet," *JBL*, Vol. LXIV (1945), pp. 241–254.

[33] See Rudolf Otto, *The Kingdom of God and the Son of Man*. It must be noted, however, that among the fragments of the Book of Enoch found at Qumran, none so far contains any of chs. 37 to 71, in which the Son of Man is prominent. So perhaps this section was added to the Book of Enoch at a date later than the ministry of Jesus.

[34] Cf. T. W. Manson, *The Teaching of Jesus*, pp. 211–236; Cecil John Cadoux, *The Historic Mission of Jesus* (London, Lutterworth Press, 1941), pp. 90–102; Bornkamm, *Jesus of Nazareth*, pp. 175 ff.

God's people Israel be roused and made ready for their true destiny? From the start—at the temptation—Jesus had rejected the way of political revolt and military action; it could not shape the springs of human living. Now the humble ministry had not achieved the goal. How could the Son of Man achieve it?

The answer of all the Gospels is that to achieve what the public ministry had not achieved the cross was necessary.[35] Jesus had to continue his urgent appeal to his people; he had to carry that appeal to the center of his people's life in Jerusalem and particularly to the center of their religious life and worship in the Temple; he had to do this knowing that there was little if any hope that this complete appeal would win Israel to the repentance, faith, and obedience that would mark the coming of the Kingdom, and knowing therefore that the power of sin being what it is, such faithful presentation of God's claim in that critical time would bring him to his death; he had to accept that death on behalf of his people and as the way to bring the Kingdom. So he began to talk to his disciples about his basic conviction, now clearly crystallized: "The Son of Man must suffer." He interpreted the Son of Man's role in the light of the Suffering Servant figure of Isa., ch. 53. But this was no message of failure and final doom. That suffering could reach men as preaching, teaching, and healing had not been able to do, and it would be followed by his vindication; the Son of Man would rise from the dead.

Doubt has been expressed whether Jesus clearly foresaw and foretold his suffering, death, and resurrection.[36] The passages that speak of this, including his words at the Last Supper, have been held to be the creation of the apostolic church. It is possible and even probable that the wording has been sharpened up by the knowledge of what actually happened to Jesus. But it is unreasonable to think that Jesus could not see what lay ahead if he persisted in his appeal to his people in Jerusalem. It is unconvincing to date in the apostolic age the most creative thinking of the Gospels. The original disciples were keenly aware that they had not understood and supported Jesus as they should have done; it would have surprised them to be credited with having created the heart of the gospel message. Equally unconvincing is the corollary that Jesus walked into the final crisis at Jerusalem with no understanding and plan, that he did

35 See T. W. Manson, *The Teaching of Jesus*, pp. 211–236; Vincent Taylor, *Jesus and His Sacrifice: A Study of the Passion-Sayings in the Gospels* (London, Macmillan & Co., Ltd., 1937); Oscar Cullmann, *The Christology of the New Testament*, Eng. tr. by Shirley C. Guthrie and Charles A. M. Hall (The Westminster Press, 1959), pp. 152–164.

36 E.g., by Rudolf Bultmann, *Theology of the New Testament*, tr. by Kendrick Grobel (Charles Scribner's Sons, 1951), Vol. I, pp. 29 ff.

nothing to prepare his followers for what was coming, and that only after his death and resurrection did his followers begin to work out the previously unexplained meaning of his method of reaching men.

Much more convincing is the view of the Gospels that Jesus foresaw and foretold in essentials the inevitable issue of his complete and final appeal to the Jews and their leaders at Jerusalem. The withdrawal period dealt basically with this entire problem. Teaching on this subject dominated the latter part of the withdrawal period, after the incident near Caesarea Philippi.

THE MEANING OF THE TRANSFIGURATION

Shortly after that decisive discussion near Caesarea Philippi the Gospels place the story of the transfiguration of Jesus on "a high mountain apart" (Mark 9:2–8 and ||s).[37] The narrative describes not an ordinary event but a vision that the three leading disciples, Peter, James, and John, had of Jesus transfigured, with his garments glistening bright in the divine light that bathed the scene. It has been thought that this is really a resurrection appearance of the risen Christ, here transferred back to the earthly ministry of Jesus. But just as in stories of Jesus' ministry the key teaching is regularly found in the saying that climaxes the report, so here the key to understanding the vision is in the closing words of the heavenly Voice: "This is my beloved Son; listen to him" (Mark 9:7).

Listen to him! He has told the disciples that he is not the commonly expected military, political Messiah; he is the Son of Man who must suffer; he can be understood best by bringing the Suffering Servant figure of Second Isaiah together with the Son of Man figure of Jewish eschatological expectation; the disciples are troubled by this teaching contrary to their personal expectation and desire; but they must recognize that Jesus is really God's Son, even if not in the way they had traditionally expected, and they should listen to him in this teaching which has troubled them since they heard it near Caesarea Philippi. The common expectation was that when Elijah came, the drama of God's powerful action to establish his Kingdom would move victoriously to its conclusion. Elijah had come, in John the Baptist. He had had to suffer. The Son of Man must suffer too, but he will rise from the dead. Listen to him; this is the path God's action will take in establishing the eternal Kingdom.

[37] See G. H. Boobyer, *St. Mark and the Transfiguration Story* (Edinburgh, T. & T. Clark, 1942).

5*

The pattern of thinking in all this outlook is foreign to modern man, but it is a consistent pattern, and it explains the events of this obscure withdrawal period better than any reconstruction which rejects this picture in the Gospels in favor of a series of conjectures more congenial to our a priori expectations.

THE DECISION TO GO TO JERUSALEM

The result of the thinking of Jesus and his conversations with the disciples was his determination to go to Jerusalem (cf. Luke 9:51).[38] This was a deliberate decision to bring things to a crisis. It took Jesus to the place where the opposition to him could muster its greatest strength. But it had for Jesus one essential advantage. It left no stone unturned to bring his message and appeal to Israel and especially to its leaders. It blocked any possible charge that he had stayed on the edge of his people's national life and had never had the courage to put the issue to a radical choice by challenging those most responsible for the religious life of Israel.

The Passover was approaching, but it was more than the usual desire of a loyal Israelite to celebrate the Passover at Jerusalem which motivated Jesus' decision to go there for that festival. At that Passover time, with great numbers of Jews present to celebrate the national deliverance from Egypt, his offer of a new deliverance through repentance and faith, and a new gift of life in the Kingdom, could be made with the greatest force to the greatest possible number.

If the Gospels can be trusted, Jesus had no real hope that such a well-timed and urgent appeal would win either the common people or the leaders. Looking back at that event, it is clear that he could not bring Israel to accept God's will without the cross. But even before the event he could have seen little if any likelihood of success. The appeal had to be made; he should have received a favorable hearing; but he was to fail. This does not mean that the appeal was wrong but only that humanly speaking it was a failure and was bound to be such. There was no easy way to fulfill God's promise of the Kingdom. "The Son of Man *must* suffer."

The disciples found it impossible to keep up with Jesus in his thinking about the crisis. The idea that God's promised leader would achieve his aim and establish the divine Kingdom by his voluntary suffering did not seem reasonable or convincing. Peter rebuked Jesus for thinking of such

38 For another analysis of the reason(s) why Jesus went to Jerusalem, see Goguel, *Life of Jesus*, pp. 392–399.

a thing—and drew a rebuke in turn for not being open to the mind of God (Mark 8:32 f.; Matt. 16:22 f.). Twice we get evidence that the disciples continued to cherish a success psychology, expecting that the promised leader of Israel would certainly triumph, so that to follow him would bring honor and privilege. The report that they disputed as to which of them was the greatest suggests strongly that they craved rank and recognition in the coming Kingdom (Mark 9:33–37 and ||s). The request of James and John for the chief places, on Jesus' right and left, in his Kingdom, and thus for honor and authority second only to his, shows that they were convinced that Jesus would establish the Kingdom but could not believe that suffering was the divine means of achieving that goal (Mark 10:35; cf. Matt. 20:20 f.).[39] It seems strange that the disciples, after specific teaching from Jesus on this point, were still impervious to its truth, but the fact that the church still tends to do as they did makes it easier to believe that they reacted just as the Gospels describe.

The route by which Jesus and his disciples went to Jerusalem is not of basic importance. From the north, where the withdrawal period was spent, the group could have moved through Galilee, though not to carry on an active ministry there; the destination was Jerusalem. Instead of going through Samaria, Jesus took the road down the Jordan valley, on the eastern side of the river, until he crossed to the west side near Jericho to follow the road up to the Mount of Olives and so into Jerusalem (Mark 10:1, 46; Matt. 19:1; Luke 19:1).

How long this journey took one cannot say.[40] There are hints that it was not hurried, and that Jesus was in touch with the people of the places passed through and also with crowds who were on the way to Jerusalem to prepare for the Passover celebration. In the presence of the crowds gathered in Jerusalem just before Passover, Jesus was to make his final appeal and require a decision from the leaders of the religious life of his people.

[39] The request of James and John for the first places was in effect an attempt to displace Peter from his leading role.

[40] In the Gospel of Luke it occupies over a third of the Gospel (chs. 9:51 to 19:28), but this "travel narrative" gives Luke a framework in which to include a great amount of teaching whose actual date and place in Jesus' ministry was not known. The journey to Jerusalem could have taken a few days or a few weeks.

Chapter 6

REJECTED, CRUCIFIED, RISEN

By A DELIBERATELY planned dramatic entry Jesus made his
arrival at Jerusalem a challenge to the Jewish leaders and people. His
entry was an acted parable of his Messianic role. The road up from
Jericho to Jerusalem passed through Bethany, rounded the southern
upper slope of the Mount of Olives, descended to the Brook Kidron, and
then led up to the eastern gate of the "holy city." As Jesus neared Bethany, where he had friends, probably from previous visits to Jerusalem,
he sent two of his disciples there to get an ass on which to ride into
Jerusalem (Mark 11:1–10 and ||s). The concise statements in the Gospels
could suggest that supernatural revelation told Jesus where the ass was
tied, but all four Gospels indicate that Jesus had friends in Bethany who
could help him in his plans.[1]

THE MEANING OF THE ENTRY

His aim was to challenge the residents and pilgrims at Jerusalem to
recognize in him the King described in Zech. 9:9: "Lo, your king comes
to you; triumphant and victorious is he, humble and riding on an ass,
on a colt the foal of an ass." Some have thought that this verse led the
later church to imagine the dramatic entry or to recast a spontaneous
acclamation by pilgrims to make it correspond to the Zechariah passage.
But Jesus himself was remarkably familiar with Scripture and regarded
his ministry as its fulfillment; he agreed with his contemporaries that
only as he fulfilled the promises of Scripture could he claim recognition
and support.

Those who acclaimed Jesus were not residents of Jerusalem, nor was
the tribute prompted by pilgrims already present there, as the Gospel
of John indicates (ch. 12:12 f.). Rather, the disciples of Jesus and the
pilgrims traveling with him to Jerusalem for the Passover feast, responding to his dramatic offer of himself as their King, accompanied him into
the city with shouts of joy and acclamation (Mark 11:7–10 and ||s). Pass-

---

[1] Cf. Lazarus, Martha, and Mary in John, chs. 11 and 12.

over recalled Israel's deliverance from Egypt, and aroused each year the hope that God would deliver his people from foreign yoke. Because this hope could stir anti-Roman demonstrations, the Roman governor, whose regular residence was in Caesarea, came to Jerusalem each Passover season to guard against riot and revolt. On the wave of this political and religious expectation Jesus presented himself to his people, not on a spirited horse and with military force, but on an ass, as an offer of leadership different from the Zealot plan to rise against Roman rule. The shouts of the pilgrims as they entered the city alerted the people to his coming.

THE CLEANSING OF THE TEMPLE

Jesus' destination was the Temple, not simply because to Jews it was the visible focus of their life as God's people, but also because he himself deeply appreciated its significance. His lament over Jerusalem, whether spoken far from Jerusalem (Luke 13:34 f.) or during his last stay there (Matt. 23:37–39; cf. Luke 19:39–44), shows how much the city meant to him, and this was largely because the Temple was there. In cleansing the Temple, he quoted Isa. 56:7: "My house shall be called a house of prayer for all the nations" (Mark 11:17). The Temple was God's house, a house of prayer. Whatever Jesus found wrong there led him not to disown the Temple but to act to remedy the evils.

But Jesus did not act immediately. He entered the Temple area, looked around, and withdrew to Bethany for the night (Mark 11:11).[2] The fact that he returned to the place from which the staged entry started shows not only that he had friends in Bethany but also that the entry had a special purpose and meaning. In it he offered himself to his people as their leader.

What he had seen in the Temple aroused him. In the outer court, the Court of the Gentiles, animals and birds were being sold for use in sacrifice, and his reference to the place as a "den of robbers" (Mark 11:17 and ||s; cf. Jer. 7:11) implied that pilgrims were being charged extortionate prices. Moreover, the confusion and din of bargaining and dispute prevented quiet worship by any Gentiles who came to the Temple for worship (this outer court was the only court which Gentiles could enter and so was their only place of worship in the Temple). The use of the

2 Matt. 21:12 and Luke 19:45 place the cleansing on the day of the entry. They probably compress the narrative to get to the climactic event as soon as possible. John 2:13–22 places it at the opening of the ministry, as a dramatic symbol of the radical correction and renewal that Jesus brought to the worship of Israel.

Temple courts as a shortcut by people going from one part of the city to another further frustrated the purpose of prayer—the very purpose that gave sanctity to the Temple (Mark 11:16).

The next day Jesus returned to the outer court. With the moral support of his disciples and many pilgrims he drove out the animals and their keepers; he also overturned the table of the money changers, who exchanged the foreign coins possessed by pilgrims for coins acceptable as Temple offerings (Mark 11:15–19 and ||s). In so doing he assumed authority and acted without consulting the priestly group in charge of the Temple area. This assertion of authority was soon to be challenged. For the moment, however, not even the Temple police could prevent it; by moral indignation, personal authority, and popular approval Jesus was able to take command. But he thereby came into direct conflict with the highest authorities of his people, the Sadducees and the Sanhedrin. It was his first open clash with the Sadducees, whose concern centered in the Temple.[3]

The next day the Sanhedrin, including the priestly leaders, confronted Jesus with the logical, inevitable question: "By what authority are you doing these things, or who gave you this authority to do them?" (Mark 11:28 and ||s). They supposedly had authority to control the Temple, and implied that Jesus had no authority to interfere. He answered by another question. It was not an evasion; it challenged the spiritual qualifications of his critics. John the Baptist had been a true prophet of God, the great final prophet to Israel, yet the leaders had not responded to his preaching. If in the case of John they had proved spiritually unfit to lead Israel, Jesus did not have to answer to them. Were they aware of God's present action? Did they see and admit that God had sent John the Baptist? This was the challenge hidden behind the question whether the baptism of John was from heaven (prompted by God) or from men (lacking divine sanction).

The leaders dared not answer. They could not call John's work divinely prompted, for they had not responded; neither could they call it a merely human invention, for they dared not fly against popular conviction that God had sent John. Their professed inability to answer, their actual unwillingness to say that they did not recognize John as divinely sent, disqualified them in Jesus' eyes, and he refused to answer their question (Mark 11:27–33 and ||s). However, his question implied his conviction that God had sent John, that he, Jesus, had the same

---

[3] In the Gospel of John, Jesus visits Jerusalem and the Temple several times during his ministry, and clashes with the Sadducees were inevitable at those times. That Jesus made such visits during his ministry is not to be denied, but the dramatic use of material and the strong interpretive element in the Gospel of John frustrate attempts to use this Gospel for detailed chronology.

authority as John (both had been sent by God), and that the Jewish leaders were not qualified to sit in judgment on Jesus. (Did he also hint, with a thought of Mal. 3:1, that he as God's Anointed was the rightful Lord of the Temple?)

A Final Teaching Ministry

From that time Jesus, teaching daily in the Temple, appealed to as many of the people as would listen. From the Gospels it might seem that Jesus taught there only two or three days before his public ministry ended. But probably the period of final teaching to the crowds was longer than this.

1. *Love of God and Neighbor.* It is not clear whether it was in these last days at Jerusalem that Jesus thus summed up the essential content of the Mosaic law (Mark 12:28–34 and ||s). Luke 10:25–28 dates this summary earlier, credits it to a Jewish scribe, and says that Jesus approved it.[4] But all three Synoptic Gospels indicate that Jesus found in these two commandments (Deut. 6:4–5; Lev. 19:18) the central meaning of the law. The first command matches in part what he did in Jerusalem in his last days; he gave the Temple a positive role put in terms of prayer. Love of God expressed in worship, without emphasis on priestly leadership and the sacrificial system, was his accent. And for him it led to active love of neighbor.[5]

2. *Taxes to Caesar.* The question concerning Jesus' authority was not the only hostile attack he met in his final days of teaching. He was asked (by Pharisees, Matthew and Mark say) whether it was lawful for a Jew loyal to the Mosaic law to pay taxes to the pagan Roman Government (Mark 12:13–17 and ||s). He had defied the Temple authorities and claimed the right to lead his people; did he plan revolt against Rome? Did he, like men of Zealot tendencies, teach that it was wrong to pay taxes to a pagan foreign power? The question was a crafty trap. If he said not to pay, he could be denounced to the Romans as a rebel; if he said to pay, he would lose the support of nationalist Jews restless under the foreign yoke. He asked for a common coin, a denarius, and by a question made his questioners say that it bore Caesar's image and inscription. They had and used Caesar's money; in government and business they lived and acted under Roman rule; let them give to Caesar obedience and taxes. This rejected the Zealot position and accepted

---

[4] In the Testaments of the Twelve Patriarchs, love to both God and neighbor is enjoined in Test. Issachar 5:2; 7:6; Test. Dan 5:3, but the Scripture passages are not cited.

[5] Cf. Ethelbert Stauffer, "Love," Eng. tr. by J. R. Coates; in *Bible Key Words*, pp. 45–53.

Roman rule, at least for the time being. But Jesus had more to say. Let them give to God the things that are God's. God's claim is primary.[6]

It is often said that Jesus here prescribed separation of church and state, but this is not true. He says nothing here about the church; he is talking of man's primary duty to God; either the church or the state could obscure that duty; but here he speaks only of the state and God. He did not divide life into two separate realms, one political and the other religious. He meant, rather, that although man owes a real obligation to the political power, his primary obligation in all of life is to God.

3. *The Resurrection.* The Sadducees also attempted to discredit Jesus by a crafty question. They denied a bodily resurrection, and had devised a test case that they thought would make Jesus look ludicrous if he tried to defend this belief (Mark 12:18–27 and ||s). Their attitude suggests that they knew he believed in the resurrection and so agreed on this point with the Pharisees (Acts 23:8). They told a story of seven brothers. The oldest married and died childless. This brought the levirate law into force (Deut. 25:5 f.). The next brother married the widow; the aim of the law was for the widow to have a son who would be regarded as the son of the dead husband, and thus the dead man's family line would continue. This second brother, and in turn all the others, married the widow and died leaving no son for the oldest brother. The question was: Of which of the seven brothers would this woman be the wife in the resurrection state? The implication was that she could not be the wife of all seven at once, and so the resurrection idea was nonsense.

The reply of Jesus was, first, that in the resurrection state the physical marriage relation has no place. As Paul later put it, "Flesh and blood cannot inherit the kingdom of God" (I Cor. 15:50); in the transformed conditions of life in the Kingdom no problem will arise; the brothers and the woman can live together without clash of interests. Then Jesus gives an argument for the resurrection taken from Ex. 3:6, where God is called "the God of Abraham, and the God of Isaac, and the God of Jacob." These men had been dead for many generations, yet God says to Moses that he *is* their God; they still live by his will and power. If, then, they have survived the experience of physical death, it must be God's purpose to raise them and give them a place in his eternal Kingdom.[7]

4. *The Relation of the Messiah to David.* The activity of Jesus in his final days was by no means limited to defense. He took the initiative in

6 See Cecil John Cadoux, *The Historic Mission of Jesus,* pp. 172 f.
7 See A. Michael Ramsey, *The Resurrection of Christ* (Board of Christian Education, Presbyterian Church U.S.A., 1946), pp. 105 f.

discussing expectations concerning the Messiah. The usual view was that
the Messiah was to be David's son. This was not the only view. Some
Jews, it seems, did not expect a personal Messiah to come and establish
God's Kingdom. Others in recent generations had regarded the Maccabean rulers, who were of priestly descent, as proper kings of God's
people, and so they accepted the idea of a priestly Messiah. The Qumran
sect evidently expected two Messiahs, a priestly Messiah of Aaron with
first rank and a Davidic Messiah of Israel as governor.[8] So the main view
in Jesus' day was not the only view.

Jesus, however, aimed not to promote an alternate view but to correct
a flaw in the current view. Using Psalm 110:1, thought to be written by
David and to refer to the Messiah, he interpreted it to mean: "The Lord
God said to my Lord the Messiah, Sit in the place of honor and authority
at my right hand, till I put all your enemies under your feet and you
rule unchallenged over your Messianic Kingdom." On this view, David,
author of the psalm, calls the Messiah "my Lord," who thus is conceded
to be superior to David. The Messiah may be descended from David, but
his task is not to imitate the career of David. Jesus did not accept and
try to fulfill the political, military, nationalistic picture of the Davidic
Messiah.

The alternate interpretation of this passage is that Jesus flatly denied
the Davidic ancestry of the Messiah. But the genealogies in Matt. 1:1–17
and Luke 3:23–38 and the references to Davidic descent in the early
speeches of The Acts (chs. 2:30; 13:23) are confirmed by Rom. 1:3, an
early item of tradition received by Paul from the earliest Christians.
Jesus' aim was to reject false ideas of the Messiah's work, rather than
to discuss his physical ancestry. As the Son of Man and Suffering Servant
he was making real alterations in current Messianic ideas, and Ps. 110:1
gave him some Scriptural warrant—but only by assuming an (improbable) Davidic authorship.[9]

Teaching in Parables

To the last, Jesus used parables to indict the Jewish leaders for rejecting his message and leadership.

1. The *parable of the two sons* was aimed at the respectable Jews and
particularly at the Jewish leaders (Matt. 21:28–32). They professed faith

---

[8] See Karl Georg Kuhn, "The Two Messiahs of Aaron and Israel," in *The Scrolls and
the New Testament*, pp. 54–64; Matthew Black, *The Scrolls and Christian Origins*,
Ch. VII.

[9] The essential thing is that accepting the promise of a leader descended from David
he nevertheless found in Scripture a nonmilitary, nonnationalist picture of the ministry of that leader.

and outwardly participated in their people's traditional religious life; like the first son in the parable, they glibly promised obedience to God's will. The careless, wicked living of tax collectors and immoral women was a refusal to follow that divine will. But now Jesus, sent by God, was being rejected by the "good" people while the outcasts were responding to his preaching. It was the outcasts who were really doing the will of God; they at first had rejected his will but now were doing it. This parable reflects Jesus' firm conviction that he brought God's authentic, crucial word for Israel; men would be judged not by outer respectability but by their response to his ministry and message.[10]

2. The *parable of the wicked tenants* (Mark 12:1–12 and ||s) was aimed at the leaders in charge of God's vineyard Israel (cf. Isa. 5:1 ff.). They are the last in a series of disobedient leaders. Now confronted by God's Son, they are bent on putting him out of the way to preserve their position. If they persist, God will judge them and give his people new leaders. This parable has allegorical features, it speaks of Jesus as God's Son, and it points to his death, so it is regarded by some as a later creation of the church.[11] Quite possibly, to say the least, its wording has been sharpened in the light of later events. But the allegorical features do not mean that it cannot come from Jesus. A parable, as was noted in Chapter 4, could be a proverb, a comparison, an illustrative story with a single point, or a story with allegorical features.

That Jesus thought of himself as God's Son is indicated in other passages (Matt. 11:27; Mark 13:32), and we must not read the full later Nicene Christology into the word "Son." He could have spoken of his death; he expected death as the practically inevitable outcome of his challenge to the Jerusalem leaders. Moreover, had the early church created this parable or radically recast it, the resurrection and future authority of the Son would have been its climax; but the quotation of Ps. 118:22 f., which concludes the story, has no clear reference to the resurrection. We need not doubt that Jesus spoke this parable. Inherent in it is the same high claim by Jesus that we have met before.

3. The *parable of the marriage feast* given by a king for his son, in the form given by Matt. 22:1–14,[12] reflects the same consciousness of

10 This parable shows once more how deep was the cleavage between Jesus and the Jewish leaders.
11 Cf. Werner Georg Kümmel, "Das Gleichnis von den bösen Weingärtnern (Mark 12:1–9)," in *Aux Sources de la Tradition Chrétienne* (Paris, Delachaux & Niestlé, 1950), pp. 120–131. But see Vincent Taylor, *The Gospel According to St. Mark*, pp. 472–477.
12 The Matthean form has allegorical touches, and adds in ch. 22:11–14 what was probably a separate parable originally, concerning a man found at a wedding feast without the proper "wedding garment." It warns men to prepare for the coming of the judgment and the Kingdom.

Jesus that he had a unique and climactic role in God's plan. But its specific aim is to indict the people, including the leaders, for rejecting the message of the Kingdom, which was often referred to in Jewish imagery as a feast. A parable similar but different in details occurs in Luke 14:16–24, and its wording and its setting earlier in Jesus' ministry may be more reliable. But the crucial importance of responding promptly to the gospel was a point that Jesus obviously emphasized throughout his ministry, and perhaps even more urgently toward its close.

In connection with Jesus' eschatological teaching, Matt., ch. 25, gives two additional parables. The *parable of the ten maidens* teaches forward-looking preparedness for the coming of the final Kingdom (ch. 25:1–13). The *parable of the talents* teaches the duty of faithful, fruitful use of the gifts with which one is entrusted; each person will have to give account of his use of his gifts (ch. 25:14–30; cf. Luke 19:12–27).

Rebuke of the Scribes and Pharisees

All three Synoptic Gospels place a summary rebuke of the scribes or Pharisees at the close of the public ministry. Luke gives part of this material at an earlier point (Luke 11:37–52), but he like Mark has a criticism of the scribes (most of whom were Pharisees)[13] at the close of the Jerusalem ministry (Mark 12:38–40; Luke 20:45–47). This climactic position of the rebuke reflects the awareness of the early church that the Pharisees were the radical foes of Jesus. The Sadducees opposed Jesus largely to protect their position and prestige, whereas the Pharisees opposed him because they had deep and radical criticisms of his message and way of life.

That Jesus spoke such an indictment at the close of his ministry is denied mainly on two grounds. One is that the rebuke of the scribes in Mark and Luke for parade and self-seeking is a brief passage; only in Matthew has editorial work heaped up a long discourse that presents a collection of sayings originally unconnected. The other is that Jesus was more friendly to Pharisees than Matthew indicates, and that the apostolic church, in its conflicts with Jewish leaders, elaborated sayings of Jesus and made them much more severe than his actual words. No doubt Matthew assembles sayings spoken at different times; this is his editorial method. The real question is whether Jesus spoke at various times the individual sayings found in Matt., ch. 23. They certainly reflect the conflict of the apostolic age, but essentially they reflect also his own conflict with the Pharisees.

13 Luke calls them "lawyers" rather than "scribes." He wants to use a term that to Gentiles will be more familiar than "scribes," but he means the same thing.

These are the charges in Matt., ch. 23: The scribes and Pharisees preach what they do not practice; they require legal obedience of the common people but give no pastoral help; they love parade and public recognition; they reject Jesus' message and keep others from following him; they show great proselytizing zeal but make their converts narrow-minded; they are hair-splitting in distinctions between oaths that are binding and others that are not; they are meticulous about petty legalistic rules but neglect justice, mercy, and faith; they are careful about externally correct behavior but not about inner purity and integrity; they use external piety to cover inner corruption; they honor prophets of earlier generations but cannot identify one in their midst, and thus are heading toward judgment. The charges made here have a sweeping range that neglects the rabbis and leaders of whom such things could not rightfully be said; the meaning is that these are real and chronic faults characteristic of the group. The faults were there; as Klausner has noted,[14] there was truth in the charges; passages in Rabbinical literature voice similarly sweeping condemnations.

The puzzling thing is that Matt., ch. 23, has no clear mention of the deepest issue between Jesus and the Pharisees, his insistence on going to the people and eating with them regardless of ceremonial rules and accepted standards for social relations. Even had every scribe and Pharisee lived faithfully by the law, this issue would still have divided them from Jesus; two mutually exclusive ways of religious living and social relations here confronted each other (see Chapter 2). Each appealed to the Scripture. Each was bound to lead to a different religious community— one to Rabbinic Judaism, the other to the Christian church (which often fails to discern and hold to the basis Jesus gave it for personal and social life).

Teaching About the Future

In each Synoptic Gospel, Jesus gives an eschatological discourse at the end of his public ministry (Matt., chs. 24 f.; Mark, ch. 13; Luke 21:5–36).[15] He had begun his ministry by announcing that the coming of the Kingdom of God was close at hand. He spoke often of its coming during his ministry. But now he had special reason to speak in more detail of what lay ahead. For one thing, Jerusalem and especially its leaders had

14 *Jesus of Nazareth*, p. 321: "Much of this criticism was certainly justified. . . . Yet Jesus (or the Gospels) errs by unfair generalization."
15 For a study of this subject by use of Mark, ch. 13, see G. R. Beasley-Murray, *Jesus and the Future*. John A. T. Robinson, *Jesus and His Coming* (Abingdon Press, 1957), finds no real apocalyptic element in Jesus' teaching.

rejected Jesus' final appeal. It was a disobedient city. Divine judgment was to strike it. Furthermore, Jesus, now that his appeal to Jerusalem had been rejected, faced outward defeat and he had to say what lay ahead.

It was the Herodian architecture of the Temple buildings that impressed the disciples. But to Jesus the situation spoke rather of the impending fall of Jerusalem and of the way God's purpose would be realized even though the message of the Kingdom had fallen mainly on deaf ears. Here again the teaching has been editorially grouped. Can the points Jesus taught be discerned?

Two questions trouble scholars. One is why this material has so many parallels in earlier writings, such as The Book of Daniel. This is not a serious problem. Language and imagery used in early Jewish writings about the future were continually taken over, recast, and used by later teachers and writers. Jesus used the Old Testament in all his teaching. So here he could have adopted and adapted traditional material in depicting future events. His words in any case were imaginative and pictorial; he described the future not by a literal blueprint but in figurative language that pictured the impending clash of forces and the final victory of God over evil.

The other question is whether the church has taken over and ascribed to Jesus traditional material that he never spoke. Few doubt that we owe to Jesus at least the parts of the chapter that speak of the impending fall of Jerusalem and the need for every disciple to be alert and faithful. But did the figurative passages that describe the cosmic conflict and the end of the world come from some apocalyptic pamphlet taken over by the church and combined with the teaching of Jesus?[16]

There is no sound reason to deny that Jesus spoke at least the great bulk of this passage. Its essential teaching is his, although it is radical distortion to interpret such imaginative language as literal prose. The passage is an editorial combination of his sayings concerning the end of the world, sayings spoken for the most part toward the end of his ministry.

The initial announcement is that Jerusalem will fall as a judgment for its hardness of heart (Mark 13:2 and ||s). Little that follows, however, refers to this event. Mark 13:14–20 may do so, but even these verses may be rather a figurative description not of the specific fall of Jerusalem but of the extreme hardship God's people will undergo in the last days.

16 The theory of a "little apocalypse" consisting of or rather embedded in Mark, ch. 13, goes back to Colani (1864). For the advocates of this theory and attempts to reconstruct the conjectured writing, see Vincent Taylor, *The Gospel According to St. Mark*, pp. 498 f. Mark 13:7 f., 14–20, 24–27, are most often assigned to this written source. If it ever existed, it could have preserved in part sayings of Jesus.

For the most part, the discourse talks of these final days. Jesus emphasizes that the disciples cannot tell when the end will come. They must reject those who insist it is certainly coming at once. There will be some little delay at least, although the delay will not be long and its exact length is not known (Mark 13:5–8 and ||s). Even the Son himself does not know the time of the end; much less can his disciples know the exact day (Mark 13:32 and ||).

Times of hardship will precede that end. Such references no doubt describe experiences of the persecuted apostolic church, but this does not prove that these sayings were created after Jesus' death. He had seen synagogues closed to him, opposition had gathered, Herod Antipas had been suspicious of him, and plans to discredit and destroy him were advancing, so it is not surprising that he drew the inference that his disciples also would have hard times if they proved faithful in preaching and life (Mark 13:9–13 and ||s). The disciples were to see signs of the approaching end, but must remember the warning that they could not know the exact time. The end would come, come soon (Mark 13:30 and ||s), and at a time they could not discover in advance.[17]

It is Matthew, always assembling related material on a topical basis, which here groups teaching as to how the disciple is to live while waiting for the end. Faithfulness even under persecution, watchfulness for signs that the end and the return of the Son of Man are approaching, fruitfulness in the use of one's abilities and opportunities, and service to the Son of Man, the King, by kindly helpfulness to those in need—these are the marks of the loyal disciple (Matt. 24:37 to 25:46).[18]

What really concerns Jesus (and the writer of Matthew) is not a program of the final events but the way the disciple can constantly be ready for what is to come. There were men whose aim was to calculate the time of the end. Jesus' interest lay elsewhere. He was interested in what the end would bring: God's perfect and eternal Kingdom; every hostile force defeated and destroyed; God's faithful believers given security and blessedness. He was far more interested in how his disciples should live in the world while witnessing to him and waiting for the end than he was in the timetable by which the final order would come.

[17] A great deal has been said about Jesus' emphasis on the nearness of the end. This note occurs (e.g., Mark 9:1; 13:30), but Jesus says much more about delay and about the uncertainty as to the exact time of the Last Day.
[18] The pictorial account of the Last Judgment in Matt. 25:31–46 seems to tell primarily how God will judge the Gentiles; their treatment of humble and needy folk will determine the divine judgment. See Joachim Jeremias, *Jesus' Promise to the Nations*, pp. 47 f. But this teaching was inevitably instructive also to the disciples as a guide for living.

The Passion and Resurrection Narrative

The story of Jesus' death and resurrection always received special attention in the apostolic church. Each Gospel reflects this by the formal way in which it begins to tell of the events that immediately preceded the arrest, trial, and death. It is widely agreed that the earliest portion of our Gospels to take definite form as a connected narrative was this passion story. There were good reasons for this. It was not enough here to tell isolated stories. The meaning of the death of Jesus could only be shown by a connected story. So although individual units of tradition no doubt were inserted into the written passion narratives after their general pattern had taken form, the main outline of the passion story had been a part of the earliest church tradition for some time before our Gospels were written.

Good reasons prompted this development. The passion story was of course a vital part of the gospel narrative. It was necessary for apologetic reasons to make clear that although the lawful government had condemned Jesus, he was guilty of no crime or wrongdoing. (The later doctrine of his sinlessness has its practical beginning in this apologetic aim.) The often ill-treated disciples in the apostolic age gained courage to be faithful from his example of courage and integrity. And from the earliest days they held the conviction that his death was a benefit to them; interest in an incipient doctrine of atonement prompted special attention to the passion story.

Judas Plots to Betray Jesus

The story begins with the decision of Jewish leaders to have Jesus put to death. They thought this necessary for the peace and good of their people. Since so many thousands of pilgrims were in Jerusalem for the Passover festival and excitement over Jesus was at a high pitch, they planned to seize him at a time and place when crowds would not be present to resist the arrest. A way to do this soon opened. A grateful woman had anointed Jesus at a dinner at Bethany (Mark 14:3–9 and ||s). Jesus had defended her act as a preparation of his body for burial, and thus had spoken again of his impending death. Then Judas Iscariot went to the leaders and offered to betray Jesus to them in a way that would avoid public protest or resistance (Mark 14:10 f.).

It is not clear why Judas did this.[19] Perhaps he realized that he was

---

[19] See Kurt Lüthi, *Judas Iskarioth in der Geschichte der Auslegung* (Zürich, Zwingli Verlag, 1955).

out of sympathy with Jesus' basic message. Perhaps he saw disaster approaching and with worldly prudence thought it best to break with Jesus in a way that would assure him protection and advantage. Perhaps he had been hoping that Jesus would lead a bold revolt against Rome and scorned Jesus' obvious willingness to suffer for his cause rather than fight fiercely for it by organizing pilgrims for revolt. Whatever his reasons, Judas took the initiative in seeking out the Jewish leaders. The explanation that he did this for money is plainly inadequate, at least if Matt. 26:15 is correct and he received only thirty pieces of silver.[20] Such a pittance could not explain the betrayal. Even if greed had been a factor, it could not have moved Judas had he still retained his earlier loyalty to Jesus.

What did Judas betray? One suggestion is that he revealed to the leaders that Jesus claimed, though he had never openly confessed it, to be the promised Messiah of Israel. But this is unconvincing; in the trial scenes Judas does not testify to this claim. Rather, it seems, Judas promised to help the leaders seize Jesus without provoking a public commotion. Jesus had been spending the night at Bethany with friends, and the daytime with pilgrims in the Temple courts. Judas was to find a quiet time at some other place where Jesus could be seized.

Judas dealt with Sanhedrin leaders. They held some authority under Rome for the government of Jerusalem. They regarded Jesus as a troublemaker, and thought they should act before he sparked an active rebellion (his cleansing of the Temple suggested to them that greater disturbances might come). It is possible that Pilate, the Roman governor, in Jerusalem alert for signs of trouble at Passover time, had been consulted and knew what was being planned.[21]

THE LAST SUPPER

These plans were made just before the Passover, which was celebrated on the evening following the fourteenth day of the first month, Nisan (March–April). Aware of impending trouble, Jesus planned to observe the Passover so as to bind his disciples to him and interpret to them what was taking place. Many have thought that he ate the Last Supper the evening before Passover, since John 18:28 implies this; in this Gospel, Jesus died while the Passover lambs were being slain and prepared for the Passover feast, and like the Passover lamb (Ex. 12:46), of which not

---

20 A reminiscence of Zech. 11:12 f., so the amount may not be meant literally.
21 For a compact study of Pontius Pilate, Roman governor of Judea, Samaria, and part of Idumea from A.D. 26 to 36, see S. Sandmel's article, "Pilate, Pontius," *IBD*, K–Q, pp. 811–813.

a bone was broken (John 19:36), he was the true "Lamb of God, who takes away the sin of the world" (ch. 1:29). Paul's reference to "Christ, our paschal lamb," would fit well with this view (I Cor. 5:7). But the Synoptic Gospels clearly designate the Last Supper as a Passover and describe it as a meal at night, eaten reclining, with red wine, and with customs that recall the Passover observance. If, as seems probable, they are right, Jesus and his disciples ate the Passover meal in a room in Jerusalem provided by a friend.[22] See Matt. 26:17–30; Mark 14:12–26; Luke 22:7–39; cf. John 13:1 to 18:1.

In telling of that Supper, however, the church was interested not in the traditional details of the Passover meal but rather in two special occurrences during the Supper. For one thing, Jesus announced that one of the group would betray him. Judas, like the others, expressed surprise; he pretended to be loyal. When he left the group is not clear; probably it was after the meal had been eaten and when it was clear where the group was to go to spend the rest of the night.

The other special event was a symbolic action performed by Jesus and accompanied by words that interpreted it. His immediate purpose was not to give the later church a sacrament to observe, but to interpret his impending death to his disciples. No doubt in thus explaining what was to come he intended that his followers should later remember his action and words and understand his death in the light of them. But his immediate aim was to give to his disciples the help they needed at the moment.

Two problems make it difficult to determine exactly what Jesus did and said. One is that some early manuscripts omit Luke 22:19b, 20. In this shorter form of Luke, Jesus first took a cup, gave thanks, and gave it to the group; then he took bread, gave thanks, broke it, and gave it to them, saying, "This is my body"; but there is no word about a cup after the bread or about repeating the rite. Although some think this shorter text was the original form of Luke, the longer text, including ch. 22:19b, 20, is probably original.[23] It is much more like the other three reports of this event (Mark 14:22–25; Matt. 26:26–29; I Cor. 11:23–25), and especially resembles in wording Paul's report, written earlier than any of the Gospels.

22 This is the view of A. J. B. Higgins, *The Lord's Supper in the New Testament* (London, SCM Press, Ltd., 1952); Joachim Jeremias, *The Eucharistic Words of Jesus,* Eng. tr. by Arnold Ehrhardt (The Macmillan Company, 1955).

23 See Goguel, *Life of Jesus,* pp. 458 f., and the books listed in note 22. The omission of Luke 22:19b, 20, may have occurred because a second cup seemed to a scribe out of place. He may not have known that there were four successive passings of the cup in the Passover celebration.

The other problem is that no two of the accounts agree as to what Jesus said to interpret his action. On one solid fact all accounts, including the shorter text of Luke, agree: Jesus took bread, gave thanks, broke it to symbolize his death, and distributed the pieces to his disciples, saying, "This is my body." "Is" must mean "represents" or "symbolizes" my body, since the bread obviously was not identical with his actually present physical body. It was a way of saying that his impending death would not defeat and end his cause, but would benefit his disciples as bread benefits the body. If we accept the longer text of Luke, all four accounts add the cup, and interpret it, too, as representing or symbolizing his death as a benefit for his disciples and as establishing a (new) covenant.[24]

This last assertion is of epochal importance. The establishing of a new covenant through his death meant that henceforth God's covenant with Israel was centered in him and his work for Israel. His disciples thus were not separated from Israel; they became the nucleus and spearhead of the new and true Israel; they were to center their life in Jesus, and their fellow countrymen should do the same to be loyal to God's covenant with them.

Whether or not Jesus commanded his disciples to observe this Supper regularly,[25] his intention was that they should remember this Supper and its interpretation of his death; henceforth they could not share a common meal without recalling his death and its benefits for them.[26]

Prayer and Arrest in Gethsemane

Those who celebrated the Passover in Jerusalem could not leave the city for another town until day came, but could only move about in or near the city.[27] This explains why Jesus did not return to Bethany, where

24 Matthew and Mark probably did not contain originally the word "new" before "covenant"; the manuscript evidence is divided, but these two Gospels probably lacked "new" when first written. This reminds us that Jesus considered that his work was linked with the earlier covenant(s) of God with Israel. But his death did establish a new covenant relation of God with his people, as the longer text of Luke and Paul's account indicate.

25 As the longer text of Luke and Paul's account explicitly commands; Matthew and Mark seem to know of no such command.

26 The Gospel of John has no parallel to the Synoptic and Pauline account of the special breaking of bread and drinking from the cup as an interpretation of the death of Jesus and its benefits to his disciples. It has already interpreted the death of Jesus in the discourse on the bread of life in John, ch. 6, and in chs. 13 to 17 gives the foot washing, the farewell discourses, and prayer. These chapters are so shot through with theological interpretation that we deal with them in Chapter 14.

27 See Klausner, *Jesus of Nazareth*, p. 330.

he would have been safer among his friends, but went instead to Gethsemane, a garden on the lower western slopes of the Mount of Olives.[28]
It was within the limits of permitted travel. At some time before the
group reached the place, Judas left them to tell the Jewish leaders where
Jesus could be seized without an uproar. Jesus knew that he was in
danger, but his full testimony could not be given if he fled; he was
determined to face the issue to the last. It was not easy.

His disciples were fearful but tired. Jesus left eight at the edge of the
grove of trees; with Peter, James, and John he went into the grove; then,
leaving the trio to watch, he went aside for prayer. The trio were awake
enough to know what he prayed. They already knew that the central
prayer of his life was "Not what I will, but what thou wilt" (Mark
14:36), but they could have heard his words that night.

Then Judas came and with him an armed party from the Jewish
leaders. Judas identified Jesus by a kiss, and the party seized him and
led him away. The eleven disciples, fearful of being seized as leaders in
Jesus' movement, took fright and fled. Peter was the most courageous
of the group. He followed the arresting party to see what would happen.
He had no plan; he knew no way to help Jesus. But he was trying to be
loyal. This must be remembered to his credit when later, with his life
in danger, he denied knowing Jesus (Mark 14:66–72 and ||s).

THE HEARING BEFORE JEWISH LEADERS

A great deal has been written about the trial of Jesus,[29] and much of
it is irrelevant, because it assumes that the legal regulations of the later
Mishnah and Talmud were in force in Jesus' day and that what took
place was a formal trial under Jewish law. Under that law a prompt
death sentence would have been illegal. But what took place at night
was an informal hearing before Jewish leaders, who examined Jesus to
decide how best to formulate their charges against him.[30] Their concern was not with Jesus' ethical teaching or his interpretation of
Scripture; it was not with general theological heresy. They discerned
that he was making an immense personal claim, which in their view was
wrong, dangerous, and even blasphemous; he set himself above the

28 See Gustav Dalman, *Sacred Sites and Ways*, Eng. tr. by Paul Levertoff (The Macmillan Company, 1933), pp. 320–327.
29 See Paul Winter, *On the Trial of Jesus* (Berlin, Walter de Gruyter & Co., 1961);
Matthew Black, "The Arrest and Trial of Jesus," in *New Testament Essays: Studies
in Memory of Thomas Walter Manson, 1893–1958*, edited by A. J. B. Higgins (Manchester University Press, 1959), pp. 19–33.
30 For a Jewish scholar's view of the trial, see Klausner, *Jesus of Nazareth*, pp. 339–348.

recognized religious and civil leaders and identified himself as so related to God and so indwelt by God's Spirit that he was entitled to acceptance and obedience by all of God's people, including their leaders.

This attitude implied superiority to the Roman rulers as well, and if this threat to Roman rule could be proved, the basis for the desired Roman action against him was solid. To Pilate religious disputes would seem to deal merely with Jewish "superstition," and Jewish leaders would be unable to get him to take action against Jesus on that ground. These leaders wanted Pilate to impose the death penalty. Whether under Rome they had legal right to execute Jesus is disputed but seems quite doubtful (cf. John 18:31).[31] In any case, however, the effective way to deal with the situation was to involve Pilate in it and play up the political aspects, and this was the strategy of the Jewish leaders from the start. They thought that their stable administration of Jewish affairs, their leadership among the people, and the stability of Pilate's province required the final removal of Jesus from the scene. This could only or best be done by Pilate's condemnation of Jesus.

In the hearing before the Jewish leaders one question emerged as the key issue: "Are you the Christ, the Son of the Blessed?" (Mark 14:61). He was asked whether he claimed to be the promised Messiah of the Jews, and also whether he claimed to be the Son of God, a title that meant the Messiah, but also implied a unique relation to God. Only in Mark does Jesus answer with an explicit affirmative, "I am" (ch. 14:62); Matt. 26:64 and Luke 22:67 f. indicate that Jesus said in effect, "I could say yes if I could give my meaning to the terms you use, but since you give those titles a meaning that I do not intend, I cannot give a clear affirmative answer." Jesus went on to declare that as the Son of Man he would sit in the position of unique honor and authority at the right hand of God, and would then come to judge his people and deliver his followers. The background of this promised judgment was his present rejection by his people. This claim of Messiahship and unique authority, even if cautiously worded, was unwarranted and blasphemous to his hearers. But they discerned in it a political claim that could be used as the basis for bringing Pilate into the case.[32]

Probably a formal meeting of the Sanhedrin was held at daybreak to formulate specific charges against Jesus (cf. Luke 22:66). As given in Luke 23:2 they wrongly assert that Jesus opposed paying taxes to the

31 See, however, C. K. Barrett, *The Gospel According to St. John* (London, S.P.C.K., 1955), pp. 445 f.
32 One could not expect Pilate to distinguish clearly between spiritual and political aspects of Messiahship. Indeed, Jewish leaders could easily regard the two aspects as inseparable.

Romans, but the indictment there given rightly recalls that before Pilate the charge had to specify political crimes. The charges there listed are disturbing the peace, opposing payment of taxes, and claiming to be the king of Israel. This last was the political twist given to the claim to be the Jewish Messiah; the Messiah was expected to be the spiritual and political leader of his people; if Jesus was aiming at military revolt and political rule, that would arouse Pilate to action.

JESUS CONDEMNED BY PILATE

Pilate was in Jerusalem for the period of the Passover and Feast of Unleavened Bread; he had come there from his regular residence in Caesarea to make sure that no uprising or riots occurred and got out of hand. He probably was staying not in the Tower of Antonia at the northwest corner of the Temple area, but in the castle built by Herod the Great on the western hill of Jerusalem.[33] When the Jewish leaders pressured him to put Jesus to death, he examined Jesus. He probably knew already of the excitement that had accompanied Jesus' arrival in the city, and may have wondered whether Jesus' activities in the Temple marked him as dangerous. Personal inquiries convinced him that Jesus was not of the Zealot type bent on stirring up armed revolt against Rome.

The Gospels may deal leniently with Pilate, but they report that though he did not regard Jesus as dangerous (Matt. 27:18; Mark 15:10; Luke 23:4; John 18:38; 19:4, 6), he condemned him rather than arouse the Jewish leaders and their yes-men by refusing their demand for Jesus' condemnation. To quiet the agitation at his palace gate he condemned Jesus to death for claiming to be King of the Jews and so a rebel in revolt against Rome. All this is no credit to Pilate.

Only Luke 23:6–11 says that Herod Antipas, tetrarch of Galilee and Perea, was drawn into the proceedings at one stage because Jesus was a Galilean. Herod is said to have treated with contempt and ridicule the idea that Jesus was a dangerous claimant to kingship. If this happened, it shows that the issue at the trial was not Jesus' religious and moral teaching but his personal claim and its possible threat to Jewish and Roman rulers.

Jesus was condemned on the basis that his claim to be the Messiah was a political crime and so a "clear and present danger" to the existing authorities. This came out in his being mocked by the soldiers (Mark 15:18 and ||) and was meant in the title that Pilate put above Jesus'

[33] See Wright and Filson, *The Westminster Historical Atlas to the Bible*, Plate XVII, C.

head on the cross: "The King of the Jews" (Mark 15:26 and ||s). The church later saw in this placard irony and real truth. Jesus was the rightful King of the Jews, and his claim for faith and loyalty, if accepted, would have condemned the existing authorities, though it did not contemplate military or political action to achieve that end.

CRUCIFIED, DEAD, AND BURIED

Roman soldiers executed the sentence pronounced by Pilate. In keeping with custom, execution was by crucifixion and was preceded by scourging. During the scourging, the soldiers, to make sport of Jesus' claim to be a king, clothed him in a purple robe, put a scepter in his hand, and paid mock homage to him (Mark 15:16–20 and ||s). Then, putting his own clothes back on him, they led him out of the city to the place of execution, called Golgotha (Mark 15:22 and ||s).[34] The name means "skull," and probably implies not that this place was skull-like in shape but that skulls had been found there or that the place was a known place of execution or burial. It evidently was outside the walls of Jerusalem on the north side.

The present Church of the Holy Sepulcher,[35] which tradition says marks the site of Jesus' execution, burial, and resurrection, is now inside the city, but it is argued that in the days of Jesus this site, which includes a small hillock, was just outside the wall of Jerusalem.[36] But a wall is for city defense, and a hillock just outside the wall would give an attacker a vantage point from which to launch an effective attack; sound defense would enclose such a hillock inside the walled area. So the view that Golgotha was a hillock and that the city wall ran close to its east and south sides is not convincing. But the place was not far from the city on its north side.

The soldiers required Jesus to carry his own cross, or at least the crossbeam on which his arms would be stretched out. On the way his strength gave out, and Simon of Cyrene, otherwise unknown except as the father of two later Christians, Alexander and Rufus (Mark 15:21), was impressed into duty and forced to carry it for Jesus. Having arrived at the site, Jesus was offered a drink of wine mingled with myrrh (ch. 15:23 and ||), intended to lessen the pain of the crucifixion, but he refused it, determined to stay conscious to the end. With him were crucified two

---

[34] On "Golgotha and the Sepulchre," see Gustav Dalman, *Sacred Sites and Ways*, pp. 346–381; Goguel, *Life of Jesus*, pp. 546–551.

[35] See notes 33 and 34.

[36] The New Testament does not describe Golgotha as a hillock.

other men condemned for brigandage (ch. 15:27 and ||s). Their lives had been a combination of lawless plunder and hostility to Rome. After Jesus had been fixed to the cross by ropes and nails,[37] the inscription prepared at Pilate's command was nailed over his head: "The King of the Jews."

The story of the crucifixion contains reminiscences of Old Testament passages. Those who told the story saw parallels to statements found in Ps. 22 and 69 and other Scripture passages.[38] This was a way of saying that the event was included in God's plan, recorded in Scripture, and so did not discredit Jesus or indicate that God's cause was being defeated.

Men crucified hung on the cross for hours, sometimes for days, before dying. According to Mark 15:25, 33 f., Jesus lived no more than six hours after being fixed to the cross. The Gospels give seven "last words" that he was said to have spoken in that time: one found in Matt. 27:46 and Mark 15:34, "My God, my God, why hast thou forsaken me?" (Ps. 22:1, quoted in faith but in desperate inability to understand completely what was happening); three found only in Luke (ch. 23:34, 43, 46), "Father, forgive them; for they know not what they do,"[39] "Truly, I say to you, today you will be with me in Paradise," and "Father, into thy hands I commit my spirit"; and three found only in John (ch. 19:26 f., 28, 30), "Woman, behold your son," "Behold your mother"; "I thirst"; and "It is finished." The failure of the Gospels to agree on what Jesus said raises doubt as to the authenticity of these reported sayings. The anguished quotation of Ps. 22:1 is least likely to be later invention.

Women who had followed Jesus (cf. Luke 8:3) stood "looking on from afar" (Mark 15:40 and ||s; but cf. John 19:25). They were not in danger from the authorities as the disciples of Jesus would have been had they been present. They could attest later the facts of the crucifixion, death, and burial.

When Jesus died about three P.M. on that Friday afternoon, Pilate probably thought it an acceptable conclusion of a distasteful incident. He had to get along with the Jewish leaders; Jesus was not deserving of death but he had caused some disturbance; Pilate was not one to brood long over one life sacrificed to obtain quiet at an explosive time and place. The priestly and other leaders at Jerusalem no doubt considered the movement of Jesus effectively crushed. Some of the public thought

---

[37] On "Crucifixion," see Pierson Parker's article in *IDB*, A–D, pp. 746 f.

[38] Cf. C. H. Dodd, *According to the Scriptures* (Charles Scribner's Sons, 1953), pp. 57–60, 96–98, 108.

[39] There is some strong evidence for omitting this saying from Luke; it is lacking from some important early manuscripts. But it probably was original; some scribes may have omitted it with the feeling that the crucifiers of Jesus should not be forgiven.

it a disgraceful injustice. To the followers of Jesus it must have seemed an irreparable loss bringing an almost hopeless situation.

At least Jesus must be buried. The Jewish law required the burial of an executed criminal before nightfall (Deut. 21:22 f.). Since the coming day was a Sabbath, this duty was particularly urgent. The task was undertaken by Joseph of Arimathea, a Jew and a member of the Sanhedrin (Mark 15:42–46 and ||s); he was not necessarily at that time a follower of Jesus, but was "looking for the kingdom of God" (ch. 15:43). Pilate gave Joseph permission to take down the body and bury it, and he did so with haste, since the Sabbath would begin at sundown. Wrapping the body in a linen cloth, he placed it in a tomb near Golgotha and rolled a stone against the door of the tomb.[40] The women who had watched Jesus' execution and death saw the place of burial and laid plans to return when the Sabbath was ended and give the body the neglected preparation for burial (ch. 15:47 and ||s).[41] The important fact for later developments was that Jesus actually died and was buried. The story was so told as to leave no doubt about that.

THE RISEN CHRIST

Had the story ended there, later generations might have heard of Jesus as a great prophet and martyr whose claim to greater distinction was barred by his rejection and death. But the story thus far told only what "Jesus began to do and teach" (Acts 1:1). Within less than two months, his followers were preaching that God had raised him from the dead, made him Lord, and was offering salvation through him.[42] The apparent defeat had become a stage on the way to further advance.

The almost delirious enthusiasm of the disciples in those early days after the resurrection makes it hard to reconstruct a picture of what happened. The disciples, shattered in spirit, had been scattered by the rejection, arrest, and crucifixion of Jesus. He had taught them the way of suffering service, but it had not become real to them; they had kept hoping for an easier kind of victory. Without his leadership they had no hope. But within three days they were electrified by meeting the risen Christ. It is impossible to regard this testimony as conscious de-

[40] The tomb was cut into the side of solid rock. The round, flat stone, which stood on its rim, rolled in a groove that let it either stand in a slot at one side of the tomb entrance or roll into position and cover the entrance.
[41] In John 19:39 f. Joseph of Arimathea and Nicodemus, with spices and linen cloths, follow "the burial custom of the Jews." The Synoptic account is preferable. Haste prevented the usual rites.
[42] See A. Michael Ramsey, *The Resurrection of Christ*.

ception; they were completely convinced that they had seen their risen Master.[43]

One may ask two questions. Where did the Eleven first see him? Matthew 28:7, 16 f. and Mark 16:7 indicate that it was in Galilee; Luke 24:13–36 and John 20:19, however, say that it was in Jerusalem (John 21:1 occurred later). It does not solve the problem to say that they saw him in both places; the question is where they saw him first. And a strong case can be made for the conclusion that it was in Galilee.[44] Later, when the details were less clear, the facts that he had been crucified in Jerusalem, and that the apostolic church had received the Spirit in Jerusalem and then centered its life there, led some to omit the flight to Galilee and the return to Jerusalem. But the main point is that the disciples saw Jesus alive and conversed with him after he had been crucified and buried.

A second question concerns the nature of this confrontation by the risen Jesus. Did he appear with the actual physical body of his ministry? The experiences of disciples who failed to recognize Jesus at once (Matt. 28:17; Luke 24:16; John 20:14; 21:4), the ability of Jesus to appear in various places and mysteriously disappear (Luke 24:31, 36; John 20:19, 26), and the clear argument of Paul in I Cor., ch. 15, all indicate a changed form of life in this resurrection state. It was the same Jesus; he was able to make his presence real to his followers and communicate with them; but he was free from limitations of a flesh-and-blood body.

Is it then right to say that it was the same body? The strongest reason for saying so is the empty tomb. Attempts have been made to base the resurrection faith entirely on appearances completely unrelated to his earthly body. But the early tradition is firm about the empty tomb. The reference to the resurrection on a definite day, the third day, suggests a specific time when the tomb was discovered to be empty.[45] Jewish opponents of the early church never challenged the resurrection message by showing the body or denying the story of the empty tomb. There is no sound reason to doubt that the tomb was found empty and that the disciples were convinced that they had been in touch with the risen Christ.

It is an act of faith to conclude that the disciples really did meet the risen Christ, or rather that he met and communicated with them. But this conclusion makes sense of the entire Christian message and story;

---

[43] So Klausner, *Jesus of Nazareth,* pp. 357, 359.
[44] For the opposite view, see Johannes Weiss, *The History of Primitive Christianity,* Eng. tr. by Frederick C. Grant *et al.* (Wilson-Erickson, Inc., 1937), Vol. I, pp. 14–18.
[45] This dating is found in I Cor. 15:4 as well as in the Gospels.

the resurrection was central in the Christian gospel from that time on; it alone enables the student to understand how the Christian movement developed with integrity from the ministry of Jesus to the establishment of the apostolic church. The Jesus of history rose from the dead, was exalted, and became active as the Lord of the church. It was in the light of the resurrection that his followers henceforth understood his life and death, his teaching and purpose.

The period during which Jesus appeared to his followers was relatively short. If we except the appearance to Paul (Acts 9:3–6; I Cor. 15:8), which Paul insisted was as real as the earlier ones to the Twelve, that period covered only a few weeks.[46] It was enough to steady the disciples and prepare them for their active witness to the Jesus of history as the Christ of Jewish expectation and the Son of Man who had suffered for the benefit of his followers. He had now become the exalted Lord of his church, and was to lead the cause of God to final victory and give his followers eternal life in the Kingdom of God.

[46] Luke 24:50 seems to date the parting (or ascension) of the risen Jesus from his disciples on the night following the resurrection. Acts 1:3 says the period before the ascension was forty days, a traditional round number. See Philippe H. Menoud, " 'Pendant Quarante Jours' (Actes i 3)," in *Neotestamentica et Patristica: Freundesgabe Oscar Cullmann*, edited by W. C. van Unnik (Leiden, E. J. Brill, 1962), pp. 148–156.

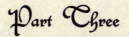

Part Three

THE JERUSALEM CHURCH

Chapter 7

BEGINNINGS IN JERUSALEM

*T*HE GOSPEL STORY does not end with the death of Jesus. Had
he been only a teacher or prophet, his work would have been done
when he died on the cross. But the personal claim inherent in his ministry, his interpretation of his death as destined to further his cause, and,
above all, his resurrection gave him a continuing role. In the Christian
understanding, this continuing role of the risen Christ is an integral part
of the gospel story, so the New Testament adds the history of the
apostolic age to its story of the earthly career of Jesus. The New Testament canon thus reflects the Christian conviction that to understand
the gospel we must combine the witness and work of the apostolic church
with the story of Jesus' ministry, death, and resurrection. In that total
story the resurrection is the hinge event that unifies the story.

THE HISTORICAL BACKGROUND

To understand the continuing story requires some knowledge of the
historical background. The next stages of the Christian story developed
almost entirely within the Roman Empire. To the east of Palestine and
Syria lay Arabia and Mesopotamia, regions not under the rule of Rome.
The Parthian empire extended as far west as Mesopotamia. The Nabatean empire, not yet subject to Rome, centered in Petra and stretched
northward toward Damascus; it lay directly to the south and east of
Palestine and the Decapolis region.

These eastern regions play little part in the history of the church in
the apostolic age, though perhaps more took place in those regions
than the New Testament reports. The gospel could have gone east from
Antioch into eastern Syria; it could even have reached Mesopotamia
during the apostolic age; but no clear information attests this. Numerous
Jews lived in that eastern region, which is included by Acts 2:9–11 in
its list of places from which Jews were present at Pentecost, and so there
were lines of communication along which the gospel story could move
eastward. However, our only explicit information relates to the Roman

153

Empire, and we turn our immediate attention to the political and religious situation there.

For the period covered by the book of The Acts, the Empire enjoyed a stable rule. Augustus, the real founder of the Roman Empire, had been succeeded by Tiberius (A.D. 14–37). The ministry of Jesus and the beginnings of the church fell during his reign. At his death Caligula became emperor (A.D. 37–41). His unstable personality and craving for divine honors led him into open clash with the Jews, but his early death freed them from a serious threat.[1] His successor Claudius was a fairly effective but not brilliant ruler (A.D. 41–54). During his reign, the Roman historian Suetonius reports,[2] he ordered all Jews expelled from Rome (Acts 18:2) because the Jews were rioting at the instigation of a certain Chrestus. This may indicate that although some Jews in Rome were vigorously pressing the claims of Jesus as the Christ, other Jews were violently rejecting their message, and so Claudius wrongly saw in the tumult an incipient uprising of the Jews under a troublemaker named Chrestus.[3] Claudius was succeeded by Nero (A.D. 54–68), in whose erratic reign occurred a great fire that destroyed much of the city of Rome. Nero, apparently seeking a scapegoat, accused the Christians of arson and led a fierce persecution against them, possibly to divert attention from his own role in starting the fire.[4]

The Empire was divided into provinces for administrative purposes. The more stable provinces (e.g., Asia, Cyprus, Achaia) were under control of the Senate, which sent out governors called proconsuls for terms of one year; the appointment could be renewed. Provinces where there might be a threat either to Rome's food supply (e.g., Egypt) or to the Empire's peace and stability (e.g., Syria) were under direct control of the emperor, who sent out legates or procurators directly responsible to him. He also could take control of a senatorial province if special trouble arose.[5]

Palestine was a special case. It was of great importance because it lay on the Empire's eastern border and was open to incursions from the Nabateans and Parthians. It offered special problems; it was largely inhabited by Jews, who had kinsmen in Parthia and throughout the Roman Empire, and so were a particularly sensitive political group;

---

[1] Josephus, *War* II.10.1–5; *Ant.* XVIII.8.2–9.

[2] *The Lives of the Caesars: The Deified Claudius*, Ch. 25: *"Iudaeos impulsore Chresto assidue tumultuantis Roma expulit."*

[3] Goguel, *Life of Jesus*, pp. 97 f.

[4] So Tacitus, *Annals* XV. 44.

[5] Cf. G. H. Stevenson, "The Administration of the Provinces," in *The Cambridge Ancient History*, Vol. X, pp. 205–217.

and their monotheistic faith was a puzzle to the polytheistic Romans.

The Romans governed newly acquired regions through native governors when possible. In this way they capitalized upon local patriotism and the knowledge of local affairs that such governors possessed. Thus in Palestine the Romans had first used the Idumean Antipater and the Hasmonean high priests to govern the land; then Herod the Great had been Rome's puppet king; following his death his sons were entrusted with the rule. But this broke down, especially in Judea, and beginning in A.D. 6 the emperor sent Roman governors to rule Judea, Samaria, and Idumea.[6] After the Herodian tetrarch Philip died in A.D. 34 and the emperor deposed Philip's brother Herod Antipas on suspicion of disloyalty in A.D. 39, new arrangements were necessary.

In A.D. 41 a grandson of Herod the Great, named Herod Agrippa I, was made king of all of Palestine. He "killed James the brother of John" the son of Zebedee, imprisoned Peter, and died in A.D. 44 after a spectacular quarrel with the people of Tyre and Sidon (Acts, ch. 12).[7] The heir apparent, Herod Agrippa II, was only seventeen years old, so the Romans placed Palestine under a Roman procurator, an arrangement continued from A.D. 44 to the outbreak of the Jewish revolt against Rome in A.D. 66.

The most noted of these governors in the Christian story are Felix, who took office in A.D. 52 and continued in it until at least A.D. 55 and possibly until A.D. 60, and Festus, who succeeded Felix and governed Palestine until his death in A.D. 62. Under Felix and Festus, Paul was in prison in Jerusalem and Caesarea (Acts 23:24 to 26:32). Between the death of Festus and the arrival of his successor Albinus later in A.D. 62 occurred the mob murder of James the brother of Jesus by Jewish opponents.[8]

RELIGIOUS AND CULTURAL LIFE

Of great importance for the development of the church was the linguistic, cultural, and religious life of the Empire and especially of Palestine. Acts 2:5–11 may seem to suggest that the Jews in each region of the Near East and Mediterranean area spoke a different language. Such an idea would be quite erroneous. No doubt local languages and dialects lingered on, as Acts 14:11 illustrates, but three languages dominated

[6] See Chapter 1.
[7] See also Josephus, *Ant.* XIX.8.2.
[8] On Felix, see Josephus, *War* II.12.8 to 13.7, and *Ant.* XX.7.1 and 8.5–7. On Festus and Albinus, see Josephus, *War* II.14.1 and *Ant.* XX.8.9 and 9.1–2. The execution of James the brother of Jesus is reported in *Ant.* XX.9.1.

the entire Roman Empire. Least important in the everyday life of the people was Latin, the original language of Rome and still widely in use, especially for certain official papers. In Palestine, Syria, and Mesopotamia, Aramaic, the basic language of Jesus and his original disciples,[9] was widely used. But throughout the Empire, and to a considerable extent in Palestine, Greek was the common language. In any part of the Empire one could communicate in Greek with leaders and a large proportion of the population. The Christian gospel could move to Syria and eastward by the use of Aramaic, but even there, and certainly in northern Africa, Asia Minor, and southern Europe, Christian preachers used mainly Greek. The future of the church was to be in the hands of those who could speak Greek and deal with Greek-speaking members of the Empire.[10]

Judaism had preceded the Christian preachers throughout the Empire. Jews were found in Mesopotamia, where since the exile there had been a continuous, vigorous Jewish life under the Babylonians, Persians, Seleucids, and Parthians. They were found also in Egypt, Cyrene, Syria, Asia Minor, Cyprus, Macedonia, Achaia, Italy, and regions farther west. Some Jews, for example in Asia Minor, fell into syncretistic adaptation to pagan environment, but for the most part the Jews took their faith with them and in spite of ridicule and opposition maintained their special worship and community practices.

In every city of importance a Jewish synagogue could be found; pilgrimages were made to Jerusalem; the Law and the Prophets were read; and the distinctive Jewish rites were practiced, with emphasis on precisely those features of their way of life that marked them off from other peoples.[11] In every major city the synagogue also had a group of Gentiles who shared in its worship.[12] Each loyal Jew paid the annual Temple tax and looked to Jerusalem and especially to the Temple as the visible

---

9 Harris Birkeland, *The Language of Jesus* (Oslo, Jacob Dybwad, 1954), argues that although many Jews in Palestine spoke Aramaic, the common people used dialectal Hebrew, and in certain studious circles (we may consider Qumran in this connection) classical Hebrew was used, at least in writing.

10 The classic study of the use of Hellenistic Greek, especially in the papyri, which show the use of Greek in the everyday life and business of common people and thus contribute greatly to New Testament study, is Adolf Deissmann, *Light from the Ancient East,* tr. by Lionel R. M. Strachan (George H. Doran Co., 1927). Greek was also the language of most of the literature of the first century A.D., though Latin was also widely used.

11 On "The Jewish Diaspora at the Time of the Rise of Christianity," see Joseph Klausner, *From Jesus to Paul,* tr. by William F. Stinespring (The Macmillan Company, 1943), pp. 7–30.

12 On "The Proselytes and the 'God-Fearers' at the End of the Period of the Second Temple," see Klausner, *From Jesus to Paul,* pp. 31–49.

focus and rallying point of Jewish royalty. The daily offerings and special festivals were celebrated there for him as well as for his widely scattered fellow Jews; their geographical dispersion did not destroy their sense of cohesion and unity.

From the Gentile viewpoint the Jews were a small and negligible fraction of the life of the Empire. Jewish culture was integrally bound up with the Jewish religion. In general Jews held aloof from pagan life —they had to do so to be true to their religion.

The chief characteristic of pagan life was its broad tolerance and great variety of religious faiths. It was essentially a polytheistic culture. Each person was free to believe in as many gods as he chose. A man might regard the gods of other men as his gods with different names; he might hold personally to a monotheistic faith; or he might be skeptical of the existence or importance of any god. But he still recognized the right of others to their various faiths. The gods as usually worshiped represented in a pantheon the many aspects and interests of human life—war, love, etc. Poetry, drama, sculpture, and architecture expressed this polytheistic culture and its rites. Social clubs and ancient predecessors of our labor unions had their patron deities. Civic duty and activity likewise involved recognition of the appropriate gods and goddesses. Community life had a polytheistic religious and cultural atmosphere with practices hostile to both Jewish and Christian faith.[13]

The religious aspects of loyalty to the Empire were bound to clash with Jewish and Christian life. Among ancient men it had long been common to regard rulers as divine descendants of the gods. Early Roman leaders could not make this claim. The republic elected its representatives; they were human and held office for a limited time. With the coming of the Empire the ancient combining of political and religious status was used to support imperial prestige. At first it was considered sufficient to deify the emperor upon his death. This led the Roman emperor Vespasian to say as he lay dying, "I think that I am becoming a god."[14] He knew that proclamation of his divine status would follow his death. But the urge to ascribe divine nature to the reigning emperor soon was felt. It was furthered by the habit of honor-

[13] A considerable element of skepticism and a philosophical outreach toward agnosticism or monotheism are factors to remember, but they did not represent the common spirit of the time. On "The Hellenistic Preparation" in religion, philosophy, and social thought and institutions, see G. H. C. Macgregor and A. C. Purdy, *Jew and Greek: Tutors Unto Christ* (London, Ivor Nicholson & Watson, Ltd., 1936), pp. 215–272.

[14] Suetonius, *Lives of the Caesars: The Deified Vespasian*, Ch. 23, last line. See Deissmann, *Light from the Ancient East*, pp. 338 ff., for extensive papyrus and inscriptional evidence of divine honors paid to Roman emperors.

ing the emperor and Rome with what was at least a quasi-religious veneration; the emperor and *Roma* became a pair of deities, one male and one female. This tendency first became strong in the eastern part of the Empire, where ascribing deity to the ruler was a long-standing practice. It was promoted discreetly by the emperors, and in time patriotism and emperor worship became almost inseparable. Caligula was widely considered deranged, and part of his abnormality was his rabid desire for divine honors.

The Jews attempted to divert the crisis of demand for emperor worship by offering sacrifice regularly on behalf of the emperor. The Christians prayed for him (I Tim. 2:2; cf. Rom. 13:1–7; I Peter 2:17), but that did not prevent the charge of disloyalty and atheism.[15]

SOURCES FOR EARLY CHRISTIAN HISTORY

In this total setting the church emerged. What sources enable us to trace its emergence? Only meager information comes to us from Roman historians. Suetonius,[16] as noted above, may have referred to agitation in Rome between Jews preaching Jesus as the promised Messiah and Jews who rejected that claim. Tacitus[17] tells of the execution of Jesus by Pontius Pilate, the persistence of the Christian movement, and the persecution of the Christians of Rome in A.D. 64. This tells practically nothing about the first two decades of the church, and little more about following decades.

Jewish sources (see Chapter 3) yield some facts concerning the ministry and death of Jesus, but they give practically no definite information about the first decades of the church. They reflect disputes between Jewish Christians and other Jews which led to the banning of such Christians from the synagogues by the latter part of the first century, but they tell little more.

CHRISTIAN SOURCES

Thus our knowledge of the beginnings of the church comes almost entirely from Christian sources. Studies in form criticism have made it clear that the Gospels reflect the life of the early church, and so each Gospel can be used with caution as evidence of Christian faith and teaching in the region and time of its writing.[18] If we admit, as we

---

15 Because they used no images or idols and did not join in such pagan worship, the charge of atheism was made against both Jews (Josephus, *Against Apion* II.15) and Christians (*Martyrdom of Polycarp* III.2; IX.2).
16 See note 2 above.   17 *Annals* XV.44.
18 See Chapter 3.

should, that the Gospels also tell us about the life and work of Jesus and that the disciples had a real sense of history, we will not credit the apostolic church with creating the essential material of the Gospels, but we will see that the church selected and shaped the tradition and used it to guide its life and teaching.

The Gospels, therefore, and the tradition they preserve, reflect the centering of the church in Jesus Christ; they show a concern for what he taught and the way he lived; and thus they attest a real continuity between Jesus of Nazareth and the earliest church. The disciples were concerned about what Jesus said and did, and about the interpretation of the Scripture worked out in connection with the gospel tradition.

The Gospel of John differs greatly from the Synoptic Gospels in vocabulary, style, events reported, and advanced interpretation. It shows, even more than do the Synoptic Gospels, that the early Christians did not try to preserve the exact wording of what Jesus said and the exact chronology of events. The new material of the Gospel of John must come from independent lines of information;[19] the Synoptic Gospels did not exhaust the store of gospel tradition available in the early church.

Since the Gospels date from about A.D. 65–100, they are not contemporary with the earliest generation or two of the church. Those earliest years are of the greatest interest for historical study of Christian beginnings. Hence the letters of Paul to churches have special importance. Their dates range over a dozen years beginning about A.D. 50; so they are earlier than any of our Gospels. Paul shared personally in the leadership of the church in its very early years. He was converted to the Christian faith not later than A.D. 36 and quite possibly a few years earlier, and he indicates points of agreement and difference between himself and the other early church leaders. His letters to churches therefore aid greatly in understanding the history of the first three decades of the church. Since the book of The Acts tells of the preaching and spread of the gospel but adds little about the daily life of the Christians, Paul's pastoral letters to local churches are the chief witness to the faith and attitudes of such churches.[20]

The other New Testament letters were written too late to give contemporary evidence for the first two generations of the church. They

---

[19] Critical study in recent years shows a strong willingness to recognize this fact. But acquaintance with one or more of the Synoptic Gospels need not be denied, even though the Gospel of John shows knowledge of additional gospel tradition shaped by other factors than those which dominated the shaping of the Synoptic tradition. See C. H. Dodd, *Historical Tradition in the Fourth Gospel.*

[20] Since even Paul's churches differed from one another in the problems faced, we must not assume that other churches faced precisely the same range of problems his churches show. We can only assume a general similarity.

date from the latter third of the first century A.D. This includes I and II
Timothy and Titus, which in their present form date late in the first
century. Some have dated The Letter of James about A.D. 45 or 65, and
The Letter to the Hebrews just before Jerusalem fell in A.D. 70. But
probably both writings date later in the first century. The other New
Testament letters likewise come from that later period, except that
at least II Peter may date in the early years of the second century. They
thus help little in the study of the first two generations of the church.[21]

THE BOOK OF THE ACTS

For the first decades of the church, the main source of specific information is the book of The Acts.[22] It is the only connected account of this
crucial period of the church and so gives limited but much needed
background for understanding the life and letters of Paul. It is also a
resource in study of the Gospels, especially in understanding the author
and literary features of the Gospel of Luke. It was a new step in the
literature of the church. As Luke 1:1 states, gospel narratives had been
written before the Gospel of Luke appeared. But no one, as far as we
can tell, had told the gospel story in a way that continued past the
resurrection. Luke saw that to tell the basic gospel it was necessary to
include the apostolic witness and the emergence of the church. So, as
Acts 1:1 makes clear, he wrote one work, in two parts, to tell the full
story. It was thus a document of faith, written by a Christian to further
the witness and work of the church.

What sources he had is difficult to say.[23] His main and possibly only
written source for the book of The Acts was a travel diary, which probably he himself had kept; he shows his presence at some of the events
narrated by using "we" in reporting them (chs. 16:10–17; 20:5–16; 21:
1–18; 27:1 to 28:16). If he knew other written records telling about the

---

21 These non-Pauline letters will be considered later, especially in Chapters 12 and 13.
22 Highly instructive for the study of The Acts are two books by Henry J. Cadbury,
The Making of Luke-Acts (The Macmillan Company, 1927), and *The Book of Acts
in History* (Harper & Brothers, 1955). The best comprehensive commentary in English is F. J. Foakes-Jackson and Kirsopp Lake, eds., *The Beginnings of Christianity:
Part I, The Acts of the Apostles*, 5 vols. (London, Macmillan and Co., Ltd., 1920–
1933); Vol. IV, *English Translation and Commentary*, and Vol. V, *Additional Notes*,
are by Kirsopp Lake and Henry J. Cadbury. Two leading recent commentaries are
F. F. Bruce, *The Acts of the Apostles*, 2d ed. (Wm. B. Eerdmans Publishing Company, 1952), critical but conservative, and Ernst Haenchen, *Die Apostelgeschichte*,
10th ed. of the Meyer *Kommentar* (Göttingen, Vandenhoeck & Ruprecht, 1956).
An excellent survey of the literature on The Acts and the problems to be faced is
Étienne Trocmé, *Le "Livre des Actes" et l'Histoire* (Paris, Presses Universitaires de
France, 1957).
23 See Trocmé, *Le "Livre des Actes,"* pp. 122–214.

early church, he no doubt used them; we know that he was willing to use written sources, for in writing the Gospel of Luke, the first part of his total work, he used Mark and at least one other written source. But perhaps for the early chapters of The Acts all he had was a number of stories that were circulating orally in the church; he then gave them written form and adapted them to the narrative into which he placed them.

Compactness and conciseness had marked his report of the words and actions of Jesus in the Gospel of Luke. The same author wrote the book of The Acts,[24] for the two parts of the total work show the same style throughout. But The Acts shows greater literary freedom in telling the story and especially in wording the speeches. Here Luke was working not so much from written sources as from stories told him as he journeyed about the church and especially as he inquired at Jerusalem concerning what had happened.

The care with which he used Mark and Q in writing his Gospel argues that he was a responsible reporter of the life of the earliest church. He clearly knew the latter part of his story much better than he did the early years of the Jerusalem church. In any case he so wrote as to bring out his interpretation of the events. But it may fairly be concluded that he gives a generally dependable account of the church's first years.

The date when he wrote is hard to fix. His Gospel must be later than the Gospel of Mark, which he used as a source. If Mark is dated between A.D. 65 and 75, Luke-Acts may be dated between A.D. 80 and 95.[25]

Like the Gospels, the book of The Acts reflects the interests of the writer and of the church in the days when he wrote. In particular, it reflects interest in Paul and in the spread of the gospel westward to Rome. Its narrative is selective. In describing the churches of which it speaks, especially those which Paul founded, it tells mainly how they were founded and began their life, and how the apostle came to leave for another place of work. It thus tells little of the internal life of any church except that at Jerusalem, for which the author has a special interest.[26] Its theme is, rather, the spread of the gospel and its universal outreach. It expresses that universality by showing how the gospel was

24 This has occasionally been disputed, e.g., by A. C. Clark, *The Acts of the Apostles* (Oxford, Clarendon Press, 1933).

25 The simplest way to explain the ending of The Acts, with Paul in prison and his fate undetermined, would be to date The Acts at the end of that two years of his imprisonment in Rome; see Bruce, *The Acts of the Apostles*, pp. 10–14. This would require dating Mark in the (early?) fifties, which seems too early.

26 For an extreme statement of the emphasis of The Acts on the Jewish nature of Christianity, see Burton Scott Easton, "The Purpose of Acts," reprinted in Frederick C. Grant (ed.), *Early Christianity* (The Seabury Press, Inc., 1954), pp. 33–118, especially pp. 56 f.

planted in leading Roman provinces and in Rome, the center of the world for a Roman citizen. But it does not say whether the gospel spread to eastern Syria and Mesopotamia, as may have happened, and—most remarkable of all—it says not a word of how the gospel came to Egypt, where it probably was carried without much delay.[27] It tells what the writer knew by personal experience or careful inquiry, and it includes what the writer thought essential for his purpose.

That Luke, the beloved physician, wrote Luke-Acts is the unbroken and unchallenged tradition of the ancient church, and there is no good reason to deny him the credit.[28] His two-part work binds the New Testament story together to give one message of "the salvation of God" provided for "all flesh" through Jesus Christ, the promised Christ and the rightful Lord of all men (Luke 3:6). Largely on the basis of his writing, we are able to sketch the story of the early church.

THE RESURRECTION THE STARTING POINT

The starting point of that story, after the gospel account of the ministry and death of Jesus, is his resurrection.[29] It is the climax of the gospel and the starting point of the history of the apostolic church. The attempt has been made to picture the church in its first years as just a Jewish sect that made no unique claim for Jesus or for itself. On that view it was just another sect within Judaism until someone, perhaps misled into using Greek thought, altered its views and created the idea that Jesus was unique and divine. This distorts the available evidence. In the Gospels, Jesus announced a unique and decisive action of God, for whom he acted with authority; and he made a unique claim for himself. He used, though with caution, the Messianic idea, for he fulfilled God's promises to Israel and stood in a direct and unique relation to the Father. He applied to himself the Suffering Servant passages, and expected the advancement of God's purpose by his suffering and ensuing triumph.

27 On this possibility, see S. G. F. Brandon, *The Fall of Jerusalem and the Christian Church* (London, S.P.C.K., 1951), pp. 221–225.

28 In Foakes-Jackson and Lake, *The Beginnings of Christianity* (see note 22 of this chapter), the case for and against the tradition is stated in Vol. II, pp. 265–348. The chief reason for its being questioned is that the writer of The Acts allegedly does not understand Paul and particularly presents an unacceptable view of the conference at Jerusalem in Acts, ch. 15. But see the discussion of this problem in Chapter 9 of the present book.

29 See Maurice Goguel, *The Birth of Christianity*, tr. by H. C. Snape (The Macmillan Company, 1954), pp. 29–86; also, A. Michael Ramsey, *The Resurrection of Christ*, Ch. 1.

His resurrection vindicated his teaching and expectation. It rallied his disciples and gave him a permanent place at the center of their faith, thought, and life. For them his role was the decisive role of history; he had acted for God, and God by the resurrection had given him full vindication. Their life henceforth was a Christ-centered life. The idea that at the outset they had no Christology is quite mistaken. From the first their whole way of life centered in him, and they had to give him a worldwide role.[30] Thus the Gospels indicate that during his ministry he made an implied claim of immense scope, and both the Gospels and the book of The Acts indicate that the resurrection at once gave him the central place in the faith, thought, and life of his followers. Christology, church, mission—all were involved in the resurrection and its effects; the beginning of the church can only be understood in the light of the resurrection.

The resurrection involves a theological view of history. The living God acts in unparalleled ways to forward his purpose. Students of history hardly know what to do with such a claim. They can treat it purely in terms of human experience without breaking their familiar pattern of history. Then they speak only of the experience of the disciples, who claimed renewed contact with Jesus of Nazareth after his crucifixion and burial. This experience is part of the story; the disciples were convinced that the same Jesus they had known during his earthly ministry had appeared and spoken to them; this honest conviction shaped their entire later life and message. But to treat this as merely a psychological experience, a recovery of love and confidence in the Jesus they had known, but not a real contact with him, denies the validity of the conviction that was the driving force of the apostolic church.

Rejecting fraud and self-deception as explanations of the resurrection story, two problems still remain. One is the nature of the resurrection life of Jesus. Was it simply the resuscitated body known during his ministry?[31] That hardly seems the case; sudden, mysterious appearance and disappearance do not fit that idea (e.g., Luke 24:31, 36). Was it simply a spiritual presence or experience of fellowship with the spirit of Jesus, independent of any tie with the previous body of Jesus of Nazareth? Paul may seem to give some basis for this view (I Cor. 15:50), but he really rejects it. The changed form of life of the risen Jesus had a real continuity with the earthly Jesus, and for the Jew Paul this meant con-

30 The titles "Messiah" and "Lord," used from the start, imply such a role. See my book *Jesus Christ the Risen Lord* (Abingdon Press, 1956).

31 Such passages as Luke 24:38–43 and John 20:20, 27, seem to imply this, but are probably graphic ways of emphasizing the reality of the resurrection, without intending to deny its mystery.

tinuity with his earthly body. This is hard to conceive, for the resurrection is a unique event, but what is described is continuity with and yet transformation of the earthly body of Jesus.

The basic affirmation is that the new form of life was perfect and suited to the new mode of existence of the risen Christ, but was nevertheless truly continuous with the life of the earthly Jesus. This is a mystery. But it is what the resurrection accounts and references describe, and it is the one explanation of the survival and advance of the movement of Jesus that is adequate to interpret what happened in the lives of the disciples.

The other main question is where the disciples first saw the risen Christ. The Gospel of Mark implies that the place was Galilee (chs. 14: 28; 16:7). In Matt. 28:16 the Eleven first see him on the appointed mountain in Galilee. In Luke 24:13, 34 and John 20:14, 19, however, the first appearance is in Jerusalem (or Judea). No doubt appearances occurred in both regions, but on the question where they first occurred the evidence is divided. More likely the first appearances were in Galilee,[32] where the disciples fled after the crucifixion of Jesus.

Once rallied by meeting the risen Christ, the disciples returned to Jerusalem. Since Jesus was crucified in Jerusalem and the church began its active ministry there, it was possible for the flight to Galilee, the appearances there, and the return to Jerusalem to drop out of the story, as in Luke, ch. 24, and John, ch. 20. The basic fact is that in these meetings with the risen Christ the apostolic church had its rallying experience and the basis of its further life as a group.

Thus the specific event that proved the starting point of the church was the resurrection. There is real point in calling Pentecost the birthday of the church, but Pentecost was possible only through the resurrection. The next event of the emerging church after the resurrection was the establishment of the disciples in Jerusalem. Whether or not the first resurrection appearances occurred in Jerusalem, some at least of them did occur there, and the striking fact is that the disciples, who as a group were Galileans (cf. Acts 2:7), promptly settled in Jerusalem and continued there even when hostility became open and extreme (Acts 8:1).

They had a reason for making Jerusalem their place of residence and base of operations. Jesus himself had climaxed his ministry by going to Jerusalem for a final urgent appeal to his people and especially to their leaders. The center of his people's life was there; only there could full acceptance of his message and claim occur. Now that the resurrection

---

[32] This is the view of Maurice Goguel, *The Birth of Christianity*, p. 59. See also note 44 in the preceding chapter.

had vindicated his claim, there was renewed reason to urge it on the leaders and people. The risen Jesus was Israel's Christ (Acts 2:36). Their rejection of him had been condemned and overruled by his resurrection. The leaders and people of Israel should face and accept that fact.

The disciples did not seek merely to win scattered individuals, nor could they abandon their people and go elsewhere with their message. Jesus was the fulfillment of God's promises to Israel; he had tried to win Israel; not he alone but Israel was called to be the Suffering Servant of God; to the end of his life he had persisted in his appeal to his people; and his disciples' immediate duty was to renew his appeal and work for a favorable response. Their return to Jerusalem and their preaching in the Temple expressed their conviction that their movement continued God's dealings with Israel and that they were the true core of the renewed Israel.

This embodied a great claim: Jesus was the Christ of Israel; all the life of Israel should center in him; the leaders of Israel should believe in and follow him; the disciples were the nucleus of the renewed Israel that should now take form. Implicit in all this was the downgrading of the recognized leaders of Israel, both priests and Pharisees, and the claim that the disciples could speak for the true and rightful Head of God's people. There was no thought of rejecting the Temple and other features of Israel's life and worship, but the disciples could speak for God and for his Christ with an authority that really undermined the authority and prestige of the official leaders and institutions of current Judaism.

An elusive question is the role that the ascension should play in a history of the apostolic church. This story, told in the briefest possible form in the longer text of Luke 24:51,[33] appears in more detail in Acts 1:9–11, but finds no place in any other New Testament passage. However, eleven New Testament books, by at least seven different writers, say that Jesus is at the right hand of God or has been exalted to his right hand.[34] One suggestion is that this exaltation was really identical with the resurrection; Jesus was raised and exalted to God's right hand in one act, and only later did the church divide this one act into two parts

---

[33] In a number of verses, especially in Luke, chs. 22 to 24, the so-called "Western" text of this Gospel omits phrases, clauses, or sentences found in most early manuscripts. It is probable that these "Western noninterpolations," as Westcott and Hort have called them, do not belong in the true text of Luke. This means that in Luke 24:51 we probably should omit "and was carried up into heaven."

[34] Matthew 22:44; 26:64; Mark 12:36; 14:62 (ch. 16:19); Luke 20:42; 22:69; Acts 2:34; 5:31; 7:55; Rom. 8:34; I Cor. 15:25; Eph. 1:20; Col. 3:1; Heb. 1:3; 8:1; 10:12; I Peter 3:22; Rev. 3:21. See Oscar Cullmann, *Christ and Time*, p. 151.

and separate them by an interval of time.[35] In fact, however, no New Testament passage clearly identifies the two events or places them at the same time. A series of resurrection appearances separates them.

Whether we speak of ascension or exaltation, however, the New Testament uses pictorial language to describe a significant event. It assumes the reality and victory of the resurrection, and describes its meaning and sequel. In the New Testament the resurrection means not merely that Jesus survived the experience of physical death and now continues a rich personal life, but that thus vindicated by God he is the Lord and Christ of his people (Acts 2:36). The imagery of sitting at the right hand of God, as John Calvin said, is "a metaphor" denoting "God's Deputy," "the power that is next to God."[36] This expresses the honor paid to the risen Christ, but it expresses far more; as the "right-hand man" next in rank to the Father, he has authority to further and realize the purpose of the Father. He enters upon a continuing ministry that will lead to his final and complete victory over all hostile forces (cf. I Cor. 15:25). He exercises the authority of God, his rank is unique, and his role is decisive for the future of mankind.

There is here a twofold claim: Jesus, risen and thus exalted, is not an ordinary human leader but has a close tie with the Father, and so the germ of a high Christology is inherent in the early church's conviction that he has been exalted; and his followers, united in faith in him and in loyalty to his cause, are set apart in a brotherhood that is the supreme social bond in their life. The essential reality of the church is present in this central relationship to the risen, exalted Christ, who as the living Lord claims full loyalty from his followers.[37] The group will consist of all Israel—without speaking yet of possible inclusion of all peoples—if they respond and center their lives in Jesus Christ the risen Lord. But should Israel—or at least most of them—reject his claim, his followers will still have to maintain full loyalty to him and the result will have to be a separate Christian fellowship.

In this nucleus of the New Israel the chosen disciples of Jesus, now the Eleven, have a crucial role. At the beginning they are the rallying center, the spearhead of the group. This is not because they have proved so steady, courageous, and resourceful as to earn this position. Rather,

---

35 Philippians 2:9, where exaltation follows the cross, and Heb. 13:20, which is vague, have been noted as possible indications of this.

36 *Commentary on a Harmony of the Evangelists Matthew, Mark, and Luke,* tr. by William Pringle (Wm. B. Eerdmans Publishing Company, 1949), Vol. III, pp. 70, 258, 393.

37 The effects of the resurrection for his followers are usually thought of in much too individualistic a manner.

their flight at the time of Jesus' arrest had highlighted their great limitations (Mark 14:50 and ||), and Peter's denial of Jesus had discredited even their spokesman and natural leader (Mark 14:66–72 and ||s). If now they are entrusted with a special role, it is by forgiveness and the gift of a new chance. For them the germ of the later doctrine of grace, which some have credited to Paul and to which he gave classic expression, was present from the first. Following the resurrection of Jesus they assume leadership, and Peter continues to be their spokesman and leader.

By the defection of Judas Iscariot, the Twelve had become the Eleven (Acts 1:13). Jesus had chosen twelve, so Peter proposed, and the others agreed, that Judas should be replaced and the full number of twelve restored (vs. 15–26). If the Twelve were symbolic of the twelve tribes of Israel and represented the nucleus of the New Israel, we can understand that the leaders thought it important to have the full number. In one ancient Jewish view one hundred and twenty (cf. Acts 1:15) were necessary for a "small sanhedrin" and the officers of a community should number one tenth of the group.[38] This view, if relevant here, would support the idea of restoring the group to full strength by selection of a twelfth member to replace Judas.

Acts 1:21 f. states the qualifications of such a person. He must be a witness of the resurrection; he must have seen the risen Christ. In addition he must have been a witness of the gospel history from the ministry of John the Baptist to Jesus' resurrection. Few of Jesus' followers could have met such a test. It implies that the Eleven had been with Jesus throughout his ministry and had even known John the Baptist, so that Jesus drew the nucleus and leaders of *his own group from those who first had responded to John the Baptist. This may be too rigid an interpretation and may not fit the facts, but this is what the reported words of Peter imply. They suggest that Jesus and the men later chosen as the Twelve spent some time with John the Baptist and became acquainted with one another during that time (cf. John 1:29 ff.).

The choice of Matthias is described as made in two stages. The entire group of disciples, the one hundred and twenty of Acts 1:15, nominated or "put forward" two of their group, Joseph Barsabbas Justus and Matthias (v. 23). After prayer they used the Old Testament method of casting lots to learn the divine choice, and Matthias was chosen.[39] This is the first and last appearance of Matthias in the New Testament story.

38 *Beginnings of Christianity*, Vol. IV, p. 12.
39 On casting lots, see F. D. Gealy's article entitled "Lots" in *IDB*, K–Q, pp. 163 f.

It must be remembered, however, that of the Eleven only Peter, James, and John appear in The Acts outside of ch. 1:13. As a group the Twelve gave important leadership at Jerusalem in the early apostolic church, but as far as the narrative tells us, only Peter exercised individual leadership. (James the son of Zebedee must have been a vigorous and active leader, for ch. 12:2 tells us that he was singled out for martyrdom, but just what he did we never hear, and of his brother John we hear only that he went with Peter on the occasions mentioned in chs. 3:1; 4:13; 8:14.) Peter was the effective leader of the church in its crucial earliest days, and deserved the title of foundation rock (cf. Matt. 16:18).

Thus far the group had not begun its active witness to the resurrection. Its total number of one hundred and twenty included not only the Twelve but "the women"—evidently the group mentioned in Luke 8:3; 23:49, 55—and also the mother and brothers of Jesus (Acts 1:14). There is no good evidence that his brothers had been his followers during his ministry; indeed, Mark 3:21 f., 31–35 and John 7:5 indicate that they were not. When did they change their attitude? The early tradition of resurrection appearances handed on to Paul at the beginning of his Christian life said that the fourth appearance was to James (I Cor. 15:7), and this must mean James the brother of Jesus. Perhaps by the end of Jesus' public ministry the attitude of his brothers had begun to change. In any case, when the risen Christ appeared to James, James could lead his brothers into the group of disciples and he himself was in a position to become in time the leading figure of the Jerusalem church (Acts 12:17; 15:13; 21:18; Gal. 2:9).[40]

The life of the waiting group was one of faith, prayer, and expectation. They had been promised Christ's continuing gifts, and specifically the gift of the Holy Spirit, who was to be given to God's people in the "last days" (Acts 2:17; Joel 2:28–32). The fulfillment of that Scriptural promise, which Jesus had renewed (Luke 24:49; Acts 1:4 ff.; cf. John 15:26; 16:7; 20:22), came on the Day of Pentecost. This Day was the second great festival of the Jewish year (Lev. 23:15–21; Deut. 16:9 f.). It followed the Passover festival by about fifty days (the word "Pentecost," of Greek origin, means "fifty"). Originally the feast had marked the end of the grain harvest, but by the time of Jesus it celebrated, though not because any specific Old Testament reference to this feast so instructed, the giving of the law on Mt. Sinai. It was thus a high point in the Jewish religious year, a time of spiritual memory and expectation at which the disciples, fully alive to their Jewish heritage, would

40 Nothing is said as to where James saw the risen Christ. It could well have been in Galilee. On this event, reported in the Gospel of the Hebrews, see M. R. James, *The Apocryphal New Testament*, p. 3.

be particularly receptive to God's new gifts to his people. It is not said where the one hundred and twenty assembled in prayer and expectation, but since "they were all together in one place" (Acts 2:1), and a "multitude" could gather and watch the group, they probably were in the outer court of the Temple area, where they often were found later (ch. 5:12).

The gift of the Holy Spirit to ten of the Twelve (Judas had defected; Thomas was not present) is dated by John 20:22 on the evening of the resurrection day. This seems to contradict Acts 1:4–8; 2:4. But the Gospel of John, concerned to show essential connections rather than mere chronological date, wants to make it clear that the Holy Spirit is the gift of the risen Christ, so it presents the risen Christ as actually giving the Spirit immediately after the resurrection. The book of The Acts agrees that the Spirit is the direct gift of the risen Christ (ch. 2:33), but is no doubt correct in dating the gift a few weeks after the resurrection.

Attention usually focuses on the speaking with tongues by the group of disciples.[41] It was not merely the Twelve who received the Spirit; the use of "all" in ch. 2—all were together; all were filled with the Spirit; Joel had promised the gift to all men and women of all ages; and Peter in his ensuing sermon promised that the Spirit would be given to all who repented and were baptized—indicates that the entire group received the Spirit, and all spoke with tongues.

The gift of speaking with tongues is described as though the disciples spoke various languages,[42] and to Luke this symbolizes the world outreach of the gospel. But Paul in I Cor., chs. 12 to 14, regards speaking with tongues as ecstatic speech not intelligible to others unless someone present has a special spiritual gift to explain the otherwise unintelligible sounds. Paul, it seems, is the clue to the real nature of speaking with tongues in the early church.[43] It was a highly emotional ecstatic expression of Christian joy. Paul recognized it as a sincere and legitimate though primitive and relatively inferior expression of faith and joy; he preferred the gifts that required the conscious use of the mind (I Cor. 12:10; 14:18 f., 39).

Possibly those who thus spoke with tongues used snatches of languages other than their normal speech, but the group did not receive the temporary or permanent gift of speaking fluently languages they had never

41 See Kirsopp Lake, "The Gift of the Spirit on the Day of Pentecost," in *Beginnings of Christianity*, Vol. V, pp. 111–121.
42 See P. G. S. Hopwood, *The Religious Experience of the Primitive Church* (Edinburgh, T. & T. Clark, 1936), Ch. 7, especially pp. 146 f.
43 I Thess. 5:19 ff. shows that such expressions were widely found in Paul's churches; cf. Acts 10:46; 19:6.

known. Indeed, the list of regions in Acts 2:9–11 may give a false impression; it may suggest that each region used a different language. Almost without exception Jews coming from those regions would speak one of two languages, Aramaic or Greek; these were the languages spoken by the .excited and joyous group of disciples that day in Jerusalem.

But the discussion of the speaking with tongues should not distract attention from the full meaning of the event. The gift of the Spirit meant an inrush of thrilling joy; faith is not a matter of intellect alone; it concerns the entire person and satisfies fully the emotions. The gift of the Spirit also meant the end of waiting; from that time the disciples were to speak, to give their witness, to present the claim of Christ to their countrymen. The gift of the Spirit also meant the promised gift of power (Acts 1:8). The deepest meaning of the Pentecost experience lay not in emotional joy but in this power to witness, to heal, and to withstand hostility and ill-treatment. It was not yet clear to the disciples how far the gift would take them. Without excluding other peoples from ultimate participation in the gift of salvation, they knew that for the present their work was to preach and appeal to their own people, beginning in Jerusalem.

More than once the book of The Acts notes that the disciples gathered in the Temple (chs. 2:46; 3:1; 5:12; cf. 6:7). This probably means in the outer court, the largest court of the Temple area, although Jews could go into the Court of the Women and Jewish men could go also into the Court of Israel. It was not merely convenience that led to this continual use of the Temple for gathering of the disciples. Nor was it merely the fact that this was where they would find the most Jews gathered in circumstances favorable for preaching and discussion; this was a fact, however, for when the people came there, they were free from work and family duties and could listen to the gospel message. There was a further reason for gathering in the Temple. When Jesus drove the money changers and the sellers of sacrificial animals from the Temple, he implied that he was authorized by God to control the Temple. Now, as the risen Christ and Lord he was the rightful Lord of the Jews and in particular of the Temple.[44] Malachi 3:1 may well have been in the minds of the disciples; they looked forward to the time when their Lord would come and take effective control of the Temple and the life of his people.

Since neither Jesus nor any of the Twelve, as far as we can tell, were priests, this attachment of the group to the Temple is striking. It points

---

[44] For a study of this theme in a wider setting, see Ernst Lohmeyer, *Lord of the Temple*, tr. by Stewart Todd (John Knox Press, 1962).

to the claim that Jesus had made and the disciples echoed. They were bound to the life of their people; they shared its loyalty to the Temple; the Temple as the central place of their people's religious life was the center of their interest and the place where the Lordship of Christ should be accepted and respected. They had full right to be there; their message was entitled to priority over the leadership and ideas of the Temple authorities.

First on the Day of Pentecost, and then on other occasions, such as the healing of the lame man (Acts, ch. 3) and the defense before the Sanhedrin (Acts, ch. 4), Peter preached to the people and their leaders. The book of The Acts includes reports of these speeches. Indeed, about one fifth of The Acts consists of speeches by Christian leaders, especially by Peter and Paul.[45] Such speeches are often called "sermons," as though they were exact reports of the very words spoken on those occasions. But these "sermons" as given in The Acts are brief; they vary in length from half a minute to perhaps eight minutes. Obviously the sermons of Peter and Paul were longer than this. At best these reports in The Acts are but compact summaries of what Luke understood was said. Moreover, the speeches are in Luke's vocabulary and style; he has written them in their present form. For this reason, it is sometimes thought that he composed them without any knowledge of what was actually said. More likely he as an eyewitness of part of the story and as an inquirer into its earlier stages knew the typical message of the Christian leaders, and something of the emphasis of each, and so could work into these summaries essentials of their typical preaching.

The failure to recognize the summary nature of the so-called "sermons" has caused some misunderstanding of the preaching and teaching work of the leaders. C. H. Dodd has led scholars to distinguish between the *kērygma*, the evangelistic preaching that stated the gospel message and appealed for repentance and faith, and the *didachē*, which gave ethical teaching, apologetic argument, and theological discussion.[46] It is usually thought that such teaching included details about the ministry and teaching of Jesus, whereas the kerygma was a simple evangelistic

---

[45] See Henry J. Cadbury, "The Speeches in Acts," in *Beginnings of Christianity*, Vol. V, pp. 402–427; Martin Dibelius, "The Speeches in Acts and Ancient Historiography," in his *Studies in the Acts of the Apostles*, Eng. tr. by Mary Ling (Charles Scribner's Sons, 1956), pp. 138–185; F. F. Bruce, *The Acts of the Apostles*, pp. 18–21.

[46] Dodd, in *The Apostolic Preaching and Its Developments* (London, Hodder & Stoughton, 1936), pp. 25–29, gives the content of the *kērygma* as found in Acts, chs. 2 to 4. He finds that in large part Paul and the Gospels have the same content for the *kērygma* as do these passages in The Acts. The definition of the content of the *didachē* as including the three aspects noted above (pp. 1 f. of his book) is striking for its omission of the teaching of the Lord (which he mentions on p. 3, however, as though a part of the *didachē*).

appeal, with no details about his earthly life. The brief sermon summaries perhaps do most to give this impression.

These short summaries, however, represent sermons which in delivery were usually as long as a half hour, an hour, or even more. In speaking at such length, the preacher had to give details about Jesus' message and ministry; in other words, teaching must have had an integral place in the actual preaching of the church; it was necessary to give concrete illustration and include explanation of the essential points of the evangelistic message. The gospel was the message of what God has done through Jesus Christ—through his ministry, death, and resurrection— to make possible the salvation of all who would repent and believe and enter the Christian fellowship. God had acted through a historical person (cf. e.g., Acts 2:22–36), and to tell what that person had said and done was necessary as a factual basis for faith that in him God had acted to save men. The preacher had to teach as he preached; the two tasks could not be separated; it was all a part of the task of giving a Christian witness; as form criticism has made clear, the gospel tradition that we find written down in the Synoptic Gospels was preserved and used in the life of the church, and part of this use was as illustrative material in the evangelistic preaching of Christian leaders.

The "sermons" of The Acts make clear to the reader that the central interest of the story of The Acts is not in the human actors. It is, rather, in the living Christ, who through the Holy Spirit active in the disciples carries forward his work of winning men to accept the gospel, enter the fellowship of God's people, and so prepare for the coming of God's final Kingdom. The "sermons" focus attention on the gospel, on Christ and the work of the Spirit, and prevent the reader from regarding the story as just a human venture.

A notable fact about Pentecost is that Peter's preaching led a large number to believe in Christ. The book of The Acts uses round numbers, but the references to three thousand believers added at Pentecost (ch. 2:41) and to a total of five thousand (ch. 4:4) after the healing of the lame man (ch. 3), indicate the rapid increase of the group of disciples. The core of this group was the group of Galileans who had been with Jesus (ch. 2:7), but the fact that they could meet for common meals in homes in Jerusalem shows that very soon, if not from the very beginning, settled residents of Jerusalem were found among the disciples (v. 46).

From time to time summaries in The Acts describe the common life of the disciples (chs. 2:43–47; 4:32–35; 5:12–16, 42).[47] They were widely

47 Henry J. Cadbury, "The Summaries in Acts," in *Beginnings of Christianity*, Vol. V, pp. 392–402, is rather suspicious of the summaries, which of course are editorial compositions, but may contain good tradition.

respected by the people; their leaders earnestly and continually preached and taught in the Temple and in homes of disciples; the apostles were able to do "wonders and signs" of healing which to those with spiritual discernment indicated that God's power was back of their preaching and works; the disciples lived together in close fellowship, going together to the Temple and meeting in homes for common meals; their joy and dedication led them to care for one another's needs so that no one suffered want.

The selling of property by some disciples to meet the urgent needs of destitute comrades has often been called "communism." This is a misleading description of a voluntary sacrifice. No disciple was compelled to surrender his property (cf. Acts 4:36 f.; 5:4). Some did so out of loyalty to Christ and his disciples, and not as part of such a compulsory and atheistic government system as the word "communism" suggests to us. Their gifts were needed not because of faulty economic theories but because the core of the group were Galileans without economic roots in Jerusalem. The group as a whole had few financial resources to begin with; the concern to preach the gospel and win others to faith prevented thought of long-term economic plans; and the entire economic need was increased almost at once by the hostility of Jewish leaders in Jerusalem and—a little later—by famine (ch. 11:28). The sharing of resources was not communism; it was a voluntary sacrifice by disciples who refused to see their comrades starve. It was a practical and effective expression of brotherhood and mutual helpfulness.[48]

The life of the group of disciples centered in their common Christ-directed faith and loyalty. Its central public expression was worship and preaching in the Temple area. There the group met in worship and in mutually encouraging fellowship, and there they found hearers for the gospel message. Another part of this fellowship was the common meals (ch. 2:46).[49] They recalled the meals, especially the Last Supper, which some of them had had with Jesus; they also met the needs of those disciples who lived in deep poverty.

If one faces the immensity of the claim that the disciples made for Jesus Christ, and realizes the startling enthusiasm and urgent insistence with which they presented their message at the very center of their people's life, it is not surprising that the reactions included not only glad acceptance of their message but active resentment and hostility. The hostility was expressed mainly by official groups, both the priestly

[48] See Cecil John Cadoux, *The Early Church and the World* (Edinburgh, T. & T. Clark, 1925), pp. 127–131.

[49] These hunger-satisfying meals constituted the earliest celebration of the Lord's Supper in Jerusalem, as later at Corinth (I Cor. 11:20–34).

leaders, responsible not only to their people for proper administration of the Temple but also to the Romans for preserving peace and order, and the Sanhedrin, the ruling body of the Jewish people in all matters not controlled by Rome.

The course of events in which this hostility developed is not entirely clear. A similarity between certain events in the narrative of The Acts led Adolf von Harnack to conclude that Luke had combined two parallel sources for the same series of events; to him Acts 3:1 to 5:16 is an excellent source, whereas chs. 2 and 5:17–42 present a legendary doublet of the same events.[50] Bo Reicke does not regard ch. 2:1–41 as a part of the story that is told in two parallel accounts, but he considers chs. 2:42 to 4:31 and chs. 4:32 to 5:42 to be parallel accounts, each with two main subjects: Christian fellowship and Sadducaic persecution.[51] Certainly these two themes stand out in these chapters, and whether the sequence of Christian growth and witness followed by official rebuke and punishment occurred once or twice, the young fellowship of disciples clearly gave an eager witness, disturbed the normal quiet of the Temple courts, aroused the suspicion and hostility of the priestly leaders and the Sanhedrin, and stoutly resisted all attempts to intimidate them and stop their public testimony to Christ.

The issue was deeper than such questions as whether the peace was being unwarrantably disturbed or whether the Romans, disturbed by events that could suggest to them political unrest, might take steps against the official Jewish leaders. Implicit in the attitude and preaching of the disciples was a transfer of the center of Jewish life from the Temple and its established leadership to Jesus Christ and those who represented him. To those who thought that the Mosaic law solidly supported the Temple regime and its established leadership, the actions of the disciples were a direct attack on the divine authority of the law given in Scripture.

This issue was ready to emerge in lively discussions between the disciples and the leaders of established Judaism. But it was not Peter and the Twelve who were to take the lead in sharpening that issue. Another group was more keenly aware of the depth of the challenge the gospel made to the established faith and life of Judaism. The Greek-speaking members among the disciples at Jerusalem were to bring that issue to a crisis.

50 *The Acts of the Apostles*, tr. by J. R. Wilkinson (London, Williams & Norgate, 1909), pp. 175–202.
51 *Glaube und Leben der Urgemeinde* (Zürich, Zwingli Verlag, 1957), pp. 55 f.

Chapter 8

OUTREACH FROM JERUSALEM

THE EXPANSION of the church, as far as we can discern, moved out from Jerusalem. No doubt our picture of the first generation of the church is incomplete. Since Jesus spent most of his public ministry in Galilee, and resurrection appearances occurred there, it must be assumed that after his death and resurrection disciples were found there. Acts 9:31, the only hint in The Acts that there were Christians in Galilee in the apostolic age, supports this view.

Ernst Lohmeyer has argued that Galilee had a strong church with views different from those held in Jerusalem.[1] But there is no conclusive evidence as to what the disciples living in Galilee thought and preached. The Twelve established their center in Jerusalem after the resurrection, and are never said to visit Galilee again (ch. 1:4, 12). The women who went to Jerusalem with Jesus settled there at the beginning of the apostolic age (v. 14). The real center of the disciples of Jesus was in Jerusalem, where the Twelve and others could present his claim at the focal center of Judaism.

It is clear from Acts 9:10, 19, that within no more than a very few years after Jesus' death there were disciples in Damascus. This group could be an offshoot of disciples in Galilee. In any case, it is plain that the new movement spread quickly to Damascus, whether from Galilee or from Jerusalem. Apart from the all-Jewish membership of the Damascus group, however, and the hint that they were in contact with Jerusalem (ch. 9:13), we know nothing about church development in the Damascus region. The expansion of the church was due essentially to leaders who went out from Jerusalem.

THE LIMITED ROLE OF THE TWELVE

That outreach did not occur in the way one might have expected. Among ancient church legends one tells how the apostles were instructed to stay in Jerusalem for twelve years, and then they were to go out into

---

[1] *Galiläa und Jerusalem* (Göttingen, Vandenhoeck & Ruprecht, 1936).

the world to spread the gospel.[2] The reality was entirely different. Most of the Twelve receive no individual mention after their brief role as a group in Jerusalem. Only Peter is reported to have had an active role in the spread of the gospel.[3] John goes with him as a silent partner on one trip, to Samaria (ch. 8:14). Peter with rare exceptions (ch. 10) preaches only to the Jews; Paul confirms this (Gal. 2:7).

Other disciples than the Twelve did most to spread the gospel. Two reasons explain this. One is that the Twelve as the responsible heads of the new church considered it their first duty to work at Jerusalem and give leadership from there. The more decisive reason is that others were better equipped for this wider ministry.

The real test was ability to speak to people in their own language. Two languages were in wide use. Aramaic was widely spoken in Palestine and Syria and regions to the east, and was the mother tongue of the Twelve. But Greek was widely used in these regions, even by Jews, and it was the common tongue in the Roman Empire as a whole. Some disciples, of course, used both languages, and provided the link between those disciples who could speak only one or the other. Most of the earliest disciples spoke Aramaic, but some spoke Greek, and some spoke both languages. The latter held a key position in the earliest years of the church.

The presence of Greek-speaking disciples in the earliest Jerusalem church comes out in The Acts in two noteworthy ways. One is the role of Barnabas, whose crucial role is too often ignored.[4] He may have been a disciple during Jesus' public ministry; a later tradition said he was one of the Seventy (Luke 10:1). Certainly from the first days of the church at Jerusalem he was an active, respected member. Though a Levite, he was from Cyprus and evidently could speak Greek well. Yet he was no recent settler at Jerusalem, for he owned a field in that vicinity (Acts 4:37). In contacts and views he was closer to the Twelve than were the Seven, and he proved able to win the confidence of both the Aramaic-speaking and Greek-speaking wings of the church.

THE SEVEN

The second impressive evidence of Greek-speaking disciples in the Jerusalem group was the appointment of the Seven.[5]

---

[2] Clement of Alexandria, *Stromateis* VI.5; Eusebius, *Church History* V.18.14.
[3] I Cor. 9:5 shows that Peter traveled about, had his expenses paid, and took his wife with him at church expense. This verse also suggests that though we cannot learn details, other apostles made preaching tours with the same expense allowances.
[4] On Barnabas, see my *Pioneers of the Primitive Church* (Abingdon Press, 1940), Ch. 3.
[5] It is possible, to say the least, that Luke used a written source for Acts 6:1 to 8:4;

It was the practice of the apostles, using in part funds offered by those who sold their property, to give daily allowances to disciples in need (cf. Acts 6:1–4). Included in this aid were numerous widows, always a concern of pious Jews (Deut. 24:19–21; 26:12 f.; Isa. 1:17). The disciples were divided into two groups, the "Hebrews," or Aramaic-speaking disciples, and the "Hellenists," or Greek-speaking members. It has been suggested that the word "Hellenists" here means Gentiles.[6] This is extremely unlikely; in the earliest days of the church only Jews, including proselytes come into Judaism from their former life in the pagan world, constituted the church. The "Hellenists" were Hellenistic Jews. Since they spoke Greek, they naturally lived somewhat apart from the "Hebrews" or Aramaic-speaking disciples. Each group worshiped in the language that they knew, and the language background no doubt determined the grouping when they met and ate in homes of disciples, somewhat as was done in the "house churches" of which Paul's letters speak (Rom. 16:5; I Cor. 16:19; Philemon 2).[7] In such circumstances a sense of division could emerge, and when the Hellenists thought their widows were being neglected in the daily distribution of food, they "murmured against the Hebrews" in protest.

Up to this time the Twelve had acted as the general administrative body of the entire group, and the daily distribution of food to the needy, it seems, was in their hands. (Later, in Acts 11:30, the "elders" handle such matters.) So the protests in effect indicted the Twelve, who thus seem essentially bound up with the "Hebrew" group. The apostles therefore convened all the disciples and proposed that they choose seven men to handle the daily administration of relief, leaving the apostles free to concentrate on prayer ånd preaching and leadership in common worship.

The entire group chose seven trusted men: Stephen, Philip, Prochorus, Nicanor, Timon, Parmenas, and Nicolaus, a proselyte originally of Antioch (Acts 6:5). All seven names are Greek, and it has been suggested that thése men were really the recognized heads of the Greek-speaking wing, which thus constituted a separate "denomination."[8] Such a view can appeal to the fact that nothing is ever said of relief work by any of

11:19–30; 12:25 to 15:35, which is called an Antiochene Source by Adolf von Harnack, *The Acts of the Apostles*, pp. 188 f. But although Luke obviously had an Antiochene source of information, it is not so certain that the material came to him in written form.

[6] On this possibility, see Henry J. Cadbury, "The Hellenists," in *Beginnings of Christianity*, Vol. V, pp. 59–74.

[7] Floyd V. Filson, "The Significance of the Early House Churches," *JBL*, Vol. LVIII (1939), pp. 105–112.

[8] Cf. Maurice Goguel, *The Birth of Christianity*, pp. 167–169.

this group, while Stephen and Philip are pictured as preaching and performing remarkable signs (chs. 6:8; 8:6). However, the idea that the Jerusalem church was split into two completely separate "denominations" seems exaggerated, though the Greek names of the Seven indicate that their ties were mainly with the Hellenists.

Chosen by the entire congregation, the Seven were set apart by the Twelve (ch. 6:6). The Seven are never called deacons, although the special work they were chosen to do resembles that of the later deacons of the church. (In ch. 11:30 the elders handle relief work.) Nor is it clear that they were "ordained" to constitute a definite permanent order. The laying on of hands signified setting apart for a specified task; for example, Barnabas and Saul were thus set apart for their evangelistic missionary task (ch. 13:3), but this does not mean that they were then ordained.[9] None of our modern polity patterns is explicitly present in The Acts. Undoubtedly the Seven were considered subordinate to the Twelve, and the laying on of hands set them apart for a definite service in the church, but the leadership of the church was not so clearly ordered then as Christians have often thought.

SIX SUMMARIES OF CHURCH EXPANSION

At key points in The Acts are found summaries of the progress of the gospel and the growth of the church.[10] At least six of these summaries deserve special notice (chs. 6:7; 9:31; 12:24; 16:5; 19:20; 28:30 f.). Acts 6:7 seems at first sight a strange place for such a summary. The Seven have just been appointed, and their work, as far as The Acts reports it, is about to be described. Why insert a summary between their appointment and their work? It is because Luke saw that the first period of the apostolic church was drawing to a close. The church thus far had centered in Jerusalem under the leadership of the Twelve. The next events were to lead to its expansion and to the emergence of new leadership. The summary signals the end of one period and points on to the next.

THE MINISTRY OF STEPHEN

At this decisive time Stephen plays the leading role. Of his background and preparation for his ministry we hear nothing. The story goes straight to his crucial work. Strangely enough, the first thing told

---

9 For the contrary view, see M. H. Shepherd, Jr., "Hands, Laying on of," *IDB*, E–J, pp. 521 f.

10 On the summaries in The Acts, see C. H. Turner, "Chronology of the New Testament," in Hastings' *Dictionary of the Bible*, Vol. I, p. 421; Henry J. Cadbury, "The Summaries in Acts," in *The Beginnings of Christianity*, Vol. V, pp. 392–402.

about him is not his relief work—nothing is ever said of that—or even his preaching, but his doing of "great wonders and signs among the people" (Acts 6:8). Implied in such miraculous deeds—no doubt healings —were the presence and working of the Holy Spirit (chs. 6:5; 7:55; cf. 1:8), noted as present also in the wisdom of his preaching and debate (ch. 6:10). The signs are mentioned as attesting God's approval and guidance of his ministry.

The scene of his preaching was mainly at least the Greek-speaking synagogues of Jerusalem.[11] Acts 6:9 refers to at least two such synagogues and probably four, one of Freedman (Jews enslaved, probably in war, and later freed by Rome), one of Cyrenian Jews, one of Alexandrian Jews, and another of Jews of Cilicia and the Roman province of Asia.[12] Some of the Jews in these synagogues clashed in debate with Stephen but could not vanquish him; since Saul (later called Paul) was from Tarsus of Cilicia, it may be, as ch. 8:1 suggests, that he was active in these attempts to refute and discredit Stephen.

When debate failed to silence Stephen, his opponents, considering his teaching erroneous and dangerous, tried stronger means. Arousing popular feeling and stirring up the Jewish "elders and the scribes," they took Stephen before the Jewish leaders. The charge was that Stephen was speaking "against this holy place [the Temple] and the [Mosaic] law," and was saying that Jesus would destroy the Temple and change the legal customs given by Moses (ch. 6:13 f.).

The charge most emphasized in The Acts concerned his criticism of the Temple. Old Testament prophets had spoken of its destruction (Jer. 26:6; Micah 3:12). So had Jesus (Mark 13:2; 14:58), and his words had aroused resentment. But in Stephen's teaching his opponents sensed an explicit disparagement of the Temple as not central or necessary for true worship of God.[13] To those who identified loyalty to the Temple with loyalty to the Mosaic law such teaching would have been also a direct attack on that law.[14] It is a question whether Stephen said that Jesus would destroy the Temple, but to the church the risen Jesus was

[11] Such a synagogue was built by Theodotus (note that he had a Greek name), and his inscription in Greek, put up on the synagogue, has been found in ancient ruins of Jerusalem. For a photograph and translation of the inscription, see Jack Finegan, *Light from the Ancient Past*, Fig. 105 and p. 228.

[12] The verse is not clear as to the number of synagogues. The interpretations range from one to five.

[13] The church later worked out a view of Christ as the Temple or as the High Priest or as the sacrifice for sins. Cf. John 1:29; 2:21; Heb. 6:20; 9:11 f.

[14] Stephen recognizes as legitimate the "tent of witness" but not the Temple (Acts 7:44). Jesus boldly interfered to cleanse the Temple of abuses, but he spoke of the Temple as a "house of prayer" and so was less radical in his criticism (Mark 11:15–17). After Jesus' final and complete rejection by priestly leaders, however, the situation was not the same as when he spoke such words.

Lord and was to come as Judge of all (Acts 2:36; 10:42), so Stephen could have held such a view, and certainly could have expected Jesus to change the ancestral ways of Jewish life and worship. To most Jews, however, Jesus had been discredited and disowned by God; God had given the law, and the Temple was his dwelling place; to oppose law and Temple was therefore blasphemous.

THE "TRIAL" AND DEATH OF STEPHEN

Stephen's "defense," the longest speech in the book of The Acts, was really a vigorous, defiant attack on his opponents (ch. 7:2–53). Like the other speeches of The Acts, it is Lucan in language and not a verbatim report of what Stephen said. But it may be taken as giving his essential criticism of the Temple and his Jewish opponents, and it was bound to enrage his accusers.[15]

In the form of a historical survey—the central Biblical message is regularly embodied in a historical account of God's dealings with his people—Stephen argued that God's revelation and man's true worship had not been bound to the Holy Land and the Temple. God had appeared to Abraham in Mesopotamia and Haran, and to Moses in Egypt and the wilderness; in the wilderness, not in the Promised Land, God gave his people the law and made himself known to them. The Temple was not needed, and God had not wanted it built; he does not dwell there (ch. 7:48) and may be worshiped elsewhere. For the Jews to make so much of the Temple was to misunderstand God's revelation and their own history. Moreover, Israel had been persistently disobedient to God and had rejected God's prophetic messengers, and have now climaxed their long record of disobedience by rejecting and executing "the Righteous One," Jesus Christ (v. 52). They resist the Holy Spirit speaking through Stephen and other Christian spokesmen (v. 51); they disobey the very law to which they make such pious appeal (v. 53).

In the main, Stephen spoke within the framework of the Jewish faith, but his disparagement of special places of worship, his denial that the Temple is a fit instrument of God's presence and will, and his rebuke of his people as persistently disobedient to God expressed an attitude of freedom toward the framework of contemporary Judaism. He did not break with Judaism or invite Gentiles into the church, but his spirit had in it the germ of a universal worship and fellowship.

It is difficult to decide how Stephen was put to death. Was his "trial"

---

15 On Stephen's speech, see C. S. C. Williams, *A Commentary on the Acts of the Apostles* (Harper & Brothers, 1957), pp. 100–111.

a formal meeting of the Sanhedrin or an informal hearing? The story begins as though describing an actual Sanhedrin meeting. But the outburst of fury at the end and the precipitate stoning of Stephen show no marks of a legal trial, condemnation, and execution; that would have taken more than one day. It was an execution by mob violence and illegal procedure, somewhat as James the brother of Jesus was executed illegally in A.D. 62. Luke suggests a remnant of legal concern by mention of witnesses present at the execution (Acts 7:58); by Jewish law they were to take the lead in an execution. But on the whole the event was not a legal action but a violent attempt to silence the Christian witness in the Greek-speaking synagogues of Jerusalem.

Thus Stephen became the first disciple to die for his witness to Christ.[16] He alone of all the speakers of the apostolic age is reported to have described Jesus as "the Son of man" (v. 56). In the tradition Luke had received, Stephen spoke of Jesus as the heavenly Son of Man who soon would come and transform current Jewish ways of life and worship, including the Temple worship and ancestral customs. The opponents of Stephen, and the Jews generally, evidently sensed in him a freer spirit and a greater threat to existing Judaism than they found in the Twelve.

Persecution broke out; Saul approved of Stephen's execution and led the persecution that followed; men and women disciples of Jesus were seized and thrown into prison; others escaped seizure only by fleeing from Jerusalem into Judea and Samaria; but—an amazing fact since the Twelve were the acknowledged heads of the church—the Twelve were not molested and could stay on in Jerusalem (Acts 8:1). Jewish opponents sensed in the Greek-speaking group rather than in the Twelve the greatest threat to the continuance of the Judaism they were determined to preserve.

THE MINISTRY OF PHILIP

Of the Seven only Stephen is said to have engaged in preaching and debate at Jerusalem. The only other member of the Seven whose individual leadership is described is Philip (not the same man as the apostle Philip). Forced to flee from Jerusalem after Stephen's death, Philip went to Samaria and preached in an unnamed city (Acts 8:5). Others also, Luke reports, preached wherever they went, but Luke regards Philip's

---

16 His death was a factor in the development of the term "martyr." The Greek word *martys* (*martyr*) meant "a witness," but because a witness who died for his cause was its outstanding witness, the word came to mean one who died for the cause or faith he supported.

work as especially significant. For one thing, it carried on the expansion outlined in Acts 1:8, in which Judea and Samaria were to be evangelized after Jerusalem.

According to the Gospel of John, the preaching of John the Baptist was done in part near Salim at Aenon, which probably was located in Samaria northeast of Shechem (John 3:23).[17] Did the preaching of John the Baptist, and then that of Jesus—note his choice of twelve to symbolize the twelve tribes of Israel—show a concern that the people of Samaria, in spite of racial intermixture, should be included in the invitation to enter the imminent Kingdom? Did this concern that Samaria should not be neglected in the preaching of the young church derive from Jesus?[18]

Certainly the Seven, if Stephen represented their thinking, were not so bound to Jerusalem and the Temple as some disciples were, and in this spirit Philip, as one of this freer group, could preach in a city of Samaria, after being driven from Jerusalem. Preaching in Samaria would go outside the usual bounds of Judaism, but since the Samaritans also accepted and observed the Mosaic law, Philip could preach there and accept Samaritans as disciples without raising all of the acute questions that the conversion of pagan Gentiles would involve. It was a step, but only a step, toward an offer of the gospel to Gentiles without requiring them to accept Judaism in order to be a Christian.

The ministry of Philip in Samaria is described in terms that resemble those used of Stephen (Acts 8:5–8). He "proclaimed to them the Christ" as the fulfillment of the ancestral hope that the Samaritans shared in some form, and he performed "signs," healings of mind and body. The impressive response in conversions included a "magician" named Simon, who had claimed to be the embodiment of the power of God and had practiced magic arts (vs. 9–13). When word of Philip's success reached Jerusalem, the apostles considered it their responsibility to investigate whether this was a proper expansion of the church. Peter and John were sent to do this (vs. 14–17). John here as elsewhere in The Acts was the passive partner; Peter was the spokesman, but John could confirm his witness. The two apostles accepted the converted Samaritans as true believers, and they prayed and laid their hands on the converts, who then received the Holy Spirit.

This may seem to imply that the Spirit was given only through this

---

17 The other possible location of Aenon is about 6 miles south of Scythopolis, at a spot where springs of water could have provided water for baptism.
18 Such a suggestion would appear more reasonable if one of the Twelve had led the preaching in the region of Samaria.

action by the apostles, but in ch. 10:44 the Spirit is given without prayer or laying on of hands by an apostle.[19] The report that the Samaritans received the Spirit indicates that when this occurred it was demonstrated by outward manifestations; by their joy and perhaps here as elsewhere by their speaking with tongues it was clear to onlookers that the Spirit was really given.

The book of The Acts reports that the convert Simon wanted to buy the right and ability to confer the Spirit (ch. 8:18 f.)[20] The incident is cited in The Acts to bring out that the Spirit is a free gift. It is not at men's disposal and cannot be bought; it is not a "monopoly" of the Twelve; they cannot give or sell the right and power to bestow the Spirit.

Philip continued his preaching ministry elsewhere (Acts 8:26–40). The story of his encounter with the Ethiopian eunuch on the way from Jerusalem to Gaza is told with dramatic flourishes, but its essential importance is clear; a Gentile, who as a eunuch could not become a proselyte, a full member of God's people (Deut. 23:1), was won to faith in Christ and baptized by Philip. The joy of the eunuch after Philip left him indicates that in Luke's view the Spirit was given to this new convert without the mediation of an apostle. The man had been a God-fearing Gentile, it would seem, interested in the Jewish faith but not a proselyte.[21] Such a conversion constituted another step toward free acceptance of Gentiles into the church.

That Philip discussed with the eunuch Isa., ch. 53, a Scripture passage regarded as fulfilled in Jesus, is a noteworthy glimpse of early Christian thought. Jesus was attentive to promises of Scripture and held that in his ministry, death, and resurrection he fulfilled God's promises. To the church this fulfillment attested his divine mission. The apostolic church continued to trace the fulfillment theme in its study of Scripture. Peter, it seems, used Deutero-Isaiah's Servant of God figure to interpret who Jesus was and what he had done (Acts 3:13, 26; 4:27, 30).[22] Acts 8:32–35 indicates that one of the Seven applied the Suffering Servant passage in Isa. 53:7 f. to the suffering of Jesus. Thus from the first the

19 In Acts 2:38 nothing is said to indicate that the laying on of hands will mediate the gift of the Spirit. Presumably Stephen received the gift at Pentecost, but that is not stated (ch. 6:3, 5). An otherwise unknown Ananias mediated the gift to Saul in Damascus (ch. 9:17). Paul laid his hands upon twelve men at Ephesus, and they received the Spirit (ch. 19:6).

20 On the at least partly legendary story of Simon as a leader in Gnosticism of later generations, see R. M. Grant, *Gnosticism and Early Christianity* (Columbia University Press, 1959), Ch. 3.

21 See Kirsopp Lake, "Proselytes and God-Fearers," in *Beginnings of Christianity*, Vol. V, pp. 74–96.

22 So Oscar Cullmann, *Peter: Disciple, Apostle, Martyr*, pp. 67–69.

preaching about Jesus interpreted his work as a fulfillment of Scripture and so as divinely approved. The story about Jesus was never told without interpretation, and that interpretation was in terms of the fulfillment of promises in Scripture.

Once the eunuch had been baptized by Philip he continued on his way home to Ethiopia, and nothing more is told of him. He is a symbol and promise of the far reach of the gospel.

Philip, however, appears briefly later. He went northward up the coastal plain from the region of Gaza to Caesarea, a Hellenistic city where the Roman governor of Judea, Samaria, and Idumea had his residence. As he went "he preached the gospel to all the towns" (Acts 8:40). Later preaching by Peter in this same region (ch. 9:32–43) is not described as an official checkup on Philip's work (contrast ch. 8:14–25). If Peter's preaching tour was in fact such an official inspection, Luke does not say so. Philip himself seems to have settled down to a ministry in the Hellenistic city of Caesarea, for when Paul, late in his career, visited Caesarea, he found Philip there (ch. 21:8).

SAUL AND THE JERUSALEM HELLENISTS

In addition to the Seven, Saul of Tarsus was another Hellenistic Jew who gave active leadership in the early church.[23] His epochal career as a missionary will occupy us in the next three chapters. Here we note only how he shared in the expansion of the church from its Jerusalem-centered ministry to its direct confrontation with the Gentile world.

Saul first appears as an opponent of the Seven. Probably he was active against Stephen in Jerusalem in the Greek-speaking synagogue of "those from Cilicia and Asia" (Acts 6:9). His share in opposing Stephen is suggested when the witnesses, who were to lead in stoning Stephen, laid their garments at his feet while they carried out their role (ch. 7:58). He approved of Stephen's execution and led active persecution of Jerusalem disciples, causing the imprisonment of both men and women (ch. 8:1–3). Then he set out for Damascus, intending to take prisoner any disciples he found there and bring them to trial before Jewish authorities in Jerusalem. His sudden and outwardly unprepared conversion put an abrupt stop to his career as a persecutor. The conversion

---

[23] Saul was his Hebrew name, and his Greek name was Paul (*Paulos;* Latin *paulus,* "small," "little"). Some have thought he took the name Paul only when he met Sergius Paulus, the Roman proconsul of Cyprus (Acts 13:7, 9). But it was common for a Hellenistic Jew to have both a Jewish and a Greek name, and this would have been true especially of one who had been a Roman citizen from birth (ch. 22:25–29).

story is told in detail three times in Acts (chs. 9:1–19; 22:3–21; 26:2–23).
This is Luke's way of saying that no other event in the apostolic age
equaled in significant consequences this dramatic conversion of the
chief persecutor.[24]

In this experience of Saul near Damascus, he saw the risen Christ, to
whom he at once submitted his life. This appearance of the risen
Christ, Paul was convinced, was as real and as basic for the life of the
church as the risen Christ's appearances to the other apostles. It enabled
him to claim to be an apostle equal in rank with any of the Twelve.
Modern study deals intensively with the preparation for this experience,
but for Saul himself no environmental, cultural, or personal background could explain the essential happening. It was God's free and
powerful act, to which Saul responded in faith. And his conversion
involved a commission. Indeed, Saul by temperament could not be a
nominal or cautious member of any group. To become a disciple was
to become active in spreading the gospel of whose truth he had become
convinced.

This fact helps us determine what happened after his conversion.
That he made contact with the disciples in Damascus is what would be
expected (Acts 9:10–19). He himself tells us that he went away into
Arabia for a short stay (Gal. 1:17). But that he spent a long period of
some three years there, as is sometimes thought, in calm, extended meditation about his new faith, is entirely unlike what we know of him.
The stay in Arabia, the region south and southeast of Damascus, was
either a short stay to collect his thoughts after a life-changing conversion
experience or a time of Christian witness and teaching of which we
know nothing more. Before long he was back in Damascus preaching
the gospel he had so fiercely opposed in Jerusalem.

Luke sums up Saul's Damascus message in the words: Jesus "is the
Son of God" (Acts 9:20; cf. v. 22). This title no doubt included the
meaning that Jesus was the expected Messiah, but we shall see that Saul
from the first avoided all ideas of political or nationalistic Messiahship.
He presented Jesus as the Son of God who was uniquely linked to the
Father in life and work and was the exalted Lord of the church.[25] If in
Saul's thought the exalted Jesus thus had an even closer link with the
Father than in the usual preaching in Jerusalem, it is not surprising
that opposition to his message soon broke out among the Jews at Damas-

---

[24] On the conversion of Paul, two able discussions are by James S. Stewart, *A Man in
Christ* (Harper and Brothers, n.d.), Ch. 3, and Johannes Munck, *Paul and the Salvation of Mankind*, Eng. tr. by Frank Clarke (John Knox Press, 1959), Ch. 1.
[25] See Chapter 9.

cus and he was forced to flee by night, as he himself confirms (Acts 9:23–25; II Cor. 11:32 f.).

From the beginning of his Christian career, and even before his conversion, Saul inevitably became a leading figure and object of dispute in the group whose faith he shared. From Damascus he returned to Jerusalem (Acts 9:26–30; Gal. 1:18–20). It was an act of courage. Perhaps his aim was in part to correct the false witness he had given before conversion. But he did not intend to stay there. His main aim, as he states, was to get to know Peter; contrary to Acts 9:27–29, he states quite clearly that he did not see the Jerusalem leaders as a group, but only Peter and James the brother of Jesus, who by then was coming into prominence in the Jerusalem church. His short stay of fifteen days supports his contention that he did not need extended instruction and did not seek commissioning by the Jerusalem leaders.

According to The Acts, Saul did preach at Jerusalem to the Hellenists, probably in their synagogues. He also found among the moderate Hellenistic Jewish Christians a friend, Barnabas, who evidently had not been a member of the group associated with Stephen but by his knowledge of Greek and of Gentile ways was able to understand the Hellenistic members of the young church. Barnabas believed in the genuineness of Saul's conversion and vouched for him with the apostles. This contact with the Jerusalem leaders was of immense importance for Saul's future work; he could not have standing in the church, even in the Hellenistic wing of it, if the Jerusalem leaders refused to recognize him.[26]

After a brief stay in Jerusalem and some unfruitful attempts to make converts among the Hellenistic Jews, danger to his life and the insistence of the harassed leaders of the church forced Saul to leave (Acts 9:30). But as he went to Caesarea and sailed back to his native Tarsus, he at least was known to the leading apostles and they recognized the genuineness of his conversion. That he preached in Tarsus anyone who understands his active nature will readily assume.

SUMMARY AND PRELUDE TO EXPANSION

With Saul's departure from Jerusalem, Luke brings the second section of The Acts to a close. From chs. 6:8 to 9:31 the Hellenistic Christians dominate the scene in the developing church. Stephen, Philip, and Saul break new paths of thought and action, the gospel spreads to Samaria and the coastal plain of Palestine, and its presence in Damascus

---

[26] See Wilfred L. Knox, *St. Paul and the Church of Jerusalem* (Cambridge, University Press, 1925).

is disclosed. Thus far the preaching has been to Jews, except in the case of the God-fearing Ethiopian eunuch (ch. 8:26–40). The next stage will offer the gospel to Gentiles who without previous connection with the synagogue come directly into the church from paganism. This will result from a cautious advance by Peter and a bolder advance by unnamed Hellenistic Jewish Christians. In the meantime things will be briefly quieter in Palestine; "the church throughout all Judea and Galilee and Samaria had peace and was built up" (ch. 9:31).

But this quiet was at a cost. Only because the Hellenistic wing of the Jerusalem church had been ejected from that city by persecution did the church there and in neighboring places have peace. It was by fitting into the conservative Jewish setting and taking a lagging role in the expanding push of the church that the Jerusalem church obtained temporary quiet. This left the future expansion of the church and its theological development in the hands of those driven from the city. Key leaders in Jerusalem were to understand the necessity of the expansion and approve it as truly Christian, but the actual expanding ministry was to be almost entirely in the hands of others than the Twelve.

PETER'S ITINERANT MINISTRY

Yet the special role of Peter as a bridge between the Twelve and the Hellenistic Jewish Christians must not be overlooked. When he and John went to Samaria to check on the work of Philip there, he preached "to many villages of the Samaritans" (Acts 8:25). This violated Jewish feelings; as a rule, "Jews have no dealings with Samaritans" (John 4:9), and Peter's action showed a spirit open to new horizons. Later he went down to Lydda, where "saints," that is, disciples, were found,[27] and he healed a man named Aeneas (Acts 9:32–35). The name suggests a Greek-speaking Jew; Peter must have been able to speak not only Aramaic but also Greek—to some extent at least—in order to do all that The Acts says he did. From Lydda, Peter went on to Joppa, a city essentially Jewish, and stayed with a man named Simon, whose trade, that of a tanner, was considered unclean by Jewish standards.[28]

Peter, thus, like his Master, went to Jews of doubtful repute, regard-

---

[27] The word "saints," used of Christians rather often in the New Testament, does not refer to the unusual moral excellence of the Christians. Basically the word *hagioi* means "persons consecrated to God." As such, they are committed to obey his will, but the religious meaning of persons consecrated to God is primary.

[28] *The Beginnings of Christianity,* Vol. IV, p. 111: "The work of a tanner was 'defiling' according to Jewish law." It seems most unlikely that Peter would have stayed with a non-Christian, so Simon the tanner must have been a disciple.

less of ceremonial rules. As noted above, Philip had preached in this region and Peter could conceivably have been checking on Philip's work, especially if Peter was dealing with Greek-speaking Jews. But the narrative of The Acts gives no hint that the previous preaching of Philip in the coastal region prompted Peter's visit to that area.

PETER AND CORNELIUS

More important for the expansion of the church was Peter's contact with the household of Cornelius at Caesarea. Acts 10:1 to 11:18 tells the story twice. This is Luke's literary way of saying that the event was of great importance in the development of the church.

Cornelius was a Roman centurion, a Gentile holding a responsible place in the Roman military system. He was an officer of the Italian Cohort stationed at Caesarea under the Roman governor, who had his residence in that city.[29] In calling Cornelius "a devout man" Luke means that he was a Gentile who, though he had not become a full proselyte to the Jewish faith, was connected with the synagogue and observed some Jewish worship practices and rules.[30]

Luke's method of bringing Peter and Cornelius together by complementary twin versions—a method used already in Acts 9:10–12 to bring the newly converted Saul into contact with the disciples at Damascus—is used to indicate that Peter's step in preaching to uncircumcised Gentiles was reluctantly taken but was divinely prompted and so should be accepted as proper by all Christians. Cornelius is led to send for Peter, who was still at Joppa and of whom Cornelius had heard.

Peter's mind was perhaps already uneasy about staying with a Jewish tanner, whose very trade was thought to be unclean. It may have become still more uneasy when he was asked to enter a Gentile home, even though it was the home of a "devout" Gentile who had connections with the synagogue. But his vision led him to recognize that contrary to inherited ceremonial laws he must not regard any food as unclean. Did he actually have this vision after the invitation to visit Cornelius came? In any case the vision was an answer to his misgivings and in effect a command to forget them and cross lines that he otherwise would not have crossed. He could go to the home of an uncircumcised Gentile and eat with him and his family.

When Peter, in response to the invitation of Cornelius, went from

---

[29] On the Italian Cohort and Cornelius, see T. R. S. Broughton, "The Roman Army," in *The Beginnings of Christianity*, Vol. V, pp. 427–445, especially pp. 441–443.
[30] See note 21 above.

Joppa to Caesarea to see the centurion, he took with him "some of the brethren from Joppa" (Acts 10:23). Later he took them (six in number) with him to Jerusalem (ch. 11:12). This shows that from the start of his trip to Caesarea he expected criticism from the Jerusalem church. But he went; he put his prestige as leader and spokesman of the Twelve back of a development that was to lead far beyond what he or the Twelve were ready personally to undertake.

Luke does not explain what Cornelius knew of Peter before this occasion. In The Acts all such knowledge comes through the vision, which constitutes a divine direction. But the real attention focuses on Peter's preaching. In the presence of Cornelius, his entire household, and his kinsmen and friends, Peter gives a typical summary of the common gospel of the early church (ch. 10:34–43): In fulfillment of God's promises to Israel and following directly upon John the Baptist's ministry, Jesus of Nazareth, anointed by God with the Holy Spirit and so with power, carried on his ministry. He did good and healed, as the apostles can witness, in Palestine and especially at Jerusalem. The Jews put him to death, but God raised him up and he appeared to chosen witnesses. They have the divinely given task, committed to them by Christ, to preach to the people (the Jews). Jesus is to judge all men; his work is attested by the prophecies of the Scripture now seen to be fulfilled in him; and forgiveness of sins, man's urgent need, is available through faith in him.[31]

This was the common Christian message, but this time the results were startling (Acts 10:44–48). These listeners were Gentiles. As Peter was finishing his message (Luke does not mean that his summary is fragmentary and that something essential has been omitted), the Holy Spirit seized the hearers. In eager excitement and almost delirious joy they spoke with tongues and praised God, thus indicating that they had accepted the message, believed in Christ, and received the Holy Spirit. The Jewish Christians who had come with Peter were amazed. They had considered the new faith a message for the people of Israel; they had not expected Gentiles to accept it and enter the church without entering Judaism first. But Peter reasoned that the Holy Spirit had directed him what to do. These people had the clear signs of the Spirit's presence and power in their lives; it was obviously God's will that they should be received into the church and be baptized. So he gave directions for their baptism (Acts 10:48).

When he returned to Jerusalem, expecting to be challenged for his

31 Martin Dibelius, "The Conversion of Cornelius," in *Studies in the Acts of the Apostles,* pp. 109–122, ascribes the speech and much of the narrative to Luke.

action and so taking with him six disciples from Joppa who had witnessed the scene at Caesarea, "the circumcision party" in that church rebuked him for eating with uncircumcised Gentiles (Acts 11:2 f.).[32] They attacked not his baptism of Gentiles but his accepting them into table fellowship without requiring them to be circumcised. Gentiles, they held, were to be accepted into Judaism and so into the church only if they were willing to be circumcised and keep the Mosaic law.

Peter did not defend himself by a systematic theological argument. Instead, he told his story (Acts 11:4–17). This is characteristic of the Biblical method; its truth is embodied mainly in history, and is understood by understanding what God was doing in the history. These Gentiles who heard the gospel believed and received the Holy Spirit before baptism and without the issue of circumcision being raised. For Peter this meant that God did not require circumcision of these devout Gentiles; it was mandatory, rather, to follow the guidance thus given by the Spirit, baptize the Gentiles, and regard them as true disciples.

In view of the strong convictions of Jews about the obligation to keep the Mosaic law, it was greatly to the credit of the Jerusalem church that they accepted Peter's story as settling the basic issue: Gentiles could enter the church without keeping the Jewish law; they were full and equal members; to enter the church they did not have to become Jews first or keep the food laws obligatory in Judaism (Acts 11:18).[33]

THE JEWISH-GENTILE CHURCH AT ANTIOCH

The approval of Peter's step was an epoch-making decision. In principle it laid the foundation for the universal church and for the mission of Paul. But it was a decision not immediately followed up by those who then approved it, and it was made concerning Gentiles already in active touch with the synagogue. The Jerusalem church did not at once organize a general mission to the Gentiles. That was left for fugitives who earlier had been associated with the Seven in Jerusalem. The work of Philip has been told. In addition, other Hellenistic Jewish Christians, their names not known, took up the preaching and independently were led to undertake a wider work.

Some of these fugitives went to Phoenicia, the region of Tyre and

---

[32] "The circumcision party" refers not to all Jewish members of the church but to those among them who insisted that only circumcised persons who accepted the Mosaic law could become Christians. This issue came to a decision in a conference at Jerusalem (Acts, ch.15; Gal. 2:1–10). It will be studied later.

[33] For a critical study of "The Conversion of Cornelius" and the "sermon" in ch. 10:34–43, see Martin Dibelius, *Studies in the Acts of the Apostles*, pp. 109–122.

Sidon; to Cyprus, where Barnabas had lived earlier; and to Antioch in Syria, where according to Acts 6:5, Nicolaus, one of the Seven, had lived (ch. 11:19). In all these places Jews were numerous and the fugitives preached to them. Of the results in Phoenicia and Cyprus we learn nothing except that later there were disciples in Phoenicia (chs. 21:4; 27:3). It would be interesting to know what success the preachers had in Cyprus, but when later Barnabas and Saul begin their missionary travel by going to Cyprus to preach, nothing is said of disciples already there (ch. 13:4–12). The one interest of The Acts at this stage is the new development in Antioch. Even there the fugitives did nothing new at first. They preached to fellow Jews. But then some of their number took the new step of preaching to Gentiles who had had no previous connection with the synagogue (ch. 11:20 f.).[34]

In this respect their action went beyond what Philip and Peter had done; Gentiles in touch with the synagogue and observing some Jewish practices were not so clearly outside the Jewish circle as were these Gentiles who now accepted the gospel at Antioch. The latter, it is implied, received the Holy Spirit and became full members of the Antioch church without observing the Jewish ceremonial law. They entered the church by repentance and faith; by the gift of the Spirit they were attested as fully Christian; evidently neither the Jewish members of the Antioch church nor the fugitive members of the Stephen group from Jerusalem raised any doubt as to their Christian status.

This was a new situation. When Philip preached to the Samaritans, he preached to people who accepted and practiced the Mosaic law. When Peter preached to Cornelius and his household and friends, the hearers were persons who had a loose connection with the synagogue and observed some practices of Judaism. But now the question was put in its extreme form. Do Gentiles with no Jewish background or connections have a place in the church without having to observe any Jewish practices as a prerequisite? The Jerusalem church naturally was concerned about the validity of this development. What is surprising is that instead of sending Peter or some other of the twelve apostles, they sent Barnabas as a one-man committee to investigate the validity of thus accepting Gentiles into the church (Acts 11:22). This was a tribute to Barnabas, and it shows that he stood closer to the Twelve than had the Seven.

---

[34] The Greek text of Acts 11:20 is uncertain. Some ancient manuscripts read "Hellenes" (*Hellēnas*); others read "Hellenists" (*Hellēnistas*). Probably "Hellenes," meaning pagan Gentiles of Greek speech and culture, is the correct reading. See note 6 of this chapter.

When he reached Antioch, he "saw the grace of God"; that is, he saw that these Gentiles were really converted (v. 23). He not only approved what had been done, but stayed on to help in this new work. Evidently he saw great possibilities at Antioch. To obtain additional help he went to Tarsus, where Saul, whom he had earlier sponsored in Jerusalem (ch. 9:27), was living and working. He induced Saul to move to Antioch and join him in presenting the gospel to both Jews and Gentiles.[35] For a year the two continued that work (ch. 11:23–26).

The Disciples Called Christians

This acceptance of Gentiles into the church led to a new name for the group of disciples. Up to this time the group had lived in the total framework of Judaism, and the disciples insisted that they represented the true Judaism and the fulfillment of God's promises to his people Israel. (The church never gave up that claim.) They were called disciples or believers, but did not feel at first the need of a separate name. Now, however, Gentiles and Jews were found together in one fellowship, separate from the synagogue. They could not be called Jews and treated as part of the synagogue. So a new name arose; the disciples began to be called Christians (Acts 11:26).

It is often said that the disciples were given this name by outsiders as a term of contempt or reproach, because they talked so much of Christ. Perhaps so, but it could have come from the disciples themselves, for it was an apt name which identified the group by their common loyalty to Jesus as the Christ sent by God. There is no evidence, however, that the name was widely used in the apostolic age; it occurs again only in Acts 26:28; I Peter 4:16.[36] The main point is that it appeared just when the church had taken a new step of accepting Jews and Gentiles into the one church on an equal basis.

The background was now present for a general mission to the world. It was soon to come. But first some developments in Jerusalem must be noted which made it more certain than ever that the church there was not to be the permanent center.

Continued Ties with Jerusalem

This removal of the center of the expanding church from Jerusalem was gradual and did not isolate the Jerusalem church and its leaders

---

35 Did he know that Paul was already doing a similar work in Tarsus? Acts 22:17–21; 26:16–23; and Gal. 1:16 would so suggest.

36 It is interesting that in the first half of the second century the name Christian, which originated at Antioch in Syria, is used freely by one writer, Ignatius of Antioch.

from the expanding church. Barnabas, the central figure of the leaders
at Antioch, was trusted by the Jerusalem church, to which he was bound
by strong ties of loyalty. Peter, who had begun to exercise an itinerant
ministry, regarded Jerusalem as the center of the church. The entire
church knew that the gospel had been preached at Jerusalem at the
beginning of the apostolic age and had moved out mainly from there.
There were differences between the Twelve and the fugitives related to
the Seven, but the churches that owed their existence to the fugitives
forced to flee after Stephen's death still felt a bond with Jerusalem.

Famine Relief from Antioch

This bond found expression when a famine made still harder the
already difficult economic situation of the disciples in Palestine (Acts
11:27–30).[87] The announcement of impending famine came from Agabus, one of a group of (itinerant?) prophets who came to Antioch from
Jerusalem. The role of these particular prophets in the life of the Jerusalem church is not known; they are known only through their appearance at Antioch.[88] Possibly their coming indicates their kinship with
the fugitives who founded the Antioch church. In any case, their coming
continued the ties of that church with Jerusalem.

When Agabus predicted extreme want due to the impending famine,
the Christians at Antioch sent a relief fund to Jerusalem. That they sent
Barnabas as the chief messenger of mercy is not surprising; the Jerusalem church had sent him to Antioch and he would be welcomed by his
old friends. That they also sent Saul is not so natural, but it indicates
his growing recognition, and expresses both his real concern for the
welfare of his fellow Christians at Jerusalem and his deep desire that
the Antioch Christians should not lose touch with the mother church.

The relief was sent to the elders at Jerusalem. This marks their first
appearance in The Acts and suggests that the Twelve were no longer
completely dominant there. James the brother of Jesus was already
prominent there when Saul visited Jerusalem some three years after conversion (Gal. 1:19), and he was destined to play a still more prominent
role. Peter had begun to itinerate in Palestine and was to expand this
kind of leadership.

---

[87] The death of Herod Agrippa I (Acts 12:20–23) is usually dated in A.D. 44. The
famine foreseen in Acts 11:28 apparently gripped Palestine in A.D. 45 or 46. See
Kirsopp Lake, "The Chronology of Acts," in *The Beginnings of Christianity*, Vol. V,
pp. 445–474, especially pp. 452–455.

[88] Prophets were prominent at Antioch (Acts 13:1) and in Paul's churches (I Cor. 12:28;
14:1–5, 19, 29; Eph. 4:11).

JAMES KILLED AND PETER IMPRISONED

The circle of the Twelve was broken by another crisis. Herod Agrippa I had been made king of all Palestine in A.D. 41. For reasons hard to discern, though prompting by Jews hostile to the church was no doubt the immediate cause, he decided to attack the leadership of the church. His first victim was James the son of Zebedee, whom he seized and killed with the sword (Acts 12:1 f.).[39] This may mean that James was beheaded, as John the Baptist had been by Agrippa's father, Herod Antipas (Mark 6:17–29). No personal leadership by James is reported in The Acts, but Agrippa would hardly have seized and executed him unless by active leadership he had distinguished himself and antagonized Jewish leaders. When Agrippa's brutal act received Jewish approval, he next arrested Peter (Acts 12:3 f.). This indicates that James and Peter had both a willingness to accept Gentiles into the church and a vigor of leadership that made them appear to Jewish leaders as the most dangerous Christian leaders.

The situation was critical for the church in Jerusalem. First the Seven and the disciples who shared their outlook had been expelled. Now the Twelve, untouched by the earlier persecution (Acts 8:1), were threatened; the inner trio, doubtless the chief source of strength among the Twelve, was being broken up. The church took to prayer; the group gathered in the home of Mary the mother of John Mark was probably not the only group thus occupied that night when through mysterious means, perhaps including the intervention of Jews who did not share the fierce determination of Agrippa and Jewish leaders to crush the church, Peter escaped from prison (ch. 12:5–11).[40] He knew where to find at least part of the disciples; he went to the home of Mary the mother of Mark, where he told his story. He himself felt that he must leave to avoid a second arrest by Agrippa, so he directed that his story be told to James the brother of Jesus and "to the brethren," that is, the rest of the Twelve or possibly the other brothers of Jesus, who with James had come to prominence in leadership at Jerusalem. From this point on, and possibly for some time previously, James was the actual head of the Jerusalem church (Acts 12:12–17).

PETER LEAVES JERUSALEM

When Peter left the house of Mary the mother of John Mark he "went to another place" (Acts 12:17). He left that house and went else-

---

39 Some scholars, using Mark 10:39 as a clue, have suggested that James's brother John was executed at the same time, but of this The Acts knows nothing.

40 Was the "angel" of Acts 12:7 a secret disciple or friend who was able to clear the way for escape? This is only a possibility and not an established fact.

where, but it is not clear whether he went to some hiding place in Jerusalem or—more likely—left Jerusalem and perhaps even Palestine to avoid arrest. He later went to Antioch in Syria (Gal. 2:11), may have visited Corinth (cf. I Cor. 1:12), and toward the end of his life probably went to Rome.[41] But inasmuch as Paul clearly states that Peter led the church's mission to the Jews (Gal. 2:7), Peter did not leave Jerusalem at the time of Acts 12:17 to take up a world mission among all races. His essential work had been and continued to be among the Jews, and so at the end of the third of the six divisions of The Acts (chs. 9:32 to 12:24) he drops out of the story, for at this point the story of the wide-ranging Gentile mission is about to begin.

Peter's departure from active leadership in Jerusalem left the dominant role there to James the brother of Jesus. He had been in the Jerusalem church from the first (Acts 1:14), and was already prominent there three years after Saul's conversion (Gal. 1:19). Perhaps he was the leading figure there even before Peter "went to another place" (Acts 12:17). Certainly after Peter's departure James was active as the real leader. Probably his brothers (cf. Mark 6:3) were with him and helped him. First Corinthians 9:5 hints that on occasion these brothers of Jesus traveled about the church, undoubtedly with special concern for Jewish Christians or to take messages from James, the oldest and most influential brother, who apparently traveled much less. Jerusalem still felt responsible for the larger church, and James as the effective head at Jerusalem kept in touch with what went on in the various church centers. His role as presiding officer at the council in Acts, ch. 15, and his prominence in the Jerusalem church at the time of Paul's last visit (Acts 21:18) will be noted later.

The point of immediate interest is the growing leadership of James the brother of Jesus in Jerusalem. After James the son of Zebedee was martyred and Peter departed for itinerating ministries, there was a lessening of the control of the Twelve in that city. This development is paralleled by the increase in importance of other Christian centers, particularly Antioch. From Antioch the expanding mission was to move out and Paul was ready to become its leading figure.

[41] See Oscar Cullmann, *Peter: Disciple, Apostle, Martyr*, pp. 41–57, 71–157.

Part Four

PAUL THE APOSTLE TO GENTILES

Chapter 9

PAUL: ORIGIN, CONVERSION, EARLY MINISTRY

MANY Jewish Christians of Hellenistic background shared in the church's active outreach into the Greco-Roman world, but Paul did the most to extend that outreach and state the gospel in world terms. His early role in that outreach was noted in Chapter 8. But as one of the greatest figures in the mission and thinking of the church he deserves detailed attention.

FAMILY BACKGROUND AND EARLY YEARS

Of Paul's family background and early years we know little. He was born of Jewish parents and proud to be of the tribe of Benjamin (Phil. 3:5). Acts 22:3 says he was born at Tarsus in Cilicia, and this is more likely than later tradition that he was born while his family lived at Gischala in Galilee.[1] His family was a loyal and strict Jewish family; his father was a Pharisee, and Paul followed his father's Pharisaic commitment (Acts 23:6). His family had standing in Tarsus. His father, as Acts 21:39 suggests, was a citizen of that city; he was also a citizen of Rome and so Paul was by birth a Roman citizen (Acts 22:28). How the father acquired this citizenship is not told. Perhaps he had been taken captive in war by the Romans and then freed; freedom thus given carried with it citizenship.[2]

From birth Paul had both the Greco-Roman name Paul (Paulus), which he uses in all his letters, and the Hebrew name Saul, by which he is known in The Acts until ch. 13:9. It has been thought that he adopted the name Paul only after he had converted the Roman proconsul Sergius Paulus in Cyprus (Acts 13:7). But it was not unusual for a Hellenistic Jew to have both a Hellenistic and a Jewish name, and Paul as a Roman citizen almost certainly had both.

[1] See Jerome, *Lives of Illustrious Men*, Ch. 5.
[2] On Roman citizenship, see Henry J. Cadbury, *The Book of Acts in History*, pp. 65–82.

199

As the son of a Pharisee, Saul was taught the Jewish law, including the oral tradition. His boyhood home Tarsus was "no mean city" (Acts 21:39).[3] Its position in Cilicia on the Cydnus River made it prominent in that region. Its "university" life and Stoic philosophers made it widely and favorably known for its Hellenistic culture. Saul could have had training in Greek literature and philosophy and could have participated in Hellenistic religions, including the worship of the prominent vegetation god Sandan.

But Saul was no detached seeker, studying all streams of thought and all religious faiths with an open mind. He was a committed Jew, trained in the ancestral faith as it was understood among the Pharisees. The focal center of his thought and imagination was Jerusalem, where he went when old enough to pursue advanced studies. In Jerusalem lived a married sister who had a son (cf. Acts 23:16). Studying under the famous rabbi Gamaliel (Acts 22:3),[4] he seemed on the way to distinction as a scholar and leader; he could say that he was outstanding among his generation in zeal and knowledge of ancestral traditions (Gal. 1:14). By disposition he would give full support to the cause he espoused; he was not made for laggard and limited loyalty.

HOSTILITY TO THE CHURCH

Nor could Saul think of opponents with indifference or mild curiosity. When he encountered disciples of Jesus, he recognized their challenge to his Pharisaic faith and gave instant resistance. He probably met the disciples mainly in the Greek-speaking synagogues (cf. Acts 6:9). He could speak Greek, Hebrew, and Aramaic, but Greek was more natural to him as a native of Tarsus, and he would naturally worship more often in a Greek-speaking synagogue. As we have indicated in Chapter 8, these Greek-speaking synagogues witnessed the sharpest expression of the newness of the Christian faith and its clearest challenge to ancestral Jewish customs.

Saul could not hear the gospel message without vocal opposition; he debated with the disciples he met, among them probably Stephen. That he was present and approved when Stephen was seized, heard, and

---

[3] On Tarsus, see W. M. Ramsay, *The Cities of St. Paul: Their Influence on His Life and Thought* (London, Hodder & Stoughton, 1908), pp. 85–244; Hans Böhlig, *Die geisteskultur von Tarsos im augusteischen Zeitalter* (Göttingen, Vandenhoeck & Ruprecht, 1913).

[4] On Gamaliel, see Emil Schürer, *A History of the Jewish People in the Time of Jesus Christ*, Eng. tr. by Sophia Taylor and Peter Christie (Charles Scribner's Sons, n.d.), Second Division, Vol. I, pp. 363–365.

executed was to be expected (Acts 7:58; 8:1). Luke does not ascribe to Saul a leading role in the agitation that led to Stephen's death. But he was more than a mere onlooker during the rising hostility against Stephen, and once that disciple had been stoned, Saul became the spearhead of the persecution. To this stage of his life he later referred with deep regret (I Cor. 15:9).

The persecution, aimed mainly at the Greek-speaking disciples allied with Stephen, led them to scatter to Judea, Samaria, Phoenicia, Cyprus, Antioch in Syria, and possibly Damascus, Egypt, and Cyrene (Acts 8:1; 11:19; cf. 9:10, 19?; 11:20?). It struck at the leaders of this group and also at other men and at the women in it (Acts 8:4). Quite likely its fury struck some Aramaic-speaking disciples as well. But it did not strike the Twelve. This shows that the fiery opponents of the Seven regarded the Twelve as less extreme and dangerous in their views (Acts 8:1).[5]

Why did Saul so bitterly oppose the young Christian movement, especially in the form represented by Stephen? To judge by his letters, his aim was not so much to defend the sanctity of the Temple as to vindicate the law and suppress what he considered blasphemous claims for Jesus. Jesus had made sharp criticisms not merely of oral traditions, which to the Pharisee Saul were an integral part of the law, but also of aspects of the written Mosaic law itself. His criticisms had evidently been echoed by Stephen and his group, and Saul sensed that Jesus was being put in the place of authority which in his view belonged to the law. This to Saul was blasphemous; Jesus had died a death which the law itself branded with a divine curse (Deut. 21:23), yet the disciples were giving Jesus honor which to say the least bordered on that due to God. Moreover, Saul rejected the disciples' witness to the resurrection of Jesus.

How far a suppressed sense of failure goaded Saul in his obedience to the law is hard to say. Romans 7:7 ff. is widely taken as his later witness to a partially suppressed sense of guilt,[6] which would go far to explain the fury of his persecution of the disciples. But Phil. 3:6 shows that Saul was outwardly loyal to the law (cf. also Gal. 1:14), and his integrity was generally recognized (Acts 26:5), so we cannot say that he already clearly saw the law's inability to meet his spiritual needs. It is hard to believe, however, that his sudden conversion, with its deep answer to his needs and its rushing release of pent-up feelings, did not

[5] Acts 8:1 indicates that not all the scattered disciples left Palestine. Probably most did not.

[6] On Rom. 7:7 ff., see Werner Georg Kümmel, *Römer 7 und die Bekehrung des Paulus* (Leipzig, J. C. Hinrichs, 1929); and for a Jewish view, H. J. Schoeps, *Paul*, Eng. tr. by Harold Knight (The Westminster Press, 1961), pp. 175, 191 f., 206.

solve an inner crisis, even if Saul had been fairly successful in suppressing his emotional conflict. That the fidelity of Stephen had shaken his confidence may also be a factor (Acts 7:59 f.).

Clearly, however, Saul did not realize that he was moving toward a sudden conversion experience. He was driven with the determination to stamp out the new faith, which threatened the Judaism he professed and the Pharisaism he so actively defended. He either knew that the new faith had for some time taken root in Damascus[7] or learned that fleeing friends of the Seven had fled there. Possibly both things were true and moved him to try to wipe out the band of disciples in Damascus. How far the high priest in Jerusalem could authorize Saul to arrest disciples in Damascus and deport them to Jerusalem for trial is not clear. The high priest and the Sanhedrin had authority over Palestine in religious matters and even in some civil concerns, and possibly the high priest could exercise some authority over the synagogue and Jews in Damascus. Damascus, a city of the Decapolis, was Greco-Roman in general administration, and groups outside of the Greco-Roman life setting might have had special arrangements to keep their group in order. The faith of the disciples was regarded as an aspect of Judaism and possibly was subject to Jewish supervision.

SUDDEN CONVERSION

As Saul drew near to Damascus, the risen Christ confronted him and Saul suddenly became committed to the faith he had tried to stamp out.[8] The date of this momentous event is uncertain; it is usually dated not earlier than A.D. 31 or later than A.D. 36. In any case, it occurred only a few years after the death and resurrection of Jesus. The story is told three times in The Acts because of its outstanding importance (chs. 9:1–19; 22:1–21; 26:2–23). The three accounts agree in essentials, but vary in details—for example, as to how far Saul's companions, who had come with him to aid in persecuting the disciples, saw and heard what occurred (cf. Acts 9:7; 22:9). The variations do not mean that Luke knew different traditions as to what took place; they are only his literary variations; they show that he did not regard agreement in detail as important.

Only Saul experienced the coming and challenge of Christ. The impression of a blinding light of which The Acts speaks has a reflection

---

[7] Possibly but not certainly from Galilee.
[8] On the conversion of Saul, see James S. Stewart, *A Man in Christ*, Ch. 3; Johannes Munck, *Paul and the Salvation of Mankind*, Ch. 1; H. J. Schoeps, *Paul*, pp. 53–55.

in words of Paul's letters (cf. II Cor. 4:6); it meant the divine presence. Jesus Christ was present and recognized as more than a teacher and prophet; he was the Christ, the Lord, the Son (Acts 9: 5, 20, 22). The recognition of his presence and the acceptance of his claim went together. Saul was converted. Whether the conversion included the immediate awareness that his main ministry was to be to the Gentiles is not certain (cf. Acts 9:15; 22:15, 21; 26:17). But beyond doubt Saul, once he had accepted the Lordship of Christ, could not withhold his active service.

What the disciple-hating companions of Saul thought of his sudden conversion we are not told; they probably were mystified and disgusted. But they fade from the story at once, and Luke moves quickly to the fact that through an otherwise unknown Ananias the disciples at Damascus made contact with the shattered persecutor and accepted him into the group that he had come to destroy (Acts 9:10–19). Saul was baptized in the name of the Jesus whom he previously had hated and denounced as the chief threat to Israel.

Did he then preach at once in the synagogues of Damascus, as Acts 9:20–22 says? He himself says later that he went to Arabia immediately after his conversion (Gal. 1:17). He said this to show that he did not hurry to Jerusalem to get the approval of the Twelve, but at once took up an independent attitude. His words, however, exclude an immediate preaching ministry at Damascus. The Arabia of Gal. 1:17 was the region south and east of Damascus. It has been suggested that Saul traveled far south to Mt. Sinai, to think out there the relation of his newly found faith in Christ to the Mosaic law given on Mt. Sinai. The less romantic answer is better; he went briefly into the desertlike region south and southeast of Damascus to rethink his faith.[9]

PREACHING IN DAMASCUS

But Saul was not one to stay long in retirement. He soon "returned to Damascus" (Gal. 1:17), a statement which shows that his conversion had occurred near Damascus, as Acts 9:3 says. On his return he began to preach, and most of the three years he spent in that region were spent in such preaching (Gal. 1:18; cf. Acts 9:20–23). By ancient reckoning, this period could have been much less than three full years, since the fragment of a year at each end of a period would be reckoned as a year. Saul boldly testified that Jesus was the Christ and the Son of God.

[9] On the meaning of "Arabia," see Arndt and Gingrich, *Greek-English Lexicon*, p. 103, *sub voce*.

This latter title shows that what he had fought in Stephen's group and what he had accepted at conversion was a high Christology.

The Damascus Jews as a group no doubt were hostile to the disciples of Jesus, but this hostility must have been multiplied many times when they heard the renegade Saul. They plotted to kill him to break the influence and growth of the group of disciples. But he fled by night and escaped, though he later regarded this flight as a humiliating experience (Acts 9:23–25; II Cor. 11:32 f.). At that time Aretas IV, king of the Nabateans (9 B.C. to A.D. 40), had some control over Damascus or at least the surrounding region. The Jews, to prevent Saul's escape from the city, enlisted the aid of officials of Aretas. But some of Saul's converts let him down in a basket from a window in the city wall; thus he escaped those who were watching the city gates to capture him, and made his way to Jerusalem.[10]

BRIEF VISIT TO JERUSALEM

Why did Saul go to Jerusalem, where danger would be as great as at Damascus? He himself gives both a negative and a positive answer (Gal. 1:18–21; cf. Acts 9:26–30). It was not because he was dependent on the Twelve to approve and authorize his ministry; had he depended on them to attest his conversion and appoint him a preacher, he would have hastened to Jerusalem immediately after conversion; since he waited three years, that could not have been his purpose. He went there, he says, to meet Peter, and of the other Jerusalem leaders he saw only James.[11] He stayed there only fifteen days. This shows that he did not go there to be trained, ordained, and have the Twelve plan his life. His going to Jerusalem showed that in fact his future role depended on contacts with the Jerusalem church and its apostolic leaders, but he insisted that the risen Christ appointed him to his ministry and that his apostleship thus was not given him from men or even mediated through men (Gal. 1:1); he was directly commissioned by the risen Christ.

The limited purpose of his visit, the limited time spent in Jerusalem, and the fact that later he was unknown by sight to the churches in Judea

10 On Aretas, cf. II Cor. 11:32 f.; Josephus, *Ant.* XVII.10.9; XVIII.5.1; Schürer, *A History of the Jewish People*, First Division, Vol. II, pp. 356–359. Either Aretas was temporarily in control of Damascus, and had his appointee in charge of it, or he controlled the country around the city and so presumably could catch a person fleeing from the city. The former view is implied in II Cor. 11:32.

11 There is no reason to doubt that Barnabas vouched for Saul at Jerusalem, as Acts 9:27 says. This prepared the way for his later invitation to Saul to help at Antioch (ch. 11:25 f.). It shows a somewhat more inclusive spirit in Barnabas than was present in many Jerusalem disciples.

(Gal. 1:22) show that Acts 9:26–30, which speaks as though Saul carried on for some time a public ministry in Jerusalem, cannot be accepted as it stands. His preaching there must have been brief and to a limited audience. The best argument that The Acts has some basis for saying that Saul preached at Jerusalem on this visit is Rom. 15:19, which clearly indicates that Paul had preached in Jerusalem.[12] This is best taken of preaching on his first visit after his conversion, and his brief and limited ministry aroused the Jews to fury when they saw him return to the Holy City to preach the faith he had sworn to exterminate. That he preached in Hellenistic synagogues reminded them that the work of Stephen was being continued just where it had seemingly been stamped out when the Hellenistic Jewish Christians had fled from Jerusalem.

Such preaching by Saul was a testimony to his courage and his determination to make up for the unjustified persecution he had led. The situation was ripe for another turbulent outbreak. The Jerusalem leaders of the church induced Saul to leave; they sent an escort with him to Caesarea, where he took ship to his native Tarsus. Then, it is said, perhaps with unintended humor, that the Palestinian church had peace (Acts 9:31, the summary that closes the second of the six main divisions of Acts). With Saul gone, the church did not seem so dangerous; the determination to stamp it out was less urgent.

A Leader at Antioch in Syria

For an undefined period, Saul lived in Tarsus. Of that period little is known, but both Acts 15:41 and Gal. 1:21–24 indicate that he spent the period in active preaching in and around Tarsus, and that the news of his effectiveness traveled back to Palestine. When Barnabas needed help at Antioch in Syria, he knew where to find a vigorous associate (Acts 11:25). Barnabas had sponsored Saul at Jerusalem (Acts 9:27), and evidently had kept in touch with him; had he not known that Saul was effectively active in Tarsus, he would not have thought him the man needed in Antioch.

How long there had been a church at Antioch before Saul came there to assist Barnabas is not clear.[13] The Jerusalem persecution that had led the Stephen group to scatter had occurred several years before (Acts 8:1); after it Saul had spent the better part of three years in Damascus

---

12 As recognized by C. K. Barrett, *A Commentary on the Epistle to the Romans* (Harper & Brothers, 1958), p. 276.

13 On Antioch and the church there, see Glanville Downey, *A History of Antioch in Syria*. On the Jewish group there, see Carl H. Kraeling, "The Jewish Community at Antioch," *JBL*, Vol. LI (1932), pp. 130–160.

and Arabia, had gone to Jerusalem, and then had spent some time in Tarsus. The church at Antioch thus must have been founded some years before Saul came there to help Barnabas. The impression given by Acts 11:19-26, that Barnabas went to Antioch immediately after that church was founded and that Saul went there shortly after Barnabas began his work there, is misleading. Saul's reference to his three years in Arabia and Damascus shows that.

So another view, that the Antioch church was founded in two stages, may be suggested. The first wave of fugitives from Jerusalem went to Phoenicia, Cyprus, and Antioch, and preached only to Jews (Acts 11: 19). This spread the gospel widely, but was not the epoch-making step. Later, others of the fugitives, "men of Cyprus and Cyrene,"[14] came to Antioch and preached also to Greeks, i.e., Gentiles (Acts 11:20). This first general public preaching to Gentiles was due not to Peter or Paul or Barnabas but to unnamed Greek-speaking Jewish Christians connected with the Stephen group and exiled from Jerusalem by persecution.

This development aroused the interest and suspicion of the Jerusalem church, and they sent Barnabas to Antioch to see whether this new development was legitimate. When Barnabas had observed the life of this church at Antioch and become convinced that it was a genuine development of the Christian mission, he saw a need for Saul. He evidently knew that Saul would approve such preaching to Gentiles; indeed, he may have known that Saul was already doing such preaching in Tarsus.

The numerous conversions of Gentiles at Antioch and their fellowship with Jewish converts created a new situation, in which the disciples were not clearly included within the bounds of Judaism. Yet, since the disciples evidently formed one group and included Jewish converts, the Antioch church was not completely separate from Judaism. Its ties with Jerusalem show this, as does its acceptance of the leadership of Barnabas, who was sent from Jerusalem.

Probably some of the converted Gentiles had had previous association with the synagogue. Such Gentiles, to make possible such association, would have observed some such regulations as the "precepts of Noah," a small number of practices that would enable conscientious Jews to associate with devout Gentiles without being offended.[15] In doing this,

---

14 Acts 11:19 f. may be taken to mean that all these fugitives arrived in Antioch at one time. But the arrival and preaching of the "men of Cyprus and Cyrene" seem to me to be dated later than the arrival and preaching of the men mentioned in v. 19.
15 Cf. the seven items in G. F. Moore, *Judaism*, Vol. I, p. 274: "1. Prohibition of the worship of other gods; 2. Blaspheming the name of God; 3. Cursing judges; 4. Murder; 5. Incest and Adultery; 6. Robbery," and also "the prohibition of flesh with the blood of life in it."

these Gentiles did not think that they were keeping the Mosaic law. Probably in the Antioch church, even though it evidently was separate from the Jewish synagogue, such Gentiles continued this keeping of such a group of minimal precepts, and their practice was adopted by Gentile converts not previously connected with the synagogue. On this basis, Jewish Christians felt permitted to associate with Gentile Christians, not only in worship services but also at common meals.

Jews who had observed the ceremonial rules of Judaism all their life could not easily enter into free table fellowship with Gentiles who paid no attention to such rules; for Gentiles to observe a few practices that would ease the conscience of Jewish disciples—though it did not make Gentiles accept and keep the law—was courteous and considerate. Thus the mixed church at Antioch, we assume, began with a mutual consideration that facilitated table fellowship between Jewish and Gentile Christians.[16] Saul and Barnabas shared in this way of preserving unity and harmony in the church.

THE FAMINE RELIEF VISIT TO JERUSALEM

The leaders of the Antioch church were called prophets[17] and teachers (Acts 13:1). Only later, when Barnabas and Saul had been sent out to preach in other regions, does Luke call them apostles (Acts 14:4, 14).[18] As prophets and teachers they were God-appointed, Spirit-endowed leaders, not ordained by the Twelve but considered fully authorized ministers of the church. This illustrates the fluid organization of the church in the apostolic age.

It was not unusual for prophets to move from place to place. One such traveling prophet, Agabus, appears twice in Acts, in ch. 11:28, when at Antioch he predicts the famine that struck Palestine about A.D. 45 or 46, and in ch. 21:10, when at Caesarea he predicts Paul's imprisonment at Jerusalem. The Antioch church, warned of approaching famine in Jerusalem and knowing the already hard situation of the church there, determined to send relief. How the collection was taken or how

---

16 This point is crucial for the view developed later in this chapter as to the conflict over the necessity of circumcision and the keeping of the Mosaic law. The assumption widely made that when Gentiles entered the church at Antioch they ignored all "kosher" food rules and showed no consideration for the long-standing habits of Jewish disciples is a fatal mistake.

17 On Christian prophets in the N.T., see Harold A. Guy, *New Testament Prophecy: Its Origin and Significance* (London, The Epworth Press, 1947).

18 On the wider use of the word "apostle," see Ernest de Witt Burton, *A Critical and Exegetical Commentary on the Epistle to the Galatians* (Charles Scribner's Sons, 1920), pp. 363–384; Karl Heinrich Rengstorf, "Apostleship," tr. by J. R. Coates, in *Bible Key Words*, Vol. II.

large it was we are not told, but the fund was raised and Barnabas and Saul were sent to carry it to Jerusalem (ch. 11:27–30).

Without explicitly saying so, The Acts implies that the help came at a particularly difficult time for the Jerusalem church. Herod Agrippa I had decided to attack the disciples. He executed James the brother of John; then he arrested Peter to execute him, but in a mysterious way Peter was freed from prison (ch. 12:1–19). The gifts and friendship of the Antioch church had special significance just when the Jerusalem church was being deprived of some of its best leaders. But of the exact synchronism of events it is hard to be sure.[19] After an apparently short stay in Jerusalem the two messengers, having delivered the relief fund to the elders of the church, returned to Antioch (Acts 12:25). If during their Jerusalem stay the leaders conferred on the place of Gentiles in the church, Luke does not know of it.[20]

BARNABAS AND SAUL SENT ON A PREACHING MISSION

The fact that John Mark went with them to Antioch may seem a minor detail. After all, he was the cousin of Barnabas (Col. 4:10), and it was only natural for him to take up active work in the church under the guidance of Barnabas. Persecution in Jerusalem offered little promise that he could develop leadership there. But his move to Antioch may throw light on the plans of Barnabas and Saul.

The chapter divisions of The Acts give the impression that their return to Antioch with Mark (Acts 12:25) was unrelated to the mission plan reported in Acts 13:1–3. But their taking of Mark to Antioch suggests that they already had in mind a ministry in which Mark could help. The decision of the Antioch leaders to send out Barnabas and Saul on a preaching mission (Acts 13:1–3) suggests that already at Jerusalem these two were at least weighing the possibility of expanding mission work, a project later approved by the other Antioch leaders at a time of special conference and prayer. In any case, it was with the backing of the other Antioch leaders that the mission was undertaken. And in the mind of the Antioch group Barnabas was the real leader of the

---

19 If Herod Agrippa I died in A.D. 44, as generally thought, the order of events in Acts 11:27 to 13:3 implies that the sending of famine relief from Antioch occurred in that year and that the mission tour of Acts, chs. 13 f., *could* have begun in A.D. 45. Probably the sending of the famine relief and the beginning of the mission tour did not occur so early. See note 37 in Chapter 8.

20 Some scholars identify this visit in The Acts with the one described in Acts, ch. 15. See discussion of this question later in this chapter.

mission. The laying on of hands was not an ordination but a formal dedication of Barnabas and Saul for this special work.

Something should be said concerning the date of this mission and how Luke describes the stages of this and later mission work. We do not know exactly when the mission started or how long it lasted. It began after the famine of A.D. 45 (or 46) and the visit to Jerusalem with the relief fund. It occurred a few years before Paul arrived in Corinth about A.D. 50 or 51. But the dates given in what follows for the various stages of the successive mission tours are at best approximate.[21] Moreover, Luke does not intend to give a complete chronology or a full report of what happened in each place visited. He tells how Paul (and his associates) came to a city, how they began their mission there—usually beginning in the synagogue and continuing there until forced to leave and work independently of the synagogue—and then how they were led to leave the city. Of the development, organization, and special problems of each new church Luke tells almost nothing. The book of The Acts reports the expansion of the gospel until it reached Rome; it does not discuss the inner life of each congregation.

PREACHING IN CYPRUS

From Antioch, Barnabas, Saul, and John Mark went to Seleucia, fifteen miles west. It was the main harbor for Antioch.[22] From there the men took ship for Cyprus (Acts 13:4). On its eastern shore lay Salamis, a city with Jewish synagogues. After preaching in them, the men traveled westward through the island and reached the capital city, Paphos (Acts 13:5 f.). Curiously, Luke says nothing of the results of preaching, and reports only one specific incident (vs. 6–12). A Jewish "magician" or "false prophet," Bar-Jesus, had impressed the proconsul of Cyprus, Sergius Paulus, but Saul shattered the self-confidence of Bar-Jesus and led Sergius Paulus to "believe."

How deeply the (Gentile) proconsul committed himself to the Christian faith is not clear, but Luke eagerly reports every indication that Roman officials approved Paul. It served to show that the Christian faith was not politically dangerous and was entitled to Roman respect and protection. The incident with Sergius Paulus was obviously significant for Luke in another respect. It was Paul who there took the lead

---

21 See the Chronology at the back of this volume.
22 Antioch was situated on the Orontes River, but the silt from the river caused navigation difficulties at the river's mouth, and Seleucia, some five miles north of the river's mouth, was used as the port for Antioch.

and won official recognition. So from that time Luke calls the apostle by his Roman name Paul rather than his Jewish name Saul. And Paul is named as the active leader of the party when it leaves Paphos to sail northwest to Perga in Pamphylia (Acts 13:13).

The ministry in Cyprus is told briefly, with mention of only one conversion (Acts 13:12). Did Luke know that Barnabas and Saul were not the first Christian preachers in Cyprus? Acts 11:19 tells that fugitives (Hellenistic Jewish disciples) went from Jerusalem to Cyprus and preached to Jews.[23] So Barnabas and Saul apparently were continuing a mission already begun in Cyprus, and it was almost entirely a mission to Jews. The distinctive things Luke could report were Paul's defeat of the Jewish magician, the winning of the Roman proconsul, and the rise of Paul to leadership. The real Gentile mission was now ready to begin.

To Southern Galatia

It is not said why Paul and his party went from Cyprus to Perga in Pamphylia, on the southern shore of Asia Minor. Evidently Perga was not the real goal, for no preaching is reported there until later (Acts 14:25). The one event noted from that first visit to Pamphylia is Mark's unexplained departure for his home in Jerusalem (Acts 13:13). It hardly seems likely that Mark returned merely because the journey was going farther than he had anticipated. More likely he resented the fact that Paul had replaced his cousin Barnabas as the effective leader of the party. But since Paul later praises Mark as a helper (Philemon 24), the real explanation may elude us.

It may seem strange that Paul and Barnabas headed northward for central Asia Minor, where Antioch of Pisidia, Iconium, Lystra, and Derbe were located (Acts 13:14). Other regions were more accessible; the trip over rugged mountainous country from Perga to Antioch was tiring and dangerous. Perhaps Paul's interest in these cities in the southern part of the Roman province of Galatia reflects his Tarsus outlook; from Tarsus a main road led northwest through the Cilician Gates to upland central Asia Minor, so this region could seem the logical next place for a westward spread of the gospel. But just possibly, as Ramsay conjectured,[24]

---

[23] Data on Jews in Cyprus and elsewhere in the Roman Empire are found in Jean Juster, *Les Juifs dans l'Empire romain: leur condition juridique, économique, et sociale*, 2 vols. (Paris, P. Geuthner, 1914).

[24] W. M. Ramsay, *St. Paul the Traveller and the Roman Citizen* (G. P. Putnam's Sons, 1896), pp. 94–97. On Gal. 4:13, see Ernest de Witt Burton, *The Epistle to the Galatians*, pp. 238 f., who notes that Paul's illness could have been epilepsy or eye trouble.

Paul suffered from malarial fever in the lowlands along the south coast of Asia Minor, and for relief went northward to the high tableland of central Asia Minor. If, as will appear later, Paul's letter to the Galatians went to these four cities in southern Galatia, his statement in Gal. 4:13 that he first preached the gospel in Galatia because of a "bodily ailment" makes this explanation possible though by no means certain.

JEWS AND GENTILES WON IN PISIDIAN ANTIOCH

The first stop in southern Galatia was at Pisidian Antioch.[25] Paul's regular practice was to begin his preaching in the synagogue. The freedom in order of worship in the synagogue gave him an opportunity to speak—with the permission or invitation of the synagogue officials. Luke gives somewhat at length—in comparison with other sermon summaries—a typical summary of Paul's message to a synagogue congregation (Acts 13:16–41). It recalls how God delivered Israel from Egypt, and sketches God's leading of his people until the time of David. Then it leaps ahead to the coming of Jesus as the promised Savior of Israel, cites John the Baptist's witness to Jesus, and next, without speaking of Jesus' ministry or teaching, tells of his death and especially of his resurrection. It is then announced that by Jesus' coming God has offered forgiveness of sins and redemption, a redemption not possible through the law of Moses.

In accenting this latter note, Luke may have intended to appeal to Gentiles not ready to accept and practice the Mosaic law. In any case, the great interest and response of both Jews and Gentile proselytes gave a good start to the mission in Antioch. But when the general interest aroused in the city led the Jewish leaders to oppose Paul, he announced that while he must first present the gospel to the Jews, he and his party would now turn to the Gentiles and preach directly to them (Acts 13:42–49).

It has been said that Paul here renounced the synagogue and turned to a Gentile mission. This is obviously wrong, for in every later mission where Paul can begin by preaching in the synagogue he does so (cf. Acts 14:1). The reason why Luke regards this mission in Pisidian Antioch as so important is that now Paul acts as the party leader and preaches to Gentiles directly. This is the first time on this journey that Paul has done this; it is by no means the last time; but it always follows preaching in the synagogue where that is possible.

---

25 See article on "Pisidia," *IDB*, K-Q, pp. 819 f., and "Antioch (of Pisidia)," *IDB*, A-D, pp. 144 f. Such articles are worth consulting on each region and city Paul visited.

This time—as often later—the initial stage of synagogue preaching and the resulting direct preaching to the Gentiles were followed by agitation among the Jews and expulsion of Paul and his friends from the city (Acts 13:50). The Jews enlisted the help both of devout Gentile women whom the synagogue had attracted and of leading (Gentile) men with whom the Jews had friendly ties. In this way they stirred up such an opposition that the preachers had to leave. But the spread of the gospel throughout the region (v. 49) implies a stay of some time before this expulsion, and it also illustrates Paul's method; he preached in an important city and let the message spread out from there into the surrounding region. Shaking the dust from their feet, as a warning to this city where their obligation to preach the gospel in that city had been faithfully fulfilled (Matt. 10:14; Luke 9:5), the party went on eastward and a little south to Iconium (Acts 13:51).

ICONIUM, LYSTRA, DERBE

Much the same sequence of developments occurred at Iconium: preaching in the synagogue, response by both Jews and Greeks (i.e., Gentiles), agitation against the preachers by Jewish leaders, a ministry of preaching and miracles by the missionaries, a decision by both Jewish and Gentile officials to stone the visitors, and a hasty flight by the latter to Lystra (Acts 14:1–6).

The preaching at Lystra led to more unusual results. Nothing is said of the usual pattern of first preaching to Jews and then preaching to Gentiles. However, disciples are mentioned (Acts 14:20); on a later visit to Lystra, Timothy was added to Paul's party as a helper (ch. 16:3), which implies that he had been converted on the first visit; and the reference to Timothy's mother as a Christian (v. 1) implies that she, too, had been converted (perhaps also his grandmother; cf. II Tim. 1:5).[26] So a ministry among Jews at Lystra is not excluded. But Luke tells only of the healing of a lame man (Acts 14:8–18).

The people excitedly thought that Barnabas and Paul were gods come to earth to help this needy man, and the local priest of Zeus saw a chance to offer a special sacrifice to the visiting gods. Because the people spoke in Lycaonian,[27] which Barnabas and Paul did not under-

---

26 If II Tim. 1:5 means to say that Timothy's grandmother had become a Christian long before Timothy had, it would favor a late date for II Timothy. Possibly II Tim. 1:5 regards the Christian faith of Timothy and his mother as continuing, in the light of Christ's coming, the ancestral faith of his grandmother, who was not a Christian before Paul's visit to Lystra.

27 This is a reminder that although Greek was commonly spoken throughout the Roman Empire, local languages or dialects continued to be used to some extent.

stand, preparations were well advanced before they realized what was happening. Then Paul with vehement speech rebuked such polytheistic ideas and spoke of the one God, the Creator, who gives all blessings. This brief statement, of course, is another typical summary. It does not mention Jesus or any specific Christian teaching, and is not meant as a complete gospel sermon, but as an example of how Paul opposed the worship of the many pagan gods by a firm preaching of monotheism as attested in God's creation.

That Paul's preaching is not given in full is clear from the reason which Luke gives for Paul's departure from Lystra; it was Jewish opposition (Acts 14:19 f.). Jews would have nothing to say against this summary of the Creation as the work of the one beneficent God; this was straight Jewish teaching. Luke simply omits the definitely Christian preaching of Paul in Lystra except in the brief reference to preaching the gospel in Acts 14:7. That the Jews stirred up such hostility that Paul was dragged from the city and stoned shows that at Lystra as elsewhere he had preached the gospel to Gentiles without requiring them to keep the Mosaic law. The stoning of Paul, who was left for dead but recovered, ended the mission in Lystra. The missionaries went on to Derbe.[28]

Paul and his friends preached at Derbe and "made many disciples," but Luke gives no details. From Derbe the party returned to Antioch in Syria (Acts 14:21–28). A shorter way, along the highway east and south through the Cilician Gates to Cilicia and then to Antioch, would have taken Paul through his native Tarsus. Instead, he and his party retraced their steps through Lystra, Iconium, and Pisidian Antioch to Perga, and then, going to the port Attalia, took ship to Antioch (or its port Seleucia). Perhaps they took this roundabout trip back to Antioch to avoid leaving strictly Roman territory, for the region just east of Derbe was in Commagene, a puppet kingdom controlled by Rome. But far more likely the apostles thought, in spite of the dangers already encountered in the cities of south Galatia, that they should visit the new Christians in those cities, encourage them to hold fast, and answer their questions. Paul is usually thought of as an evangelistic missionary, but he was equally a pastor of his converts.

THE GENTILE MISSION CHALLENGED

The missionaries returned to Antioch to report to the church that had sent them out. They could report two main results: a rather large

---

[28] On these South Galatian cities, see W. M. Ramsay, *The Cities of St. Paul*, pp. 247–419.

number of converts, and the readiness of many Gentiles to accept the gospel. This raised an issue of fundamental importance. These Gentile converts had not been required to become Jews in order to become Christians. Faith in Christ and a life of love was the basic demand of the missionaries, and they found that the Holy Spirit was given to Gentiles who thus responded to the gospel (Gal. 3:2). This could lead in a short time to a church largely Gentile in membership. Such a result had not seemed imminent when the household of Cornelius, for example, had been converted (Acts, ch. 10) or the Antioch church had been founded. But the issue could not be further postponed. The church had to face it.

This free acceptance of Gentiles was challenged by strict Jews from Jerusalem (Acts 15:1). There was continual communication between Antioch and Jerusalem, and the Jerusalem church knew from Antioch if not from other places that Gentiles in several cities had responded to the preaching of Paul and Barnabas. The "circumcision party" (Acts 11:2), that is, the disciples at Jerusalem who insisted that to be a true disciple of Christ one must accept and observe the Mosaic law,[29] had already challenged Peter for eating with the household and friends of Cornelius. From Acts 11:18 it might seem that Peter had convinced them by telling how the Spirit led him to act as he did. But although they were silenced when the apostles and the majority at Jerusalem accepted Peter's defense, they now show that they were not convinced. The situation resulting from the mission tour of Paul and Barnabas was to them even more serious than what Peter had done.

The apostle Peter had preached in the home of Cornelius, but he had not followed up this step by a general preaching to Gentiles; his act was a special case, and he remained essentially a preacher to Jews (Gal. 2:7). But now a systematic mission to Gentiles in city after city had shown that when the gospel was preached to Gentiles without requiring them to keep the Mosaic law, Gentiles would respond. The church was on the way to becoming predominantly Gentile. The "circumcision party," the Judaizers, were alarmed.

Christians often fail to realize how strong a case this party had. When they used circumcision as the test of willingness to accept and observe the law of God, they chose their ground well. Genesis 17:9–14 professes to quote the very words of God himself, and God there com-

---

29 Acts 15:5 says that "some believers who belonged to the party of the Pharisees" challenged Paul and Barnabas at Jerusalem. These Pharisees, unlike Paul, continued after becoming Christians to insist that all Christians "keep the law of Moses," at least in its written form.

mands that every descendant of Abraham, including foreigners who
become members of his household, must practice circumcision "throughout your generations" as "an everlasting covenant." These, the very
words of God, are given in authoritative Scripture; they must be observed. Gentiles are welcome in the church of Christ, as the Jews widely
welcomed proselytes to Judaism, but they must be circumcised, accept
the Mosaic law, and observe the ceremonies it prescribes.

This position of the "circumcision party" was not a capricious twisting
of Scripture, for the Scripture taken literally gave them impressive support. The opponents of Paul must be given credit for honest and intelligent thinking.[30] Only if their presuppositions were in some way open
to attack could they be vanquished in argument.

PAUL'S ANSWER TO "THE CIRCUMCISION PARTY"

The fact is that Paul gave no direct answer to those who used Gen.
17:9–14 to oppose free acceptance of Gentiles into the church. He could
not cut the church's tie with Judaism and the Old Testament. He was
a member of Israel; to him the church was the true Israel, continuous
with the Old Testament Israel; he accepted without question the Scripture of the synagogue; he recognized that his position had to be based
on Scripture.[31]

In part Paul's answer was that God's promise to Abraham, and Abraham's faith for which he was pronounced righteous by God, preceded
by centuries the giving of the law to Moses on Mt. Sinai, and therefore
the law, which came later, could not annul the promise or replace faith
as the basis of God's acceptance of men (Gal. 3:17). The "circumcision
party" could reply that it was precisely to Abraham, and not later to
Moses, that God first gave the explicit command to circumcise, not only
all descendants of Abraham, but all foreigners who became members
of their household. Paul could answer that God first gave Abraham the
promise, and justified him on the basis of his faith, before he ever gave
Abraham the command of circumcision. But it still was true that God
did command Abraham to circumcise his sons and included all later
descendants and Gentile servants in this command.

So Paul's real answer was twofold. First was a spiritual insight. He
sensed and maintained that the essential basis of God's dealings with
men was God's promise, Abraham's faith, and God's acceptance of

---

[30] This credit is far too seldom given them by modern Christians.
[31] On Paul's use of Scripture, see E. Earle Ellis, *Paul's Use of the Old Testament*
(Edinburgh, Oliver and Boyd, 1957).

Abraham on the basis of his faith without regard to ceremonial observance. These things are far more important and basic than any rite; such rites are secondary and must be kept from usurping equal importance with the spiritual basis of God's dealings with men. On a literalistic view of the Scripture this is not true; when the question is asked as to what is basic and decisive, Paul's position can be defended.[32]

The eschatological argument was perhaps even more decisive for Paul. With the coming of Christ, a new day in God's dealings with men had begun. Without questioning that during the period from Moses to Christ, God's people were to keep the Mosaic law, Paul affirmed that with the coming of Christ the period for God's people to live under the law was at an end. Christ was "the end of the law" (Rom. 10:4). Henceforth, Christ and not the law is the decisive factor. The first and central requirement is faith in Christ. Where that is found, the believer is acceptable to God and will be blessed by him. The Scripture is not discarded; it is full of promise and points forward to the day when the promise will be fulfilled and men will live under a new covenant; that fulfillment has come in Jesus Christ, and he who believes in him need not and must not accept the law as basic and decisive. Life must be centered in Christ and lived in constant obedience to him; the law can no longer play its former role.

This position of Paul is not brought out in Acts, ch. 15, but it is noted here to clarify the issue at the Jerusalem council and to show that the issue was a radical one with honest arguments on both sides.

THE DISPUTE CARRIED TO JERUSALEM

The church at Antioch, challenged by members of the "circumcision party" who came from Jerusalem, was torn by the debate that Paul and Barnabas had with the visitors. Whether the visitors claimed to represent the Jerusalem apostles and elders is not clear; perhaps they did (cf. Acts 15:24). But probably the Antioch leaders knew that Peter's action in preaching to Cornelius had been approved at Jerusalem, and suspected that the visitors would not be supported by the Jerusalem leaders. In any case, the Antioch church had no desire to take unilateral action. They felt bound to the Jerusalem church; their sense of the unity of the church suggested a consultation.

This consultation was later an embarrassment to Paul. His opponents apparently used it to argue that he was not an independent apostle but was subject to the Jerusalem leaders. But all his Christian life he looked to the Jerusalem church with respect and recognized its basic role in

[32] Cf. Ernest de Witt Burton, *The Epistle to the Galatians*, pp. lvii-lxv.

the life of the total church; neither he nor Barnabas wanted to set up a separate church cut off from the Jerusalem leaders. They shared in the decision to consult the Jerusalem leaders and were appointed by the Antioch church to lead the Antioch delegation. Paul later wrote that he had gone up in response to a revelation; his misgivings about the wisdom of this action were resolved by what he considered direct divine approval (Gal. 2:2).[33]

THE CONFERENCE AT JERUSALEM IN ACTS, CH. 15

Paul in Gal. 2:1 f. gives no details of the journey to Jerusalem, but Acts 15:3 mentions contact with churches in Phoenicia and Samaria, regions evangelized by Greek-speaking Jewish Christians who before being scattered by persecution had belonged to the Stephen group in Jerusalem (Acts 11:19).[34] Such churches no doubt heard with approval and joy the word of successful preaching to the Gentiles.

At Jerusalem the welcome was not so hearty. There is no hint of hostility toward Paul or Barnabas from James the brother of Jesus, Peter (Cephas), or John the son of Zebedee (Gal. 2:9); indeed, Barnabas was a former member and trusted representative of the Jerusalem church, and he naturally is mentioned before Paul in Acts 15: 12, 25. These two told their story to the entire Jerusalem church, according to Acts 15:4. They defended the acceptance of Gentiles into the church without requiring them to be circumcised and keep the Mosaic law. But this policy was challenged by former Pharisees who had believed in Christ (Acts 15:5); they were of the "circumcision party" (cf. Acts 11:2). So the leaders met with the Antioch delegation to discuss and settle the issue. Galatians 2:3 suggests that Titus, an uncircumcised Gentile active in Christian service, was taken to the conference as a test case.

Here as in the other speeches in The Acts we do not have verbatim reports of what was said; Luke reports the conference as he understands it occurred, and does so in his own wording. He even quotes Amos 9:11 f. according to the Greek translation of the Old Testament, although it is highly probable that the conference was conducted mainly at least in Aramaic.[35] The question is whether Luke knows essentially what hap-

---

[33] A special revelation or vision is regularly found to occur in the New Testament when the person involved has a problem or crisis to meet. The revelation in Gal. 2:2 indicates that Paul saw possibilities of misunderstanding in such a conference at Jerusalem.

[34] For mention of Christians in Tyre and Sidon, see Acts 21:3 f.; 27:3.

[35] In both the Hebrew original and the Greek translation of Amos 9:11 f., the inclusion of the Gentiles in the renewed Kingdom of David is expressed. The Greek allows more initiative and standing to the Gentiles in this new order.

pened, and we may conclude he does. In his account, Peter, speaking in reply to the demand that all Gentile Christians must be circumcised and keep the law of Moses, tells how he was led to preach to Gentiles. God guided him to do this without requiring circumcision; God gave the Gentiles the Spirit, and so showed that he accepted them on the basis of their faith without requiring them to keep the law (Acts 15:7–11).

Barnabas and Paul continued the report of what had actually happened. They told of their work among the Gentiles; the results showed that God approved their direct appeal to Gentiles and their acceptance of Gentiles without requiring them to keep the law (Acts 15:12). Then James the brother of Jesus, who for some years now had been the effective head of the Jerusalem church, pointed out that the coming of the Gentiles into God's people was predicted by Scripture (Amos 9:11 f.); James expected Jews in the church to continue keeping the Mosaic law, but he did not think it necessary to require Gentiles to do so (Acts 15:13–21). He proposed that the Gentiles be told "to abstain from the pollutions of idols and from unchastity and from what is strangled and from blood" (Acts 15:20; cf. chs. 15:29; 21:25).

This plan the group approved, and a letter carried by Judas Barsabbas and Silas stated that the Jerusalem leaders had not sent the visitors who caused the trouble at Antioch, that Barnabas and Paul were leaders approved at Jerusalem, and that Gentile Christians in Antioch and Syria and Cilicia (and by inference in churches founded by Paul and Barnabas) need not keep the law but need only abstain from the four things James had mentioned (Acts 15:22–29). This is sometimes taken to mean that the entire Antioch church, including the Jewish Christians there, were freed from keeping any of the Mosaic law, but Acts 15:20, 29 and 21:25 refer only to Gentile Christians. The letter was directed to Gentile believers.

ACTS, CHAPTER 15, AND GALATIANS, CHAPTER 2

No item in the New Testament has caused more debate than this account of the Jerusalem conference.[36] The dispute centers mainly on two questions. One is whether Acts 15:1–29 refers to the same conference that Gal. 2:1–10 describes. In Galatians this is Paul's second visit to Jerusalem after his conversion; in The Acts, however, it is his third:[37]

[36] Two noteworthy recent studies of Galatians and Acts, ch. 15, are Ernst Haenchen, *Die Apostelgeschichte* (Göttingen, Vandenhoeck & Ruprecht, 1956), pp. 401–419; Johannes Munck, *Paul and the Salvation of Mankind*, Ch. 4.

[37] The text of Acts 12:25 is uncertain. If it originally read "returned to Jerusalem," it could refer to a third visit of Saul to Jerusalem. Then Acts, ch. 15, would be his fourth visit to that city after his conversion. But probably the original text of Acts

(1) Acts 9:26–30 is clearly the same visit as Gal. 1:18. (2) Acts 11:30; 12:25 tell of a visit to take famine relief from Antioch to Jerusalem. Galatians tells nothing of this visit, unless Gal. 2:10 implies that on the visit described in Gal. 2:1–10 Paul took famine relief to the poor disciples in Jerusalem. (3) Acts 15:1–29 seems to be the real parallel to Gal. 2:1–10. Both passages tell of a conference about the place of Gentiles in the church; in both accounts the dispute arises at Antioch, is carried to Jerusalem, and is settled essentially in Paul's favor. But in Acts 15:20, 29, Gentile Christians are told to avoid four things, whereas Paul says that the Jerusalem leaders "added nothing to me" (Gal. 2:6).

This difference causes the difficulty. It is thought impossible to reconcile the two accounts, and since Paul would hardly have completely misrepresented the essential result of the conference, numerous scholars conclude that the account in The Acts must be rejected as a later attempt to conceal the deep difference between the Jewish and Gentile wings of the church.

The attempts to reconstruct what actually happened are too numerous to list. The more important ones may be noted:

1. Gal. 2:1–10, Paul's second visit to Jerusalem in Galatians, is identical with Acts 11:30; 12:25, his second visit in The Acts; Paul's gospel was approved in a conference of leaders at that time, but later, at the conference mentioned in Acts, ch. 15, he agreed that the four regulations of the "decree" (Acts 15:29) were needed to enable Jewish and Gentile Christians to eat and meet together without violating the scruples of the Jewish Christians.

2. Acts 11:30; 12:25 tell of the same visit as Acts, ch. 15; Luke wrongly thought that the famine relief trip and the conference about conditions for receiving Gentiles into the church were two separate occasions, whereas in fact both things were done on one visit to Jerusalem.

3. Regardless of how many trips Paul made to Jerusalem, the "decree" of Acts, ch. 15, was never issued; it was dreamed up in later decades in an attempt to cover up the radical divisions in the early church.

4. Regardless of whether Acts 11:30; 12:25 and Acts, ch. 15, refer to the same visit or two different visits, the "decree" was not passed so early but was issued later by the Jerusalem leaders at a time when Paul was not present; Paul heard of it only on his final visit to Jerusalem (Acts 21:25). He therefore never agreed to it.

5. Perhaps the most usual solution is that Gal. 2:1–10 tells of the same visit as Acts 15:1–29, that the "decree" was issued then with the agreement of Paul, that it was a compromise which Paul accepted to preserve

---

12:25 read that after the visit to Jerusalem reported in Acts 11:30, Barnabas and Saul "returned *from* Jerusalem" to Antioch.

the peace and unity of the church, but that when he found it used to undermine his independent ministry to Gentiles, he ignored or disowned it; this would explain why later in Corinth, when the question of eating food offered to idols was raised, he did not mention the "decree" (I Cor. 8:10).

The Solution Suggested

The simplest solution is hardly ever mentioned.[38] It is that the visits took place as The Acts reports; that in Galatians, Paul did not mention the visit of Acts 11:30; 12:25 because the issue of the place of Gentiles in the church did not arise during that visit; that Gal. 2:1–10 refers to the same visit as Acts 15:1–29; and that *Paul agreed to the "decree" not as a compromise but because it continued essentially the kind of arrangement which he had led Gentile Christians to accept from the beginning of his Gentile mission.*

It is clear that in both The Acts and Galatians the conference vindicated Paul and Barnabas. It disowned the idea that to be Christians the Gentiles must be circumcised and keep the Mosaic law. Rarely in church history has a leader or group won so sweeping a victory as Paul won at the Jerusalem conference.

This basic fact has often been obscured by calling the result a compromise. The word "compromise" implies that up to this time the Gentile mission had completely ignored all Jewish practices and that the churches which included both Jews and Gentiles, notably the church at Antioch, had previously neglected all regulations of the Jewish law. This is the common assumption that should be challenged.

How Should Jewish and Gentile Christians Live Together?

What happened when the first Gentiles believed in Jesus Christ? They believed in response to preaching from Jewish believers, and when they believed, they at once joined with such Jewish believers in worship and common life. This was obviously true at Antioch in Syria; Jewish Christians who brought the gospel there preached at first to Jews and presumably added some of them to the group of disciples; then some of these Jewish Christians began to preach to Gentiles and so added believers from among the Gentiles to the band of disciples of Jesus (Acts 11:19–21).

38 T. W. Manson is close to it in his *Studies in the Gospels and Epistles*, ed. by Matthew Black (The Westminster Press, 1962), Ch. 9. But he thinks Acts, ch. 15, may be composite and Gal. 2:3–5 refers to two different events.

What did they eat in such a racially mixed group? Did they at once begin to eat pork and other food revolting to Jews? Certainly not. Without thinking that any deep issue was involved, the group no doubt continued familiar Jewish practices as to food and daily life, not with the idea that thus they were all accepting the law and admitting that they must obey it to be saved, but simply because it was common Jewish practice and also because it served to separate the Gentile believers from surrounding paganism. When Paul went on his mission tour of central Asia Minor, he began his work in each city, as we have seen, in the synagogue, and his converts included both Jews and Gentiles. He, too, no doubt led his mixed groups in a way of life that used many common Jewish practices, not to force Gentiles to keep the law to be saved, but simply because it was the familiar pattern and enabled Jewish and Gentile Christians to eat and worship together without offending long-standing Jewish feelings.

Gentiles previously connected with the synagogue but not actual proselytes to Judaism are called "God-fearers" in the New Testament.[39] Paul found in them a source of converts to Christ. They were already living a life detached from pagan Gentile society and they conformed in some ways to Jewish practice. Upon conversion to Christ it would be easy for them to continue to adapt their way of life somewhat to common Jewish practices. It may be added that among Jews it was becoming a common thought that God had set up a limited number of things that Gentiles ought to do. These items were called the "precepts of Noah," and the idea obviously had some currency that if Gentiles were faithful to these few requirements, they would have a place in the final Kingdom of God.[40]

So if Paul and Barnabas agreed that Gentile converts should be asked to respect Jewish feelings by observing four specified items, this was nothing new to these missionaries or their churches. Paul could have agreed to this plan with a good conscience and still have said that the Jerusalem leaders "added nothing to me" (Gal. 2:6), for this sort of thing was already common practice in his churches.[41]

---

[39] See Kirsopp Lake, "Proselytes and God-Fearers," in *The Beginnings of Christianity*, Vol. V, pp. 74–96.

[40] On the so-called precepts of Noah, see note 15 in this chapter and also H. J. Schoeps, *Paul*, pp. 66 f.

[41] In I Cor. 8:1 to 11:1 Paul makes no reference to the agreement reached at Jerusalem. I take it that when "the circumcision party" agitated in his churches for the keeping of the Mosaic law by Gentile Christians, and perhaps made a legalistic use of the Jerusalem agreement, Paul made no further use of it. It was directed to a limited region that was not his real mission field (see the next chapter). But his argument in I Cor. 8:1 to 11:1 shows that he saw real wisdom in refraining from eating meat sacrificed to idols.

This view shocks the modern sense of consistency. To the modern Christian, his faith is sharply separate from modern Jewish religion; he cannot conceive that early Gentile Christians practiced any special ways of living in order to keep brotherly contacts with Jews who shared their faith. Yet in the modern Conference of Christians and Jews, a nation-wide organization, the Christian members would never think of serving ham at a common meal. The meal is always one that will not offend the Jewish members of the group. The Christians who avoid ham at such a meeting are doing exactly what was done by Paul and other first-century Christians, especially Gentile Christians, to permit all Christians, many of whom were Jews, to eat and worship and live together.

WHAT GENTILE CHRISTIANS SHOULD DO

What was asked of Gentile Christians at the Jerusalem conference was very little (Acts 15:20, 29). They should avoid food sacrificed to idols; to eat such food might seem to imply approval of polytheistic pagan religions (cf. Lev. 17:8 f.). They should not eat blood, for to Jews "the blood is the life" (Deut. 12:23; Lev. 17:11 f., 14), and in eating meat, Jewish Christians would feel at ease only when it was meat from animals so slaughtered that the blood was completely drained from the slain animal. They should not eat meat of animals that had been strangled, for this too would mean eating blood, which a Jewish Christian would shrink from doing (cf. Lev. 17:13). They should avoid unchastity, whether this meant any form of illicit sexual intercourse, or more par-ticularly the sexual orgies connected with some pagan cults, or marriages of persons closely related (cf. Lev. 18:6–18; I Cor., ch. 5). The first and fourth of these items were something that both Jews and Gentiles could accept as wise and necessary for clean life and clear Christian witness. The second and third respected a deep-seated aversion of Jewish Chris-tians to eating blood, and imposed no great hardship on Gentile Chris-tians.[42]

There is no evidence that these regulations were intended as legal rules necessary for salvation. Rather, they were things any good Gentile should do,[43] and they made it possible for Jewish and Gentile Christians to live in unity. Their observance is the only good explanation of the unity of Jews and Gentiles in the early churches in Antioch and the

[42] On the view that the original "decree" had no reference to "things strangled" and that this was added later in some manuscripts, while in others it was not added and "blood" was interpreted to mean murder and the Golden Rule was added, see James Hardy Ropes, *The Beginnings of Christianity*, Vol. III, pp. 265–269.

[43] See notes 15 and 40 in this chapter.

cities of Galatia. It was not these practices but the demand that Gentiles be circumcised and keep the Mosaic law that threatened to divide the church.

VICTORY AND MUTUAL COURTESY

Paul won his battle to reject that legalistic demand, but he knew how to adapt his life and the life of the Gentile Christians so that all the Christians of his churches could eat and worship together. He could agree to the "decree" formulated in Jerusalem and yet say in Gal. 2:6 that the Jerusalem leaders "who were of repute added nothing to me." He and his churches had lived in that spirit of mutual concern for one another from the start; the Jews accepted the fact that Gentiles were coming into the church without being required to be circumcised and keep the Mosaic law; the Gentiles accepted the facts that their Jewish fellow disciples had practices which kept them from pagan evils and that these practices included ways of eating and living that should be treated with consideration by Gentile believers.

The unity of the church was vital, and it took mutual consideration to preserve it. Once it was granted, as it clearly was at the Jerusalem conference, that Gentiles had as much place in the church as did Jews, and that Gentiles need not accept and keep the Jewish law as a condition of becoming a Christian, then the agreement accepted by Paul was not a compromise, as it is often called; essentially it continued practices already in use to preserve the unity and mutual courtesy of the church.[44]

The Jerusalem conference was of epoch-making importance because the leaders of the Jerusalem and Antioch churches agreed (1) that a Gentile need not become a Jew to become a Christian, (2) that a Gentile therefore need not be circumcised and keep the Mosaic law to be a disciple of Christ, (3) that the unity of the church is so vital that it must be preserved by mutual adaptation of each group to the other in things not essential, (4) that the Scripture is not to be interpreted with a liter-

[44] The above picture of the Jerusalem conference will be criticized at various points, and it—like every other reconstruction that has been or can be offered—is not completely convincing. But its strength is that it takes seriously the question as to what happened at Syrian Antioch and elsewhere when the first Gentiles entered the previously all-Jewish church. Did those first Gentile Christians promptly reject all dietary and ceremonial practices that were axiomatic among Jews? I have read scores of discussions of the Jerusalem conference which either ignore this question or—more often—tacitly assume that the first Gentile Christians, and Paul too, consistently avoided such Jewish practices from the beginning of the Gentile mission. Then the four items listed in Acts 15:29 look like a devastating surrender by Paul. The only sound way to seek an understanding of Acts, ch. 15, is to raise first the question stated above. Then some such reconstruction as I have offered will become necessary.

alism and legalism which tie the church permanently to all the ceremonies of first-century Judaism, (5) that Christ is the center and head
of the church and that faith in him and a life of Christian love are the
essentials, and (6) that the church is a universal fellowship in which
Jews and Christians live in brotherly unity.

The sequel of the conference, according to Acts 15:30–35, was encouraging. The letter stating the agreement reached naturally caused
rejoicing at Antioch; it vindicated the practice at Antioch and supported
the work and methods of its missionary leaders Paul and Barnabas.
Judas and Silas, who were the official bearers of the letter and were
recognized as prophets, spoke with power to confirm the written message.
Then Judas returned to Jerusalem, while Silas chose to remain at Antioch and was available when Paul needed a helper on his next missionary
journey.[45] Paul and Barnabas likewise remained in Antioch for some
time and resumed active leadership in that church.

PETER'S VISIT TO ANTIOCH

Paul in Galatians does not deny what The Acts says, but he reports
an ominous incident that may have happened somewhat later than the
time when the letter from Jerusalem was delivered (Gal. 2:11–14). Peter,
he reports, visited Antioch,[46] entered into the life of the mixed church,
and ate at the common meals, which were celebrations of the Lord's
Supper and not mere church suppers such as modern churches have.
Then "certain men came from James" (Gal. 2:12); this implies that
they could speak for him. If so, as seems probable, James the brother
of Jesus was somewhat more conservative than Peter and much more
conservative than Paul.

This is understandable, for while Paul was living at Antioch and
moving out into Asia Minor on mission work, and Peter was no longer
regularly resident in Jerusalem, James was living in Jerusalem, heading
the church there, and trying to get along even with extreme conservatives
who thought that every Christian should be circumcised and keep the
Jewish law. He was under a pressure that the leaders at Antioch did not

---

45 A "Western" reading, probably added later to the original text of The Acts, inserts
"But it seemed good to Silas to remain there" (ch. 15:34), and some Western
authorities add further "and Judas went [to Jerusalem] alone." These additions
were made to explain how, if Judas and Silas were dismissed to return to Jerusalem
(Acts 15:33), Silas is present at Antioch in Acts 15:40.

46 On the improbable view that Gal. 2:11–14 refers to an event that happened *before*
the conference of Gal. 2:1–10, see George S. Duncan, *The Epistle of Paul to the
Galatians* (Harper & Brothers, 1934), pp. xxv ff.

have to face. Under that pressure he held that although Gentiles could be received into the church without requiring them to be circumcised and keep the Mosaic law, Jewish Christians should observe not merely the items mentioned in Acts 15:29 but also all the other ancestral Jewish practices.

James really was suggesting a very modern solution: Let there be two denominations, the First Jewish Christian Church of Antioch and the First Gentile Church of Antioch! Each would be Christian; they might even have an Antioch Council of Churches and have occasional meetings together; but they could not eat together unless the Gentiles observed the Jewish food laws.[47]

Paul's Defense of the Essential Gospel

For Paul, the unity of the church was so axiomatic that he could not consider this division of the church into two parts. And his sense of the freedom of all Christians was so great that he could not consider making Gentile Christians adopt the Jewish law. Indeed, he could not concede that keeping the law was basic in the Jewish Christian's life; a Jewish Christian might keep the law, for it was the life pattern he knew, but he could not ascribe to it any saving effect nor should he keep it rigidly when to do so would break the unity of the church. It was the grace of God, accepted in simple faith and active in a life of love, which made any man a sharer in the privilege of Christian discipleship. So the Jewish Christian should not demand that Gentiles accept the Jewish pattern of life to preserve Christian unity and fellowship. The Gentile Christian should show such separation from paganism and consideration for his Jewish Christian brother as Acts 15:29 provides, but this was out of Christian charity and not because such observances were necessary to become and remain a Christian.

This was not fully clear to Peter or Barnabas. The pressure from Jerusalem was strong on these men, who were deeply attached to their fellow disciples in Jerusalem. Peter yielded to the demand that came from James; he no longer ate with the Antioch Gentile Christians (Gal. 2:12). Other Jewish Christians did the same. One was Barnabas. He had approved the Jewish-Gentile mixed church at Antioch (Acts 11:23), had led out on the mission tour to Cyprus and Asia Minor, and had returned to defend the acceptance of the Gentiles into the church without asking

---

47 In spite of what I Cor. 9:5 might suggest, it seems that James the brother of the Lord lived regularly in Jerusalem and thought of Gentile Christians as a rather separate group. He himself did not live in daily contact with Gentile Christians.

them to keep the Jewish law. Yet he was so moved by the pressure of
the messengers from James that he too—and for Paul this was the most
cruel blow—refused to eat any longer with Gentiles at the Lord's Table
(Gal. 2:13).

One might have expected Paul to report that he rebuked Barnabas,[48]
who had worked with Paul most closely, and could hardly have a clear
conscience in yielding to this pressure. But Paul tells us only that he
rebuked Peter (Gal. 2:14 ff.). Peter was the leading member of the
Twelve, his standing outweighed that of Barnabas, and he had defended
the mission to the Gentiles at the Jerusalem conference. In rebuking
Peter, however, Paul did not appeal to the conference agreement. Instead, he went to the heart of the matter. Both Jew and Gentile, in their
spiritual need, could find the answer to their need only in the grace of
God available in Christ. That being so, and the Mosaic law having no
saving power for either Jew or Gentile, it was not right for Peter to
begin observing the law again, as though it were necessary to salvation.
(Two axioms for Paul were that what is not essential for salvation must
not be made compulsory, and what destroys the unity of the church is
wrong.)

The effect of Paul's impassioned appeal to Peter is not reported.
Probably Barnabas at least saw the truth of what Paul said, since he
later considered a plan to join Paul in revisiting the churches of Cyprus
and southern Galatia (Acts 15:36–40).[49] But of Peter's response we hear
nothing. Perhaps Peter persisted, at least for a time, in his aloofness
toward the Gentile Christians at Antioch, or—more likely—Paul in
Gal. 2:14–21 was so concerned to state the basic gospel that he did not
stop to report Peter's later change of attitude. Certain it is that Paul
stood his ground; he was the one man who did so, and he thus preserved
the essential gain of the Jerusalem conference. Only upon the basis of
what Paul did and said at Antioch could the church go ahead on its
widening mission to the Gentiles. It was Paul and not Peter who was
the key leader in protecting and widening the universal outreach of the
gospel.

---

[48] Since Paul says nothing of a rebuke to Barnabas, one could suggest that Barnabas
did not himself refuse to eat with Gentiles but only defended Peter for not doing
so. But this is not convincing. Barnabas as well as Peter separated himself from
the Lord's Supper that the Gentiles ate, and Paul no doubt rebuked him. But in
Galatians, Paul mentions his rebuke of Peter because Peter was the leading one of
the Twelve and Paul was concerned in Gal., chs. 1 and 2, to show his own independence of the Jerusalem leaders.

[49] But the dispute between Paul and Barnabas about whether to take John Mark on
that next mission tour suggests that the former cordial relations between the two
leaders no longer existed.

Chapter 10

PAUL'S INDEPENDENT MISSION

THE DAYS of Paul's independent mission were now to begin. The Jerusalem leaders had agreed that Gentiles need not become Jews and keep the Mosaic law in order to become Christians. They had recognized that Paul had a commission from Christ to work among the Gentiles.

THE SPLIT WITH BARNABAS

One question still to be settled was whether Paul and Barnabas would continue to work together. Paul proposed, Acts 15:36 says, that they should revisit the churches in Cyprus and Asia Minor. Barnabas agreed. But he wanted to take with them John Mark, his cousin (Col. 4:10). Since Mark had left the party on their former journey (Acts 13:13), Paul thought that he was not the man to take into southern Galatia, where hardship, persecution, and danger might again meet them. On this issue, Paul and Barnabas separated (Acts 15:37–39). Barnabas, taking Mark, went to revisit the churches in Cyprus, his native region (Acts 4:36). Paul later spoke favorably of Mark (Col. 4:10), and Mark later wrote one of the canonical Gospels. Barnabas, it seems, was right to see more possibilities in Mark than Paul discerned.[1]

The split between Paul and Barnabas probably had still other grounds. Two other factors were involved. At Antioch, Barnabas had bowed to the pressure of men from James in a way that Paul thought wrong and traitorous to the Gentile mission. Barnabas was more closely bound to the Jerusalem church and to ancestral customs than was Paul, who could move out into a widening Gentile mission with greater freedom. This difference on an issue central to Paul rendered further teamwork difficult. In addition, Paul had proved the more forceful leader; he could no longer follow the lead of Barnabas; that had become clear during their former journey. Yet Barnabas could not easily accept a

---

[1] I Peter 5:13 indicates that Mark later worked with Peter. This recalls Acts 12:12, and is confirmed by Papias as quoted in Eusebius, *Church History* III.39.15, where Mark is called "the interpreter of Peter."

role as Paul's assistant. The break was inevitable, and served the best interests of the Christian mission.

PAUL AND SILAS IN SOUTH GALATIA

For his new fellow worker, Paul chose Silas (Acts 15:40). With Judas, he had come from Jerusalem to Antioch with the letter about the place of Gentiles in the church (Acts 15:22), and had shown himself in sympathy with Paul's work. It is not clear whether Paul sent to Jerusalem to get Silas, as Acts 15:33 suggests, or Silas had stayed at Antioch after delivering the letter, as suggested by the textually uncertain verse Acts 15:34.[2] In any case, he went with Paul on the next journey. Does the Old Testament principle that valid witness calls for two witnesses explain the practice of going out by twos (cf. Deut. 19:15)? Another interesting question is this: Was Silas, who was also called Silvanus (I Thess. 1:1; II Thess. 1:1), identical with the Silvanus who later helped Peter (I Peter 5:12)?

Paul and Silas took the land route north from Antioch and went northwest through Cilicia (Acts 15:41). In Cilicia, Paul could revisit his native city Tarsus and the Christians he had converted earlier (Acts 9:30; Gal. 1:23). Through the Cilician Gates, a strategic pass, they reached the upland regions of southern Galatia and revisited the churches in Derbe and Lystra (Acts 16:1). Of this visit only two things are said. At Lystra, Timothy was added to the party (Acts 16:1–3). He, like his mother, must have been converted on Paul's former visit to Lystra (Acts 14:6 ff.); Paul would hardly have taken a totally untried convert on his further journey.

But Timothy's presence in the party raised a question. Paul expected Jews to continue the practice of circumcision, but he was adamant that Gentiles need not and must not be circumcised. Now, Timothy had a Jewish mother and a Gentile father. Should he be circumcised? His father, a Gentile, had not permitted him to be circumcised when a babe. But Paul regularly began his mission work in a city by going to the synagogue, and he knew that Jews in those synagogues would regard the uncircumcised Timothy as a renegade. This would make trouble at the very beginning of Paul's work in every city. So Paul, whose will Timothy accepted, circumcised Timothy (Acts 16:3). This probably ex-

---

2 The fuller form of the Western reading in Acts 15:34 is: "But it seemed good to Silas to remain there, and Judas went [to Jerusalem] alone." See *The Beginnings of Christianity*, Vol. III, by James Hardy Ropes (1926), pp. 148 f., and Vol. IV, by Kirsopp Lake and Henry J. Cadbury (1933), p. 182.

plains the taunt which Paul's opponents later hurled at him in Galatia, that on occasion he could "still preach circumcision" (Gal. 5:11), though he forbade the practice when he pleased. All seemingly neat rules encounter difficulty in borderline cases.

The other thing told of this visit to southern Galatia is that Paul and Silas delivered to these churches the decisions formulated at the Jerusalem conference (Acts 16:4; cf. ch. 15:28 f.). This is often regarded as a humiliation for Paul and a compromise of his conviction that the gospel is offered to the Gentiles freely and without legal conditions. It is not enough to reply that Silas, sent from Jerusalem to Antioch to deliver the decisions, would want the churches to hear of them. Nor is it enough to say—though it is true—that once Paul left Galatia, these decisions are never mentioned again.

As noted in the last chapter, Paul in all probability had always led Gentile converts to respect the feelings of their Jewish fellow Christians by observing something like the "precepts of Noah."[3] Thus the Jerusalem decisions were not to Paul legalistic or essentially new. He had been challenged at Antioch and in Jerusalem by the "circumcision party," who insisted that Gentile converts to Christianity must be circumcised and keep the Mosaic law. This party had won partial support from James at Jerusalem; they had induced many Jewish Christians not to eat with Gentile Christians unless the latter accepted the Mosaic law; they had split the church at Antioch. They could be expected to persist in agitation against Paul and his understanding of the gospel; they could appear in Galatia and renew there the demands made at Antioch and Jerusalem. So in publicizing the Jerusalem decisions, Paul was protecting his former work and trying to prevent further trouble. Gentile Christians, Paul could report, would of course be expected to show consideration for their fellow Christians of Jewish origin, but they had the full approval of the Jerusalem conference in not accepting the obligation to keep the Mosaic law.

"COME OVER TO MACEDONIA"

Once the churches in southern Galatia had been revisited, the way was clear to undertake work in a new region. The summary in Acts 16:5 shows that a new stage of the church was now to begin.[4] But only after considerable uncertainty did Paul decide where to go. At first it seemed

3 See notes 15 and 40 in the preceding chapter.
4 Each of the six summaries in Acts (chs. 6:7; 9:31; 12:24; 16:5; 19:20; 28:30 f.) marks the end of a distinct phase of the spread of the church.

natural to travel west from southern Galatia into the Roman province of Asia, located in western Asia Minor. It contained many Jews, and Ephesus was one of the Empire's leading cities. But after thought and prayer Paul and his group concluded that the Holy Spirit opposed their going to Asia at that time (Acts 16:6).[5] So they went northward.

The road they took is uncertain. Acts 16:6 and 18:23 may mean that they went north from Antioch in Pisidia through Phrygia and then turned northeast into northern Galatia, where the chief cities were Pessinus, Ancyra (modern Ankara), and Tavium.[6] In these cities lived descendants of the Gauls who had invaded Asia Minor in the third century B.C. If these two verses mean that Paul visited northern Galatia, then his letter to the Galatians probably went to that area. But Luke tells nothing of work in that area; he seems to mean that as Paul went north from Pisidian Antioch he did no real missionary preaching, but moved northward to seek a place to work along the southern shore of the Black Sea.[7] When the group were just south of Bithynia and east of the region of Mysia (which was in northwest Asia Minor), they felt led to stay out of Bithynia and move westward to Troas, on the extreme northwest coast of Asia Minor (Acts 16:7 f.).

The result was to leave aside areas of secondary importance and move toward work in great cities of key Roman provinces. Paul's policy from this time was to take up work in new places rather than to strengthen churches he himself had not founded. Perhaps he already had worked out in his mind the strategy of moving toward Rome and the western part of the Empire. Did he also know that there were already churches in the northern parts of Asia Minor (cf. I Peter 1:1)?

At Troas, a short sea trip from Macedonia, Paul had a vision (Acts 16:9 f.). A man of Macedonia, such as he surely saw daily on the streets of Troas, summoned him to cross to Macedonia and preach there. This convinced Paul and his helpers that such a plan, already under consideration when they came to Troas, was indeed God's will for them.

---

[5] I have never seen a convincing statement of what situation made preaching in Asia undesirable at that time.

[6] Galatia was originally the name of this section in Asia Minor where Gauls settled. Their kingdom continued there until 25 B.C. Then the Romans took over this region and for administrative purposes combined it with territory of ancient Lycaonia, Isauria, Pisidia, and a bit of Phrygia. Thus in Paul's day Galatia might mean either the total Roman province of Galatia or the region where the Gauls settled (referred to above as North Galatia since it was in the north part of the Roman province, as contrasted with South Galatia, where Antioch of Pisidia, Iconium, Lystra, and Derbe were located). See *The Beginnings of Christianity*, Vol. V, Note 18, "Paul's Route in Asia Minor," by Kirsopp Lake, pp. 224–240.

[7] On Galatia and Paul's travel route, see Ernest de Witt Burton, *The Epistle to the Galatians*, pp. xvii–xliv.

Was Luke the Macedonian in the vision? That is not certain. Paul saw numerous Macedonians in Troas; their very presence could suggest a mission in Macedonia. But it does appear that Paul first met Luke in Troas and that Luke was a native of Macedonia, perhaps Philippi. Luke probably kept a diary or travel record; beginning at Acts 16:10 we find a series of passages written in the first person plural, as though the writer himself had been present at the events thus described (chs. 16:10-17; 20:5-15; 21:1-18; 27:1 to 28:16). This travel record, which Luke seems to have used later in writing The Acts, indicates that Luke went with Paul from Troas to Philippi, stayed there when Paul left, and rejoined Paul when he next passed through Philippi. This supports the view that Luke was a native of Philippi.[8]

Paul's crossing from Troas to Philippi is often dramatized as the beginning of Paul's mission in Europe. This is true from our later point of view, but it was not the first preaching of the gospel in Europe, for there was certainly a church in Rome by this time, and Paul hardly thought of the trip as bringing the gospel to a new continent. He was moving from one Roman province to another, as a part of his plan to preach the gospel where it had not yet been heard (Rom. 15:20; II Cor. 10:15 f.).

THE MINISTRY IN PHILIPPI

In one day Paul sailed from Troas to the island of Samothrace, the next day from Samothrace to Neapolis, the port for Philippi; then a nine-mile journey by land took Paul and his party to Philippi (Acts 16:11 f.). It was a Roman colony where Roman soldiers had been retired and given special privileges.[9] On the first Sabbath, Paul looked for the "place of prayer" of the Jews. The phrase could mean a synagogue, but in this instance Paul did not find one. Had there been an actual synagogue, Jewish men would have been in charge; it took ten Jewish men to make a synagogue; Jewish women could worship together but could not hold a regular synagogue service. By the riverside Paul found only a worshiping group of Jewish women and spoke to them. Lydia, a well-to-do Gentile woman already attracted by Judaism, was won to faith

---

[8] The Western manuscripts of Acts 11:28 read, "And when *we* were assembled one of them named Agabus, etc." This has led some to think that Luke was a native of Antioch in Syria. But in all probability the words "when we were assembled" are not original. On this passage and the certain "we" passages, see *The Beginnings of Christianity*, Vol. II, pp. 158 ff.; Vol. IV, p. 130.

[9] On Philippi as a colony, see *IDB*, articles on "Colony," A-D, p. 657, and "Philippi," K-Q, pp. 786 f.

in Christ (Acts 16:12–15). She invited the missionary party to her home for the period of their stay in Philippi. Luke continually notes acts of hospitality; several times he names the host who entertained Paul and his party (Acts 9:11; 17:7; 18:3; 21:8, 16).

The Acts tells nothing more about Paul's work in Philippi. Luke's usual practice in The Acts is to tell how Paul begins his work in a city, how he is led to make a direct appeal to Gentiles, and then how he is led to leave the city and move on to another place. He rarely gives clear information as to how long Paul stayed in a place, and he tells little or nothing of the life of the newly founded church. On this point the letters of Paul are our resource. His later letter to the Philippian church attests a successful ministry that led to the foundation of a strong church.

Acts tells only why Paul left Philippi. He healed a slave girl who had "a spirit of divination" and seemed able to reveal secrets (Acts 16:16–18). Her owners had used and guided her emotionally disturbed utterances to make great financial profit. Deprived of her services, they stirred up opposition to Paul and Silas as Jews who were disturbing the city (a hint of citywide interest in Paul's preaching) and living contrary to Roman customs, to which this Roman colony was loyal. Paul and Silas were seized, beaten, and imprisoned; the jailer "fastened their feet in the stocks" (Acts 16:19–24). They prayed and sang hymns (a glimpse of early Christian worship).

About midnight an earthquake freed the prisoners and opened the prison doors. The jailer knew of Paul's preaching; awed by what had happened, he was ready to listen to Paul, especially since the prisoners made no attempt to escape—an escape would have brought the jailer into disgrace (cf. Acts 16:23). He believed the gospel message, and he and "all his family" were at once baptized (Acts 16:25–34).

The next day the city officials ordered the prisoners released; indeed, there was no solid charge against them. But Paul, to rebuke the officials and protect the Philippian church from future ill-treatment, appealed to his rights. The officials, in a hasty and riotous scene, had had Paul and Silas beaten with rods. Such hasty action was wrong in any case. But Paul and Silas were Roman citizens; to beat them without fair trial in this Roman colony was particularly outrageous. (Just how Paul established his Roman citizenship is not made clear.)[10] Paul forced the officials to come to the prison, apologize, and ask the prisoners to leave (Acts 16:35–40). Then Paul and Silas, after receiving this apology and visiting

[10] On Roman citizenship and its relation to this incident, see Henry J. Cadbury, *The Book of Acts in History*, pp. 65–82.

Lydia and the church that met in her home, traveled westward on the Egnatian Way, passing through the less important cities Amphipolis and Apollonia, and reached Thessalonica.

FAITH AND HOSTILITY IN THESSALONICA

Paul's method was to work in the chief city of an area and let the gospel message spread out from there into surrounding places. Thessalonica was an important port, a key city on the main east-west road through Macedonia,[11] and lay at the south end of a fruitful river valley. Paul began as usual in the synagogue and preached there for three Sabbaths before being expelled (Acts 17:1–4). His message in such synagogues is briefly indicated. Since the Jews did not expect the Messiah to suffer and die in fulfilling his role, Paul had to show from Scripture that such suffering was in God's plan.[12] Then he could argue that Jesus was the expected Christ. He won to Christian faith some Jews, many "devout Greeks," that is, Gentiles loosely connected with the synagogue,[13] and leading (Gentile) women; here as in many other cities women of standing had been attracted by the Jewish faith.

But Paul's success led other Jews to oppose him. From Acts 17:2 it might seem that Paul had to leave Thessalonica at the end of three weeks, but a longer period of directing preaching to idol-worshiping Gentiles must have followed, for I Thess. 1:9 shows that the majority of the church in that city had "turned to God from idols," and so had not been "devout Greeks" worshiping at the synagogue. After this period of preaching to Gentiles, however, the Jews agitated against "these men who have turned the world upside down," and stirred up a mainly Gentile mob; the city officials, called politarchs,[14] took the protest seriously. Paul's strong criticism of idolatry and pagan ways of life probably had roused Gentiles to hostility. The crowd, unable to find Paul and Silas, seized Jason, Paul's host, and made him give bond that there would be no more disturbance such as Paul's urgent preaching had aroused. Jason

---

11 The Egnatian Way ran from Dyrrhachium or Apollonia on the western coast of Macedonia through Thessalonica and Philippi to Neapolis, the seaport for Philippi. Travelers from Rome crossed the Adriatic Sea from Brundisium to Dyrrhachium or Apollonia and then went east on this main road.

12 The Old Testament passages used for this purpose are not specified. See C. H. Dodd, *According to the Scriptures*.

13 On these Gentiles loosely attached to the synagogue, see Kirsopp Lake, "Proselytes and God-Fearers," Note 8 in *The Beginnings of Christianity*, Vol. V, pp. 74–96.

14 Inscriptions at Thessalonica attest the title "politarchs" for officials there. One such inscription, which was on a Roman arch at the western entrance to the city, is now in the British Museum. Cf. Jack Finegan, *Light from the Ancient Past*, p. 271.

and the other disciples sent Paul and his companions away by night; the fugitives went to Beroea, a short distance southwest of Thessalonica (Acts 17:5–10).

JEWS AND GENTILES BELIEVE IN BEROEA

Two facts about Paul's ministry at Beroea are worth noting. Though The Acts reports numerous conversions, the church there is never mentioned again in the New Testament (but cf. ch. 20:4). And the ministry was particularly effective among Jews, who showed an openness to the gospel that Jews in other cities rarely matched (Acts 17:10–12). Paul got the entire Jewish group to consider whether the story of Jesus fulfilled Scripture, and he convinced many that it did. Gentiles also, including in part at least persons already under synagogue influence, believed in Christ.

But Jewish hostility in Thessalonica pursued Paul to Beroea and stirred up opposition to him, so his friends in Beroea took him to the sea and conducted him, apparently by ship, to Athens (Acts 17:13–15). The opposition was particularly against Paul; Silas and Timothy were able to stay behind and continue the work for a time. But as soon as Paul reached Athens, he needed their help, and sent word to them to come to him as soon as possible. He evidently depended on his friends and helpers more than is sometimes realized.

PAUL IN ATHENS

Silas and Timothy came to Paul at Athens, though The Acts does not say so. Timothy he sent back to encourage the Christians at Thessalonica and then return to tell Paul how they were faring (I Thess. 3:1–5). Probably Silas was sent on a similar visit to some other church of Macedonia, either Beroea or Philippi. Paul himself of course was not idle; he worked along two lines (Acts 17:16–18). He carried on active preaching and discussion in the synagogue with Jews and "devout" Gentiles; The Acts does not report the results. He also was stirred by the idolatry everywhere manifest to engage in discussion persons he met in the marketplace.

The modern tourist who visits Athens and its Acropolis gazes with awe at the ruins of ancient art and architecture. Paul, with a more discerning eye, looked at the scores or hundreds of statues of gods and goddesses, and was vocal against such a visible denial of his monotheistic faith and his loyalty to Christ. The sophisticated Greeks became curious.

Taking him aside from the bustle of the marketplace to the Areopagus, a small hill near the Acropolis, they asked him to explain his views (Acts 17:19–21). Luke reports that some thought he was preaching two new deities—Jesus and Anastasis; the Greek word for "resurrection" is *anastasis,* a feminine noun, so they supposed that Paul, following a frequent ancient pattern, was presenting a pair of deities, the male god Jesus and the female goddess Anastasis. The resurrection was central in Paul's thinking; his hearers had sensed that, but had misunderstood his message of the resurrection.

PAUL'S SPEECH ON THE AREOPAGUS

The ten verses of Paul's Areopagus speech as given in Acts 17:22–31 are famous in literature, but it is widely held that they are Luke's free composition rather than Paul's own words.[15] Certainly so short a passage is at best a brief summary of points Paul made in preaching to a Gentile audience unacquainted with Judaism; the actual wording is due to Luke. But the thought is what Paul could have said with his rabbinic background and his roots in Hellenistic Judaism. Pagan idolatry is at best only an ignorant groping after the real God, the Creator and Lord of all things, who is terribly misrepresented by idolatrous images; repentance and turning from such pagan life is urgent in view of the certain and imminent divine judgment of the world through "a man whom he has appointed" (v. 31) and has attested by raising him from the dead.

In the King James Version (v. 22) Paul's opening sentence refers to the Athenians as "too superstitious." The Revised Standard Version is probably justified in translating the Greek word "very religious," since Paul is pictured as opening his speech with a conciliatory point of contact with his hearers. But in fact Paul did think the idolatrous Athenians very superstitious; they were concerned and active in religion, but in a miserably misguided and most regrettable way, and his aim was to effect a thorough revolution in their religious outlook.

The inscription Paul says he had seen in Athens, "To an unknown god" (v. 23), cannot be found or paralleled, but one to unknown gods (plural) has been found, and it is possible that some grateful Greek who did not know what deity to thank for a favor or deliverance received had set up an altar "to an unknown god." The quotations from Epi-

---

15 The classic study of this speech by E. Norden, *Agnostos Theos* (Leipzig-Berlin, B. G. Teubner, 1913), argues that it is a traditional missionary sermon inserted into The Acts in the second century. An intensive argument that the speech can be Pauline is given by Bertil Gärtner, *The Areopagus Speech and Natural Revelation* (Lund, C. W. K. Gleerup, 1955).

menides and Aratus in v. 28 do not indicate great familiarity with Greek literature; they were current "quotable quotes" that any intelligent writer, including Paul, could have known.[16]

It is often said that this speech, like that at Lystra (Acts 14:15–17), presents a natural theology which Paul could not have used. Both passages, however, really present the Old Testament God, the Creator, Lord, and Judge. Almost nothing is said about Jesus; but Acts 17:18 indicates that the hearers at Athens knew quite well that Jesus was central and the resurrection prominent in Paul's message (cf. v. 31), so Luke was content to give Paul's approach in vs. 22–31 and refer briefly to the specifically Christian gospel in v. 18.

To Greeks who regarded the physical aspect of life as a limitation, the resurrection seemed an absurdity. Paul later encountered this problem in an acute form at Corinth (see I Cor., ch. 15). His success in Athens, Acts 17:32–34 indicates, was limited, and indeed neither the New Testament nor any early source speaks of a church there. At Athens, Paul met pride in Greek culture and religion but very little sense of need and openness.

A Notable Ministry at Corinth

In The Acts it would seem that Paul stopped only briefly in Athens. But he waited there until Silas and Timothy came to him, and sent them back to Macedonia (I Thess. 3:1). This implies that he stayed at least some weeks at Athens before he moved on to Corinth to seek a more responsive hearing. Again Luke tells who his hosts were; at Corinth he stayed with Aquila and his wife Priscilla (Acts 18:1–3). These Jews came originally from Pontus, on the southern shore of the Black Sea, but recently had been in Rome. Because of disturbances among Jews in Rome, the emperor Claudius, about A.D. 49, expelled the Jews from the city, so Aquila and Priscilla, forced to leave, moved to Corinth.[17] These disturbances, Suetonius says,[18] were at the instigation of one Chrestus. This may well mean that the synagogues at Rome were rocked by controversy over the claims made for Christ by Christian Jews but fiercely opposed by other Jews.

Were Aquila and Priscilla already Christians at Rome? Nothing in The Acts suggests that they were converted by Paul's preaching, and by

---

[16] See Kirsopp Lake, "The Unknown God" and "'Your Own Poets,'" Notes 19 and 20 in *The Beginnings of Christianity*, Vol. V, pp. 240–251.

[17] This suggests a date about A.D. 49 or 50 for Paul's arrival in Corinth.

[18] *Life of Claudius* XXV.4. See p. 66.

the time he left Corinth they were active Christians taking a prominent role in Paul's mission (Acts 18:18 f.). Possibly, therefore, they were already Christians when Paul came to Corinth, and for this reason, as well as because they and Paul were tentmakers, Paul stayed with them.

Luke often is content to mention a fact once at some stage of his story. So here he states for the first time that Paul worked as a tentmaker to support himself.[19] His policy was not to accept money support from a church while he was with it (I Cor. 9:15), and so except when churches he had founded sent him gifts after he had left them (cf. II Cor. 11:9; Phil. 4:15 f.; I Thess. 2:9; II Thess. 3:8), he worked to support himself and even his helpers (cf. Acts 20:34; I Cor. 4:12). He felt an urge to do this for a special reason; he had persecuted the church, and when he was converted and given his mission by what he regarded as an irresistible divine compulsion, he felt that only by forgoing the support to which he was entitled could he show something of his gratitude (I Cor. 9:3–18).

At first Paul worked during the week and preached in the synagogue on the Sabbath (Acts 18:4).[20] Then Silas and Timothy rejoined him, and apparently brought gifts from the Macedonian churches (II Cor. 11:9), for after they came "Paul was occupied with preaching" to win the Jews (Acts 18:5).

As almost invariably happened, the opposition grew—in spite of or perhaps precisely because of his success in winning both Jews and "devout" Gentiles to the Christian faith. He then had to leave the synagogue and "go" directly "to the Gentiles," moving his base of operations to the home of Titius Justus, a Gentile formerly interested in the synagogue and then won by Paul to the Christian faith. This home was located next door to the synagogue. The Jewish converts included Crispus, who before conversion had been the ruler of the synagogue, and his entire household. The nearness to the synagogue and the outspoken hostility of the Jews placed Paul in a tense situation. A vision telling him to continue his work in Corinth answered the question in his mind as to what he should do, and he settled down to stay there eighteen months (ch. 18: 5–11).

19 For the view that although the etymological meaning of the Greek word *skēnopoios* is "tentmaker," the Greeks used it to mean a "leatherworker," see *The Beginnings of Christianity*, Vol. IV, p. 223.

20 An inscription found not far from the marketplace in Corinth can come from this synagogue. Though not now complete, it almost certainly read: "Synagogue of the Hebrews." See Jack Finegan, *Light from the Ancient Past*, p. 281.

Paul's Ministry Through Letters

It was at Corinth, as far as extant evidence goes, that Paul began his unique and influential writing ministry. He was deeply concerned for the churches he had founded but could not often visit. At times he could send messengers—he had sent Silas and Timothy to Macedonia—but this did not give the churches his personal help. So he often turned to letter-writing as the best substitute for his personal presence. How many letters he wrote is not known, but the fact that letters ascribed to Paul form almost half of the books of the New Testament shows their importance as an expression of Christian faith, thinking, and pastoral concern. They give a much needed supplement to The Acts, which tells mainly how the gospel came to each new region rather than how the local churches grew in faith and maturity. The letters reveal problems the churches faced, and give a splendid insight into Paul's mission work and pastoral ministry.[21]

Many of Paul's letters are hard to date, but his earliest extant letter, I Thessalonians, was written fairly early in his ministry at Corinth. It shows many features common to all his letters. It begins, as was usual in Greek letters, by giving first the name of the writer, then the name of the recipient(s), and next a greeting to conclude the opening. However, Paul here as often shares credit for the writing with his companions; he names as coauthors Silvanus (Silas) and Timothy, although he himself wrote (or rather, dictated) the letter. He usually adds to the name of the writer(s) and to the name of the recipients words that refer to their Christian situation, and instead of the word "Greeting," regularly used in the opening of a Greek letter, or the word "Peace," similarly used in a Semitic letter, he always writes the Christian greeting, "Grace to you and peace," adding in later letters some such words as "from God our Father and the Lord Jesus Christ." Next in a Greek letter would come an expression of thanks or personal appreciation. Such a thanksgiving section in a Christian form always appears in Paul's letters to churches, except in Galatians, where his urgency and indignation leads him to plunge at once into a rebuke; all his other letters express thanks for something good in the Christian life of the churches, except II Corinthians, in which Paul thanks God for his own recent deliverance from danger and anxiety. Following the opening and thanksgiving came the body of the letter, dealing with whatever subjects the writer wanted to discuss. Finally came personal remarks, greetings to friends, and a final word of farewell, which in Paul's letters was always a Christian prayer that the recipients might receive the continuing grace of God.

[21] See O. J. F. Seitz, "Letter," *IDB*, K-Q, pp. 113–115.

The letters of Paul, therefore, are not theological essays but direct responses to the situation and needs of the readers, and they are unsurpassed sources concerning the life of Paul and his churches. They were preserved and finally placed in the New Testament canon not because they dealt with general timeless topics but because they dealt with current specific situations in the light of the basic gospel, and dealt with them so helpfully that they can continually speak to the church about Christian faith and life.

THE FIRST LETTER TO THESSALONICA

I Thessalonica was written immediately after Timothy returned to Corinth from Thessalonica with the good news that the persecuted Christians there were holding fast to their faith and remembered Paul with gratitude and love (I Thess. 2:17 to 3:8). Opponents of Paul, mainly the Jews, had accused him of bad motives and suggested that if he cared for the church, he would visit them. Paul seems to have been kept from such a visit to them mainly by the bond that Jason and others had given (Acts 17:9). But he thanks God for their true faith and good life (I Thess.1:2–10), recalls his faithful and sincere ministry to them (I Thess. 2:1–16), and earnestly assures them of his love and interest. Their steadfastness, he assures them, has given him joy and courage (I Thess. 2:17 to 3:10). He closes the opening half of the letter with a formal prayer that the readers (or rather, hearers, since the letter will be read aloud at a gathering of the church) may grow in love and faithful integrity (I Thess. 3:11–13).

The second half opens with the same note of satisfaction and encouragement: "Just as you are doing, . . . do so more and more" (I Thess. 4:1). They are to follow Paul's teaching, and be pure in their sex life—a standard not common in pagan life (vs. 2–8). They are to love one another, live quietly, and work to provide for their needs (vs. 9–12). Note this latter point. Concerned about the end of the world, which Paul had taught them could be expected soon, they tended to quit work, live idle lives, and thus bring discredit on the church. Verses 13–18 shows their vivid expectation of the end. Contrary to their expectation, some of their number had died. Would their beloved dead have no part in the final triumph of Christ? Paul assures them that when Christ returns, the dead Christians will rise first, then they and the living will be caught up together to meet the returning Lord ("we who are alive," v. 17, shows that Paul expects the end to come in his lifetime); they all will share the triumph and the perfect life of God's eternal Kingdom; "and so we shall always be with the Lord."

How can they tell when the end is to come? It will come suddenly, "like a thief in the night," so they must always be ready and alert and help their comrades do the same (I Thess. 5:1–11). They must respect their leaders and live busy, helpful, prayerful, thankful, Spirit-guided lives (vs. 12–22). A second formal prayer (vs. 23 f.; cf. ch. 3:11–13) closes the formal letter; final instructions and a closing benediction then follow (ch. 5:25–28). The letter is to be read to "all the brethren." They had no church building; meetings were held in homes. No doubt several groups thus met separately; all must hear the letter and keep in touch with one another (v. 27).[22]

The notable thing about this letter is its unusually strong expectation that the end of the age and the coming of the Lord Christ were very near. The letter, urging the readers to be ready for that coming at any minute, encouraged them in such expectation, and continued persecution (II Thess. 1:4) made them ready for the Final Day. Excited idleness made the Christians suspect as a disturbing and troublesome group, and when Paul heard of the situation, he wrote them again. He was the more prompt to do this, since he feared or knew that a letter circulating at Thessalonica purported to be from him and said "that the day of the Lord has come" (II Thess. 2:2).

The Second Letter to Thessalonica

In this situation, Paul, still at Corinth, writes II Thessalonians. The usual thanksgiving expresses gratitude that God has enabled the readers to hold steadfast even under persecution. Their faithfulness is an assurance that God's judgment will soon strike their wicked persecutors (II Thess. 1:3–12).[23] But the readers must not think "that the day of the Lord has come" or will come immediately (ch. 2:1–2). A present restraining power (v. 6), a restraining person (v. 7), must be removed before the man of lawlessness, the great final expression of the diabolical forces opposing God and his church, can appear and threaten to destroy the church.[24] Only when the restrainer is removed and the man of lawlessness

22 On I and II Thessalonians, see the articles by F. W. Beare in *IDB*, R-Z, pp. 621–629, and the commentaries by James Everett Frame, *A Critical and Exegetical Commentary on the Epistles of St. Paul to the Thessalonians* (Charles Scribner's Sons, 1912), and William Neil, *The Epistle of Paul to the Thessalonians* (London, Hodder and Stoughton, 1950).

23 Not only this passage but I Thess. 2:14 shows that this young church had to withstand persecution from their fellow Thessalonians.

24 The restraining power and person are often taken to be the Roman Empire and the Roman emperor. Oscar Cullmann, *Christ and Time*, pp. 164–166, holds that the reference is to the missionary preaching and the apostle Paul. Similarly, Johannes Munck, *Paul and the Salvation of Mankind*, pp. 36–43, takes the reference to be to Paul's preaching to the Gentiles.

appears will the Lord Jesus come and defeat and slay the man of lawlessness; after that, God's perfect order will be established. Until those
final events, and especially during them, the Thessalonians must stand
firm and prove loyal to Christ (vs. 1–15). Paul here uses traditional
imagery about the great final clash between the forces of evil and the
cause of God led by the Lord Jesus. He does so to nerve the Thessalonians to stand firm and live faithfully in whatever remaining time may
elapse before the end of the age comes. Paul expected that end rather
soon.

The pattern of II Thessalonians is much like that of I Thessalonians.
The longer opening half closes with a formal prayer (II Thess. 2:16 f.).
The shorter second half gives varied practical teaching about how the
readers should live (ch. 3:1–15); Paul emphasizes their need to work and
earn their own living rather than to be idle busybodies who bring discredit on the church. The second formal prayer (v. 16) is followed by
a statement of Paul's in his own handwriting. He has dictated the main
letter; if a forged letter is in circulation (ch. 2:2), the readers can tell
this by comparing it with his handwritten greeting such as he adds in
every letter (ch. 3:17). Then comes the final benediction (v. 18).[25]

These two letters illustrate the dangers in too vivid an expectation of
the end of the age. Paul never gave up this expectation (cf. Phil. 4:5,
probably written near the close of his life). It was an essential part of
his firm Christian faith that Christ's full triumph was sure and could
come very soon. But he guided his other churches so that they did not
lose their balance, as the Thessalonians had done, over the expected
return of Christ. The heart of his gospel, as his other letters show, was
not the certain imminence of that return but the redeeming work of
Christ, accepted in faith. It made the believer capable of meeting the
present and awaiting with trust the future.

THE CRISIS IN GALATIA

In addition to I and II Thessalonians, Paul may have written from
Corinth his letter to the churches of Galatia. A definite dating of Ga-

25 The close similarity in formal pattern and the difference in the emphasis (on the
nearness of the end in I Thessalonians but on delay in its coming in II Thessalonians) have caused some either to doubt that Paul wrote II Thessalonians, or to
say that it went to a group other than those addressed in I Thessalonians (suggested
destinations: Jewish Christians in Thessalonica or Beroea, or the church in Philippi).
See the article by Beare listed in note 22. It is doubtful whether any of these hy-
potheses can explain the facts as well as the usual view, accepted above, that I and
II Thessalonians both went to all the Christians at Thessalonica. T. W. Manson,
Studies in the Gospels and Epistles, Ch. 14, argues that we can best understand the
two letters by assuming that II Thessalonians was written before I Thessalonians.

latians is not possible. If Acts 16:6 means that Paul preached in North Galatia, where Pessinus, Ancyra, and Tavium were located, then Galatians probably should be dated during Paul's long ministry in Ephesus (Acts 19:8, 10). But if, as is more likely, Galatians was written to South Galatia, to the churches in Pisidian Antioch, Iconium, Lystra, and Derbe, founded on the visit reported in Acts, chs. 13 f., then Paul may well have written Galatians from Corinth in the period of Acts 18:11. The essential meaning and message of the letter remain the same in either case.

The situation reflected in Galatians is the important thing to understand. Whatever adaptations Paul and the Gentile Christians had made to facilitate unity in the church and active fellowship between Jewish and Gentile Christians, he had not asked or permitted Gentiles to observe the Jewish law found in the Pentateuch, and of course had not imposed on them the oral traditions that to Pharisees were an integral part of the Mosaic law.

It is easy to understand how some Jewish believers in Christ thought Paul had surrendered essentials.[26] They accepted the Jewish Scripture, which included the law, as obligatory for God's people. They agreed with Paul that Gentiles of course were welcome in the church. But they held that Gentile believers should accept the Scriptures and keep the law just as Jews necessarily do. There is no salvation for either Jew or Gentile who breaks God's covenant with Abraham and refuses to fulfill the precepts of the law. So Paul's Gentile converts must be told to accept and obey the law. These legalistic Jewish Christians insisted that all Christians should observe the law; this is involved in being part of God's people.

Thus the aim of the Judaizers, the "circumcision party," was to have all Christians observe the Jewish law as well as believe in Christ. Their immediate aim when Paul wrote Galatians was to get Gentile Christians to become circumcised. This they held was prescribed by God himself (cf. Gen. 17:9–14).

It seems that in Galatia this attack on Paul and this pressure to observe the law began by inducing the Galatian Christians, most of whom were of Gentile origin, to keep the Jewish feasts (Gal. 4:10); as we might say, they had persuaded the Galatians to observe the Jewish "church year," the annual feasts such as Passover, Unleavened Bread, Pentecost, Day of Atonement, and Tabernacles.[27] Now they were insisting that the

---

26 Johannes Munck, *Paul and the Salvation of Mankind*, Ch. 4, thinks that Paul's opponents in Galatia were Judaizing Gentile Christians.
27 The "days" in Gal. 4:10 could refer to the Sabbath, Passover, and Day of Atonement. "Months" could refer to the new moon celebrations. "Seasons" could refer to

Gentile Christians practice circumcision. They argued that this was clearly prescribed in the law. This point, if accepted, would establish the principle that what the law requires the Gentile must do if he wants to be a Christian and be saved. Paul saw clearly how crucial this issue was: What is the basis of salvation?

To gain their aim, the Judaizers had to attack Paul. They attacked him on three counts: 1. He was not a true apostle and so was not an authoritative interpreter of the gospel. 2. The gospel he taught was false; it wrongly stated how one becomes a Christian and what attitude one should take toward circumcision and the keeping of the law. 3. His gospel that Gentiles were not under the Jewish law must inevitably lead to bad results in conduct.

Paul's letter in reply to these attacks was written when his opponents seemed on the verge of convincing the Galatians to renounce Paul's leadership and adopt the legal demands of his opponents. In general, he answers each of the three attacks by two chapters of his letter.[28]

PAUL'S LETTER TO THE GALATIANS

From the first line of the letter, its form is shaped by the situation. In Gal. 1:1 f. Paul asserts that all the Christian brothers with him agree with what he is to say, and that he is an apostle directly appointed by God and Christ and so his teaching is authoritative; he is not subject to the Twelve or to James. His greeting (vs. 3–5) implies that his gospel of redemption by divine grace is the only valid message for the church; Christ's death and not the keeping of the law is the means of salvation. He omits the usual Thanksgiving section; instead, he hastens to rebuke the readiness of the Galatians to abandon Paul's gospel of the free grace of God and accept the radically different message—no gospel at all— that one must keep the law to be saved (vs. 6–10). Then he begins his main argument.

He received his gospel message by direct divine revelation (vs. 11 f.). Step by step he traces the course of his pre-Christian life, his conversion, and his conduct since conversion, and shows that he had been converted by the risen Christ, had had no contact with the Jerusalem leaders at the critical initial stages of his Christian life, and could not have received his message or commission from them (vs. 13–24). Rather, he had vindi-

---

the festivals that lasted more than one day, e.g., the Feast of Unleavened Bread and the Feast of Tabernacles. "Years" could refer to the Sabbatical Year and the Year of Jubilee, or, more likely, to the New Year celebration.

28 On Galatians, see the article by J. Knox in *IDB*, E-J, pp. 338–343, and the commentaries of Ernest de Witt Burton, *The Epistle to the Galatians,* and George S. Duncan, *The Epistle of Paul to the Galatians* (Harper & Brothers, 1934).

cated his independent apostleship in the conference at Jerusalem (ch.
2:1–10) and in his face-to-face challenge of Peter at Antioch (vs. 11–21).

Christian experience, Scripture, and argument support Paul's gospel
(chs. 3:1 to 4:31). When Paul preached to the Galatians, they received
the Spirit, not because they had kept the law but because they had believed Paul's gospel; the divine Spirit thus confirmed his message (ch. 3:
1–5). Faith and not works made Abraham acceptable to God, and those
who believe in Christ are the true sons of Abraham; not physical descent
from Abraham, nor doing what the law requires, but faith makes man
acceptable to God (vs. 6–9). No man by fully obeying the law can earn
his standing before God; the law only makes clear how sinful man is
and how much he needs a Savior. God provides salvation in Christ, and
man receives it as a gift contrary to what he deserves. The one condition
that all must fulfill is grateful, wholehearted faith, and such faith marks
Christ's people as free sons of God (chs. 3:10 to 4:31).

Set free by Christ from guilt and sin, the Christian is free—not free
to do wrong, but now for the first time truly free to do the will of God
from a grateful heart. The grateful faith that gives the life to God in
Christ works out in a life of love. The Spirit produces in such a life
good fruit; the disciple is obedient to God and helpful to his fellows.
The believing Christian by this life of love now fulfills the law which
formerly could only increase his transgression and guilt. The believer
lives by the power of the Spirit; he can do the will of God, and must
dedicate himself to do so (chs. 5:1 to 6:10).

The letter, Paul realized, was urgently important, so he took the pen
and added in his own handwriting a summary of what he had dictated
(ch. 6:11–18). This shows how crucial he knew the issue was, and how
much he cared for the Galatians. The letter is one of the key writings of
Christian history. Paul had to vindicate his own apostleship because his
opponents were trying to discredit his message by discrediting him. But
his main concern was not personal vindication; it was to defend the
gospel of salvation through Christ for sinners who respond in grateful
faith and gladly live in love and obedience to God.

THE CLOSE OF PAUL'S STAY IN CORINTH

In the sinful city of Corinth,[29] widely known for its low morals, such
a gospel had special point. During a relatively long stay, Paul preached
and served as pastor to a constantly growing church that contained both

---

[29] On the Corinth of Paul's day, see O. Broneer, "Corinth: Center of Paul's Missionary
Work in Greece," *The Biblical Archaeologist*, Vol. XIV (1951), pp. 77–96.

Jews and Gentiles. After he had worked in Corinth more than a year and a half (Acts 18:11), the Jews thought they saw a chance to get rid of him. A new proconsul, Gallio, had just arrived to take up his administration of the province of Achaia (Greece), of which Corinth was the capital city. (A fragmentary inscription found at Delphi enables us to date his arrival in A.D. 51 or 52.[30]) The Jews charged Paul with teaching contrary to Judaism (Acts 18:12 f.). Since Rome tolerated only recognized religions, and Paul's message—so they claimed—was not Judaism (or any other lawful religion), it was an illicit religion; it should be suppressed and the preachers punished.

Gallio decided that the gospel was a form of Judaism, and refused to interfere (Acts 18:14–16). One can see his point, for Paul insisted that his gospel fulfilled the promises to Israel; but one can also understand the position of the Jews, for Judaism as it existed would undergo radical change if Jews accepted the gospel.

The astonishing thing in The Acts is that when Gallio rejected the Jewish charge, the Jews who had made it seized and beat Sosthenes, the ruler of the synagogue (Acts 18:17). They apparently thought that Sosthenes was too lenient toward the Christians or was ready to believe the gospel message. Some two or three years later, when writing I Cor. 1:1 from Ephesus, Paul names as coauthor "our brother Sosthenes." It would seem that the Jews had reason for their suspicion. He was the second synagogue ruler in Corinth to become a Christian (cf. Acts 18:8).

PAUL REVISITS JERUSALEM AND ANTIOCH

For a time after Paul was accused before Gallio, he continued his work at Corinth. Then he felt it necessary or advisable to revisit his original base at Antioch in Syria. His reason is not clear. But when ready to sail from Cenchreae, the eastern seaport of Corinth, Paul cut his hair in fulfillment of a (Nazirite?) vow (Acts 18:18; cf. 21:23–26). This recalls his deep ties with his ancestral faith and his own people; perhaps part of the purpose of the voyage was to complete in the Temple in Jerusalem ceremonies connected with this vow.

In any case, Paul thought he had finished his pioneer work at Corinth, and should continue his strategy of taking the gospel to every main center of the Roman Empire where it was not already established (cf. II Cor. 10:15 f.). So on his way from Corinth to Jerusalem he went to

---

[30] Jack Finegan, *Light from the Ancient Past*, p. 282, gives a translation of the now fragmentary inscription and concludes that Gallio became proconsul about July 1 in A.D. 51.

Ephesus, taking Priscilla and Aquila with him, and after speaking and
arousing interest in the synagogue there, he left these two trusted friends
to prepare for his work there when he returned (Acts 18:19–21). Then
he sailed from Ephesus, landed at Caesarea in Palestine, "went up and
greeted the church, and then went down to Antioch" (Acts 18:22). This
could mean that he greeted the church in Caesarea and at once went
north to Antioch in Syria. But the immense importance of Jerusalem
for Paul and the church argues that he "went up" from the seacoast to
Jerusalem, 2,400 feet above sea level, perhaps to fulfill ceremonies connected with his vow (Acts 18:18). The Acts mentions no welcome from
the Jerusalem church or any contact with it; this suggests that Paul's
purpose in this visit was personal or that relations between Paul and
James the brother of Jesus were not cordial.

The Acts is equally silent about Paul's welcome or contacts at Antioch.
Perhaps there too his relations were not cordial, but the omission may
only be due to the purpose of The Acts to concentrate on Paul, now
busy with his independent mission, rather than to divert attention to
regions with which Paul was no longer decisively concerned.

For Luke the important thing was to tell of the next stage of Paul's
epochal mission. It began with another pastoral visit to central Asia
Minor (Acts 18:23). If Galatia here and in Acts 16:6 refers to North
Galatia, where descendants of Gallic invaders from Europe lived, then
Paul visited not only the churches of South Galatia: Pisidian Antioch,
Iconium, Lystra, and Derbe, but also such places as Pessinus, Ancyra, and
Tavium in North Galatia. More likely Paul had never preached in
North Galatia, and on this occasion his objective was to visit South
Galatia and then go westward into the Roman province of Asia and work
in its chief city Ephesus.

APOLLOS AT EPHESUS AND CORINTH

During Paul's travels after leaving Corinth, an able Alexandrian Jew
named Apollos came to Ephesus. Possibly he came directly from Alexandria in Egypt, but since he knew of the baptism of John, and it is not
clear how much was then known of John the Baptist in Egypt, he may
have come by way of Palestine.[31] Earnest in spirit, eloquent in speech,
and unusually well versed in the Scriptures, he preached the message of
John the Baptist and apparently baptized in preparation for the Greater

---

31 We have no clear and trustworthy information on how the gospel first reached
Egypt. S. G. F. Brandon has tried to show that Egypt had a prominent role in the
early church following the fall of Jerusalem in A.D. 70; cf. *The Fall of Jerusalem
and the Christian Church*, Ch. 12.

One to follow John. The statement that he "taught accurately the things concerning Jesus, though he knew only the baptism of John," seems to mean that he knew of John but did not yet identify Jesus as the Greater One whom John had said would come (Acts 18:24-26). Obviously the disciples of John the Baptist had continued an independent movement for more than twenty-five years after his death and through Apollos, if not before, this movement had reached Ephesus. The dozen "disciples" Paul found there who did not know of Jesus probably had been taught by Apollos (Acts 19:1-7). If, as tradition says, the Gospel of John was written from Ephesus, its spirited determination to put John in a role subordinate to Jesus (John 1:6-8,15;3:27-30) would show that this movement was still present in Ephesus late in the first century.

Priscilla and Aquila, left in Ephesus by Paul, convinced Apollos that Jesus had fulfilled the prediction of John the Baptist, and Apollos henceforth preached a clear Christian gospel. Like Paul and other early Christian preachers, he moved from place to place; he soon crossed the Aegean Sea to Corinth with a letter of recommendation from the little group of disciples at Ephesus, a group probably established by Paul's synagogue preaching there and by the activity of Priscilla and Aquila (Acts 18:27 f.).

PAUL'S LONG MINISTRY AT EPHESUS

Not long after Apollos left Ephesus, Paul, coming from his visit to the churches of South Galatia, arrived and took up his ministry in the synagogue (Acts 19:1, 8).[32] That he could still work in the synagogue indicates that the "brethren" of Acts 18:27 were Jewish Christians. He had considerable success in this synagogue ministry, continuing there for three months before Jewish hostility forced him to withdraw with his converts and begin direct preaching to Gentiles.

For this wider ministry, he rented the hall of an otherwise unknown Tyrannus; according to some ancient manuscripts, he rented this hall only during the midday rest period "from the fifth hour to the tenth," that is, from about eleven A.M to four P.M. (Acts 19:9).[33] In two years of preaching and teaching in this publicly accessible hall, Paul made the gospel message generally known in Ephesus, and since Ephesus was continually visited by residents of smaller cities of the province, these visitors and Paul's helpers carried the gospel to these smaller cities throughout the province of Asia, whose chief city was Ephesus (Acts 19:8-10).

[32] On Ephesus, see Jack Finegan in *IDB*, E-J, pp. 114-118. Also, Merrill M. Parvis, "Ephesus," and Floyd V. Filson, "Ephesus and the New Testament," in *The Biblical Archaeologist*, Vol. VIII (1945), pp. 61-73 and 73-80.
[33] See F. F. Bruce, *The Acts of the Apostles*, p. 356.

This was Paul's longest ministry in any one city, and was directed to both Jews and Gentiles. Acts 19:11 f. notes that Paul was able to perform numerous miracles. There is no good reason to doubt that he, like Peter, and like Jesus before them both, was able to give health of mind and body to disturbed and diseased people (II Cor. 12:12; cf. Rom. 15:19; Gal. 3:5). The story of the seven sons of a (self-styled?) "Jewish high priest" named Sceva reflects the view that mental disturbance was due to demons, "evil spirits." The seven sons attempted to use the name of Jesus as a magical means of exorcising demons, and their failure, it is implied, was due to their failure to share the Christian faith (Acts 19:13-17).

Such stories reflect a thought world different from that of today, but they contain the solid fact that the Christian leaders with their faith in Christ and their compassion for the suffering were able to perform healings in a way that shamed those who attempted such feats merely as a business venture and to get public fame. The superstitious common people, much addicted to magical formulas and a good market for those who sold copies of magical incantations,[34] were impressed by Paul's preaching and healings; in one mass ceremony they burned a great number of such magical books (Acts 19:18 f.).

The summary in Acts 19:20 states briefly the solid effects of Paul's independent mission, and marks the end of that mission. From Acts 19:21 on, the story points to Rome.[35] But before following that story we must speak of letters written from Ephesus.

Paul's outlook always had wide horizons. From the beginning of his Christian life he thought of the gospel as destined for the world, and he soon began to find his place in the expanding mission of the church. It was essential for him in that widening ministry to keep touch with the churches he had founded. He carried their problems and needs on his mind and heart. Occasionally he could revisit them; sometimes he could send an assistant to visit and help them; but often a letter was his best way of continuing his ministry to them. While at Ephesus this ministry by letter continued. Possibly he wrote to the Galatians from Ephesus. But probably, as already noted, Galatians was written from Corinth to the churches in South Galatia. His main letters from Ephesus, as far as we know, were written to deal with a series of problems that arose in the gifted but erratic church at Corinth.

---

34 For ancient testimony that Ephesus was known for its interest in such magical practices, see F. F. Bruce, *The Acts of the Apostles*, p. 360.

35 That nine and a half of the twenty-eight chapters of The Acts deal with the journey to Rome via Jerusalem shows how important that journey was in Luke's view of the spread of the gospel.

Four Letters to Corinth

Paul's correspondence with Corinth was more extensive and tells more about his work and his churches than any other of his letters that survive. Within a year he wrote at least four letters to Corinth.[36] They repay careful study for their light on the history of the apostolic church.

I. The Lost Letter

Prior to the letter we call I Corinthians, Paul had written a letter telling the Christians of Corinth not to associate with immoral men (cf. I Cor. 5:9). He found this church too lax in its moral standards and too ready to excuse lax sex conduct. The letter no doubt dealt with other subjects, but only its instructions on this one topic are known. (It is just possible that II Cor. 6:14 to 7:1 was part of this letter.)

The Corinthians, more clever than judicious, appealed to the fact that in Corinth, notorious for its immoral practices,[37] no one who engaged in business and community activities could avoid contacts with those who shamelessly lived immoral lives. So they ridiculed Paul's letter and called his instructions impractical. Paul was concerned essentially with true standards of life and judgment within the church itself; he always insisted that Christians must live pure lives; they should of course support this standard in wider relations, but their primary duty was to teach and live by this standard in their own circle.

One purpose of Paul's second letter to Corinth, the one we call I Corinthians, was to correct the misinterpretation of his first letter. He wanted the church to refuse to associate with those in its group who committed such immorality or other serious wrongdoing. Community discipline must be maintained. Possibly it was to help correct the misunderstanding of his earliest letter to them that Paul sent Timothy to Corinth, perhaps by way of Macedonia; when Paul wrote I Cor. 16:10 f., Timothy was on his way to Corinth with some mission from Paul.

Other concerns led Paul to write a second letter. He had news from Corinth through "Chloe's people" (I Cor. 1:11). Chloe may have been

---

[36] The problems in identifying these letters and reconstructing the situation are sketched in the articles of S. M. Gilmour on I and II Corinthians in *IDB*, A-D, pp. 684–698. See also A. H. McNeile, *An Introduction to the Study of the New Testament*, 2d ed. revised by C. S. C. Williams (Oxford, Clarendon Press, 1953), pp. 132–142.

[37] The reputation of Corinth was such that a verb, "to Corinthianize," had been coined to mean "to practice fornication," and the moral danger of going to Corinth was proverbial.

a woman of Corinth or Ephesus who to foster business or family ties had representatives who traveled between the two cities. She is not said to be a Christian, but since Paul assumes that the Corinthian Christians know her, she probably was. Her people told Paul of serious defects in the church at Corinth.

He had two other sources of information. Three men, Stephanas, Fortunatus, and Achaicus, had come to Ephesus to consult Paul. They were from Corinth, and Stephanas was one of Paul's first converts there (I Cor. 16:15–18; cf. ch. 1:16). Probably they brought the letter from Corinth mentioned in I Cor. 7:1; it asked for Paul's counsel. Thus Paul wrote again to Corinth to correct a probably deliberate misunderstanding of his letter against tolerating immorality in the church, to deal with disturbing reports from Chloe's people, to give counsel as suggested by friends just come from Corinth, and to reply to a letter seeking Paul's pastoral advice. This letter is our I Corinthians.[38]

II. The Pastoral Letter

The letter opening recalls the Corinthians' high privilege; they are "sanctified in Christ Jesus, called to be saints,"[39] and as part of the one church, must share its commonly accepted teaching and standards (I Cor. 1:2). Before turning to rebuke and correction, Paul thanks God for their gifts and Christian faith; their brilliance needs discipline, but he recognizes their special gifts (vs. 4–9). Then he takes up their problems, and throws great light on the early church:

a. Partisan quarrels (chs. 1:10 to 4:21). There seem to have been four parties. One embarrassed Paul by a partisan appeal to him as their leader. Another played up the eloquence and wisdom of Apollos. A third appealed to Peter, who as one of the Twelve, even if he had not visited Corinth, might seem to Jewish Christians in particular a better guide than Paul. A fourth group made a partisan appeal to Christ; perhaps it appealed to James and his family ties with Jesus, or was "spiritualistic" and claimed special revelations and knowledge from Christ. For Paul, the church of Christ is one and cannot be divided. Divisive pride in human leaders or personal gifts has no place. Though

---

38 Useful commentaries on I Corinthians are Archibald Robertson and Alfred Plummer, *A Critical and Exegetical Commentary on the First Epistle of St. Paul to the Corinthians* (Charles Scribner's Sons, 1911), and James Moffatt, *The First Epistle of Paul to the Corinthians* (London, Hodder and Stoughton, 1938). On I Corinthians as on other N.T. books *The Interpreter's Bible* is useful, especially the Introduction on each book.

39 The Greek word for "saints," *hagioi*, does not refer to selected Christians who are especially virtuous but to all Christians as "consecrated" to God.

Apollos and Paul remained friends (ch. 16:12), Paul attacks particularly those who found in Apollos a satisfying wisdom. The real wisdom for Paul was to accept gratefully the saving work of the crucified Christ. Each Christian should benefit from the gifts of all the leaders and never let any leader take the central place, which belongs to Christ alone.

b. Problems of sex and marriage (chs. 5:1 to 7:40, except ch. 6:1–11). High standards of sex and family life were normal among the Jews, but in pagan life, with notable exceptions, there was a laxity on these points which conflicted radically with the teaching of the Old Testament, Jesus, and Paul. Paul had condemned such immorality in the Lost Letter (cf. I Cor. 5:9). Now he had learned that a man was living with his father's wife. Even if the woman was the man's foster mother and his father was dead, such a union was not wholesome.[40] Paul insisted that the church expel the guilty man (ch. 5:1–8). Some Corinthians evidently held that all things are lawful for the Christian and that physical acts are not spiritually wrong or harmful. Paul rejected this false division of life into two separate compartments (ch. 6:12–20).

In view especially of the nearness of the end of the age (I Cor. 7:26, 31), Paul thought it preferable to refrain from marriage, but he recognized that for most people marriage was better, and he considered it fully in accord with God's will (vs. 1–9). He echoed Jesus' teaching forbidding divorce (vs. 10 f., 39); however, if a Christian had a pagan marriage partner who insisted on separating, the Christian could permit this, but not remarry (vs. 12–16). In general, the Christian would do well to live until the end of the age in the condition in which he or she was when converted (vs. 17–24). An engaged man would do well to refrain from marriage, but to marry would not be wrong (vs. 25–38).[41]

c. Lawsuits before pagan judges (ch. 6:1–11). It shocked Paul that Christians had such disputes; he thought that for the sake of the gospel and the community standing of the church, Christians should submit to wrong instead of insisting on their rights. If two Christians had a dispute and could not settle it, they should let fellow Christians decide it. Christians, who are to judge the world and even angels (vs. 2 f.), should surely be able to settle trivial disputes.

d. Food offered to idols (chs. 8:1 to 11:1). Some Christians at Corinth thought that to eat meat of animals killed in pagan sacrifice would approve idolatry. Others considered that since idols are not real gods,

---

[40] It is more likely that the father was still living and the situation flagrantly immoral.

[41] There was a custom in the church later for a man and woman to live together without having normal sex relations. This was to show an ascetic superiority to physical indulgence. Some think that Paul's words in this passage show that such a practice was already known at Corinth.

the meat could be eaten. Paul urged that all Christians refrain from participation in actual feasts at idol shrines; to eat at them would subject the Christian to the demons active in idol worship (ch. 10:20 f.). But he himself saw no inherent evil in eating meat sold in the public markets after the animal had been sacrificed in a pagan cult. A Christian could eat such meat when set before him at a dinner unless informed that it had been offered to idols; in that case, he should not eat it, for he must not seem to approve idol worship; and he must not eat when to do so would lead a fellow Christian to eat such food against his conscience (chs. 8:7–13; 10:27–29). To act against conscience, even in matters indifferent in themselves, is bad, and to lead another person to go against his conscience is still worse.

As an example of giving up one's rights, Paul cites his own example in ch. 9; he was entitled to support from his churches, but he had not claimed his full rights; he had given them up to further the progress of the gospel. Christians should show a like spirit in such matters as eating meat offered to idols; even if they can eat without hurt to their conscience, they should willingly refrain if to eat would pressure another to eat contrary to his conscience.

e. Problems of worship. Paul deals with three. Some Corinthian women, glad in the freedom they had found in Christ, had begun to worship with head unveiled. This shocked many observers; the boldness recalled habits of immoral women of the day. Paul insisted that Christian women pray with heads veiled (ch. 11:2–16). His advice had wisdom in it, though it did not root in such an eternal will of God as he supposed.

Most instructive is Paul's teaching about the proper way to observe the Lord's Supper (I Cor. 11:17–34).[42] At that time it was a hunger-satisfying meal. Essential to it was a sharing of the food and wine. But at Corinth some brought abundant food and wine and shared it with their family or friends, whereas the poor were not fed or treated with brotherly concern. Such selfish enjoyment and snobbish cliques made Paul indignant. He proposed an innovation that finally separated the Lord's Supper from the church supper: Let the hungry eat something at home so as not to rush to the Supper like hungry beasts (v. 34). The essential thing for the church at the Supper is to recall what Christ's death means for his people and so continually keep this in mind until he comes again. In vs. 23–26 Paul repeats the tradition he received at his conversion a very few years after the death of Christ; it is our oldest written record of Jesus' actions and words at the Last Supper.

42 See A. J. B. Higgins, *The Lord's Supper in the New Testament.*

The third problem of worship was the right use and relative value of spiritual gifts (chs. 12:1 to 14:40).[43] Worship at Corinth was exciting but not always helpful. There was no set order; each one took part as led by the Holy Spirit. Some were proud that they could speak with tongues—unintelligible ecstatic speech, spectacular but not instructive to the hearers. Other gifts included prophecy—intelligible searching speech beneficial to those who listened with a humble and teachable spirit. Paul's concern was the right use of all such spiritual gifts. No utterance of the Spirit will belittle or denounce Jesus Christ; that is one test of alleged spiritual utterances (ch. 12:1–3). God gives varied spiritual gifts, and each must honor the gifts of others; all gifts must work together for the good and upbuilding of the community (vs. 4–31). No gift benefits the possessor unless exercised in the spirit of love; only actions springing from love have value and permanence (ch. 13). Prophecy rates above speaking with tongues, because it benefits others, and that is the test of the worth of a gift (ch. 14:1–25). Finally, Paul urges orderliness and courtesy in worship; "All things should be done decently and in order" (vs. 26–40).

f. The resurrection of the dead (ch. 15). Doubts were being expressed in Corinth about the resurrection of the dead. The doubters held, not that physical death ended man's existence, but that in the perfect future life only the spirit will live on. Paul strongly opposes this view.[44] He recalls the tradition of the resurrection appearances of Jesus (vs. 3–7), another bit of tradition received at his conversion and handed on to his churches. The resurrection of Jesus is an essential part of the gospel story. Paul does not mean that man will rise with the same body he had during his earthly life (v. 50). Just as the risen Christ who appeared to Paul had a spiritual body, so his people will be transformed at the Last Day. The resurrection will give to them a perfect body or form of existence in which they will live with God and Christ in the eternal Kingdom. Paul is opposing the idea that only a part of man will survive. Man will have a full and perfect life in a form suited to eternal fellowship with God and God's people.

g. The collection for the Christians in Jerusalem (I Cor. 16:1–4). To express Christian brotherhood, to bind the Gentile churches to the Jewish Christians in Palestine, to show the Jerusalem church the truly Christian concern of the Gentile Christians, and to keep his agreement

---

[43] On "Spiritual Gifts," see E. Andrews' article in *IDB*, R-Z, pp. 435–437.
[44] His view and that of the New Testament as a whole is presented by Oscar Cullmann, *Immortality of the Soul or Resurrection of the Body?* (The Macmillan Company, 1958).

(Gal. 2:10), Paul asked his churches to take a collection for the poor Christians ("saints") in Jerusalem. He asks each Corinthian to set aside something for this fund on the first day of every week. Sunday, he indicates, was a time of regular worship and fellowship in his churches, no doubt because it was known as the day on which Jesus rose from the dead (cf. Rev. 1:10).

h. Travel plans and conclusion (I Cor. 16:5–24). Paul writes at Passover time in the spring (ch. 5:7). He plans to stay in Ephesus, where he writes, until Pentecost (ch. 16:8). Then he intends to go to Macedonia and on to Corinth for a visit (v. 5). And so with personal news, an expression of love, and a prayer for their good he closes this notable Pastoral Letter.

PAUL'S FUTILE VISIT TO CORINTH

I Corinthians did not solve the problems at Corinth. After it was received, criticism of Paul and opposition to his leadership continued. Visiting teachers, Jewish Christians who called themselves apostles[45] and brought with them letters of recommendation, worked craftily to undermine the influence of Paul (II Cor. 3:1; 11:4–6); they said he was not a true and authorized apostle. If Timothy visited Corinth (cf. I Cor. 16:10), he failed to remedy the crisis. To hold the church steady and undercut the influence of the visiting teachers, Paul made a visit from Ephesus to Corinth (cf. II Cor. 12:14; 13:1 f.), but he was rebuffed and returned to Ephesus defeated. On leaving Corinth, however, he threatened to return soon and visit the Corinthians on his way to Macedonia (II Cor. 1:15 f.).

Refusing to give up his role as founder and authorized leader of the Corinthian church, he wrote a sad but stern letter, rebuking the church and insisting that they punish the leader who had insulted him on his short recent visit to Corinth (II Cor. 2:3–9). This letter he sent by Titus, who by his personal ministry was to attempt to lead the church to renew its loyalty to Paul.

Paul was ready to leave Ephesus and revisit Macedonia while waiting for the stern letter and Titus to win back the Corinthians. So he arranged for Titus to meet him at some point on the route; Titus would travel north from Corinth and east through Macedonia, and cross to Troas if he had not yet met Paul; Paul would go north to Troas and cross to Macedonia if he had not yet met Titus (II Cor. 2:12 f.; 7:5–16).

45 On these visiting apostles, see Johannes Munck, *Paul and the Salvation of Mankind*, Ch. 6, "The True and the False Apostle."

III. The Stern Letter

It is not certain that any of the Stern Letter has survived. Our II Corinthians contains, at least for the most part, what Paul wrote from Macedonia, and so dates later than the Stern Letter. But II Cor. 10:1 to 13:10, with its stern rebuke of the Corinthians and the persons who are troubling them, recalls the circumstances of the Stern Letter. It is widely held—probably rightly—that these four chapters, though they do not contain Paul's demand that the ringleader opposing him be punished, are part of that Stern Letter written just before Paul left Ephesus.[46] After Titus had reconciled the rebellious Corinthians to Paul, Paul would hardly have broken out in such stern denunciation. The chapters have the tone of the Stern Letter and assume that the church is still rebellious.

These four chapters are valuable above all for what they reveal of Paul and his ministry. They show his deep and persistent concern for even his erratic churches. They confess his unimpressive personal appearance and poor speaking manner (II Cor. 10:10), and mention his persistent and painful physical ailment, "a thorn . . . in the flesh" (ch. 12:7), which dogged him during his amazingly active ministry.[47] The list of his hardships and sufferings shows that we know but a small fraction of his missionary experiences (ch. 11:23–28). His words also show what a privilege it was to him to be a Jew, and how conscious he was of God's commission and approval in his apostolic ministry, attested as it was by the "signs and wonders and mighty works" he had been able to do (chs. 11:22; 12:12). He threatens stern action if he comes again to Corinth and finds the church still disobedient (ch. 13:2), but he closes with a renewed appeal to them to change their attitude and accept his leadership (vs. 5–10). He is unselfishly concerned for their welfare.

GOOD NEWS FROM TITUS

The fierce rebuke of the Stern Letter was at best a calculated risk. It might harden the Corinthians in opposition to Paul and lead them to

---

[46] Two helpful commentaries on II Corinthians are Alfred Plummer, *A Critical and Exegetical Commentary on the Second Epistle of St. Paul to the Corinthians* (Charles Scribner's Sons, 1915), and R. H. Strachan, *The Second Epistle of Paul to the Corinthians* (London, Hodder and Stoughton, 1935). I have presented my understanding of II Corinthians in my Introduction and Commentary in *The Interpreter's Bible*, Vol. 10.

[47] Gal. 4:13 probably refers to the same physical ailment. See note 24 in the preceding chapter of this book.

follow the visiting teachers who were working to undermine his influence. As he left Ephesus after a long and fruitful ministry and traveled north to Troas, he was tormented by fears that it had been a mistake to write such a letter (II Cor. 7:8).

This inner torture was not his only problem. At the end of his stay in Ephesus or on his way to Troas he faced some great danger, so ominous that he despaired of escaping alive (II Cor. 1:8 f.). This probably was not the riot described in Acts 19:23–41; at that time Paul did not fall into the hands of the mob. It seems to have been some other sudden danger in which death seemed certain. Deliverance came when Paul had ceased to think it possible—he felt as though raised from the dead—and he went on to Troas comforted by the saving power of God.

At Troas the prospect of a fruitful ministry opened to him, but he could not settle down; he had to know as soon as possible whether his Stern Letter and the appeal of Titus had won the Corinthians. So he crossed to Macedonia (II Cor. 2:12 f.). There, probably at Philippi, he met Titus and heard the thrilling news that the Corinthians regretted their rebellion, had punished the Corinthian ringleader opposing Paul,[48] and wanted him to forgive them (II Cor. 2:6 f.; 7:5–16). Overjoyed and relieved, Paul at once wrote a thankful letter to the church, which he loved in spite of their unpredictable fickleness.

IV. The Thankful Letter

If we leave aside II Cor. 10:1 to 13:10, which probably was part of the Stern Letter, this Thankful Letter (chs. 1:1 to 9:15; 13:11–14) consists of four main sections:

a. II Cor. 1:1 to 2:13 reviews recent events and explains Paul's part in them. After the address, which includes "all the saints who are in the whole of Achaia" and so gives a hint of how widely the gospel has spread out through Greece from Corinth, Paul speaks of his recent deliverance from death and the comfort this has given him (ch. 1:3–11). Then he insists that his changes of plans have not been due to fickleness. He at first planned to go through Macedonia and then come to Corinth (I Cor. 16:5–7); then, on his hurried visit to Corinth before writing the Stern Letter, he promised the Corinthians to visit them on his way to Macedonia, and return to see them on his way from Macedonia to Jerusalem; later, however, he decided not to visit them again while they

---

[48] The fact that the Corinthians could and did discipline the ringleader of the rebellion shows that he was a member of the church in Corinth and not a visiting apostle.

were rebellious but to wait until the visit could be more pleasant and profitable. This change was not due to fickleness or indecision but to his desire not to visit them again under conditions in which he would have to be stern.

Now satisfied with the punishment inflicted on the ringleader of the anti-Paul movement, Paul wants the church to forgive and comfort the punished man (II Cor. 1:12 to 2:11). He then tells how he could not settle down to any other work until he met Titus (ch. 2:12 f.). But just when he is ready to tell of meeting Titus in Macedonia, his joy over the happy news Titus brought and his sense of immense privilege in his apostolic ministry overpowers him, and he goes off on one of the most significant digressions in world literature.

b. This digression (II Cor. 2:14 to 6:10) deals with his triumphant apostolic ministry (ch. 2:14–17). It is attested by the very existence and faith of the Corinthian church (ch. 3:1–3), and is far more glorious than the ministry of Moses, since the new covenant in Christ is far superior to the Sinai covenant (vs. 4–18). Amid unjustified criticism and continual hardship, Paul carries on his work (ch. 4:1–18): "For what we preach is not ourselves, but Jesus Christ as Lord, with ourselves as your servants for Jesus' sake," and "so we do not lose heart" (vs. 5, 16). The wearing physical strain and threat of death do not discourage him; he has the assurance of an eternal spiritual body if only he is faithful and meets his test before the judgment seat of Christ at the Last Day (ch. 5:1–10). He carries on a reconciling ministry on behalf of the reconciling Christ, and as an ambassador for Christ undergoes any hardship in order to get as many as possible to accept the grace of God (chs. 5:11 to 6:10).

c. Returning to the current situation, Paul appeals to the Corinthians for a complete reconciliation (chs. 6:11–13; 7:2–4. II Cor. 6:14 to 7:1 either belongs to the Lost Letter or is a parenthetic appeal not to associate with unbelievers in lax relations that would discredit the church and damage the Corinthian Christians). He reports his glad meeting with Titus in Macedonia and the joy he and Titus felt over the new attitude of the Corinthians (ch. 7:5–16). The crisis is past; he can say, "I rejoice, because I have perfect confidence in you" (v. 16).

d. Before the crisis at Corinth, Paul had urged regular collections of relief money to send to Jerusalem (I Cor. 16:1–4). These collections had been discontinued during their rebellion against Paul. Now that the church is again loyal, he urges that they proceed without delay to prepare the collection and make it as generous as they can (II Cor. 8:1 to 9:15). He plans to go to Jerusalem after he visits Macedonia and Achaia, and he wants the collection ready before he makes his final visit to Corinth. The churches of Macedonia have been giving with magnificent liberality and a sacrificial spirit, and Paul urges the Corinthians to match that record. He induces Titus to take the Thankful Letter to Corinth and reinforce by his personal plea its appeal to complete the collection and make it as liberal as possible. Loyalty to Paul, brotherly sympathy for the needy Christians in Palestine, and gratitude to God "for his inexpressible gift" in sending Christ as men's Lord and Savior (ch. 9:15) should lead them to respond willingly. Paul hopes that the appeal of Titus and two other unnamed Christian leaders (ch. 8:16–24) will move the Corinthians to eager participation in this great collection, which will show the brotherly love of his Gentile churches for the Jewish Christian church in Jerusalem and Palestine.[49]

The suggestion has been made that chs. 10 to 13 of II Corinthians are a fifth letter, still later than chs. 1 to 9, and written when further news came to Paul that the supposedly complete reconciliation had not in fact been completed and men hostile to Paul were still exercising great influence against him at Corinth.[50] But it is probable that these four chapters are part of the Stern Letter.

After writing the Thankful Letter, Paul continued through Macedonia, making what he then thought was his final visit to these churches. From there he went south into Achaia, the Roman province of which Corinth was the capital and leading city. In Achaia he spent three months (Acts 20:2 f.). No doubt it was the winter season, when ships did not brave the stormy seas. Paul was concluding his independent mission in Asia Minor, Macedonia, and Achaia, and was planning the next great stage of his broad plan to spread the gospel throughout the Roman Empire.

---

49 This collection is discussed in Johannes Munck, *Paul and the Salvation of Mankind,* Ch. 10, "Paul and Jerusalem." Note also John Knox, *Chapters in a Life of Paul* (Abingdon-Cokesbury Press, 1950), Chs. 3 and 4.
50 Hans Windisch, *Der zweite Korintherbrief* (Göttingen, Vandenhoeck & Ruprecht, 1924), presents this view.

Chapter 11

TO PRISON, ROME, AND DEATH

The Days of Paul's independent mission lay behind him. He did not yet know this. During his three months in Greece, mainly at Corinth (Acts 20:3), he was planning for the future. His churches had taken a collection for the poverty-stricken Jewish Christians in Jerusalem.[1] This was an important expression of the unity of the church, and Paul was determined to go to Jerusalem with the representatives of the churches and be present when they handed the gifts over to the Jerusalem leaders. The gift would recognize a debt of the Gentile churches, who had received the gospel from their Jewish Christian brothers (Rom. 15:27). It would fulfill Paul's pledge that he would keep in mind the poor in the Jerusalem church (Gal. 2:10). He hoped that both he and his churches would be regarded as Christian brothers by the Jewish Christian church at Jerusalem.

Paul's Plan to Visit Rome

From Jerusalem, Paul intended to go to Rome. He had long wanted to do that (Rom. 1:13), but had felt that he could not leave the eastern part of the Empire until he had preached the gospel wherever it had not yet been firmly established. (This implies that others had already preached with success in Egypt, Cyrene, Pontus, and Bithynia.) He did not plan to settle in Rome, where he knew a strong church already existed (Rom. 1:8),[2] but he did want to preach there. As a Roman citizen, he realized Rome's central role in the Empire, and he wanted to visit the church and witness to the gospel in the capital city.

His ultimate plan was to go on to Spain. His aim, clearly stated in II Cor. 10:14–16, was mission preaching in areas where no church had yet been founded. So Spain, still unevangelized, captured his imagination as the westernmost point of the Empire. His plan was to visit Rome, preach there, win the Roman church's friendship and support for his

---

[1] See note 49 in the preceding chapter.
[2] On the origin and early history of the Roman church, see the next chapter.

further work, and then go on to Spain as his new mission field (Rom. 15:18–29).

PAUL WRITES TO THE ROMAN CHURCH

With this in mind he wrote his great letter to the Romans.[3] He did not want to arrive in Rome without notice or without doing all he could to assure a warm welcome. He knew that everywhere Jews worked to nullify his preaching of the gospel, and many Jewish Christians thought he had betrayed his Jewish heritage by his free attitude toward the Mosaic law. So at Rome he might meet suspicion if not actual opposition. The church there was too important to ignore, and he set himself to win its friendship and support.

To do this he wrote his most formal letter. It is the nearest thing to a systematic statement of his gospel that has survived. His aim was not to clarify his own thinking or to provide the church with an ecumenical theology, but to introduce himself to the Roman church and win its understanding and friendship. To a minor extent he deals with situations in Rome, but his central aim is to present clearly and persuasively how he understands his gospel in relation to Judaism and the Gentile world.

THE CONTENT OF THE LETTER

Since Paul has never visited the Roman church, his opening lines are more detailed and formal than in his other letters. In Rom. 1:1–7 he sums up essential features of his gospel and defines his role in its spread. Next, he thanks God for the widely known faith of the Roman church and tells them that he has long desired to visit them and preach in Rome (vs. 8–15). Then he states his main theme: righteousness given and effected by God in all who believe in Jesus Christ (vs. 16 f.).

In his first main section (chs. 1:18 to 3:20) Paul states that though righteousness is necessary to avoid spiritual ruin, since God judges all sin and wickedness, yet all men lack this righteousness, for they have sinned and deserve condemnation. Contrary to what some think, Paul does not here blame the sin of Adam for this dark situation, nor does he excuse sin as something that men must do because of Adam's sin. He

---

[3] F. W. Beare, "Romans, Letter to the," *IDB* (1962), R-Z, pp. 112–122. Commentaries: William Sanday and Arthur C. Headlam, *A Critical and Exegetical Commentary on the Epistle to the Romans*, 14th ed. (Charles Scribner's Sons, 1913); C. H. Dodd, *The Epistle of Paul to the Romans* (London, Hodder and Stoughton, 1932); Anders Nygren, *Commentary on Romans*, tr. by Carl C. Rasmussen (Muhlenberg Press, 1949); C. K. Barrett, *A Commentary on the Epistle to the Romans*.

points to the actual present situation. Both Jews and Gentiles are sinners; all have enough knowledge of God to be responsible (ch. 1:19–21), but they all sin. God's judgment is already active and he will judge all men at the end of the age. The Jews are not saved by possession of the law and other advantages; these gifts only make it crystal clear that they have gone against God's will and deserve condemnation. The fact of universal sinfulness is attested by Scripture (ch. 3:10–18).

The righteousness that all lack (vs. 19 f.) is offered to all as sheer gift.[4] This free grace of God is promised in the Old Testament; both the Law and the Prophets attest it. It is a redemption secured through the death of Jesus Christ. No one earns or deserves it, since all have sinned and fall short of what they should be to pass God's judgment. But whoever believes in Christ receives this grace as free gift (vs. 21–31). This way of faith is exemplified in Abraham; it is thus older than the law and is not superseded by the law (ch. 4). It opens to man the way to reconciliation with God and continued blessing through the risen life and ministry of Christ (ch. 5:1–11). Just as since the sin of Adam death has reigned in the world, and all men by their own sin have ratified their destiny of death for their sin (v. 12), so all men who believe receive grace and life through Christ (vs. 12–21).

This new life is not a pretense. Some have thought that when Paul emphasized justification, the judicial decision by which God forgives sinful men and receives them into good standing with him, he did not think that any real change took place in the believer; the believer remains a sinner and yet by God's gracious decision is treated as righteous. Paul would have been shocked to hear it suggested that justification has no effect in actual living. Of course he emphasized that God's grace is free. Man deserves condemnation for his sin, but through the death of Christ, God provides forgiveness to those who believe, in spite of their sinful record. But justification is more than clever divine bookkeeping that cancels the debt to God while leaving man as sinful as before. For Paul, faith is vital and creative. To believe means not merely to accept the gospel as true by an act of the mind, not merely to accept a forgiveness not deserved; it means also trust in the gracious God active in Christ, grateful commitment of the life to the God who in Christ has given freedom not merely from the guilt but also from the grip of sin; it means willing surrender of the life to the will and purpose of God. No one understands Paul who does not realize how deep and transforming faith was to him.

4 On "Righteousness," see the study by Gottfried Quell and Gottlob Schrenk, in *Bible Key Words*, Vol. I. Eng. tr. by J. R. Coates (Harper & Brothers, 1951).

Romans, chs. 6 to 8, attest this transforming power of God's grace received in faith. The Christian dies to sin; there is a real and decisive break with his sinful past; he can do the will of God in a way not possible before (ch. 6). The law could command, but it gave no power to fulfill the command. Grace enables man to do freely what the law commanded in vain. Life under the law, as described in ch. 7:7–25, sees the right but cannot do it; it knows wrong is wrong but cannot keep from doing it.[5] But in the Christian life there is a note of victory. Not by an external law, but by the inner power given by God in the continuing outpouring of divine grace, man can do the will of God and triumph over all the forces that would defeat man's good intent or drag him down to sin (ch. 8).

"Newness of life" even now (ch. 6:4) and final victory through the love of God continuously active in Christ (ch. 8:31–39)—this is the picture Paul gives of the Christian life. The grace of God through Christ gives to the believer renewal of life and power to fulfill God's will. This way of life, life by the power of God's Spirit, is vastly more effective in moral fruits than is obedience to law.

One problem that Paul faced was that whereas numerous Gentiles accepted the gospel, the Jews largely rejected it. This problem may have been under discussion in the church at Rome. As a Jew loyal to his people, Paul was deeply troubled to see most of his fellow Jews reject the gospel message (ch. 9:1–5). So after presenting the universal need of the gospel, God's free grace open to all through faith in Christ, and the moral renewal effected by God's grace received in faith, Paul discusses how this refusal of most Jews to believe fits into God's plan (chs. 9 to 11).[6] They were the very people who by background and advantages might be expected to believe the gospel.

Paul deeply believed that God is the effective Lord of his world and his people. So his first main point is that God is sovereign and in his election of some persons rather than others he is free and is not to be criticized by men who do not understand God's ways (ch. 9:6–29). This does not mean that God is capricious; in his wise administration of his-

---

[5] Romans 7:7–25 is widely taken as Paul's description of his Christian life. But in the first place, although he writes in the first person and perhaps with conscious reference to himself, he regards this picture as typical of man's dilemma. In the second place, it is a picture of life under the law, and this is not the position of the Christian. Paul is describing life under the law as he now sees it from his Christian outlook. The best detailed study of this passage is by Werner Georg Kümmel, *Römer 7 und die Bekehrung des Paulus* (see note 6 in Chapter 9 of the present book).

[6] For a Jewish scholar's interpretation of these chapters, see H. J. Schoeps, *Paul*, pp. 235–245.

tory his will prevails, but the sin of man is a fact, and the Jews cannot complain of their rejection, for they have been a persistently "disobedient and contrary people" (chs. 9:30 to 10:21). Yet God has not finally rejected his people Israel. Already a remnant has been saved. The unbelief of the Jews has driven the gospel preachers to go to the Gentiles, and so has been the means of the wider spreading of the gospel. But the time will come, Paul believes, after the Gentiles have heard the gospel, when Israel will turn to Christ and so all mankind will be united by the grace of God in the one fellowship of faith in Christ (ch. 11).

Paul held that divine grace and grateful faith effect moral renewal; this is clear from the closing chapters of Romans. Paul first urges a consecration of the entire life, including the body, to the service of God (ch. 12:1 f.). A life of helpfulness and mutual love will overcome evil just as Christ, by his willing death for men, overcame sin (vs. 3–21). All are to respect and obey the lawful civil authorities,[7] love their neighbors, and live alert lives while awaiting the imminent coming of complete salvation (ch. 13). In matters where a moral issue is not clear and some Christians think it right to do some act, such as eating meat, which others regard as wrong,[8] Paul obviously sides with the former group but thinks that they should refrain rather than pressure those weak in conscience to do what they think is wrong (chs. 14:1 to 15:13). Concern for the effect of one's actions on others is a guiding principle for Paul.

Paul then tells the Roman church that he has completed his pioneer work in the east. He now plans to visit Rome and ask their help in his new work in Spain. He tells of the collection he is ready to take to Jerusalem, and since he knows that he will be in danger there from enemies of his preaching, he asks the Roman Christians to pray for his safe journey to Jerusalem and to Rome (Rom. 15:14–32).

THE ENDING AND EARLY USE OF ROMANS

With a prayer that God's peace may be with all in the Roman church, the letter may have ended (v. 33). Romans, ch. 16, with its recommendation of Phoebe and its long list of greetings to friends of Paul, seems a strange way to conclude a letter to a church he has never visited. Probably, therefore, vs. 1–20 is a letter sent originally to Ephesus to recommend Phoebe, to add greetings to his many friends in Ephesus, and

---

[7] See Clinton D. Morrison, *The Powers That Be* (London, SCM Press, Ltd., 1960).
[8] Why some objected to this is not clear. Did they fear it had been sacrificed to an idol (cf. I Cor., chs. 8 to 10)? Or were they Jewish Christians who had scruples about eating "nonkosher" meat? Or were they vegetarians? (This last seems the least likely answer.)

to warn against divisive people of sensual lives who were trying to gain influence in the Ephesian church.[9] It is possible, however, that Paul sent these recommendations and greetings to Rome because although he had never been there, he knew many Christians who had moved there from eastern cities, and he wanted to use every available tie to win a friendly reception.[10]

That the letter to Rome was altered and added to is suggested by two curious facts. The words "in Rome" (Rom. 1:7, 15) are lacking in a few manuscripts. The benediction, unlike any other in Paul's letters, is found at the end of the letter in most manuscripts (ch. 16:25–27), after ch. 14:23 in others, in both places in another, in neither place in a few others, and after ch. 15:33 in the third-century papyrus P[46]. Note that there are also benedictions in ch. 15:33 and ch. 16:20, and in some manuscripts in ch. 16:24. It appears from these facts that Romans later circulated in more than one form. At times the references to Rome in ch. 1 and the personal notices and greetings in chs. 15 and 16 were omitted so that the letter could circulate generally in the ancient church. Paul himself wrote to Rome (and probably wrote ch. 16 to Ephesus), but it was soon seen that his letter would give valuable help to other churches, and so slightly altered copies were made in which the general message stood out and local details were omitted.[11]

PAUL'S LAST JOURNEY TO JERUSALEM

The collection taken, the representatives of the contributing churches appointed, the letter to Rome sent off, and the spring sailing season

---

9 On the tendency in Paul's churches to use Christian freedom as an excuse for sensual living, see Phil. 3:19. Cf. Gal. 5:13, 16; 6:7 f.

10 The following points make an Ephesian destination of Rom. 16:1–20 seem probable to me: Prisca and Aquila were at Ephesus when last mentioned in The Acts (ch. 18:18 f., 26); Epaenetus as "the first convert in Asia" would normally be found in Ephesus rather than Rome; it was in Ephesus rather than in Rome that Paul would have known so large a number of Christians as Paul names—and he knows not only the individuals but also how they group together in family circles or house churches.

11 Paul himself may have sent his letter not only to Rome but also, with different personal notes and benedictions, to various other churches. Then when his letters were collected for general church use, the editor(s) preserved the closing material and benedictions of various conclusions that were in circulation, and included Rom. 16:1–20, the note to Ephesus. But more likely the various shortened or altered forms of Romans were made after his lifetime, to give more general use to the letter; then when his letters were collected for reading in the churches, the endings of these various forms were combined, Rom. 16:1–20 was included, and vs. 25–27, whose vocabulary and style are not characteristic of Paul, was added, since in the early collection of his letters, it seems, Romans stood last, and this formal ascription of praise was added as the conclusion of the entire collection.

come, Paul was ready to leave Corinth for Jerusalem. His plan was to
sail from Cenchreae, the eastern seaport of Corinth, to Syria (Acts 20:3);
that is, he intended to land at some port of Phoenicia or Palestine, regions reckoned as belonging to Syria for purposes of Roman administration. But Jews who regarded Paul as a renegade made a plot to kill him
during the long journey on the crowded ship. To avoid this danger, Paul,
when he learned of the plot, revised his plans, went north and then east
through Macedonia to Philippi, and crossed to Troas (Acts 20:3–6). Perhaps the Corinthians selected to carry the Corinthian collection did sail
directly to Palestine, for though Achaia, whose capital was Corinth, had
its collection ready (Rom. 15:26) and must have sent a representative to
Jerusalem, Acts 20:4 mentions no Corinthian in the group of church
representatives that assembled at Troas.

The Macedonians, no doubt informed of Paul's changed plan, gathered with others at Troas to await Paul; Sopater of Beroea[12] and Aristarchus and Secundus of Thessalonica were in the group, and as the "we"
passage beginning in Acts 20:5 indicates,[13] so was Luke, probably as the
representative from Philippi. At Troas were also Gaius of Derbe and
Timothy (of Lystra). Thus the churches of Galatia were represented;[14]
this indicates that Paul's strong letter to the Galatians had kept them
loyal to him. The others in the group were Tychicus and Trophimus
of Asia, that is, from Ephesus (cf. Acts 21:29).

Thus the trip from Corinth to Jerusalem began with a swing northward through Achaia and eastward through Macedonia to Philippi.
There Paul observed the Passover and Feast of Unleavened Bread; then,
with Luke and perhaps others, he went to its port Neapolis and sailed
to Troas. This voyage, completed with favorable winds in two days in
the other direction (Acts 16:11), took five days at this spring season
(cf. Acts 20:6). The party waited seven days at Troas for a ship going
southward. Paul's desire was to reach Jerusalem in time to observe Pentecost there (Acts 20:16).[15]

At Troas a meeting was held on the first day of the week to break
bread. This is another indication of the early practice of a special service
of worship on the day of the resurrection (cf. I Cor. 16:2), and it recalls
that the formal remembrance of the Last Supper occurred at a real meal

[12] This reference to Sopater attests a live church at Beroea. Cf. Acts 17:12.

[13] The "we" passages are Acts 16:10–17; 20:5–16; 21:1–18; 27:1 to 28:16.

[14] Since Timothy's native city is not named here, it is not certain that he was acting
as a representative of the Galatian churches, but Gaius was. The reading that Gaius
was a Douberian (i.e., from Doberus in Macedonia) rather than from Derbe is
poorly attested. But see Ernst Haenchen, *Die Apostelgeschichte*, p. 46 n.

[15] This no doubt means mainly at least the Jewish Feast of Pentecost rather than an
annual celebration of the gift of the Holy Spirit to the church, but for Paul the two
aspects could have been combined.

of worshiping disciples. The all-night meeting of Paul and his companions with the Troas Christians carried the added atmosphere of a regretful farewell (Acts 20:7–12).

More than once The Acts mentions in passing a church whose existence had not been mentioned before; Luke does not intend to tell of every church Paul founded. When the party sailed the next morning from Troas, Paul went southward on foot to previously unmentioned Assos, where the ship was to stop for freight or passengers (Acts 20:13). Paul was no tourist; he did not go overland to admire nature or study ancient ruins; there must have been at Assos a church that Paul wanted to visit. From Assos the ship worked its way down the western coast of Asia Minor, stopping to anchor at night in the lee of a convenient island. The first stop was Mitylene, the next was "opposite Chios," the third at Samos. On the next day the ship put in at Miletus, an important harbor about thirty miles south of Ephesus (Acts 20:14 f.).

The ship had business at Miletus, and this gave Paul time to send for the elders of Ephesus (called "bishops," i.e., "overseers," in Acts 20:28) and talk to them. In a typical farewell speech[16] Paul recalls the diligence and integrity of his ministry, urges the elders to be faithful leaders, and warns that "fierce wolves," false teachers with destructive teaching, will come to Ephesus and find allies in local leaders ambitious for power (Acts 20:17–38). Paul's words were so focused by Luke as to condemn later developments at Ephesus.

From Miletus the ship sailed south to the island of Cos, then south and east to Rhodes, and eastward to Patara, a port in Lycia. At Patara the group found a ship sailing to Phoenicia. It was a ship of some size, for it sailed directly southeast, going past the west end of Cyprus, and made port at Tyre (Acts 21:1–3). Seven days' delay at Tyre while the ship unloaded its cargo permitted Paul and his party to visit the church there (Acts 21:4–6). The ship then sailed southward to Ptolemais, where Paul and his party spent a day with the church there (Acts 21:7). Then they moved on (by land?) to Caesarea, where the group were guests of Philip, one of the Seven whom Paul had once persecuted. Luke, in both his Gospel and The Acts, mentions women who exercised leadership in the church; he here notes that the four unmarried daughters of Philip were prophetesses (Acts 21:8 f.).

During the stay at Caesarea, Agabus, who in Paul's presence had predicted the famine at Antioch in Syria (Acts 11:28), came down to Caesarea from Judea and predicted that Paul would be put in chains at

---

[16] Such farewell speeches were used by ancient writers to sum up the work and significance of the speaker.

Jerusalem and turned over to the Gentiles (i.e., the Romans). Paul's friends tried to dissuade him from going there, but taking the collection to Jerusalem and maintaining friendly relations with church leaders there meant so much for the unity of the church that Paul refused to cancel his plan (Acts 21:10–14). The warning reminds us that all the churches thus far visited on this trip to Jerusalem were Hellenistic congregations, founded by Paul or by those who fled from Jerusalem after Stephen's death; the Jerusalem church, led by James the brother of Jesus, was more conservative and to say the least less friendly to Paul.

Some of the Caesarea disciples accompanied Paul and his party to Jerusalem, where Mnason, one of the earliest members of the church, became Paul's host (Acts 21:15 f.).[17]

PAUL'S CONFERENCE AND VOW AT JERUSALEM

Upon arrival at Jerusalem, Paul and his companions met with the church, and on the following day Paul conferred with James and the elders (Acts 21:17–19). Not a word is said about presenting the collection. Indeed, The Acts never says that Paul and those named in Acts 20:4 brought a collection to the church. In Acts 24:17, Paul says that he came to Jerusalem "to bring to my nation alms and offerings." This evidently refers to the collection, but so vaguely that the words could mean an offering given to the Jewish authorities. Only from Paul's letters do we learn how much this collection meant in his strategy to foster brotherly unity between the Jewish and Gentile wings of the church. We must assume that as soon as possible after arrival Paul and his party presented the collection to the church, probably to the elders, as in Acts 11:30.[18]

James and the elders were concerned to avoid the hostile reaction that Paul's visit might cause in the Jerusalem church. They told Paul with pride how many Jews in Jerusalem were believers in Christ, but they added that these Christians were zealous for the Mosaic law, which, they had heard, Paul taught Jews in the Dispersion not to observe. If Paul wanted to foster church unity, James told him, he should perform an act that would show his loyalty to the law. They had a plan. Four disciples had taken a vow and were now in the Temple, needing expense

17 The Western text of Acts 21:16 seems to say that Mnason lived at the place where Paul and his party stopped for the night on their way from Caesarea to Jerusalem. See F. F. Bruce, *The Acts of the Apostles*, pp. 389 f.

18 On the collection, see Johannes Munck, *Paul and the Salvation of Mankind*, Ch. 10, "Paul and Jerusalem."

money for the ceremonies to conclude the vow.[19] If Paul would provide these expenses, purify himself, go into the Temple with the four men, and join in the offering that would conclude the ceremonies, this would demonstrate his loyalty. James reminded Paul that an earlier agreement (Acts 15:28 f.) protected Gentile Christians from having to keep the law; they need only keep the minimum list of four things.

Paul, who felt free to observe the law or not as the occasion suggested (I Cor. 9:20 f.), agreed to the plan. He purified himself as required, entered the Temple,[20] and began the wait for the required seven days to pass before the final offering could conclude the period of the vow (Acts 21:20–26).

THE RIOT AND PAUL'S SPEECH IN THE TEMPLE

The plan failed of its purpose. Some Jews of the Roman province of Asia, present in Jerusalem, as was Paul, to celebrate the Feast of Pentecost, saw him in the Temple. They knew he preached to Gentiles without requiring them to keep the law and did not strictly keep the law himself. They had previously seen him in Jerusalem with the Gentile Trophimus of Ephesus, one of those who brought the collection to Jerusalem. They assumed, wrongfully but probably honestly, that he had brought the Gentile into the inner Temple court, where only Jews were permitted. In fanatical zeal for the Temple they raised a cry against Paul for defiling the Temple, and their impassioned cries set off a riot. Paul was seized, dragged into the outer Court of the Gentiles, and beaten. The Jewish Temple police closed the gates to the inner courts to keep them from being profaned by riot and murder. A Roman soldier, on watch from the top of the north wall of the Temple area, sent word of the riot to the centurion in the Tower of Antonia, at the northwest corner of the Temple area, and the centurion with a detachment of soldiers rushed down and rescued Paul from the angry mob (Acts 21: 27–32).

The tribune, thinking Paul the instigator of the riot, had him arrested, bound, and taken to the barracks in Antonia. The mob followed; swirling around the soldiers and Paul, they tried to seize the apostle. As the soldiers started to take Paul up the steps to the lower entrance, he asked permission to speak to the mob. The tribune had thought Paul an

19 This seems to have been a Nazirite vow. Cf. Num. 6:1–21. For a vow taken by Paul, see Acts 18:18.
20 Paul and the four men were not in the Court of the Gentiles but in an inner court where only Jews could go. This is the background for the misunderstanding of Acts 21:28.

Egyptian Jew who recently had led some Jews to resist Roman rule.[21] But when Paul spoke Greek and declared that he was a Jew and a citizen of Tarsus, a leading city of the Empire, he was allowed to speak (Acts 21:33–40).

Paul thus was able to describe his conversion and his gospel to his fellow Jews at Jerusalem. The speech is Luke's composition, but he was in Jerusalem at the time and could know something of its content. Speaking in Aramaic, Paul told how God had guided him, a loyal Jew, into the Christian faith and into a ministry to Gentiles (Acts 21:40 to 22:21). This last point, involving as it did the acceptance of Gentiles into the church without making them keep the Mosaic law, led the mob to renew their demonstration against Paul. To the tribune, who did not understand Aramaic, the whole scene was a mystery, but since Paul seemed to be arousing the mob, he determined to have Paul scourged to make him tell what his scheme was (Acts 22:22–24). Three times Paul had been beaten with rods (II Cor. 11:25); to be scourged with leather thongs with pieces of lead attached was perhaps still more dangerous. So for the second time he appealed to his Roman citizenship,[22] which he had held from birth, since his father had already possessed it (cf. Acts 16:37). Thus he escaped scourging (Acts 22:25–29).

Paul's last journey to Jerusalem and his arrest, hearings, and voyage to Rome were highly important to Luke. One third of The Acts deals with this segment of Paul's life (chs. 20 to 28). It takes up over one half of the space The Acts gives to Paul. We might have expected his missionary travel and preaching to receive by far the most attention. But his witness before Jewish and Gentile officials, the recognition by Roman leaders that no real ground existed for action against Paul, and his preaching in Rome seemed so important to Luke that he makes the detailed story of these events the climax and conclusion of Luke-Acts.

The Hearing Before the Sanhedrin

The first hearing at which Paul had opportunity to give his Christian witness was arranged by the tribune before the Sanhedrin, to find out why the Jews had rioted against Paul. The apostle protested that he had done nothing for which he had a bad conscience. When the high priest Ananias had him struck illegally for this, he rebuked Ananias, but then

---

21 Josephus, *War* II.13.5; *Ant.* XX.8.6, speaks of thirty thousand followers, whereas The Acts says four thousand. On this "Egyptian," an Egyptian Jew, see Kirsopp Lake and Henry J. Cadbury in *The Beginnings of Christianity*, Vol. IV, pp. 276 f.
22 See note 10 in the preceding chapter.

apologized for his angry, disrespectful outburst.[23] He pointed out that it was because he believed in the resurrection that he was now on trial; the Pharisees present also believed in the resurrection of the dead, but did not accept his basic Christian message that God had raised Jesus. It is doubtful how far the Pharisees in the Sanhedrin defended Paul; in any case, the hearing had no clear result and gave the tribune no help (Acts 22:30 to 23:10).

The vision of Paul the following night recalls that at decisive points in The Acts visions came to him; the vision reassured Paul and underlined the importance of what Paul was facing; his witness in Rome was to be the climax of The Acts (ch. 23:11). We need not doubt that Paul had such visions, even if Luke uses them for literary emphasis.

The Plot Against Paul's Life

A plot to arrange another hearing before the Sanhedrin and kill Paul as he was being taken to the hearing became known to Paul's nephew, who lived in Jerusalem; whether the nephew was a Christian is not said. Paul, when told of the plot, asked a centurion to take his nephew to the tribune, who decided to refer the matter to Felix, the Roman governor of Palestine (Acts 23:12–22).

To avoid possible ambush, Paul was started to Caesarea on horseback, guarded by two hundred infantrymen, seventy horsemen, and two hundred spearmen. They proceeded at night to Antipatris; then, the danger of ambush being past, the soldiers returned to Jerusalem, and the horsemen took Paul to Caesarea, where the governor had his official residence. Claudius Lysias, the tribune, had sent an explanatory letter to Felix, stating the situation as he understood it. It is highly doubtful that Luke had a copy of the letter, but he could represent the situation as the tribune would describe his own role in it. The governor, learning for the record the name of the native province of Paul (Cilicia), held Paul in custody in the praetorium, which Herod the Great had built (Acts 23: 23–35).

The Hearing Before Felix at Caesarea

Five days later the high priest Ananias arrived; with him were elders of the Sanhedrin and Tertullus, a professional pleader. Tertullus indicted Paul as a disturbing agitator throughout the (Roman) world and

23 This Ananias was high priest during part of the reign of both Claudius and Nero. Cf. Josephus, *Ant.* XX.9.2.

a ringleader of the sect of the Nazarenes who had tried to profane the Temple.[24] The Jews supported these charges (Acts 24:1–9). But Paul, when permitted to speak, denied them. He had followed his ancestral religion, of which "the Way" was the true fulfillment,[25] so his worship was legal under the Empire; he had been in Jerusalem but a few days;[26] he had come to bring to his own people alms and offerings, and as he was in the Temple, making no tumult, he had been seized by some Jews from Asia on a false charge. Those Jews were not present to renew their charge, so it must be false. He was under attack because he preached the resurrection of Jesus, but his accusers (actually not all of them; only the Pharisees) accepted the doctrine of resurrection, so the dispute was only over a specific case, the resurrection of Jesus (Acts 24:10–21).

This summary of Paul's case by Luke is most suspicious in saying that the alms and offerings were for the Jews (Acts 24:17); however, Luke could have reasoned that the gifts were for Jewish Christians and so for Jews, and the purpose of Paul's visit at the Pentecost season could have included Temple offerings even before James suggested one for the four Jewish Christian disciples who wanted to complete their vow (Acts 21: 23 f.).

Felix found no reason to condemn Paul, but he put off his decision to avoid offending the Jewish leaders, with whom he had to work in the administration of Palestine. That he was interested in Paul, heard Paul present his case more than once, and was open to a bribe to release him is quite credible (Acts 24:22–26). The case dragged on for two years; Paul had no political influence, and as long as he was in prison his foes were somewhat satisfied. The situation did not change until Festus replaced Felix, perhaps in A.D. 60 (Acts 24:27).[27]

---

24 The word "tried" is puzzling. If Paul as charged in Acts 21:28 had taken a Gentile into the inner court of the Temple, he had in fact profaned it in Jewish eyes. If that charge was false, as The Acts implies, the riot against Paul was unjustified. By the word "tried" Luke may be hinting at the latter point without clearly making it.

25 On "the Way" as one of the early names for the Christian movement, see Kirsopp Lake and Henry J. Cadbury in *The Beginnings of Christianity*, Vol. IV, p. 100.

26 Acts 24:11 says that Paul reached Jerusalem only twelve days before this hearing. It is hardly possible to fit the events of The Acts into this brief period: ch. 21:17, Paul arrives at Jerusalem; v. 18, sees James; v. 26, goes into the Temple; v. 27, riot near the end of seven days; ch. 22:30, hearing the next day; v. 12, plot and departure for Caesarea; v. 32, arrival at Caesarea; ch. 24:1, hearing before Felix five days later.

27 The date when Festus replaced Felix is much disputed. Kirsopp Lake, "The Chronology of Acts," in *The Beginnings of Christianity*, Vol. V, note 34, p. 466, favors A.D. 55, as does Ernst Haenchen, *Die Apostelgeschichte*, pp. 68 f. Other scholars have favored A.D. 56, 59, or—most often—60.

PAUL APPEALS TO CAESAR

Three days after Festus reached Palestine and took up official residence in Caesarea, he went up to Jerusalem, the center of Jewish life and the chief potential threat to the peace of the province. The Sanhedrin leaders, on the arrival of the new governor, reopened the case against Paul, and asked that he be brought to Jerusalem for trial. Festus instead invited the accusers to make their charges before him at Caesarea in the prisoner's presence (Acts 25:1–5). When they did this, Paul insisted that he had done nothing against the Jewish law, the Temple, or the emperor; he should be released (Acts 25:6–8).

Festus did not want to begin his administration by a break with the Jewish leaders, so he asked Paul to agree to a trial before him in Jerusalem. This indicated an inclination to favor the Jewish leaders; it convinced Paul that he could not count on justice from Festus. He therefore appealed to Caesar; he asserted his right as a Roman citizen to have his case settled at Rome by the emperor or the emperor's personal representative. Festus consulted his council of advisers and granted Paul's appeal (Acts 25:9–12).[28]

THE HEARING BEFORE FESTUS AND AGRIPPA

Before being taken to Rome, Paul received one more hearing, unofficial but important in Luke's view because it occurred before one who knew more of Judaism than did Festus. Herod Agrippa II and his wife, Bernice, made a courtesy visit to welcome their new neighbor Festus. (This Agrippa was then Rome's puppet king over parts of Galilee and Perea and the region to the northeast of Galilee.) When told of Paul, Agrippa expressed a desire to hear him. Festus was the more ready to do this, since he needed to know more about the case for the report he must send to Rome with the prisoner (Acts 25:13–27). So the reader of The Acts hears for the third time the story of Paul's faithful Jewish life in earlier years, his persecution of the disciples, his conversion near Damascus, his call to preach to Jews and especially Gentiles,[29] and the Scriptural basis of this Gentile mission (Acts 26:1–23).

The story impressed Festus as the words of a deranged man (Acts 26:

[28] Henry J. Cadbury studies the legal situation of an appeal to Caesar in *The Beginnings of Christianity*, Vol. V, Note 26, "Roman Law and the Trial of Paul," pp. 312–319.

[29] In view of Gal. 1:22 f., the statement of Acts 26:20 that Paul had preached "at Jerusalem [cf. Acts 9:28 f.] and throughout all the country of Judea" is to say the least exaggerated.

24). Agrippa, appealed to by Paul because he knew Jewish life, deftly escaped Paul's attempt to get him to commit himself, but agreed with the others that Paul was guilty of no crime and that only his appeal to the emperor prevented his acquittal (Acts 26:25–32). This testimony that Paul was innocent and that being a Christian was not ground for Roman condemnation had strong apologetic value for Luke and the early church. Luke sprinkles such testimonies throughout his narrative.

THE VOYAGE AND SHIPWRECK

The voyage from Caesarea to Puteoli is one of the fascinating sea stories of world literature.[30] It gives little new information about the early church, but it describes how God's providence brought Paul to Rome and how Paul was a leader even as a prisoner.

Julius, a Roman centurion of the Augustan Cohort, was sent by Festus to take Paul and other prisoners to Rome. There was no ship sailing directly from Caesarea to Italy, but a ship of Adramyttium, on the northwestern shore of Asia Minor, was leaving Caesarea for ports in Asia, that is, western Asia Minor. Julius put his prisoners on board (Acts 27:1 f.). Luke was allowed to go with Paul (cf. the "we" in Acts 27:2), as was Aristarchus of Thessalonica, who had been with Paul since he helped take the collection to Jerusalem (Acts 20:4). The ship sailed north and put in at Sidon. There Paul had friends—so a church existed there—and Paul was permitted to visit them (Acts 27:3).

To get to its destination on the west coast of Asia Minor, the ship could not sail northwest from Sidon and pass west of Cyprus; facing westerly winds, it had to run northward, pass east of Cyprus, and then work westward, near the coast of Cilicia and Pamphylia, to reach Myra in Lycia (Acts 27:3–5). Anchored there was one of the many ships that took grain from Egypt to Rome. To get to Rome it had sailed northward from Alexandria and was now planning to work its way westward from Myra. The centurion put his party on this ship, and it sailed westward with difficulty until it reached Cnidus, on the southwestern tip of Asia Minor. The west winds did not permit sailing straight west from Cnidus, so the ship sailed southwest, passed Salmone, on the east tip of Crete, and sailed along the south side of Crete to Fair Havens, an anchorage near Lasea (Acts 27:6–8).

Here a crucial decision had to be made. The "fast," that is, the Day

---

[30] The classic study is by James Smith, *The Voyage and Shipwreck of St. Paul* (London, Longmans, Green & Co., 4th ed., 1880). See W. M. Ramsay, *St. Paul the Traveller and the Roman Citizen*, pp. 314–346.

of Atonement, in October, was already past, and weather was becoming dangerous for sea travel. In such conditions ships anchored in a safe harbor for the winter. But Fair Havens was only an anchorage, in which ships could be badly battered by winter storms. So the captain and owner of the ship wanted to get to Phoenix, some fifty miles west on the southern shore of Crete; it had an excellent harbor for wintering. Paul, knowing that the stormy season was at hand, advised against this (Acts 27:9–12). But when a gentle south wind offered apparently perfect conditions for sailing west to Phoenix, the attempt was made.

A sudden change of weather came; the ship was hit by a tempestuous northeaster and driven westward and a little southward. Getting behind the small island called Cauda (or Clauda), the crew pulled aboard the small boat ordinarily towed by the ship. Then they undergirded the ship by passing ropes under the hull,[31] and lowered the gear used in sailing. The crew feared that they were being driven southwest into the treacherous quicksands of the Syrtis, near the African coast west of Cyrenaica; their actual course, it proved later, was westward. They threw overboard cargo and ship tackle, and lost hope of survival (Acts 27:13–20). A vision assured Paul that the company would reach land safely (Acts 27:21–26).

On the fourteenth night of the storm the experienced seamen sensed that land was near. They were drifting in the sea of Adria, which included the present Adriatic Sea and the expanse between Crete on the east and Malta and Sicily on the west, and were approaching the island of Malta, though they did not know where they were. Taking soundings, they learned that the water was getting shallower. Thinking they might be heading for a rocky coast, they threw out anchors and waited for daylight to show them their situation. The sailors planned to let down the small boat and escape, leaving the soldiers and prisoners at the mercy of the storm, but at Paul's warning the boat was cut loose and the 276 men had to face the danger together (Acts 27:27–32).[32] As dawn approached, Paul induced all to eat something, to gain strength for whatever exertion the crisis might soon require (Acts 27:33–38).

At dawn they did not recognize Malta, but they saw a sandy beach where they might beach the ship and save their lives. So they cast off the anchors, hoisted the foresail, and made a run for the beach. The ship, however, grounded on a shoal and began to break up under the

[31] Henry J. Cadbury, in *The Beginnings of Christianity*, Vol. V, Note 28, pp. 345–354, concludes that we cannot determine just how the sailors undergirded the ship.

[32] Though Codex Vaticanus and the Sahidic Version read "seventy-six," the reading "two hundred and seventy-six" in Acts 27:37 is to be preferred. The overwhelming majority of manuscripts have the latter reading.

pounding of the waves. The soldiers, responsible for the prisoners, wanted to kill them to avoid blame for their escape, but the centurion blocked that plan, in part at least out of friendship for Paul, and the entire group reached land by swimming or floating on planks or other wooden pieces from the ship (Acts 27:39–44). Once ashore they received a friendly welcome from the natives. Acts reports two further items: a viper, warmed by the fire when the wood to which it clung was thrown into the fire, bit Paul, but he was not harmed; and Paul healed sick natives, including the father of Publius, chief man of the island (Acts 28:1–10).

ARRIVAL AT ROME

When spring weather permitted sea travel, the party sailed for Italy aboard another Alexandrian ship, which had wintered at Malta. After stops at Syracuse on Sicily and Rhegium on the tip of Italy, the ship made port at Puteoli, close to Naples. Paul and his companions found Christians in Puteoli, and by permission of the centurion stayed there seven days (Acts 28:11–14). Some of the Christians in Rome were friendly to Paul, for two delegations came and met him on the way, one at the Forum of Appius and the other nearer to Rome at Three Taverns. When Paul reached Rome and the centurion delivered him to the proper military authority, he was permitted to stay by himself in a rented home (or was he the guest of some Christian?). A soldier guarded him, but he could see visitors (Acts 28:15 f.).

PAUL AND THE JEWISH LEADERS AT ROME

In view of Paul's expressed and long-standing desire to make the acquaintance of the Roman church and preach to them (Rom. 1:11–15; 15:23 f.), it is astounding that apart from Acts 28:15 Luke says nothing of Paul's contact with the Roman church. Was that church as a whole not so friendly as he had hoped? Did they hesitate to associate closely with the prisoner bitterly opposed by Jews and accused of crime against the Empire? Luke does not say, but their coming to meet him does indicate courageous friendliness.

Luke reports that Paul as usual first made contact with the synagogue. Since he was a prisoner, he asked the Jewish leaders to come to him, and expressed to them his concern for his people, his innocence of wrong-doing, and his desire to tell them his message. They had had no word about him from the Jerusalem leaders; apparently they also lacked direct contact with the Christians in Rome; but they knew that the Christian sect was everywhere opposed (Acts 28:17–22). So they set a day, came to Paul, listened to his gospel, and debated it with him. Some believed; but when most of them rejected his message he declared that he would preach to Gentiles (Acts 28:23–28). For two years Paul lived in his private residence, free to receive and speak to all who came to see him. During that time he preached the gospel without hindrance (Acts 28:30 f.).

Here then, without telling the results of that preaching or what happened to Paul at the end of two years,[33] Luke ends his story.

PAUL'S PRISON LETTERS

From Paul's arrest in Jerusalem until the close of The Acts he had been a prisoner for almost five years, two of them at Caesarea and two after he reached Rome. At both Caesarea and Rome he could receive visitors and send messages. Since he never forgot or ignored his churches, he must have kept in touch with them, in part at least by letters. The New Testament contains five letters carrying Paul's name and written from prison: Ephesians, Philippians, Colossians, II Timothy, and Philemon. II Timothy, by almost universal agreement, dates later than the period covered by The Acts. Whether Paul wrote it as it stands is disputed; probably, as explained later in this chapter, it contains fragments from Paul which a follower expanded to the present form late in the first century; but in any case it was not written during the period covered by The Acts. The other four prison letters are usually dated in the years which The Acts describes.

Three questions have been raised about these four prison letters:

1. Did Paul write them? Although doubts have been expressed about all four, it is now agreed that Paul wrote Philemon and Philippians. It is also widely and rightly agreed that he wrote Colossians, which is closely bound to Philemon in situation and purpose. Far more objections have been raised to the Pauline authorship of Ephesians, whose general character and more laborious style differ from Paul's other letters to churches. On the whole, however, it is easier to accept it as Pauline than to explain how, if Paul did not write it, it was accepted as his so early and so easily.[34]

2. Where did he write them? Three answers have been urged: (a)

---

[33] This must mean that the very fact of Paul's preaching in the capital city, Rome, to all who would listen had climactic importance for Luke.
[34] This question is discussed later in this chapter.

Ephesus. Though The Acts does not say Paul was imprisoned there, II Cor. 11:23 shows that he suffered imprisonments never mentioned in The Acts, and letters to Asia Minor and Philippi can be explained more easily, it is argued, when thought of as written in Ephesus.[35] (b) Caesarea. Paul was in prison there for two years (Acts 24:27); he received visitors, and could have sent letters to churches. (c) Rome. The references to the praetorian guard and to Caesar's household (Phil. 1:13; 4:22) do not prove that this letter was written at Rome, but they fit best this view, which tradition has always favored for all four letters. It is assumed in what follows.

3. In what order did Paul write them? Their personal references show that Philemon, Colossians, and Ephesians were written and sent at the same time, while Philippians was written separately. No decisive argument is available, but in Philippians, Paul seems to have been in prison for quite a while, so this letter may be dated last and the other three dated somewhat earlier in the Roman imprisonment.

THE LETTER TO PHILEMON

The letter to Philemon is a priceless reflection of Paul's spirit and his personal concern for his converts.[36] It is not written, as is usually said, to one person, Philemon, but is addressed also to Apphia, Philemon's wife, and Archippus, perhaps his son, and to the church in Philemon's house. The entire church that meets in his house will hear the letter and know whether Philemon grants the request Paul makes.

Philemon, who lived at Colossae,[37] was converted by Paul, probably while Philemon was visiting in Ephesus (Philemon 19), for Paul had not visited Colossae (Col. 2:1). A slave of Philemon, Onesimus, had run away, apparently taking property or money of his master. He had known where to find Paul, news of whom reached Colossae from time to time, and so he had sought Paul out in Rome and Paul had converted him (Philemon 10). Paul would have liked to have Onesimus stay with him (v. 13), but he thought, and Onesimus agreed, that the slave should

---

[35] See George S. Duncan, *St. Paul's Ephesian Ministry* (London, Hodder and Stoughton, 1929).

[36] See C. F. D. Moule, *The Epistles of Paul the Apostle to the Colossians and Philemon* (Cambridge, University Press, 1957); John Knox, *Philemon Among the Letters of Paul*, rev. ed. (The University of Chicago Press, 1959).

[37] Edgar J. Goodspeed thinks that Philemon lived at Laodicea and that "the letter from Laodicea" in Col. 4:16 is the letter to Philemon; see *The Meaning of Ephesians* (The University of Chicago Press, 1933). But Col. 4:9 indicates that Onesimus (and so Philemon his master) lived in Colossae, and Col. 4:17, compared with Philemon 2, locates Archippus at Colossae.

10

go home and seek forgiveness from his fellow Christian and master, Philemon. The master could punish the slave almost at will; Paul was really risking the life of Onesimus. So he wrote to appeal to Philemon to forgive the converted Onesimus and recognize him as a Christian brother.

Paul uses a word play. Onesimus means "profitable," and although the slave had not been profitable before, he now has become so (v. 11). Still using financial language, Paul says that if Onesimus has robbed his master, he (Paul) will repay it, though he adds that Philemon owes Paul for his whole Christian life, since Paul had converted him (vs. 18 f.). Paul appeals to his age (v. 9)[38] and his friendship with Philemon, and even resorts to subtle threat, for when he asks for a guest room to be prepared (v. 22), he hints that it will greatly embarrass Philemon if Paul comes and finds that the master has been harsh to the returning slave.

What did Paul want Philemon to do? Certainly to forgive Onesimus and treat him as a Christian brother (vs. 15 f.). Did he want Onesimus returned to take care of Paul on behalf of Philemon, as v. 13 would suggest? Perhaps; this may be the "even more than I say" in v. 21. Did he expect Philemon to set the slave free? This is a modern view to which Paul gives no support. In fact, writing to the same city of Colossae, Paul takes care to discourage agitation for emancipation; he urges slaves to obey their masters (Col. 3:22), as he had said in I Cor. 7:20: "Every one should remain in the state in which he was called."

Paul did not agitate against slavery. Conversion made the slave worthy of brotherly respect; the master should treat the slave as a brother; differences in life situation were not to influence relations within the Christian community. Paul's expectation of the near end of the age kept him from any long-term social program, but his attitude made slavery incongruous in human society and ultimately doomed it where the gospel was taken seriously.

The Letter to the Colossians

The letter to the Colossians[39] was written to the city in which Philemon lived, but the two letters differ amazingly in content. The problem of the runaway slave Onesimus is not discussed in Colossians. He is

---

[38] The manuscripts read "an old man." The conjecture that Paul wrote or meant "an ambassador" is not necessary.

[39] See G. Johnston, "Colossians, Letter to the," *IDB*, A-D, pp. 658–662; E. F. Scott, *The Epistles of Paul to the Colossians, to Philemon and to the Ephesians* (London, Hodder and Stoughton, 1930); C. F. D. Moule (see note 36 above).

treated as a member of the Colossian church; converted by Paul, he must be accepted as a fellow Christian (Col. 4:9). But note that when Paul discusses the duties of the members of households, one sentence each suffices for wives, husbands, children, fathers, and masters, while four emphatic sentences insist that slaves faithfully obey their masters (chs. 3:18 to 4:1). Paul does not want his kind treatment of Onesimus to lead slaves to restlessness and disobedience.

The church at Colossae included other groups besides the small house church that met in the home of Philemon (Col. 4:15).[40] Archippus was now the leader of the Colossian church (v. 17). It seems to have been founded by Epaphras; Col. 1:7 probably indicates that he had ministered in Colossae (and in nearby Laodicea and Hierapolis) under the direction of Paul, who sent out such helpers from Ephesus to preach the gospel in neighboring cities.[41] This tie with Paul explains the apostle's personal concern and his sense of responsibility for the Colossians (cf. chs. 1:24 to 2:5).

The faith of the Colossian church and its love for other Christians gave Paul joy (ch. 1:3–8). But teaching being given there disturbed him. During his years in prison, teachers with at least some Jewish background had come to Colossae claiming to have a special knowledge, a philosophy that would make the Colossians more mature (ch. 2:8).[42] It emphasized angel worship (v. 18) and so gave to Christ a lesser role than Paul could approve. This new teaching included legal practices and an ascetic emphasis, as though by legalistic and ascetic practices one could earn better standing with God and keep free from evil (vs. 16–23).[43]

For Paul, any attempt to earn or improve one's standing with God by legalistic living or ascetic disciplines is misguided. Salvation is God's free gift through Christ; all idea of merit must be excluded from the Christian life. Paul strongly opposed the dualistic idea that the natural world is inherently evil and that therefore asceticism, abstaining from physical enjoyments to be more "spiritual," is necessary.

But Paul's answer to the new teaching in Colossae was not so much

---

[40] Otherwise, Paul would have had no reason to write Colossians as a separate letter.
[41] The above statement assumes that in Col. 1:7, Paul spoke of Epaphras as "a faithful minister of Christ on *our* behalf"; that is, the Colossians learned the gospel from Epaphras, who preached to them under Paul's direction and became their minister. Many good manuscripts, however, read "on *your* behalf," meaning that Epaphras was a Colossian acting for the Colossians; and Col. 4:12 may mean that Epaphras was a native of Colossae and not the founder of the church there.
[42] Col. 1:27 indicates that most of the Colossian Christians were Gentiles.
[43] Disparagement of the physical aspects of life indicates a pre-Gnostic mood combined with a legalistic attitude that used certain Jewish regulations to discipline the physical life.

negative as positive. Jesus Christ is central; what he has done, is doing, and will do for his people fully meets their needs. He is the divine Son, the Father's agent in creating, upholding, and redeeming all things (ch. 1:13–23).[44] He even created and redeemed the angels (vs. 16, 20), so it is wrong to push Christ aside to worship angels, as the Colossians were being urged to do. "In him the whole fulness of deity dwells bodily" (ch. 2:9); he is risen and seated at the right hand of God, and will appear in glory (ch. 3:1–4). The church is the body of Christ, "in whom are hid all the treasures of wisdom and knowledge" (ch. 2:3); it receives from him all needed grace and knowledge. It is not true philosophy but sheer nonsense to diminish his place in Christian faith and worship and turn to angels for help that only Christ can give.

The Christian has died to the world of sin and been raised with Christ (ch. 3:1); his hope is in this link with the risen, exalted Christ. He must break with all sin and live in love (vs. 5–16); "whatever you do, in word or deed, do everything in the name of the Lord Jesus, giving thanks to God the Father through him" (v. 17).

How Paul continued his ministry though in prison is clear from personal notices at the close of Colossians. Tychicus will deliver the letter, explain Paul's situation, and encourage the Colossians; Onesimus will go with Tychicus and confirm the news (ch. 4:7–9). Aristarchus, Mark (now back in good standing with Paul and about to travel in church work), Epaphras (now with Paul, at least for a time), Luke the beloved physician, and Demas send greetings (vs. 10–14). These people are with Paul; Aristarchus is actually sharing prison life with Paul (voluntarily?); all are concerned for the welfare of the churches. Paul's ministry continues from its "executive office" in the Roman prison.

THE GENERAL LETTER CALLED "EPHESIANS"

With the letters to Philemon and the Colossians, Paul probably sent also the letter we call "Ephesians."[45] It too was written from prison and carried by Tychicus (Eph. 4:1; 6:21 f.; cf. Col. 4:7–9). The language and thought of Ephesians and Colossians have so much in common that the most natural way to explain the close relationship is to say that Paul wrote and sent both at one time. But at least the title "Ephesians" is misleading. The oldest manuscript evidence shows that the words

44 On this "Logos" idea, cf. I Cor. 8:6; John 1:1–18; Heb. 1:1–3.
45 On Ephesians, in addition to books by John Knox, Edgar J. Goodspeed, and E. F. Scott (see notes 36, 37, and 39 above), see G. Johnston, "Ephesians, Letter to the," *IDB*, E–J, pp. 108–114; C. Leslie Mitton, *The Epistle to the Ephesians* (Oxford, Clarendon Press, 1951); E. Percy, *Die Probleme der Kolosser- und Epheserbriefe* (Lund, C. W. K. Gleerup, 1946).

"in Ephesus" were not original in ch. 1:1; the address is quite general, "to the saints who are also faithful in Christ Jesus." Even more important is the fact that though Paul spent most of three years at Ephesus and knew that church's problems well, this letter has no local color and deals with no local problems. Paul with his pastoral spirit could not have written so general a letter to a church he knew so well.

So it is often doubted that Paul wrote Ephesians. It is a general letter; the letters that surely come from Paul deal with specific church situations; even Romans, written to a church he had never visited, contains specific personal and local information. Ephesians is marked by long, meandering sentences, rich in meaning but lacking incisive style. The vocabulary includes noteworthy words not found in assured letters of Paul. The curious similarity to Colossians may be explained, if Paul wrote it, by the fact that Paul wrote both letters at the same time and so used the same ideas and expressions in both, but it may also be explained by saying that since Colossians is the more clearly Pauline, Ephesians comes from an admirer of Paul who made Colossians his pattern in presenting Pauline ideas to a later generation.

These arguments have real force. But on the whole we can best understand Ephesians as a letter written and sent by Paul when he wrote and sent Philemon and Colossians from his Roman prison. It was a general letter written mainly to churches near Ephesus that Paul had not founded but in which he had a special interest, since their founding resulted through his mission outreach from Ephesus (cf. Epaphras in Colossae). Since Paul does not know in detail the inner situation of the churches addressed and the situation varies from city to city, he writes less specifically. Among the cities to which Ephesians went were Laodicea and Hierapolis. It was to be read also in Colossae, just as Colossians was to be read in those two neighboring cities (Col. 4:13, 16).

Possibly the use of another scribe, who was given some freedom as to final wording, helps to account for the more involved style. The vocabulary and style, however, are essentially Paul's.[46] The similarity to Colossians is best explained if Paul wrote the two letters at the same time, writing Colossians first, and in the general letter we call Ephesians used many ideas and expressions already used in Colossians. As far back as evidence goes, Ephesians was accepted as written by Paul. When his letters were collected toward the close of the first century, it was included without question.

If, then, we conclude that Paul wrote Ephesians, we learn important

---

[46] Though not made for this purpose, the diagrams in P. N. Harrison, *The Problem of the Pastoral Epistles* (Oxford, University Press, 1921), show that in test after test the vocabulary and linguistic traits of Ephesians are Pauline.

things about him, for it represents some of his most mature thinking about the gospel and the church. It tells little about the churches addressed, except that they were in friendly touch with the church at Colossae and presumably also with Ephesus, for probably it was because a copy of the letter was preserved in Ephesus that the idea arose that Paul had written it to the church there. The letter was written to churches essentially Gentile in membership (Eph. 2:11).

Its theme is the worldwide outreach of the gospel of God's grace in Christ to all men, Jew and Gentile alike, so that there is one world church in which all men find their place through faith in Christ. This was God's plan "before the foundation of the world" (ch. 1:4). Paul calls it a mystery (v. 9), that is, a purpose of God once hidden from men but now made known by his redeeming action in Jesus Christ. It is God's sheer grace to undeserving sinners (ch. 2:4–8). The Gentiles have now been brought into the people of God and added to the Old Testament people of God, the Jews. Jews and Gentiles thus form one church, one body of Christ, one household, one temple (vs. 11–22). The ministry committed to Paul is to "preach to the Gentiles the unsearchable riches of Christ" (ch. 3:8), and he prays that the readers may be given insight to understand fully this gospel which is the hope of the world (vs. 14–19).

Of the leadership of the church, Paul mentions apostles, prophets, evangelists, pastors, and teachers (ch. 4:11). In two other passages Paul mentions apostles and prophets (chs. 2:20; 3:5). The leadership of the church is still mainly in the hands of traveling Spirit-guided men rather than in the hands of the authoritative resident local church officers who soon after Paul's day began to gain in power.

In Colossians, Paul had stressed the cosmic Lordship of Christ. He had done this to exclude any significant role for angels, whom the Colossians seemed ready to worship and trust for much of their spiritual help. In Ephesians the same cosmic role of Christ is asserted (ch. 1:10, 20–22), but the emphasis is on Christ's worldwide Lordship over the one universal church, in which there must be no divisions based on previous religious privilege or lack of it. Christ is the head of the church (ch. 1:22); the church is and must be one (ch. 4:4–6); life in the body of Christ, the church, erases all dividing walls between men (ch. 2:14) and unites all men in common loyalty to the common Lord in the one church. This loyalty must be expressed in moral obedience and integrity in all of life, especially in view of the active hostility of evil powers (chs. 4:17 to 6:20).

Perhaps there was a special need of such teaching in the churches to which the letter was sent. Throughout Paul's ministry it was his constant aim to reconcile Jews and Christians and all classes in one fellowship of faith and love.

THE LETTER TO THE PHILIPPIANS

In addition to Philemon, Colossians, and Ephesians, all written and sent at the same time in Paul's Roman imprisonment, he probably wrote Philippians toward the end of this imprisonment.[47] It clearly was written while Paul was in prison (Phil. 1:7, 13). The Philippian church had heard of Paul's imprisonment; they had sent a gift by Epaphroditus to help meet his needs; Epaphroditus had fallen sick and almost died; the Philippians had heard of this sickness; Epaphroditus had heard of their concern over his illness and had been troubled at their anxiety (ch. 2:25–30). All these developments show that Paul had been in prison at Rome for some time when he wrote this letter.

As was true of Philemon, Colossians, and Ephesians, there are three views as to when and where Paul wrote Philippians. (The answer to this question for Philippians need not be the same as for the other three letters.) One view is that Paul wrote it while in prison in Ephesus. There is no certain evidence of an imprisonment there, and for all the events connected with the Philippians' gift and the sickness of Epaphroditus, an imprisonment of several weeks or months would seem necessary. This makes it quite unlikely that this imprisonment was at Ephesus, where according to The Acts, Paul was active and remarkably effective in spreading the gospel by continual public preaching. Still less likely is the view that the imprisonment was at Caesarea (Acts 23:35; 24:27). Much the most likely view is that Paul was in prison at Rome. Mention of the praetorian guard (Phil. 1:13) and Caesar's household (ch. 4:22) points naturally to Rome, and ancient tradition from the time of Marcion (ca. A.D. 140) supports the Roman prison as the place of writing.

The Philippians had sent Paul a gift by Epaphroditus, who had fallen sick. This was not their first gift to Paul. To avoid the suspicion that his aim was personal profit, he never accepted support from a church while he was with it. But he let them support him in later work in other places, and the Philippians had sent gifts to him at Thessalonica (Phil. 4:16) and Corinth (Phil. 4:15; II Cor. 11:9). The words "now at length" and "in the beginning of the gospel" (Phil. 4:10, 15) show that

---

47 On Philippians, see George S. Duncan, "Philippians, Letter to the," *IDB*, K–Q, pp. 787–791; J. Hugh Michael, *The Epistle of Paul to the Philippians* (London, Hodder and Stoughton, 1929); F. W. Beare, *The Epistle to the Philippians* (Harper & Brothers, 1959).

some years have passed since those earlier gifts. (This favors the Roman
rather than the Ephesian origin of the letter.) But Paul knows of their
constant willingness to help, and his gratitude for the gift is genuine.

So he writes in part to thank the church for their love and generosity
(ch. 4:10–20), and to report on the sickness and recovery of Epaphroditus
(ch. 2:25–30). Perhaps Epaphroditus had been sent not only to carry
the gift, but also to stay and minister to Paul; Paul explains that he is
sending Epaphroditus back to let them see that their messenger has recovered (and perhaps because the man still needs to convalesce rather
than share prison life with Paul).

Paul has other reasons for writing. The Philippians, concerned for his
safety, are anxious about the outcome of his impending trial. He can
report that he has used his situation to spread the gospel among the
praetorian guard (ch. 1:12–14). Others have been spurred by his imprisonment to more urgent preaching; some have done it "from envy
and rivalry" (v. 15), to draw attention from Paul and to themselves,
but they are preaching the gospel, so Paul rejoices in that (v. 18). The
words "joy" and "rejoice" occur sixteen times in this short letter; Paul
is not defeated in spirit, and he wants the Philippians also to live glad
lives.

His case has not yet been decided, but he has hope of release. To die
and be at once with the exalted Lord Christ would mean for him a
special privilege and a relief from hardship, but he hopes to live and
continue to minister to the Philippians and others (vs. 19–26). He still
expects the return of the Lord in the near future (ch. 4:5), but he is
more ready to think that his death may come before that event than
he was in earlier letters.

Paul writes also to admonish and warn the Philippians. Their faith,
love, and loyalty give him joy (ch. 1:3–11). But there is dissension or
friction in this church, and a rivalry and pride instead of humility and
mutual helpfulness (chs. 2:1–4; 4:2). To emphasize this essential role
of humility Paul appeals to the humility of Christ (ch. 2:5–11). This
classic statement of Christ's preexistence, incarnation, Servant life, death
on the cross, and exaltation as Lord of all creation may have been a
very early hymn or confession of the church.[48] Its use here reminds us
that throughout his ministry Paul held a high Christology and shared
this faith with other early Christians.

The Philippians, like other churches (I Thess. 2:14), had undergone
persecution (Phil. 1:29). But the danger Paul fears comes from narrow

48 So Frank Chamberlin Porter, *The Mind of Christ in Paul* (Charles Scribner's Sons,
    1932), pp. 204–228.

Jewish Christians who demand circumcision and boast of their Jewish background and advantages. Paul insists that he could boast of more advantages than these opponents, but none of such things really count; the only solution for human need is the gospel, and so Paul concentrates on "the surpassing worth of knowing Christ Jesus my Lord" and presses earnestly toward the goal of complete loyalty to Christ (ch. 3:2–14).

The sensual people against whom Paul warns the Philippians (vs. 18 f.) are probably not the same as the circumcision promoters of v. 2. These sensualists abuse their Christian freedom to indulge their worst appetites. Perhaps they taught that what men do in the physical life does not affect their spiritual life. For Paul, as for Jesus and the Old Testament, man is a unity; his entire life should express consistent obedience to the will of God. High Christology and spiritual zeal are no substitute for moral integrity as an integral part of the Christian's service to God.

Thus even as a prisoner Paul continued his preaching and his pastoral care of his churches. If Philippians dates near the end of his two-year imprisonment in Rome, had his situation changed for the worse? Paul speaks as a prisoner with the praetorian guard in charge of him (Phil. 1:13 f.); Acts 28:30 says that he lived in his own quarters. But in The Acts, though he could receive visitors, a soldier constantly guarded him; and in Philippians, though he is in prison, he can receive visitors and write letters, and is in touch with the local church (Phil. 4:22); so there seems to be no radical change of situation. Nothing indicates that death is at hand.

WAS PAUL RELEASED FROM PRISON?

The ending of The Acts leaves unanswered the question as to what happened to Paul. There are at least four possibilities:

1. Luke could not tell more because he wrote at the end of the two years mentioned in Acts 28:30; Paul's case had not yet been settled. On this view, Luke-Acts probably was written as a background document for Paul's trial, to show that his faith was not politically dangerous and that he had committed no crime. This would be the neatest explanation of why The Acts ends as it does.[49] It would identify Theophilus as the Roman judge appointed by the emperor to hear Paul's appeal. But Theophilus appears to be rather a Christian patron of Luke (Luke 1:4),

---

[49] F. F. Bruce, *The Acts of the Apostles*, dates The Acts about A.D. 62 but does not urge that its purpose was to support Paul at his trial; see pp. 10–14, 29–34, 481. For a discussion of possible explanations of why The Acts ends as it does, see Kirsopp Lake and Henry J. Cadbury, *The Beginnings of Christianity*, Vol. IV, pp. 349 f.

and to date The Acts so early would mean dating Luke a little earlier, and since Luke uses Mark as a source, this would require a date in the fifties for Mark; this dates Mark and Luke too early.

2. Luke intended to write a third part of his work to tell of Paul's further career and report the further spread of the church. But such a third writing would have been an anticlimax, with nothing to match the story of Jesus' ministry, death, and resurrection and the spread of the gospel from Jerusalem to Rome.

3. Paul suffered martyrdom at the end of his two-year imprisonment in Rome; Luke's purpose was fulfilled in telling of the spread of the gospel until Paul reached Rome and preached in the capital city; this symbolized the spread of the gospel throughout the world; Luke did not make Paul's martyrdom the climax of The Acts, for the center of his story was Jesus Christ, so he merely hinted at Paul's martyrdom in Acts 20:25 and closed his book with the summary statement of Paul's free preaching at Rome. This may be so, but the hint of martyrdom in Acts 20:25 is faint; one could expect a clearer reference to it.

4. Paul was freed after two years, under a law that required prosecution within two years or the prisoner must be released.[50] Luke hinted at this by referring to the two-year period (Acts 28:30), and closed his story with the basic point—the preaching of the gospel in the capital of the Empire; to have told of Paul's release would have focused final attention on the apostle rather than on the freedom of the gospel to spread from Rome throughout the world. This may be correct, but a brief report of Paul's release could have been given and then followed by a final statement of the free preaching of the gospel after Paul's vindication.

THE FURTHER MINISTRY OF PAUL

No explanation of why The Acts ends as it does is entirely satisfactory. But the ancient church held, probably rightly, that Paul was released and traveled further in mission work. Perhaps the first evidence for this is the Pastoral Letters. These three writings, I and II Timothy and Titus, were accepted as from Paul and included in the collection of his letters, probably by the end of the first century. They refer to movements of Paul that have no place in his travels as found in The Acts. If they come

---

50 On the possibility of such a release, which would not have been a decisive climax for The Acts and so might not have seemed useful to Luke, see *The Beginnings of Christianity*, Vol. V, pp. 325–332, where Henry J. Cadbury quotes Kirsopp Lake's statement of the theory.

from Paul, or even if their biographical data come from Paul while the letters took their present form a generation or two after Paul's death, he made trips in the eastern Mediterranean that must be dated after the end of the story of The Acts.

Support for this view can be drawn from I Clement, written about A.D. 96.[51] This writing, composed in the name of the Roman church and ascribed by credible tradition to Clement, then the leader of that church, says that Paul in his travels went to the boundary or limit (*terma*) of the west. For a Roman, the boundary of the west would not be Rome, the westernmost point to which Paul goes in The Acts, but Spain. Clement thus says that Paul went to Spain. Either he deduced this from Rom. 15:24, 28, or it was known in Rome to be a fact. Against Clement's statement, one may argue that it refers to a preaching ministry in Spain, while the biographical notes in the Pastoral Letters reflect travels in the eastern Mediterranean area, including Crete, Ephesus, Troas, Macedonia, and Nicopolis. Already in The Acts, Paul seems to be an old and battle-scarred veteran (II Cor. 11:23–27; Philemon 9). To add the hardships of a preaching mission in Spain and further work in the East may seem too great a burden for his battered and "thorn"-tortured body (II Cor. 12:7). But the evidence seems to favor the conclusion that he was freed and engaged in further ministry.

The sequence of this further ministry eludes us. What Paul did in Spain is not known. We catch only glimpses of his eastern travels. We get no clear evidence of his later thinking; the statements of the Pastoral Letters about Christian doctrine and church polity are the very part of these writings whose Pauline origin is disputed.[52]

EVIDENCE FROM THE PASTORAL LETTERS

The Pastoral Letters purport to be written by Paul, and were accepted into the canon as his work. But their vocabulary and style are quite unlike the admittedly genuine letters of Paul; their emphasis on good works has a different ring from Paul's grace-given, faith-received, and Spirit-directed life of love and Christian freedom; the stress on sound

---

[51] See Cyril C. Richardson, *Early Christian Fathers* (The Westminster Press, 1953), pp. 33–73, for Introduction, translation, and notes on I Clement.
[52] For a concise discussion, see J. C. Beker, "Pastoral Letters, The," *IDB*, K-Q, pp. 668–675. See also P. N. Harrison, *The Problem of the Pastoral Epistles;* Walter Lock, *A Critical and Exegetical Commentary on the Pastoral Epistles* (Charles Scribner's Sons, 1924); E. F. Scott, *The Pastoral Epistles* (London, Hodder and Stoughton, 1936); Burton Scott Easton, *The Pastoral Epistles* (Charles Scribner's Sons, 1947).

doctrine has a conservative and defensive note unlike Paul's flashing theological brilliance; the formal church polity is unlike the priority Paul gives to charismatic leadership. In short, Paul hardly wrote the letters as they stand.

But the view that he had nothing to do with their writing has to explain the biographical references as mere fictional dress, and fails to explain how the church accepted the Pauline authorship so early and unhesitatingly. So a third view, though not entirely satisfactory, has much in its favor: Paul, after release from prison at Rome, wrote brief letters during his final visit to the East; these letters contained the biographical notes now found in the letters; a generation or so after Paul's death one of his disciples revised and enlarged them to say what he thought Paul, if still alive, would say about the dangers of false teaching and the need of discipline in the church. This means that the Pastoral Letters throw light mainly on the church toward the close of the first century.

The biographical notes that survive in them, however, indicate that Paul revisited many of his old churches—Ephesus, Miletus, Troas, the Macedonian churches, and Corinth (I Tim. 1:3; II Tim. 4:13, 20; Titus 1:5; 3:12). He also visited places not previously evangelized, e.g., Crete; and perhaps he now first visited Nicopolis in northwest Achaia, though Rom. 15:19 indicates that during his missionary travels before his long imprisonment Paul visited more cities in Achaia and Macedonia than The Acts specifically mentions, and Nicopolis could have been among them. But how many places Paul now visited and with what results we cannot tell.

If Paul was released after his two-year imprisonment in Rome and traveled in Spain, Crete, Asia Minor, Macedonia, and Achaia, he was again arrested and taken to Rome as a prisoner (II Tim. 1:17; 4:16). This time his words express no hope for release. He assumes that he faces martyrdom. The personal notes about himself and his friends and helpers reflect his difficulties on his recent travels and his readiness to die (II Tim. 4:6–16).[53]

THE MARTYRDOM OF PAUL

Ancient Christian tradition says that Paul died as a martyr at Rome.[54] This may have been in A.D. 64, in the persecution headed by the Em-

[53] II Tim. 4:18 does not mean that he will never die but that whatever outward treatment comes, the Lord will keep him safe.
[54] For a summary of ancient traditions about the death of Paul, see W. J. Conybeare and J. S. Howson, *The Life and Epistles of St. Paul* (Charles Scribner's Sons, 1892), Vol. II, pp. 487–490.

peror Nero; an alternate date A.D. 67 is sometimes given; but the date may well have been before A.D. 64. As a Roman citizen he could not lawfully be crucified, as Peter was reported to have been. A tradition says he was beheaded outside the Ostian Gate. Today the traditional spot is marked by the Church of St. Paul Outside the Walls.

On what charge was he executed? So severe a penalty suggests a more severe charge than disturbing the peace. Was he accused of preaching an illicit religion, separate from Judaism? Did Jews with influence at Rome press such a charge? Was the preaching of Christ as Lord and King treated as treason? Or—if Paul died in A.D. 64—was Nero looking for a scapegoat and ready to crush the Christians to draw attention away from his own misrule? Such was the rumor at Rome, according to the Roman historian Tacitus.[55] Paul's life ended in considerable obscurity, but what counted for him was the preaching and spread of the gospel. To that work he gave his active mission life; for that gospel he was willing to give his life in martyrdom, and he did so.

THE ACHIEVEMENT OF PAUL

1. *His personal life.* He had a persistent physical ailment, his "thorn in the flesh" (II Cor. 12:7), and he faced continual opposition. But he stood firmly and actively for his faith. He had none of the cautious, calculating minimum loyalty that blocks the way to achievement for so many men. With unrelenting courage, not always expressed in the most lovely way, he stood for his cause and was ready to make any sacrifice to advance it.

2. *His missionary career.* Essentially Paul was an evangelist, committed to the preaching of the gospel. He was a missionary, concerned to spread the gospel as widely as possible. His strategy was to plant the church in great centers and let it move out, chiefly through his converts and his helpers, into surrounding regions. He aimed to preach the gospel throughout the world wherever it had not yet been heard, and for him as a Roman citizen this meant primarily to cover the Roman Empire by his expanding ministry. His particular role in this expansion program was to preach to the Gentiles. He was not the first to preach to them, but he alone in the apostolic age conceived, carried out, and defended a systematic and comprehensive program of evangelizing Gentiles.

3. *His intellectual leadership in the development of Christian theology.* He did not begin that development. It began with the thinking of Jesus, and inevitably continued in the earliest church, for the disciples could not believe in the crucified and risen Christ and speak of him to others

[55] *Annals* XV.44.

without thinking of God's purpose and how it had been fulfilled in the decisive events they had witnessed. But in the apostolic age, Paul was the outstanding leader in facing and answering the basic theological questions that the gospel story raised. (Some would give this honor to the author of the Gospel of John.)

His theology was never a carefully formulated system; his letter to the Romans comes nearest to such a system, but even it is not a complete statement of Paul's thinking, and we most nearly capture all aspects of his theology by using all his letters. His profoundest insights and classic statements emerge from his grappling with urgent church situations, to which he spoke with relevance because he faced each passing situation in the light of the basic gospel. Much of his most important thinking comes out in only one passage of one letter. That a crucial phase of his thinking survives in but one letter, or that it is omitted in some other highly valued letter, does not cast a shadow on it. We get no clear, neat, consistent system of theology in these letters, written as they are for immediate needs, nor do we find a progressive chronological development in theology from one letter to the next. We receive the materials for a theology, glimpses of at least most of the vital aspects of Paul's thinking; and his theology is always linked with the life and needs of the Christian and the church.

We cannot here sum up the theology of Paul but may note great themes not to be ignored by those who want to understand him. God was the axiom of his thinking as of his worship. His thinking dealt with realities known in faith and worship. He thought as a member of Israel; he was convinced that God had chosen and called Israel, revealed himself to Israel, and given to Israel and now to the church its Scripture (our Old Testament). He was keenly aware of the sinfulness of all men; the basic democracy of mankind for Paul rests not only on creation of all by the one God but also on the common and radical need of all men for a spiritual help they cannot provide for themselves. To that common need there was a common answer. The undeserved grace of God provided in Christ and available on the simple condition of sincere and grateful faith is the one answer for all men. Jesus, the promised Messiah of the Jews, is the Son of God and the Lord of all men and all the creation. He has brought and now provides new life, new power for good living. Crucified, risen, and exalted to honor and power by the Father's will and plan, he is the head of the church, and by the gift of the Holy Spirit he actively rules and leads the one church. The newness of life made possible by the work of Christ and the power of the Spirit leads men in the church to a mutual ministry of love and unselfish service.

What God has done and is doing through Christ and the Spirit guarantees the full and final triumph of God's eternal purpose and so enables the believer to live in hope and eager anticipation.

4. *His letters.* More than one third of the books of the New Testament come from Paul. No other figure of the apostolic age is so well known, and probably no other leader in church history has played so great a role in determining the interpretation of the gospel in the church. He influenced some of the later New Testament writers, for example the editor of the Pastoral Letters and the writers of Hebrews and I Peter. In the second century, when the conflict with syncretism and Gnosticism led the church to form the New Testament canon, the result, to put it in one legitimate way, was to give Paul's understanding of the gospel a classic role. The immense influence of Paul's life and writings on such outstanding later leaders as Augustine is well known. At the Reformation, Luther, Calvin, and others found largely in Paul the stimulus for their decisive and original thinking. In recent times such men as Karl Barth have found in Paul's letters the stimulus to a fresh grasp of the essential gospel. Thus to Paul's unique ministry to his own generation must be added his continuing ministry to the church through his letters and the story of his life. He spoke and wrote for his own day, but the church has found that he speaks also to succeeding generations. The record of his achievement is not yet complete.

Part Five

THE CHURCH ANCHORED
IN HISTORY

Chapter 12

THE OBSCURE DECADES

THE BOOK of The Acts closes with Paul in prison at Rome. Up to that point, The Acts furnishes something of a connected history of the church. To be sure, it gives at best a sketch. Of many regions, such as Egypt and northern Asia Minor, it tells nothing, and of most other regions it presents but passing glimpses. But it provides our only connected narrative. All later writers of the history of the early church use the book of The Acts for their framework. When The Acts closes, this one resource is lacking, and a connected account of the next few decades of the church cannot be written. Only after several generations is it again possible to write anything like a consecutive narrative. From the closing days of The Acts to the end of the first century we get only occasional glimpses of events.

The importance of this obscure period is immense. In it were written almost all the New Testament writings except the letters of Paul. The message and form of the church were developing, as were contacts and conflicts with the Jewish and Gentile societies and their governing authorities. The outreach of the church was enlarging. New leaders were emerging.

But who these new leaders were is almost entirely unknown, and the external events in the ongoing life of the church almost entirely escape us. So it is impossible to trace clearly the stages of development and assign definite dates to individual New Testament writings. Though scholars often date one writing in the seventies and another in the eighties, we cannot write the Christian history of either decade, so such datings have no solid basis and rest mainly on the degree of church development that each writing seems to show. This is a subjective and treacherous procedure; we cannot assume that all parts and persons of the church developed at an equal pace, so that simpler ideas must be dated earlier than more developed ones. In many respects Paul, the earliest Christian writer whose works survive, is as advanced in thought as any other New Testament writer.

The Method Here Followed

Since no connected history of the church in these crucial decades can be traced and the specific settings of the individual New Testament writings elude us, it may seem that we can only discuss each writing separately, and abandon any attempt to write a connected narrative. But one other method, honest in facing the limitations of the sources, can yield a sketchy historical picture. We can study first the historical background of the period and then consider in turn each region in which there is evidence that the gospel was preached and churches founded. This is the method we shall follow.

What is known of the church between the end of The Acts and the middle of the second century takes place within the Roman Empire. In an apocryphal correspondence between Jesus and Abgar, king of Edessa, Abgar invites Jesus to visit his kingdom; Jesus promises to send one of his followers, and Thaddeus is supposed to have gone to Edessa later.[1] Edessa, it seems, was the first kingdom in which the ruler became Christian and Christianity became the official religion, but it is not clear when this took place, whether in the first century or only in the second.[2] Important trade routes ran east from Antioch in Syria to the region of Edessa, and it is possible—we can say no more—that the gospel traveled that way before the end of the first century. For attested history, we must look within the Roman Empire, and as background for that study we must survey briefly the political setting.

From Nero to Antoninus Pius

The boundaries of the Empire remained much as they had been in the days of Jesus and Paul, but the succession of emperors began with violence. Nero (A.D. 54–68) was egotistical, capricious, ambitious to excel in the arts, and suspicious of whoever might threaten his life or purpose. Some people at Rome held him responsible for the great fire that destroyed Rome in A.D. 64.[3] They said that he wanted to rebuild the city and took this method of "slum clearance." He blamed the Christians for the catastrophe.

Like Herod the Great, he was forceful in government but was dogged

---

[1] Edgar Hennecke, *New Testament Apocrypha*, Vol. I, pp. 437–444; Montague Rhodes James, *The Apocryphal New Testament*, pp. 476 f. Cf. Eusebius, *Church History* I.13.1–22; II.1.6 f.

[2] Hugh Jackson Lawlor and John Ernest Leonard Oulton, *Eusebius* (London, S.P.C.K., 1928), Vol. II, p. 57, put the evangelization of Edessa "not earlier than the middle of the second century."

[3] Cf. Tacitus, *Annals* XV.44. Suetonius, *Life of Nero*, Ch. 38, says flatly that Nero was responsible.

by family troubles; he even killed his own mother. He was both disliked and feared by the people. When he died, they hardly dared to rejoice; rumor had it that he was only in hiding and would return to wreak vengeance on his enemies; in one form it asserted that he was biding his time in the East and would return from Parthia to regain his throne.[4]

Toward the end of Nero's reign the Jews in Palestine revolted against Roman rule. Herod Agrippa II was Rome's puppet ruler over territory east and north of the Sea of Galilee, and over parts of Galilee and Perea; he appointed the Jewish high priest.[5] But since A.D. 44 procurators sent by Rome had governed most of Palestine. They did not understand the Jews and had increasing difficulty in keeping order. Finally, under Florus in A.D. 66, open revolt occurred, signaled by cessation of the regular sacrifices offered in the Temple on behalf of the emperor.

Though Jewish resistance was heroic and tenacious, it was slowly beaten down by superior Roman force, aided by dissension within the Jewish ranks. Jerusalem, which held out much the longest, finally fell in A.D. 70, and the city and Temple were destroyed.[6] Judaism was forced to reorganize, with the synagogue rather than the Temple as the focus of its religious life. Johanan ben Zakkai, a rabbi of Pharisee position, escaped from Jerusalem before it fell and led in this reorganization at Jabneh (Jamnia).[7]

Early in the revolt the Jerusalem church, responding to a prophetic utterance from one of their number, left the city and fled to Pella, a few miles southeast of the Sea of Galilee.[8] By this series of events, Jerusalem ceased to be the center of the religious life and outlook of both Jews and Christians.

In the confusion that followed Nero's death, four aspirants to the imperial throne came forward in one year; each was supported by a portion of the Roman armies. Galba, Otho, and Vitellius made successive but futile attempts to gain complete power (A.D. 68–69); Vespasian, who when Nero died was in Palestine quelling the Jewish revolt that had started in A.D. 66, won the throne and held it until his death (A.D. 69–79). His son Titus, who completed the subjugation of Palestine,[9] succeeded him for a brief reign (A.D. 79–81).

4 See, e.g., A. Momigliano in *The Cambridge Ancient History*, Vol. X, pp. 741 f.
5 See Stewart Perowne, *The Later Herods* (Abingdon Press, 1958), *passim* (see Index).
6 The detailed source is Josephus, *War*. On the cessation of Temple sacrifices, see II.17.2.
7 On Johanan ben Zakkai, see George Foot Moore, *Judaism*, Vol. I, pp. 83 ff.; Vol. II, p. 116.
8 Eusebius, *Church History* III.5.3. On his sources, see Lawlor and Oulton, *Eusebius*, above in note 2, Vol. II, pp. 81 f.
9 The hostilities did not end when Titus captured Jerusalem in A.D. 70. Jewish resistance continued, and the last of the revolt may be dated in A.D. 73, when the

The next emperor, Domitian (A.D. 81–96), troubled the Christians by his claim to divinity[10] and his attempts to suppress opposing views. Rather late in his reign he gave up hope of having a son to succeed him, and designated two sons of T. Flavius Clemens and Domitilla to succeed him, but in the last year of his rule, after Clemens had served four months as consul, Domitian executed him and exiled his wife Domitilla for *atheotēs,* failure to practice properly the religion of the Empire. It is possible, if not probable, that Clemens was a Christian; the evidence that his wife was one is even stronger.[11]

On Domitian's death, Nerva took the throne for a brief reign (A.D. 96–98). His successor, Trajan (A.D. 98–117), extended the Empire eastward. In A.D. 106 he annexed Arabia and made it a province, which included the former Nabatean kingdom and, in addition, some cities of the Decapolis. In A.D. 114 he added two more provinces, Armenia and Mesopotamia.

It proved too difficult, however, to maintain this eastward thrust, and Trajan's successor Hadrian gave up the added territory. Among the governors appointed by Trajan was the younger Pliny, who went to Bithynia in Asia Minor in A.D. 111 and died two years later. As we shall see, his exchange of letters with the emperor Trajan throws light on the state of the church in Bithynia and on Trajan's opposition to the Christians.[12] Trajan also had troubles with the Jews—witness their uprising in the years A.D. 115–117 in Cyrene, Egypt, and Cyprus.[13]

His successor, Hadrian (A.D. 117–138), had even more difficulty. About A.D. 130 he gave orders that a city to be called Aelia Capitolina be built on the site of Jerusalem. It was to have a temple dedicated to Jupiter Capitolinus in which Hadrian would be honored.[14] This bold disregard of Jewish feelings led to a revolt under Bar-Cochba (A.D. 132–135). Rabbi Akiba hailed Bar-Cochba as the expected Jewish Messiah. Bar-Cochba is said to have harassed the Jewish Christians.[15] When the revolt was crushed by Rome, only Gentiles were permitted in Jerusalem; the church there after A.D. 135 was Gentile rather than Jewish.

The reigns of Antoninus Pius (A.D. 138–161) and the philosopher-king

---

Romans captured Masada, on the west side of the Dead Sea. See Josephus, *War* VII.8.1 to 10.1.

[10] Suetonius, *Life of Domitian,* Ch. 13.

[11] Cf. M. P. Charlesworth in *The Cambridge Ancient History,* Vol. XI (1936), pp. 31 f., 41 f.; B. H. Streeter, *ibid.,* p. 255.

[12] Pliny the Younger, *Letters,* Book X, xcvi and xcvii.

[13] See Victor A. Tcherikover and Alexander Fuks, *Corpus Papyrorum Judaicarum,* Vol. I, pp. 85–93.

[14] See Wilhelm Weber in *The Cambridge Ancient History,* Vol. XI (1936), pp. 313 f.

[15] So Justin Martyr, *Apology,* Ch. 31. Yigael Yadin, *The Message of the Scrolls* (Grosset & Dunlap, 1962), pp. 71 f., is not certain that this report is true.

Marcus Aurelius (A.D. 161–180) are less important for our study. The ways in which the Roman rule affected the church will be noted in the following survey of how the church developed in the various regions of the Empire. In general, the Empire in A.D. 60–150 was under a strong central rule whose stability depended on the support of the army. The economic crises led to considerable dependence on the emperor for relief, especially in Rome. One sees a strong tendency to promote emperor worship, particularly in the eastern provinces, and some emperors, notably Domitian, took the claim of divinity seriously. The claim was taken less seriously by most subjects, but their polytheistic or sophisticated outlook permitted them to participate in the state cult, and they could regard it as an expression of imperial authority and unity.

In spite of much skepticism among the cultured classes and superstition especially among the common people, there was still wide adherence to the inherited classical faiths of Greece and Rome, and a turning to mystery religions was under way. A marked tendency to syncretism was observable, and particularly in the Near East, including Asia Minor, this trend was present. The movement toward what took form as Gnosticism in the second century was already active in the latter half of the first century and was beginning to seize upon the Christian gospel to crystallize and gain strength. In such a time of totalitarian rule, weakening of the old standards, skepticism, and ferment, the moral fiber of society could not stay strong.[16]

In this period, outward organizational expression of the unity of the church was lacking. The church generally sensed its unity; those who shared the faith in the one basic gospel generally regarded themselves as members of one church. But this unity was not expressed in outward form. The only first-century Christian known to have planned a broad and systematic spread of the gospel was Paul. The church's mission was carried on by numerous preachers, almost all nameless to us; no discernible master plan knit their work together.

THE CHURCH IN PALESTINE

Our survey of the founding and early growth of Christianity in various parts of the Roman Empire may well begin with Palestine. Church history there differed from that of other regions. In the period following The Acts it was at first mainly a phase of Jewish Christianity. This Jewish Christianity in its characteristic form was composed of Christians of Jewish (or Samaritan) ancestry who shared with their people the

16 See Samuel Dill, *Roman Society from Nero to Marcus Aurelius* (London, Macmillan & Co., 1905).

conviction that they all should observe the Mosaic law. There is no good evidence that in Palestine the church in our period included Gentiles previously unconnected with the synagogue.[17]

Almost nothing is known of the church in Galilee, where the ministry of Jesus had centered.[18] The book of The Acts only once mentions the existence of the church there (Acts 9:31). However, the tradition of Galilean appearances of the risen Jesus most likely was handed down by Galilean Christians, and perhaps the church in nearby Damascus (Acts 9:10, 19) was founded by early preachers from Galilee. In the reign of Domitian (A.D. 81–96) two grandsons of Jude the brother of Jesus were brought before the emperor on suspicion of plotting rebellion.[19] They were accused of teaching that Jesus as Messiah would be an earthly king and throw off Roman rule. But they convinced Domitian that the kingdom of Jesus was not political in character and that they were no threat to the Empire, and so were freed. Probably the small plot of land they owned and tilled was in Galilee; if so, there were Christians in Galilee late in the first century, and references in rabbinical literature to disputes between rabbis and Jewish Christians support this conclusion.[20]

Samaria plays a clearer role in the first-century church.[21] Hellenistic Jewish Christians, especially Philip, one of the Seven, preach there (Acts 8:1, 5); Peter and John confirm and expand this mission. The later church fathers regard Simon Magus, with whom Peter has an encounter (Acts 8:9–24), as the origin and cause of later heresies, especially the Gnostic heresy. It is difficult to tell how far Simon deserves this dubious honor, but he and Menander were active in Samaria in developing ideas that later proved heretical.[22] Not all the products of Samaritan Chris-

---

[17] The converts of Philip in Samaria and Caesarea (Acts 8:5–40; 21:8) probably had a freer attitude toward the law than that which prevailed at Jerusalem, but they did not reject the law.

[18] Ernst Lohmeyer, *Galiläa und Jerusalem*, argues for a strong church in Galilee independent of Jerusalem. The theory may show the existence of a Galilean wing of the church but rests on too many shaky deductions to be convincing as a whole.

[19] See Eusebius, *Church History* III.19 to 20.6, who quotes Hegesippus.

[20] After A.D. 70 the rabbis could not live in Jerusalem. Their first center was Yabneh (Jamnia), but after the Jewish revolt of A.D. 132–135 Galilee became a prominent center of rabbinical study and life. Rabbinic references are not conclusive proof of an active Galilean Christianity in the late first century, but go well with such a view.

[21] On "Samaria and the Origins of the Christian Mission," see Oscar Cullmann, *The Early Church*, edited by A. J. B. Higgins (London, SCM Press, Ltd., 1956), pp. 183–192.

[22] On "The Samaritan Gnosis," see Johannes Weiss, *The History of Primitive Christianity*, Vol. II, pp. 756–766. Cf. also R. M. Grant, *Gnosticism and Early Christianity*, Ch. 3, "Simon Magus and Helen, His Thought."

tianity were bad, however; Justin Martyr, a prominent and effective second-century apologist for the Christian faith, was born in Samaria about A.D. 100.

Possibly Caesarea was the most enduring center of Christianity in Palestine. It early became a center of a free Hellenistic Jewish Christianity. Philip, one of the Seven, centered his ministry there for years (Acts 8:40; 21:8). Peter preached there to Cornelius and his household (Acts 10:1 to 11:18). Paul passed through Caesarea more than once, and during his two years in prison there, he was free to keep in touch with Christian friends (Acts 24:23). The later work of Origen and Eusebius in Caesarea suggests a long history of Greek-speaking Hellenistic Christianity in that city, though breaks in the continuity of the church there may well have occurred during the Jewish revolt of A.D. 66–70 and in later periods of tension between the Empire and the Jews.[23]

THE JERUSALEM CHURCH

We hear also of Christians at Lydda, Joppa, and Ptolemais in the apostolic age (Acts 9:32–43; 21:7), and may assume that the gospel was preached in numerous other Jewish cities and towns of Palestine. But we really know very little of Palestinian Christianity outside of Jerusalem during the last third of the first century. By the end of The Acts, James the brother of Jesus was the unchallenged leader in Jerusalem. The brothers of Jesus were active both in Jerusalem (cf. Acts 1:14) and as traveling leaders (I Cor. 9:5). Stephen and James the son of Zebedee had been martyred (Acts 7:58–60; 12:2). Peter had been imprisoned and when released had left the city (Acts 12:17); he had returned to be present at the Jerusalem conference (Acts, ch. 15), but was no longer resident there. The rest of the Twelve, or most of them, seem to have left also; the leaders were now James and the elders (Acts 21:18).

Only by faithful adherence to the Mosaic law had the church there escaped devastating attack. Stephen and even Peter had been too liberal for Jerusalem Jews. James the brother of Jesus was known for his devout Jewish piety, but finally even he was martyred. After the death of the Roman procurator Festus (A.D. 62), and before the arrival of his successor, Albinus, Annas the high priest brought about the death of James. Since James believed that Jesus was the risen Christ and the way to salvation, and had agreed with Paul that Gentiles need not keep the law to be

23 On the recent exploration of the Caesarea harbor, see Charles T. Fritzsch and Immanuel ben-Dor, "The Link Expedition to Israel," in *The Biblical Archaeologist*, Vol. XXIV (1961), pp. 50–59.

saved, the fact that he himself faithfully observed the law did not save him.[24]

His successor as leader of the Jerusalem church was Symeon, a cousin of Jesus and James. He was chosen leader, Eusebius says, by the apostles and disciples and the family of Jesus.[25] The belief that Jesus would rule God's people in an earthly kingdom evidently gave special importance to his family; in the kingdom the royal family would naturally be prominent. (Paul had no such idea of the role of Jesus' family, nor did Jesus himself.) Symeon is said to have led the Jewish Christian wing of the church for decades, until martyred under Trajan. This martyrdom is added evidence that Jesus' family was long under suspicion of being political rebels; at least some Jewish Christians gave the impression that Jesus would throw off the Roman yoke and set up an earthly kingdom.

THE JEWISH REVOLT: THE CHURCH LEAVES JERUSALEM

But long before Symeon's martyrdom came the Jewish revolt against Rome. Angry at what they considered the unjust and unjustified rule of God's people by Rome (the blunders of the last Roman procurators added fuel to the flame of hate), the Jews ceased to offer sacrifices on behalf of the emperor and revolted against him.[26] The Christians faced a hard decision. They did not expect Christ's rule to be established by revolt against Rome. They had a saying of Jesus warning them, rather, to flee when such a crisis arose (Mark 13:14 and ||s). Also, Eusebius reports that an oracle of the Lord directed them to flee from Jerusalem; probably some Christian prophet spoke to the church there when the siege was beginning, and they fled across the Jordan River to Pella, a city of the Decapolis, where they quite likely knew that other disciples were living.[27]

This flight from Jerusalem had two momentous consequences. For one thing, the fugitives must have seemed to their fellow Jews to be deserters. They lost any tie they had had with the Jerusalem leaders of Judaism. In addition, their flight ended the era in which Jerusalem was the church's visible center and symbol of unity. As long as the Jerusalem church was continuously active, even the Gentile churches looked up to it, and Paul could lead his churches to send help to it (Rom. 15:27).

---

24 See Josephus, *Ant.* XX.9.1, and Eusebius, *Church History* II.23, which quotes Hegesippus at length.

25 Eusebius, *Church History* III.11. Eusebius reports Symeon's martyr death in III.32. 1–4.

26 See note 6 of this chapter.

27 Eusebius, *Church History* III.5.3. S. G. F. Brandon, *The Fall of Jerusalem and the Christian Church*, pp. 168–173, rejects this tradition.

Now Jewish Christianity was separated from both Jerusalem and the Gentile churches. It was destined to dwindle slowly away; henceforth it had no noteworthy influence on the church at large.

Not that the Jewish Christian church immediately withered and faded from sight. It lived on for centuries, and won many Jews to faith in Christ. Such passages as Matt. 10:17–39 reflect an active and brave ministry of Christian witness to Jews in the face of fierce opposition and active persecution. References in rabbinic literature point to a continual controversy for decades between Jewish Christian preachers and rabbinic opponents. Evidently toward the close of the first century one of the Eighteen Benedictions used in the synagogue worship was so formulated that no Christian could join in it.[28] This was to exclude the still-existing Jewish Christian group from participation in the synagogue; it shows that they still seemed to Jewish leaders a real threat.

It would appear that sometime after the fall of Jerusalem the Jewish Christian group, or at least part of them, returned from Pella to the neighborhood of Jerusalem. When the Messianic message of the group and its emphasis on the coming earthly (Jewish) Messianic Kingdom aroused Trajan to execute Symeon, the leader of the church, his successor was Justus or Judas.[29] Little is known of the later history of this group, but when Bar-Cochba revolted against Rome and was recognized as Messiah by Rabbi Akiba, he appears to have been actively hostile to the Jewish Christians, whose claim for Jesus clashed with his own claim.[30]

The views of the surviving Jewish Christians were not uniform. Many but not all of them rejected the virgin birth of Jesus (it was not part of the earliest public gospel tradition). Paul was an ogre to many; they regarded him as a renegade who taught freedom from the Mosaic law, and the typical Jewish Christian of this period stood firmly by that law. One wing of the Jewish Christians followed Gnostic tendencies, and the *Clementine Homilies* and *Recognitions* embody—in revised and developed form—material that attests this. But the history of this tendency as it affects Jewish Christian circles extends into the next two centuries and we cannot follow it further.[31]

28 So G. F. Moore, *Judaism*, Vol. I, p. 91; but Israel Abrahams, *A Companion to the Authorised Daily Prayer Book*, pp. lxiv f., denies that Benediction xii was directed against Christians.

29 Eusebius, *Church History* III.35; IV.5.3. On the problems raised by the lists of Jerusalem bishops in Eusebius, see Hugh Jackson Lawlor and John Ernest Leonard Oulton, *Eusebius*, Vol. II, pp. 167–170.

30 See note 15 above.

31 On Jewish Christianity after the flight to Pella, see Johannes Weiss, *The History of Primitive Christianity*, Vol. II, pp. 712–739.

THE CHURCH IN EGYPT

.During the apostolic age and for some time afterward the Christians in Palestine had their closest ties with Syria. There is no evidence of vital ties to the south. The hint in Acts 8:26–39 that the gospel was early carried to Ethiopia stands isolated. Information as to how and when the gospel reached Egypt is also strangely lacking. It seems certain that this occurred in the first century, and one suggestion is that when in A.D. 66 the Jews revolted against Rome, some members of the Jerusalem church fled to Egypt. Indeed, it may well be conjectured that even earlier the gospel was preached not only in Alexandria and other Egyptian cities where Jews were found[32] but also in Cyrene, just west of lower Egypt (Acts 2:10; 11:20; 13:1). Possibly Apollos heard the gospel in Egypt and went from there to Ephesus (Acts 18:24 ff.). But perhaps more likely he first heard of Jesus in Palestine or, especially if Acts 19:1–7 reflects his early preaching in Ephesus, learned in Palestine only what John the Baptist had preached about the Greater One who was to follow him (Acts 18:25). The tradition that John Mark, after writing his Gospel, was the first to preach in Egypt and that he founded churches in Alexandria lacks early support.[33]

But however the gospel reached Egypt, it did so in the first century, and made rapid headway. The Rylands Papyrus fragment of the Gospel of John may be dated about A.D. 130, or possibly even earlier.[34] The so-called Fragments of an Unknown Gospel, to be dated before the middle of the second century A.D., come from a work that depends on our canonical Gospels.[35] These manuscripts, discovered in Egypt, show that the gospel was known, churches existed, and gospel materials were being copied and rewritten in Egypt in the first half of the second century. Other papyrus fragments confirm this statement. Gnostic documents in Coptic, recently discovered near modern Nag Hammadi, are mostly Coptic translations and revisions of Greek writings dating from A.D. 150 and later; they show that an extensive Christian literature, some of it quite heretical by usual standards, was already being produced in Egypt by A.D. 150.[36] Back of such literary activity lay decades of Christian

---

[32] S. G. F. Brandon, *The Fall of Jerusalem and the Christian Church*, Ch. 12, argues that the gospel reached Alexandria before A.D. 50 and that the church there was greatly increased by Jewish Christians who came from Jerusalem about A.D. 70.

[33] See Eusebius, *Church History* II.16.1.

[34] C. H. Roberts, *An Unpublished Fragment of the Fourth Gospel in the John Rylands Library* (Manchester University Press, 1935).

[35] H. Idris Bell and T. C. Skeat, *Fragments of an Unknown Gospel and Other Early Christian Papyri*. The editors wrongly inclined to date this "Unknown Gospel" so early that it could be a source of the Fourth Gospel.

[36] For description and introduction, see Jean Doresse, *The Secret Books of the Egyptian Gnostics*.

preaching and worship in Egypt. The apocryphal Gospel of the Egyptians also indicates that in the second century the gospel was widely preached and believed in Egypt.[37]

All these data show that the foundation of the church in Egypt goes back into the first century, possibly into the middle third of that century. But of the history of the earliest church there we know nothing certain.

To the east and south of Palestine lay Arabia. Paul reports that he went to Arabia, and he may have preached there, but his passing reference in Gal. 1:17 is our only hint of possible early spread of the gospel into the Nabatean kingdom.[38]

The Church in Syria

As we have said, it was in Syria that the gospel first took deep root outside of Palestine. Soon after Pentecost it reached Damascus in southern Syria, for Jewish Christians were there when Saul was persecuting the church (Acts 9:1–25), but whether the gospel came there from Jerusalem or from Galilee is not known, nor can we trace the later history of the Damascus church. Fleeing Hellenistic Christians preached in Phoenicia after Stephen's death (ch. 11:19), and there were churches at Tyre and Sidon toward the end of Paul's career (chs. 21:2–6; 27:3), but their further history escapes us.

The real center of Christian life in Syria was Antioch on the Orontes River.[39] This large and important city had a mixed population and wide contacts in every direction. It thus was uniquely fitted to be the base for the widening church's first far-reaching mission program. As Acts 11:19–26 implies and ch. 15:1 makes certain, the Gentiles there who became Christians were not required to be circumcised and keep the Mosaic law as a condition of entering the church, and the Jewish disciples accepted this situation and even ate with their Gentile fellow Christians (Gal. 2:12). Led by "prophets and teachers," with Barnabas as the trusted key leader at the first (Acts 11:22–26; 13:1), the first really "ecumenical" church developed. It sponsored the first planned mission outreach (Acts, chs. 13 ff.), and defended the spread of this "ecumenical" form of church life when it was attacked (Acts 15:1 ff.).

Evidently the Jerusalem church and its leaders had vital ties with the Antioch church for decades. They had sent Barnabas to Antioch as their representative. Peter visited there and perhaps stayed there for some

---

[37] See Montague Rhodes James, *The Apocryphal New Testament*, pp. 10–12; Hennecke, *New Testament Apocrypha*, Vol. I, pp. 166–178.

[38] See Johannes Weiss, *The History of Primitive Christianity*, Vol. I, p. 197.

[39] Glanville Downey, *A History of Antioch in Syria*.

time (Gal 2:11); indeed, Eusebius refers to him as the first bishop of Antioch.[40] Messengers from James the brother of Jesus were able to break the unity of the Antioch church when James decided that the Jewish disciples there were too lax in observing the Jewish law (Gal. 2:12). To Antioch, Syria, and Cilicia was sent the agreement reached at the Jerusalem conference (Acts 15:23), and The Acts gives the impression that Paul, after the Jerusalem conference, his dispute with Peter over eating with Gentiles (Gal. 2:11 ff.), and his break with Barnabas (Acts 15:36–41), had no influential role in the church at Antioch, although he later revisited it (Acts 18:22 f.).

There is little further information about Antioch until the first decade of the second century. Eusebius says that Evodius was the first bishop of Antioch (or was the second bishop, after Peter), and he dates the entrance into office of the next bishop, Ignatius, in or shortly after A.D. 69.[41] But the Antioch church had no bishop in its early years; it was led by "prophets and teachers" (Acts 13:1), and only after several decades did it develop the monarchical episcopate that was in effective operation at the end of Ignatius' life. His significance in the development of church order and Christian thought requires special notice.

IGNATIUS OF ANTIOCH

Ignatius, seized in a persecution about A.D. 107,[42] was taken to Rome with other victims to be thrown to the wild beasts in the arena. As he passed through Asia Minor, he was met in Smyrna by bishops and other representatives of churches in that region. From Smyrna he wrote not only to the churches in Ephesus, Magnesia, and Tralles—cities not on his travel route—but also to the Roman church, to beg it not to work to prevent his martyrdom. Later, at Troas, he wrote to the churches in Philadelphia and Smyrna, and also to Polycarp, the bishop of Smyrna.

These letters are highly instructive and immensely important for three reasons: (1) They are a remarkable testimony of a dedicated Christian eager to face martyrdom for Christ. (2) They show clearly that when he wrote, Antioch and a number of cities in western Asia Minor had churches led by a monarchical bishop, with the definitely recognized threefold church order of bishop, elders, and deacons (*To the Smyrnaeans*, ch. 8). (3) They make it clear that both the churches in Asia Minor

---

[40] *Church History* III.36.2; cf. III.22.
[41] This rests upon Eusebius' *Chronicle.* See John Lawson, *A Theological and Historical Introduction to the Apostolic Fathers* (The Macmillan Company, 1961), p. 103.
[42] See note 41, and for alternative dates, Hugh Jackson Lawlor and John Ernest Leonard Oulton, *Eusebius*, Vol. II, p. 108. Dates about A.D. 110 or 115 are often suggested.

and the Antioch church were facing at least two types of teaching that Ignatius considered heretical and dangerous: a Judaistic trend that emphasized Jewish practices and lacked an adequate view of Jesus Christ (*To the Philadelphians*, ch. 6); and a Gnostic movement that denied that Christ had actually come in the flesh and lived and died (*To the Smyrnaeans* 5.2).

In opposing such teachings, Ignatius emphasized the role of God as Creator, Lord, Redeemer, and Judge; the virgin birth of Jesus; his true humanity and full deity; redemption through his death and resurrection available to believers in the church under the bishop through the working of the Spirit in baptism and the Lord's Supper; the unity of the church, given only through the bishop; and the necessity for all the Christians in a church to live in vital unity with the bishop and in faithful loyalty to the true teaching as the bishop attests it.[43] Such vigorous theology and church organization show Ignatius as a powerful leader.

The vigor with which he defended the monarchical episcopate suggests strongly that it was a relatively recent establishment and not so generally accepted as he would have liked. Indeed, he mentions no bishop at Rome; the monarchical episcopate evidently was not so explicitly recognized there as at Antioch in Syria.[44] (The letter that Polycarp, bishop of Smyrna, wrote to the church at Philippi shortly after Ignatius passed through these cities mentions no bishop at Philippi; there too the church had no such episcopal system as did Syria and Asia Minor.)

Apart from Antioch, almost nothing is known of the early development of churches in Syria. Some information is available if, as seems probable, the Gospel of Matthew[45] and The Letter of James[46] were

---

43 On his theology, see Virginia Corwin, *St. Ignatius and Christianity in Antioch* (Yale University Press, 1960), and John Lawson, *A Theological and Historical Introduction to the Apostolic Fathers,* pp. 145–152.

44 I Clement, written from Rome about A.D. 95, gives no hint of the existence of a monarchical episcopate in Rome.

45 The Gospel of Matthew is discussed in Chapter 14.

46 The "Letter" of James opens in letter form, but is really an excellent example of wisdom literature, and makes much use of questions and direct commands. It deals with the benefits from trials endured in faith (James 1:2–18), being doers of God's word (vs. 19–27), worship without social snobbery (ch. 2:1–13), faith and works (vs. 14–26), wisdom in speech and peaceable life (ch. 3:1–18), disciplined, humble, trustful living (ch. 4:1–17), woe to the rich (ch. 5:1–6), and patience, truthfulness, prayer, and help to the erring (vs. 7–20). Some would date the work ca. A.D. 45 and ascribe it to James the brother of the Lord (but he emphasized the ceremonial law, and this epistle does not). Others would date it in the early sixties as James's reply to Paul. But it really answers a garbled Paulinism, which may better be found later in the first century. See Joseph B. Mayor, *The Epistle of St. James,* 3d ed. (London, Macmillan and Co., 1910); James Hardy Ropes, *A Critical and Exegetical Commentary on the Epistle of St. James* (Charles Scribner's Sons, 1916).

written somewhere in Syria in the latter part of the first century. These writings show a strong Jewish background but do not come from a Jewish Christian circle devoted to the strict keeping of the Jewish ceremonial law. These Jewish authors belonged to the Hellenistic wing of Jewish Christianity. Such strong contact with Judaism, freedom from narrowness, and vital tie with Gentile Christians seem most likely to have existed in the region of Syria.[47]

CHRISTIANITY IN ASIA MINOR

For the period between the ending of The Acts and the middle of the second century we know more about Asia Minor than about any other region of the ancient church. But we get few added facts about Cilicia, Cyprus, Pamphylia, and Galatia, which Paul visited on the journey of Acts, chs. 13 and 14. The fact that Philo, a deacon from Cilicia, accompanied Ignatius to Rome to minister to him[48] suggests a close connection between Syrian Antioch and Cilicia. And since Gaius of Derbe went with Paul to Jerusalem on his final visit to take the collection (Acts 20:4), it would seem that after Paul's departure, Galatia continued to regard him as their apostolic guide.[49] We get more detailed information, however, concerning the church both in the Roman province of Asia in western Asia Minor, and also in Bithynia and Pontus.

THE CHURCH IN THE PROVINCE OF ASIA

Paul's work in Asia had centered in Ephesus, and had been highly successful. From Ephesus the gospel preaching had reached out into surrounding cities. Visitors to Ephesus from these outlying regions heard Paul and carried the gospel back to their home; thus Philemon of Colossae seems to have been converted in Ephesus by Paul (Philemon 19). Helpers of Paul went to other cities of Asia and preached there; Epaphras seems to have gone to Colossae (Col. 1:7),[50] and also to

---

[47] Some would say that both The Letter of James and the Gospel of Matthew were written in Palestine, but we find no evidence of a vigorous Hellenistic Jewish Christianity there in the later decades of the first century, and attempts to date either book before Jerusalem fell are not convincing: S. G. F. Brandon (see note 32) suggests Egypt as the place of writing of both works, but we have no solid facts about early Christianity in Egypt to support this view. Syria is to be favored.

[48] Ignatius, *To the Philadelphians* 11.1.

[49] But this Gaius is by some considered a Macedonian, on the basis of a Western reading in The Acts: "Gaius of Doberus." See F. F. Bruce, *The Acts of the Apostles,* pp. 370 f.

[50] This is so if we accept the reading: "a faithful minister of Christ on *our* behalf." Some ancient manuscripts, however, read "on *your* behalf." See note 41 in Chapter 11.

Laodicea and Hierapolis (Col. 4:13). Paul himself, on his visits to Troas, may have founded the churches at Troas and Assos (Acts 16:8; 20:1–14). The exaggerated summary of Acts 19:10, "that all the residents of Asia heard the word of the Lord," sums up this intensive ministry of Paul and his assistants in the province of Asia.

His letter to Philemon and to the church meeting in Philemon's home (Philemon 2) illustrates how early churches, without church buildings, held their meetings for worship and common meals;[51] and it shows that Christian converts included slaves. The letter to the Colossians illustrates how strange teaching—asceticism, angel worship, and other syncretistic practices—was already appearing in churches of this region; this was a prelude of Gnostic teaching to come. If, as argued earlier, Ephesians was a general letter to be taken to a group of Pauline churches in Asia Minor, that letter attests the strength of the church in that region at the end of Paul's ministry. And the instruction Paul gave that the letters he wrote were to be sent from church to church, with churches exchanging letters (Col. 4:16), shows how the collection of Paul's letters began naturally during his lifetime.

After Paul's death definite detailed information about the churches of Asia is lacking for nearly thirty years. The collection of his letters must have continued in this period; at the end of the first century at least ten had been collected, and the final expansion of the Pastoral Letters into their present form probably had occurred. If, as seems probable, the Pastorals were given their final form in Asia, they give us important information about the condition and leadership of the church there at that time; they show that in the three decades following Paul's death the church in Asia showed concern for sound teaching and for stable and authoritative local leadership.[52]

THE BOOK OF REVELATION

The book of Revelation gives considerable information about the churches of Asia Minor.[53] It was written about A.D. 95 by one John, who describes himself as a servant of God and a prophet (Rev. 1:1–3; 10:11;

[51] See my article, "The Significance of the Early House Churches," in *JBL*, Vol. LVIII (1939), pp. 105–112.

[52] On the Pastoral Letters, see note 52 in the preceding chapter.

[53] For a recent summary of study of this book, see J. W. Bowman, "Revelation, Book of," *IDB*, R-Z, pp. 58–71. See also Isbon T. Beckwith, *The Apocalypse of John* (The Macmillan Company, 1919); R. H. Charles, *A Critical and Exegetical Commentary on the Revelation of St. John*, 2 vols. (Charles Scribner's Sons, 1920); Martin Kiddle, *The Revelation of St. John* (Harper and Brothers, n.d.).

11

22:6–9, 18 f.). He writes to churches facing severe persecution. The
church has already passed through one time of suffering and martyrdom;
one martyr, Antipas of Pergamum, is named (ch. 2:13; cf. ch. 6:9). John
anticipates a terrible and immediate spread of persecution, due in part
to the refusal of the Christians to worship the emperor as divine; apparently Jewish hostility has urged on the persecutors (chs. 2:9; 3:9).
The author writes to encourage the threatened churches to stand fast no
matter what they may have to suffer.

He writes to seven churches (chs. 1:11; 2:1 to 3:22). His prophecy
shows a great liking for groups of seven, so this number is probably sym-
bolical and shows that the writing was intended for all the churches in
the region. Five of the seven had not been mentioned in what The Acts
tells of Paul's work in Asia; Smyrna, Pergamum, Thyatira, Sardis, and
Philadelphia now appear in addition to Ephesus and Laodicea.

Part of the problem of these threatened churches is that they are not
fully faithful and loyal. Those at Smyrna and Philadelphia, though
weak and harassed by hostile Jews, have held fast to their faith and
receive praise (chs. 2:8–11; 3:7–13). But Ephesus has lost much of its
original love and loyalty (ch. 2:4), and Ephesus, Pergamum, and Thyatira
tolerate the teaching of the Nicolaitans and Balaam and "Jezebel" (an
evil woman nicknamed after the Old Testament queen who in Elijah's
time—see I Kings 18:4, 13—opposed God's true prophets); these seducers
teach people to eat food sacrificed to idols and practice immorality (ch.
2:6, 14 f., 20).[54] Sardis and Laodicea are described as "dead" (with few
exceptions) or "lukewarm" (ch. 3:1–4, 15 f.).

This is a picture of churches founded many years before, with a record
of earlier faith and courage, but now lacking spiritual resources and
loyalty sufficient to withstand fierce persecution. These "letters" were
not sent separately to the churches addressed; the entire writing was
sent to these and other threatened churches of Asia to nerve them for
the coming test.[55] The province of Asia was a stronghold of Roman
emperor worship, and intensified demands for worship of the emperor

[54] Cf. Acts 15:29.
[55] The Revelation, chs. 4 to 22, portrays in traditional symbolic language the final
drama in which God defeats and permanently banishes the devil and his forces and
sets up the eternal Kingdom in which his faithful people will be forever blessed.
Prominent in the action are the seven seals (chs. 6:1 to 8:1), the seven trumpets
(chs. 8:2 to 11:19), and the seven bowls (chs. 15:1 to 16:21). The Lamb, the Word
of God, has a part in this defeat and punishment of evil (chs. 5; 14:1–5; 19:11–21).
The fall of Babylon (=Rome) is depicted (chs. 17:1 to 18:24), and the special privilege of the martyrs in their thousand-year reign with Christ before the last and
decisive battle with evil is portrayed (ch. 20:1–10). This portrayal of final victory is
intended to nerve the threatened churches to face even martyrdom if necessary.

Domitian, who liked to be called *dominus et deus*, "Lord and God," were largely responsible for the crisis.[56]

THE SETTING OF I PETER

It is difficult to date I Peter.[57] It anticipates persecution in Asia Minor, but not because the Christians refuse to worship the emperor; that demand does not seem to have been made when this letter was written. So it probably dates from a time earlier than the crisis of which Revelation speaks. It hardly dates in the time of Nero, for as far as we know, his persecution in the sixties did not affect Christians outside of Rome. If Silvanus (I Peter 5:12) actually wrote the letter, he may have done so after Peter's death, perhaps in the seventies but more likely in the eighties. In any case, the writer, although he knows that persecution threatens the churches of Asia Minor,[58] still hopes that worthy living and tested integrity will convince outsiders that Christians are not evil and really deserve respect (I Peter 3:13). "But if not" (cf. Dan. 3:18), the Christians must "not be surprised at the fiery ordeal" and must "share Christ's sufferings" (I Peter 4:12 f.).

The danger does not come—at least primarily—from state officials; Christians are to pray for and obey them (ch. 2:13–17). It comes rather from popular dislike of the Christians, who criticize pagan ways of life (chs. 2:12, 15; 3:15–17; 4:4). It must be remembered that the Christian gospel was an indictment of the first-century world, whose normal reaction to such criticisms was resentment and hostility.

THE GOSPEL AND LETTERS OF JOHN

It is usually conceded that the Gospel of John and the three Letters of John originated in Asia Minor toward the end of the first century. Those who think that this Gospel was originally written in Aramaic

---

[56] See R. M. Grant, *The Sword and the Cross* (The Macmillan Company, 1955); Ethelbert Stauffer, *Christ and the Caesars*, tr. by K. and R. Gregor Smith (The Westminster Press, 1955).

[57] Basic commentaries are Edward Gordon Selwyn, *The First Epistle of St. Peter* (London, Macmillan & Co., 1947); Francis Wright Beare, *The First Epistle of Peter*, 2d ed. (Oxford, Basil Blackwell, 1958).

[58] The churches addressed were in the Roman provinces of Pontus, Galatia, Cappadocia, Asia, and Bithynia. This included all of Asia Minor except a strip along the south coast where Lycia, Pamphylia, and Cilicia were located. The address to "exiles of the Dispersion" could mean Jewish Christians, but probably refers to Christians as a minority in a pagan world where they cannot feel at home.

suggest Syria or Palestine as its place of writing,[59] and those convinced of its ties with Philo and Egypt sometimes suggest that it perhaps was written in Egypt, but strong ancient tradition supports its origin in the region of Ephesus. But if so, its date cannot be the same as that of the book of Revelation, whose background of persecution has no real parallel in the Gospel and Letters of John. The writer of the Gospel and Letters, who describes himself as "the Elder" (II John 1; III John 1), probably wrote several years earlier than A.D. 95, the approximate date of Revelation.[60]

The nonapocalyptic viewpoint of "the Elder" is so different from that of Revelation that he cannot be the John who wrote that book. He faces a situation in which persons in the church—some have even left the church to take a more "advanced" position (I John 2:19)—are denying that Jesus really lived a physical human life. They thus were taking a Docetic view (cf. John 1:14; I John 4:2; II John 7). They were arrogant toward Christians of more "simple" faith and so were lacking in brotherly love (I John 3:11, 23).[61]

I John was written as a general letter to be read in many churches; II John was sent to a certain church, not now identifiable, designated as the "elect lady"; III John was sent to Gaius, a Christian loyal to the Elder but living in a church whose local leader, Diotrephes, refused to let the Elder's messenger be heard in that church.

The title Elder has here a far wider reference than it generally has in the modern church; it refers, not to an officer in a local church, but to a prominent leader exercising authority over a considerable region. Strong ancient tradition identifies this Elder with the apostle John, said to have lived long and died in Ephesus. A considerable number of modern scholars, however, distinguish the Elder John (or the Elder) from the Apostle John, and point out rightly that Papias knows of an Elder John separate from the Apostle John.[62] In any case, the Elder must

---

[59] Cf. C. F. Burney, *The Aramaic Origin of the Fourth Gospel* (Oxford, Clarendon Press, 1922), pp. 127 ff. (Antioch in Syria); Charles Cutler Torrey, *The Four Gospels*, pp. 263 f. (Jerusalem).

[60] It has generally been thought that the writer of the three letters also wrote the Gospel of John. Cf. A. E. Brooke, *A Critical and Exegetical Commentary on the Johannine Epistles* (Charles Scribner's Sons, 1912); R. H. Charles, *A Critical and Exegetical Commentary on the Revelation of St. John*, Vol. I, pp. xxxviii-xliii. But C. H. Dodd, *The Johannine Epistles* (London, Hodder and Stoughton, 1946), represents a recent tendency to ascribe these letters to a writer other than the author of the Gospel.

[61] I John emphasizes two points: the actual human life and death of Jesus Christ as the basis of the gospel message of salvation (chs. 1:1, 7; 4:2; 5:6), and the necessity of mutual love among Christians (chs. 2:9–11; 3:11–18, 23; 4:7–21). II John emphasizes the same two points (vs. 5, 7).

[62] Papias is quoted in Eusebius, *Church History* III.39.4.

be clearly distinguished from the prophet John who wrote the book of Revelation.[63]

IGNATIUS ON THE CHURCHES IN ASIA

Important new information about churches in Asia comes from the letters that Ignatius, bishop of Antioch, wrote from Smyrna and Troas when he passed through Asia Minor on his way to Rome to suffer martyrdom. These letters, to Ephesus, Magnesia, Tralles, Rome, Philadelphia, Smyrna, and Polycarp bishop of Smyrna, include two Asian cities not previously mentioned, Magnesia and Tralles. Written about A.D. 107, they tell us more about Ignatius than about the churches of Asia. But they make clear that churches along the route he traveled, and some not on that route, rallied to honor and hear the condemned prisoner. This reflects a sense of unity and morale.

His letters indicate that the Docetic tendency in Asia, noted in the Johannine Letters fifteen or more years earlier, was still strong enough to require militant opposition. The urgent insistence of Ignatius on the essential role of the bishop and on the necessity of the threefold order of bishop, elders, and deacons suggests that this church order, obviously solidly established in Syria (and Cilicia), had also been generally accepted in Asia, but so recently and with enough resistance that Ignatius is led to emphasize repeatedly how essential this order is.[64]

Ignatius wrote four letters from Smyrna and three from Troas (about A.D. 107). A few weeks or months later, the church at Philippi wrote to Polycarp, bishop of Smyrna, asking him to forward their letter to Antioch in Syria. (When Ignatius passed through Philippi on his way to Rome, he asked the Philippian church to send an encouraging message to his church at Antioch.) They also asked for copies of any letters of Ignatius that Polycarp had.[65] This shows that the keeping, copying, and circulation of letters by outstanding church leaders was a known practice; probably Paul's letters had been collected by such a gradual process (cf. Col. 4:16), and this had set the pattern of collecting letters of Christian leaders.

Polycarp's reply, still extant, notes that he is sending the letters (he does not say how many, but there are several), and he asks (ch. 13) for news of Ignatius; he still does not know the whole story of Ignatius' martyrdom. Polycarp's letter is remarkable for its quotations from or

[63] The Gospel of John is discussed in detail in Chapter 14.
[64] See, e.g., Ignatius, *To the Trallians*, ch. 2; *To the Smyrnaeans*, ch. 8.
[65] The situation is indicated in the Letter of Polycarp, bishop of Smyrna, *To the Philippians*, ch. 13.

allusions to many New Testament writings; it points forward to the coming formation of the New Testament canon.

It has been suggested that Polycarp wrote only chs. 13 and 14 in A.D. 107, and that chs. 1–12 were a separate writing, composed not long before Polycarp's martyrdom at Smyrna about A.D. 156.[66] But if, as is probable, the entire letter was written about A.D. 107, it is a notable testimony to the early knowledge and use of most of the New Testament books.

PAPIAS AND PHILIP IN ASIA

Another prominent Christian leader of Asia in the first half of the second century was Papias, bishop of Hierapolis, noted for having written, perhaps in the reign of Hadrian (A.D. 117–138), the (now lost) five books of Expositions of the Sayings (or Oracles) of the Lord. He speaks of knowing John the Elder, and he values highly the oral tradition about the apostles' teaching as given him by their followers, but he accepts Mark's Gospel as a faithful report of what Peter taught about Jesus, and he hands on the view that "Matthew compiled the oracles (sayings of Jesus?) in the Hebrew language."[67] This and his own writing show his interest in the words and deeds of Jesus. He had great interest in a materialistic eschatology. We know his ideas mainly through Eusebius.

Eusebius reports that Philip, one of the twelve apostles, spent the closing years of his life in Hierapolis, where his four daughters continued to prophesy (cf. Acts 21:9). Eusebius seems to mean that their activity extended into the early years of the second century. He seems, however, to have confused Philip the apostle with Philip of the Seven (Acts 6:5; 8:5–40; 21:8); apparently the latter left Caesarea, perhaps at the time of the Jewish revolt against Rome in A.D. 66–70, and settled in Hierapolis.[68] The report that in the late first century and perhaps in the early second century the daughters of Philip prophesied in Hierapolis, not far from Phrygia, is an interesting background to the role that prophetesses play in the Montanist movement in Phrygia in the middle of the second century.

66 See P. N. Harrison, *Polycarp's Two Epistles to the Philippians* (Cambridge, University Press, 1936).
67 Preserved in Eusebius, *Church History* III.39.16.
68 See Eusebius, *Church History* III.31.2–5; 39.9; V.24.2.

THE CHURCH IN BITHYNIA: PLINY'S LETTER

Just when Christianity reached northern Asia Minor is not clear. Possibly, to say the least, this occurred by A.D. 50, for when Paul thinks of going to Bithynia to preach, he is mysteriously barred (Acts 16:7), and the best reason, in view of his policy of going where others had not yet preached (Rom. 15:20), is that he knew the gospel was already being preached in Bithynia. I Peter 1:1 refers not only to Galatia and Asia but also to Pontus, Cappadocia, and Bithynia. This clearly implies that at the time of writing, possibly in the sixties but more likely in the seventies or eighties, the gospel had been preached there for some years. The letter makes no claim that Peter had founded or preached to these churches; he certainly had not founded the churches in Galatia or Asia, but he may have visited the churches addressed.

The first clear picture of Christianity in Bithynia comes from about A.D. 112. The emperor Trajan had sent Pliny the Younger as governor of Bithynia. Pliny found the church strong in both cities and rural regions; it obviously had been there for decades. The pagan temples and worship were being neglected. There were bitter criticisms of the Christians, wild charges against them, and demands that they be condemned.

It was clear to Pliny—we do not know why—that the Christian faith was not to be permitted. If those reported to be Christians were Roman citizens, he sent them to Rome for the emperor to judge; noncitizens who denied being Christians and offered incense to the emperor he dismissed, but he punished those who admitted being Christians and persisted in their Christian confession. Perplexed when he received an anonymous document naming many other Christians, he wrote to the emperor Trajan for advice on what to do. His letter and Trajan's reply are extant.[69] Trajan approved Pliny's method, except that he told him to pay no attention to anonymous charges.

But clearly, Christians were numerous. The church had been in Bithynia for decades. Many were ready to suffer martyrdom, although they insisted that their faith and life gave no reason for condemnation; they told Pliny that they gathered at dawn on a certain day (no doubt Sunday, the day of Christ's resurrection), sang hymns to Christ as to God, then dispersed and reassembled in the evening for a common meal, and pledged themselves in their worship to do no wrong or crime.

How long the persecution lasted is not known, but since Pliny went to Bithynia in A.D. 111 and died two years later, it probably was a short

---

[69] Pliny the Younger, *Letters*, Book X, xcvi and xcvii.

period. But the official policy was clear; Christians could be condemned, with imperial approval, whenever hostility arose against them.

CHRISTIANITY IN PONTUS

I Peter 1:1 refers to Christians in Pontus, but the origin and early days of the church there are unknown. Aquila and Priscilla came from Pontus to Rome and later to Corinth (Acts 18:2), but nothing proves that they were Christians before leaving Pontus.

The most notable figure from Pontus in the early church was Marcion.[70] His father was bishop of the church at Sinope, and from there Marcion came to Rome about A.D. 139. By then his religious views were no doubt well formed, although the Gnostic teacher Cerdo may have sharpened his thinking after he reached Rome. He rejected the Old Testament, held that the righteous, wrathful God of the Old Testament was a different being from the gracious Father of Jesus Christ, and put together a canon consisting of the Gospel of Luke and ten letters of Paul (he excluded the Pastoral Letters). He "restored" all eleven writings to their original form by excising passages that tended to identify the Father of Christ with the God of the Old Testament. Marcion was trying to do full justice to Paul's gospel of divine grace freely given apart from works of the law, but he distorted Paul's gospel, which was rooted in the Old Testament. The impetus Marcion gave to the formation of the New Testament canon will be noted later.

THE CHURCH IN MACEDONIA

The history of the church in Macedonia and Achaia is obscure after Paul's departure. In Macedonia he had founded churches in Philippi, Thessalonica, and Beroea (Acts 16:11 to 17:14). At some time during his ministry, his mission in Macedonia also extended still farther west, for he tells the Roman church that he has preached the gospel as far as Illyricum (Rom. 15:19), and the statement in II Tim. 4:10 that Titus went to Dalmatia is another indication that Paul's interest extended to western Macedonia and north into Dalmatia-Illyricum.

Of the next decades in Macedonia, however, we have definite knowledge only of Philippi. Ignatius, when taken through Philippi on his way to martyrdom about A.D. 107, met the leaders and some members of

---

70 Adolf von Harnack, *Marcion: Das Evangelium vom fremden Gott* (Leipzig, J. C. Hinrichs, 1924); John Knox, *Marcion and the New Testament* (The University of Chicago Press, 1942); Edwin Cyril Blackman, *Marcion and His Influence* (London, S.P.C.K., 1948).

that church. Ignatius asked them to send encouraging word to his home church at Antioch in Syria; his arrest had left its members without a bishop to lead them. They wrote a letter, and sent it to Polycarp, bishop of Smyrna, asking him to forward it to Antioch and also to write them.[71] His reply, still extant, was written before he received definite news of what had happened to Ignatius at Rome.

Polycarp's letter shows that the church at Philippi had no bishop; its leaders were elders and deacons (ch. 5:3). One elder, Valens, had taken church funds entrusted to him, and Polycarp's prayer that the Lord may grant to Valens and his wife true repentance suggests that she shared the guilt (ch. 11). Since the church is said to have power to restore them, it must have been the assembled church which deposed Valens and excluded them both from its fellowship.

In his letter, Polycarp says nothing of danger from Jewish sources such as Paul mentioned in Phil. 3:2 f. The danger now comes rather from Docetic ideas. Polycarp speaks of "false brethren" who "bear the name of the Lord in hypocrisy" (ch. 6), and he says, apparently reflecting I John 4:2 f. and II John 7, that such people deny that Jesus Christ came in the flesh, refuse to confess the testimony of the cross, and deny the resurrection and the judgment (ch. 7.1). This denunciation reflects in part the situation in Asia Minor, but such earnest tones and general terms indicate that a similar danger threatens the Philippian church.

As noted earlier, Polycarp sends to the Philippian church a copy of the letters of Ignatius which he has, and in his own letter quotes or reflects most of the New Testament writings.[72] Just as a church in one province was getting letters of Ignatius from a church in another province, so the letters of Paul were being exchanged, other Christian letters were circulating, and probably churches were already exchanging written gospels.

THE CHURCH IN ACHAIA

Of the churches in Achaia our knowledge is meager. There was a church in Athens in the first part of the second century, since Quadratus wrote his Apology from there ca. A.D. 125. A tradition states that Dionysius the Areopagite was the first bishop at Athens.[73] Such traditions cannot be verified, but this one, if it were true, would imply a continuous

[71] See note 65 of this chapter.
[72] John Lawson, *A Theological and Historical Introduction to the Apostolic Fathers*, pp. 157–165.
[73] Cf. Eusebius, *Church History* III.4.10; IV.23.3.

history of that church from the days of Paul (Acts 17:34), though nothing proves that it was a strong or prominent church.

Apart from Athens, our information about Achaia after Paul's day deals with Corinth. There, as at Philippi, the church was led by elders and deacons (I Clem. 42:4 f.; 44:1–16; cf. Polycarp, *To the Philippians* 5:3). About A.D. 95 a controversy arose and the church deposed certain elders. Then the church of Rome intervened with a letter called I Clement. A probably correct tradition says that Clement wrote it, and this shows that he held a position of influence and leadership at Rome, but it is written in the name of the Roman church and never mentions Clement.

The church at Rome intervened in the quarrel at Corinth on the basis of a definite theory of church order (I Clement, chs. 42; 44). In fact, it seems that only church order, and not the right or wrong of the dispute, concerned the Roman church. I Clement never tells what was under dispute at Corinth, or why the elders were in the right. Its one clear point is that God sent Christ, Christ appointed the apostles (who are said to include Paul), the apostles appointed their successors,[74] and so an unbroken succession runs from God and Christ on to the presbyters at Corinth, who should hold office for life and cannot rightly be deposed by the congregation. Though the majority of the church at Corinth had acted to depose the elders, I Clement blames the action on certain ringleaders, who are urged to withdraw from the church or repent and submit to the wrongfully deposed elders (chs. 54; 57). I Clement makes no mention of a bishop at Corinth—or at Rome; but the importance of its theory of succession for later church polity is apparent.

THE CHURCH IN CRETE

Closely connected with Achaia was Crete. Paul never preached there before the end of The Acts, but if released, as he probably was, Titus 1:5 ff. shows that he then visited Crete and established churches. Of their later history we know that their leading officers were elders (Titus 1:5), and we may also conclude from the Letter to Titus, whose present form we date late in the first century, that they needed strong teaching and moral discipline. Crete emerges again in Christian history about A.D. 170, when Dionysius of Corinth writes letters to such Cretan churches as Gortyna and Cnossus.[75] He seems to imply that these churches had long existed.

---

74 These successors are called bishops or overseers in I Clem. 42:4 f.; 44:1, and elders in I Clem. 44:5; 54:2; 57:1. The two terms are interchangeable in I Clement.
75 Mentioned in Eusebius, *Church History* IV.23.5–7.

THE CHURCH IN ROME

The other important center of Christian life in the period before A.D. 150 is Rome. When Paul was taken to Rome as a prisoner, there were Christians at Puteoli, near the site of modern Naples (Acts 28:13). No doubt there were Christians in other Italian towns, such as Ostia, the port of Rome. But of them we hear nothing in the period following the close of The Acts. The story centers on Rome.

No one knows how the gospel first reached Rome. "Visitors from Rome" in Jerusalem at Pentecost could have taken the gospel story back home (Acts 2:10). As Rom., ch. 16, may suggest, Christians from other churches, especially Pauline churches, could have moved to Rome and through their Christian witness founded a church there. In any case that church was founded quite early in the apostolic age. When Paul writes Romans, it is a strong church whose "faith is proclaimed in all the world" (Rom. 1:8).

Perhaps it was spirited disputes between Christian and non-Christian Jews in the synagogues of Rome that led Claudius to banish the Jews from the city (Acts 18:2).[76] Possibly Aquila and Priscilla were members of the Roman church before they went to Corinth and met Paul. Certainly this banishment of Jews helps to explain how when Paul wrote to the church it was predominantly Gentile, and why the synagogue leaders, when Paul reached Rome, were quite out of touch with the Christian movement. The latter point can hardly be discounted by saying that the writer of The Acts completely misunderstood the situation in Rome; the "we passages" of The Acts extend to the time of Paul's arrival in Rome (Acts 28:16); the writer evidently knew what happened at that time.

If, as seems probable, Paul wrote Philippians from prison in Rome, we learn that he had been making converts there among the "praetorian guard," and there were Christians in "Caesar's household"; some of the Roman Christians were friendly to Paul, but others "preach Christ from envy and rivalry," thinking by their partisan preaching to cause the authorities to make the conditions of his imprisonment more severe (Phil. 1:12 f., 15–17; 4:22). The "saints" (i.e., the Christians) of Caesar's household probably included not only slaves and freedmen but also others of higher standing. From the founding of the Roman church to the middle of the second century it was a Greek-speaking church. Latin became its language only at a later time.

[76] See Suetonius, *Life of Claudius* XXV.4. On later supporting statements by Dio Cassius and Orosius, see F. F. Bruce, *The Acts of the Apostles*, pp. 342 f.

PETER IN ROME

It seems almost certain that Peter came to Rome and died there as a martyr, probably when Nero persecuted the Christians. His travels after he left Jerusalem and visited Antioch (Gal. 2:11) cannot be traced. It is improbable that he went east to Mesopotamia and Babylon (cf. I Peter 5:13, where "Babylon" more likely refers cryptically to Rome). He may have visited northern Asia Minor (I Peter 1:1) and Corinth (I Cor. 1:12).

When he came to Rome is not known; there is no evidence that it was before Paul came or while Paul was in prison there. He certainly did not found that church; Paul must have mentioned him had he been the leader at Rome when Paul wrote to the Roman church; The Acts could hardly have ignored him had he been in Rome when Paul arrived (Acts, ch. 28). But he probably came there for a brief stay before his martyrdom. His visit and martyrdom have early and strong attestation, beginning about A.D. 95 (I Clem., ch. 6) and continuing with Ignatius,[77] Papias,[78] and other ancient Christian writers. It is likely that the church preserved a continuous tradition as to the place of his martyrdom or burial; the spot is under the present St. Peter's Church at the Vatican.[79]

According to Tacitus, Nero's persecution of the Christians occurred in A.D. 64.[80] Nero was being blamed for the great fire that destroyed much of Rome. To divert attention from himself he chose as scapegoat the church. It was already an object of public contempt for its strange and insistent preaching and perhaps also for its mainly lower class membership. Numerous Christians fell victim to Nero's cruel and fiendish tortures; even the public, originally unfriendly, began to sympathize with them.

There is no evidence that Nero's persecution extended beyond Rome, but it was ominous that the executions were not directly based on the original charge of incendiarism, but Christians as such could be condemned by police action. This meant that at any time the authorities could harass and execute the Christians by simple exercise of police authority, without proving any treasonable or criminal act. The specific action against Peter is nowhere described, but I Clem., ch. 6, indicates that jealousy led certain other Christians at Rome to give information or

---

77 *To the Romans,* ch. 4. This seems to imply that Peter and Paul had been martyred at Rome.

78 See Eusebius, *Church History* II.15.2. This passage attests Peter's presence in Rome, whether or not its statement that Peter himself wrote I Peter is accepted.

79 The best documented discussion of Peter's stay, martyrdom, and burial in Rome is by Oscar Cullmann, *Peter: Disciple, Apostle, Martyr.*

80 Tacitus, *Annals* XV.44. Cf. Suetonius, *Life of Nero,* ch. 38.

direct attention to Peter and so contributed to his seizure and death (cf. earlier about Paul in Phil. 1:15–17).

RENEWED PERSECUTION

There is no clear evidence that either Vespasian or Titus persecuted the church. But Domitian did, in Rome and in Asia Minor. I Clem., ch. 1, written about A.D. 95, refers without details to "sudden and repeated calamities and reverses which have befallen us" in Rome as the reason the Roman church has been slow to write to Corinth. Eusebius refers definitely to persecution at Rome by Domitian.[81]

T. Flavius Clemens, who had just ended a short term as consul, was executed, and Domitilla, his wife (or according to another report his niece), was banished. Both were close relatives of Domitian. Domitilla, it appears, was a Christian and the highly placed Clemens probably was. The charge against them was "atheism," failure to acknowledge and worship the pagan gods of Rome and take part in emperor worship.[82]

THE ROMAN CHURCH WRITES TO CORINTH

When the persecution subsided, the Roman church, disturbed that the majority of the church at Corinth had deposed some elders, wrote to Corinth. Such a wide-ranging interest of the Roman church appeared early; "from the beginning" they sent relief to needy Christians in other places.[83] They now feel led to intervene in Corinth and urge that the deposed elders be restored to office. The leaders opposed to the elders should either withdraw from the church or repent and ask forgiveness for their unjustified action (I Clem., chs. 54; 57). Tradition quite likely is correct that Clement wrote this long and somewhat ponderous letter, called I Clement though it never mentions him and is written in the name of the Roman church. It perhaps is the earliest noncanonical Christian writing we possess.

I Clement is important: (1) For its attitude to Scripture. It accepts the Old Testament as giving the pattern of life for the church; it shows knowledge of letters of Paul, I Peter, and Hebrews (this may support the Roman origin of the last two writings); but its use of Christian writings is meager compared with its copious Old Testament quotations.

---

81 *Church History* III.17.
82 See note 11 of this chapter.
83 So says Eusebius, *Church History* IV.23.10.

(2) For its doctrinal tendencies. It emphasizes God's created order, stresses unity, humility, and repentance, accents obedience in faith, and emphasizes works and especially hospitality without discarding grace or ignoring the saving role of Christ's death and resurrection. (3) Especially for its emphasis upon divinely prescribed church order. Not that it supports the later Roman hierarchical system, or even the monarchical episcopate; such an episcopate is lacking in this letter even where it would have strengthened the argument; the Roman church knows only elders (also called *episkopoi*, "overseers") and deacons as appointed by the apostles (this was also the case, the letter indicates, at Corinth, as it was at Philippi about A.D. 107 when Polycarp wrote to that church).

I Clement's basic argument is that God sent Christ, Christ chose and sent the apostles, the apostles chose and set apart elders and deacons, and no local church can depose them (chs. 42; 44). Such church officers, it is implied, serve for life. When they pass on, successors are appointed "by other men of repute with the consent of the whole church" (ch. 44.3). The church ratifies the choice, but does not make it and cannot revoke a choice once ratified. This theory, once the monarchical bishop emerges from the group of elders and the bishop of the church becomes allegedly the bishop of the entire church, can lead to the modern hierarchical system of the Roman Catholic Church. But there is no evidence that the apostles always chose the elders in the apostolic age.[84]

I Clement thus indicates that the Roman church did not have a monarchical bishop about A.D. 95, but we should note the usual view of the succession of early bishops at Rome. Ancient tradition held (wrongly) that Peter came to Rome in the reign of Claudius (A.D. 41–54);[85] he and Paul were martyred under Nero (A.D. 64); Linus was the first bishop of Rome after that (cf. II Tim. 4:21?); after twelve years Anencletus succeeded him for twelve years; then Clement was bishop for nine years or less (until the third year of Trajan), and was succeeded by Evarestus.[86] The evidence is not so clear as this might suggest. There are, in fact, conflicting traditions about the identity and order of the first Roman bishops, including a difference as to whether Anencletus and Cletus were the same person.[87]

84 In Acts 14:23 "the apostles Barnabas and Paul" (ch. 14:14) appoint elders. However, the place of Barnabas and Paul in the theory of ecclesiastical succession is not clear. Neither belonged to the Twelve; neither is said to have been given episcopal office by the Twelve. Cf. also Titus 1:5.

85 This view is found in the fourth century; see Oscar Cullmann, *Peter: Disciple, Apostle, Martyr*, p. 113, especially note 72.

86 See Eusebius, *Church History* III.2; 4.8 f.; 13; 15; 21; 34; IV.1; V.6.1–5.

87 Cf. Jules Lebreton and Jacques Zeiller, *The Emergence of the Church in the Roman World* (Collier Books, 1962), p. 105, especially note 8.

THE ROMAN CHURCH UNDER LATER EMPERORS

Whether Trajan persecuted the Roman Christians is disputed, but Ignatius was taken from Antioch to Rome about A.D. 107, during Trajan's reign, to be fed to the wild beasts in the arena, so Trajan could hardly have favored or been neutral toward the Christians. (His approval of Pliny's persecution of Christians in Bithynia has been noted above.) But the letter of Ignatius to the Roman church suggests another point. Ignatius begs and almost commands the Roman church to do nothing to prevent his martyrdom at Rome.[88] He assumes and seems to know that the Roman church has ways of influencing the imperial authorities. There must have been Christians—slaves, freedmen, and quite possibly citizens of social and political rank—who could influence legal processes. It was a strong, active, and outreaching church, despite the persecutions it suffered.

The emperor Hadrian (A.D. 117–138) dealt with popular clamor against Christians in Asia Minor by forbidding accusations except before regular courts or tribunals,[89] but his attitude toward Christians in Rome is not known. His successor, Antoninus Pius (A.D. 138–161) did not persecute the Christians. A letter to the Commune of Asia highly favorable to the Christians purports to be from him, but is probably not genuine, at least in the form Eusebius preserves.[90]

The reign of Antoninus Pius is noteworthy in church history for at least three things:

1. The Shepherd of Hermas, a pedestrian work, promises a second forgiveness of sins committed after baptism (Mandate IV.3), opposes double-mindedness, and insists on continence, uprightness, and faithfulness in good works; it was written in Rome and is usually dated in the reign of Pius (ca. A.D. 145?). But it was highly esteemed in the church (some thought it worthy to be in the New Testament canon). It reflects a nonepiscopal church order (no monarchical bishop, but rather elder-bishops and deacons), so some date it at the end of the first century.[91]

2. Marcion came to Rome from Sinope about A.D. 139 and taught that the Creator God, the righteous God, is different from the gracious God, the Father of Jesus Christ, who was not incarnate by birth but only came to earth at the beginning of his ministry. Rejected by the Roman church about six years later, Marcion founded a separate church and

---

88 *To the Romans*, chs. 1, 2, 4, 8.
89 See Eusebius, *Church History* IV.8.6–9.3.
90 *Ibid.*, IV.13.
91 Lawson, *A Theological and Historical Introduction to the Apostolic Fathers*, pp. 224 f., discusses both views without a clear decision.

made a canon of Christian writings. It excluded the Old Testament and used only the Gospel of Luke and ten letters of Paul (it omitted the Pastoral Letters). From these eleven writings he deleted those passages which identified the Creator God with the Stranger God who sent Christ; he regarded them as later insertions.[92]

3. Justin Martyr addressed one of his two famous Apologies to Pius. This shows that the church was now fully conscious of its duty to present the gospel to all classes, including the ruling class.

Here we may conclude our survey of the regions where the church was found. By the middle of the second century there probably were churches in the Carthage region of northern Africa and also in Spain and in Gaul. We have no definite early evidence of them, but since a little later they show such strength and signs of established status, their origin must date in the first half of the second century, or possibly even earlier. Of all the church centers at the end of our period we know Rome the best and its church was destined to play a central role. When the book of The Acts closes, that church is on the western edge of the Christian world. But as other churches emerge in the West, the one in Rome occupies a more central position, and its position in the imperial capital helps to focus upon it the attention of other Christian churches.

[92] See note 70 of this chapter.

Chapter 13

TRENDS IN THE DEVELOPING CHURCH

THE PRECEDING chapter surveyed by regions the growth of the church in its first century. It became clear that we cannot write a connected history of the church in the period after the end of The Acts. This proved especially true of the years from A.D. 65 to 95. We may draw some inferences concerning these three decades from the situation that existed at the close of The Acts and from conditions we find in the decades immediately after A.D. 95.

In that shadowy period before A.D. 95 much of the New Testament was written, but the specific setting of these writings eludes us. Their exact date cannot be fixed, since we cannot trace a continuous history into which to fit them. Often their place of writing is uncertain. For example, we cannot say definitely where Luke-Acts, Hebrews,[1] II Peter and Jude[2] were written. Because of such uncertainties we can only infer or conjecture the actual setting of such writings.

[1] Hebrews is not so much a letter as a message written by an absent church leader to be read to a local church or special local group of Christians in Italy, probably Rome (Heb. 13:24). He wrote to nerve this group, already once persecuted (ch. 10: 32–34), to stand fast as persecution again threatens them. He saw no hope for those who in fear renounced their faith (chs. 6:4–6; 10:26–31), for they would be turning from Jesus Christ, the Son of God, the one source of salvation. He is superior to the prophets (ch. 1:1), to angels (chs. 1:5 to 2:18), to Moses (chs. 3:1 to 4:13), to Joshua (ch. 4:8), and to the Old Testament high priests and the sacrifices they offered (chs. 4:14 to 10:25). The readers are urged to show faith, which includes faithfulness in trial (ch. 11). The writer of Hebrews was not Paul, though he was of the Pauline group (cf. ch. 13:23). He wrote in the latter third of the first century. (He never refers to the Jerusalem Temple, but only to the Tabernacle of the days of Moses; cf. Ex., chs. 35 to 40.) See James Moffatt, *A Critical and Exegetical Commentary on the Epistle to the Hebrews* (Charles Scribner's Sons, 1924); William Manson, *The Epistle to the Hebrews* (London, Hodder and Stoughton, 1951); C. Spicq, *L'Épitre aux Hébreux*, 2 vols. (Paris, J. Gabalda et C¹ᵉ, 1952–1953).

[2] Jude and II Peter are related; it seems that the unknown writer of II Peter used Jude as the basis of his ch. 2. (Both are "Catholic Letters," written for the church at large.) Jude, probably written late in the first century, opposes false teachers of immoral life (Jude 4) who threaten to corrupt the thinking and conduct of the churches. Divine judgment strikes the wicked (vs. 5–23), but God can keep his loyal people from falling (v. 24). Jude the brother of Jesus is the traditional author

Our best procedure is to study in a topical way the chief trends and emphases that we find in these and later writings. Wherever the place and approximate date of a writing can be determined or reasonably inferred, we may use such data as clues for a tentative sketch of church development. Our main purpose, however, since we cannot write a connected and comprehensive history of the period, is to survey the chief trends discernible in the church between the end of the period covered by The Acts and the middle of the second century A.D.

THE CENTRAL ROLE OF JESUS CHRIST

The first noteworthy fact about the church in the period under study is the central role that all Christians gave to the risen Lord Jesus Christ. Faith in God the Father was of course basic, but God had acted in Jesus Christ, had raised him from the dead, and had made him Lord and Christ. The gospel was a message about God and his work, but since God's central action was through Jesus Christ, the gospel necessarily told of Christ, and particularly so since the risen Christ was now the living Lord of the church. The development in thought about Jesus was not so bold among Jewish Christians, but they too knew that he was the Messiah, the Christ, and they gave him the central role in history.

That he preexisted (Col. 1:15–17; John 1:1; Heb. 1:2), that he was the Logos or Son of God, that he was born of a virgin, that he was the Christ of Israel, that his death was more than a martyr's death and had meaning for man's salvation, that he was raised, that he was now the exalted Lord of the church, that he was to be the Judge at the end of history—this was the common view.[3] The church never considered Jesus

---

of this open letter. II Peter also opposes immoral false teachers and appeals to the righteousness of Christ and the prophetic word of the Old Testament (II Peter, ch. 1). The writer also opposes the cynicism of those who use the delay in Christ's return to prove that he will not come (ch. 3:1–13). The letter claims to be by Peter (chs. 1:1; 3:1), but this means that he writes in the name of Peter, probably early in the second century. See Joseph B. Mayor, *The Epistle of St. Jude and the Second Epistle of St. Peter* (London, Macmillan and Co., 1907); J. W. C. Wand, *The General Epistles of St. Peter and St. Jude* (London, Methuen & Co., 1934).

[3] The confession of his preexistence is as early as Paul (Phil. 2: 5–7; Col. 1:15–17) and occurs in John 1:1 f. and Heb. 1:1 f. The "Logos" idea is found in John 1:1, 14 (Heb. 4:12 and Rev. 19:13 are not fully parallel), but the title "Son" is far more widely used to express preexistence, unique relation to the Father, and unique role in redemption. The virgin birth appears in Matt. 1:18–25 and Luke 1:34 f., and in Ignatius, *To the Ephesians* 19.1; *To the Smyrnaeans* 1.1. The detailed passion narratives of the Gospels, including the interpretation given at the Last Supper, and the very early tradition that "Christ died for our sins" (I Cor. 15:3), show the attention to his death, and this never occurred without the thought of his resurrection. That Jesus is Lord is the early and continuing confession of the church, and of his role as judge Acts 10:42 stands as a witness (cf. also Matt. 25:31 ff.). The church's Christology, although not uniform, was consistently a high Christology.

as merely a noble man, a prophet, a great teacher. Christians generally gave him the crucial and decisive role in history and made him central in their worship and life.[4]

THE CHURCH'S USE OF THE OLD TESTAMENT

This centrality of Jesus Christ found expression in the church's use of Scripture. The Old Testament was Scripture to all followers of Christ except Marcion and his followers.[5] Since this Scripture was authoritative, the events of Jesus' life, his teaching, and his present role must conform to and fulfill that Scripture. Christians were firmly convinced that these events did fulfill it, and to make this clear a Christological interpretation of Scripture inevitably developed.

It is often held, with considerable reason, that Christian leaders made written collections of Old Testament passages which they saw that Jesus had fulfilled. A small group of Messianic Scripture passages found among the Dead Sea Scrolls furnishes a precedent for such a practice.[6] Indeed, one view of the origin of our canonical Gospels is that they arose from the practice of gathering together Old Testament passages and showing how they had been fulfilled by Jesus; from this beginning, it is argued, the disciples then began to report Jesus' deeds and words more directly and use the Scripture passages, which earlier had been the starting point, in a supporting role to show that his unique career fully conformed to Scripture and its promises.[7]

The regular practice was to regard the Old Testament as a real history that prepared for and pointed forward to the coming and work of Christ. The Jewish Christians emphasized not only this continuity with the life of Israel but also the importance of the Mosaic law as guidance for Christian living.

Marcion, reacting against a tendency to subject the gospel to the Old

---

[4] Col. 2:8 shows a tendency in Colossae to seek angelic help to supplement Christ's saving work. Paul insists that these angels were both created and redeemed by Christ, who alone is the head of the church (Col. 1:15–20). There are hints, however, that angel worship was occasionally found and opposed in later decades (Heb. 1:4–14). Angelic powers sometimes played a role in later Gnosticism.

[5] Two recent books on Marcion and his view of Scripture are John Knox, *Marcion and the New Testament*, and Edwin Cyril Blackman, *Marcion and His Influence*. Basic for thorough study is Adolf von Harnack, *Marcion: Das Evangelium vom fremden Gott*.

[6] See J. M. Allegro, "Further Messianic References in Qumran Literature," *JBL*, Vol. LXXV (1956), pp. 174–187, especially pp. 182–187 (Deut. 5:28 f.; 18:18 f.; Num. 24:15–17; Deut. 33:8–11; Josh. 6:26).

[7] Cf. the emphasis on Christian interpretation of the Old Testament as the predecessor of the gospel sources and our Gospels in B. P. W. Stather Hunt, *Primitive Gospel Sources*.

Testament, cut this line of continuity. As we must note again at the end of this chapter, he rejected both the Old Testament and the view that Old Testament history led up to and prepared for the Christian story. The Epistle of Barnabas[8] denied that Israel had ever accepted the covenant that God offered (ch. 14:1); it insisted that the law was never meant to be observed by Israel (ch. 9:4); Israel entirely misunderstood the Scripture.

But to every New Testament writer, and to the overwhelming majority of the church, the Old Testament was Scripture, the history of Israel was the history of God's people, and the work of Christ and the life of the church fulfilled God's promises and climaxed God's redemptive dealings with Israel.[9] It was their axiom that Scripture referred to Christ and the church. It was their concern to find in Scripture promises and specific prophecies fulfilled in Christ.

Although as a rule they respected the literal historical sense of Scripture, they developed an amazing ability to find in Scripture types of Christ.[10] In Hebrews, for example, Melchizedek is a type of Christ the great High Priest, and the annual offering by the high priest on the Day of Atonement is a type of the perfect self-offering of Jesus the Son of God, an offering made not on earth but in the heavenly tabernacle, where the exalted Christ now continually intercedes for the Christians (Heb. 7:1 to 10:25). Allegory also was used to apply Old Testament stories and passages to Christ and the church (cf. Gal. 4:21–31).

The entire Scripture was considered a witness to Christ, and Scripture was interpreted to bring out this continual reference to him. It was also applied to the Christian life, and this had a fateful effect, for the church applied to the Christians numerous legal provisions of the Old Testament, with the result that a legal note not found in Jesus' own attitude or in the earliest preachers crept back into the thinking of much of the church.

THE RELATION OF THE CHURCH TO JUDAISM

The relation of the church to continuing Judaism was constantly an issue in the period following The Acts. The Christian movement rose

---

8 This writing is dated earlier than the Didache by John Lawson, *A Theological and Historical Introduction to the Apostolic Fathers*, pp. 193–201, and by W. Eltester, *IDB*, A-D, pp. 357 f. This priority is not certain, but the Epistle of Barnabas, with its use of allegory and typology, probably dates in the first half of the second century.

9 See Raymond Abba, *The Nature and Authority of the Bible* (Muhlenberg Press, 1958), Ch. 6.

10 See Robert M. Grant, *The Bible in the Church* (The Macmillan Company, 1948), Chs. 4, 5.

among the Jews, and at first seemed to outsiders to be simply a Jewish sect. Only when numerous Gentiles were converted and accepted as true disciples without being required to keep the Jewish law did it become clear that here was a new faith; this occurred first at Antioch in Syria (Acts 11:21, 26). The Christians themselves made it difficult for this point to be grasped, for they claimed to be the true Israel to whom Israel's Scripture and promises belonged. This was not only a basic theological claim but also a useful apologetic point; in the Roman Empire only recognized religions were permitted; if the Christians were properly called Jews, if their faith and life represented the climax and fulfillment of Israelite faith, they were entitled to imperial protection,[11] but if their continuity with Judaism was denied, they were open to attack and prosecution as an illicit religion.

The motto "To the Jew first and also to the Greek" or Gentile (Rom. 1:16) had described the ministry of Paul and the general policy of the early church. Jerusalem held a central place in Christian thought and imagination. Even when the Twelve no longer held the leadership in Jerusalem, and James the brother of Jesus had become the recognized leader there, Jerusalem was the geographical focal point in Christian thought. James the brother of Jesus was somewhat conservative in his Christian views; though he approved the mission of Paul, he thought that Jewish Christians should observe the Jewish law. For this reason and for his earnest piety he was widely respected among both Jews and Jewish Christians, and when he was martyred at priestly instigation, some Jewish leaders protested to the Roman governor.[12]

The legal tone in James's life, however, did mark his distance from the Gentile churches, and when, about A.D. 66, the Christians of Jerusalem, acting upon an oracle or prophecy (was it a saying of Jesus?), fled from that city and went to Pella,[13] east of the Jordan River and a few miles southeast of the Sea of Galilee, the leading role of Jerusalem in the church was ended and the life of the Jewish Christians lost regular contact with the Gentile churches.

Under Symeon, said to be a cousin of Jesus, part at least of the group of fugitives later returned to the region of Jerusalem, for he is said to have headed the church in Jerusalem,[14] and these law-observing Jewish Christians carried on a vigorous evangelistic program among the Jews. This is evidenced in the Rabbinical literature, which records disputes

11 It appears likely that a minor purpose of Luke in writing Luke-Acts was to make this point.
12 Josephus, *Ant.* XX.9.1. But there is no hint that James did any act of friendship for Paul after Paul was imprisoned at Jerusalem.
13 Eusebius, *Church History* III.5.3.
14 Eusebius, *Church History* III.11.22.

of followers of Jesus with Jewish rabbis and indicates that the Christian faith won many Jews. Toward the end of the first century the Jewish leaders inserted into the Benedictions (called the Amidah) a curse upon apostates, *notsrim* (Nazarenes), and *minim* (heretics); since a follower of Jesus could not repeat this benediction, he could no longer participate in Jewish synagogue worship.[15] Christian preachers must have had considerable success or Jewish leaders would not have taken such a drastic step.

Other Jewish Christians were attracted by speculative, more or less heretical tendencies found especially among Jews east of the Jordan and in Syria.[16] In the period under study, this region was marked by speculative, syncretistic, and Gnostic-tending activities. Into such speculative developments Jews as well as Jewish Christians entered. One noted prophet of that period was Elkhasai.[17] Such syncretistic tendencies, however, were a minor feature in the total life of both Judaism and Jewish Christianity. Most Jewish Christians scrupulously followed the law of Moses, connected their Christian faith with the prophecies of Scripture, and regarded the church as the fulfillment of their ancestral heritage.

As time passed, the name Ebionites was used of these Jewish Christians who continued loyal to Jewish legal practices. The name was not the name of a leader Ebion, as was once asserted; it was the Hebrew word for "poor," and was used to designate the law-loyal Jewish Christians. Cast out by their own people and out of touch with their Gentile fellow Christians, they had a dwindling significance. Symeon, their leader, was martyred about A.D. 104 or not long thereafter, and Justus, not a relative of Jesus, succeeded him.[18] For many generations the group continued, but it had a small and decreasing part in the total impact of the church on the ancient world.

That the Jews continued hostile to the Christians wherever the issue arose is clear both in and outside of Palestine. Activities of the Jews against Christians in Asia Minor are reported in Rev. 2:9; 3:9. The sharpness with which Ignatius rebukes the readiness of some Christians to practice Judaism[19] indicates that he had observed in Syria and perhaps in Asia Minor the pressure that Jews exerted to get Christians to practice the legal prescriptions of the Jewish law. At the martyrdom of Poly-

15 See G. F. Moore, *Judaism*, Vol. I, pp. 91, 292; cf. note 28 in Chapter 12.
16 For one reconstruction, see H. J. Schoeps, *Theologie und Geschichte des Judenchristentums* (Tübingen, J. C. B. Mohr, 1949).
17 See Hippolytus, *Refutation of All Heresies* IX.8–12. Elkhasai is said to have been active in the reign of Trajan (ca. A.D. 100).
18 Eusebius, *Church History* III.32.1–3; 35.
19 *To the Magnesians* 8.1; 10.3; *To the Philadelphians* 6.1.

carp the Jews, it is said, were especially zealous in gathering the wood
for the fire; this event dates later than the limit of our study, but the
report is relevant, since the *Martyrdom of Polycarp* XIII.1 says that such
zeal of Jews against Christians was "their custom."

Such evidence indicates that down to the middle of the second century,
clashes occurred between the Jews and the Christians. In that period the
Christians could not defend themselves by legal means or by force, but
the Jews at times could persecute the Christians or stir up official or
Gentile hostility toward them.

This action was not merely a power struggle or an expression of
jealousy. From the outset the claim of Jesus Christ put before the Jews
a basic choice. They could accept that claim and become followers of
Jesus, or they could react with horror and indignation against him and
his followers who gave him a more than human role. The basic clash
was not due to any later alteration of the gospel to make it attractive
to Gentiles of Hellenistic culture; it occurred from the first in Palestine
and occurred even between law-observing Jewish Christians and opposing
Jews. The original message of Jesus and the earliest Christians contained
a claim that no Jew could accept without becoming an active part of
the church.

The World Outlook of the Church

One prominent emphasis during this entire period, notwithstanding
the ties with the Old Testament and Judaism, was the world outlook
of the church. Such an outlook has been noted in the period covered by
The Acts. It was clearest in the Gentile mission of Paul, but it was
present even in the Jerusalem church from its early days. The Jewish
Christians might have questioned as to how soon and on what terms the
gospel was to be preached to Gentiles, but they saw the world outreach
implicit in the gospel and expected God's final kingdom to include people
of other nations.

The flight of the Jerusalem church to Pella (ca. A.D. 66) and the resulting increased separation between Jewish and Gentile Christianity
no doubt diminished the universalistic outlook among Jewish Christians.
However, after the ministry of Paul and the fall of Jerusalem, the church
was largely Gentile, and the world outlook of the Gentile churches was
explicit, clouded occasionally, it seems, by the conviction that since official Judaism had rejected Christ, Jews had forfeited their place in the
church.[20]

[20] Such a passage as Matt. 27:25 could express and further this view.

The inclusive outlook of the church excluded class barriers. In this later period, as in the time of the Pauline mission, the poor and the slaves were numerous in the church.[21] People of social standing and financial means found a place in the church, which, as time went on, had leaders with education and intellectual vigor. But the gospel was preached to all; the converts represented all classes; and the majority of Christians belonged to the lower classes in the social and economic scale. Warnings not to show partiality to persons of wealth and position indicate that the church stood for close brotherhood of all members regardless of class. These warnings show that the ideal was not always reached, but the leaders denounced and did not tolerate such infiltration of worldly standards of judgment (cf. I Tim. 6:17–19; Heb. 13:5; James 1:9–11; 2:1–7; 4:13 to 5:6).

Frequent meetings of each Christian group and active helpfulness to one another according to the resources and abilities of each kept the Christian from thinking in individualist terms. Almsgiving, directed as a rule to needy fellow Christians, was generally stressed.[22] Especially in times of persecution—when to be seen in the Christian group was to invite attack—the importance of regular meetings was emphasized (Heb. 10:25).

This outgoing spirit was needed in the cities, which so easily became impersonal and hostile to needy people. The church in the first generations was mainly an urban church,[23] a minority group in the cities of the Empire; but it worked to establish and maintain personal ties between the Christians of each local church. The gospel was carried out from large cities into the surrounding areas; Paul had adopted this procedure as his strategy for extending the church as rapidly as possible, and his method, it seems, was not forgotten. Every city had a surrounding area tied to it by economic, political, and cultural relations, and the church, following the radiating travel routes, carried the gospel into the neighboring regions.

The sense that the gospel was for the world was clear even in the apostolic age; the only questions were whether all Jews should hear the gospel before the Gentiles did and on what basis Gentiles might come into the church. In the period that followed the end of The Acts, the surviving writings reflect the clear sense of the world mission of the church. Along the routes of travel and trade went the preachers, prophets, and teachers who succeeded the apostles in furthering the expanding

[21] On poverty and slavery in the church of this period, see Cecil John Cadoux, *The Early Church and the World*, pp. 129–135, 196–200, 284–286.

[22] See Cecil John Cadoux, *The Early Church and the World*, pp. 130 f., 198 f.

[23] The Letter of James reflects an outdoor and agricultural background more than do the other extant writings of this period; cf. chs. 1:9–11; 5:4, 7.

mission.[24] The scattered little churches kept in touch with one another through itinerant preachers, "lay" Christians traveling on business, messengers sent on specific church errands, and letters from churches and leaders in other cities. There was no authoritative overall organization, but the church had a sense of essential unity and worldwide mission.

These ties between churches were made possible by the common-language basis. In Palestine, Syria, and eastward from Syria, Aramaic was widely used and enabled Christians who spoke it to keep in touch with other Aramaic-speaking disciples. In the Roman Empire, however, Greek was the common tongue. It was extensively used in Palestine and Syria. Even in the city of Rome, where Latin had an official role, Greek was the language of the church from its beginning to the middle of the second century.[25] This oneness of language over so wide an area was the key to the ecumenical interchange which contributed greatly to the sense of belonging to a world church.

THE RELATION OF CHURCH AND STATE

The relation of the church to the governing power concerns essentially relations within the Roman Empire. Almost no evidence exists of the spread of Christianity elsewhere before A.D. 150.

Church relations with the Jewish authorities in Palestine in the apostolic age were under the general supervision of the Romans, but the imprisonment of the apostles in Jerusalem was not Rome-inspired but was due either to Jewish leaders who saw the extent of the claim being made for Christ (Acts 4:1-3; 5:17 f.), or to Herodian leaders influenced by Jewish officials. Herod Agrippa I executed James the son of Zebedee and imprisoned Peter (Acts 12:1-3); he was king of Palestine under the Romans, but these acts were done on his own initiative and to please the Jews. The execution of James the brother of Jesus in Jerusalem occurred when no Roman governor was present in Palestine. It was the work of the Sanhedrin led by the high priest Ananus, and was condemned by many non-Christian Jews.[26]

Apart from such acts and the Jewish agitation against Christians in

---

[24] A glimpse of the activity of traveling teachers, apostles, and prophets, and a hint of frequent appearance of other traveling Christians, are found in the protective measures prescribed in the Didache, chs. 11 and 12. The date of the Didache is much disputed. A date between A.D. 50 and 70, proposed by Jean-Paul Audet, *La Didachè: Instructions des Apôtres* (Paris, J. Gabalda et Cⁱᵉ, 1958), is too early; a date late in the first century or early in the second is more attractive.

[25] Perhaps Latin first came into use by Christians in Africa, in the general region around Carthage. But the beginnings of the church in that area are too obscure to permit confident statements.

[26] Josephus, *Ant.* XX.9.1.

Gentile cities, the relation of the church to the government involves essentially its relation to the Roman emperors, their provincial governors, and the Gentile leaders in cities under Roman administration.

It is often asked when Christianity ceased to be legal and became subject to official suppression. The question is wrongly stated. As long as the Christians were Jews and appeared to be part of Judaism, they were protected by the official recognition that Rome gave to Judaism. Since the Christians maintained that they were the true Israel, they considered the church permanently entitled to the protection that Judaism enjoyed.[27] But the Roman recognition applied only to the established official Judaism, and as soon as Rome decided that the Christian faith differed from official Judaism, the Roman recognition of Judaism no longer protected the Christians, and Christian assemblies were considered illicit. With the coming into the church of numerous Gentiles, who by agreement of all the apostolic leaders were not required to practice the Jewish ceremonial law, the situation existed in which the new faith had no legal status, due to its difference from official Judaism.

In addition, the Christians lacked influence; they were mostly poor people and slaves who worked long hours, met at night, and sometimes held closed meetings whose emotional enthusiasm made outsiders suspect that the group was sharing immoral orgies. Moreover, the gospel preaching aroused public resentment because it indicted polytheistic and immoral life and rejected emperor worship. It had no visible forms of worship (such as the Jewish Temple sacrifices, which included an offering on behalf of the emperor), and so was charged with "atheism," refusal to share in worship of the accepted gods.[28]

It is thus easy to see how Christians came under official and popular criticism. Such hostility was strengthened when gospel preaching hurt business, as at Ephesus in the days of Paul (Acts 19:24–26) or in Bithynia, where Pliny says that the spread of Christianity almost ended the demand for sacrificial animals.[29] The Christian church inevitably became the object of Gentile denunciation and condemnation.

The church, faced by such hostility, had two possibilities open to it. One was to trust the state to preserve order and protect Christians. Those who included in the Gospels the saying of Jesus, "Render to Caesar the things that are Caesar's" (Mark 12:17 and ||s), agreed with Paul that "the governing authorities . . . have been instituted by God" (Rom. 13:1); they hoped, with the author of I Peter 3:13, that no one

[27] Luke in the book of The Acts has as a secondary purpose the vindication of the church as the true Judaism entitled to Roman recognition and protection.
[28] Cf. *Martyrdom of Polycarp* III.2: "Away with the Atheists" (i.e., the Christians). This dates ca. A.D. 156, but this was then an established view and not a new idea.
[29] *Epistles* X.96.

would harm the Christians if they were zealous for what was right. This attitude found expression in the second-century apologists, who hoped that the governing powers would be reasonable, just, and not swayed by popular slander against the Christians. But in times of cruel persecution the cry could arise among Christians that Satan and his demonic aides were in control of the human rulers. Then the church, enduring unjust suffering, could only witness to their faith and hope for early vindication by God.[30]

It is not clear how often and how widely persecution struck the church before A.D. 150. Nero's persecution, about A.D. 64, was fierce and deadly but apparently brief and confined to Rome. As Tacitus describes it,[31] it condemned the Christians not for their faith but because they criticized the pagan life of Rome and so were haters of the human race. The claim that Vespasian and Titus persecuted the Christians is very poorly supported.

The next definite persecution by an emperor was by Domitian.[32] The book of Revelation is vivid testimony to this; it reflects the crisis in Asia Minor that was caused by the insistence that everyone worship the emperor. But the fact that Domitian's close relatives in Rome, Clemens the ex-consul and his wife (or was it his niece?) Domitilla, were punished (Clemens by execution and Domitilla by banishment) suggests that Domitian struck at Christians nearer home than Asia Minor.[33]

Trajan is sometimes regarded as a mild emperor, very fair to the Christians, but in his reign Symeon was martyred in Palestine (not directly at Trajan's will), Ignatius was taken from Antioch in Syria to Rome to be thrown to the wild beasts as a martyr, and when Pliny asked Trajan how to proceed against the numerous Christians in Bithynia, Trajan said that Pliny should investigate every public charge that a person was a Christian and punish (execute?) everyone who persisted in his Christian confession.[34]

Hadrian too has been regarded as a mild emperor in this matter, but it is not clear that he respected Christians. He simply advocated formal court procedures instead of irresponsible actions and public clamor for mob violence.[35]

On the whole, the church as a group separate from official Judaism

---

[30] On these views, see Cecil John Cadoux, *The Early Church and the World*, pp. 166–183, 247–268.

[31] *Annals* XV.44.

[32] See Maurice Goguel, *The Birth of Christianity*, pp. 528–537, on "The Persecution of Domitian."

[33] See note 11 in Chapter 12.

[34] Pliny, *Epistles* X.97. Cf. Goguel, *The Birth of Christianity*, pp. 537–544.

[35] Cecil John Cadoux, *The Early Church and the World*, p. 250. Eusebius, using Justin Martyr, gives Hadrian's rescript in his *Church History* IV.9.

had no effective protection but was dependent upon the fair-mindedness and moderation of the rulers. At times official and popular action flared up against the defenseless Christians; but for the most part the Christians, considering their anomalous position before the law, enjoyed a remarkable degree of freedom from persecution.

THE LESSENING OF ESCHATOLOGICAL EXPECTANCY

In the century that followed the career of Paul, the theme of eschatology still held a somewhat prominent place. The message of Jesus that the Kingdom was at hand and that through him God was beginning to establish it made that theme a permanent part of the gospel. The vivid expectation of the early church that the end was near was connected not only with the teaching of Jesus but perhaps even more with the fact of his resurrection; in his miracles, and especially in his resurrection, the power of the new age had begun to manifest itself. Paul shared in this eager expectation. For the greater part of his ministry he confidently expected to be still living when the great final day came, and even when he saw that his death might come before that day he continued to be assured that "the Lord is at hand" (Phil. 4:5). Eschatology was central and pervasive in the original gospel.

At no stage of the New Testament story was this eschatology an entirely future thing. Jesus sensed the actual presence and working of the Kingdom in his ministry, especially in his healings (Matt. 12:28; Luke 11:20). To the church the resurrection of Jesus and the gift of the Spirit proved that the final drama was under way. Christians who at conversion died to sin and rose to "newness of life" (Rom. 6:4) had part in this new order. So there is solid truth in the idea of "realized eschatology," widely accepted since C. H. Dodd made it popular.[36] The purpose of God to establish his Kingdom has already been realized in part.

But only in part. An eschatology completely realized would not be an eschatology; it would be merely a description of accomplished facts. The New Testament church never lost the note of expectancy. So it is not surprising to find in the period now under study a persisting note of eschatology.

At least three things explain this persistence of a strong hope for the full realization of God's purpose and plan. One basic factor was the teaching of Jesus and the apostles. Even before the New Testament canon was formed, indeed even before the Gospels were written, the

---

36 See *The Apostolic Preaching and Its Developments* and *The Parables of the Kingdom* (Charles Scribner's Sons, 1936).

words of Jesus were steadily shaping the thought of the church.[37] The preaching of the apostles also kept this hope vivid; it stressed the resurrection, the decisive action of God that opened the way to the final realization of God's plan. The gift of the Spirit was a confirming factor; it was to be given in "the last days" (Acts 2:17).

A second reason for the continued eschatological expectation was the inherent frustration that God's people continually experienced in a largely hostile world. They had a tenacious desire for God to complete his plan and rescue his people.

The third reason for the persistence of strong eschatological hope, or for the recurrent upsurge of such hope, was the series of urgent crises that Christians had to face. They suffered social and economic discrimination; political action against them was always possible and sometimes occurred, with arrests, imprisonments, and martyrdoms; then the eager and often fierce expectation arose that this time God would surely act and Christ would come to rescue and reward his own. The book of Revelation illustrates this burning expectation. Thus eschatology was always present in the church's basic teaching, hope was an inherent necessity for Christians in a harassingly imperfect world, and each recurrent crisis renewed the waning flame of hope.

Yet in the century now under study, eschatology did not hold the prominent place that it had in the message of Jesus and the apostolic age. This was due to a variety of reasons. One was the corroding effect of the steady passage of time. The end was at hand, it had been said, but year after year brought no fulfillment of that promise. Perhaps then, after all, it would not come soon. Some waning of that hope is felt in the Pastoral Letters. II Peter, perhaps written at the end of the first century but more likely in the first decades of the second century,[38] clearly reflects a current disappointment; "scoffers" were saying, "Where is the promise of his coming? For ever since the fathers fell asleep, all things have continued as they were from the beginning of creation" (II Peter 3:4). Apparently, they implied, things will go on as they are for an indefinite time. The unknown writer of II Peter may be satisfied with his solution, that "with the Lord one day is as a thousand years, and a thousand years as one day" (ch. 3:8), and so every Christian must constantly be alert, since though the end may come in the far future it may come any day. But this was not the vivid expectation that the

---

[37] A sane emphasis on the preservation, use, and influence of the tradition of Jesus' deeds and words is found in C. F. D. Moule, *The Birth of the New Testament* (Harper & Row, Publishers, Inc., 1962), e.g., on p. 147.
[38] See note 2 of this chapter.

church in earlier days had known. The mere passage of time had reduced greatly the alert expectancy of the earnest Christian.[39]

This lessened role of eschatology in Christian thinking was also due to the grateful sense of promises already fulfilled, eschatological hopes already realized. By the death and resurrection of Jesus, God had provided redemption; the resurrection of Jesus, his exaltation to effective Lordship, and the gift of the Spirit were eschatological events that created a new situation. The Christian's blessings were not merely future; in part they were already realized; the more he sensed the greatness of his present privilege, the less prominent could be his emphasis on what was still to come.[40]

The prominence of eschatology in the Christian attitude may have been reduced also by the acceptance of the nature-religion mentality. In that outlook, the life of the believer was linked with the annual cycle of nature, the yearly death and revival of vegetation, and the concern for continued fertility of flocks and herds. The mystery religions of early Christian centuries embodied, transformed, and largely ennobled this ancient way of worship, so familiar to the Old Testament prophets in the worship of Baal.

Such a religious concern could exist on a high level, coupled with an expectation of still greater blessings from God in the future. The Jewish "church year" illustrates this. An observance such as the Passover combined annual nature aspects with the memory of God's deliverance of Israel from Egypt and so kept alive, especially when Israel was a subject people, the hope and conviction that he would again redeem them; the annual cycle and the hope for a great future event were combined, and the history-grounded hope held the dominant place. This could happen also in the church. The annual celebration of the decisive events in the life of Jesus could recall gratefully what God had done in Jesus Christ and thus stimulate faith that he would complete his promise of complete redemption. For Paul the Passover annually recalled Jesus' death (I Cor. 5:7), and such usages no doubt were common in the church.

But the annual cycle could also fit into the pattern of nature religion; the believer's main impression could be that "it happens this way every year." To the extent that God's saving work becomes an annual series of events the edge of eschatological expectation is dulled. The Gentile

---

[39] Martin Werner, *The Formation of Christian Dogma,* tr. by S. G. F. Brandon (Harper & Brothers, 1957), makes the fading of this hope the key to the development of early Christian theology. He greatly exaggerates the change of outlook.

[40] Albert Schweitzer, in *The Mysticism of Paul the Apostle,* tr. by William Montgomery (Henry Holt and Company, 1931), sees in this aspect of Paul's experience the preparation for escape from a rigid eschatology.

world lacked any such sense of history as Israel had from the Old Testament and as the first Christians brought with them into the church. Thus, in the Gentile world this exchange of eschatology for an annual repetition of God's redemptive work was a constant danger and at times a fact.

The urgent need to promote a worthy and useful way of life was another factor that contributed to the waning of the eschatological emphasis. Anyone who has held himself ready for the imminent arrival of an important expected visitor knows how little one gets done in such a situation and how hard it is to carry on normal tasks when the visitor's arrival is delayed a little. Paul had to deal with this problem of people who quit work and waited for the expected Lord to come. That was in the early days of the Thessalonian church (II Thess. 3:6-12). As decades passed, this breathlessly expectant posture grew harder and harder to maintain. Responsible leaders like Paul wanted Christians to be faithful in work, worship, and daily duty. The important thing for a leader or disciple was to be found doing his own task well whenever his Lord should return (Matt. 24:46). This emphasis dampened eschatological excitement and focused attention on regular work.

The continual pressure to conform to the world also tended to lessen the eschatological note in Christian life. Christians were torn by two imperatives: they must not be part of the ungodly world but must separate from it; yet their mission was to evangelize the world, and they were not inherently better than other men, so they had to go to others and befriend them in a spirit of brotherliness. To be in the world, to feel oneness with all men, and yet not to be worldly was not (and is not) easy. Nor was it easy to maintain without compromise family ties with pagan relatives, and community ties with pagan people, in a polytheistic environment where moral standards usually were lax. Christians could overvalue the pleasures and comforts of life; they could seek respectability and acceptance in the pagan community; they could relax their standards; then they would not feel sharply the tension between God's people and the world, nor would they long so keenly for the total victory of God's cause.

Probably the accent on the blessings already given to Christians did most to lessen the eschatological emphasis. The Old Testament was their Scripture; they saw that it pointed to Jesus Christ and his accomplished work; they often, as time went on, saw in it the law of the ongoing Christian life; it no longer spoke to them an eschatological cry of promise. The accomplished work of God in Christ was so crucial that the focus of attention tended to rest on it rather than on the great victory to come (cf. the "realized eschatology" condemned in II Tim. 2:18: "the resurrection is past already"). The church could and sometimes did loom so large in the thought and loyalty of believers that it seemed to be permanent rather than merely the temporary home of God's people while they carried out their urgent witness to the world and waited for God's final Kingdom. For this and the other reasons named, the period under study shows, on the whole, a substantial decrease in eschatological expectation. That hope was never surrendered, but it was no longer so controlling.

EARLY CONFESSIONS OF FAITH

Among the trends in the developing church was that toward a more regular pattern of worship[41] and leadership. This trend must not be overstated. As late as A.D. 150 there was still a remarkable variety. But the churches scattered over the Empire kept in touch with one another, and as problems arose within the churches and hostile forces threatened from without, the church slowly felt its way toward a common facing of its task and problems.

In this period we find no developed creeds. None appear in the New Testament writings, most of which were produced in this period (A.D. 60–150). Not even the Apostles' Creed had taken form by A.D. 150. Its nucleus had probably taken form by then, but many generations elapsed before that creed attained its present form. New Testament passages often called creeds are rather brief confessions.[42] Some of these affirmations of faith were widely used in the church; others were the writer's own wording in his specific situation. None of them was officially formulated by any church authority.

These New Testament confessions have two main characteristics: they are Christological, and in almost all cases they use Old Testament terms to express Jesus' role in redemption and his relation to God the Father. Some of the confessions are brief: "Jesus is Lord" (I Cor. 12:3), "Jesus Christ is Lord" (Phil. 2:11), "Lord and Christ" (Acts 2:36), "the Christ, the Son of the living God" (Matt. 16:16), "the Lamb of God, who takes away the sin of the world" (John 1:29), "My Lord and my God" (John 20:28), "Christ Jesus our Savior" (Titus 1:4), "the Word of God" (Rev. 19:13; cf. John 1:1, 14), etc. Others, such as Phil. 2:5–11, are expanded statements of what he is and has done for men.[43] In general the titles

---

[41] See C. F. D. Moule, *Worship in the New Testament* (John Knox Press, 1962); *The Birth of the New Testament*, Ch. 2.

[42] See Oscar Cullmann, *The Earliest Christian Confessions*.

[43] It is widely thought that Phil. 2:5–11 was a confessional hymn taken over by Paul from the early Christian church. Frank Chamberlin Porter, following Lohmeyer, develops this view in *The Mind of Christ in Paul*, pp. 204–228.

used of him are attempts not to describe his nature or person but to express the greatness and effectiveness of his work in redeeming men and bringing them to God. Since his work fulfills the promises of Scripture, it is not surprising to find it described almost entirely in terms provided by Scripture. Some of the terms, such as Lord, Son, and Word, were already used in pagan circles and so were useful in expressing Christ's significance to Gentiles, but the Old Testament roots of a true and adequate understanding of Jesus were never forgotten.[44]

COMMON WORSHIP AND SPECIAL DAYS

Such confessions had an essential role in Christian worship.[45] The worship of which the New Testament and other early Christian writings speak is almost always common worship. The private worship of individuals receives occasional notice (e.g., Matt. 6:6; Rom. 1:9), but it is taken for granted that those who believe in Jesus will gather regularly in common worship. Even in persecution, as Heb. 10:25 recalls, or perhaps especially then, the need for common worship was great. Faith brought the believer into the family of God; there he found the essential setting of Christian worship and witness.

From the days of Paul, the first day of the week was a special day for worship (I Cor. 16:2). It was an appropriate day for the prophet John, exiled to Patmos, to see his vision of the risen Christ as he remembered and prayed for his fellow Christians in Asia, with whom he would be worshiping were he not in exile (Rev. 1:9 f.). Pliny, writing to Trajan of Christian meetings in Bithynia, mentions meetings "on a fixed day," which almost certainly was Sunday.[46] Such special worship on the first day of the week must have been connected with the gospel tradition that Jesus' resurrection occurred on that day of the week, and these facts may well have led to the custom of observing Easter each Sunday.

If the resurrection was remembered weekly, that must have diminished the need and importance of an annual festival. The weekly observance was at first the main thing; in this, the earliest church was quite unlike the modern church. But the annual observance of Easter was bound to come. I Cor. 5:7 may indicate that the annual remembrance of the Last Passover of Jesus with his disciples began early, and in that case the annual remembrance of his resurrection could hardly have been lacking. But a difference arose over how to choose the day for this annual ob-

---

[44] Oscar Cullmann uses the main titles used of Jesus as the organizing basis of his book, *The Christology of the New Testament.*
[45] See the books mentioned above in note 41.
[46] *Epistles* X.96.

servance. The custom in Asia Minor in the mid-second century was to observe Easter on the day of Passover, no matter on what day of the week it fell. The practice of always observing Easter on Sunday was championed in Rome and soon became quite general.[47]

Of annual festivals in remembrance of other key events in the life of Jesus there is no clear record in our period. In view of the Pentecost date of the gift of the Holy Spirit, however, every Pentecost must have recalled that gift wherever Jewish Christians were present, and this must have been an effective impetus to the entire church to recall that gift every year.

PATTERNS IN COMMON WORSHIP

A study of the nature and parts of the worship services of the church in the century after Paul's ministry leads to the basic observation that here, as in so many other aspects of the church's life, there was no uniformity or fixed pattern. Scholars today often describe passages of the New Testament and other early Christian writings as "liturgical." This would suggest not merely that they were used in public worship but also that they had been so used before being written down in the New Testament writing that now preserves them. But there is no clear evidence that the solemn, sonorous, confessional passages thus singled out had been used repeatedly in just this wording in public worship and then echoed by the writer who presents them to us.

That such passages were used later in public worship is not the point. To deserve the name liturgical the passage should have been used as a regular pattern in public worship *before* being written down, and then written down under the influence of that repeated public use. But we cannot demonstrate that this happened except in the case of the Lord's Prayer.[48] To be accurate we should avoid the word "liturgical" in speaking of famous New Testament passages unless we are ready to maintain that before they were written down the church made regular public use of them in precisely the New Testament wording.[49]

---

[47] The Quartodeciman controversy was strong by the middle of the second century, and was a point on which Polycarp, bishop of Smyrna, and Anicetus, bishop of Rome, could not agree. The Asia Minor Quartodeciman practice of observing Easter on the fourteenth of Nisan must have its roots very early in the church; the use of the Jewish calendar indicates that. See Eusebius, *Church History* V. 23–25.

[48] And we receive even the Lord's Prayer in two considerably differing forms: Matt. 6:9–13; Luke 11:2–4!

[49] On the overuse of the liturgical theory of the origin of New Testament passages, see C. F. D. Moule, *The Birth of the New Testament*, pp. 11 f.; also W. C. van Unnik in "Dominus Vobiscum: The Background of a Liturgical Formula," in *New Testament Essays: Studies in Memory of Thomas Walter Manson, 1893–1958*, p. 272.

It is certain that Scripture, that is, our Old Testament, was used in Christian worship. We do not know that any fixed pattern or cycle of readings, such as was being developed in the synagogue, was yet in use, but the example of the synagogue, the appeal the church made to the gospel as the fulfillment of Scripture, and the use of the Old Testament in almost every New Testament writing make it practically certain that the Old Testament was read and discussed regularly in Christian worship assemblies.[50]

The use of hymns was also a common feature of such worship, although we cannot say how many were Old Testament psalms and how many were fresh Spirit-prompted creations of Christian authors (cf. I Cor. 14:26; Eph. 5:19; Col. 3:16; and the hymns in Luke, chs. 1 f., and in Rev., chs. 4; 5; 11; 15). When Pliny says about A.D. 112 that the Christians of Bithynia sang hymns to Christ as to a god,[51] he was testifying to an established feature of Christian worship. Prayer was offered in every worship meeting of Christians. What we call preaching was an important normal part of such worship.

The word "preaching" is used in the New Testament of evangelistic preaching to win outsiders to faith in Christ. The challenging, teaching, and inspiring of the Christian group itself is called prophecy, teaching, speaking with tongues, exhortation, etc.[52] The teaching no doubt included instruction on how to live, similar to the commands and exhortations that we find at the close of New Testament letters and in the section on the Two Ways in the Didache (Teaching of the Twelve Apostles), chs. 1–6, and the Epistle of Barnabas, chs. 18–20.[53]

CHRISTIAN BAPTISM

A special service of worship was baptism.[54] There is no early evidence that it was limited to the Easter season, as there was a tendency to do later in the church. It was a time of special prayer; the one baptized was being received into the church, and so the service concerned not simply

---

[50] See Adolf von Harnack, *Bible Reading in the Early Church*, tr. by J. R. Wilkinson (G. P. Putnam's Sons, 1912), Ch. 1.

[51] *Epistles* X.96.

[52] See C. H. Dodd, *The Apostolic Preaching and Its Developments*, and my book, *Three Crucial Decades: Studies in the Book of Acts* (John Knox Press, 1963), Ch. 2, "Preaching and Teaching in the Apostolic Church."

[53] Note the passage on the two opposed spirits in man in the Manual of Discipline 3:13 to 4:26 of the Dead Sea Scrolls.

[54] See H. G. Marsh, *The Origin and Significance of Christian Baptism* (Manchester University Press, 1941); W. F. Flemington, *The New Testament Doctrine of Baptism* (London, S.P.C.K., 1948); Oscar Cullmann, *Baptism in the New Testament*, tr. by J. K. S. Reid (London, SCM Press, Ltd., 1950); G. R. Beasley-Murray, *Baptism in the New Testament* (St. Martin's Press, Inc., 1962).

an individual but the church. Just how baptism was administered is often disputed. In the Didache (ch. 7), baptism in running water, recalling Jesus' baptism in the Jordan River, was preferred. If necessary, baptism in a pool of standing water was quite proper. If the candidate could not safely undergo a plunge into cold water, warm water could be used, and if none of these alternatives met the situation, water could be poured upon the candidate(s) three times.

More important was the reference to Christ in the baptism. In The Acts, baptism is simply in the name of Jesus. Matt. 28:19 and the Didache 7:1, however, prescribe baptism in the name of the Father and the Son and the Holy Spirit. There was good reason for this. In the Gentile world, monotheistic faith in God the Father could not be assumed, as it could where the Jewish background was strong, and the work of the Spirit needed to be clearly tied to the work and Lordship of Christ. So the practice arose of baptizing with the use of the trinitarian formula as noted in Matthew and the Didache.[55]

The Lord's Supper

Difficult as it is to follow the developments in the observance of the Lord's Supper, great developments certainly took place. According to the dominant tradition, Jesus ate the Passover meal with his disciples (Matt. 26:17–19; Mark 14:12–16; Luke 22:7–13),[56] and used it to interpret the meaning and benefit of his impending death.

The early church shared a common meal, described as the breaking of bread (cf. Acts 2:42, 46); it was a time that recalled Jesus' Last Supper and his death and his risen life; it expressed a faith-based fellowship in Christ the risen Lord and was a brotherly sharing of food by the disciples. Paul's churches too had a common meal, though in his indignation at the selfishness and drunkenness of some, who had no thought for their hungry fellow Christians, he demanded that those who were too hungry to wait and eat with others should eat something before they left home, so that at the meeting they could wait patiently and eat the common meal with their comrades (I Cor. 11:34). This instruction started

[55] On infant baptism in the early church, see the books cited in note 54 and also Joachim Jeremias, *Infant Baptism in the First Four Centuries*, tr. by David Cairns (The Westminster Press, 1961); Kurt Aland, *Did the Early Church Baptize Infants?*, tr. by G. R. Beasley-Murray (The Westminster Press, 1963).

[56] For this view, see A. J. B. Higgins, *The Lord's Supper in the New Testament;* Joachim Jeremias, *The Eucharistic Words of Jesus.* For the Last Supper as a fellowship meal given new meaning, see Neville Clark, *An Approach to the Theology of the Sacraments* (London, SCM Press, Ltd., 1956).

the process that separated the remembrance of Christ's death and its benefits from the sharing of food at a hunger-satisfying meal. The mere token use of bread and "wine" in the usual Protestant Communion service today has a very limited resemblance to the common meal of the apostolic age.

The process of separating the remembrance ceremony from the hunger-satisfying meal occurred mainly in the period after Paul, the period for which we have little clear evidence. The accounts of the Last Supper in Matthew, Mark, Luke, and I Corinthians, however, show that for a time the church continued to observe a Supper in remembrance of Christ's death and its benefits for his followers. The Supper recalled his death and its benefits and the victory of his resurrection; it expressed the faith, fellowship, and thankfulness of the worshipers; and it looked to Christ's final and complete victory at the end of history. (As the sacramental celebration of the Lord's Supper took definite form apart from a common meal, the church developed a fellowship meal which, among other things, provided food for the needy.)

The greater attention to the work of Christ in his death seems to have been accompanied by a development of sacrificial theories to explain the meaning of Christ's death. Sacrificial imagery from the Old Testament was used from the first, but it later became more literal, formal, and dominant, and called for a more formal ministry. In time, the service of worship became an offering conducted by the proper minister.[57] We need to study the development of church leadership in order to understand this trend.

FLUID PATTERNS OF LEADERSHIP

At the end of The Acts, there is still no fixed form or order in the church.[58] In Jerusalem, James and the elders had taken over the leadership that the Twelve led by Peter had exercised at the beginning. Peter is the only one of the Twelve reported to have carried on an active ministry outside of Jerusalem; all that John did in Samaria was to support Peter (Acts 9:32 to 11:18). Nothing is told of Peter's ministry after Acts 12:17. Barnabas, appointed by the Jerusalem church to investigate

[57] This view was not clearly developed until after the first century. See Alan Richardson, *An Introduction to the Theology of the New Testament* (Harper & Brothers, 1958), Chs. 13, 16.

[58] See Burnett Hillman Streeter, *The Primitive Church* (The Macmillan Company, 1929); Eduard Schweizer, *Church Order in the New Testament* (London, SCM Press, Ltd., 1961). He examines the evidence down to the middle of the second century A.D. See also Alan Richardson's book cited in note 57.

the preaching to the Gentiles at Antioch (Acts 11:22), stayed there to become the active leader, but after his mission with Paul and his failure to defend the unity of the Antioch church (Gal. 2:13), he worked again in Cyprus (Acts 15:39). Of his further work nothing definite is known. It was Paul who spearheaded the Gentile mission. He is the sole object of attention in the latter half of The Acts.

The idea that all leaders were responsible to the Twelve and commissioned by them never occurred to Luke when he was writing The Acts (or if it did, he rejected the idea). The theme of The Acts is that the Spirit freely guided men to assume leadership and spread the gospel. The Twelve are important. They are called apostles, but so are Barnabas and Paul (Acts 14:4, 14), and Rom. 16:7 names others. Led by Peter, the Twelve take the lead in the crucial first years. But the leadership of the Jewish Christian group at Jerusalem slips into the hands of James the brother of Jesus, and not by any action of the Twelve, and the leadership of the Gentile mission develops in a progressively independent way from the Hellenistic wing of the Jerusalem church and it later centers in Paul.

The churches of Paul as seen in his letters show no sign of a fixed and imposed order. There are leaders, but they fall into no pattern. At Thessalonica there are "those who labor among you and are over you in the Lord and admonish you" (I Thess. 5:12); no formal title or position is given. In Galatia we hear nothing of local leaders from Paul (Acts 14:23 says that Paul and Barnabas "appointed elders for them in every church"). At Corinth the household of Stephanas "have devoted themselves to the service of the saints" (I Cor. 16:15), but apparently they hold no official position, and the Spirit-prompted leadership that is suggested in I Cor. 12:28 permits no formal pattern. Ephesians, a general letter, speaks of churchwide leaders and of pastors and teachers (Eph. 4:11), but suggests no fixed local pattern.

Phil. 1:1 shows that the Philippian church has "overseers and deacons"; here, for once, local leaders are mentioned in the address, but the word *episkopoi*, "overseers," refers to a group of leaders in the one church; to call them "bishops" is misleading, for their role is essentially that of local pastors or elders. At Colossae, Archippus is charged to "fulfil the ministry" he has "received in the Lord" (Col. 4:17), but his ministry is not defined. When Paul writes to Rome, a church he has never visited, he mentions no leaders; we can only say that Peter is not there and the Roman church is not under Peter's leadership, for otherwise Paul must have mentioned him. (Acts 20:17 calls the leaders at Ephesus elders; v. 28 calls these elders "overseers," *episkopoi*, a description that indicates not their formal title but their function.)

Other New Testament writings give much the same indefinite picture. Of the Gospels, Mark speaks least of church leaders; it simply tells of the choice of the Twelve and their mission during Jesus' lifetime (Mark 3:13–19; 6:7–13). Matthew has most interest in church leadership; it tells of the Twelve (Matt. 10:1–4), states that "in the new world" they "will also sit on twelve thrones, judging the twelve tribes of Israel" (ch. 19:28), and gives Peter a leading role as the rock on which Christ will build his church (ch. 16:18).[59] Luke has the choice of the Twelve (Luke 6:13–16) and of the Seventy (ch. 10:1), the role of the Twelve in judging Israel (ch. 22:30), and the promise that Peter will take the lead and rally his comrades after Jesus' death (v. 32). The special relation of the Twelve to Israel is worth noting in these Gospels; the number twelve probably recalls the twelve tribes of Israel. The Gospel of John never lists the Twelve; it never speaks of successors, but, like Matthew and Luke, it has (in the appendix) a special charge to Peter; he is to feed Christ's sheep (John 21:15–17). Local church officers are not mentioned.

In Rev. 21:14 the twelve foundations of the New Jerusalem bear the names of the twelve apostles of the Lamb. This gives them a wider basic role as foundation of the entire church. Eph. 2:20 partly supports this, but includes the prophets in the foundation. Of successors of apostles there is no word.

The later New Testament letters and epistles give meager information. The Pastoral Epistles, revised into their present form a generation or more after Paul's ministry,[60] speak of definite officers in the local church: elders and deacons. I Tim. 3:1 and Titus 1:7 do speak of a bishop or overseer, but it is clear from the word "for" in Titus 1:7 that the "bishop" is one of the group of elders mentioned in Titus 1:5; and in I Tim. 4:14 (cf. II Tim. 1:6) it is clear that it is the elders who lay hands on the young man being set apart for the ministry. So here again the "bishop" is an elder. The use of the term "bishop" is coming in, but the bishops, as in Phil. 1:1 and Acts 20:28, are elders; they are called "bishops" because that word describes their function; they are "overseers," as the word *episkopoi* means.

(The nearest New Testament approach to a bishop in the modern episcopal sense is found not in the *episkopoi*, who are elders, but rather in Timothy and Titus, who are thought of as succeeding Paul and carrying forward his work. However, it is the elders who lay hands on Timothy in I Tim. 4:14; the idea of episcopal succession is not present;

---

[59] On Matt. 16:17–19, see Oscar Cullmann, *Peter: Disciple, Apostle, Martyr*, 2d ed., pp. 161–242.

[60] See P. N. Harrison, *The Problem of the Pastoral Epistles;* Burton Scott Easton, *The Pastoral Epistles.*

and the work of Timothy and Titus is not a settled episcopal administration in a limited region, but a roving ministry. The Pastorals do not yet know the monarchical episcopate.)

Hebrews, perhaps written to Rome, speaks of past "leaders . . . who spoke to you the word of God" (Heb. 13:7) and present ones who "are keeping watch over your souls" (v. 17). No titles are given. James 5:14 speaks only of elders. I Peter, apparently written from Rome to northern, central, and western Asia Minor, refers only to elders in the churches addressed; the writer calls himself a "fellow elder" and thinks of the elders as shepherds (I Peter 5:1 f.). II Peter, I John, and Jude name no local church leaders. II and III John are written by the Elder, who is no mere local official, but a prominent aged church leader with influence over a wider area; in church tradition he is the apostle John the son of Zebedee. He writes letters, sends messengers, and makes visits to a region that seems to be in Asia Minor. But his letters ascribe no formal title or office to the writer, and they show concern not for formal succession but only for trustworthy leaders who will hold and teach the true gospel.

The foregoing sketch shows that the New Testament depicts no fixed church order. Church leadership takes a variety of forms. There are apostles, the Twelve and others. They play a basic role and exercise real influence and authority; but they have no formal successors. There are the Seven, and they have no successors. There are elders and deacons; to indicate their function, the elders sometimes are called "overseers." There are prophets, teachers, and other gifted leaders, but they fit into no formal pattern. James the brother of Jesus takes a leading role, and is called an apostle in Gal. 1:19; and he and his brothers form a known group of leaders (I Cor. 9:5). This James seems to have remained regularly in Jerusalem, and of the New Testament leaders he is the nearest to a monarchical bishop; actually to call him one, however, would be too hasty; it would assume a more explicit polity than yet existed. James's successor, Symeon, continued the influence of Jesus' family in church leadership, and shows the continuing tendency to episcopacy in Jerusalem.

The Emergence of the Monarchical Episcopate

The monarchical episcopate, the next decisive development in church order, appears in Antioch in Syria and in Asia Minor. Ignatius in his letters reflects the fact that he was the established and recognized bishop of Antioch. (His *To the Romans* mentions no bishop at Rome.) At the same time, Polycarp was the bishop of Smyrna in Asia Minor (cf. the address in *To Polycarp*), and Ignatius mentions bishops in all the churches he addresses in western Asia Minor. The very vehemence with which Ignatius repeatedly insists on centering the life of the local congregation in the bishop strongly suggests that in Asia Minor the monarchical episcopate was not fully accepted.[61] Ignatius seems to be arguing for something not so firmly established in Asia as in Antioch. His visit was a strong factor in completing this process in the province of Asia.

The monarchical episcopate was not so quickly accepted in other prominent churches. When about A.D. 107,[62] Polycarp, bishop of Smyrna, writes to the Philippian church, he gives no hint that this church had a bishop. I Clement, written to Corinth about A.D. 95, speaks of elders who had been deposed by the majority of the Corinthian church. The picture leaves no place for a bishop in the church of Corinth at that date.

The most striking thing is that at Rome, traditionally known for its line of popes beginning with Peter, I Clement gives no hint of a bishop. It speaks of elders, whom it also calls "bishops," i.e., "overseers," and it speaks of deacons, but there is no threefold ministry of bishop, elders, and deacons. So about A.D. 95 at Rome the monarchical bishop still is not mentioned.[63] Indeed, the Shepherd of Hermas, traditionally dated shortly before the middle of the second century, seems not to know the monarchical bishop, and largely for this reason some would date this writing about A.D. 100.[64]

Regardless of this dating, the general fact is clear: in the New Testament and down toward the middle of the second century there is no evidence of general concern for a fixed episcopal order; church polity is still a variable; no order is an essential in the New Testament doctrine of the church. That there must be Spirit-led leadership is an accepted fact, but no specific order emerges as necessary; indeed, no uniform fixed order exists.[65]

[61] *To the Ephesians*, chs. 1–6; *To the Magnesians*, chs. 2–4; 6 f.; 13; *To the Trallians*, chs. 1–3; 7; 12 f.; *To the Philadelphians*, chs. 1; 3; 7; *To the Smyrnaeans*, chs. 8 f.; *To Polycarp*, ch. 6. One can say that this is the dominant theme of these letters, and that it is a view not universally accepted in Asia Minor at the time.

[62] On the possibility of a date about A.D. 117–118, see John Lawson, *A Theological and Historical Introduction to the Apostolic Fathers*, pp. 104, 157 f.

[63] Ignatius, so careful to build up the authority of the bishop in every letter to Asia Minor, writes to the Roman church ca. A.D. 107 with no mention of church officers.

[64] See John Lawson, *A Theological and Historical Introduction to the Apostolic Fathers*, pp. 224 f. The usual date for the Shepherd of Hermas, the date supported by ancient tradition in the Muratorian canon, is in the time of Pius I (A.D. 140–155).

[65] I am fully aware that a strong later tradition tells of an established episcopal and even papal succession of authoritative leaders reaching back into the first century A.D. For almost every main Christian center, tradition lists a chain of bishops connect-

12*

GNOSTICISM'S CHALLENGE TO THE CHURCH

Another development in the century following the ministry of Paul was the emergence of Gnosticism, which attempted to transform the gospel and take over the Christian movement. To discuss Gnosticism helpfully we must first make clear the sense in which we use the word. The term has so many shades of meaning that it is elusive and often quite misleading.[66]

The word comes from the Greek word *gnōsis*, "knowledge." Gnosticism therefore is a teaching that professes to give trustworthy knowledge. Since all philosophies and religious messages make this promise, the word in itself is rather neutral. It is necessary to know what knowledge is offered. In the Gnostic movement the word did not refer to such knowledge as man can acquire by diligent human observation and by study of the natural world. It referred, rather, to a knowledge of the nature and meaning of life that gives understanding of God, of man's nature and dilemma, and of the answer to man's needs. This knowledge man receives by revelation; *gnōsis*, then, was revealed knowledge of God and man's nature and the right way of life; since man was seen to be in an unhappy state, it was knowledge of the way of salvation.[67]

In long-standing usage, Gnosticism has referred to a revealed knowledge and understanding of the world and man as preached by Gnostic leaders in the second century and later. These Gnostics caused the church great trouble, especially in the second and third centuries. This Gnosticism was long known from the denunciations of it by church fathers, and the fury of their attacks raised doubts whether they were fair to their opponents—in fact, one felt sure that their reports were one-sided and not entirely accurate.

Essential to the developed Gnostic view was a radical dualism; matter was thought to be inherently evil. The good God therefore could not have created this material world; it must be the work of an inferior or evil spirit. Man cannot trust or worship the Old Testament God who

---

ing back to an apostolic sponsor. It is astounding that the actual writings from the period we are studying do not support these traditions. Some would argue that the extant contemporary writings I have used do not tell the whole story. But they at least prevent the assumption that there was a fixed and uniform church order in the first century or more of the church.

66 On the definition and date of emergence of Gnosticism, see Johannes Munck, "The New Testament and Gnosticism," in *Current Issues in New Testament Interpretation,* edited by William Klassen and Graydon F. Snyder (Harper & Row, Publishers, Inc., 1962), pp. 224–238. See also R. M. Grant, *Gnosticism and Early Christianity,* Ch. 1.

67 See Rudolf Bultmann, *"Gnosis,"* in *Bible Key Words,* Vol. II.

created the material world. Man, composed of matter and soul or spirit, belongs to two realms; the material part of him comes from the evil realm and cannot be redeemed; only the soul or spirit can be saved, and it is saved by being released from matter and taken back to the pure realm of light, from which by some mishap it fell and became mired down in evil matter. Man must learn who he is—a spark of the divine enmeshed in an evil material body. He must learn the way to salvation; by revelation he can learn how the divine spark can make its way back to the realm of light.

Gnostic teaching of the second century and later often included the story of the divine Redeemer who comes down from the pure realm of light, rouses the fallen divine sparks, reveals to them the way back to their true home, and leads them back. The God and Father of Jesus Christ is the true God; he has sent Christ to show men the way home; since matter is evil and Christ is divine and perfect, he could not actually enter a physical body; that would have involved him in evil; he only *seemed* to have a real physical body (this view is called Docetism); in fact, he did not have one; but he came and took this apparent form in order to reach men and arouse them to seek and follow the way home which he came to show them.

This is approximately what Gnosticism was in the second century and later when the church fathers attacked it as fatal to the true Christian gospel.[68] Its view that man's real problem is his physical nature rather than a sinful will; its rejection of the Old Testament; its denial that the Redeemer God, the Father of Jesus Christ, is identical with the Creator God, the God of Israel; its denial that Jesus actually lived a physical human life; its view that man's true self is untouched by sin and needs only to know the way home, wake up, and take that way—all these views were radically at variance with what Jesus and the apostles taught, and the church fathers were right in holding that the very nature of the gospel was at stake in this controversy.

Was Gnosticism Pre-Christian in Origin?

It was long held that this Gnostic teaching was an alteration of the gospel message. The church fathers insisted that the Gnostics had twisted and debased the gospel, and their assertion was accepted. But in recent decades an earlier, independent origin of Gnosticism has been proposed

[68] For a selected bibliography on Gnosticism and its relation to Judaism and Christianity, see R. M. Grant, *Gnosticism: A Source Book of Heretical Writings from the Early Christian Period* (Harper & Row, Publishers, Inc., 1961), pp. 245–248.

and widely accepted. It has been maintained that in the ancient Near East, even before Jesus and Paul lived, Gnostic teaching was current. It had even made inroads into some areas of Jewish thought. Then when the disciples of Jesus began to think of the meaning of his ministry and message, they applied to Jesus some features of the Gnostic teaching and especially of its myth of the descent of the Redeemer to rescue the divine sparks from the realm of evil matter.

Paul, on this view, took up and made use of some, but not all, of the Gnostic ideas. So did other writers of the New Testament books, notably the author of the Gospel of John. Gnosticism was thus a tool used in the apostolic age and later to interpret and make persuasive the message of Jesus. The New Testament writers, possessing a message originally stated in Jewish terms, seized upon Gnosticism as the best available means to make their message clear and effective in the wider world—to make it "relevant," as we say today. It was really Paul and other New Testament writers who imported into Christian teaching the essentials of the Gnostic myth and terminology against which the church fathers later raged so violently.[69]

If we ask how this new view of the time and method by which Gnostic teaching entered the church is defended, how the pre-Christian origin of Gnosticism and its use by Paul and others is supported, the answer is that it is an inference based largely on later evidence, some of it as late as the ninth century. It is argued that a series of writings from the second to the ninth century reflect Gnostic features whose origin must have been at least as early as the first half of the first century A.D. Indeed, individual points of Gnosticism are found in pre-Christian writings, including Jewish writings.

But the question is whether these elements of Gnosticism had crystallized into a system before the days of Paul and other apostolic writers. There does not appear to be any proof that this crystallization occurred so early.[70] The New Testament writers lived when this Gnostic movement was ready to take form. In Jewish literature, including the Dead Sea Scrolls and various apocalyptic and wisdom writings, lay items of later Gnosticism which the early Christian teachers and writers used. But the distinctive features of developed Gnosticism—radical dualism of matter and spirit; the rejection of the Old Testament and of the Creator God of Israel; the assigning of the redemption of men through Christ to another God, the stranger God who was the Father of Jesus Christ; and

[69] See Rudolf Bultmann, *Theology of the New Testament*, Vol. I, pp. 164–183.
[70] Note the argument of Johannes Munck in the essay listed in note 66 of this chapter.

the definition of salvation as essentially liberation from the evil world of matter—these features and their combination into a system appear to be later than the New Testament period and independent of the New Testament writers.[71]

GNOSTIC LEADERS

The church fathers ascribed the beginning of Gnosticism to Simon Magus of Samaria, the self-asserted and widely acclaimed "power of God which is called Great" (Acts 8:9–24).[72] Later legend said that he confronted Peter and was defeated in his attempt to match Peter's wonder-working power. He was even equated with Paul in later Jewish Christian legendary lore, and the charges against each were combined in one mass of condemnations. Another early Gnostic teacher was a Samaritan named Menander. These Samaritans did not hold the ancient Samaritan religion; they probably were Gentiles who promoted a Gnostic-type teaching and tried to influence the church.

Antioch of Syria was another center for Gnostic teachings. Menander took up residence there and led a school of Gnostic teaching. He seems to have been followed by Satorninus, who in turn was followed by Cerdo, who held the doctrine of the two gods, one just and the other gracious. Cerdo went to Rome about A.D. 140. At about the same time, Valentinus of Egypt went to Rome and tried in vain to win acceptance and leadership there. It is widely thought that he or one of his disciples wrote the recently discovered Gnostic work, *The Gospel of Truth*. The noted Gnostic leader Basilides, perhaps connected for a time with the Antioch Gnostic School, worked mainly in Egypt.[73]

MARCION AND HIS CHURCH

Of unusual importance for the history of the church was Marcion.[74] It has been questioned whether he is rightly called a Gnostic, but it seems that he had connections with Gnostics, especially with Cerdo, and by his rejection of the Old Testament, his distinction between the just

---

[71] On the recent discovery of Gnostic documents in Coptic at Nag Hammadi in Egypt, see W. C. van Unnik, *Newly Discovered Gnostic Writings* (London, SCM Press, Ltd., 1960); Jean Doresse, *The Secret Books of the Egyptian Gnostics;* and my article, "New Greek and Coptic Manuscripts," *Biblical Archaeologist*, XXIV (1961), pp. 1–18.

[72] On "Simon Magus and Helen, His Thought," see R. M. Grant, *Gnosticism and Early Christianity*, Ch. 3.

[73] On these Gnostics, see R. M. Grant, *Gnosticism and Early Christianity*, Chs. 3 to 5.

[74] See note 5 of this chapter for books on Marcion.

Creator God and the gracious Stranger God who sent Jesus Christ, and his denial of the actual birth and physical life of Jesus he appears to belong in the Gnostic group. He came to Rome from Pontus shortly before A.D. 140, and is said to have given a large gift to the Roman church, which that church returned to him when it learned better what he taught. He soon organized his own church, which his zeal, ability, and high moral standards enabled him to build into a real threat to the opposing churches.

Convinced that the Old Testament was not Scripture from the gracious Father of Christ, Marcion made his own Scripture, consisting of the Gospel of Luke and ten letters of Paul. From these writings he deleted passages that he thought had been added; actually he disliked most of such passages because they tied Jesus and the church to the Old Testament and the Creator God. He put squarely before the church the question as to its Scripture. Would it keep the Old Testament? Would it add to the canon any Christian writings? If so, which ones? He made the church see that the content of the gospel and the extent of the Scripture were interrelated questions.

Marcion put squarely before the church another question: What was the role of the historical Jesus, and what use was the church to make of the records of his life? We must consider this question. It was crucial for the emergence of the church in definite form.

Chapter 14

ANCHOR IN HISTORY

THE CHURCH could not take stable form until it clearly affirmed in the face of opposition its permanent anchor in concrete events of history. The rise of Gnosticism, discussed in the preceding chapter, forced the church to reaffirm the importance of key historical events for Christian faith and life. Gnosticism rejected the Creator God, the Old Testament, Israel's role as God's people, and the physical life of Jesus Christ. The church could not tolerate this radical denial that Israel and the historical Jesus had a positive role in the gospel story.[1]

THE GOSPEL MORE THAN A HUMAN HISTORY

But from the beginning the question had existed of how far the Christian message rooted in human history. By its very emphasis on the transcendent divine factor, the gospel raised this question; such an emphasis could easily lead some to belittle or even exclude human action. The preaching of John the Baptist, the message of Jesus, and the gospel preached by the apostles all had a dimension that transcended the area of "objective" history and science. They spoke of God's judgment, of the coming of his Kingdom, of his coming into human life to save men and fulfill his purpose, of the beginning now of a new age different from that in which men had been living. They announced Jesus as the central figure of a series of events which they confessed to be acts of God, but which the historian and scientist could not verify as God's working.

Particularly after Christ's resurrection this added dimension dominated the experience and message of his followers. Jesus was risen; he was now the exalted Lord of the church and the world; he would judge the world and bring all things under God's effective rule.[2] The earthly career of Jesus of Nazareth could easily seem unimportant or embar-

---

[1] On this subject, see the closing part of the preceding chapter.
[2] On the full scope of the church's gospel message, see Chapter 3. That message was never a mere report of the ministry and teaching of Jesus.

355

rassing in the face of this cosmic sweep of the risen and reigning Christ, whom Christians confessed to be the Son of God.

Yet the church could not forget or ignore the historical Jesus. The first disciples had known this man and lived with him. The earliest converts in the apostolic church, even those who had not known Jesus personally, inevitably learned of his earthly life from those who had actually seen and heard him. It is part of the merit of form criticism that it points back of our written Gospels and their written sources to the earliest oral period of reports about Jesus. It assumes, with good logic, that the church remembered and continually repeated items about what Jesus did and said during his ministry and especially at its end, when the cross inexorably drew near. This continual use of the gospel tradition means that the church was never content to speak of the risen Christ and forget the historical Jesus.

A further indication of historical interest is found in the written sources reasonably supposed to lie back of our Synoptic Gospels. These sources were written because the church continually used the gospel tradition and needed it in clear and convenient form. The very production, preservation, and collection of our canonical Gospels gives further evidence that interest in the historical Jesus continued in the decades after the end of The Acts. The Christian message emphasized the risen Christ and his Lordship present and future, but it likewise recalled as basic the earthly life and ministry of Jesus of Nazareth.[3] The Gnostic disrespect for the historical Jesus was radically wrong.

MEAGER REFERENCE TO WHAT JESUS DID AND SAID

But it still was possible to give a meager and inadequate place to the deeds and words of the historical Jesus. Let us survey briefly the New Testament apart from the Gospels.

The sermon summaries in The Acts, whose writer knew all the details about the life of Jesus which he had recorded in the Gospel of Luke, center on the Old Testament prophecies pointing to Christ and on his death, resurrection, and present meaning for faith. That Jesus did "mighty works" and "went about doing good" is noted (Acts 2:22; 10:38), but the facts of his ministry, his specific actions and sayings, are not recounted; the saying in Acts 20:35 is the only exception to this lack of specific information about his ministry. Taken alone, the sermon summaries could suggest that the apostolic preaching concentrated almost

[3] On the oral and written preservation of the gospel tradition, see Frederick C. Grant, *The Gospels: Their Origin and Their Growth*, and the other works cited in Chapter 3.

entirely upon the redemptive drama rather than upon details of Jesus' public ministry.[4]

The letters of Paul likewise lack detail about what Jesus did and said during his earthly ministry. Paul must have given more teaching on such matters than his letters contain.[5] But the fact is that apart from references to Jesus' birth (Gal. 4:4) and Last Supper, death, and burial (I Cor. 11:23–26; 15:3 f.), Paul's letters direct attention to the risen Christ and not to Jesus of Nazareth. They tell of the preexistent Son, but they never mention the Galilean ministry of Jesus (I Cor. 8:6; Gal. 4:4; Phil. 2:6 f.; Col. 1:15–17).

The situation is even more striking in The Letter to the Hebrews. It is the only New Testament book outside of the Gospels which refers specifically to the temptation that Jesus underwent (Heb. 2:18; 4:15; 5:7–9). But it usually is overlooked that for this writer the earthly life is not the time or scene of the high-priestly ministry of Christ. It is, rather, the time of training in preparation for his real ministry. That ministry consists of two parts: first, his one effective offering for sin (ch. 9:11 f., 24–26), and second, his continual intercession for his people (ch. 7:25; cf. Rom. 8:34). Both these ministries are exercised not on earth but in the heavenly tabernacle. There he offers his own blood as the one sufficient and effective sacrifice for sin, and there he "always lives to make intercession for them." There is no earthly ministry of Jesus in Hebrews.[6]

The Letter of James is a little more favorable to the earthly ministry. Its author reflects knowledge of several sayings of Jesus known to us from the Gospels. But they are not quoted as sayings of Jesus, and there is no reference to specific events of his ministry. One noted scholar contended that this letter was originally written by a non-Christian Jew and then taken over by some Christian who inserted the name of Jesus Christ in two passages (James 1:1; 2:1).[7] That anyone could suppose this shows how little specific reference the letter makes to Jesus' historical career.[8]

I Peter has specific references to the suffering and death of Jesus (e.g., I Peter 3:18; 4:1, 13; 5:1). But it does not report his ministry and teach-

---

[4] To avoid misunderstanding, it must always be remembered that these so-called "sermons" in The Acts are very meager summaries of the chief points of early Christian preaching. In such summaries, historical detail could not be given. Even so, the almost complete absence of references to Jesus' public ministry and teaching is significant. See my book *Three Crucial Decades*, Ch. 2.

[5] See Elias Andrews, *The Meaning of Christ for Paul* (Abingdon-Cokesbury Press, 1949), pp. 28–32.

[6] See Maurice Goguel, *The Life of Jesus*, pp. 128 f.

[7] F. Spitta, *Der Brief des Jakobus* (Göttingen, Vandenhoeck & Ruprecht, 1896).

[8] For parallels with passages in the Gospels, see Joseph B. Mayor, *The Epistle of St. James*, 2d ed. (London, Macmillan and Co., 1897), pp. lxxxiv ff.

ings as one might expect the author to do if he had been an eyewitness of Jesus' ministry. II Peter and Jude, which share a fierce opposition to false Gnostic teachings and immoral tendencies in the church, do not support the Christian faith and standards by appeal to sayings or actions of Jesus. II Peter refers to the transfiguration of Jesus on the mountain (II Peter 1:17 f.), an incident found in the Synoptic Gospels, but it does not report other actions or quote any sayings of the historical Jesus.[9]

The three letters of John likewise have no detail about Jesus' earthly life. They insist on the actual physical life of Jesus on earth (I John 4:2 f.; II John 7), for they know that the Gnostic denial that Jesus has come in the flesh would prove fatal to the Christian gospel. But they do not support this point by reporting specific events and teachings that would attest concretely Jesus' physical historical life.[10]

The book of Revelation deals with the church of its day (late first century) and the future (imminent) coming of the risen Christ, and so has little place for references to the earthly life of Jesus. It speaks of him as the Lamb that was slain (Rev. 5:6), and knows that he was of Davidic descent (chs. 5:5; 22:16), but it tells nothing of his actions and teaching during his public ministry.[11]

That these twenty-three writings of our New Testament contain so amazingly little about the earthly Jesus usually escapes the notice of Christians; their minds are conditioned by the presence and importance of the four Gospels in the New Testament. Had it not been for the Gospels, Christians of the late first and early second centuries could easily have focused attention almost entirely on the risen Christ rather than equally on the public ministry of Jesus.

The Jewish Jesus Strange to Gentile Christians

Jewish disciples could more easily understand Jesus within the framework of Judaism. Gentile Christians could find it more difficult to do justice to the earthly Jesus. The very fact of human limitations could seem to them unworthy of a divine Lord. His Jewish manner of life could embarrass Gentile believers and hinder them from a clear and grateful acceptance of his human life. The joyful emphasis on the resur-

9 On the meagerness of the information about Jesus in I and II Peter, see Maurice Goguel, *The Life of Jesus*, p. 129. Jude, traditionally written by a brother of Jesus, gives no information about events and sayings of Jesus' ministry.

10 This is the more striking in view of the claim of the author in I John 1:1 that he proclaims what "we have heard" and "seen" and "looked upon and touched with our hands."

11 See Maurice Goguel, *The Life of Jesus*, pp. 129–133.

rection and present Lordship of Christ could overshadow reports of his earthly life. The sense of present privilege and imminent future blessings could so sharply focus attention on present and future as to discourage attention to the historical past.

Where Gentile Christians gave attention to the Old Testament as Scripture, its fulfillment could be seen mainly in the death, resurrection, Lordship, and coming triumph of Christ. Attention could easily be drawn from Jesus' earthly career and teaching ministry to the triumphant aspects of the gospel story, and the humble life in Galilee, the puzzling rejection by most Jews, and the official rejection in Jerusalem could seem no essential part of the gospel message. As time went on, this tendency to underestimate his earthly life reached its climax in the Gnostic outlook which denied that Jesus really lived in the flesh and suffered and died.[12] There was on this latter view no earthly life of Jesus.

THE NECESSITY OF THE GOSPELS

Yet a sound historical and theological basis for the church required respect for and attention to the historical Jesus. First of all, that earthly life was a stubborn fact of history. It was not a neutral fact. Either it had a constructive place in the gospel message or it challenged the truth and relevance of the gospel itself. If Jesus' early life, his deeds and teaching, did not fit into the gospel story, then that story was indefensible. For Jesus did live a human life. He lived a humble life. He met opposition and increasing rejection. He finally suffered official rejection and was executed as an impostor. This story of apparent failure could not be ignored; too many people knew it. If the gospel had no place for that puzzling human life, it was false at the center and doomed to defeat wherever the facts became known. The church had to have an adequate anchor in history.

The essential and only possible basis for the continuing spread of the gospel was an understanding of Jesus' life which would make clear his ties with Israel, his expression of the deepest meaning of the Old Testament, his authentic teaching of the truth and will of God, his loyalty to the highest purpose of God, his achievement of God's purpose precisely through a humble and apparently futile life, and the organic link of his present life and Lordship with his earthly ministry. The miracle and

---

12 Gnostics did not always take this extreme view. For example, it might be held that Jesus lived a human life, but the spiritual Christ descended from heaven and entered this human life at the beginning of the ministry and left it before the crucifixion. See R. M. Grant, *Gnosticism and Early Christianity*, Chs. 1–2.

majesty of a human life of ministry and suffering, the coming of God
into a human life which incarnated the Suffering Servant portrait of
Second Isaiah, the victory and triumph of suffering love, the redeeming
power of the seeking love of God in this key life of history—all this
had to come to light not by ignoring the earthly life of Jesus but by
putting it boldly forward so that the basis and reason for the present
gifts and promised future of God's people could be gratefully grasped.
In the long run, there could be no gospel without the Gospels.

THE NATURE AND FUNCTION OF A GOSPEL

What we have said does not mean that the Gospels are mere historical
narrative. They are not merely, as they are so often called, biographies,
lives of Jesus. There had been no writings like them in the world's literature.[13] Here was a unique story, that in a specific human life and ministry God had acted to fulfill his divine promises and give men the
redemptive help they desperately needed. This outwardly unimpressive
human career was the basic and central historical action of God. It was
a story told, not to interest the curious or to increase men's knowledge
of human history, but to announce and explain that in this human life
God had acted for men and that the only right response to this story is
faith, obedience, witness to Jesus, and confident hope that through him
God's cause will reach its full and final triumph.

Since God's central and decisive action occurs in Jesus, since this life
is the key by which to understand God's ways with men and man's need
and prospects, faith in God must take the form of faith in this historical
(and risen and exalted) figure. The church must face its situation in the
light of what God has done and revealed in Jesus. It must continually
return to the Gospels, to their account of this unique career, in order
to understand its own situation and find out how to worship and live.

This does not mean that the other writings in the New Testament
are of no value and should be discarded. It means that they can be understood rightly and used helpfully only if they are understood and used
in the light of the story the Gospels tell. The Gospels give the basis and
tell the story on which the apostolic witness rests. The apostolic witness
interprets this historical life as the central and decisive action of God.
The Gospels anchor the church in history, a special history in which
God is the key actor and Jesus Christ is his unique agent. Thus they give
the church its durable and true basis for its faith and life. Each Gospel
in its own way ties the church to the historical Jesus and to the work of
God in and through him. The Gospels as a group indicate that the

13 On the Gospel as a literary form, see K. Grobel, "Gospels," *IDB*, E-J, p. 449.

church cannot understand the gospel message and live faithfully under Christ except by constant link with their strange and haunting story.

We must consider the Gospels to see how they speak to their own day and how they give to the later church the needed anchor in history.

MARK WROTE THE EARLIEST GOSPEL

It became clear in Chapter 3, when we studied the Gospels to learn what they teach concerning the life of Jesus, that Mark wrote the earliest Gospel. The alternative view, that Matthew was written first and that Mark used Matthew as a source for his Gospel,[14] is much less likely. John Mark, cousin of Barnabas and assistant in turn to Paul and Peter (Col. 4:10; I Peter 5:13),[15] wrote his Gospel shortly after the death of Peter in Rome. Within a few years, probably in the period A.D. 62–64, Peter, Paul, and James the brother of Jesus had been martyred. It is probable, to say the least, that others of the Twelve were still living; tradition says that John the son of Zebedee lived on for several decades more. But the period dominated by the great leaders known from The Acts had ended.

The message of the church was now mostly in the hands of second-generation Christians, who had not known Jesus or taken part in the life of the Jerusalem church. The gospel tradition had been handed on by numerous preachers and teachers. It had taken form in the telling, and was a more or less definite body of material. In recent years, perhaps, Christian teachers had begun to write down parts of that tradition: the passion story (cf. Mark, chs. 14 to 16), collections of Old Testament prophecies fulfilled by Jesus, a group of controversies bringing out Jesus' position on disputed subjects (Mark 2:1 to 3:6; 11:15–17, 27–33; 12:13–40),[16] a collection of parables (Mark 4:1–34), and a collection of Jesus' teaching about the impending end of the world (cf. Mark, ch. 13).[17] We cannot prove that these things were already set down in writing, but it is reasonable to think that at least some of them were.[18] Certainly such groupings of material had occurred in the teaching of the church.

---

14 This is the usual Roman Catholic view. See John E. Steinmueller, *A Companion to Scripture Studies*, Vol. III, pp. 66, 128.
15 It has been questioned whether both passages refer to the same Mark. But it is clear from Acts 12:12, 25; 13:5, 13; 15:37–39 that Peter and Paul knew the same Mark, and there is no evidence in the history or tradition that points to two prominent Marks in the apostolic age.
16 See Martin Albertz, *Die synoptischen Streitgespräche* (Berlin, Trowitzsch & Sohn, 1921); Vincent Taylor, *The Gospel According to St. Mark*, pp. 91 f., 101.
17 See Vincent Taylor, *St. Mark*, pp. 498–500, 636–644.
18 On theories of Marcan sources, see Vincent Taylor, *St. Mark*, pp. 67–77; Frederick C. Grant, *The Gospels: Their Origin and Growth*, pp. 108–116.

But the church still lacked a well rounded written record of the basic gospel story on which all of its preaching and teaching was based. It was not enough to read the Old Testament and identify single passages as fulfilled in the life and work of Jesus. It was not even enough to gather together all the passages of that sort and arrange them in an order that would throw light on his career.[19] The story itself, supported by Old Testament references, but with primary attention centered throughout on Jesus and his work, needed to be clearly told. The purpose was not to satisfy historical curiosity or to create classic literature. It was to meet the needs of the church in its worship, preaching, and teaching.

No one was better equipped to do this than was John Mark. He had lived in Jerusalem in the earliest days of the church (Acts 12:12). Quite possibly he had seen Jesus. He had known Barnabas and, no doubt, Peter at Jerusalem (Acts 12:12–25). He had worked with Barnabas and Paul in the earliest mission of the Antioch church (Acts 13:5, 13). At Antioch and elsewhere he had seen the gospel accepted by Gentiles. In touch with Paul and Peter, he had reached Rome (Col. 4:10; I Peter 5:13). He knew Luke, one of those who saw how important a record of the gospel story would be (Col. 4:10, 14). But from all appearances, Mark was ahead of Luke in seeing this importance and meeting this need.

FEATURES OF THE GOSPEL OF MARK

Mark set the pattern and scope of the gospel type of writing. He held to the scope of the gospel preaching of the apostolic age, as illustrated in Acts 10:34–43 (and other typical sermon summaries of The Acts). His gospel story recalled God's preparatory work with Israel. It referred to the Old Testament as Scripture and quoted specific passages as fulfilled in the gospel story. It referred also to John the Baptist as the one who prepared the way for Jesus. But its main story extended from the baptism of Jesus through his ministry to his death, resurrection, and recognition as exalted living Lord.[20] This is the basic pattern and scope which is common to all four canonical Gospels, and this written pattern was set by Mark.

[19] See B. P. W. Stather Hunt, *Primitive Gospel Sources*.

[20] It is certain that Mark 16:9–20 was not a part of the original Gospel of Mark but was added a few generations later. Some think that this Gospel is complete at ch. 16:8, but it is usually held—and rightly—that Mark wrote more, which has been lost. On this question, see Vincent Taylor, *The Gospel According to St. Mark*, pp. 609–615.

Within this pattern there is noteworthy emphasis on the closing events of Jesus' earthly career. This is true in all four Gospels. Each gives from one fourth to one half of its total space to the last week of Jesus' life. Mark no doubt had a special reason for this. When he wrote, about A.D. 65–70, the Roman church had just passed through trying days. The persecution by Nero, with numerous brutal executions of Christians, including quite likely the crucifixion of Peter and the beheading of Paul, had left the Roman church weakened by losses and shaken by such fierce and cruel imperial hostility. In this situation it must have steadied and encouraged that church to have Mark's Gospel with its emphasis on what Jesus had suffered and what a benefit and example his suffering gave to them.[21] Mark's immediate aim in writing was thus to nerve and steady the Roman church.

But he did not do so by distorting the truth. He was able to achieve his aim by showing faithfully that the shadow of the cross had, in fact, lain over the entire second half of the gospel story (from Mark 8:31 on), and that Jesus' death and resurrection occurred on behalf of the Roman Christians and their fellow believers in other cities. The detailed story of the last week of Jesus' life showed the innocence of Jesus; it reminded Christians of the benefits of his death and resurrection; and it gave them an example to follow.

In other respects, the Gospel of Mark stakes out the lines that the other Gospels follow. It—and they—bring out clearly the Jewishness of Jesus and the limitation of his ministry almost completely to the Jews.[22] Since our earliest Gospel appeared in Rome after the Gentile mission was widely developed and since Jesus could have been presented to Gentiles more easily if he could have been pictured in frequent and friendly relations with them, this feature is the more striking. But it was solid historical fact that in family background, religious heritage, and general outlook Jesus was a Jew, and he worked almost entirely with Jews.

Moreover, Mark and the other Evangelists agree that Jesus' real clash was with the Jewish leaders. Jesus, though living as a Jew, differed radically with the accepted Jewish leaders of his day. The official leaders disowned him, and at their request the Roman governor executed him. This is attested by all four Gospel writers; it did not make it easy to present Jesus either to Jews or to Romans, but it is the common testimony

21 For emphasis on "the martyr motif" as "one of the two most notable aspects of the Marcan gospel," see Donald Wayne Riddle, *The Gospels: Their Origin and Growth* (The University of Chicago Press, 1939), p. 140.
22 Joseph Klausner, *Jesus of Nazareth*, emphasizes Jesus' Jewishness and its limits from the modern Jewish viewpoint; see pp. 363 ff.

of all four Gospels. Related to this official rejection is the fact that the movement Jesus led was a lay movement. Mark and the other Gospels emphasize in varying degrees Jesus' Davidic descent,[23] in which they saw his qualification to be the King of the Jews. But Jesus had no recognized office in the religious life of his people, nor did his twelve disciples. They had no official role in the organized religious life of Judaism.

Each of the four Gospels in its own way brings out the uniqueness of Jesus and his right to faith and loyalty from all men. But Mark was the one who set this basic pattern. It is wrong to think that while the Gospel of John is theological, the Synoptic Gospels, especially Mark, are merely historical. All four center in a Christological message. Mark uses four prominent titles on which all four agree: Son of Man, Christ, Son of God, and Lord.[24] Outside of the four canonical Gospels, Acts 7:56 is the only other New Testament use of the title "the Son of Man," and in all four Gospels it is always used by Jesus as his favorite self-designation. Thus, it would appear, Mark set the pattern: he told the gospel story with this strong emphasis on Jesus as the Son of Man, and reflected in this title (used fourteen times) Jesus' awareness of being both the humble Suffering Servant of God and the heavenly figure who will come at the end to complete God's plan. Mark leads the other Evangelists in identifying Jesus as the Christ, the expected Jewish Messiah (Mark 1:1; 8:29; 14:61 f.). In addition, Mark accented the title Son of God (chs. 1:1?; 1:11; 3:11; 15:39), and in so doing he was using a high title found throughout the New Testament. Another common key title boldly used by Mark is Lord (e.g., ch. 12:36 f.), a title that occurs in almost every New Testament book and reminds the reader that the humble human Jesus is now the risen, exalted, reigning Lord.

In these ways Mark set a pattern followed by all three of the other Evangelists. In other ways, however, he set a pattern followed by the other two Synoptic Gospels but not by the Gospel of John. The Galilean center of Jesus' ministry occurs also in Matthew and Luke, though in Luke the travel narrative (Luke 9:51 to 18:14; it is not paralleled in Mark) somewhat limits the scope of the Galilean ministry. The message of the Kingdom is the central theme in all three Synoptic Gospels. The extensive use of parables is another common feature of these three Gos-

---

23 Mark puts little stress on this (chs. 10:47 f., 11:10), and in ch. 12:35–37 Jesus rejects at least the popular meaning of this title to describe a political and military leader. But it is wrong to think that he completely rejected it or that Mark did so. It was the general view, when Mark wrote, that Jesus was descended from David; cf. Rom. 1:3.

24 See Vincent Taylor, *The Names of Jesus* (St. Martin's Press, Inc., 1953), for the use of these and several dozen other titles in the New Testament.

pels, and so is the picture of the ministry of Jesus as in one respect a conflict with demons. The note of Jesus' message as a secret is not lacking in the Gospel of John—in it only those who believe know the truth—but Mark's thought that Jesus deliberately used secrecy as a teaching method to prevent outsiders from understanding him (Mark 4:10–12) is particularly common to the Synoptics. Thus there are ways in which Mark sets the pattern for Matthew and Luke but is not followed by the writer of John. These patterns and those in which Mark sets the pattern for the other three canonical Gospels show the epoch-making significance of his Gospel.

THE GOSPEL OF MATTHEW

How rapidly and widely the Gospel of Mark became known in the church we do not know. In any case the Gospel of Mark, written originally for the Roman church, was known and used a generation later by other writers in other parts of the church. This suggests rather wide use and high regard. Somewhere in Syria or Phoenicia (or possibly Palestine) a Jewish Christian teacher, keenly aware of the Jewishness and the Jewish roots of his gospel, but equally convinced that the gospel should be preached to all Gentiles (Matt. 28:19), wrote what we call the Gospel of Matthew. Its unknown author probably used as a source a document by the apostle Matthew, either a collection of Scripture passages seen to be fulfilled by Jesus, or a collection of Jesus' teachings used also by Luke and commonly known as Q. Use of such a source, written by Matthew not earlier than A.D. 50 and perhaps a decade or two later, could explain how Matthew's name became attached to this Gospel.

The writer's use of Mark as a basic source indicates that he was not an eyewitness apostle but a teacher who depended on good sources for his material. He writes after the apostles have passed from the scene of leadership. He has the teacher's mind and interest—he arranges material in an order that will promote memory and understanding and comparison; he uses topical grouping of material; he makes groups of threes or fives or sevens and so uses numerical grouping to aid memory and promote effective teaching.[25] He writes mainly for teachers of the church. Few individual Christians or inquirers would own a copy of a Gospel. Copies would be in the hands of teachers and leaders, and continual use by teachers would be the main use of such a writing, in worship, in

[25] See the lists in Willoughby C. Allen, *A Critical and Exegetical Commentary on the Gospel According to S. Matthew* (Charles Scribner's Sons, 1907), p. lxv.

dealing with inquirers, in instructing new Christians, and in guiding all Christians to face the varied problems of Christian living.[26]

When this Gospel was written, the relation of the gospel to the Old Testament and to Judaism was much discussed. The writer was a Jewish Christian grateful for his Jewish heritage. But he has to condemn the Jewish leadership for its continued rejection of Jesus Christ, and he clearly supports the world mission of the church. That Jesus' life and ministry fulfilled Old Testament prophecy had special importance for him, and he either made or took over from someone of like interest a collection of passages that made this fulfillment clear. Possibly, as has been contended, he belonged to a "school" of Christian teachers who studied the Scripture to show how the gospel story fulfills what Scripture promised.[27] His Gospel reflects an intensely active study of prophecy in the church of his region.

The relation of Moses and the law to Jesus and the gospel was a vital issue for him. The famous five "discourses" of Matthew assemble on a topical basis Jesus' teaching on the life of the disciple (chs. 5 to 7), the mission of the disciples (ch. 10), the parables of the Kingdom (ch. 13), relations between disciples (ch. 18), and the end of the age (chs. 24; 25). This fivefold pattern recalls the five books of Moses and may have been meant to suggest that Jesus is the new Moses, whose teaching supersedes the law of Moses and gives the new law by which the disciple is now to live.[28] This is not certain, for the Old Testament, including the law of Moses, was still Scripture to this Gospel writer and he knew it was not discarded by Jesus. But the immense importance and clear superiority of Jesus' teaching does seem to be a point in this Gospel. Its writer was not really a legalist, but his orderly way of arranging teaching and stating what Christ wants of his disciples tends in that direction and could easily further a legalistic way of living.[29]

THE CHURCH IN THE GOSPEL OF MATTHEW

There is in Matthew a special accent on the people of God. The writer, like Mark and Luke, knows that the Kingdom was central in

26 Its obvious special suitability for use in the life of the church is suggested by Frederick C. Grant's designation of this Gospel as "The Ecclesiastical Gospel" in *The Gospels: Their Origin and Growth,* Ch. 11.

27 See Krister Stendahl, *The School of St. Matthew* (Lund, C.W.K. Gleerup, 1954).

28 So Benjamin W. Bacon, *Studies in Matthew,* pp. 81, 165 ff.

29 See Gerhard Barth, "Matthew's Interpretation of the Law," in *Tradition and Interpretation in Matthew,* by Günther Bornkamm, Gerhard Barth, and Heinz Joachim Held, Eng. tr. by Percy Scott (The Westminster Press, 1963). Barth thinks this Gospel is opposing antinomian teaching.

Jesus' teaching. But only Matthew has the phrase "Kingdom of Heaven" (thirty-three times; he also has "Kingdom of God" four times). He thus shows a Jewish shrinking from frequent use of the word "God"; the word "heaven" was often used in ancient Jewish circles to point to God; it was a Jewish expression of reverence, but one that Jesus himself did not think necessary. The Kingdom has more imperfect features in Matthew than in the other Gospels. With the writer's emphasis on the Kingdom as already present in small beginnings goes his recognition that not all who enter into the Kingdom movement live worthily: some are weeds (darnel, Matt. 13:25), and lack the proper wedding garment (ch. 22:11). The Kingdom is thus pictured as being much like the church, an imperfect group of God's people gathered around Christ.

The church is a special interest of this Gospel. Not only does the writer aim to serve the church by effective writing and teaching, but he alone of the four Gospel writers uses the word "church." In Matt. 18:17 it refers simply to a local congregation, but in ch. 16:18 it means the whole group of followers of Christ. Many scholars consider this verse an intrusion into Jesus' teaching. They claim he never spoke of "my church"; they argue that the writer and his associates inserted the verse into the original gospel tradition. But if we do not read into the word the meaning it later acquired, there is no reason why Jesus could not have spoken of the church, i.e., the congregation of his followers united by their faith in him. The Gospel of Matthew attests that it was in Syria or Phoenicia that this church idea of Jesus was best preserved in the gospel tradition.[30]

Another noteworthy difference between Mark and Matthew is that Matthew includes birth and infancy stories (Matt., chs. 1; 2). This same development occurred independently in Luke. These two Gospels thus reflect a general tendency in the late-first-century church to emphasize that aspect of the story, even though it was absent from the early apostolic preaching. The reason for the addition was not merely biographical or devotional or legendary interest. The church was convinced by then that the birth of Jesus deserved an essential place in the gospel story of the church. Jesus could not be explained by environment, heredity, or training; in him had occurred God's unique invasion into human life, an invasion that began not at his baptism but at his conception and birth.[31]

[30] For an extensive study of Matt. 16:17–19, concluding that it came from Jesus, see Oscar Cullmann, *Peter: Disciple, Apostle, Martyr*, 2d ed., pp. 161–242. Cullmann gives extensive bibliographical references.

[31] On the significance of the birth studies in Matthew and Luke, see J. Gresham Machen, *The Virgin Birth of Christ*, 2d ed., and Thomas Bosslooper, *The Virgin Birth*.

THE GOSPEL OF LUKE

While Mark was almost certainly written in Rome and Matthew probably was written in Syria or Phoenicia, it is uncertain where Luke and The Acts were written. Rome, Corinth, Philippi—none of these suggestions has solid support. What is clear and important is the new atmosphere in the preface (Luke 1:1-4). Such a careful literary preface reflects a literary purpose, a concern for cultural contacts, an awareness of the world around the church as worthy of attention. Mark and Matthew show no such clear concern for respect and standing in the world outside the church. To say this does not question Luke's Christian dedication and purpose. It implies, rather, that he thought literary standing and cultural contacts would serve the church and further the spread of the gospel. It also implies some fading of the vivid eschatological expectation of the apostolic age; Luke wants to help the church learn how to live in this ongoing world.

Luke-Acts constitutes essentially a single two-part work.[32] To be sure, in Luke the author follows the pattern already set by Mark. Indeed, he uses Mark as his basic source in writing his Gospel; and like Mark, he weaves together numerous specific events and concise sayings of Jesus. This may obscure the oneness of Luke's total work, for in writing of the apostolic age he has no such abundance of specific events and sayings and so writes in a less concise way. But a careful reading of Luke-Acts shows its unity. Luke did not set out merely to write another Gospel like Mark. His purpose was to trace the rise and spread of the church until it had become the world church.

The Acts was thus a new project in Christian literature. It is still our only independent story of the preaching and expansion of the apostolic church; all later histories of this period are based on The Acts. As the next chapter will emphasize, the thesis of the writer of Luke-Acts was the basis on which the New Testament was built: the gospel story included not only the ministry, death, and resurrection of Jesus as given in Mark but also the witness of the apostles in their expanding mission.

Like Matthew, Luke contains birth and infancy stories (Luke, chs. 1 f.). This shows more biographical interest than Mark had, and attaches theological importance to Jesus' human birth. What is new in these stories is Luke's attention to the birth and growth of John the Baptist.[33]

---

32 The unity of Luke-Acts and the literary methods of Luke and his contemporaries are most effectively presented in Henry J. Cadbury's book, *The Making of Luke-Acts.*

33 On the importance and subordinate role of John the Baptist, see A. R. C. Leaney, *A Commentary on the Gospel According to St. Luke* (Harper & Brothers, 1958), pp. 41-43, and Hans Conzelmann, *The Theology of St. Luke*, pp. 22-27.

Luke is the only Gospel in which we find this strong interest in the Baptist's family and background. This, however, is not mere biographical interest. Luke senses in the entire gospel story, from the birth of John the Baptist and Jesus to Jesus' resurrection and the work of the Spirit, a divine purpose and working which gives the entire story its real meaning.

Luke brings this out in the hymns of chs. 1 and 2.[34] Perhaps they are not original with Luke but were known in the church before he wrote. But probably Luke himself, alive to God's special working in these background events of the central historical narrative, wrote these hymns to express what he discerned. His deep roots in the Old Testament show in the numerous Old Testament allusions and phrases that these hymns contain.

The Gospel for All

One pervasive and prominent note in Luke-Acts is its persistent emphasis on the universality of the gospel. This note is clear and explicit in The Acts. It is just as truly present in the Gospel of Luke, but is differently expressed. Luke knew that Jesus had limited his ministry almost entirely to his own land and people, and he reports this fact. But he finds ways to indicate that this geographically and racially limited ministry was essentially universal in content and aim and so was rightly carried to the wider world in the apostolic age.

One way in which Luke brings out this universal note is in his selection of Scripture passages. In Luke 2:29–32, with allusion to Old Testament passages, Simeon speaks of Jesus as "a light for revelation to the Gentiles, and for glory to thy people Israel" (v. 32; cf. Isa. 49:6; 52:10). In ch. 3:4–6, Luke, quoting Isa. 40:3–5, gives the quotation a universal outreach by ending with the words: "and all flesh shall see the salvation of God."

Another way by which Luke shows the universal spirit of Jesus is by repeated indications that Jesus sought out those who needed help. He went to the outcasts, the tax collectors and sinners, whose company respectable people avoided. Luke pictures Jesus eating in the homes of Pharisees (Luke 7:36; 11:37; 14:1) and ready to help people of (social or) financial standing (ch. 19:2), but he shows Jesus to be actively interested in all classes of people and especially in those with the greatest need (e.g., ch. 15:1 f.). Jesus was concerned for the poor and was critical of the rich who deprived the poor of justice; he criticized wealth and em-

---

34 They are known from the opening word or words of the Latin version: *Magnificat* (Luke 1:46–55); *Benedictus* (Luke 1:68–79); *Gloria in Excelsis* (Luke 2:14); *Nunc Dimittis* (Luke 2:29–32).

phasized its damage to faith and brotherhood (chs. 6:20, 24; 12:13–21).

Women had an inferior position in Jesus' day, but Luke portrays Jesus' friendship for women as another feature of his concern for all people (chs. 8:2 f.; 10:38–42; 23:49).

Luke also emphasized the widening outreach of the gospel by reporting Jesus' interest in the Samaritans. Mark lacks this emphasis, and in Matthew, Jesus even warns his disciples to let the Samaritans alone (Matt. 10:5). In Luke, however, Jesus goes to a village of the Samaritans to seek lodging (Luke 9:52). In the parable of the good Samaritan the Samaritan proves to be a real neighbor when the Jewish priest and Levite do not (Luke 10:33). Of the ten lepers healed, only the one who was a Samaritan returns to thank Jesus (Luke 17:16). Just as in Acts, ch. 8, the Samaritans are the first non-Jewish group to receive the gospel, so in the Gospel of Luke the Samaritans are the one non-Jewish group who on occasion respond to Jesus and so symbolize the wider response that the Gentile world will make to the gospel.

In these ways Luke, while respecting the gospel tradition that Jesus confined his ministry almost entirely to Jews, pointed to the universalist spirit in Jesus' ministry and prepared the reader for the Gentile mission which he describes in the book of The Acts.

THE GOSPEL OF JOHN

The Gospel of John is unique, though it is similar to the Synoptic Gospels in many ways. It too embodies the basic gospel message in a historical narrative. Here too John the Baptist is the forerunner of Jesus and Jesus' career is described from his baptism to his resurrection. The Gospel of John early underwent alteration, which certainly included the addition of ch. 21 and may also have involved minor revisions or additions at other points.[35] But this revision did not alter the Gospel's essential content and scope. It was a true Gospel and parallel in most essentials to the Synoptic Gospels.

Yet it is different in many ways.[36] The writer is independent in choice of material and wording.[37] It has been estimated that only eight percent

[35] John 20:30 f. is the original and remarkably fitting and effective conclusion of the original draft of the Gospel.

[36] See C. K. Barrett, *The Gospel According to St. John*, pp. 34–45.

[37] It is usually held that the writer of this Gospel knew at least one or two of the Synoptic Gospels, and this seems probable. But since P. Gardner-Smith wrote *Saint John and the Synoptic Gospels* (Cambridge, University Press, 1938), there have been persistent attempts to maintain that the author did not know the Synoptic Gospels and could have written much earlier than often supposed. Clement of Alexandria, cited in Eusebius, *Church History* VI.14.7, says that John wrote after the other Gospels were written and became known to him.

of his material is paralleled in any of the other three Gospels. And whatever the author tells, he expresses in his own words. The discourses of Jesus are not crammed, as are the Synoptic Gospels, with brief compact sayings on a variety of spiritual and ethical subjects, but are usually longer discussions which always have Jesus Christ as their central theme. Some historical themes and leading ideas of the Synoptics vanish or occur only in a minor way.[38] For example, in this Gospel, Jesus' baptism is mentioned only indirectly (John 1:31–34); Jesus does not expel demons from tortured people; he refers to the Kingdom, the central theme of the Synoptics, only in ch. 3:3, 5; he uses almost none of the many parables found in the Synoptics; the Twelve are rarely mentioned (only in chs. 6:67, 70, 71; 20:24) and their names are never listed; the Galilean ministry largely fades from view; the institution of the Lord's Supper is not mentioned.

A formal theological prologue opens the Gospel (ch. 1:1–18); the high Christology of the Gospel appears from the first chapter; Judea and especially Jerusalem are the usual geographical setting of the ministry; a selection of seven particularly striking miracles is given (chs. 2:1–12; 4:46–54; 5:2–9; 6:1–14; 6:16–21; 9:1–11; 11:1–44); extended discourses on the person of Jesus occur, sometimes as an outgrowth of a miracle; and a noteworthy extended farewell discourse and prayer mark the Last Supper (chs. 14 to 17). This highly selective and uniquely Christ-centered story constitutes one of the world's greatest religious documents.

It seems highly probable that this Gospel was written in Asia Minor, in or near Ephesus.[39] It is one of five Johannine writings which church tradition has always connected with that region. Of these five, the book of Revelation differs in style and apocalyptic urgency from the other four, and was hardly written by their author.[40] But the three Letters of John and the Gospel of John are bound together not only by tradition but also by vocabulary, manner of thinking, and situation reflected.[41]

---

[38] Note the leading ideas of this Gospel discussed by C. H. Dodd in *The Interpretation of the Fourth Gospel*, p. ix.

[39] Such is the overwhelming tradition. Two other places have been proposed. Syria, at Antioch, may be proposed if one takes seriously the theory that the Gospel of John was written in Aramaic; cf. C. F. Burney, *The Aramaic Origin of the Fourth Gospel*, pp. 127 ff. Or, since our earliest extant manuscripts of the Gospel of John are from Egypt, and kinship of this Gospel with Philo is found by many scholars, origin in Egypt is proposed. See C. K. Barrett, *The Gospel According to St. John*, pp. 109 ff.

[40] A recent defense of the traditional view that John the apostle wrote all five is found in Ethelbert Stauffer, *New Testament Theology*, Eng. tr. by John Marsh (The Macmillan Company, 1955), pp. 39 ff.

[41] So A. H. McNeile, *An Introduction to the Study of the New Testament*, 2d ed., pp. 300–305. C. H. Dodd, *The Johannine Epistles*, pp. xlvii ff., assigns the three Letters to an author other than the Gospel writer.

None of these four writings names its author. In II and III John the author identifies himself only as "The Elder," an aged Christian leader whose influence extended over a considerable area in western Asia Minor. In John 1:14 and I John 1:1–4 he seems to say that he was an eyewitness of the life of Jesus (but some take these passages to mean only that "we" Christians as a group can give eyewitness testimony to Jesus).

The Author of the Fourth Gospel

The writer seems to be a Jew originally from Palestine, and from the minor role he gives to Galilee as compared with his emphasis on Judea and Jerusalem, he would seem to have lived in Judea during Jesus' ministry. If we ask his name, church tradition, reaching back to the second century, rather strongly—though some aspects leave room for hesitation—inclines to the answer that he was John the son of Zebedee. If we ask the Gospel itself, we get a different answer. John the son of Zebedee is not named; "the sons of Zebedee" are mentioned only in the appendix (John 21:2). The Gospel gives no sign that its author was the Galilean "son of thunder" named John (Mark 3:17). In fact, the original Gospel, including chs. 1 to 20, makes no statement about the author.

The appendix, however, states that the author was the beloved disciple (John 21:24). This raises a conflict between the church tradition, which has identified the beloved disciple as John the son of Zebedee,[42] and the original Gospel, which has no such idea. In fact, the original Gospel has a quite different idea. It mentions the beloved disciple in chs. 13:23; 19:26 f.; 20:2–10; 21:7, 20–24; but it does not name him.[43]

However, we must ask whether before ch. 13:23 this Gospel has already identified any disciple of Jesus as the disciple whom Jesus loved. To this crucial question we get a clear answer. One and only one disciple has been so identified. His name is Lazarus. Four times in ch. 11 his special relation to Jesus has been stated: "Lord, he whom you love is ill" (ch. 11:3); "Jesus loved Martha and her sister and Lazarus" (v. 5); "Our friend Lazarus has fallen asleep" (v. 11; the word "friend" has the same root "love" that occurs in the verb "love" in vs. 3 and 36; Lazarus is, as we might say, the "beloved friend" of Jesus); "See how he loved him" (v. 36). Of no other individual man does the Gospel say even once that Jesus loved him; of Lazarus this special relation comes out in four passages.

In chs. 11 and 12—the climax of Jesus' ministry in this Gospel—not

---

42 For a discussion of the tradition, see McNeile, *An Introduction to the Study of the New Testament*, pp. 279 ff. He notes the difficulties in the traditional view.

43 The title prefixed to the Gospel names John, but this title was no part of the original Gospel. It was prefixed when the fourfold Gospel collection was formed.

only Lazarus but also his sisters, Martha and Mary, are prominent. Martha is the only one in the Gospel who makes the confession about Jesus which the Gospel was written to promote: "You are the Christ, the Son of God" (ch. 11:27; cf. ch. 20:31). In ch. 12:2, Lazarus is noted as present at the anointing scene, when his sister Mary anoints Jesus and Jesus recognizes her act as a preparation for his burial (ch. 12:7). Thus this family dominates the story at the climax of the public ministry and beginning of the passion story. Moreover, it is of the utmost importance to note that Lazarus' resurrection is the acted parable of the theme of the Gospel: Life through Christ (ch. 20:31).

So after the prominence of Lazarus and his sisters in chs. 11 and 12, and the fourfold indication that Lazarus is the disciple whom Jesus particularly loved, the remarks in ch. 13:23 and later passages about the disciple whom Jesus loved can only point to Lazarus. He was the beloved disciple of whom the Gospel speaks. He lived in Bethany, a suburb of Jerusalem (ch. 11:1). It fits the Jerusalem-centered nature of this Gospel if a Bethany resident, who later lived in Ephesus, wrote it or —as may be more likely—was the witness whose testimony lies behind it.

We touch here an elusive phase of early Christian history. If Lazarus was the beloved disciple, as the Gospel of John clearly indicates, how did John the son of Zebedee come to be named as the author of this Gospel? Was it because it was known in the region of Ephesus that this apostle John wrote the book of Revelation, and so this Gospel from the Ephesian region could be ascribed to him? Certainly some John wrote Revelation (Rev. 1:1, 4, 9; 22:8), and Justin Martyr, in his Dialogue with Trypho 81:4, said it was "John, one of the Apostles of Christ." Did Lazarus have some connection with the circle of the apostle John, so that as time passed the name of John became attached to the Fourth Gospel? Certainly at some time the church became convinced that the apostle John was the beloved disciple and had written the Gospel, and if Lazarus had had some connection with the apostle John in Palestine or in Asia, this conviction would be easier to explain. Perhaps this identification was made early, before the appendix was added to the original draft of the Gospel (John 21:24).[44]

[44] The troublesome questions that remain are: (1) Was Lazarus an actual historical person or just a symbolic figure to represent the true disciple as given life by Christ? (2) Why do we hear nothing of the activity of Lazarus in the apostolic age? (3) What became of him? It may be replied: (1) It is characteristic of the Gospel writer to find his symbolism in actual events. He believed Lazarus had been raised from the dead. (2) Lazarus is pictured as a retiring figure rather than an aggressive public leader. (3) We have little reliable information as to what became of the early Christian leaders. In the case of Lazarus, John 12:10 suggests that Jewish leaders effected his death, but it does not say when or where. It may be added that no view of the origin of the five Johannine writings is without difficulties. The view sketched

The Purpose of the Fourth Gospel

Our task now is to understand why the author of the original Gospel wrote and what aim he had in mind. His purpose was not merely or mainly negative. He had polemic aims, and opposed wrong ideas, but his best answer to wrong views was to state positively the gospel message in such a way as to exclude the false views bidding for acceptance by Christians. He left no doubt as to his purpose; he stated it at the end of his original draft of the Gospel: "that you may believe that Jesus is the Christ, the Son of God, and that believing you may have life in his name" (John 20:31). He writes to bring out the significance of the historical Jesus. He implies that men have a radical spiritual need that only God can meet. He is certain that God has met this need by sending his Son into human life, so that the coming and work of the Son, incarnate in Jesus of Nazareth, provides the one real answer to man's needs. The gospel offers eternal life to those who believe in the historical Jesus as the expected Christ of the Jews and the divine Son of God. To those who will say sincerely, "My Lord and my God" (ch. 20:28), this priceless gift of life is available.

The importance of believing is clear in the author's presentation. When he wrote, some were putting great emphasis on knowledge. The Christian message always claimed to give knowledge of God and of the way of salvation, but as Gnostic tendencies grew, the idea gained ground that what counted was to know the facts about the spiritual world, the imprisonment of the soul in the evil matter of this created world, and the way to escape from this imprisonment and return to the Father. Faith could easily become identified with acceptance or possession of this revealed knowledge. But if man's problem is not his imprisonment in a material world but his sinful imagination, will, and actions, he needs more than knowledge; he needs to realize and confess his sin and helplessness, and put his trust in the God who sent his Son into human life to redeem men.

Thus, believing is basic. So this writer never uses the noun "knowledge" or the noun "faith"; he uses verbs; he speaks of believing, active believing, and of knowing, a gaining of understanding which comes only through believing in Jesus Christ. He indicates also that there are stages in the life of believing;[45] one must continually renew his active believing

---

above has the solid merit that it takes seriously what the Gospel of John says about the beloved disciple; that Gospel points clearly to Lazarus as that disciple.

[45] For example, Samaritans believed first "because of the woman's testimony" but later because of direct relation to Jesus (John 4:39–42). The man born blind at first

and grow in the clarity of his commitment to Jesus Christ.

All this will yield a real knowledge, but this knowledge given through faith anchors in the historical Jesus. It recognizes that he really lived in the flesh (ch. 1:14), and so it avoids the supercilious and misguided views of the emerging Gnostics who thought that the divine Son was too spiritual to become incarnate in a physical body and live and die as a real man. Such believing also avoids unbrotherly separation from other "common" Christians; it preserves the unity and mutual love of the brotherhood of Christ (ch. 13:34 f.).

To center the gospel message in the historical Jesus does not mean to believe less than the Gnostics; it means to believe more. This Jesus is not only the Christ (ch. 1:41), the Son of God (v. 34), the Lord and God of the believer (ch. 20:28); he is the incarnation of the divine Word (ch. 1:1, 14), through whom the Father not only created the world (vs. 3, 10) and enlightens all men (v. 4) but also saves and eternally blesses all men who truly believe (chs. 3:17; 4:42; 10:9). Thus, to believe is to know the one true God and the one divine Son, Jesus Christ, sent by the Father; and this is eternal life (ch. 17:3).

In carrying out his essential purpose to state the gospel in a positive way, the author's real concern was not to use or oppose Greek philosophy and culture. Even in his use of the word *Logos*, "the Word," this is not his purpose.[46] The background of this term, used in ch. 1:1, 14, was varied. *Logos* was a Greek word used in Greek philosophy, notably in Platonism and Stoicism, but the Word of God was a prominent concept in the Old Testament, and even before this Gospel was written the Hellenistic Jew Philo had used the term to bring out the meaning of Judaism in terms congenial to persons of Hellenistic culture.

What the Gospel of John does is to take a word widely used in both Jewish and Hellenistic circles and say that the historical Jesus was the unique embodiment of this *Logos,* this divine reason and utterance, of which people often spoke. It was a way of saying that the message of Jesus Christ could be expressed in both Jewish and Gentile ways of thinking. But this was a minor point in this Gospel, which makes no real use

---

accepted Jesus as a prophet and later came to call him Lord (John 9:17, 38). A believing based on seeing the signs Jesus did is worth something, but is not yet full believing (John 10:38).

[46] On the meaning and background of the word *Logos* in John 1:1, 14, see Edwyn Clement Hoskyns, *The Fourth Gospel*, ed. by Francis Noel Davey, 2d ed. (London, Faber and Faber, 1947), pp. 154–163; Rudolf Bultmann, *Das Evangelium des Johannes* (Göttingen, Vandenhoeck & Ruprecht, 1950), pp. 5–15, 38–43; C. H. Dodd, *The Interpretation of the Fourth Gospel* (Cambridge, University Press, 1953), pp. 263–285.

of the term Logos after this introductory use in the prologue. The term is used in I John 1:1 in a sense essentially the same as that in John 1:14.

Now that the positive purpose of the Gospel is clear, it still is necessary to note that the author vigorously opposes wrong ideas which threaten the church. In particular, we see from the Gospel and especially from the Letters of John that the church in Asia Minor faced a threat from an incipient form of Gnosticism. It is significant, in view of the claim some make that Gnosticism antedated the apostolic age, that the Synoptic Gospels show no clear signs of such a threat. But toward the end of the first century, in Asia Minor, that threat was becoming real and strong. The syncretistic tendency that was about to crystallize into real Gnosticism was not basically an expression of Greek philosophy or Greco-Roman culture. It was the result of Semitic, Oriental, and Hellenistic forces meeting in the Near East and amalgamating in a way that produced a real rival to the historical gospel message.

The threat, as the Elder in Asia Minor saw it, centered in a denial of the flesh-and-blood life of Jesus of Nazareth.[47] That Jesus was the Son of God (John 3:18; 10:36), that he came from the Father to bring salvation to men (ch. 16:28), that he is the true Way to eternal life with the Father and the Son (ch. 14:6)—this was common ground for this author and his Gnostic-type opponents. But this author differed from them in his insistence that the divine Word became flesh (ch. 1:14), grew tired on his travels (ch. 4:6), hungered and thirsted (ch. 19:28), suffered, and actually died (ch. 19:30, 34). The gospel would be lost if the life of Jesus on earth were reduced to a mere phantom appearance. The author rejected the Gnostic view that matter is evil and so cannot have been created by the true God, man's Redeemer. Indeed, the divine Word who came to give men life was the divine agent in creating the world on behalf of the Father (ch. 1:3).

The author thus was defending the historical reality and physical life of Jesus Christ the Son of God. The author also was troubled by the arrogance of his opponents. They claimed to have a superior knowledge and thus lived with contempt for and in separation from other Christians (I John 2:19; II John 9; III John 10); to the author, this loss of love for other Christians was a fatal fault and marked these opponents as radically wrong in their views and attitude.[48]

With these opponents in mind the author wrote his Gospel; he aimed,

47 He saw that this denial left the church with a phantom Jesus, a Docetic figure whose life was not real and whose death lacked reality and power to save men.

48 John 13:34 f. makes mutual love among believers their authentic identifying mark and their effective way of witness to the world.

not primarily to win new converts or to convince his opponents, but to state the role of Jesus Christ in such a way that his role as Son of God, as the Father's agent in creating and upholding the world, and as the Savior and Lord of the world, would be plain, and so the church would be saved from despising or disparaging the historical Jesus.

Apart from opposing the threat from emerging Gnosticism, the polemic aims of the Gospel of John are directed mainly at Jewish and Samaritan groups. He condemns "the Jews." This does not mean that the writer wants to keep Jews out of the church. Quite the contrary. He himself is a Jew; "salvation is from the Jews" (ch. 4:22); everyone, Jew or Gentile, who believes will be saved and have eternal life (ch. 3:16).

But the great majority of the Jews, including the official leadership, had rejected Jesus; all four Gospels as well as The Acts make this clear. Moreover, when the Gospel of John was written the Jews of Asia Minor, a numerous group, were actively hostile to the Christian church. This is clear from Rev. 2:9; 3:9, written about the situation in Asia Minor at a date not too far from that of this Gospel (cf. the *Martyrdom of Polycarp* XII.2; XIII.1, a few decades later). To the author of the Gospel of John this was a bitter tragedy; Jesus, born as a Jew, came to "his own home" and "his own people," and yet they "received him not" (John 1:11). They placed themselves outside the church by rejecting him during his ministry and by rejecting the apostolic preaching.

About sixty-five times the writer calls them "the Jews." His basic reason for using this phrase is not racial prejudice or anti-Semitism,[49] for he himself is a Jew and wants the Jews to believe in Christ and enter the church. Indignation at those who rejected and opposed Jesus may creep into his tone, but essentially he means to say (1) that Jesus came to the Jews and they should have been quick to believe in him, and (2) they have culpably put themselves outside the true people of God, the group of those who believe in Jesus. Perhaps this Gospel's great emphasis on the Jerusalem ministry of Jesus and on his clash with the Jewish leaders there was intended to underline their stubborn rejection of Jesus.

Another polemic note in this Gospel is its insistence that John the Baptist was inferior to Jesus and was sent to point men to Jesus. It was a fact that John appeared first and baptized Jesus. This might suggest that John was the superior and that Jesus had so recognized by being baptized by John (cf. John 1:31–34). Moreover, even after John was imprisoned, his disciples continued as a separate group (Mark 6:29).

[49] For a different view, see Frederick C. Grant, *The Gospels: Their Origin and Growth*, p. 164: "There is a bitter hatred of 'the Jews' (i.e., the Jewish Leaders)."

They had their forms of prayer (Luke 11:1) and habits of fasting (Mark 2:18). Whether their group spread to Alexandria we do not know, but possibly it was there that Apollos heard of John's message (Acts 18:24 f.). Certainly there were in Ephesus in Paul's day twelve people, no doubt Jews, who had received John's baptism (Acts 19:1–7).

If these twelve who first received John's baptism and then believed in Jesus were only part of the Baptist movement in Asia Minor, and the Baptist movement continued there till the late first century when the Gospel of John was written, this would explain why this Gospel so emphatically insists that John was inferior to Jesus (John 1:8, 15, 19–36; 3:25–30). The Baptist movement was continuing and it seemed to the Gospel writer a threat that needed explicit undermining, so he stated clearly that John's role was preparatory and inferior to that of Jesus.[50]

The great care taken to refute any idea that Samaritan worship preserved the true Mosaic religion is another polemic note in the Gospel of John. The Samaritans are welcome in the church; Jesus himself began the preaching of the gospel to them. But "salvation is from the Jews," not from the Samaritans, and this Gospel strongly opposes any tendency, Gnostic or otherwise, to make the Samaritan center of worship on Mt. Gerizim the starting point for a sectarian form of the gospel (John 4:20–22). From Luke-Acts and from the early history of Christianity and Gnosticism we know that Samaria had an active role in the first and second century in religious developments within and related to the church.[51] But the church had its center in Jesus; his background and roots were in Judaism and in the Jewish worship which had its visible center in Jerusalem. The apostolic church moved out from Jerusalem. So this Gospel warns that whatever message does not anchor in the Jerusalem witness of the apostles is on the wrong track.

Quite possibly the Gospel of John was aimed also against the uncontrolled enthusiasm of people who claimed they were guided by the Holy Spirit.[52] We remember that at Corinth, Paul had to curb a tendency to such wild utterances as "Jesus be cursed!" (I Cor. 12:3). Some converts at Ephesus "spoke with tongues and prophesied" (Acts 19:6). In the middle of the second century, Montanism arose in Phrygia, east of the

50 On "The Later History of the Baptist Movement," see Carl H. Kraeling, *John the Baptist*, Ch. 6.

51 Acts 1:8 indicates that Samaria had an important role in the early spread of the church, and Acts 8:5–40 attests such a development. That the Hellenists of Acts 6:1 ff. carried the gospel to Samaria is a key fact in Oscar Cullmann's picture of "Samaria and the Origins of the Christian Mission," in *The Early Church*, pp. 185–192. Samaria in later decades was a center of Gnostic developments.

52 C. K. Barrett sums up the Fourth Gospel's teaching on the Holy Spirit in *The Gospel According to St. John*, pp. 74–78.

Ephesus region in Asia Minor, and its extravagant emotionalism subordinated the work of Jesus to the supposedly greater work of the Spirit.[53] These facts suggest that late in the first century the Gospel writer saw a tendency to belittle the historical career and work of Jesus Christ and exalt the more "spiritual" and powerful work of the Spirit. He emphasizes that the Spirit was not given to the church until Jesus was glorified (John 7:39), and it was the risen Christ himself who gave the Spirit to his disciples (ch. 20:22).

In the farewell discourse to the disciples on the last evening of his earthly life, Jesus taught them that they would receive the Spirit from him or from the Father at his request; the Spirit would bear witness to Jesus, recall his message, interpret his work, and so promote faith in him. Thus all that the Spirit does will always respect Jesus' central and basic role and will continue and develop Jesus' work (John 14:16, 26; 15:26; 16:7–15). No supposed utterance or guidance of the Spirit which belittles the role of Christ or obscures his central and decisive work is really from the Holy Spirit. The work of the historical Jesus lies at the basis of all future witness and work of the Spirit and the church.

In particular, Christians must reject the emerging Gnostic attempt to deny that Christ, the Son of God, actually came in the flesh. Such an attempt might seem to glorify Christ by freeing him from physical limitations to act as a purely "spiritual" being. Emphasis on the Spirit might seem to support the Gnostic view, which belittled the human life of Jesus and tended to deny that he had lived a physical human life. But the true work of the Spirit will always be to attest and interpret the historical life of Jesus, in whom the Word became flesh.

This was also the basic aim of the Gospel. It was not primarily apologetic or polemic, even in its opposition to the tendency to deny the physical life of Jesus. Its chief aim was to state positively that eternal life with God the Father and his Son Jesus Christ is freely available to all who will "believe that Jesus is the Christ, the Son of God" (John 20:31).

The Contribution of the Gospels

The four Gospels thus make a basic and crucial contribution to the understanding of apostolic Christianity. Study of the oral and written sources back of them reveals that active concern for the historical Jesus was a continual fact in the apostolic age. The writing and canonizing

[53] On the Montanist movement, see Eusebius, *Church History* V.16–19.

of these Gospels ensured the continued recognition of this historical ground of Christian faith. Through them the church was permanently anchored in this one life in first-century Palestine.

The historical account was told in such a way that the unique redemptive mission of Jesus and his unique relation to the Father were an integral part of the story. For the Gospels were not written out of historical curiosity. They were written to express the church's faith and to give the church a tool to use in its worship, preaching, teaching, and study. They are documents of history, a history whose most important feature is the working of God. They are documents of faith, a faith rooted in a historical life in which God was uniquely and redemptively at work. When the church gave them the prominent place in the emerging New Testament canon, it rejected the Gnostic threat and gave all its future worship and life the necessary solid anchor in history.

Chapter 15

ANCHOR IN SCRIPTURE

THIS BOOK has tried to trace the emergence of the church. To tell this story has meant essentially to tell the New Testament story. In doing this, we had to give the historical background of New Testament events and look briefly at what immediately followed the central New Testament period.

The need for historical background was clear. To understand a story so unique and so rich in meaning as the New Testament history, it was important to know the political, cultural, and social conditions and especially the religious setting in which the church took its rise. Only against that background could we understand the uniqueness and distinctive newness of the Christian faith. The basic meaning of the Gospel and the overtones of the language in which it found expression could be grasped only by knowing something of the life, ideas, images, burdens, and hopes of the first-century world.

THE KEY ROLE OF THE MACCABEAN REVOLT

To reconstruct that setting, we had to begin with the Maccabean uprising in the fourth decade of the second century B.C. This event brought a creative renewal in the life of the Jews. Under the threat of pagan syncretism and Syrian suppression of the Jewish faith, Judaism rose to its best, and through loyal suffering and fierce defense the Jews preserved and purified their heritage. Out of this time of persecution and struggle developed the party groupings and special teaching that prepared for Rabbinic Judaism. Gradually there emerged, essentially through Pharisaism, the synagogue worship and oral tradition which, after the destruction of the Temple, developed into Rabbinic Judaism, later into the Talmud, and still later into the synagogue-centered orthodox Judaism of later centuries.

The period from the Maccabean uprising to the middle of the second century A.D. was the decisive period in the formation of the Judaism of

381

today.[1] This development of Judaism not only preceded but in part paralleled the emergence of the church. Indeed, it likely took its permanent form to a minor degree in reaction against the emerging Christian faith and fellowship.

It is universally recognized that Christianity cannot be understood without a knowledge of its original Jewish setting. But it is unreasonable to think that the later orthodox Judaism took form without any reaction to the challenge with which Jesus, the apostles, and the emerging church confronted it. By the middle of the second century A.D., Judaism had excluded Jewish Christians from its fellowship, had drawn back from previous tendencies to cultural interchange with the Greco-Roman world, and had disowned the Jewish literature in Greek.[2] The period we have been studying was thus the formative period for later rabbinical Judaism; the period from the Maccabean revolt to the middle of the second century A.D. was crucial for this development as well as for the emergence of Christianity.

WHERE SHOULD WE END OUR STORY?

But if the Maccabean uprising is the clear starting point for our study of the emergence of Christianity, it is not so easy to determine where to end the story. This is due in part to the fact that the story of the church still continues, and no sharp division exists between the New Testament story and the following history of the church. But there is another reason. Our knowledge of the period in which we must seek the closing point of our story is meager and full of gaps, and no single decisive event stands out as the unmistakable terminal point.

THE STORY CONTINUES PAST THE CLOSE OF THE ACTS

As our study advanced, it became clear that we could not end it at the close of the period covered by The Acts. Even to understand that early period it was necessary to continue the story farther. In some parts of the Roman Empire, such as Egypt and northern Asia Minor, Christianity probably had taken root by the time The Acts ends, but it was only by looking at the later history of those regions that we could form even a tentative idea as to when and how the church began

---

[1] The classic work of G. F. Moore, *Judaism*, is invaluable especially in the study of the latter half of our period.

[2] This literature was preserved to modern times by Christian interest in it and use of it.

there. Even more important reasons compel us to continue our history beyond the early sixties of the first century. At that time, when the latest events of The Acts occurred, most of the New Testament books had not yet been written.[3] Thus, to sketch as far as possible the setting of those later books of the New Testament we had to continue the story for several decades at least. Moreover, issues shown to be in ferment by the letters of Paul and the narrative of The Acts continued to confront the church in the period during which the other New Testament books were written. Examples are the form of leadership of the church and the rise of tendencies to Gnostic thinking. The impact and changing formulation of such issues had to be followed, and new issues reflected in later books, such as the Christian attitude to emperor worship, had to be identified and their place in the total history explored.

It is true that with the end of the period covered by The Acts the great central figures of the first thirty years of the church pass from view, and a new era opens. James the brother of Jesus at Jerusalem, Paul the founder of widely scattered Gentile churches, Peter—the one known spokesman and outreaching member of the Twelve—these all leave the scene, and the leadership of the church is no longer in apostolic hands. But emergence of new leadership had already characterized the period covered by The Acts. Change in the personnel and method of leadership continued in the next decades, and such leadership found expression particularly in writings destined to find a place in the New Testament and so play a normative role in the later church. The decisive period of the emergence of the church continued past the end of The Acts.

WHY THE STORY CONTINUES PAST A.D. 100

Neither is it possible to end our story at the close of the first century. To be sure, by that time almost all the New Testament books had been written. Some scholars, indeed, defend a later dating for some New Testament books. We find proposals to date one or more of the following writings in the first half of the second century: the Gospels of Matthew and John; Luke-Acts; the Pastoral Letters; James; I Peter; the Johannine Letters; and Jude.[4] But it is highly probable that all these writings date from the first century, or at least very early in the second century. II

---

[3] Probably ten letters of Paul were the only books of our New Testament already written by that time.

[4] To assess trends in the dating of these writings, see the articles on them in *IDB* and Peake's *Commentary on the Bible*, rev. ed. edited by Matthew Black and H. H. Rowley (London, Thomas Nelson and Sons, 1962).

Peter, quite likely the latest of the New Testament writings to be composed, seems most likely to date as late as the first half of the second century. Thus, to get the setting of almost all the New Testament writings, we would not need to go beyond A.D. 100.

But two further facts, apart from the search for the likely setting of II Peter, make it advisable to continue the story to the middle of the second century. One is the regrettable but highly important fact that we know almost nothing definite of the external history of the church from about A.D. 65 to 95. We must pick up the story at the end of the first century, follow it for a few decades, and then look back and try to see what must have happened in that dark period. Moreover, the material for writing the history of the first decades of the second century is still very meager. So it is necessary to follow the clues to the middle of the century to get as good a basis as possible for concluding what must have followed the end of The Acts and led to the emergence of the church in its later form.

The other further fact that makes this terminus advisable is that by following the story to the middle of the second century we get a picture of the developing forces against which the church had to contend. The later writings of the New Testament contain many references to false and harmful teaching. It is not always clear what is meant. By noting the early-second-century clues to the character of such hostile movements and teaching, we are able to understand better what the New Testament writers were opposing and what issues were rising to face the church at the end of the New Testament period.[5]

The creative and buoyant forces of the apostolic age were tending to give way to legalistic and pedestrian ways which were honest and loyal but lacked the lift and power of the apostolic gospel. The expectation that the end of the world was surely close at hand was largely replaced by the acceptance of this world as destined to continue through the foreseeable future. The productive freedom of the Spirit-prompted life of the earliest church tended to give way to a plodding moralism. The fearless freedom which was not afraid of fresh new starts led by the Spirit gave ground before the determination to conserve the priceless gifts of the gospel by authoritarian fences and control. The down-to-earth realism of the gospel story of Jesus of Nazareth, who, though he was the Son of the Creator God, lived a truly human life, faced a desper-

[5] For an account of the first two centuries of the church, see Hans Lietzmann, *A History of the Early Church*, Eng. tr. by Bertram Lee Woolf, rev. ed., 2 vols. (London: Lutterworth Press, 1953); on the second century, see Robert M. Grant, *Second Century Christianity* (London: S.P.C.K., 1946).

ate struggle with a syncretistic movement which denied that Jesus came in the flesh or that the Redeemer God was the Creator of this world or that the whole man, body and soul, could be redeemed to serve his Creator and Redeemer.[6]

These were aspects of a crisis that evidently was gathering in the closing decades of the first century and took clearer form in the early decades of the second. To follow the story to the middle of the second century helps us to see by extension and by contrast what the New Testament has to say. It helps us make inferences as to what went on in the closing third of the first century, when over half of the New Testament writings may best be dated.

THE NEED FOR A NEW TESTAMENT CANON

The usefulness of a history that is extended to the middle of the second century may be observed in another way. By that time the New Testament writings not only had been written but in most cases had become fairly well known, and the situation was emerging in which they as a group could make a basic, decisive, and permanent contribution to the further history of the church. We have already noted how the writing of the Gospels served to anchor the gospel permanently in that unique history of Jesus of Nazareth. At the end of the first century and in the first half of the second, evidence begins to accumulate that most of the New Testament writings have come into public—though not yet universal—use in the public reading and teaching of the church. The church was being forced to consider its situation. How could it build solidly for the ongoing generations that now seemed to lie ahead? How could it discern and reject false trends and at the same time confirm and strengthen loyalty to its true heritage? As it faced these questions, the significance of the writings now included in the New Testament became increasingly apparent.

This appreciation did not occur as a sudden flash of insight. These writings had first been preserved and found helpful in the places where they first appeared. They were read in services of public worship and were used by teachers of the church. As their usefulness became clear and the need for trustworthy guidelines for Christian faith and life became more keenly felt, they had begun to circulate more widely. This process began in Paul's day (Col. 4:16) and increased in importance in later decades. Out of this development grew the conviction that the future health and growth of the church depended on giving this written

[6] See R. M. Grant, *Gnosticism and Early Christianity*.

form of the apostolic witness the permanently decisive role in guiding the church's life.[7]

There were three main ways by which the church could guide its life to keep true to its Lord. All three played a part in its search for integrity and stability, but we must ask which one had the basic role and proved best able to render the decisive service. None of the three was free from the possibility of misuse, but the crucial question was which one could most faithfully provide the needed control of continuing developments in the church.

The Place of Creedal Confessions

One way to guide and control the church was by a clearly formulated creed that could be used to test the life and changes in the church. From the earliest days the church had something of a creed, although it would be far more accurate to call it a confession, for during the entire period of our study the church never reached agreement on a formal creed that all Christians were asked to accept.

The nearest approach to a common creed in the apostolic age seems to have been the common confession, "Jesus Christ is Lord" (Phil. 2:11; cf. I Cor. 12:3).[8] Since from the very beginning of the church the resurrection was basic in Christian thought about Jesus, this confession meant that Jesus Christ is the risen, exalted, and actively authoritative Lord. There were other ways of stating and confessing the central role of Jesus; for example, he was acknowledged to be "the Christ, the Son of the living God" (Matt. 16:16), "the Christ, the Son of God" (John 11:27; 20:31), "Lord and Christ" (Acts 2:36), and "the Lord Jesus Christ" (e.g., I Thess. 1:1; James 1:1).

These confessions did not yet take trinitarian form. They did not speak explicitly of "the God and Father of our Lord Jesus Christ" (II Cor. 1:3). They invariably assumed that in some active and purposeful sense "God was in Christ" (II Cor. 5:19) and through Christ was carrying out his divine will, but their actual wording centered attention on Jesus Christ. Nor did they refer to the Holy Spirit, who was thought to carry forward and witness to the central work of God in Jesus Christ. In later generations it was necessary to include in such confessions an explicit reference to the Father and the Spirit, but in the earliest confessions it was considered sufficient to make clear and grateful confession of Jesus Christ the risen Lord.

7 See my book *Which Books Belong in the Bible?*, especially Ch. 5.
8 See Oscar Cullmann, *The Earliest Christian Confessions.*

In the second century more detailed confessions were developed. It is rather surprising how slowly this process proceeded. In popular modern church thought, the so-called "Apostles' Creed" is assumed to go back to the apostolic age.[9] In fact, however, that creed, as we know it, does not go back even to the second century; it did not take final form until perhaps the fourth century. The most that can be said is that by the middle of the second century, probably at Rome, the nucleus of the "Apostles' Creed" had taken form. In both its conjectured earliest wording and its final form it still bears the marks of the early tendency to center attention on the person and work of Jesus Christ; at every stage the reference to him takes much the larger place.

In the first half of the second century, however, that creed was just taking its early form, and there is no evidence that its use extended throughout the entire church. Such a confession was useful in expressing the essential faith of the church, but there is no sign that the church saw in it the decisive basis of the church's unity, integrity, and stability. The real days of the creeds were not to come until the fourth century.

If, then, we ask on what basis the church emerged, the answer in part must be that the basis was not a dominant, authoritative creed. There was no fixed and normative creed in the second century. Even the so-called "Apostles' Creed" was not yet fully formulated. Simple and earnest confessions were in use, and they took many forms, none of which was universally used or regarded as a formal authority. But the church did not emerge and stabilize its life on the basis of such varied and vital confessions. No fixed confession or creed was the formal norm or control of the church. And it was in the writings that were making their way to a place in the New Testament that the church was finding the confessions that were basic in its worship.

THE ROLE OF THE EPISCOPATE

A second way by which the church has tried to be true to its Lord and its faith has been by formal organization. For many people the church emerged and attained stability when it developed a structure or form of organization by which it could unify its worship and life, discipline unworthy members, and rally the Christians for effective

[9] On early forms of creedal confession, see Hans Lietzmann, *A History of the Early Church*, Vol. II, pp. 105 ff. Lietzmann points out that "all the doctrinal articles to be found in the Apostles' Creed appear about the end of the first century in the formularies of the Church" (p. 108). But they occur separately, not yet as a unified confession. See also J. N. D. Kelly, *Early Christian Creeds* (London, Longmans, Green & Co., 1950).

witness and steadfast living in the face of a hostile world.

It is clear that strong organization has played a prominent and necessary role in the life of the church through the centuries. In particular, the episcopal form of organization has proved rather effective in furthering inner unity and in defending the church against hostile attacks. But it was not the basis on which the church emerged. Even in the middle of the second century, when our study ends, it still is clear that the episcopal system has not prevailed throughout the entire church. And there is no clear evidence of such a system in the first century. The graded ranks of episcopal ministry do not appear until the opening years of the second century, in Ignatius and Polycarp. The militant insistence of Ignatius on the necessity of the episcopate reflects the fact that this polity was not yet universally accepted or axiomatically established, and other writings indicate that in part of the church the presbyter-deacon type of polity known from earlier decades still continued.[10]

The New Testament provides no evidence of episcopal polity and succession. It is misleading in New Testament passages to translate the Greek word *episkopos* as "bishop." This gives the impression that in the apostolic age there were bishops in the hierarchical sense. In the New Testament, however, the word *episkopos* is not a formal title and does not designate a formal office; it describes elders as "overseers" or "supervisors." In Acts 20:28 and in the Pastoral Epistles (I Tim. 3:2; Titus 1:7) the word is clearly used of elders, and when the leaders at Philippi are called by Paul "overseers and deacons" (Phil. 1:1), the fact that these *episkopoi* or overseers are mentioned as a group in the one church shows that they are local elders rather than bishops in the later episcopal sense.

The New Testament has no officials who have the official title of "bishop" and hold an episcopal rank superior to that of the teaching elders of the church. We hear of the apostles,[11] but not a word indicates that they had formal episcopal successors; the role of the apostle in the

10 On this point, consult Chapter 13. Cf. Burnett Hillman Streeter, *The Primitive Church*, p. 267: "In the Primitive Church [by which Streeter seems to mean "the first hundred years of Christianity"] there was no single system of Church Order laid down by the Apostles; . . . the Church was an organism alive and growing—changing its organization to meet changing needs." For a somewhat stronger feeling that with all the variation there *was* a real and indispensable structure, see Kenneth M. Carey (ed.), *The Historic Episcopate in the Fullness of the Church* (London, Dacre Press, 1954), and for a vigorous insistence upon the necessity of the apostolic succession through the historic episcopate, see Kenneth E. Kirk (ed.), *The Apostolic Ministry* (London, Hodder & Stoughton, 1946).

11 On "The Apostolate," see T. W. Manson, *The Church's Ministry* (The Westminster Press, 1948), pp. 34–56; cf. also Karl Heinrich Rengstorf, "Apostleship," in *Bible Key Words*, Vol. II, Part IV.

basic witness to the gospel is unique. We hear of the Seven (Acts 6:3, 5), but they have no successors; even if the later deacons were chosen to carry out duties similar to those of the Seven, no link between the Seven and such deacons is ever stated. We note that Paul was an apostle; he maintains, and the Twelve seem to agree, that he is an independent apostle (Gal. 1:1; 2:7); he is not a successor of or subordinate to the Twelve. We see James the brother of Jesus take the lead in Jerusalem (Acts 15:13–21; 21:18), but he is not one of the Twelve and he takes the lead not by appointment of the Twelve but by the authority that the brothers of Jesus were recognized to have. In The Acts we see the Twelve fade from the position of leadership and control, not by formal transfer of office, but by the emergence and recognition of other leaders who are prompted by the Spirit to assume leadership.

We find mention of elders in Jerusalem and elsewhere (Acts 11:30; 14:23; 15:2, 4, 6, 22 f.; 20:17; 21:18; I Tim. 5:17; Titus 1:5); we hear of deacons (Phil. 1:1; I Tim. 3:8); and it is hinted in Titus 1:7 that one of the elders is emerging as the prominent one of the group of elders in the local church. But there is no indication that this one is to be over a diocese of some extent; even he is simply the most prominent of the pastoral and teaching leaders of that local church. We see Timothy and Titus sent by Paul to carry on his work while he is alive, and it is implied that they are to continue that ministry after he is gone, but they are traveling missionary leaders; they do not hold a formal episcopal position or represent a link in a formal chain of succession. We hear of an elder in the Letters of John (II John 1; III John 1), and he acts, though not without opposition (III John 9), as the leader over an area in Asia, but there is no indication that he has a formal episcopal position or that he appoints or ordains successors.

The New Testament is anything but a picture of episcopal organization and succession.[12] There is freedom and variety, and apart from the apostles, who are unique, the elder holds the dominant official position. But no clear system of polity appears. In fact, the prominence and significance of the prophet in the New Testament period bars the way to any theory of fixed and formal offices and succession. The true prophet speaks and acts at God's command and without regard for formal organization. The later church has persistently ignored this fact, and has looked for a fixed polity and external continuity which the New Testament neither embodies nor approves.

---

12 Of course the gospel was handed on from each generation to the next, and there was continuous leadership in the church. The point is that there is no evidence in the first century or in the New Testament that an unbroken chain of bishops was in fact or in theory the way that the truth of the gospel was preserved or the unity of the church was expressed.

This does not deny the importance and the contribution of the historic episcopate. It played an important role from the second century on. But its place was not unchallenged in the early part of the second century, and there is no clear evidence at all for it in the first century.

This is the point for our present discussion. When one seeks the trustworthy permanent tie with Jesus and the apostles, the historic episcopate fails us in the crucial early decades. The historic episcopate, as traditionally understood, includes the idea of apostolic succession, that is, the theory that the later bishops connect back to the apostles by an unbroken line of episcopal ordination and so give a guarantee that the gospel and the authority of the church have passed by unbroken succession from the very beginning to the present day. The stubborn fact is that this theory breaks down at the decisive point, in the first decades of the church. No clear line of episcopal succession can be traced from the apostles to the second-century bishops. The idea that such a line of formal succession is necessary does not appear in the first century or even in the first half of the second century. The church emerged without any fixed polity and in particular without any theory of continuous episcopal leadership.

The Basic Role of the Apostolic Witness

The third way by which the church could keep its life continuously true to its Lord and its entrusted heritage was by testing every stage of its development by the basic apostolic witness to Christ. In our study extending to A.D. 150, the church did not realize and protect its unity and continuity by agreement on a common creed. Nor did it do so by appeal to an unbroken line of episcopal control of its worship, life, and teaching. It was by continual attention to the apostolic witness that the church kept alive to what it was and what its task and privileges were. At first that witness was orally known and could be attested by those who had heard apostles or their personal assistants. As time went on, more emphasis inevitably was placed on the apostolic writings that continued that witness.

Stages on the Way to the Canon

This process began early. Even in the days of Paul, his churches began to exchange copies of his letters (Col. 4:16). The death of Paul must have stimulated increased attention to his letters, which at his death became the only way by which people could continue to hear his own words.[13] This must have caused further exchange of his letters and led his churches to make collections of them. Probably the earliest collection did not have the Pastoral Letters.[14] But before the end of the first century, it would seem, the Pastoral Letters had been given their present form, to take account of disturbing tendencies facing the church. So Paul's message, thus brought up to date and adapted to later needs, became widely available and increasingly used. The church was now almost entirely a Gentile church; Paul was the most prolific writer and clear exponent of that Gentile church; his writings could not be neglected in seeking the apostolic witness.

Four Gospels likewise came gradually but surely to a place of unchallenged influence. Each must have been influential at first in the region where it was written. But as is shown by the use of Mark as a source by the writers of Matthew and Luke, these Gospels soon began to circulate more widely. The church realized, not merely as a compromise but as a fruitful fact, that the four Gospels could say more to the church and express better the witness of the apostolic age to the historical Jesus than any one of them alone could do.[15] So perhaps by A.D. 125,[16] and certainly well before the middle of the second century, this group of four Gospels was generally recognized to have a basic importance.[17]

The book of The Acts then took a key role in the further development of the New Testament canon. When Luke was separated from The Acts and made part of the fourfold Gospel collection, it might have seemed that The Acts was doomed to be discarded. But the reverse proved true. The Acts provided the link to give unity to the emerging New Testament canon. Luke-Acts had expressed the position that the full gospel message must include not only the Gospels with their story but also the witness

[13] So H. E. Dana, *A Neglected Predicate in New Testament Criticism* (Blessing Book Stores, 1934), pp. 14–21.

[14] So Edgar J. Goodspeed, *New Solutions of New Testament Problems* (The University of Chicago Press, 1927), Ch. 5, and C. Leslie Mitton, *The Formation of the Pauline Corpus of Letters* (London, The Epworth Press, Publishers, 1955), Ch. 2.

[15] See Oscar Cullmann, "The Plurality of the Gospels as a Theological Problem in Antiquity," in *The Early Church*, pp. 39–54.

[16] Edgar J. Goodspeed, *An Introduction to the New Testament* (The University of Chicago Press, 1937), p. 314, places the formation of the Fourfold Gospel A.D. 115–125.

[17] It is rightly pointed out by Wilhelm Schneemelcher, in Edgar Hennecke, *New Testament Apocrypha*, Vol. I, p. 33, that the Gospel of John still met objection toward the end of the second century. But as Schneemelcher notes and as Tatian's *Diatessaron* (ca. A.D. 170) reflects and as the statements of Irenaeus (ca. A.D. 185) and the Muratorian canon (ca. A.D. 200 or earlier) make clear, the four Gospels were generally recognized as a group during the second half of that second century.

and work of the apostolic leaders in the emerging church. Similarly, the church came to see that its authoritative writings must include not only the Gospels but also the witness of the apostles. The book of The Acts gave one expression of that witness and its narrative provided the historical setting for the inclusion of letters that contained that apostolic witness. It showed how the apostolic church and preaching developed out of the work of Jesus.

Thus, The Acts furnished the background for inclusion of the New Testament letters in the canon.[18] Its references to the Twelve and to other leaders showed their importance and made it natural to include in the canon not only Paul's letters, which were the only letters in Marcion's canon, but also letters ascribed to other apostolic leaders. Some early manuscripts express this point of view. They group with The Acts the so-called Catholic Letters,[19] supposed to be written by various apostles to the whole church. To this witness of The Acts and the Catholic Letters they then add the Letters of Paul. This gives the essential structure of the New Testament canon: Gospels, Acts and Letters—the Catholic Letters and the Letters of Paul.

The right of the book of Revelation to a place in this canon was long disputed (and has been disputed repeatedly to modern times). But there was a widespread and ultimately dominant readiness to include it. It served to attest the Christian hope that following the period of the church, in which the apostolic witness is authoritative and the work of the Christian mission calls for the church's faithful dedication, God's plan will reach its full realization. His perfect eternal Kingdom will come, and God's people will be given eternal security, free from the trials and sufferings that their faithful witness must endure in this present age.

When Did the Canon Outline Emerge?

The church had taken its essential form once it had separated from Judaism, accepted its world mission, and identified the written apostolic witness as the necessary and permanent basis of its future life and work.[20] Just when the church clearly realized the necessity for the New Testament canon as the only trustworthy way to preserve and hand on this

18 Cf. A. H. McNeile, *An Introduction to the Study of the New Testament*, pp. 346 f.
19 James, I and II Peter, I, II, and III John, and Jude.
20 This statement reflects the conclusion previously drawn from the New Testament that although the church inevitably has structure, no specific structure is prescribed and the structure of the church can be altered to enable the church better to fulfill its task in changed circumstances.

basic apostolic witness is not certain. Quite likely it had begun to realize this necessity even before Marcion, about A.D. 140, rejected the Old Testament and, to replace it, formed a new canon by putting together the Gospel of Luke and ten letters of Paul (he did not include the Pastoral Letters). These eleven writings he edited to restore what he thought must have been their original text. What he actually did in this editing was to eliminate the passages that showed the close ties of these writings with the Old Testament story and teaching. He was determined to show that the gospel was a new message and that the Father of Christ was not the Old Testament God.[21]

What Marcion did is clear. What is not clear is whether the idea of forming a New Testament canon first occurred to Marcion and was then taken over and developed by the church, or whether even before Marcion the church, which from the first had accepted the Old Testament as Scripture, was already consciously developing the New Testament canon. It is hard to believe that the idea of forming a New Testament canon was completely new with Marcion. The church was already moving in that direction, and even before Marcion's bold action, the Gnostic Basilides was treating both Gospels and Letters of Paul as authoritative. The Letters of Paul had been collected decades before Marcion, about A.D. 140, made his canon, and the four Gospels had already been linked together as a unified though multiple witness to the historical Jesus and his decisive work. It seems likely that the germinal idea of a New Testament canon antedated Marcion.

Just possibly, however, this process of forming a New Testament canon and adding it to the Old Testament to form one Scripture, even if already under way, had not crystallized in an explicit form before Marcion boldly rejected the Old Testament, selected one Gospel and ten Letters of Paul, "corrected" their text, and made them the Scripture of his movement. However, even if such an explicit step had not yet been taken, the church at the least had the materials ready at hand for a countermove. It could counter at once with a larger canon, which would keep the Old Testament, include all that Marcion had and present it in its original complete text, and add other works to give a broader presentation of the apostolic witness. In any case, whether the church was already on the way to a fuller canon before Marcion appeared, or first took conscious action after Marcion presented his canon, the idea of that larger canon and its essential structure took form in the church by the middle of the second century.

21 Recent works on Marcion: John Knox, *Marcion and the New Testament;* Edwin Cyril Blackman, *Marcion and His Influence.*

It was to be many generations before the church reached final agreement on the exact number and the identity of the books that should be included in the New Testament. But by the middle of the second century the basic structure of the Christian canon of Scripture was emerging. The Old Testament must be kept. The fourfold group of Gospels has an essential place. The Acts vindicates for the apostolic witness an integral role in the canon, and shows how reasonable it is to include letters by apostolic figures of the church. The Christian hope must find expression in the canon, either in the other books already found essential or by the addition of the book of Revelation.

In forming the New Testament canon, the church said that for the future its basic charter for its worship, life, and mission would be the apostolic witness as given in writings whose content went back directly or indirectly to apostolic figures. These writings could be misused; against such misuse the church had no sure protection. Not every writing included was written or directly approved by an apostle; the claim could, in fact, only be that they all preserved dependably the apostolic witness. But the church knew no better way to found its faith and life and witness on the true gospel. That gospel was attested in apostolic form in these writings, and the formation of the canon meant that the church was henceforth to shape its life and form and thought by this authoritative deposit of the apostolic witness. Not in a creed or in an official organization, but in the New Testament canon read and used under the guidance of the Holy Spirit, the church found its fundamental point of reference for the future. To be the church meant henceforth to be true to the apostolic witness preserved in the canon and interpreted and attested by the Spirit.

This is not to say that the New Testament is the final authority of the church. Final authority belongs to God, and the Christian who knows that "God was in Christ reconciling the world to himself" (II Cor. 5:19) confesses that God has acted in Jesus Christ and makes his will and authority effective through the gospel message that centers in Jesus Christ. The Christian's outlook is theocentric with a Christocentric focus; his life centers in God and he knows God through Jesus Christ and through the Holy Spirit given to the church by Jesus Christ the risen Lord. But the way to get back to that basic story, discern its essential content and meaning, and identify and reject its perversions is by gratefully accepting the canon and continually responding to the apostolic witness it preserves.

Chronology

Many of the dates are uncertain or approximate. None of the events of the first-century church can be dated with certainty. But it may be of value to see approximately where these events fit into the outline of ancient history. No attempt is made to date all the events and leaders of the period covered.

General History	B.C.	Jewish and Christian
Reign of Alexander the Great	336–323	
Ptolemaic Empire in Egypt	323–30	
Seleucid Empire in Syria, etc.	312–64	
Antiochus III (The Great)	223–187	
Ptolemy V Epiphanes	203–181/0	
Seleucids take Palestine from the Ptolemies	200 (or 198)	
Seleucus IV Philopator	187–175	
Ptolemy VI Philometor	181/0–145	
Antiochus IV Epiphanes	175–163	
	167	Temple at Jerusalem desecrated
		Maccabean revolt against the Seleucids
	166–160	Judas the Maccabean Leader
	166 (or 165)	Book of Daniel written
	164	Temple purified and re-dedicated
Antiochus V Eupator	163–162	
Demetrius I Soter	162–150	
	160–142	Jonathan, high priest
Alexander Balas, king of Syria	150–145	

396

General History	B.C.	Jewish and Christian
Demetrius II Nicator	145–139/8	
Antiochus VI Epiphanes	145–142/1	
Trypho, claimant of Syrian throne	142/1–138	
	142–134	Simon, high priest
Antiochus VII Sidetes	139/8–129	
	134–104	John Hyrcanus, high priest (and king?)
Demetrius II Nicator (again)	129–126/5	
Antiochus VIII Grypos	125–96	
	104–103	Aristobulus I, high priest and king
	103–76	Alexander Janneus, high priest and king
Aretas III, Nabatean king	85–60	
	76–67	Alexandra, Hasmonean queen
	76–67	Hyrcanus II, high priest
	67–63	Aristobulus II, king and high priest
Antipater, the Idumean, active in Palestinian affairs	67–43	
Pompey captures Jerusalem	63	
Julius Caesar defeats Pompey at Pharsalus	48	
Julius Caesar assassinated	44	
Octavian and Mark Antony defeat Brutus and Cassius at Philippi	42	
Parthian thrust into Palestine	41–37	
Herod, king of Palestine	40 (37)–4	
Battle of Actium; Octavian defeats Antony	31	
Octavian (Augustus), Roman ruler	31 B.C.–A.D. 14	
	ca. 20 B.C.– ca. A.D. 50	Philo Judaeus of Alexandria

General History	B.C.	*Jewish and Christian*
	20–19	Herod begins to rebuild the Jerusalem Temple
Aretas IV, Nabatean king	9 B.C.–A.D. 40	
Census in Palestine?	ca. 8–6	
	ca. 5–4	Birth of Jesus of Nazareth
Archelaus, ethnarch of Judea, Samaria, and Idumea	4 B.C.–A.D. 6	
Philip, tetrarch of Ituraea and Trachonitis	4 B.C.–A.D. 34	
Herod Antipas, tetrarch of Galilee and Perea	4 B.C.–A.D. 39	
	A.D.	
Census in Palestine by Quirinius, legate of Syria	6	
Coponius, procurator of Judea	6–9	
	6–15	Annas (Ananus), high priest
Marcus Ambibulus, procurator of Judea	9–12	
Annius Rufus, procurator of Judea	12–15	
Tiberius, Roman emperor	14–37	
Valerius Gratus, procurator of Judea	15–26	
	18–36	Caiaphas, high priest
Pontius Pilate, procurator of Judea	26–36	
	26–27 or 27–28	Ministry of John the Baptist
	ca. 27 or 28	Baptism of Jesus by John
	ca. 30	Crucifixion of Jesus
	ca. 33	Martyrdom of Stephen at Jerusalem
	ca. 34	Conversion of Saul (Paul) of Tarsus
	ca. 36	Paul visits Jerusalem

General History	A.D.	Jewish and Christian
Caligula, Roman emperor	37–41	
Claudius, Roman emperor	41–54	
Herod Agrippa I, king of Palestine	41–44	
	ca. 44	Martyrdom of James son of Zebedee at Jerusalem; Peter leaves Jerusalem
Roman procurators govern Palestine; Cuspius Fadus first	44–46	
	ca. 45	Barnabas and Paul take famine relief to Jerusalem
Tiberius Alexander, procurator of Palestine	46–48	
Ventidius Cumanus, procurator of Palestine	48–52	
	47–48	Mission of Paul and Barnabas in Cyprus and Asia Minor
	49	Apostolic conference at Jerusalem
	49	Claudius expels the Jews from Rome
	49(50)–52	Paul's mission in Asia Minor, Macedonia, and Achaia
Herod Agrippa II, king of former tetrarchies of Philip and Lysanias (and, beginning in 53, of parts of Galilee and Perea)	50–?	
Gallio, proconsul of Achaia	51–52	
Felix, procurator of Palestine	52–60?	
	53–58	Paul's mission in Asia Minor (Ephesus), Macedonia, and Achaia
Nero, Roman emperor	54–68	
	58	Paul arrested in Jerusalem

General History	A.D.	Jewish and Christian
	58–60	Paul in prison at Caesarea
Porcius Festus, procurator of Palestine	60?–62	
	60–61	Paul's voyage to Rome; shipwreck
	61–63	Paul in prison at Rome
	62	Martyrdom of James the brother of Jesus at Jerusalem
		Symeon, leader of the Jerusalem church
Albinus, procurator of Palestine	62–64	
	63	Paul released from prison?
	64	Fire in Rome; Nero blames the Christians
	64 (67?)	Martyrdom of Paul and Peter at Rome
Gessius Florus, procurator of Palestine	64–66	
	66	Jewish revolt against Rome; Jerusalem Christians flee to Pella
Galba, Otho, Vitellius fail in attempts to seize Roman rule	68–69	
Vespasian, Roman emperor	69–79	
Jerusalem captured by the Romans (last remnants of resistance crushed ca. 73)	70	
	ca. 75	Josephus' *Jewish War* published
Pliny the Elder published his *Natural History*	ca. 77	
Titus, Roman emperor	79–81	
Domitian, Roman emperor	81–96	
	ca. 95	Josephus' *Antiquities* published
	ca. 96	I Clement written from Rome to Corinth

General History	A.D.	Jewish and Christian
Nerva, Roman emperor	96–98	
Trajan, Roman emperor	98–117	
	ca. 100	Elkhasai active
	ca. 100	Didache written
	ca. 107	Ignatius of Antioch taken to Rome for martyrdom; writes seven letters from Asia Minor
	ca. 107	Polycarp writes *To the Philippians*
Pliny the Younger, governor of Bithynia	111–113	Pliny writes to Trajan concerning Christians in Bithynia
	115–117	Jewish uprisings in Cyrene, Egypt, Cyprus
Tacitus' *Annals* published	ca. 116	
Suetonius' *Lives of the Caesars* published	ca. 120	
Hadrian, Roman emperor	117–138	Papias, bishop of Hierapolis in Hadrian's time
Quadratus' *Apology* written at Athens	ca. 125	
	ca. 130	*Letter of Barnabas*
	132–135	Jewish revolt led by Bar-Cochba
Antoninus Pius, Roman emperor	138–161	
	ca. 139	Marcion comes to Rome
	ca. 145	Shepherd of Hermas written (some date it ca. 100)
	150–160	Justin Martyr's *Apology* and *Dialogues* written
	ca. 156	*Martyrdom of Polycarp* written shortly after his death
Marcus Aurelius, Roman emperor	161–180	
	ca. 185	Irenaeus' *Against Heresies*
	ca. 200	Muratorian canon

The Herodian Family

(The following statement gives information on those Herodians involved in the story of this book; we give in parentheses New Testament references. The basic source is Josephus. A detailed Index, Genealogy, and Chronology of the Herodian family is given in Hastings' *Dictionary of the Bible*, Vol. II, pp. 353–355.)

I. The Herodian line as we know it was founded by Antipater, who had sons Antipater and Joseph.

II. This second Antipater had four sons: Phasael, Joseph, Herod (the Great), and Pheroras; and a daughter Salome, who married in succession Joseph, Costabar, and Alexas.

III. Children of two of the four sons of Antipater should be noted:

    1. Phasael had a son Phasael, one of whose sons was Cypros.

    2. Herod the Great (Matt. 2:1; Luke 1:5), married ten times, had children as follows:

        a. by Doris: Antipater.

        b. by Mariamne of the Maccabean family: Alexander, Aristobulus, Salampsio, and Cypros.

            (1) children of Aristobulus: sons Herod of Chalcis and Herod Agrippa I (Acts 12:1), and daughter Herodias (Mark 6:17), who married first Herod of Rome (Herod Philip? cf. Mark 6:17), and later Herod Antipas (cf. Mark 6:14 ff.).

                (a) children of Herod Agrippa I: Herod Agrippa II (Acts 25:13), Bernice (Acts 25:13), and Drusilla (Acts 24:24).

        c. by Mariamne, daughter of the high priest Simon: Herod of Rome (Herod Philip? cf. Mark 6:17), who with Herodias had a daughter Salome (cf. Mark 6:22).

        d. by Malthace: Archelaus (Matt. 2:22) and Antipas (Mark 6:14; Luke 3:1).

        e. by Cleopatra of Jerusalem: Philip (Luke 3:1).

Indexes to Text

PERSONS AND SUBJECTS

403

14

Parables, 79 f., 104 f., 133 ff.
Parker, 83, 147
Parthians, 17, 23 ff., 153 f., 156
Parvis, 247
Passion narrative, 82, 139 ff.
Passover, 39, 47 f., 126 ff., 140 ff., 265, 341
Pastoral Letters, 160, 286 ff., 309, 347, 391
Patara, 266
Paul, 58, 109, 159; name, background, early years, 50, 72, 184, 199 ff., 210; tentmaker, 237; persecutor, 181, 184 f., 200 f.; conversion, relation to historical Jesus, 70 f., 150, 185, 201 ff., 357; in Arabia, 185; at Damascus and Jerusalem, 185 f., 203 ff.; at Tarsus, 186; at Antioch, 178, 192 f., 205 ff.; famine relief, 207 f.; mission to Cyprus, Pamphylia, South Galatia, 209 ff.; miracles, 106, 248, 255; Gentile mission challenged, 215 ff.; Jerusalem conference and agreement, 216 ff.; rebuke of Peter at Antioch, 225 f.; independent mission to Macedonia, Achaia, 226 ff.; letter writer, 159, 238 ff., 291, 357; crisis in Galatia, 241 ff.; to Jerusalem and Antioch, 245 f.; ministry in Ephesus (visit to Corinth), 247 ff.; plan to visit Rome, 248, 259 ff.; to Jerusalem, 264 ff.; vow, riot, prison, 267 ff.; hearings and appeal to Caesar, 269 ff.; voyage and shipwreck, 273 ff.; at Rome, 275 ff.; released?, 285 f.; martyr, 288 f.; achievement, 289 ff., 346
Pella, 297, 302 f., 329, 331
Pentateuch, 4, 37 f., 49
Pentecost, 48, 153, 164, 168 ff., 265, 342
Percy, 280
Perga, 210, 213
Pergamum, 310
Perowne, 29, 297
Perrin, 95
Persecution, 138, 174, 180 f., 200 ff., 240, 311, 320 f., 333 ff., 363
Peter, 58; call, 99; Messianic confession, 121 ff.; prominence among the

Twelve, 108 ff., 122 f., 127, 143, 168, 176, 345 f.; denial of Jesus, 167; role in The Acts, 168; sermons, 171 f.; preached to Jews, 176, 191; itinerant ministry, 182, 184, 187 ff., 193 ff.; Cornelius, 188 ff., 214; in prison, leaves Jerusalem, 155, 194 f., 208; at Jerusalem conference, 217; at Antioch, 224 ff.; at Corinth?, 250; in Rome, 320 ff.; source for Mark, 83. See also Twelve disciples
Peter, the First Letter of, 311, 357 f.
Peter, the Second Letter of, 160, 325 f., 337, 348, 358, 383 f.
Petra, 20
Pharisees, x f., 9, 18 ff., 26 f., 45, 47 ff., 57, 73, 93, 113 ff., 135 f., 200 ff., 214, 217, 270
Phasael, 22 f.
Philadelphia, 306, 310
Philemon, 277 ff.
Philemon, Letter to, 276 ff., 309
Philip, of the Seven, 109, 177 f., 181 ff., 186, 300, 314
Philip, of the Twelve, 314
Philip, son of Herod, 28, 30 f.
Philippi, 231 ff., 316 f., 349
Philippians, 283 ff.
Philo, 53 f., 312
Phoebe, 263
Phoenicia, 25, 35, 118, 190 f., 201, 206, 217, 305, 365
Phoenix, 274
Phrygia, 230
Pilate, Pontius, 32 f., 66, 140, 144 ff., 158
Pliny the Elder, 53 f.
Pliny the Younger, 66, 298, 315, 334 f., 341, 343
Plummer, 250, 255
Politarchs, 233
Polybius, 6
Polycarp, 306, 313 f., 317, 330 f., 342, 348 f.
Polycarp, Letter of, 313 f., 317 f.
Polycarp, Martyrdom of, 330 f., 334, 377
Polytheism, 157
Pompey, 13, 20 ff.
Pontus, 236, 259, 311, 316, 354

REFERENCES TO SCRIPTURE AND APOSTOLIC FATHERS

414

BRITISH EDITIONS

In addition to the British books mentioned in the text, these editions are also available.

THE HISTORICAL BACKGROUND 175 B.C.–A.D. 30

The Westminster Historical Atlas to the Bible. SCM Press.

Works of Josephus, ed. H. St. J. Thackeray. Loeb Library. Heinemann.

Corpus Papyrorum Judaicorum, ed. V. A. Tcherikover and A. Fuchs. Oxford University Press.

J. A. Montgomery, *The Book of Daniel*. T. and T. Clark.

John Bright, *A History of Israel*. SCM Press.

The Scrolls and the New Testament, ed. K. Stendhal. SCM Press.

Matthew Black, *The Scrolls and Christian Origins*. A. and C. Black.

G. F. Moore, *Judaism in the First Centuries of the Christian Era*. Oxford University Press.

The Interpreter's Dictionary of the Bible. Nelson.

Stewart Perowne, *Life and Times of Herod the Great*. Hodder and Stoughton.

Maurice Goguel, *Life of Jesus*. Allen and Unwin.

THE RELIGIOUS SETTING

New Testament Apocrypha, ed. E. Hennecke. Lutterworth Press.

A. B. Davidson, *Theology of the Old Testament*. T. and T. Clark.

G. E. Wright, *Biblical Archaeology*. Duckworth.

Jack Finegan, *Light from the Ancient Past*. Oxford University Press.

Oscar Cullmann, *The State in the New Testament*. SCM Press.

Millar Burrows, *The Dead Sea Scrolls*. Secker and Warburg.

F. M. Cross, *The Ancient Library of Qumran*. Duckworth.

Charles Scobie, *John the Baptist*. SCM Press.

THE HISTORICAL JESUS

J. Jeremias, *Unknown Sayings of Jesus*. SPCK.
J. Doresse, *Secret Books of the Egyptian Gnostics*. Hollis and Carter.
R. McL. Wilson, *The Gospel of Philip*. Mowbray.
The Gospel According to Thomas, ed. A. Guillaumont, etc. Collins.
The Secret Sayings of Jesus, ed. R. M. Grant, etc. Collins.
W. C. van Unnik, *Newly Discovered Gnostic Writings*. SCM Press.
Rudolf Bultmann, *History of the Synoptic Tradition*. Blackwell.
C. H. Dodd, *New Testament Studies*. Manchester University Press.
Günther Bornkamm, *Jesus of Nazareth*. Hodder and Stoughton.
Frederick C. Grant, *The Gospels*. Faber and Faber.
Floyd V. Filson, *St. Matthew*. A. and C. Black.
Hans Couzelmann, *The Theology of St. Luke*. Faber and Faber.
Thomas Boslooper, *The Virgin Birth*. SCM Press.

THE GALILEAN MINISTRY

Oscar Cullmann, *Christ and Time*. SCM Press.
Matthew Black, *An Aramaic Approach to the Gospels and Acts*. Oxford University Press.
Gerhard von Rad, *The Kingdom*. Bible Key Words. A. and C. Black.
Norman Perrin, *The Kingdom of God in the Teaching of Jesus*. SCM Press.
C. H. Dodd, *The Parables of the Kingdom*. Fontana Books. Collins.
J. Jeremias, *The Parables of Jesus*. SCM Press.
E. Stauffer, *Jesus and His Story*. SCM Press.
Oscar Cullmann, *Peter: Disciple, Apostle, Martyr*. SCM Press.
G. R. Beasley-Murray, *Jesus and the Future*. Macmillan.
The Interpreter's Bible. Nelson.
Oscar Cullmann, *The Christology of the New Testament*. SCM Press.
Rudolf Bultmann, *Theology of the New Testament*, 2 vols. SCM Press.

REJECTED, CRUCIFIED, RISEN

E. Stauffer, *Love*. Bible Key Words. A. and C. Black.
A. M. Ramsey, *The Resurrection of Christ*. Fontana Books. Collins.
Vincent Taylor, *The Gospel According to St. Mark*. Macmillan.
John A. T. Robinson, *Jesus and His Coming*. SCM Press.
J. Jeremias, *The Eucharistic Words of Jesus*. SCM Press.

BRITISH EDITIONS

BEGINNINGS IN JERUSALEM

H. J. Cadbury, *The Making of Luke-Acts*. SPCK.
H. J. Cadbury, *The Book of Acts in History*. A. and C. Black.
F. F. Bruce, *Acts of the Apostles*. Tyndale Press.
Ernst Lohmeyer, *Lord of the Temple*. Oliver and Boyd.
Martin Dibelius, *Studies in the Acts of the Apostles*. SCM Press.

OUTREACH FROM JERUSALEM

C. S. C. Williams, *Acts of the Apostles*. A. and C. Black.
James S. Stewart, *A Man in Christ*. Hodder and Stoughton.
Johannes Munck, *Paul and the Salvation of Mankind*. SCM Press.

PAUL: ORIGIN, CONVERSION, EARLY MINISTRY

H. J. Schoeps, *Paul*. Lutterworth Press.
C. K. Barrett, *Romans*. A. and C. Black.
T. W. Manson, *Studies in the Gospels and Epistles*. Manchester University Press.
G. S. Duncan, *Galatians*. Hodder and Stoughton.

PAUL'S INDEPENDENT MISSION

C. H. Dodd, *According to the Scriptures*. Nisbet.
William Neil, *Thessalonians*. A. and C. Black.
A. Robertson and A. Plummer, *I Corinthians* and *II Corinthians*. T. and T. Clark.
Oscar Cullmann, *Immortality of the Soul or Resurrection of the Body?* Lutterworth Press

TO PRISON, ROME, AND DEATH

W. Sanday and A. C. Headlam, *Romans*. T. and T. Clark.
A. Nygren, *Romans*. SCM Press.
G. Quell and G. Schrenk, *Righteousness*. Bible Key Words. A. and C. Black.
John Knox, *Philemon*. Collins.
F. W. Beare, *Philippians*. A. and C. Black.

The Obscure Decades

Stewart Perowne, *The Later Herods*. Hodder and Stoughton.
J. H. Ropes, *Epistle of St. James*. T. and T. Clark.
E. Stauffer, *Christ and the Caesars*. SCM Press.
A. E. Brooke, *The Johannine Epistles*. T. and T. Clark.

Trends in the Developing Church

James Moffatt, *Hebrews*. T. and T. Clark.
Raymond Abba, *The Nature and Authority of the Bible*. James Clarke.
C. J. Cadoux, *The Early Church and the World*. T. and T. Clark.
M. Goguel, *The Birth of Christianity*. Allen and Unwin.
C. F. D. Moule, *The Birth of the New Testament*. A. and C. Black.
M. Werner, *The Formation of the Christian Dogma*. A. and C. Black.
A. Schweitzer, *The Mysticism of Paul the Apostle*. A. and C. Black.
C. F. D. Moule, *Worship in the New Testament*. Lutterworth Press.
O. Cullmann, *The Earliest Christian Confessions*. Lutterworth Press.
G. R. Beasley-Murray, *Baptism in the New Testament*. Macmillan.
J. Jeremias, *Infant Baptism in the First Four Centuries*. SCM Press.
Kurt Aland, *Did the Early Church Baptize Infants?* SCM Press.
Alan Richardson, *An Introduction to the Theology of the New Testament*. SCM Press.
Rudolf Bultmann, *Gnosis*. Bible Key Words. A. and C. Black.
R. M. Grant, *Gnosticism and Early Christianity*. Oxford University Press.

Anchor in History

Vincent Taylor, *The Names of Jesus*. Macmillan.
G. Bornkamm, etc., *Tradition and Interpretation in Matthew*. SCM Press.
A. R. C. Leaney, *St. Luke*. A. and C. Black.